ALFRED JARRY
A CRITICAL AND BIOGRAPHICAL STUDY

Keith Beaumont

ALFRED JARRY
A Critical and
Biographical Study

ST. MARTIN'S PRESS   New York

© Leicester University Press 1984

All rights reserved. For information, write
St. Martin's Press, Inc., 175 Fifth Avenue, New York, NY10010
Printed in Great Britain
First published in the United States of America in 1984

ISBN 0-312-01712-X

Library of Congress Cataloging in Publication Data
Beaumont, Keith, 1944–
Alfred Jarry: a critical and biographical study.
Bibliography: p.
Includes index.
1. Jarry, Alfred, 1873–1907.   2. Authors, French – 19th century –
Biography.   I. Title.
PQ2619.A65Z58   1984   842'.8 [B]   84-40443

ISBN 0-312-01712-X

Contents

Illustrations

Bibliographical note

Quotations from Jarry's work refer to the following editions:

Oeuvres Complètes, ed. Michel Arrivé. Paris: Gallimard, Bibliothèque de la Pléiade, vol. I, 1972.
La Chandelle verte, lumières sur les choses de ce temps, ed. M. Saillet. Paris: Livre de Poche, 1969.
Léda, ed. N. Arnaud and H. Bordillon. Paris: Christian Bourgois, 1981.
Le Manoir enchanté et quatre autres oeuvres inédites, ed. N. Arnaud. Paris: La Table Ronde, 1974.
Messaline, ed. T. Foulc. Paris: Eric Losfeld, 1977.
L'Objet aimé, ed. R. Shattuck. Paris: Éditions Arcanes, 1953.
Le Surmâle, ed. T. Foulc. Paris: Eric Losfeld, 1977.
Ubu, ed. N. Arnaud and H. Bordillon. Paris: Gallimard, Collection Folio, 1978.

All other references are to the earlier edition of Jarry's complete works: *Oeuvres Complètes*, ed. R. Massat. Monte Carlo: Éditions du Livre and Lausanne: Henri Kaeser, 8 vols., 1948.

Note on translations

Translations from the French appear in square brackets throughout the text; all translations are by Keith Beaumont.

Abbreviations

The following abbreviations are used:

C.C.P.	*Cahiers du Collège de 'Pataphysique*
D.C.P.	*Dossiers acénonètes du Collège de 'Pataphysique*
O.C., Éditions du Livre	Alfred Jarry, *Oeuvres Complètes*, ed. R. Massat (Monte Carlo: Éditions du Livre and Lausanne: Henri Kaeser, 8 vols., 1948)
O.C., Pléiade, I	Alfred Jarry, *Oeuvres Complètes*, ed. Michel Arrivé, vol. I (Paris: Gallimard, Bibliothèque de la Pléiade, 1972.

Acknowledgments

The author wishes to thank the following for their help: M. Patrick Besnier; M. François Caradec; Mr Stanley Chapman; Mademoiselle Marie-Françoise Christout of the Bibliothèque de l'Arsenal, Paris; M. Raymond Fleury; M. Paul Gayot; Mr Peter Harlock of the Royal Shakespeare Company; Mrs Franciszka Themerson; Mrs Barbara Wright.

Introduction

The Jarry Revival

DESPITE a large and amazingly varied output, ranging from Symbolist verse through half-a-dozen novels to over a dozen farces and musical comedies, Alfred Jarry appeared to most of his contemporaries as primarily the author of one outrageous farce, *Ubu Roi*, which provoked a near-riot in the Paris theatre in 1896, and as a thoroughgoing eccentric in an age of eccentricity – the clowning incarnation of his own creation of 'Père Ubu'. His contemporaries, not to mention many of his friends, even created the legend of a Jarry 'victim' of Ubu, 'devoured' by Ubu, 'killed' by his own imaginative creation. Their consequent attitude was one of pity and condescension, expressed in such phrases as 'pauvre petit Père Ubu', 'le pauvre Père Ubu' and 'pauvre Jarry'.[1] Little read and even less understood, rarely did any of his books sell more than a few hundred copies at most. In the eyes of friends and contemporaries alike, Alfred Jarry *homme de lettres* was – with the possible exception of *Ubu Roi* – a failure.

Yet beneath the surface of the apparent oblivion which followed his death in 1907, the memory of Jarry's work and of the spirit which he had embodied survived. Something of that spirit was reincarnated in the fantasy-play of his friend Guillaume Apollinaire, *Les Mamelles de Tirésias*, whose first performance created a major stir in the theatrical world in 1917. A grimmer, less fantastic side of his work was recalled by the anarchism and nihilism of Dada, the artistic – or anti-artistic – movement founded by Tristan Tzara in 1916 in the midst of the disgust and disillusionment born of the First World War. A few years later Jarry was 'rediscovered', and again proclaimed as a forerunner, by Dada's heirs in the Surrealist movement, whose founder, André Breton, in a short essay of 1918 held out the promise of a new understanding of his work.[2] The promise, alas, was not realized, and Breton, in his first *Manifeste du surréalisme* of 1924, whilst seeming to follow Jarry in equating the two categories of 'imagination' and 'reality', ultimately fell back like so many others on the more colourful aspects of his life and personality, contenting himself with the declaration that 'Jarry est surréaliste dans l'absinthe'.[3] (In Breton's second Manifesto of 1930, he received a mention only twice, sharing the status of predecessor and patron saint with Hegel, Feuerbach, Marx, Lautréamont, Rimbaud, Freud, Chaplin and Trotsky.) A more significant contribution, ultimately, to his fame was made by Antonin Artaud and Roger Vitrac, both of whom had for a time been associated with Surrealism, who founded in 1937 the short-lived Théâtre Alfred Jarry which they dedicated to the destruction of the conventional theatre.

The 1920s and 1930s had also seen the first stirrings of critical and academic interest, though the results as yet were meagre. But it is only since the Second World War that Jarry has truly come into his own and that his work has begun to receive the attention it deserves. The *Ubu* plays have been translated into many languages and *Ubu Roi* has become part of the established theatrical repertoire, and several of his novels and fragments of other works also have been translated into English. A number of serious critical studies, and the first volume of a major biography, have appeared, together with a steady stream of new published and republished works. Instrumental in this process has been the work of the 'Collège de 'Pataphysique', founded in 1948 by a group of academics, writers and artists, whose members have included such notable figures as Raymond Queneau, Jacques Prévert, Boris Vian, Eugène Ionesco, Max Ernst, Marcel Duchamp, Francis Picabia, Jean Dubuffet and René Clair. The Collège, particularly in the person of its late founder and moving spirit, 'His Magnificence Dr I. L. Sandomir' has devoted itself to a study and elucidation of the work of Jarry and in particular to the exposition and illustration, in his work and in that of a host of others, of his 'science' of pataphysics. The groundwork done by the Collège has proved invaluable to later scholars and editors of Jarry's work, and all students of Jarry remain deeply indebted to it.

From the activity of the last 30 years, a new picture of Jarry has emerged – no longer that of a colourful eccentric or of the embodiment of his own creation, Ubu, nor even that of a 'metaphysical rebel' determined to confront the absurdity of the world with his own brand of absurdity, but that of a rich and complex personality, having less in common with the blundering monstrosity of Ubu than with the partly autobiographical heroes of such books as *Les Jours et les Nuits*, *L'Amour absolu*, *Le Surmâle*, *La Dragonne* and – last but by no means least – his *Gestes et opinions du docteur Faustroll, pataphysicien*. He can be seen also as not just the author of a single explosive play, but as dramatic theorist, poet, novelist, journalist and 'philosopher' – a writer whose true posterity is to be found at one and the same time in the whole 'anti-realist' revolution in the theatre of the twentieth century; in the anarchism and nihilism of Dada and its heirs; in the explorations of dream and the world of the subconscious by the

Surrealists; in a long line of writers of fantasy literature from Roussel to Vian; and in a host of modern writers who lightheartedly play with language, and who tend to conceive of literature itself as a vast, elaborate and fascinating 'game'.

Chapter One

Childhood and youth

A STUDY OF Jarry's early years is crucial to an understanding of his development as a writer and as a man. Like Baudelaire a generation and a half earlier, and like his contemporary Proust also, throughout his adult life Jarry looked back with nostalgic regret on the lost magical world of childhood. Scenes from his childhood are transposed into such novels as *Les Jours et les Nuits*, *L'Amour absolu* and *La Dragonne*, enabling us to piece together fragments of a portrait of those years. And whilst Jarry's transposition of such memories nowhere allows us to read these and other works as *romans à clef* – since nowhere is there an exact identity between novelist and fictional protagonist, these recollections being fused into an autonomous imaginative whole – the recurrence of such memories, and of familiar objects from his childhood, testifies to the continuing importance for him of his early years. Above all else, throughout his adult life Jarry clung resolutely to the *spirit* of childhood, both in the form of the child's sense of wonder at the strangeness of the world, and in that of the irreverence of the precociously intelligent and rebellious schoolboy.

Alfred-Henry Jarry was born on 8 September 1873 in the quiet, sleepy provincial town of Laval (Mayenne), on the borders of the ancient province of Brittany. His father, Anselme Jarry, was descended from a long line of artisans, but had broken with the family tradition, beginning his working life as a commercial traveller and then, by the time of his marriage, setting himself up in business with a small textile-manufacturing concern. His mother, *née* Caroline Quernest, was the daughter of a magistrate at Hédé in the Ille-et-Vilaine. Three children issued from the marriage: Caroline-Marie (known as Charlotte), born in 1865; a boy, Gustave-Anselme, born in 1870, who survived only two weeks; and Alfred-Henry who, nine months after his birth, was baptized in Laval Cathedral.

The marriage was not a particularly happy one. Tensions arose between the couple, owing to differences both of temperament and social origin and, before long, to the family's financial circumstances.

As a result of the negligence of a business-partner, in 1879 Anselme Jarry's business collapsed with the loss of 40,000 francs, and he was forced into a humiliating return to his former employment as a commercial traveller. Thereupon Caroline Jarry left Laval and her husband, taking her two children with her, to take refuge with her father in the small Breton seaside town of St-Brieuc, where they were to remain for the next nine years.

The exact nature of the boy's relationship with his father is difficult to determine. Certainly this was distant, since father and son saw little of each other in the course of the next few years. Whether it was as antagonistic, at least on Alfred's side, as his first biographers suggested, is open to some doubt. Some time after Anselme's death in August 1895, his son is reported to have declared of him – in an *ubuesque* manner no doubt deliberately intended to shock – 'Notre père était un bougre dénué d'importance, ce qu'on appelle un bien brave homme. Notre mère et lui décédèrent à huit jours de distance, très régulièrement, pour nous laisser leurs sous . . .' ['Our father was an utterly insignificant fellow, what is known as a thoroughly good chap. Our mother and he passed away within a week of each other, in an orderly manner, so as to leave us their money . . .'].[1] Evidence assembled more recently by Noël Arnaud, however, in his vast but chaotic biography of Jarry, suggests that relations between father and son were by no means as antagonistic as the above remark implies.[2] Anselme Jarry not only continued loyally to support his estranged wife and his children in St-Brieuc and then Rennes, but later supported his son financially during the several years in which he was a student in Paris, and Alfred on several occasions visited his father in Laval from Paris.

What is however certain is that the boy's attachment to his mother was deep and lasting. She was a high-spirited woman, strong-willed, and of a decidedly whimsical if not eccentric turn of mind (according to Jarry's first biographer, he later admitted that she 'was fond of dressing up').[3] She may well also have inherited something of the instability inherent in her family: her mother had been placed in an asylum some time before Caroline was married. She was proud, too, of her Breton ancestry and of the belief, passed down from one generation to another, that her family was of noble ancestry. Both son and daughter were later to give her family name as 'Kernec'h de Coutouly de Dorset' (Kernec'h was a bretonized form of Quernest, while Coutouly had been the maiden name of Caroline's mother), and Alfred was to claim ancestry from Herbrand Sacqueville (or Sackville), one of the companions-in-arms of William the Conqueror.[4] The boy's love for his mother was later transposed and dramatized in the poetic fantasy-novel *L'Amour absolu*, written early in 1899. One of the forms of 'absolute love' portrayed here is that of incestuous love between mother and son – a love which is obscurely linked to the suggestion of feelings of fear and guilt. Though it would be rash to infer from Jarry's treatment of this theme in *L'Amour absolu* the existence of a similar relationship between the boy and his mother, the work does clearly reflect his strong and passionate attachment to her – an attachment which probably has much to do with his later homosexual inclinations and fierce misogyny.

It was against this provincial bourgeois family background, set at first amid the narrow streets of the old medieval town of Laval, that the young Alfred spent his early years. In May 1878, at the age of four and a half, he was enrolled in the *classe des minimes* at the Petit Lycée de Laval. A passage in *L'Amour absolu* recaptures with whimsical humour the naïve view of the world of the child at the moment of his first schooling; it also reveals the closeness of his attachment to his mother and the painfulness of separation:

> Quand il eut quatre ans, Mme Joseb le conduisit tous les matins, elle-même, à la classe des *Minimes* du lycée de la ville.
> Par une côte escarpée, praticable qu'à force de spirales, un ruisseau pavé noyau de la vis, et qu'on appelait le Roquet.
> Puis, par une petite ruelle tortueuse aussi, où il s'enorgueillissait de la sureté nouveau-née de sa marche à suivre la bordure du trottoir, lui semblant, à longer le ruisseau, côtoyer un gouffre.
> Et, la porte ferrée franchie, dans le jardin fleuri qu'on disait la cour, sa solitude s'affirmait du baiser de départ de *sa mère*.

> > [When he was four years old, Madame Joseb herself took him every morning to the nursery class of the town's *lycée*.
> > Up a steep slope, negotiable only by a series of spirals, a cobble-bedded stream forming the centre of its screw-thread, called Le Roquet.
> > Then, along another winding little lane, where he swelled with pride in the new-born confidence of his step as he balanced on the edge of the pavement, believing, as he followed the edge of the stream, that he was skirting an abyss.
> > And, once through the iron gate, in the flower garden which they called the playground, his solitude made itself felt with the farewell kiss of *his mother*.][5]

He was taught at the school by the stern Mme Venel (or Venelle), a strict disciplinarian who, to call distracted pupils to attention, used a long switch of hazel – an object which became, in the imagination of the child, 'quelque chose comme la baguette des fées'.[6] According to the reminiscences of his sister (which, despite their incoherence – Charlotte had literary pretentions which were sadly misplaced – are a valuable source of information about her brother's childhood), Alfred was a favourite pupil: 'Mais Fredo . . . je l'aime bien; il est toujours appuyé sur mes genoux et apprend vite ce qu'il veut!' ['But Fredo . . . I'm very fond of him; he is always resting on my knees and he learns quickly what he wants to!'].[7] The last phrase – assuming it to be reliably reported – suggests that he was already showing signs of a keen intelligence allied to a wilful and headstrong temperament.

The child remained at the school only until July 1879. Then, in October, following Caroline's move to St-Brieuc, he was enrolled at the Lycée de St-Brieuc where he remained until the end of his *classe de seconde* in 1888, in addition to receiving private tuition in German and English. He does not appear to have liked the town much. One of his earliest extant poems is a charmingly naïve satire upon St-Brieuc and its inhabitants, which begins with the lines:

A Saint-Brieuc des Choux tout est plus ou moins bête,
Et les bons habitants ont tous perdu la tête.

The same poem contains also the first expression of a feeling of solitude which is to become a frequent theme in his work:

Ce qui me plaît le plus, c'est, pendant les vacances,
D'aller me promener, mais non d'aller aux danses;
Et, si vous m'en croyez, répétez avec nous:
'Ah! quel triste pays que Saint-Brieuc des Choux!'

> [*In Saint-Brieuc of the Cabbage-patch everything is more or less stupid,*
> *And the good citizens have all gone off their heads.*
>
> *What I like most is, during the holidays,*
> *To go for walks, but not to dances;*
> *And, if you believe me, repeat with us:*
> *'Oh! what a sad place is Saint-Brieuc of the Cabbage-patch!'*][8]

This theme of solitude takes two forms – that of a deeply felt and painful sense of isolation, such as he experienced at the moment of early separation from his mother; and that of a solitude and independence deliberately sought after and cultivated. For, in the solidly *bourgeois* setting of his mother's family in St-Brieuc, surrounded by grandfather, great-uncles, aunts and cousins, the boy had no objective reason to feel lonely or cut off, and his feeling, and then cultivation, of solitude was therefore a matter of individual temperament.

Allied to this sense of solitude was a deep love for the wild and picturesque landscape and rugged coastline of Brittany, coupled with a delight in the world of nature in general. Charlotte recalled her brother fishing for shrimps and shell-fish in the rock-pools along the coast, and chasing and collecting insects, butterflies, frogs and other creatures 'with all the seriousness of a naturalist'.[9] Reminiscences of the sights and sounds of the Breton landscape are a familiar feature of his mature work. A passage in *Les Jours et les Nuits* describes its hero's (and no doubt author's) delight as a child in the tiny creatures he found in ponds and ditches:

Et il y avait au pied de l'escalier, sur une route droite, des fossés avec des mares et des grenouilles bleues, et Sengle aimait beaucoup les mares, parce qu'on ne sait jamais les bêtes qu'on y trouvera, ni même, avec le tarissement solaire, si l'on retrouvera des mares ou les mêmes mares, et on croit toujours les avoir rêvées.

> [And there were, at the foot of the steps, running alongside a straight road, ditches with pools of water and blue frogs, and Sengle loved pools, because you never know what creatures you will find in them, or even, with the sun's evaporation, if you will find any pools or the same pools again, and you always think you have dreamed them.][10]

The hero of *La Dragonne* recalls the time when, visiting his maternal grandfather's house as a child, 'il laissant pendant ses vacances échapper des crabes, des escargots et des bernard-l'hermite' ['during his holidays he let escape crabs, snails and hermit-crabs'.][11] And *L'Amour absolu* offers us glimpses of the adolescent Jarry walking alone amidst bracken-covered heaths and forests, and spending long periods watching the world from the seclusion of a deserted customs officer's observation hut. Indeed, until we reach *La Dragonne*, with its depiction of Jarry's favourite fishing-grounds on the Seine south of Paris, the only landscapes to figure in his literary works are, with one or two brief exceptions, Breton ones. And many of the familiar plants and animals associated with his Breton childhood were to provide recurring images in his later work, forming part of his strange and private *herbiaire* and *bestiaire* of mandrakes, owls and the like.

Closely related, in turn, to this feeling for the landscapes, flora and fauna of Brittany was a deep attraction to its religious beliefs and customs. Brittany was not only one of the most staunchly traditionalist provinces of France, but also one of the most fervently Catholic. It is difficult to assess exactly how pious Jarry's childhood was. The (somewhat idealized) images of childhood which we encounter in *La Dragonne* are suffused with piety. And *Les Jours et les Nuits* contains a detailed reminiscence of a childhood pilgrimage to Saint-Anne-d'Auray – the leading centre of pilgrimage in Brittany and, before its eclipse by Lourdes, one of the most important centres in France – which is recounted with a mixture of nostalgia and whimsical humour deriving from a fusion of the viewpoints of the child and the adult narrator:

Sengle avait été conduit tout petit enfant à ce pèlerinage de Sainte-Anne, et en gardait des souvenirs qui étaient plusieurs.
. . . on arrivait dans des cercles sacrés de pierre grise, et tout le monde montait à genoux des marches douloureuses, jusqu'au sommet d'un triangle

de granit; et il jouait debout parmi, parce qu'il était tout petit enfant. . . .

Il y avait de l'eau aussi, mais sans herbes ni bêtes, dans les trois bassins de pierre de la fontaine. Des vieilles offraient et vantaient des bolées de l'eau miraculeuse et vous les jetaient aux talons quand on passait outre, et maugréaient. L'une, à qui il refusait l'aumône, lui dit:

'Que le bon Dieu vous bénisse . . . que le bon Dieu vous bénisse, la paille au cul et le feu dedans.'

> [Sengle had been taken as a small child on this pilgrimage to Sainte-Anne and retained several memories of it.
>
> . . . one entered sacred circles of grey stone, and everyone climbed on their knees up the steps which were painful, right up to the top of a granite triangle; and he played amongst them, standing up, because he was a little child. . . .
>
> And there was water too, but without plants or creatures, in the three stone basins of the fountain. Old women held out and sang the praises of bowls of the miracle-working water and threw their contents at your heels when you ignored them, and grumbled. One of them, to whom he refused to give alms, said to him:
>
> 'May the Good Lord bless you . . . may the Good Lord bless you, with straw up your arse set on fire.']¹²

Yet at the same time, an oddly incongruous image of the piety of his family is provided by the fact that, although Alfred was baptized shortly after his birth, his sister Charlotte was not baptized until the age of nine, and that on the same occasion as her brother in order that she might be his godmother![13] Despite these ambiguities, it does seem that Jarry's childhood was immersed in the fervour of Breton piety, and – although he was to cease to be an orthodox believer – his religious upbringing was to leave a deep imprint upon his imagination. Jarry's Bretonism – of which Catholicism was an integral part – was to form a recurrent and increasingly important element in both his life and work.

It was while at St-Brieuc that Jarry began to write, producing a series of poems and playlets a selection of which has survived. Among his papers deposited in the offices of the *Mercure de France* after his death, Maurice Saillet in 1947 found a *dossier* of some 260 pages, comprising 48 separate poems and dramatic fragments written between December 1885 and June 1890, when he was aged between 12 and 16. About half of these texts had been recopied by the adult Jarry, perhaps around 1897–8, and all were carefully dated and arranged in chronological order. To this collection, its author had given the curious title, at once modest and pretentious, of *Ontogénie* – in English, ontogenesis, a term derived from the biological sciences where it denotes the development of the individual organism from birth to adulthood. This was followed on the sleeve of the *dossier* by the words: 'Pièces antérieures aux *Minutes* [his first book to be published], quelques-unes postérieures à *Ubu Roi*, et qu'il est plus honorable de ne pas publier.' ['Texts predating *Les Minutes* [his first book to be published], some of them dating from after *Ubu Roi*, and which it is more honourable not to publish.'] Why this collection was put together is uncertain. Did Jarry at some point hope to have it published? At the very least, his attitude towards these texts was ambiguous. For, 'dishonourable' though publication may have been, it is impossible to escape the conclusion that this *dossier* was compiled as a tribute to his own burgeoning creative genius. And, although we cannot know to what extent Jarry has carried out a process of selection of his early work in compiling it, it is striking to see just how much of the mature writer can already be seen in this literature of his boyhood and adolescence.

The poems and dramatic sketches comprising *Ontogénie* can be divided into four broad groups. The first is a small group of playlets written in 1885 and early 1886 inspired jointly by the traditions of the *guignol* and the *commedia dell'arte*, and of Gothic romanticism. The second is a collection of satirical poems and dramatic sketches featuring teachers or supervisors (*surveillants*) and pupils at the Lycée de St-Brieuc. The third is a group of poems on philosophical, mythological or literary themes, many of them inspired by the boy's study of the classics and of German and English literature (for example, Goethe's *Faust*, or Coleridge's *Rime of the Ancient Mariner*), or by the traditions, once again, of Gothic romanticism. The last group comprises two short satirical comedies which show a precocious talent for social satire – a vein which will not reappear in his work until *L'Amour en visites* of 1898 – and two further dramatic fragments featuring teachers and fellow-pupils (only the first of these four texts having been written at St-Brieuc). Of the texts written at St-Brieuc, it is the second and third groups – examined here in reverse order – which are of the most interest. Radically different in content and in mood, together they reveal two deeply contrasting but complementary sides of their author's character which will re-emerge periodically throughout his literary career.

In both content and style, there is clearly much in Jarry's poems of the period 1887–8 that is imitative, to the point where imitation merges with pastiche (Jarry himself later recalled that he and his fellow-pupils 'composaient force pastiches, suffisamment réussis d'ailleurs, de Victor Hugo ou du Parnasse' ['composed a great many pastiches, quite successful moreover, of Victor Hugo or of the Parnassians'.][14] Nevertheless they display considerable technical virtuosity, even if they cannot be put on a par with the productions of the adolescent Rimbaud (although one wonders, in Rimbaud's case, whether these poems would have created such a stir had it not been for the subsequent career of their young author). Their chief interest however lies in the insight which they afford us into the mind and imagination of their adolescent author. For, despite their varied sources, these poems present a surprising thematic unity, almost all of them centring on the themes of death, destruction and damnation. The treatment of these themes reaches a particularly macabre and gruesome pitch in an unbroken series of 13 poems written between March and September 1888, which deal with such subjects as the destructiveness of the forces of nature (storm winds, hurricanes, volcanoes, fire), a man buried alive, the dissection of corpses, murder, skeletons hanging from gibbets, the four scourges of the Apocalypse, witches' sabbaths and the Dance of Death. There is also the complementary theme of the impotence and vulnerability of man, which reaches a culmination in three sonnets grouped under the Pascalian title of 'Misère de l'homme'. These paint a bleak and despairing portrait of human existence (reminiscent of the young Laforgue's *Le Sanglot de la terre*, written only a decade or so earlier), which is seen as a constant and losing battle against hostile nature and against the approach of death. The first stanza of the last sonnet will serve as an example:

Car pour lui [Man] sur la terre il n'est point d'espérance.
Il pleure, et c'est justice. Il doit pleurer, celui
Qui commence une vie où toujours la souffrance,
La misère et la mort s'acharnent après lui.

> *[Because for him [Man] on this earth no hope exists.*
> *He weeps, and it is right that he should. He must weep, he*
> *Who is beginning a life in which suffering,*
> *Wretchedness and death pursue him relentlessly.][15]*

Behind the obvious naïvety and adolescent romanticism, there is evidence also of a veritable obsession on Jarry's part with the idea of death, and evidence also that he was passing through a profound religious and philosophical crisis at this period of his life. With the sole exception (and here only briefly) of the poem 'La Seconde Vie ou Macaber', nowhere is there any trace of a positive religious faith to temper this outlook of pessimism and despair. Both the outlook of Jarry in these poems, and the themes and imagery through which it is expressed, are remarkably consonant with those of his first book, *Les Minutes de sable mémorial*, published in 1894; while the pessimistic view of mankind displayed here is that which underlies also his vision of Ubu.

'La Seconde Vie ou Macaber' is also of interest as a precursor of things to come. Inspired initially by Goethe's *Faust*, this long poem recounts the descent into death, through suicide, of a certain Aldern (a Breton form of Alfred, which was to be used again by Jarry in his partly autobiographical drama *Haldernablou*), in order to 'sonder, comme Faust, de la mort/L'insondable mystère', and his subsequent journey through the 'ether' of eternity. Whether the *éthernité* of Jarry's Dr Faustroll owes something to this poem must remain an open question, but the episode strangely prefigures the 'descent' towards death – this time through drinking – of the hero of his last novel, *La Dragonne.*

No less interesting (and certainly more entertaining) is the second broad group of *Ontogénie*, the poems and dramatic sketches featuring teachers and fellow-pupils at the Lycée de St-Brieuc. Most of these centre on the almost legendary *pompe Rouget* – alias the *Antlium* (a dubious latinization of the Greek word for pump), alias *Le Taurobole*. This was originally the newly-installed sewage pump of the town of St-Brieuc, invented by a certain Rouget of Lorient, which fascinated the pupils of the Lycée. In their fertile and imaginative minds it became transformed into a machine of war operating rather like a modern water-cannon, but firing something other than water. Paradoxically, this fearsome instrument also took on in the minds of the pupils both musical and religious associations, both serving as an organ to accompany the hymns of praise to its inventor (perhaps inspired by the curious coincidence of his name with that of Rouget de Lisle, creator of the *Marseillaise*, recently restored to its full glory as the official anthem of the newly established Third Republic) and, through the name *Taurobole*, recalling the sacrificial rites of the ancient Mithraic religion (did this name arise from the gurgling sound made by the pump, reminiscent in the schoolboy imagination of the sound uttered by a dying bull?). In a series of dramatic sketches written in mock-heroic verse, beginning with the Homerically-entitled *L'Antliade* and culminating with *Les Antliaclastes*, Jarry recounts the exploits of Rouget and of his devoted servants, the 'Antliatores', in their battles against the pump's enemies, the 'Antliaclastes', led by Sicca (the nickname of one of the *surveillants* at the school). Most of these sketches date from 1886, when Jarry was aged 12, but at the beginning of 1888 he wrote – in the space of three days – a completely new, three-act version of *Les Antliaclastes*. Here, more than ever, the theme of the 'pump' is treated in a way which looks forward to that of the conflict between the old, 'artisanal' methods of sewage disposal and the new 'scientific' method in both the *Guignol* of 1893 and the work from which it was extracted, *Ubu Cocu* – the Antliaclasts' resolve being expressed in the terms:

Nous avons décidé qu'avant que de permettre
Que l'ennemi Rouget, acharné, puisse mettre
En ces lieux l'Antlium, nous tous, jusqu'au dernier,
Nous devons le combattre . . .

[We have decided that, rather than allow
Our bitter enemy Rouget to install
In these premises the Antlium, we must all, to the last man,
Fight him . . .][16]

Apart from this parallel with the theme of sewage-disposal which will recur in *Ubu Cocu*, these poems and dramatic sketches prefigure Jarry's later work in four other important respects. Firstly, the relationship between Rouget and his devoted followers, as also that between Sicca and his henchmen, prefigures in an uncanny way that between Père Heb and his faithful *palotins*, even down to the latter's singing of choruses in praise of their master. Secondly, the association here of the religious and the scatological parallels the association in the person of Ubu of the scientific and the scatological. Here, as to a lesser but still important extent in the *Ubu* plays, scatology is one of the chief sources of comedy. But this preoccupation on Jarry's part is not simply evidence of a juvenile obsession; on the contrary, throughout his life he was to use elements of scatology as a means of expressing his uncompromising rejection of and contempt for the values of a world from which he felt himself estranged. Thirdly, these early dramatic sketches with their wordplay and proliferation of humorous and frequently scabrous names and nicknames, especially those based on translation from one language to another – the *Antlium* and its derivatives, the *Taurobole*, *Sicca* (a latinization of 'Crotte-Sèche'), *Roupias Pet-Sec*,[17] and the like – show a love of linguistic invention and deformation which is to be a permanent feature of Jarry's work. Lastly, it is striking that all of these early plays and dramatic fragments, without exception, carry detailed stage-directions. Whether or not they were ever performed we shall probably never know, but it is significant that Jarry conceived of them all as being performable, revealing from an early age a profound interest in the mechanics of the theatre. All of these characteristics and tendencies present in this, his earliest extant work, reveal Jarry to have been fully prepared, even before his historic encounter with the prototype of his most famous creation, for his exploitation of the figure of Ubu.

This abundance of literary activity does not appear to have seriously affected the boy's performance at school: in his last three years at St-Brieuc he carried off a string of prizes – in Latin prose and translation, in English, in reading and recitation, and in French composition[18] – much to the delight of his mother, who began to conceive on her son's behalf the ambition of a university degree. To this end, Mme Jarry decided to move with the children to the administrative and intellectual capital of Brittany, Rennes. Here, the family seems to have been rather unsettled: at least three different addresses in Rennes are known, a reflection perhaps of Caroline Jarry's character. Meanwhile, in October 1888, at the age of 15, Alfred had been enrolled as a pupil at the Lycée de Rennes. It was the beginning of a sequence of events that was to become a part of history; for it was at the Lycée de Rennes that Ubu was born.

At the Lycée, Jarry encountered the person of M. Hébert, the physics master, an enormously fat, ridiculous and ineffectual figure. Generations of cruel and malicious schoolboys had ridiculed and terrorized this pathetic victim by their projectiles, pranks and practical jokes, with that intense impersonal cruelty of which boys are so capable. Jarry was here in his element. The figure of M. Hébert exercised a peculiar fascination over him. Watched by his entranced class-mates, he carried the attack to a new level, harrassing Hébert with a grim determination which far surpassed the pranks of the others. One of his fellow-pupils later described his behaviour in these terms:

Il entrait dans le jeu, à la fin, comme le matador dans l'arène, pour le coup de grâce. Grand silence. Avec froideur, à l'emporte-pièce, il posait au père Heb des questions insidieuses, abracadabrantes, qui rompaient ses périodes, qui rompaient son onction. Il l'encerclait et l'étourdissait de sophismes. Il le surmenait. Le père Heb se décontenançait, battait des paupières, bégayait, faisait le sourd, perdait pied. En fin de compte, se dérobant, il s'effondrait sur la table . . .. La classe regardait Jarry vainqueur avec émerveillement.

Avec crainte et recul aussi. Car on sentait bien que son sarcasme dépassait la turbulence commune, que quelque chose, en lui, prenait part à ce combat, quelque chose d'autre, une injonction aiguë qui pressait sa tactique.

> [He entered the fray at the end, like a matador in a bull-ring, for the death-blow. Complete silence. Coldly, incisively, he put to Père Heb insidious, preposterous questions, which caused him to falter in mid-sentence and shattered his composure. He encircled him and made him giddy with his sophistry. He wore him out. Père Heb became disconcerted, batted his eyelids, stammered, pretended not to hear, lost ground. Finally, giving way, he collapsed onto the table . . .. The class looked upon the victor Jarry with wonder.
>
> With fear and a sense of recoil also. For there was the distinct feeling that his sarcasm went beyond the general unruliness, that something deep down inside him was taking part in this battle, something different, that his tactics arose from some powerful impulse.][19]

Long before Jarry's arrival at the school, Hébert – under the names of *le Père Heb*, *Eb*, *Ébé*, *Ébon*, *Ébouille* and *le P. H.* – was already the hero-villain of a vast and diffuse body of schoolboy legend, epic and farce. With the passage of time, and the accretion of new details drawn from countless school texts (in particular Rabelais and Le Sage), the gap between reality and fantasy widened progressively. At first, the legend took shape in oral form; it was only with its increasing complexity that parts of it came to be written down. These told of the birth of *le P. H.* on the banks of the Oxus, of the copulation of a member of the race of the *Hommes-Zénormes* and a Tartar witch from the Aral Sea. He was born with his bowler hat, woollen cloak and check trousers, with a single extendable ear on the top of his head, and with his enormous *gidouille* or belly. He had in addition three teeth, of stone, iron and wood. Some time after his birth he was baptized with 'essence de pataphysique'. Later, fleeing from the pursuit of the 'Hommes-Zénormes', *le P. H.* crossed the mountains into China, whence he made his way through Mongolia, Manchuria and Siberia and across the Bering Straits. Here he was trapped in an iceberg where he remained for a thousand years. Released following an exceptionally mild winter, he crossed the Atlantic and made his way along the coasts of Norway and France to the mouth of the Seine, which he swam up until caught by a fisherman near the Pont du Louvre. Shortly after, he obtained his *baccalauréat* by dint of terrorizing his examiners. Then, at the head of a band of brigands, he captured the château of Mondragon in the south of France which became a base for his expeditions of plunder and looting. In his lust for plunder (or *finance*), he dispatched his enemies with a 'disembraining spoon' (later industrialized into the *machine à décerveler*), and loaded his loot into an enormous sack, his *poche*, which he dragged along behind him. Eventually he made his way to Spain, where he usurped the throne of Aragon, whence he was expelled to Poland, to become a captain of the King's dragoons . . . and the rest is history.

Such was the cycle of adventures woven around the legendary figure of *le Père Heb* in existence when Jarry arrived at the Lycée de Rennes – a cycle to which untold numbers of unruly and imaginative schoolboys had made their contribution. It was out of this shapeless mass of schoolboy legend that *Ubu Roi* was created – though precisely by whom is a question which has never been totally resolved.

In 1921, a rather naïve (but not wholly scrupulous) teacher of English and former pupil of the Lycèe de Rennes, named Charles Chassé, published a small book entitled *Sous le masque d'Alfred Jarry(?): les sources d'Ubu-Roi*,[20] in which he maintained that *Ubu Roi* was not the work of Jarry, who had pirated it from its original authors, and that the play was originally no more than a grotesque schoolboy farce. Behind this attack on Jarry's literary integrity lay the avowed twofold aim of demonstrating that the notorious first performance of *Ubu Roi* in Paris in 1896 was an enormous hoax and, thereby, that the enthusiasm with which the play was received by the whole Symbolist generation therefore served merely to reveal the 'stupidity' of a whole era. The upshot was a veritable furore of charge and counter-charge, with Jarry's former friends, led by the 'Prince of Poets', Paul Fort, springing to the defence of both his and their slighted honour. As one observer put it at the time: 'On a versé plus d'encre à écrire qu'*Ubu Roi* est ou n'est pas l'oeuvre d'Alfred Jarry qu'à rechercher si Naundorff est bien le fils de Louis XVI.' ['More ink has been spilt in arguing that *Ubu Roi* is or is not the work of Alfred Jarry than in seeking to determine whether Naundorff is indeed the son of Louis XVI.']21 Twenty-six years later, in 1947, Chassé, slightly more wary but still undeterred, returned to the attack with a book entitled *Dans les coulisses de la gloire: D'Ubu-Roi au douanier Rousseau* – a reissue of the earlier volume along with the text of a number of articles attempting to prove that Jarry's alleged 'discovery' of the painter Henri Rousseau (in itself, in fact, an erroneous belief) was equally a hoax.

According to Chassé, in 1885–6 two brothers, Charles and Henri Morin, had written down and elaborated upon some of the adventures of *Père Heb* under the titles of *Les Héritiers*, *La Bastringue*, *La Prise d'Ismaïl*, *Le Voyage en Espagne* and – last but not least – *Les Polonais*, the text of which was contained in a notebook of about 30 pages. It was the latter that Jarry had seized upon and renamed *Ubu Roi*, his sole contribution having been – according to Charles Morin – to change a few names and to add a few minor and insignificant details. Charles Morin, the principal author, left Rennes in October 1888 to begin preparation at the Collège Stanislas in Paris for entry to the École Polytechnique, entrusting the manuscript of *Les Polonais* to his younger brother. It was Henri, who became an intimate friend of Jarry, who communicated the manuscript of the play to him.

Though Chassé's book contains a mine of valuable information about the origins of the figure of Ubu, his general thesis is both confused and erroneous. That Jarry was not the sole author of *Ubu Roi* is disputed by no-one. That he tried to hide this fact is quite false. Most of his friends were well aware of the origins of the play, and Alfred Vallette, editor of the *Mercure de France*, in an obituary notice on Jarry mentioned almost casually that 'la plus connue de ses oeuvres, *Ubu Roi*, fut écrite au collège, en collaboration avec deux camarades' ['the best known of his works, *Ubu Roi*, was written at school, in collaboration with two schoolfriends'.]22 On Chassé's own evidence, the version of *Les Polonais* written down by Charles Morin could not have been (despite Morin's later attempts to disguise the fact) more than, at the very most, half the length of the eventual *Ubu Roi*. It seems probable – if we are to give any credence at all to Jarry's description of the play on the title page of its first published edition in 1896: 'Restitué en son intégrité tel qu'il a été représenté par les marionnettes du Théâtre des Phynances en 1888' ['Restored in its entirety as it was performed by the marionnettes of the Théâtre des

Phynances in 1888'] – that the text of Charles Morin underwent a major reworking at the hands of Jarry and Henri Morin in the winter of 1888–9. Even so, Jarry must have continued to modify and to add to elements of the play in the years that followed (the *name* Ubu, for example, had not yet been invented), though his exact contribution to its elaboration will doubtless never be known.

In any case, this whole debate about the play's authorship is misconceived. For neither *Les Polonais* nor the Morin brothers' other plays would or could ever have come into being without the vast body of anonymous legend and fantasy which preceded them. Jarry's comments in the article 'Les Paralipomènes d'Ubu' of 1896[23] make it clear that he and the other pupils of the Lycée regarded the whole of the Hébert 'cycle' as common property – as a common fund which could be drawn upon and added to at will. *Ubu Roi* is thus in the fullest sense the product of a schoolboy collaboration, an authentic product of a collective schoolboy imagination.

Notwithstanding this, there are three respects in which Jarry, and he alone, has the right to a claim upon the play. Firstly, whereas Charles Morin, upon leaving the Lycée de Rennes and on the threshold of the 'serious' world of adulthood (as represented by the École Polytechnique) was only too willing to leave behind for good this 'couillonnade' and 'bêtise' of childhood (as he described it to Chassé), it was Jarry alone who was responsible for saving the play, along with other elements of the Hébert saga, from the oblivion into which it, M. Hébert, the Morin brothers, and possibly even M. Chassé, would otherwise have fallen. Secondly, it was Jarry alone who realized the dramatic or theatrical potential of the play, a realization which culminated in the notorious *première* of *Ubu Roi* in December 1896 which forever established its fame. And, thirdly, it was he and he alone who invented the *name* Ubu. This fact was readily admitted by Henri Morin, who put the date of its invention at around 1893 or 1894: 'Le nom d'Ubu est entièrement de l'invention de Jarry et il nous était parfaitement inconnu avant l'année 1894 . . . .. La paternité lui en revient absolument.' ['The name Ubu is entirely Jarry's invention and it was completely unknown to us before 1894 . . . .. Its authorship is his and his alone.'][24]

The question of the way in which the various deformations of Hébert came to be transformed into Ubu is a fascinating one. Jarry himself is not much help, and is even deliberately misleading in 'Les Paralipomènes d'Ubu', where he speculates on a possible derivation from *Ybex*, the vulture. The most likely (and certainly the most satisfying) explanation is that given by J.-H. Sainmont in the *Cahiers du Collège de 'Pataphysique*.[25] Among the miscellaneous fragments of the Hébert cycle was a song entitled *Tudé* – transformed by Jarry into the *Chanson du Décervelage* – whose chorus ran:

Voyez, voyez la machine tourner,
Voyez, voyez la cervelle sauter,
Voyez, voyez les rentiers trembler,
Hurrah, cornes au cul, vive le père Ébé.

> [*See, see the machine go round,*
> *See, see the brains spurt out,*
> *See, see the* rentiers *tremble,*
> *Hurrah, horns on your arse, long live Père Ébé.*][26]

Ébé thus formed a rather unsatisfying weak rhyme with *trembler*, until Jarry hit upon the brilliant idea of converting the word into *Ubu* to give to this splendid classical alexandrine an internal rhyme – *Ubu* rhyming, appropriately, with *cul*, the furthest extremity of Ubu's *gidouille* or belly, concerning which Jarry wrote in 'Les Paralipomènes d'Ubu': 'Des trois âmes que distingue Platon: de la tête, du coeur et de la gidouille, cette dernière seule, en lui, n'est pas embryonnaire.' ['Of the three souls perceived by Plato – those of the head, of the heart and of the *gidouille* – the latter alone, in him, is more than embryonic.'][27] The very *name* Ubu is therefore linked by Jarry with that which is most base and physical in man – standing at the opposite pole to his intellectual and emotional faculties. It is a name whose magic is undeniable. Indeed, it is the resonance and expressivity of the name Ubu, with its suggestion of something at once primitive and monstrous, which, perhaps more than any other single feature, is responsible for the appeal of the play.

It is worth examining more closely, in the light of this transformation, the question of Jarry's attitude towards his physics master. That attitude was compounded in part, no doubt, of the mixture of amusement and contempt with which his fellow-pupils regarded M. Hébert; but it also went far beyond this. Two complementary clues were given by Jarry himself, the first in a description of the figure of Ubu as 'la déformation par un potache d'un de ses professeurs qui représentait pour lui *tout le grotesque qui fût au monde*' ['the imaginative distortion by a schoolboy of one of his teachers who in his eyes represented *everything in the world that was grotesque*'],[28] and the second in a reference to 'le principe de synthèse que trouve l'enfant créateur en ses professeurs' ['the principle of synthesis which the imaginatively gifted child finds in its teachers'].[29] The implications are clear: just as children tend to see in their parents and teachers a model of the whole adult world, so too this precociously misanthropic 15-year-old, newly arrived at the Lycée de Rennes, came to see in the monstrously fat and pathetically incompetent and ineffectual figure of his physics master a symbol of the grotesqueness and hideousness of mankind itself.

Ubu Roi was, however, far from being the only product of Jarry's years at Rennes – and M. Hébert by no means the only one of his teachers to be thus satirized. Sometime during the school year 1888–9, he began work on what was eventually to become the second Ubu play, *Ubu Cocu*. Its first sketch (the surviving fragments of which were included in *Ontogénie*) bore the title *Onésime ou les tribulations de Priou. Pièce alquemique*. It loosely combines a number of disparate themes – ribald scenes of drunken monks (transpositions of his fellow-pupils), probably inspired partly by Rabelais, partly by the history of the Lycée de Rennes, whose premises had once served as a Jesuit College; *le P. H.* in his laboratory counting his 'finance' and talking nonsense-physics and -chemistry; and satire upon a pupil named Priou (here transformed into 'Onésime O'Priou'), an abominable dunce whose repeated failures were legendary and who here becomes the unwitting lover of *la mère EB*. Even more than *Ubu Roi* in its final version, *Onésime* is an authentic product of the schoolboy imagination at the Lycée de Rennes in its 'raw' state, striking both for its wealth of scatological detail and for the range of its linguistic invention – a profusion and variety which are considerably attenuated in both *Ubu Roi* and *Ubu Cocu*. Two other fragments from this period also survive and were included by Jarry in *Ontogénie*: *Le Futur malgré lui*, the first (and perhaps only) act of a scathing satire upon bourgeois customs and conventions, written in 1889–90; and *Les Alcoolisés*, a dramatic sketch dated June 1890. This combines the alcoholic theme of *Onésime* with further scatological elements in a laboratory setting which offers further scope for satire upon teachers and fellow-pupils (the teacher in question here being a M. Legris, whose name is transformed into Lesoûl). The play reveals also Jarry's liking for scientific and technical terms, which was to be a prominent feature of his later work, and it develops also the curious theme of a human foetus preserved in alcohol which will mysteriously recur in *Les Minutes de sable mémorial*. It is interesting also as a first attempt to produce a libretto, a vein to which Jarry was to return in the middle years of his literary career – the play actually being sub-titled 'opéra chimique'.

Sometime during the period 1888–90, Jarry also produced a first version of *Ubu Cocu*, possibly under the title of *Les Cornes du P. H.* This, at least, is the case according to the description which accompanied the title of the play in its first finished version, identical to that which accompanied the title of *Ubu Roi*: 'Restitué en son intégrité tel qu'il a été représenté par les marionnettes du Théâtre des Phynances' ['Restored in its entirety as it was performed by the marionettes of the Théâtre des Phynances'] (though once again, it is doubtful whether this description can be taken wholly literally). In *Ubu Cocu*, the scatological element is both increased, relative to *Ubu Roi*, and reinforced by the addition of sexual themes (much to Charles Morin's disapproval). Indeed, the whole play is a much more 'personal' work than *Ubu Roi*: where the latter was the result of a collaboration between Jarry and Henri Morin working on a text written by Charles Morin, *Ubu Cocu* is principally Jarry's own work, and in any case certainly owes nothing to Charles Morin.

Although a detailed discussion of *Ubu Cocu* is given in Chapter Five, some explanation of the sources of its principal themes and characters is appropriate here. In it, the theme of Ubu's cuckoldry, first enunciated in *Onésime*, is more fully developed and the name of Mère Ubu's lover, originally O'Priou, becomes first Barbapoux – the nickname of a *répétiteur* at the Lycée – and then, in a subsequent version, Memnon, who is attributed with the function of *vidangeur* (night man). The implied link between sexual and faecal themes is further developed when the two lovers arrange a tryst in the latrines. Ironically, the inspiration for this scene may well have come from none other than the greatest of French tragedians, Racine. The schoolboy mind is adept at reading obscene or ambiguous meanings into the most innocent of texts – and the more sacrosanct the author, the greater is the temptation to look for such meanings. Thus the scene of Mère Ubu's rendezvous with her lover 'dans les cabinets' was quite probably inspired by the opening lines of *Bérénice*:

Arrêtons un moment. La pompe de ces lieux,
Je le vois bien, Arsace, est nouvelle à tes yeux.
Souvent ce cabinet, superbe et solitaire,
Des secrets de Titus est le dépositaire.
C'est ici quelquefois qu'il se cache à sa cour,
Lorsqu'il vient à la reine expliquer son amour.

> [*Let us pause a moment. The pomp of this place,*
> *I can see clearly, Arsace, is new to your gaze.*
> *Often it is to this room, magnificent and solitary,*
> *That the secrets of Titus are confided.*
> *It is here sometimes that he hides from the court,*
> *When he comes to explain to the queen the reasons for his love.*][30]

The most important new characters in *Ubu Cocu*, however, are those of Achras, the unfortunate 'collector of Polyhedra' whose home is invaded and taken over by Ubu, and of Ibu's Conscience. The first is an innocent and amusing parody upon Jarry's mathematics teacher, M. Périer (Périer = Poirier = Achras, the Greek word for pear-tree), who was notorious for his mannerisms of speech and his fondness for complex geometrical forms.[31] Out of these 'polyhedra' the fertile schoolboy imagination had made living creatures who were carefully nurtured and whose habits were studied by Achras. They, together with his 'treatise on the surface of the square', are his lifelong passion, as Achras tells us in his opening speech:

O mais c'est qué, voyez-vous bien, je n'ai point sujet d'être mécontent de mes polyèdres: ils font des petits toutes les six semaines, c'est pire que des lapins. Et il est bien vrai de dire que les polyèdres réguliers sont les plus fidèles et les plus attachés à leur maître; sauf que l'Icosaèdre s'est révolté ce matin et que j'ai été forcé, voyez-vous bien, de lui flanquer une gifle sur chacune de ses faces. Et que comme ça c'était compris. Et mon traité, voyez-vous bien, sur les moeurs des polyèdres qui s'avance: n'y a plus que vingt-cinq volumes à faire.

> [Oh, but it's that, look you, I've no reason to be displeased with my polyhedra: they have little ones every six weeks, they're worse than rabbits. And it's quite true to say that the regular polyhedra are the most faithful and the most devoted to their master; except that the icosahedron rebelled this morning and I was obliged, look you, to give him a slap on each of his faces. And that way he got the message. And my treatise, look you, on the habits of polyhedra, which is coming along: there are only twenty-five more volumes to write.][32]

Ubu's Conscience, on the other hand, represents a satire upon Jarry's philosophy teacher during this year, M. Bourdon – latinized to become 'B. Bombus' – the name possibly suggesting to the pupils the 'buzz' or 'hum' of conscience, as expressed in Bourdon's moral philosophy, as a passage from the play would seem to indicate:

LA CONSCIENCE, *émergeant comme un vers au moment où Memnon plonge*: Ouf! quel choc! mon crâne en bourdonne!
MEMNON: Comme un tonneau vide.
LA CONSCIENCE: Le vôtre ne bourdonne pas?

> THE CONSCIENCE, *emerging like a worm as Memnon plunges in*: Ow! what a blow! my head's buzzing from it!
> MEMNON: Like an empty barrel.
> THE CONSCIENCE: Isn't yours buzzing?[33]

The fact of the presence in *Ubu Cocu* of Bourdon/Bombus is again an indication of the curiously impersonal nature of this parody. For Jarry referred to him twice in later life with considerable respect, remembering him as 'l'auteur de livres excellents',[34] and as having expounded to his pupils the philosophy of Nietzsche even before Nietzsche's works had been translated into French.[35] Here, notwithstanding, he appears as a tall, thin figure clothed only in a shirt, whom Ubu carries about with him in a suitcase, whom he consults concerning the fate to be meted out to the unfortunate Achras, and whose highly moral advice he then proceeds to use in a quite unintended way. The scene of this interview is one of the most brilliantly satirical passages of the play, and was considered by André Gide, along with

Ubu's first dialogue with Achras, to be 'un extraordinaire, incomparable et parfait chef-d'oeuvre'[36] (the opening words of the Conscience and Ubu's reply are a verbatim reproduction of an actual classroom scene involving Bourdon and a pupil who was adept at imitating the voice and manner of M. Hébert[37]):

PÈRE UBU: Avons-nous raison d'agir ainsi? Cornegidouille, de par notre chandelle verte, nous allons prendre conseil de notre Conscience. Elle est là, dans cette valise, toute couverte de toiles d'araignée. On voit bien qu'elle ne nous sert pas souvent.
   Il ouvre la valise. Sort la Conscience sous les espèces d'un grand bonhomme en chemise.
LA CONSCIENCE: Monsieur, et ainsi de suite, veuillez prendre quelques notes.
PÈRE UBU: Monsieur, pardon! nous n'aimons point à écrire, quoique nous ne doutions pas que vous ne deviez nous dire des choses fort intéressantes. Et à ce propos je vous demanderai pourquoi vous avez le toupet de paraître devant nous en chemise?
LA CONSCIENCE: Monsieur, et ainsi de suite, la Conscience, comme la vérité, ne porte habituellement pas de chemise. Si j'en ai arboré une, c'est par respect pour l'auguste assistance.
PÈRE UBU: Ah ça, monsieur ou madame ma Conscience, vous faites bien du tapage. Répondez plutôt à cette question: ferai-je bien de tuer Monsieur Achras, qui a osé venir m'insulter dans ma propre maison?
LA CONSCIENCE: Monsieur, et ainsi de suite, il est indigne d'un homme civilisé de rendre le mal pour le bien. Monsieur Achras vous a hébergé, Monsieur Achras vous a ouvert ses bras et sa collection de polyèdres, Monsieur Achras, et ainsi de suite, est un fort brave homme, bien inoffensif, ce serait une lâcheté, et ainsi de suite, de tuer un pauvre vieux incapable de se défendre.
PÈRE UBU: Cornegidouille! Monsieur ma Conscience, êtes-vous sûr qu'il ne puisse se défendre?
LA CONSCIENCE: Absolument, Monsieur. Aussi serait-il bien lâche de l'assassiner.
PÈRE UBU: Merci, Monsieur, nous n'avons plus besoin de vous. Nous tuerons Monsieur Achras, puisqu'il n'y a pas de danger, et nous vous consulterons plus souvent, car vous savez donner de meilleurs conseils que nous ne l'aurions cru. Dans la valise!

Il la renferme.

[PÈRE UBU: Are we right to act in this way? Hornbelly, by our green candle, we'll consult our Conscience. There it is, in that suitcase, all covered in cobwebs. You can see that we don't make use of it often.
   He opens the case. The Conscience emerges in the form of a tall fellow in shirt-tails.
THE CONSCIENCE: Sir, and so forth, be so good as to take some notes.
PÈRE UBU: Sir, we beg your pardon! we are not partial to writing, although we do not doubt that you would tell us some most interesting things. And by the way, I would ask you how it is that you have the cheek to appear before us in shirt-tails?
THE CONSCIENCE: Sir, and so forth, Conscience, like truth, is usually naked. If I have donned a shirt, it is out of respect for your august person.

PÈRE UBU: Really, sir or madam Conscience, you are making a lot of fuss. Answer me rather this question: would I be right in killing Monsieur Achras, who has dared to come and insult me in my own home?
THE CONSCIENCE: Sir, and so forth, it is unworthy of a civilized man to repay good with evil. Monsieur Achras has given you shelter, Monsieur Achras has placed at your disposal himself and his collection of polyhedra, Monsieur Achras, and so forth, is a perfectly decent chap, quite inoffensive, it would be an act of cowardice, and so forth, to kill a poor old man incapable of defending himself.
PÈRE UBU: Hornbelly! Sir Conscience, are you sure he's quite incapable of defending himself?
THE CONSCIENCE: Absolutely, Sir. Therefore it would be cowardly indeed to murder him.
PÈRE UBU: Thank you, Sir, we have no further need of you. We shall kill Monsieur Achras since there is no danger, and we shall consult you more often, for you give better advice than we would have thought. Into the suitcase!

He locks him up again.][38]

The love of linguistic invention and wordplay seen here in the names of Achras and B. Bombus is nowhere more graphically illustrated in these plays than in the oaths employed by Ébé/Ubu, many of them part of the original schoolboy 'fund' from which the character emerged. Though such obscenities may constitute initially a source of humour (through the creation of a sense of liberation from accepted taboos), they quickly become tedious unless reinvigorated by linguistic inventiveness. The celebrated *merdre* with which *Ubu Roi* opens is a typical example of this process: the deformation by the pupils of the Lycée de Rennes of the *mot de Cambronne* through the addition of an 'r', far from camouflaging or euphemizing the word it replaces, draws attention to it through the derisory nature of its apparent camouflage and acquires an additional comic force from its very parody of such euphemizing processes. The combinations *bougre de merdre*, *merdre de bougre*, *cornegidouille* and the *pissemerdre* of *Onésime*, as well as words such as *oneille*, *tuder* and the many terms for Ubu's belly or intestines – *gidouille* itself, *giborne*, *boudouille*, *bouzine* – are other examples of the same linguistic distortion and inventiveness. The same applies to the mysterious *côtes de rastron* of the banquet scene in *Ubu Roi*, which mystified the audience at the play's performance in 1896 and which constituted originally the subject of a joke for initiates: one of the pupils of the Lycée, named Lemaux, who lived in the rue du Chapitre in Rennes, was given the nickname of 'Chapistron', which was then abbreviated to 'Chastron' before becoming finally (since *chat* and *rat* are opposites) 'Rastron'![39]

In addition to this linguistic deformation and invention which – in *Ubu Roi* at least – confused and upset his first adult audiences, Jarry also makes use in all these plays and fragments of a number of elements which derive from the original schoolboy folklore of Rennes and whose meaning, once they are removed from this context, is puzzling if not outright incomprehensible. The title of 'Maître des Finances' derives from the name *finance* (later to become *phynance*, a spelling possibly inspired by Jarry's favourite author, Rabelais) given to the loot or plunder of Père Heb. In the many tales and sketches comprising the Ébé legend, it became a kind of official title given to the character, and in turn gave rise to other terms denoting objects associated with his illustrious (and then regal) person: *casque à finances, cheval à finances, voiturin à phynances, pistolet à finances*, as well as to such expletives as *corne finance* and *sabre à finance*. The term *phynance* was also adopted by Jarry and Henri Morin for their marionette-theatre in 1888–9, which became the 'Théâtre des Phynances'. The loyal servants and henchmen of Père Heb, responsible for the collection of *phynance* and for brutally punishing those who refused to pay up, were the *palotins* or *palotins à phynance*. The name (which replaced the original *salopins à finance* used by Charles Morin) was probably derived from a fusion of *salopin, palatin* and *paladin* with overtones also of the *pal* – a stake upon which their victims were impaled – and of phallus. In *Ubu Roi* and *Ubu Cocu* their number has been reduced to three (and, in the former, their role considerably modified); in *Onésime* however they are 'une infinité de Palotins'. In origin, these *palotins* were the pupils of the Lycée themselves, in particular the boarders (of which Jarry was not one), as the several songs which they sing clearly reveal. In the first *Ubu Cocu*, for example, they introduce themselves singing the lines:

Dans de grandes boît's en fer-blanc
Empilés la semaine entière,
C'est le dimanche seulement
Qu'on peut respirer le libre air.
L'oreille au vent, sans s'épater,
On marche d'un pas assuré
Et les gens qui nous voient passer
Nous prennent pour des militaires.

> [*Kept in big tin boxes*
> *Stacked up all week,*
> *It's only on Sundays*
> *That we can breathe free air.*
> *Our ears to the wind, keeping close together,*
> *We walk with a confident step*
> *And the folks who see us go by*
> *Take us for soldiers.*][40]

The *palotins*' chief victims were the *rentiers* (those who live from property or investments – evidence of a nascent socio-political commitment amongst the pupils of the Lycée de Rennes?) upon whom they inflicted unspeakable tortures, such as the extraction of their brains, upon which Père Heb breakfasted. In particular, they were associated with three ingenious instruments of torture which represent a strange mixture of farce and sadism. The first of these was the *pal*, to which the unfortunate Achras falls victim on the orders of Ubu. Even more gruesome is the *machine à décerveler*, an object which even figures in the list of *dramatis personae* of *Ubu Roi* and which, with its attendant ceremonies, seems to embody the epitome of sadistic cruelty and horror. Its praises are sung in the *Chanson du Décervelage* which was inserted by Jarry into *Ubu Cocu* and which contains an accumulation of grotesque and horrific details ('voyez la cervell' sauter', 'pour pas salir mes godillots dans l'sang', 'bientôt ma femme et moi nous somm's tout blancs d'cervelle') ['see the brains spurt out', 'so I don't mess up my boots in the blood', 'soon my wife and I are white with spattered brains'].[41] Does this song, with its specific references to the topography of Rennes and the surrounding district, refer originally to some real public event which took place on Sundays (the 'jour de décervelage') and which was subsequently elaborated upon, constituting a denunciation of the cruelties of the adult world?[42] Or is the event purely a figment of a lurid schoolboy imagination? In either case, one can see the same imaginative processes at work here as in the invention of the *pompe Rouget* (it may even be that the *machine à décerveler* is an imaginative fusion of a guillotine and the machinery of a basement printing-works in Rennes which fascinated the pupils of the Lycée). It is also linked to the third object in this gallery of torture instruments, the *trappe*, which figures in both *Ubu Roi* and *Ubu Cocu*. Through its various associations, among them the 'trou' into which the unfortunate 'ouvrier ébéniste' is hurled head-first in the *Chanson du Décervelage* and the 'trou entre deux semelles de pierre' into which Achras is thrown in *Ubu Cocu*, it is evident that the *trappe* was originally some vague and horrible cess-pit (the same seems to be true of the *Chambre à sous* and *Pince-Porc* of both plays), becoming subsequently closely associated with the *machine à décerveler*. Other items deriving from the original folklore which are worthy of mention for one reason or another are: the crocodile (of *guignol* origin), which appears suddenly and mysteriously at the end of *Ubu Cocu* to produce a completely arbitrary *dénouement* of the intrigue (and which also figures in one of Jarry's woodcuts of his 'Symbolist' period); the *chiens à bas de laine*, referred to in passing in *Ubu Roi* and one of which figures in the list of characters of *Ubu Cocu*, whose function was to divest the *rentiers* of their shoes and stockings; the *chandelle verte*, made famous by Ubu's oath 'de par ma chandelle verte', which was originally a signal used by Père Heb to correspond with his henchmen, the candle being placed at his window; and the 'vingt-cinquième heure sidérale', the hour of Mère Ubu's tryst with her lover, which will reappear amid the apocalyptic outpourings of Jarry's 'Symbolist' drama, *César-Antechrist*. The inclusion or retention by Jarry of these and other such details without any attempt to render them more comprehensible to the uninitiated raises a tantalizing problem to which we shall have occasion to return. Was it the result of a desire to preserve authentic features of the original schoolboy folklore in their pristine purity? Or of a desire to mystify adult theatre audiences and readers?

All of these early plays and fragments of the Ébé/Ubu 'cycle' were given performances by Jarry, either live, or in his marionette-theatre, or in the shadow-theatre which succeeded it. No sooner had Henri Morin first shown him the manuscript of *Les Polonais* in the Winter of 1888 than Jarry, fired with enthusiasm, suggested adapting the play for the stage and performing it. The Morin family lived in a large house, the huge attic of which was admirably suited to such a purpose. Jarry himself painted the scenery, and both actors and audience were easily recruited from among their fellow-pupils (it says a great deal for the impersonal nature of this satirical fantasy that among the actors was the eldest daughter of M. Hébert himself).[43] The first performance by their 'Théâtre des Phynances' was given in December 1888, with Henri Morin in the role of Père Heb, whose enormous *gidouille* was filled out with pillows. It was a riotous success, and numerous other performances followed. Then, at the beginning of the Summer of 1889, the family moved to a smaller house. Jarry, thrown back upon his own resources, turned from the live theatre to the world of marionettes. The puppet-theatre was enormously popular in the nineteenth century with audiences of both children and adults alike, and no fair was complete without its *guignol*. Jarry had from a very early age been fascinated by this theatre, and as a small child he had played with his sister Charlotte at dressing up skittles as puppets. Now he, Charlotte and Henri Morin together fashioned a set of marionette characters for *Les Polonais*; Charlotte moulded out of clay a magnificent bust of Père Heb, *gidouille* and all (M. Hébert passed by her window every day, and she was able to capture a perfect likeness), while between them they also produced a splendid Tsar, looking like a jack-in-the-box.[44] The manipulation of these marionettes, however, proved to be too complicated, and in the winter of the same year Jarry turned instead to the creation in his own home of a shadow-theatre devoted primarily to further manifestations of Père Heb. This too proved to be extremely popular with friends and fellow-pupils at the Lycée. Despite the abandonment of the marionette experiment, it is significant that the idea of performing the future *Ubu Roi* and other works of the same 'cycle' as puppet-plays was present in Jarry's mind from the beginning. Indeed, a number of scenes, particularly in *Ubu Cocu* – for example, that in which Ubu is caught in the *trappe*, that of the impaling of Achras, and that in which Ubu's Conscience jumps in the air and is caught by the feet – suggest that such scenes were originally conceived for performance by marionettes. And, as we have already seen, when the text of *Ubu Roi* was eventually published in June 1896 (and when he came to write a final version of the first *Ubu Cocu*), it was to these early marionette performances alone that Jarry chose to refer.[45]

What sort of youth had Jarry developed into during these years at Rennes? He had lost none of his love of pranks and practical jokes: Charlotte relates two of his escapades, one an occasion on which he and Henri Morin, dressed up as monks, waylaid people on their way to the market in Rennes, the other a disastrous chemistry experiment which ended by burning the whole of the guttering of the family home with acid. He had now acquired a passion for fencing to add to his earlier passions for fishing, boating and cycling. At school, he was a brilliant and eccentric, rather than good, pupil. Though popular with his classmates, he nevertheless remained distant and, with the exception of Henri Morin, with whom his relations were particularly close, seems to have had few, if any, close friends. He was given to long cycling trips through the countryside (Charlotte refers to him cycling to the Mont St-Michel and back), and one wonders whether these feats of physical prowess were not, in part at least, a form of sublimation of some hidden adolescent distress. He was probably painfully self-conscious of his small stature: unusually short and thick-set, he was nicknamed by his schoolmates 'Quasimodo', after the hunchback of Hugo's *Notre-Dame de Paris*. Generally, in fact, both parents and pupils looked upon him with reserve and some apprehension; the tone is given by one former school-fellow, Henri Hertz, looking back many years later:

C'était un fort en thème. Mais pas un de ces forts en thème douillets, facilement monnayables. Les professeurs, les pères de famille hochaient la tête, d'un air débordé, en le nommant. On ne pouvait se servir de son exemple. Il montait de sa personne quelque chose d'acerbe.

Les parents en parlaient à voix basse. Élève remarquable, mais sans règle et sans sagesse. Pire qu'un mauvais élève, oh! oui, pire. Et précoce! En ses curiosités et ses moeurs, terrible précocité.

[He was a clever pupil. But not one of those goody-goody, easily manipulated clever pupils. Teachers and parents shook their heads, with an exasperated look, when they spoke of him. One could not cite him as an example to others. There was something caustic in his character and attitudes.

> Parents spoke of him in hushed tones. An outstanding pupil, but
> undisciplined and unruly. Worse than a bad pupil, oh indeed, worse! And
> precocious! In his interests and his behaviour, terribly precocious.][46]

According to another testimony recorded by Chassé, his speech was
deliberately coarse and full of sexual allusions.[47] Charlotte portrays
him rising at 5 a.m. to read and study, in his bedroom which he had
himself painted with white skeletons on a black background, surrounded by his dictionaries, guitar and rifle.[48] When he arrived at the
school in the morning, however, haggard and dishevelled, the story
he told was a different one, declaring with his staccato diction: 'Je vi
. . . ens des . . . bor . . . dels . . .'.[49] Of his unconventional methods
of study, Jarry himself later wrote that he had followed the advice of
his philosophy teacher, Bourdon, who allegedly told his pupils: 'Pour
vous préparer à un travail . . . commencez, plusieurs jours et au
besoin plusieurs mois à l'avance, par ne rien faire, ne rien étudier, ne
rien lire ou ne lire que des matières futiles et récréatives n'ayant
aucun rapport avec l'épreuve à subir.' ['To prepare yourself for an
examination . . . begin, several days and if need be several months in
advance, by doing nothing, studying nothing, reading nothing or
reading only trivial and light-weight things having nothing to do with
the examination to be sat.'][50]

Many of these retrospective views of Jarry need, however, to be
treated with some scepticism (Hertz, for example, was not in the
same class as Jarry). There is evidence also that, both at this time and
for some years to come, Jarry was to remain a loyal and devoted son,
brother and nephew, by no means as ready to throw over all the
conventions of respectable 'bourgeois' society as these accounts
suggest. It seems highly probable that the authors of these accounts
unwittingly exaggerated certain features of his character and behaviour in the light of what he was later to become and of the 'legend'
thus created. Amidst this uncertainty, however, one thing in particular seems indisputable. By the end of his second year at the Lycée de
Rennes, Jarry, whose seventeenth birthday was only a month or so
away, was at an age at which others (such as the Morin brothers)
were beginning to leave 'childish' things behind them and to set forth
on the path to a career in the 'serious' world of adulthood. But where
others rapidly left behind and forgot the activities and productions of
these years, Jarry – precocious, intelligent, wise beyond his years in
many respects – nonetheless remained extraordinarily attached to the
figure of Ébé/Ubu and to the various legends surrounding that
figure. His attachment to this creation of his boyhood years, and to
the *spirit* which it incarnated, is and will remain one of the most
constant and striking features of his whole career.

Jarry passed the first part of his *baccalauréat* (then an examination

in two parts) without distinction in July 1889. Perhaps a more accurate reflection of his abilities was his performance in the 'Concours
Général des Départments' for that year, in which he was runner-up in
Latin Unseen Translation – clear evidence of what he could achieve if
he chose to make the effort. A year later, in July 1890, both he and
Henri Morin obtained the second part of their *baccalauréat*, this time
with credit (*mention Bien*). From this point, his movements are
uncertain. Did he stay on at the Lycée de Rennes for a third year?
What seems in any case certain is that he used the year 1890–1 to
prepare for entry to one of the Parisian *grandes écoles* – though the
question of which one had caused him to hesitate for some considerable time. Up to the end of his first year at Rennes, his work in the
sciences and mathematics had been every bit as good as that in the
humanities, and his mother wished him to try for entry, like his
friend Henri Morin, to the École Polytechnique, most prestigious of
all the *grandes écoles*. This at least is the testimony of Morin – looking
back many years later from the standpoint of a middle-aged army
officer and respectable citizen:

Jarry lui-même était un esprit très clair – il était à dix-sept ans aussi bon
mathématicien que rhétoricien brillant et, après avoir passé son bachot ès
lettres 1re partie, il fut sur le point de se tourner vers les études scientifiques,
ce qui aurait été beaucoup plus conforme aux désirs de sa famille que la voie
qu'il suivit par la suite – mais en même temps qu'un esprit clair, c'était un
grand pince-sans-rire et un grand mystificateur.

> [Jarry himself had a very good mind – at seventeen, he was as good at
> mathematics as he was brilliant in the humanities, and, after taking the first
> part of his *baccalauréat* in the humanities, he was on the point of turning
> towards the sciences, which would have been much more in keeping with the
> wishes of his family than the path which he took subsequently. But while
> having a good mind, he was also a great practical joker and a great hoaxer.][51]

Instead, Jarry chose the humanities, and in June 1891 sat the *concours
d'entrée* of the École Normale Supérieure for the first time, though
failing to pass even the written examination. Undaunted, he persuaded his mother to let him enrol in 'Rhétorique supérieure' (as it
was then called) at the prestigious Lycée Henri IV in Paris, in order to
continue preparation for the entrance examinations to Normale
Supérieure. And so, in the late summer or early autumn of 1891, Jarry
left Rennes for good to make his mark upon the capital.

Chapter Two

Paris, poets and artists

PARIS, for Jarry, would come ultimately to represent freedom – an escape from the narrow provincialism of Rennes and from the restrictions of home and family – and to constitute the centre of his existence. But for the moment, such a development still lay in the future. At the Lycée Henri IV, he applied himself seriously to his studies and was a conscientious worker, despite a talent for jokes and witty remarks which often had the class in an uproar (and which led one former fellow-pupil to speak of 'son incapacité apparente d'aborder quoi que ce soit autrement que par l'ironie' ['his apparent inability to approach any subject other than in a spirit of irony'].[1]) Here, too, he listened attentively to the philosopher Henri Bergson, whose first major work, *Essai sur les données immédiates de la conscience*, had appeared only a few years earlier, in 1888. Jarry was later to describe Bergson's philosophical teaching as 'précieux entre tous', and to recall Bergson '[improvisant] devant ces adolescents s'éveillant au sérieux, sa théorie du rire' ['precious above all others'; '[improvising], before these adolescents awakening to seriousness, his theory of laughter'][2] – a theory fully formulated in *Le Rire, essai sur la signification du comique*, published in 1900. Jarry's knowledge of the classics was exemplary if unconventional; when on one occasion his Latin teacher congratulated him on his style in composition and ventured to ask which author Jarry had modelled himself upon, he was astonished to receive the reply that it was Aristophanes – not the Greek text, but the many footnoted translations and explanations in Latin of obscene passages in the original.[3] He was also developing a reputation among his fellow-pupils as a strange and compelling *raconteur*, whose mind ranged rapidly over widely disparate areas of knowledge.

Jarry remained at Henri IV for two years, his second year somewhat interrupted by illness, leaving at the end of the school year 1892–3. His examination results at Henri IV show him to have been a good, but by no means outstanding, pupil. The same is true of his results in the very difficult competitive entrance examination for the

École Normale Supérieure. He made three attempts to pass this examination, each of them unsuccessful; he also enrolled for a fourth attempt, but did not sit the examination. (It is interesting to note that in each examination his marks in history were uniformly lamentable. Perhaps this lack of success is a pointer to the lack of interest in, and indeed contempt for, the specificity of history which he was to display throughout his later life.) After his repeated failure to enter the École Normale Supérieure, he made two further attempts to obtain a higher educational qualification: in March, and then again in October 1894, he sat for the examinations for the Licence-ès-Lettres at the Sorbonne, but again failed. It is striking that even after the death of his mother, Jarry continued for a time to harbour academic ambitions. The fact once again reveals him to have been at this time by no means the anti-Establishment rebel he has so frequently been portrayed. Indeed, the picture which emerges of him during this period is on the whole that of a somewhat reserved, respectful and even shy young man, conventional in his dress and sober in his habits. Charles-Henry Hirsch, who knew him around 1892, remembered him as 'cet adolescent à la parole douce et réfléchie', whose conduct was 'sage et fort ordonnée' and whose outlook was still both provincial and *bourgeois*;[4] whilst the sheaf of letters published by Noël Arnaud in his biography of Jarry reveals him to be a loyal and warm-hearted friend, polite, courteous and considerate – a far cry from the image he was deliberately to create in the wake of the scandal of *Ubu Roi* in 1896.

Although Jarry and Henri Morin (who had also gone to Paris) remained close friends and continued to see each other at intervals, it was Léon-Paul Fargue, who arrived at Henri IV in the spring of 1892, who soon became his most intimate friend. Much remains obscure in their relationship, and Fargue himself is an extremely unreliable source of information: many of his friends in later life, and even his wife, attested to his extraordinary capacity for deforming truth at will.[5] Despite his repeated assertions, they were never in the same class together at Henri IV, and could not have been: Fargue at this time had not even obtained the first part of his *bacculauréat*, at which he was to fail lamentably in July 1893. On the other hand, his fictions may reveal something of the closeness of their association: not only did Fargue through Jarry meet many of the latter's classmates, and possibly even attend some of the classes of Bergson, but also, looking back in later years, perhaps came really to believe that he had been one of them. The reaction of Fargue's parents to Jarry is also a matter of some confusion. Fargue later maintained that Jarry visited the family frequently and that his parents were very fond of him.[6] But his mother has been quoted as referring to Jarry as a 'mauvaise fréquentation' of her son;[7] and in April 1893, Fargue was banished by his father to Germany where he was placed under strict supervision, not only for the sake of his studies, but also to remove him (in the words of a letter from his father) from 'la société d'un jeune homme beaucoup trop âgé pour toi'[8] – an almost certain reference to Jarry, who was two and a half years his senior. The association, and even the 'identification', of the two young men is a theme that was to be exploited by Jarry in both *Haldernablou* and *Les Jours et les Nuits*.

That the relationship between Jarry and Fargue (several of whose friends testified to his strikingly handsome appearance at this time) was a homosexual one is certain, both from a number of snide references made by mutual friends and acquaintances, and from Jarry's own dramatization of that relationship in *Haldernablou*. Of the two, Jarry (as *Haldernablou* clearly indicates) was undoubtedly the more possessive, Fargue refusing to limit his friendship exclusively to Jarry. Their relationship was as a result an intense but turbulent one, involving frequent quarrels and even a number of actual fights. It was to end abruptly towards the end of 1894 or early in 1895, and was followed by a refusal ever to speak to each other again. Nevertheless it was to leave a deep impact on both young men, an impact which can be gauged, in Jarry's case, from the pages of *Haldernablou* and *Les Jours et les Nuits*, and in that of Fargue from his life-long reluctance to discuss the subject of their friendship.

Nevertheless, Fargue has left us a valuable portrait of his former friend at this period:

Alfred Jarry était déjà un poète ingénieux, précis, très artiste, et, comme homme, affectueux et même sentimental. Il parlait vite, d'une jolie voix nette et qui n'avait rien encore de cette sécheresse fabriquée, de cet accent ubuesque, de ces attitudes qu'il devait adopter par la suite. Il était seul à Paris, il venait souvent chez mes parents et nous l'aimions beaucoup.

> Alfred Jarry was already an ingenious, precise, very artistic poet, and, as a man, was affectionate and even sentimental. He spoke rapidly, in a clear, pleasant voice which as yet had nothing of that artificial harshness, of that *ubuesque* accent, of those attitudes which he was to adopt subsequently. He was alone in Paris, he often visited my parents' house and we were fond of him.][9]

The two young men were both indefatigable sightseers, and together they tramped and cycled the length and breadth of Paris on a voyage of discovery of the capital – a foreshadowing of the journey 'from Paris to Paris by sea' undertaken by Jarry's Dr Faustroll. Fargue, a Parisian by birth and upbringing, was undoubtedly the leader in these expeditions. He was, however, less fanatical about cycling than Jarry, and is probably the object of the latter's reproaches in *Les Jours et les Nuits* directed at those who 'ne [savent] pas cycler assez pour jouir de la vitesse'.[10] Amongst their favourite haunts were the cafés and bars of Montparnasse, then one of the centres of the artistic 'Bohemia' of Paris, and the area stretching along the banks of the Bièvre, recently celebrated by Huysmans in a little work of 1890 entitled *La Bièvre*. Bordered on both sides by grim tanneries with their tall chimneys, its foul-smelling and murky waters, now covered over and forming part of the underground sewerage network of Paris, but then still flowing openly through one of the most depressed and poverty-stricken areas of the capital, conjured up in their minds visions of some fantastic hell.[11]

No less fantastic was Jarry's abode during part of this time. Until her death in 1893, he lived with his mother, who had left Rennes in order to be near her son, in an apartment at No. 84 Boulevard de Port-Royal. He continued to live here for some time thereafter as well. A short distance away, however, at No. 78 Boulevard de Port-Royal, he had rented a tiny apartment at the end of an alley-way no more than four feet across at its widest point, which he used as an art studio, as a store-room, and as a place for receiving his friends. Giving free rein both to his imagination and to a talent for mystification, Jarry baptized this his 'Calvaire du Trucidé'. Everything about its décor was deliberately contrived to create an air of mystery and of the sinister. The walls were hung with black cloth; a skeleton and assorted bones were suspended from the walls and ceiling, which were illuminated by a candle placed in a skull; and the imprints of blood-stained hands were to be seen in the narrow, winding staircase. Here, too, he kept his beloved owls, prized because they were regarded by the 'stupid herd' as maleficent creatures and because their nocturnal habits matched his own.[12]

More importantly, perhaps, both here and in an apartment at 162 Boulevard St-Germain to which he subsequently moved, Jarry set up a makeshift puppet-theatre. With Henri Morin, and then with Fargue and others, he recited and organized performances of the future *Ubu Roi* and *Ubu Cocu* before enthusiastic audiences of fellow-students from Henri IV and other friends. He so 'saturated' Fargue, in fact, with Ubu during the period of their friendship that some 40 or 50 years later, Fargue could still perfectly remember and reproduce the diction of Hébert/Ubu which he had learned from Jarry as well as those of Achras and Ubu's Conscience, and could recite long extracts from *Ubu Cocu* (the text of which was not published until 1944).[13] He also continued to work on the two plays from time to time, developing, adapting, rearranging. It was at some time during these early years in Paris – and by the beginning of 1893 at the latest – that the name 'Ubu' was discovered.

It was with Fargue also that he made a discovery which constituted for the young man from the provinces a veritable 'New World' and a 'revelation', and which was to have a determining influence on his career – that of the new literature of Symbolism. Jarry's arrival in Paris happily coincided with the most active phase in the history of the Symbolist movement. Starting in the mid-1880s as the banner of one among several warring literary factions, by the beginning of the 1890s the term 'Symbolism' had come to designate a broad front of self-consciously 'modernist' writers hostile to the hitherto dominant doctrines of 'realism' and 'naturalism' and united above all by a common devotion to the all-consuming cause of 'Art'. The atmosphere of excitement which accompanied the discovery of the new literature, made all the greater by the efforts of school and university authorities to keep their charges in ignorance of it, was evoked by Jarry in an article written towards the end of his life:

On imagine à peine aujourd'hui, où les révolutionnaires d'un peu lointain passé sont des gloires admises, l'éblouissement que ne connurent peut-être point d'autres générations et qui, vers 1892, transporta maints jeunes hommes de vingt ans, amoureux de belles lettres et croyant alors ne les point ignorer, quand leur fut révélée une littérature qui s'avisait manifestment l'unique – au moins – à leurs enthousiasmes d'alors. . . . Et c'est vers ces temps-là que la révélation eut lieu, le verset de l'Apocalypse n'est point trop grandiloquent: 'le ciel se replia comme un livre qu'on roule'.

> [It is difficult to imagine now, when the revolutionaries of a not-too-distant past are accepted and hallowed figures, the sense of wonder which other generations have perhaps not experienced but which, around 1892, enraptured many young men of twenty, enamoured of literature and believing that they had discovered it all, when there was revealed unto them a literature which manifestly appeared to be the only one – at least – in their enthusiastic eyes at that time. . . . And it was around that time that the revelation occurred, the verse from the *Book of Revelation* is not too grandiloquent to describe it: 'And the heaven departed as a scroll when it is rolled together'.][14]

Among those whose work was part of this discovery, Jarry lists Verlaine, Mallarmé, Rimbaud, Laforgue, Lautréamont, Tailhade, Kahn, Régnier, Viélé-Griffin, Louys, Quillard, Maeterlinck, Van Leberghe, Verhaeren, Saint-Pol Roux, Renard and Samain. Of those still alive – the majority – almost all were soon to become acquaintances, and many of them friends, of Jarry himself.

The flourishing of the Symbolist movement was accompanied by a vast proliferation of literary reviews, numbering well over a hundred and perhaps as many as several hundred in all. Though small and all too often emphemeral, these played a vital part in the literary life of the time; to be published in their pages was the ambition and consecration of many an aspiring young writer on the path to higher things. Amongst this plethora of literary reviews, three were of paramount importance: the *Mercure de France*, founded in 1890 in a successful attempt to bring together all the leading figures associated with Symbolism (and which was to survive, as a broader-based literary journal, until 1965); the *Revue Blanche* (1891–1903), like the *Mercure* at the forefront of Symbolism and sharing many of its collaborators, but leaning also towards politics and in particular towards the fashionable 'anarchism' of the period; and, on the fringes of the movement, the somewhat eclectic *La Plume* (1889–1904). All three were to play a crucial role in the life and literary career of Jarry, the *Mercure* and the *Revue Blanche* publishing between them the majority of his literary works, and the latter, together with *La Plume*, providing his chief source of financial support in return for his 'journalistic' work between 1900 and 1903.

The immediate excitement of this discovery, however, was soon dissipated by other events. From January to March 1893, Jarry lay seriously ill – at death's door, according to his sister[15] – nursed devotedly by his mother. Scarcely had her son recovered when Caroline Jarry, presumably worn out by her labours, died, on 10 May 1893, at the age of 49 years. It was a loss from which her son never fully recovered. Among his papers, he carefully preserved the receipt for a grandiose memorial service, paid for by his father, celebrated on 11 May 1894 in the church of St-Jacques du Haut Pas.[16] The theme of death which runs so insistently through his literary work from beginning to end undoubtedly owes something, and probably a good deal, to the loss of his mother.

By an irony of fate, Jarry's illness and the death of his mother coincided with his first literary successes. Since September 1892, the prestigious and highly influential *Écho de Paris* had held a monthly literary competition which offered to aspiring young writers the prospect of four valuable and much coveted prizes of 100 francs each – one for poetry, the other three for short prose works – and a guarantee of publication in the paper's weekly illustrated literary supplement. Between February and August 1893, Jarry was to win outright or to share five such prizes, with poems or prose texts which would be republished the following year in his first book, *Les Minutes de sable mémorial*. The first of these was the poem 'Châsse claire où s'endort mon amour chaste et cher', probably written by Jarry and Fargue in collaboration[17] and which exhibited a superabundance of (deliberately forced) alliterations. The second, and most significant, was a three-part text in prose entitled *Guignol*, published in the *Écho de Paris littéraire illustré* of 23 April 1893, the first and third sections of which were composed of extracts from the future *Ubu Cocu*, portraying respectively Ubu's invasion of the home of Achras and the latter's subsequent impaling, and – under the sub-title of 'L'Art et la Science' – the secret rendezvous of Mère Ubu with her lover. Jarry's choice of these scenes as his first prose entry for the competition –

and therefore almost his first aspiration to appear in print – was certainly no accident; and nor was the fact that it was in the first part of *Guignol* that his 'science of pataphysics' was first introduced, in the immortal lines:

M. UBU: Ceci vous plaît à dire, monsieur, mais vous parlez à un grand pataphysicien.
ACHRAS: Pardon, monsieur, vous dites? . . .
M. UBU: Pataphysicien. La pataphysique est une science que nous avons inventée, et dont le besoin se faisait généralement sentir.

> [M. UBU: It pleases you to say so, Sir, but you are speaking to a great pataphysician.
> ACHRAS: I beg your pardon, Sir, you said? . . .
> M. UBU: Pataphysician. Pataphysics is a science which we have invented and for which a general need was felt.]

L'Écho de Paris included on its board of directors Marcel Schwob, Catulle Mendès, Henry Bauer, Jean Lorrain, Armand Silvestre and Octave Mirbeau, all of whom were to become firm friends and supporters in his campaign for the staging of *Ubu Roi*. His next most immediate stepping-stone, however, was to be a monthly literary review entitled *L'Art Littéraire*, founded in 1892 by Louis Lormel (*alias* of Louis Libaude), a young auctioneer turned man of letters – according to Fargue, he specialized in the sale of horses.[18] Jarry became a regular contributor to the review from December 1893 onwards, in the wake of Fargue who had probably been responsible for introducing him to Lormel, with a supply of poems, literary and art criticism, 'philosophical' texts, and the first act of the future *César-Antechrist*, his contributions appearing alongside those of Remy de Gourmont, Fargue, René Ghil, Gustave Kahn, Saint-Pol-Roux and, on one occasion, Mallarmé. He also became – particularly following the receipt of an uncle's legacy in 1894 – a valued financial contributor to *L'Art Littéraire*, whose financial support came mainly from its literary contributors. Though desperately poor for much of his life, Jarry spent recklessly and gave generously on those occasions when he had money. He was also a frequent attender of the cafés and other haunts where the editorial staff and contributors of the journal met, and where he rubbed shoulders with many other promising young men of letters. In fact it was as much in bars, cafés and restaurants as in the offices of publishers and editors and at literary gatherings that Jarry met his future literary colleagues and associates, a fact which serves to highlight the spirit of joyous *camaraderie* which pervaded much of the literary and artistic life of the age. Lormel, looking back some 13 years later, recalled Jarry at these gatherings in terms which betray his own sense of bewilderment and fascination:

J'y vois encore Jarry, petit et nerveux, brun et pâle, dont les yeux sombres, dans la face immobile, flambaient, articuler lentement, avec la prononciation accentuée du Père Ubu [?] et l'intonation bizarre qu'il s'amusait souvent à prendre, quelque paradoxe qu'il cherchait ensuite à démontrer à grand renfort d'erudition. Il voulait étonner et déconcerter. . . . Il aimait les traditions archaïques, les cas étranges, les faits sans explication.

> [I can still see Jarry there, short and highly-strung, with black hair and a pale complexion, whose dark eyes shone out of his motionless face, slowly enunciating, with the staccato delivery of Père Ubu [?] and the weird intonation which he often enjoyed adopting, some paradox which he then sought to prove with the aid of a great display of erudition. He wanted to surprise and to disconcert. . . . He loved archaic traditions, strange events, unexplained facts.][19]

The two men quarrelled, and Jarry's contributions ceased, in the second half of 1894, followed not long afterwards by the disappearance of the review. (Jarry, whose susceptibilities were particularly acute, had a talent for quarrelling with his friends.) But *L'Art Littéraire* had never been for him more than a stepping-stone to higher things. While contributing to it, he had also begun to publish in the rival *Les Essais d'Art Libre*. In the meantime, his and Fargue's contributions in *L'Art Littéraire* had brought them to the attention of the founder-editor of the *Mercure de France*, Alfred Vallette. They were soon invited to attend, and became regular visitors to, the celebrated Tuesday evening gatherings of the *Mercure*, held above its offices in the old and narrow Rue de l'Échaudé-Saint-Germain and presided over by Vallette's witty and attractive young novelist-wife, Marguerite Eymery, who wrote under the name of Rachilde. On 3 April 1894, Jarry became a share-holder in the 'Société anonyme du Mercure de France' with the purchase of four 100-franc shares. The receipt, signed by Vallette, reveals that he had already adopted the title of *homme de lettres*.[20]

It was under the aegis of the *Mercure* that the greater part of Jarry's early literary activity was conducted. The years from 1894 to 1899 – when he was aged between 20 and 26 – constituted a period of remarkable creativity in his career, and during this time all but one of his books, and many smaller-scale works, were either published by the Éditions du Mercure de France or appeared in the pages of its review. In March 1894, Jarry had sent to Vallette a translation of Coleridge's *Rime of the Ancient Mariner* under the title of *Le Dit du Vieux Marin*. Though Vallette refused the manuscript, he did accept for publication in the edition of the review for July 1894 the poetic drama *Haldernablou*. This was incorporated into *Les Minutes de sable mémorial*, published by the Éditions du Mercure de France in October 1894, in a small but respectable edition of 216 copies and – as was the custom – at the author's expense. Jarry's first book to be published, it was enthusiastically reviewed in the October issue of the *Mercure* review by Remy de Gourmont. Further contributions from Jarry followed, culminating a year later in the publication of his second book, the 'apocalyptic' drama *César-Antechrist*, the last major work of his 'Symbolist' phase.

Jarry's relations with the Vallettes form a curious chapter in his career. For the rest of his life, Vallette and his wife were to prove to be among his most staunch friends (despite profound misgivings on Vallette's part in his role as editor and publisher), and were to be at times almost a second family to him. Yet Vallette, an energetic and shrewd businessman, methodical, unimaginative and eminently rational (Fargue called him 'un des hommes les plus raisonnables que j'eusse connus'[21]), could scarcely have been further removed in character and temperament from Jarry himself. Even more surprising is the relationship which grew up between Jarry and Rachilde. She was a fashionable and successful novelist, who turned out novels almost at the rate of one a year on subjects both in vogue and, preferably, tinged with a vague aura of vice or scandal (for example, *Les Hors-Nature, roman de moeurs contemporaines* appeared in 1897, shortly after the Oscar Wilde/Lord Alfred Douglas scandal). Yet she seems to have been the only woman whom Jarry respected intellectually and whom he deigned to treat as an equal. He reviewed her books enthusiastically as they appeared, and even went so far as to pronounce the words 'genius' and 'masterpiece' with regard to her work.[22] The misjudgment seems to have been mutual: Jarry (due to his ignorance of womankind in general?) consistently overestimated her talents, while she, in spite of her claim to have known him more intimately than anyone else, totally failed, as her interesting but largely anecdotal biography, published 21 years after his death, reveals,[23] to grasp the real motivations underlying his eccentric behaviour. In fact, throughout her book she *never* has Jarry speak in other than a deliberately stilted, *ubuesque* manner. Was it really the case that he never once lowered his mask throughout the many years of their friendship? It scarcely seems credible, however much Jarry may have played a game with his friends and hosts. The inability of friends such as Vallette and Rachilde to penetrate beneath the mask is all the more regrettable in view of the fact that others, such as Fargue and Gourmont, who knew him intimately and who might have provided some insight into his mind and character, are strangely reticent, both about Jarry himself and about their relationship with him.

Alongside Vallette and his wife, two other figures stand out as friends, mentors and 'patrons' of Jarry in these early years of his literary career. The first is Marcel Schwob, whom he and Fargue had first met through *L'Écho de Paris*, of which he was literary editor. One of the most erudite of writers associated with the Symbolist movement (Jarry in his *Almanach du Père Ubu* of 1899 referred to him as 'celui qui sait'), his breadth of learning and taste for the fantastic had immediately appealed to the two young men. Schwob had invited them to his home where he had enchanted them by his conversation and read to them from little-known English works belonging in particular to the Gothic horror tradition and from such imaginative works as *The Thousand and One Nights*.[24] *Ubu Roi* was dedicated to him by Jarry on its publication in 1896, while by a curious parallel Paul Valéry dedicated his *Une Soirée avec M. Teste*, also published in 1896, to the same man.

But the man with whom Jarry's intellectual and working relations were closest during the years 1894 and 1895, and whose influence was one of the determining factors in his career, was undoubtedly Remy de Gourmont. The extent of his debt was implicitly acknowledged by Jarry himself in the dedication which followed the title of *Haldernablou*: 'Appartient à Remy de Gourmont'. The two probably met in 1893 through Lormel: Gourmont was one of the patrons of *L'Art Littéraire*, as well as a co-founder and guiding spirit of the *Mercure de France* to which he was a regular and invaluable contributor, and it may well have been he who first drew Vallette's attention to Jarry. By the time of their meeting, Gourmont was well on the way to establishing a reputation as an important essayist and novelist, as a scholar with wide-ranging and idiosyncratic interests, and as one of the most perspicacious critics associated with the Symbolist movement. His publications included a novel, *Sixtine, roman de la vie cérébrale* (1890), a vast and erudite collection of studies and translations of medieval Latin mystical and religious verse from the fifth to the twelfth centuries entitled *Le Latin mystique* (1892), a number of dramatic prose-poems, and a large number of influential literary and philosophical essays including several published as a volume by the Éditions du Mercure de France in 1893 under the title *L'Idéalisme*. (He was also the author of a scathingly satirical pamphlet entitled *Le Joujou patriotisme*, whose publication in 1891 caused him to lose the administrative post which he had held at the Bibliothèque Nationale since 1884.) Gourmont's interests and writings held an immediate appeal for the young Jarry. He and Fargue were frequent visitors to Gourmont's home in Paris, where he lived almost as a recluse since his affliction in 1891 with a painfully disfiguring skin disease, attended by his mistress and self-styled 'cousin' Berthe (de) Courrière – the ennobling *particule* was of her own invention. The full extent of his profound influence on the ideas of the young Jarry will be seen in the following chapter.

At the *soirées* of the *Mercure*, Jarry met many of the leading or up-and-coming writers associated with Symbolism – among them the poets Henri de Régnier, Francis Viélé-Griffin, Paul Fort, Paul Valéry, Gustave Kahn and Laurent Tailhade, and the novelists or prose-writers Jean de Tinan, Louis Dumur, André Gide (who felt little sympathy for him), and the passionate Catholic novelist Léon Bloy, whose fiery temperament and bluster Jarry obviously appreciated.[25] He also made the acquaintance of a number of men with whom he was later to be in one way or another closely involved, among them A.-Ferdinand Hérold, poet, playwright and translator of texts from Greek, Latin, German and Sanskrit, who was to introduce him to the young theatre director, Lugné-Poe, and whom he was later to work alongside in the 'Théâtre des Pantins' in 1897–8; Pierre Quillard, erudite poet, translator and critic, who was to be the author of one of the first and most lucid, if brief, studies of his work;[26] and Eugène Demolder, a Belgian writer who was to become a regular fishing and cycling companion in later years. Many of these men were amongst the audience to whom Jarry read aloud, probably at a number of the *Mercure's soirées*, extracts from or the complete text of *Ubu Roi*, which was thus known to the *habitués* of the review long before its publication and first live performance.[27]

By the end of 1894 or early in 1895, therefore, Jarry had succeeded in penetrating the most important of the literary *milieux* of the age and in becoming one of its regular members. Important as the *Mercure* and its circle were to him, however, they were by no means the only pole of attraction in these early years. Alongside his acquaintance with a number of leading theatre critics, mentioned earlier, he also made that of Félix Fénéon, one of the most perspicacious literary and art critics of the time and editor from 1894 of *La Revue Blanche*, who quickly perceived the merits of his work and opened the pages of the review to him. And in the offices of the *Revue Blanche* he met its proprietors, the three Natanson brothers ('ceux qui Revuent Blanche', in the *Almanach du Père Ubu* of 1899), of whom Alexandre and above all Thadée were to prove to be among his most loyal and generous friends in the last years of his life. Above all else, some time in 1894 Jarry and Fargue succeeded in penetrating the Symbolist holy-of-holies itself, the *mardis* of Mallarmé, the uncontested master of a whole generation of young poets and prose writers who regarded him with an almost religious veneration. Fargue refers to 'several visits' which he and Jarry made together,[28] and it is possible that Jarry, for a time at least, alternated these visits with attendances at the receptions of the *Mercure*. Like most aspiring young writers who attended these gatherings in the rue de Rome, he was fascinated and beguiled by Mallarmé, who through his conversation as much as his writings exercised an enormous influence over the whole of the younger literary generation; and, on one occasion at least, he was among the last to leave, remaining listening to the master until

2 a.m.[29] The cordial relations between the two men are attested to also by their correspondence: five letters from Mallarmé to Jarry have survived, written in response to the latter's gift of each of his early books to be published, in which the poet warmly praised the work of his young disciple.

But Jarry's interests and acquaintances at this time were by no means restricted to the world of letters. Both he and Fargue were passionately interested in art, and spent many hours visiting exhibitions and the studios of painters. Here too it may well have been the Parisian Fargue who led the way, although it had been Gourmont, together with his late friend and colleague G.-Albert Aurier, who had first singled out for praise the work of a number of emerging young artists who were to become favourites of Jarry. One of their favourite haunts was the small private gallery of Le Barc de Bouteville, a patron and exhibitor of many of the younger artists: here they saw works by Gauguin, Sérusier, Bonnard, Denis, Vallotton and Vuillard, among others. Together, too, they tried their hand at art criticism: Fargue's first article was published in *L'Art Littéraire* in December 1893, while a number of articles by Jarry entitled 'Minutes d'Art' were published in the issue of *Les Essais d'Art Libre* dated February-March-April 1894 and in *L'Art Littéraire* of March–April and May–June 1894. In part, of course, the two young men were following a fashion: such was the tradition of mutual interest and support between men of letters and painters that had existed in France since Baudelaire that the Symbolists, once they had established themselves, cast around for artists whose work appeared to parallel their own, and the young intellectuals of the movement devoted a great deal of time to, and exercised a considerable influence in, the field of art criticism. But Jarry's interest was also genuine and lasting, and his articles and reviews of exhibitions, though written in the often wilfully obscure and contorted style popular among the Symbolists, reveal a profound sympathy for and understanding of the works they describe. During these years, too, he maintained an active correspondence with a large number of artists; among those whose letters to him have survived are Filiger, Seguin, Alphonse Osbert, Henri Rousseau, Pierre Bonnard, Paul Ranson, the Dutch painter Léonard Sarluis (the 'Raphaël Roissoy' of *Les Jours et les Nuits*), and the engravers Hermann-Paul and Maurice Delcourt.[30] Indeed, one fact which emerges from this correspondence is the closeness of Jarry's relations with his chosen painters – to the point where Armand Seguin, for example, could write to him asking for his help in 'placing' his paintings, and Filiger could write begging for a loan of 1,000 francs, a loan which was obviously not the first which he had requested of Jarry.[31]

Jarry's career as art critic thus began almost before he established himself as a writer. Although that career proved to be short-lived – after 1894 he published only a further two short articles – his reticence was probably due to the fact that the position of art critic on those reviews with which he was associated, other than *L'Art Littéraire*, which ceased publication towards the end of 1894, was in all cases already filled, often (as was the case most notably with the *Mercure de France*) by men of decidedly lesser talent and perception. Such was his artistic understanding and sympathy that it was he whom Gourmont chose to assist him, in the place of the now-departed brilliant art critic Aurier, in editing the sumptuous publication which he founded in 1894, entitled *L'Ymagier*. And in addition to his reviews of exhibitions and his art criticism as such, Jarry sought in his literary work to recapture the atmosphere and characteristics of this art, creating in the process what was in effect a new literary genre which reaches its culmination in his brilliant evocation of the imaginative and pictorial universe of painters in the *Gestes et opinions du docteur Faustroll, pataphysicien* of 1898.

The most famous of Jarry's acquaintances and of the painters he admired was Gauguin who, since his establishment in 1886 in the artistic colonies of Pont-Aven and Le Pouldu in south-western Brittany and his visit to Tahiti, had become something of a cult-figure among the Symbolists, in whose work they believed that they could see an embodiment of the ambiguity, mystery and invitation to search for a hidden meaning which was their own artistic goal. Jarry probably met Gauguin in the offices of *Les Essais d'Art Libre*, to which the painter also contributed, and in June 1894 during a visit to Brittany he stayed for several days with him at the Pension Gloanec in Pont-Aven – by this time something of a Mecca of the world of art.[32] He also visited the painter's great Tahitian exhibition which had opened in the Galerie Durand-Ruel in November 1893, which directly inspired three poems bearing the dedication 'd'après et pour Paul Gauguin' whose titles were borrowed from three paintings by Gauguin: 'L'Homme à la hache', 'Ia Orana Maria' and 'Manao Tùpapaù'.[33] These poems represent an attempt to render in words – not by means of a literal description, but through the creation of a series of evocative and interrelated images – the exotic or fantastic world of Gauguin's paintings. The same effort was continued some years later in a chapter of *Faustroll*, also dedicated to Gauguin, which is devoted to an evocation of the fragrant and exotic world of his Tahitian paintings.

Another noteworthy acquaintance was the fiery and gifted young artist Émile Bernard, a friend since their schooldays of Louis Lormel, and closely associated with *L'Art Littéraire*. A former friend, and later bitter enemy, of Gauguin, Bernard had arrived in Pont-Aven in 1886.

It was he who had been the initiator of 'Symbolism' in painting and who had pointed the way forward to Gauguin before becoming a religious convert as a result of his sojourn in Brittany. In *Faustroll*, Jarry was to seek to evoke impressionistically the world of his paintings also in a chapter entitled 'Du Bois d'Amour', the name of a local beauty-spot near Pont-Aven which figures in several of Bernard's canvasses along with scenes from the popular festivals and dances which were held there, and which was made famous by a painting by Paul Sérusier. Yet another artist with whom he was associated was Charles Filiger, a painter of Alsatian origin who had illustrated Gourmont's *Le Latin mystique* and *L'Idéalisme* and who was one of the strangest figures associated with the colonies of Pont-Aven and Le Pouldu, where he had arrived in 1890 and where Jarry visited him in 1894. Of profoundly mystical inclinations, he retreated increasingly into paranoia and drink, writing from the depths of his reclusion long, mystico-philosophical letters to friends in Paris, Jarry among them. Jarry was among the first and most appreciative critics of Filiger's work, and the only one to write at length about him, in an article inspired by his encounter with the painter at Pont-Aven which was published in the *Mercure de France* in September 1894.

A more famous acquaintance was Henri Rousseau, familiarly but incorrectly known to his contemporaries as the 'douanier'. The story (which appears to have been put about by Jarry's friends, among them Lormel and Apollinaire, and which was swallowed whole by Charles Chassé) that Rousseau was first 'discovered' by Jarry, who had decided to publicize his work as a huge practical joke, is totally without foundation: Rousseau had been exhibiting at the Salon des Indépendants since 1886. Though Fargue maintains that he and Jarry together first encountered Rousseau in the course of their walks around Paris,[34] it is equally possible that the two men met in 1893 when they were for a time near-neighbours on the Boulevard de Port-Royal. Both natives of Laval, where their respective families had long had links, they quickly became close friends despite the almost 30 years difference in age, and when Jarry was expelled in 1897 from his lodgings he sought refuge with the older man, who generously gave up half of his bed for a period of several weeks. Jarry praised Rousseau's *La Guerre* in two of his reviews of 1894, and Rousseau painted a portrait of Jarry which was exhibited at the Salon des Indépendants in April 1895 (where, because of the young man's long hair, it was wrongly entitled in the catalogue *Portrait de Madame A.J.*). Beneath the portrait, a deplorably bad quatrain was inscribed on the frame. A lengthy description by a critic of *Le Temps* attempted, with an ironical dig at the contemporary mania for discovering 'symbols' everywhere, an interpretation of the painting:

Sur le balcon près duquel le poète est assis, un hibou, une chouette sont posés. Quantité d'emblèmes, autour de lui, disent que ses préoccupations habituelles ne sont pas celles du vulgaire et qu'il se plonge dans les méditations les plus hautes. Une plume passée sur son oreille indique qu'il fait métier d'écrivain. Son oeil noir, fixe et rond, ses cheveux implacablement noirs, son complet de cérémonie, noir aussi, accentuent encore le sérieux de ses habituelles pensées.

> [On the balcony near which the poet sits are placed two owls. Numerous symbolic objects surrounding him indicate that his customary concerns are not those of the common man and that he is absorbed in thoughts of a higher order. A pen placed behind his ear indicates that he is a writer. The fixed gaze of his dark, wide-open eyes, his implacably black hair, his formal suit, also black, further emphasize the seriousness of his customary meditations.][35]

The portrait unfortunately has been lost or destroyed. According to one of several legends surrounding it, Jarry burned away the background and kept only the head, in his later lodgings in the Rue Cassette.

In addition to these four men, Jarry was also on friendly terms with a number of other, more minor painters, among them Alphonse Osbert who, like Filiger, exhibited at the Salon de la Rose+Croix of the 'Sâr' Péladan, and Félix Vallotton, who between 1890 and 1900 made a series of notable wood-engravings – among them one of Jarry himself – developing a technique made fashionable by Gauguin. A further acquaintance was the English illustrator Aubrey Beardsley, who painted a portrait of Jarry which also appears to have been lost. Probably both the wilful cruelty and perversity of the imaginative world of Beardsley's drawings, and his delicate use of line and contrast, appealed to Jarry, who dedicated to him a chapter of *Faustroll* appropriately entitled 'Du Pays de Dentelles'. Lastly, he was also to become particularly closely associated with a band of young men united by a common rejection of both academism and naturalism and by a common enthusiasm for the work of Gauguin, who had adopted the grandiose and ironic name of 'les Nabis' – derived from the Hebrew word for a divinely inspired prophet. He had first discovered their work with Fargue in 1893 and had commented enthusiastically on a number of paintings; both young men had made the acquaintance of several members of the group. The leading figures among the Nabis – Sérusier, Maurice Denis, Pierre Bonnard, Édouard Vuillard, Karl-Xavier Roussel – were also close friends of the young actor-director Aurélien Lugné-Poe, and were responsible for many of the sets of his productions at the Théâtre de l'Oeuvre. Here Jarry was to work closely with them, on the set for *Ubu Roi* in 1896, and he was again to be closely associated with several of them in his Théâtre des Pantins in 1898 and with Bonnard in the production of his two *Almanachs du Père Ubu*. Chapter XXXII of *Faustroll* was dedicated by Jarry first to Sérusier and then to Bonnard.

What was it in the work of these various painters that attracted Jarry? From the evidence of his writings on art and of his own literary work, it can be seen that four characteristics in particular appealed to him. Firstly, he was attracted by the apparent 'naïvety' of this art. Gauguin's rejection of the laws of perspective and his non-realistic use of colour, for example, give to his paintings just such an air of deliberate unsophistication. Jarry himself referred approvingly to the apparently crude and primitive draughtsmanship of Filiger. And in the paintings of Rousseau he was undoubtedly drawn to the seemingly childlike vision with its strange combination of incongruous elements. The same juxtaposition of incongruities is a feature of his own work of his 'Symbolist' phase; while his interest in the naive and childlike in art parallels his attachment to the naïvely crude and grotesque in his own work, as represented above all by the figure of Ubu.

Secondly, Jarry was attracted by the Breton and Breton-religious elements in many of the paintings of these men. Brittany had become in the last decades of the nineteenth century a source of inspiration for a small but growing number of painters and writers, who had been entranced by its rugged coastline, turbulent seas and sandy beaches, and by the strangeness and 'primitiveness' of its customs. More than any other region of France at this time, it had succeeded in preserving its traditional culture and language; while alongside its fervent Catholicism and a plethora of local saints and shrines, it offered evidence also in its menhirs and dolmens of a pre-Christian Celtic past. Simple peasant-folk, local saints, calvaries and Breton landscapes form the subject-matter of many of the works of Gauguin, Bernard, Sérusier, Filiger and others associated with Pont-Aven and Le Pouldu. To the young *littérateurs* of Paris their work seemed to portray the very essence of Brittany; to none more so than Jarry, with his own Breton origins. Indeed, his love of his native (or part-native) Brittany seems to have grown, as so often happens, with distance and the passage of time: an acquaintance who visited him in 1894 or 1895 described the walls of his apartment as being hung with pictures of saints, crucifixes, censers and other religious objects, all of Breton origin and characteristic of the popular art of the province, and referred also to the way in which Jarry's normally withdrawn and reserved manner could give way to sudden enthusiastic and voluble outbursts on the subject of Brittany.[36] Several times in his reviews of the work of his favourite painters, it was the Breton elements in their work which he singled out for comment – drawing attention, for example, to Filiger's 'Bretons résignés' with their oval faces, 'encadrés aux portes de verdure des fermes et des noces, faits pour le supplice dont ils ne bougeront pas' ['framed by the doorways of greenery of farms and wedding-festivities, made for the suffering of life from which for them there is no release'], and to 'les paysannes de Trégunc, les silhouettes de danseurs de gavottes et joueurs de biniou, les hauts arbres fusées et lombrics de la route de Clohars' ['the peasant women of Trégunc, the silhouettes of gavotte-dancers and bagpipe-players, the tall, spindle-like trees and earthworms of the road to Clohars'] of Seguin.[37] All the same, the fact that, amongst the Nabis, it was with Bonnard that he came to form the closest relationship rather than with the more 'mystically' inclined members of the group (Sérusier and Denis, described in the *Almanach du Père Ubu* of 1899 as 'celui qui mystique', for example, were fascinated by occultism, medievalism, neo-Catholicism and other cults of the time) suggests that it was the more specifically Breton rather than the religious elements in their work which most appealed to him, and indicates something of his own scepticism towards such 'mysticism'.

The third reason for Jarry's attraction to this art, and to the ideas of the Nabis in particular, lay in its and their resolute hostility to all forms of realism and naturalism. Where both academic art and Impressionism, whatever their differences in other respects, had aimed at the reproduction on the canvas of 'nature' or 'reality', the avowed aim of the Nabis – and with them, generally speaking, of the Symbolist movement in art and literature as a whole – was to turn their backs on realism, if not on reality itself, and to affirm the primacy of *imagination*. Thus Maurice Denis could look forward to the 'triomphe universel de l'imagination des esthètes sur les efforts de bête imitation, triomphe de l'émotion du beau sur le mensonge naturaliste' ['universal triumph of the imagination of aesthetes over attempts at stupid imitation, triumph of the sense of beauty over the naturalist lie'].[38] And Jarry praised Filiger for being above all 'un *déformateur*, si c'est bien là le conventionnel nom du peintre qui fait ce qui EST et non ... ce qui est conventionnel' ['a *deformer*, if that is indeed the conventional name for the painter who paints what IS and not ... according to convention'].[39] Less paradoxically, what the Nabis were aiming at was to affirm the essentially 'pictorial' qualities of art as against the pre-eminence of 'subject', moving in the direction of abstract art and asserting the autonomy or independence of reality of the work of art. This is the point of Denis' celebrated statement of 1890: 'Se rappeler qu'un tableau – avant d'être un cheval de bataille, une femme nue ou une quelconque anecdote – est essentiellement une surface plane recouverte de couleurs en un certain ordre assem-blées' ['Remember that a painting – before being a war-horse, a naked woman or the illustration of some story – is in essence a flat surface covered with areas of paint arranged in a certain order'] – a view echoed some years later in the definition of Georges Braque: 'Le peintre ne tâche pas de reconstituer une anecdote mais de constituer un fait pictural' ['The painter does not try to recreate a story but to create a pictorial fact'].[40] Again, as we shall see, there is a parallel between these artistic aims and ideas and those of Jarry in the field of literature.

Finally, Jarry was attracted by the idea of 'synthesis' held by Gauguin, Bernard and the Nabis. According to this doctrine of 'syntheticism', the artist should, by a process involving deliberate simplification and stylization, seek to combine elements chosen from different facets or areas of the 'real' world and to produce a new, subjective, non-'realistic' or 'synthetic' vision – a vision which, in the view of some, would itself constitute a new, separate, self-sufficient 'reality'. Jarry, in one of a series of direct or oblique references to this doctrine, cites Filiger and Bernard as examples of painters in whose work 'de la synthèse du complexe se refait la simplicité première' ['from a synthesis of the complex is created fundamental simplicity'].[41] For the Symbolists generally, this view was the source of the belief that the work of Gauguin and others contained some mysterious and hidden 'meaning'. In the context of Jarry, more specifically, it has two important applications concerning the figure of Ubu. In their set for the production of *Ubu Roi* in December 1896, the Nabis sought to realize, through simplification and stylization, just such a 'synthesis' of disparate elements. And in Jarry's own view, Ubu himself represented just such a 'simplicité première' in which, by 'la synthèse du complexe', was embodied a multiplicity of possible allusions.

In addition to his work as critic, Jarry was also himself active as an artist and illustrator, working in a number of different media. His output in the course of his life was quite prolific: if we include a number of rapid sketches contained in letters and manuscripts, some one hundred separate examples of various kinds are known (they are reproduced in *Peintures, Gravures et Dessins d'Alfred Jarry*, edited by Michel Arrivé). The extent of this output is matched by the variety of techniques and media employed, from pen- and pencil-drawings through woodcuts and lithographs to four known oil paintings. Jarry's adoption of a wide range of artistic forms parallels, in fact, the remarkable variety of forms in his literary work.

The years 1894–5 constituted his most prolific period as an artist. During this time he produced some 28 works, the majority woodcuts (enormously popular at the time among men of letters with an artistic bent), the others drawings and a few lithographs. Many were published as illustrations to *Haldernablou*, *Les Minutes de sable mémorial* and *César-Antechrist* – lavishly reproduced in five separate colours – or in the pages of the two art reviews which he edited or co-edited,

L'Ymagier and *Perhinderion*. Their subject matter is for the most part closely related to that of his literary works, embodying personages (such as Antichrist, or popular Breton saints), animals (owls, chameleons, snakes) and other objects and motifs (the Cross, Breton calvaries, instruments of the Passion and of torture) which figure in his writings. They range from the simple and purely illustrative to the extraordinarily complex and highly symbolic, all display the same technique of extreme stylization, and a number involve also the technique of 'synthesis': a typical example is an elaborate representation of the Cross in which the latter is surrounded by other objects relating to the Passion, and by a number of strange birds and animals. The effect of such a combination of apparently disparate objects and motifs is bizarre to say the least (Apollinaire found in some of Jarry's woodcuts 'un caractère de singularité presque cabalistique'),[42] and closely parallels, as we shall see, Jarry's procedure in *Les Minutes de sable mémorial* and *César-Antechrist*.

Lastly, his artistic interests found expression also in the editing of two luxurious art journals. Following his break with Lormel, he became co-director with Gourmont of a quarterly 'revue d'estampes' entitled *L'Ymagier*, the first issue of which appeared in October 1894. The two men shared a common love of ancient woodcuts and *images d'Épinal*, proudly affirming their love for such popular and supposedly 'naïve' art forms in the face of official 'bourgeois' culture. Though Jarry's co-editorship ceased after only five issues following a quarrel with Gourmont, and *L'Ymagier* itself ceased publication after eight issues, it was more enduring than most of its rivals and set a pattern which was soon to be followed by other publications. Its ambitious and costly programme – which it came close to realizing – was described by the editors as being to produce annually a volume of some 300 pages in 4°, containing over 200 engravings and at least eight authentic *images d'Épinal*.[43] Amongst its reproductions were works by Gauguin, Bernard, Filiger and Rousseau, and a number of engravings by Dürer, whose celebrated *Melancolia* was an object of fascination for the Symbolists and to whose popularity Jarry and Gourmont helped to contribute. In addition to several of his own works, Jarry also contributed a total of five articles, all abundantly illustrated with reproductions of ancient woodcuts, lithographs or *images d'Épinal*, devoted respectively to the subjects of the Passion of Christ, martyrs, monsters, the Virgin and Child and, once again, the Passion, in an article sub-titled 'Les Clous du Seigneur'.

The break with Gourmont was followed by the founding, in competition with *L'Ymagier*, of an even more luxurious publication entitled *Perhinderion* – a Breton word for pilgrimage. An important factor in its foundation, as in other activities during this period, was Jarry's inheritance of substantial sums of money from his uncle,

Julien-René Jarry, who died in June 1894, and his father, who died in August 1895 and whose estate was divided between Alfred and his sister (who retained the family home in Laval) in December of that year. These legacies enabled him for a time to enjoy the privileged rank of 'symboliste financeur' (the works of most of the aspiring young poets of the Symbolist movement were published at their own expense, and Jarry was no exception). It was a situation which, while it lasted, enabled him to look with contempt upon the commercial and practical concerns of publishers and to regard the creative artist as infinitely far removed from such pedestrian matters. Keenly sensitive, as were others among the Symbolists – most notably Mallarmé – to the *appearance* of the printed page, Jarry had specially cast for his new review a fount of type in imitation of an elaborate fifteenth-century design, and proudly announced his intention of reproducing old prints in the original format on laid paper resembling as closely as possible the original.[44] *Perhinderion* was to comprise six issues annually, and was to be devoted to reproducing the earliest *images d'Épinal* and to a systematic reproduction of the entire work of Dürer. Alas, only two issues appeared, in March and June 1896, by which time Jarry's inheritance had been used up. (A plan to publish an 'album en couleurs' entitled *Petits Crayons des Gestes plus notoires de M. Ubu, Maître des Phynances*, announced in the first issue of *Perhinderion*, came to nothing, possibly for the same reason.)

Jarry's break with Gourmont was occasioned by a farcical incident involving the older man's mistress, Berthe (de) Courrière. A lecherous, priest-chasing woman (according to legend she was several times locked up as a nymphomaniac), over 20 years Jarry's senior, she had been a model for the sculptor Clésinger, had then served as the model for the eponymous heroine of Gourmont's novel *Sixtine*, and was later used as a model by Huysmans for his portrayal of Mme Chantelouve in his 'satanic' novel *Là-bas*. The subject of ribald jokes amongst the *habitués* of the *Mercure de France*, she was commonly referred to as 'la Vieille Dame'. According to Rachilde, she and Jean de Tinan decided to engineer a practical joke (pranks and practical jokes were a regular feature of this milieu), and told Berthe that Jarry was secretly and passionately in love with her. She in turn promptly conceived a boundless passion for Jarry, whom she importuned with repeated requests for a rendez-vous and to whom she addressed, slipped between the pages of a book, a long, turgid, mystico-erotic poem entitled 'Tua res agitur'. Jarry savagely spurned her advances and wrote (though – fortunately for him – did not publish) an obscene satirical poem entitled 'Inscription mise sur la grande histoire de la Vieille Dame'.[45] A few years later this practical joke almost turned to disaster: Jarry recounted the incident in a savagely satirical chapter of *L'Amour en visites* (1898), in which he published Berthe's poem as well as a string of letters and telegrams which she had sent him – and almost landed himself in prison as a result.

The incident, though trivial in itself, throws a sharp light on Jarry's susceptibilities and, even more important, on his attitude towards women and the nature of his sexual inclinations. If we except his – highly implausible – schoolboy boasts concerning visits to brothels, there is no evidence of any sexual involvement whatsoever on Jarry's part with women. Most of his writings, and reported pronouncements, moreover, exude a spirit of extreme misogyny. Rachilde reports him as having declared haughtily that 'l'honneur des femmes est une chose essentiellement négligeable puisqu'elles n'ont point d'âme' ['the honour of women is an essentially trivial matter, since they have no soul'], and he is also supposed to have confided to her, referring to Berthe's poem (and with a savage dig at Gourmont):

Ça manque vraiment de technicité, et nous ne lui confierons point nos personnels boutons à recoudre. Libre aux gens de génie de coucher avec leur cuisinière, nous, nous ne tenons pas à avoir du génie à ce prix-là. Nous n'aimons pas les femmes du tout, mais si jamais nous en aimions une nous la voudrions notre égale, ce qui ne serait pas rien!

> [It really does show a lack of technical accomplishment, and we shall not entrust her with the sewing on of our personal buttons. Geniuses are free to sleep with their housekeepers if they wish, but *we* have no desire to be a genius at that price. We do not love women at all, but if ever we did love one we would wish her to be our equal, which would be no small matter!][46]

Rachilde also maintains (not wholly convincingly) that the only woman apart from his mother to have escaped his general misogyny was she herself, to whom he is supposed to have paid the backhanded compliment: 'Ma-da-me! vous avez un bien mauvais caractère! Vous êtes une quantité négligeable d'atomes crochus. Mais nous vous accordons une qualité: *vous ne raccrochez pas!*' ['Ma-dam! you have a distinctly bad character! You are an insignificant bundle of atoms clinging together. But we grant you one quality: *you do not cling to us!*'][47] This misogyny is matched by clear evidence of homosexual inclinations. Rachilde insinuates that the relationship between Jarry and Henri Morin was homosexual in nature, and Louis Lormel somewhat belatedly 'denounced' the character of his relationship with Fargue in a satirical short story of 1897 in which Jarry and Fargue appear thinly disguised under the names, respectively, of 'la Tête de Mort' and 'l'Androgyne'.[48] Lugné-Poe comments snidely in his memoirs that Jarry in 1896 '[traînait] maintes histoires derrière lui' and claims to have seen him at the Théâtre de l'Oeuvre in the company of Oscar Wilde's notorious friend, Lord Alfred Douglas.[49] Yet Jarry made no more secret of his homosexual leanings than of his

misogyny, frankly dramatizing in *Haldernablou*, through the characters of the Duke Haldern and his page Ablou, his own relationship
with Fargue. Indeed – apart from exemplifying some of the worst
excesses of Symbolism and revealing the influence upon Jarry of
Lautréamont – the chief interest of *Haldernablou* lies in the light it
throws upon the nature of that relationship and upon Jarry's own
intimate personality.

The frankness of Jarry's dramatization was such as acutely to
embarrass Fargue. The title of the play, and the name of the page, in
the manuscript sent to Vallette in March 1894 was *Cameleo*. So obvious
was the reference to Fargue, who then went by the name of 'Léon'
and was even nicknamed 'Caméléo' by his friends on account of the
changeability of his character, that he begged Jarry to 'debaptize' him.
On the advice of Gourmont, Jarry wrote to Vallette requesting him to
substitute for the names Henrik (an obvious reference to his own
second name, Henry) and Cameleo those of Haldern (a Breton form
of his first name, already used in *Ontogénie*) and Ablou – the
conjunction of the two names in the new title suggesting the union of
the play's two protagonists.[50]

It would be wrong, however, to see in *Haldernablou* purely the
expression of homosexual love. The play opens, in fact, with a
profession by the Duke Haldern of his equal contempt for women
('J'aime en les femmes – carie et scorie que Dieu extirpa de la grille de
leurs [i.e. of men] côtes – leur servilité, mais je les veux muettes'
['What I like in women – blight and dross which God extracted from
the grid of their [men's]ribs – is their servility, but I want them
silent']) *and* men. His own desire, as expressed to his page, is for a
spiritualized, asexual form of love:

Hors du sexe seul est l'amour; je voudrais . . . quelqu'un qui ne fût ni homme
ni femme ni tout à fait monstre, esclave dévoué et qui pût parler sans
interrompre l'harmonie de mes pensées sublimes; à qui un baiser fût stupre
démonial.

> [Only outside of sex does love exist; I wish for . . . someone who would be
> neither man nor woman nor wholly a monster, a devoted slave who could
> speak without disturbing the harmony of my sublime thoughts; to whom a
> kiss would be a demonic depravity.][51]

Yet for all Haldern's search for a purely spiritual relationship, the
'love' of which he dreams is inseparable from the will to dominate
and to humiliate:

HALDERN: . . . Quelque homme t'a-t-il dit qu'il t'aimait, Ablou?
ABLOU: S'il avait été assez hardi – j'aurais fouetté sa joue de mes cinq doigts
de pieuvre, ou tout au moins je l'aurais tué.
HALDERN: Je t'aime et te veux à mes pieds, Ablou.

ABLOU: Plaisanterie!
HALDERN: Du nord, du sud, de l'est, de l'ouest, tous ont rampé autour de
moi en étoile de sphinx accroupis. Tu es au-dessus des autres, tu deviendras
plus vil qu'eux tous.

> [HALDERN: . . . Has any man told you that he loved you, Ablou?
> ABLOU: If he had been so bold – I would have whipped him across the cheek
> with my five octopus fingers, or at the very least I would have killed him.
> HALDERN: I love you and I want you at my feet, Ablou.
> ABLOU: You jest!
> HALDERN: From the north, from the south, from the east, from the west, all
> have crawled at my feet, squatting around me like the arms of the sphinx-
> star. You are above all others, you will become baser than them all.][52]

The page accepts this relationship; but soon the roles become
reversed, as Ablou's frankly sado-masochistic declaration clearly
indicates: 'D'agressif deviens victime, intervertissons les rôles. Haldern, je t'aime.' ['From being aggressive, become a victim, let us
reverse roles. Haldern, I love you.' As the play unfolds, moreover,
Haldern's dream of a pure relationship free from any sexual basis
proves to be impossible to realize. Despite an awareness that a
physical relationship would destroy their friendship –

ABLOU: . . . Le jour ou nous coucherons ensemble . . .
HALDERN: Nous irons chacun de notre côté, nous irons chacun de notre
côté.

> [ABLOU: . . . The day we sleep together . . .
> HALDERN: We shall each go our own way, we shall each go our own way.]

– the physical attraction is too strong to be resisted. Separation
ensues, amidst remorse and violent hatred, culminating in Haldern's
outburst:

Je le tuerai: car je le méprise comme impur et vénal: – car la beauté ne doit, à
peine de déchéance, même pour esclave élire qu'une beauté pareille; – car fier
encore il faussera l'aventure; – car il faut, en bonne théologie, détruire la bête
avec laquelle on a forniqué . . . .

> [I will kill him: for I despise him as impure and venal: – for beauty must, on
> pain of corruption, elect, even as a slave, an equal beauty; – for, still proud,
> he will pervert the experience; – for one must, in accord with true theology,
> destroy the beast with which one has fornicated . . . .][53]

And the action ends mysteriously but violently, with Haldern strang-
ling his former lover.

Quite how closely the action of *Haldernablou* traces the course of
the affair between Jarry and Fargue is impossible to determine with
certainty (the rupture between them certainly did not go so far as

murder)! It seems highly improbable that the writing of the play, in the first few months of 1894, followed the break between them; it would seem therefore to have been a prophetic work, anticipating the development of their relationship. Indeed, it is even possible that the publication of the work may have contributed to that break. Much, too, in the play must be treated with some scepticism. In writing *Haldernablou*, Jarry was in part undoubtedly responding to a vogue: the themes of homosexuality, narcissism, androgyny and other 'abnormal' forms of love were favourites in the last two decades of the nineteenth century, while homosexuality itself strangely enjoyed a place of honour among men of letters in France in this period – the names of Count Robert de Montesquiou, Jean Lorrain and (in Jarry's own generation) Gide and Proust, are but the most prominent that come to mind. But his association of the themes of love and physical contact with those of fear, remorse and death suggests at the same time a more deep-seated, personal preoccupation, and seems to reveal a haunting *fear* of love, or at least of physical contact. *Haldernablou* must be read, in fact, alongside such texts as 'Les Prolégomènes de Haldernablou' (in *Les Minutes de sable mémorial*) and *César-Antechrist*, in the latter of which the injunction: 'Phallus déraciné, NE FAIS PAS DE PAREILS BONDS!' ['Uprooted Phallus, DO NOT LEAP ABOUT SO!']⁵⁴ clearly refers back to the mysterious line from *Haldernablou*: 'Est-ce lui qui là-bas fait des bonds énormes, comme pour rattraper un retard inexpliqué?' ['Is it he who, over there, is making huge bounds, as if to make up for unexplained time lost?'].⁵⁵ Such sexual symbols as these, and in particular the association of such symbols with the themes of guilt and destruction, suggest both a fascination with and a deep-rooted fear of unbridled sexual urges in the young Jarry.

But this cross-referencing also opens up a new dimension in *Haldernablou*, that which has been designated in modern criticism by the name 'intertextuality'. The phrase 'ne fais pas de pareils bonds' was itself borrowed from *Les Chants de Maldoror* of Isidore Ducasse, who wrote under the name of 'Comte de Lautréamont' (the words are addressed in the third *Chant* by God to a hair left behind in a brothel). First published in 1869 in Brussels but totally ignored, it was republished in Paris in 1890 at the initiative of a young Belgian publisher and rescued from total oblivion by the eagle eye of Gourmont at the Bibliothèque Nationale, who revealed the existence of this extravagant work to the literary world in a celebrated article in the *Mercure de France* of 1 February 1891, entitled 'La Littérature Maldoror'. (It was subsequently 'rediscovered', and its author hailed as a precursor, some 30 years later by the Surrealists.) In an extraordinary profusion of apostrophe and imagery, Maldoror, a demonic figure, pours out his loathing of both God and mankind and expresses his love for all that is hideous, monstrous and cruel in nature. The work is an expression of Romanticism at its most paroxysmic (so much so as to read almost like a parody of the worst excesses of Romantic emotionalism and posturing) as well as expressing, paradoxically, in many respects an inversion of Romantic values. It is easy to see what elements of it appealed to Jarry, who incorporated many of them into *Haldernablou* and a number of texts included in *Les Minutes de sable mémorial* – amongst them such features as the self-consciously declamatory, and even hysterical, tone; the 'hallucinatory' imagery (Gourmont described the work as an example of 'les hallucinations servies par la volonté'); the deliberately outrageous sadism and cruelty of Maldoror; his blasphemy and stance of superhuman arrogance; the profusion of strange or horrific animal images; and even certain turns of phrase (such as the expression 'beau comme', repeated in Jarry's metaphor 'beau comme un hibou pendu par les griffes' in 'Les Prolégomènes de Haldernablou'). Indeed, the very subject of *Haldernablou* is suggested in a reference in the fourth *Chant*: 'Deux amis qui cherchent obstinément à se détruire, quel drame!'. And Jarry's work even contains an *explicit* reference to Lautréamont (who was born in Montevideo in Uruguay) in Haldern's words (which also allude to an episode in the fourth *Chant*):

Serait-il lâche? Plût au ciel qu'il le fût, et ne pérît point comme cet autre page que mon ami le Montévidéen lança contre un arbre, ne gardant dans sa main que la chevelure sanglante et rouge, abusant de la suprématie de sa force physique.

> [Could it be that he is a coward? Please God that he be so, and that he may not perish like that other page whom my friend the Montevidean hurled against a tree, retaining in his hand only the red and bleeding crop of his hair, taking undue advantage of the supremacy of his physical strength.][56]

And yet, the very self-consciousness of Jarry's borrowings from Lautréamont leaves one wondering as to his real intentions here. Such self-conscious 'quotation' from the works of other writers, and even from his own, is to be a recurrent feature of his work, one which forces us to ponder upon the nature of Jarry's conception of 'literature' and to call into question the whole concept of literary authenticity and originality – a question to which we shall have occasion to return in the final chapter. While such features of *Haldernablou* as its strangely incongruous setting in which moated medieval manorhouses and forests are juxtaposed with city trams and railway stations, its 'invisible and inconceivable' Chorus, its deliberate and macabre sadism (Haldern feeding his pet owls upon live cockchafers found feasting on human corpses), its flamboyantly sado-masochistic presentation of love, and its use of the mysterious letter 'x' to separate scenes, lead us to ask whether the work is not – in part – something of a pastiche and spoof upon many of the commonplaces of both Gothic Romanticism and the more macabre forms of Symbolism. The question takes us to the heart of the complex question of Jarry's relationship to the Symbolist movement.

Chapter Three

Symbolism and its subversion

JARRY'S work of the years 1893–5 has to be seen against the background of the Symbolist movement and of the impact of a host of cults and fads (neo-Platonic idealism, occultism, medievalism, 'neo-Christianity', anarchism, to name but a few) which in their turn helped to mould it. The contours of the movement are charted retrospectively in his *Gestes et opinions du docteur Faustroll, pataphysicien* of 1898: of the authors comprising the good doctor's library, just under half are chosen from among the ranks of the Symbolists or of their recognized precursors, among them Baudelaire, Max Elskamp, Gustave Kahn, Lautréamont, Maeterlinck, Mallarmé, Régnier, Rimbaud, Schwob, Verlaine and Verhaeren. Jarry's encounter with Symbolism had a determining influence both upon his thought and upon his style in prose as well as in verse – the idiosyncratic syntax and slightly precious vocabulary of Mallarmé tempering a natural ebullience and verbal inventiveness nourished on Rabelais. Yet though he rapidly absorbed these and other influences of his time, the use to which he put them remains peculiarly his own.

The Symbolist movement in literature and painting was a complex phenomenon whose roots were at once literary, social and political. In part, it sprang from a deep-seated hostility to the prevailing literary doctrines of realism and naturalism. In part, too, it was an elitist reaction against contemporary 'materialism', that is, the effects of accelerating industrialization and the beginnings of a 'mass' culture; against literary 'commercialism'; and against widespread 'mediocrity', a notion which included the democratic and egalitarian ideals of the age. And in part its sources were political – it sprang from a sense prevalent among intellectuals of alienation and exclusion from the forefront of public life, coupled with a political disillusionment which was exacerbated by the scandals and corruption of contemporary political life. Thus Gourmont saw his generation, in retrospect, as 'une génération lassée d'avance des lourdes querelles politiques et sociales' ['a generation tired in advance of ponderous political and social disputes'];[1] while the young literary critic, and future socialist

Prime Minister, Léon Blum, in his first published article in 1892, lamented the 'désintéressement et indifférence pour tout ce qui touche la politique' ['lack of interest in and indifference towards everything of a political nature'] of young intellectuals.[2] The corollary of this revulsion against the 'vulgar' reality of the modern world was an attraction to the past, and to the exotic and mysterious; a turning towards religious or vaguely 'mystical' ideas; a cult of rarefied poetic 'Beauty'; and a professed concern for universal and eternal, as opposed to merely contemporary and ephemeral, values and concerns. The same impulse led also to the development of a cult of aristocratic and anti-social individualism which, in its theoretical expressions at least, far surpassed that of the Romantics; to the development, out of the Baudelairian cult of the dandy, of a doctrine of aestheticism; and, above all, to a view of the creative artist – the ultimate consequence of the Romantic exaltation of individual genius and of imagination – as a superior being, a High Priest of culture amidst the ignorant and uncultured herd of his fellow-men.

Alongside these political and social factors, however, other, more purely intellectual, factors were present which helped to confirm the Symbolists in their opposition to the spirit of materialism, rationalism and 'positivistic' science which in the second half of the nineteenth century had come increasingly to dominate intellectual life in France. Particularly important were a group of developments known collectively as the 'anti-positivist reaction' or 'idealist revival' of the 1880s and 1890s, which profoundly influenced their view of the relationship between reality and imagination, and which led to the creation in the minds of many educated non-specialists of the idea that the physical sciences were somehow incapable of guaranteeing the accuracy, and even the reality, of their picture of the external world.[3] At the same time as these developments, a ferment of new and exciting ideas was taking place in the field of psychology, including the first systematic explorations of the strange and mysterious world of the subconscious (and, incidentally, the elaboration of techniques of analysis which were to inspire the young Sigmund Freud whilst a student in Paris.)[4] Of equal significance was the fact that the relatively new science of psychology was increasingly threatening the traditional pre-eminence of the physical sciences. This shift of emphasis can be seen in the work of Hippolyte Taine and Henri Bergson, probably the two most influential thinkers of their respective generations in France. For where Taine, one of the chief spokesmen for the doctrines of 'positivism', takes as his starting point the data of the physical sciences, accepting their materialistic and deterministic view of the world and attempting to integrate the human mind into this scheme – the result being the 'disintegration' of the 'self' and, logically, a denial of its freedom[5] – Bergson on the contrary takes as his starting point the immediate experiences of the individual consciousness, whence the title of his first major work, *Essai sur les données immédiates de la conscience* (1889).

This is not to suggest, as has sometimes in the past been all too rashly maintained, that the Symbolist movement sprang directly from the ideas of Bergson. Bergson was himself symptomatic of a general shift of ideas which was gradually taking place away from the materialist and determinist doctrines which had dominated the minds of the leading French thinkers during roughly the third quarter of the nineteenth century. The evolution was a slow and by no means universal one; Roger Martin du Gard's powerful novel *Jean Barois* (1913) testifies to the continuing strength of such materialist and determinist conceptions of the world around the turn of the century. But it was the new ideas, springing in part from the growing pre-eminence of the new science of psychology, which, filtering through to the Symbolists, helped, alongside the other influences mentioned, to shape their thinking. Out of them, the more philosophically-minded constructed a doctrine to which they gave the name of 'idealism', and which the poet Henri de Régnier claimed to constitute 'la clé métaphysique de la plupart des esprits de la génération qui compose l'école symboliste' ['the metaphysical key to the minds of most of those of the generation making up the Symbolist school'.[6] The doctrine was summed up in the aphorism of their favourite, much quoted but little understood philosopher, Schopenhauer: 'The world is my representation', to whose *The World as Will and Representation*[7] they appealed for authority as well as to such works as Théodule Ribot's *La Philosophie de Schopenhauer*[8] (and, by a supreme irony, to the monumental *De l'intelligence* of Taine himself). Resolutely taking the experiences of the individual self as the starting point of all knowledge, the Symbolists went on to develop the view that we can never have any direct knowledge of the external world, but only of our own thoughts and perceptions, whose exact correspondence to any external, supposedly 'objective', reality must remain uncertain. The idea was clearly formulated by Gourmont, commenting on the above-quoted aphorism of Schopenhauer in his small volume of philosophical essays published in 1893 under the title of *L'Idéalisme*:

Les conséquences logiques de ces aphorismes sont nettes: on ne connaît que sa propre intelligence, que soi, seule réalité, le monde spécial et unique que le moi détient, véhicule, déforme, exténue, recrée selon sa personnelle activité; rien ne se meut en dehors du sujet connaissant; tout ce que je pense est réel: la seule réalité, c'est la pensée.

[The logical consequences of these aphorisms are clear: one knows only one's own mind, one's self, the sole reality, the special and unique world of which the self is in possession, for which it serves as a vehicle, which it distorts, exhausts, recreates in accordance with its own unique activity; nothing exists outside of the individual consciousness; everything which I think is real: the only reality *is* thought.][9]

Gourmont's brilliant paradoxes were joyfully and lovingly indulged in (a trait of character which he shared with Jarry), whilst he was careful to avoid pushing his arguments into too evident absurdity. Some among the Symbolists, however, with equal enthusiasm but less critical acumen, pushed this idea to the extreme of solipsism, a doctrine which actually denies the reality of the external world and asserts that the individual 'self' alone is real. But almost all adopted, explicitly or implicitly, a philosophical view which encompassed a series of fundamental oppositions, between 'life' and 'art', 'living' and 'being', 'time' and 'eternity', and 'reality' and 'imagination' respectively.

Whatever the philosophical basis (and inherent contradictions) of such ideas, however, it was their *aesthetic* consequences which were of most importance to the Symbolists, since they appeared to them to justify their rejection of the doctrines of realism and naturalism in which they saw the literary expression of the rationalistic and materialistic spirit they so abhorred.[10] It was this which led Gourmont to describe the new gospel of idealism in ecstatic terms as 'cette vérité évangélique et merveilleuse, *libératrice et rénovatrice*' ['this wonderful, gospel-like, *liberating and renewal-bringing* truth'],[11] in which he claimed to find a justification for the individual artist to turn away from the 'problématiques contingences' of the world to a contemplation of the riches of his own 'self' and to the cultivation of pure imagination. Far from being, as in naturalist theory (if not practice), the description of a more or less objectively perceived external world, art is and can only be the self-projection or *self-representation* of the artist: 'La seule excuse qu'un homme ait d'écrire, c'est de s'écrire lui-même, de dévoiler aux autres la sorte de monde qui se mire en son miroir individuel.' ['The only excuse which a man has for writing is to write himself, to reveal to others the kind of world which is reflected in the mirror of his own mind.'] The chief aim of art is therefore originality and, conversely, 'le crime capital pour un écrivain c'est le conformisme, l'imitativité, la soumission aux règles et aux enseignements' ['the cardinal sins for a writer are conformism, imitativeness, submission to rules and precepts']. And thus Symbolism, in which Gourmont sees the 'expression artistique' of this idealism, becomes a doctrine of absolute artistic individualism: 'le symbolisme, c'est, même excessive, même intempestive, même prétentieuse, l'expression de l'individualisme dans l'art' ['Symbolism, even in its most extreme, most excessive, most pretentious forms, is the expression of individualism in art'].[12] Symbolism is synonymous with total free-

dom, and even with anarchy: 'Le Symbolisme . . . se traduit littérale-
ment par le mot Liberté et, pour les violents, par le mot Anarchie.'
['Symbolism . . . can be translated literally by the word Freedom and,
for those of a violent disposition, by the word Anarchy.']13

Where does Jarry stand in relation to such ideas? He appears in his
early work to accept by and large the basic premises of this idealism.
He shares the general aristocratic disdain for any literature of social
involvement or concern. He shares (or appears to share) the Symbolists' preoccupation with artistic 'Beauty'. He not only shares their
exalted view of the creative artist as a being infinitely superior to his
fellow men, but surpasses the majority of his contemporaries in the
haughtiness and arrogance of his expressions of this view and in his
scathing contempt for 'the mob' (*la foule*). He resolutely espouses the
doctrine that the true aim of artistic creation is not a reproduction of
reality but the expression of the artist's own original, personal vision.
And he adopts the view that there exists a radical opposition between
life and art, living and being, time and eternity – to which he adds
moreover a number of new antitheses of his own invention. There is a
curious passage in the programme notes for *Ubu Roi* in 1896 which,
despite the deliberately paradoxical nature of the context, tells us a
great deal about the ideas of its author: 'nature' is here opposed to
'art', 'le moins de compréhension' (that is, the level of understanding
of 'the mob') is contrasted with '[le] plus de cérébralité', 'la réalité du
consentement universel' is opposed to 'l'hallucination de l'intelligent', and 'les honneurs' (that is, recognition in the eyes of the world
at large) are contrasted with 'la satisfaction de soi pour soi seul' and
the rewards of 'la compréhension des intelligents'.14 An equally
categorical expression of this dualism is expressed in the opening
words of his article of September 1894 on the painter Filiger, which
echo the contemptuous dismissal of 'life' by the hero of Villiers de
l'Isle-Adam's *Axël* (one of the Symbolists' most cherished works):
'Vivre? les serviteurs feront cela pour nous.':

La banalité de la mode étant à qui parle d'art de répondre qu'il vaut mieux
vivre . . ., il est permis, nos serfs pouvant suffisamment cette chose, d'exister
dès maintenant en l'éternité, d'en faire de notre mieux provision, et de la
regarder chez ceux qui l'ont su mettre en cage, surtout discolore de la nôtre.

> [The banality of fashion decreeing that one should reply to anyone who
> speaks of art that it is better to live . . ., we have the right, our serfs being well
> able to carry out such an injunction, to live from this moment on in eternity,
> to lay in as best we can a stock of it, and to contemplate it in the work of those
> who have managed to capture it, especially if their cage is of a different colour
> from ours.]15

Nowhere, in fact, is the fundamental egotism of Symbolist doctrine
better exemplified than in the grandiosely rhetorical declarations of

his own Caesar-Antichrist, in a passage which exalts the creativity, freedom and power of the imagination and which expresses also the theme of a narcissistic delectation in the 'elixir' of the 'self':

Je n'ai que faire de cette extérieure représentation et je passe aveugle et sourd sur la terre, me contemplant moi-même, sûr qu'on ne peut rien m'adjoindre d'externe . . . Je suis César il est vrai, non des hommes que je méprise et pour qui je ne veux user les courts moments de mon séjour terrestre, mais de l'Univers et de l'Absolu . . . . Dieu – ou moi-même – a créé tous les mondes possibles, ils coexistent, mais les hommes ne peuvent même en entrevoir un. . . . Je suis l'Orgueil absolu parce que je suis la Force suprême; et c'est pourquoi je ne dominerai pas, car ma domination ne serait pas comprise (laissons cela aux faux Césars), et aussi tout ce qui est moi est un élixir précieux qui ne doit pas être follement perdu.

> [I have nothing to do with this outward appearance and I pass blind and deaf over the earth, contemplating my own self, certain that nothing external can be added to me . . . . I am Emperor, it is true, not over men whom I despise and on whose behalf I have no wish to expend the brief moments of my earthly sojourn, but of the Universe and the Absolute . . . . God – or myself – has created all possible worlds, but men cannot even catch a glimpse of one of them. . . . I am absolute Pride because I am absolute Power; and that is why I shall not rule, for my rule would not be understood (let us leave that to false Caesars), and moreover everything which is myself is a precious elixir which must not be extravagantly wasted.][16]

Of these various ideas adopted by Jarry, none is more important than the Symbolist belief in the primacy of imagination. He surpasses, here also, the majority of the Symbolists in his contemptuous dismissal of both realism and naturalism, and of the work of Zola in particular.[17] In the previous chapter, it was seen that his artistic preferences were for the work of such deliberately non-'realist' painters as Rousseau, Gauguin and the Nabis; while in his article on Filiger he stated categorically that it is the artist's *imaginative deformation* of reality which represents *true* reality. This belief in the primacy of imagination – soon to be given a new formulation in his 'science' of pataphysics, the 'science of imaginary solutions' – together with an unrelenting hostility to all forms of realism, was to be a constant theme in his work, profoundly influencing the nature of his poetry, of his novel-writing, of his journalism and, not least, of his theatre.

Yet, for all Jarry's adherence to certain fundamental points of Symbolist doctrine, in other ways he departs singularly from the views of his contemporaries. And, by a supreme paradox, it is the very nature of his view of imagination which accounts for his seemingly paradoxical, if not self-contradictory, treatment of other cherished concepts of Symbolism. Nowhere is this treatment more apparent than in the short philosophical essay *Être et Vivre*, published in *L'Art Littéraire* in March–April 1894, which constitutes one of the most revealing philosophical 'statements' ever made by him.[18]

Être et Vivre deals with the neo-Platonic opposition between Being and Living (to which Jarry adds, once again, that between Thought and Action, Eternity and Time, the Idea and the Real). Despite (or because of?) its profusion of hyperbolic and abstract terms, the essay has the appearance of a serious if rather abstruse philosophical meditation. Yet the epigraph chosen by Jarry must put the alert reader on his guard: it consists of those lines from the *Guignol* published in *L'Écho de Paris* in which Ubu first presents to us his newly invented science of pataphysics. Moreover, quite apart from the strangeness of certain allusions, the very structure of Jarry's argument flies in the face of the most elementary logic: beginning with an apology for Being, he moves suddenly and quite arbitrarily to a celebration of Existence and to a call to 'destroy Being'. The justification of this 'casuistique licite', as he calls it, is to be found in a principle to which only a passing reference is made here, but which will play a crucial role in his work, that of the 'identity of opposites'. It serves here to reduce all oppositions to a common meaninglessness and, ultimately, to reduce the elaborate argument of *Être et Vivre* to the level of a sustained philosophical hoax. The essay hints at the ambiguous nature of Jarry's adherence to much of Symbolist doctrine and – with its evidence of an impish delight in juggling with grandiose metaphysical abstractions which he implicitly chooses to regard as all equally 'imaginary' – offers an indication of things to come.

The same ambiguity, springing from the same source, is present in his attitude to religious matters also. Contemporary with the flowering of Symbolism was a revival of interest in Christianity coupled with an upsurge of interest in Oriental religious and metaphysical thought, much of it stemming from the publication of Édouard Schuré's *Les Grands initiés* in 1889. Simultaneously there was a renewed interest in such subjects as theosophy and occultism, culminating in the revival of the Rosicrucian order by Joséphin Péladan and Stanislas de Guaïta in 1888. One upshot of this was the development of a dilettante and largely aesthetic 'mysticism' focussing on the traditional paraphernalia of religious worship and belief and on the more esoteric forms of religious symbolism. No better example exists of this 'aesthetic' Christianity than Gourmont's *Le Latin mystique* of 1892 (which, by a nice double irony, was provided with a preface by the novelist J.-K. Huysmans which castigated the very 'pseudo-mysticism' of contemporary aesthetes and men-of-letters which the work embodied, and whose adherents were in any case merely following in the footsteps of Huysmans' own model of 'decadent' aestheticism, Des Esseintes, in his novel *A rebours* of 1884).

A related phenomenon was the development among many of the Symbolists of a belief in a Swedenborgian 'universal analogy', for which a source was found in Baudelaire's celebrated sonnet 'Correspondances'. This vague but influential belief in the existence of a mysterious relationship between the material and spiritual worlds expressing itself in a system of universal symbolism helped to shape the Symbolist view of literature as containing hidden levels of meaning.

Jarry shared the general fascination with such ideas, including their more extravagant manifestations. It is no accident that included among the writers represented in Dr Faustroll's select library is the self-styled prophet and *magus* who went by the name of the 'Sâr' Péladan. But Jarry's delight in the colourful absurdities of occultism is matched by evidence of a deep interest in the religious beliefs and practices of Christianity also. In his graphic work – particularly in *L'Ymagier* and *Perhinderion* – and in his writings of this period, there is a striking concentration upon religious subjects. To an extent, as we have seen, this can be accounted for by the Breton associations of much of the religious art with which he deals, by his love of the latter's features of simplification and stylization, and by the associations of religion with his own childhood. But there is also a deeper and more complex reason; alongside elements of deliberate impiety and anti-clericalism, Jarry's attitude towards Christianity at this period embraces also a mixture of reverence and fascination born of his delight in the richly imaginative, the fantastic and the bizarre. Nowhere in fact is his tendency to treat religion (as he had done with abstract metaphysical concepts in *Être et Vivre*) as a pure manifestation of the human imagination more clearly evident than in two articles in *L'Ymagier* devoted to the Passion of Christ – 'Le Christ en croix' and 'Les Clous du Seigneur'. The first describes various primitive representations of the crucifixion; the second is devoted to a lengthy and erudite examination of the question of whether Christ was actually *nailed* to the Cross and, if so, whether by three nails or four. The discussion is conducted with a profusion of references to and quotations from the Church Fathers, medieval Latin authors, ecclesiastical tradition and early Christian iconography. He concludes in the second article that four nails were in fact used, a conclusion based not on historical evidence but on an appeal to the visions of saints and to the traditions of iconography – just as previously he had appealed for evidence of the appearance of Christ to 'divers portraits du Christ, *par quoi seuls nous le connaissons*' ['various paintings of Christ, *which are our only source of knowledge of him*'] and which will give us 'ses aspects divers et ce que *les Évangélistes, trop proches, n'ont point vu*' ['his different characteristics, and what *the Evangelists, too close, failed to see*']¹⁹ Jarry is clearly not concerned here to establish any historical or theological truth; but nor, despite a slight element of tongue-in-cheek humour behind the deadly serious façade of the argument, is his intention chiefly satirical. On the contrary, his whole argument is simply based on an extreme and paradoxical application of the Symbolist belief in the primacy of imagination. Not only does he accept the Symbolist view that 'Beauty' is a product of the creative imagination; he is asserting here, implicitly, that 'truth' also, far from residing in historically ascertainable or scientifically verifiable facts, is to be found in the creations of the imagination. Such a notion (which was to receive a 'theoretical' outline in *Faustroll* in 1898) is typical of the tightrope which Jarry sought to walk throughout much of his life, between the banal 'commonsensical' view of the majority of his contemporaries and total absurdity.

A similar perspective governs his attitude to political issues as to philosophical and religious subjects. This can be most clearly seen in his attitude towards the 'anarchism' fashionable in literary milieux in the 1890s – a subject of particular significance in view of the debate which was to be aroused by his production in 1896 of *Ubu Roi*. Between 1892 and 1894, a terrified Paris was shaken by a series of anarchist bomb-outrages. The most celebrated (or notorious) of their perpetrators were Ravachol, Auguste Vaillant, who in December 1893 threw a bomb into the crowded *Chambre des Députés*, and Émile Henry, a young bourgeois intellectual who in February 1894 threw a bomb into a crowded café at the Gare St-Lazare. Many among the Symbolists were secretly or openly sympathetic to the ideas, and in many cases the actions, of such men. Jarry's friends Marcel Schwob and Pierre Quillard wrote articles in defence of them, and Paul Adam in 1892 published an 'Éloge de Ravachol' in which he presented the terrorist as a saint and a martyr and implicitly identified him with the figure of Christ. Cries of 'Vive l'anarchie, vive le vers libre!' rang out from the *impériale* (upper storey) of horse-drawn omnibuses. The Symbolist review *La Plume* devoted a special issue in May 1893 to the subject of anarchy. *Les Entretiens politiques et littéraires*, under the direction of the young poet Francis Viélé-Griffin, published extracts from the writings of Bakunin and Max Stirner and contributions by the French anarchist theoreticians Élie and Élisée Reclus alongside literary contributions by Valéry, Régnier, Gourmont and Mallarmé. In its turn, the *Revue Anarchiste* in 1893 published previously unpublished works by Jules Laforgue alongside its political contributions. And the future editor of the *Revue Blanche*, Félix Fénéon (on whose behalf Mallarmé testified in court), was arrested and put on trial in the famous 'Procès des trente' of August 1894, along with 18 anarchist theoreticians and propagandists and 11 common criminals.[20]

But whereas most of these self-styled anarchists were men moved by a deeply humanitarian sense of outrage at the injustices of the existing social order, the 'anarchism' of some (though not all) in the literary community was in reality an aristocratic, and even nihilistic, individualism, equally contemptuous of both conservative and 'progressive' ideologies. The 'tyranny' which they rejected was not that of capitalism or of the bourgeoisie, but of 'le nombre'. The attitude expressed (though fully meant?) by Louis Lormel in *L'Art Littéraire* of March–April 1894, referring to Ibsen's play *An Enemy of the People*, was typical:

Que nous importe l'affranchissement du plus grand nombre? Notre individualisme est celui du Docteur Stockmann, l'Ennemi du peuple. Il tend . . . à la glorification du génie. . . . Notre anarchisme est tout aristocratique . . . . Napoléon 1er est un admirable prototype: il a soumis l'Europe à son moi . . . .

> [What does the emancipation of the majority matter to us? Our individualism is that of Dr Stockmann, the Enemy of the People. It tends . . . towards the glorification of individual genius. . . . Our anarchism is wholly aristocratic . . . . Napoleon the First is an admirable prototype: he subjected the whole of Europe to his own ego . . . .]

A similar nihilistic individualism was expressed by Jarry's future friend Laurent Tailhade in a flamboyantly provocative assessment of Vaillant's deed: 'Qu'importent les victimes si le geste est beau? Qu'importe la mort de quelques vagues humanités si, par elle, s'affirme l'individu?'. ['What do the victims matter if the deed is aesthetically pleasing? What do the deaths of a few vague embodiments of mankind matter if, through them, the individual asserts himself?'][21] Something of this aestheticism pervades the attitude of Jarry also, who similarly chose (or feigned to choose) to exalt purely artistic values above all else. In an article of May 1894 entitled 'Visions actuelles et futures', he dismisses the anarchist theories of Émile Henry as merely the 'apparente logique éblouisseuse de potaches, absurdité guerroyant contre l'absurdité' ['obvious pseudo-logic of schoolboys, absurdity waging war against absurdity'], concluding with the remark: 'Qu'il est plus beau d'étudier les conjonctions!' He exalts as superior to both the bomb and the guillotine the 'Machine à décerveler' and its faithful servants, the 'Palotins' – 'les seuls/*Parfaits pour qui veut que sa Volonté s'érige loi souveraine*' ['the only/Perfect instruments *for him who wishes to establish his Will as supreme law*'].[22] While in a review in the *Mercure de France* two years later, in May 1896, of a well-intentioned but naïve novel by Augustin Léger entitled *Journal d'un anarchiste*, he concludes with the contemptuous remark that the book simply tended to prove 'que les "overriers" anarchistes sont de mauvais littérateurs', and that its hero is in the end 'appropriately' guillotined. With the ideas of such self-styled 'anarchists', he contrasts 'l'Anarchiste propre', at whose orders are both 'le Naturel et le Surnaturel' and to whom 'pour un laps de vie, Dieu . . . a cédé sa place de Synthèse' – that is, the literary 'genius'.[23] In short, above all other forms of activity stands the *creative imagination*, and the theories of 'anarchism' no less than those of its opponents – and no less also than the fundamental concepts of philosophy and religion – are to be regarded merely as 'imaginary solutions'. Obscure though such pronouncements as these may have been to Jarry's contemporaries (at least, to those few who read them), they constituted a warning to all those who, in December 1896, were to give a 'political' interpretation to the theatrical bomb of *Ubu Roi.*

In all of these respects, then, Jarry's thought is profoundly influenced by, yet at the same time tends to undermine, the ideas of the Symbolists. Alongside his views on imagination, however, one other closely related subject remains to be examined, that of his views on the nature of *language.* For here too his attitude, far more radical than that of any of his contemporaries, was to profoundly affect the nature of his literary work for the rest of his life.

The Symbolists' treatment of language was in fact the feature of their work which most struck (and most outraged) their more conservative contemporaries (causing, for example, in the 1880s, poets such as Verlaine, Laforgue and Mallarmé to be denounced as 'decadents'). Their attitude to language sprang from a number of different sources, among them an aristocratic indifference to the needs of the vulgar 'mob', and an attempt to apply their view of art as the expression of an absolute individualism. One result was the frequent adoption of an idiosyncratic and even deliberately contorted syntax. Another was the creation of a flood of neologisms, many of which have since found their way into general usage. So great was the wave of linguistic invention that in 1888 the novelist Paul Adam published, under the pseudonym of 'Jacques Plowert', a *Petit glossaire pour servir à l'intelligence des auteurs décadents et symbolistes* in which he attempted, not without an element of tongue-in-cheek humour, to catalogue the most common forms of word-creation. They include the fusion of two or more existing words; the creation of new nouns from existing verbs and adjectives by the addition of suffixes such as *-ance*, *-ure* and *-ité*; that of adjectives by the addition of suffixes such as *-aire* and *-oire*; of new verbs deriving from existing nouns and adjectives; and of entirely new words derived from Latin and Greek roots. A third, and even more significant, development concerned the meaning and function of words. A characteristic of the work of many of the Symbolists is a tendency to choose words first and foremost for their sound and shape – an attitude admirably summed up by Gourmont (whose own *Le Latin mystique* contains a veritable treasure-house of strange and sonorous terms) in an article of 1892 with the telling title of 'L'Ivresse verbale':

Les mots que j'adore et que je collectionne comme des joyaux sont ceux dont le sens m'est fermé, ou presque, les mots imprécis, les syllabes de rêve, les marjolaines [*sic*] et les milloraines, fleurs jamais vues. . . . Quelle musique est comparable à la sonorité pure des mots obscurs, ô cyclamor?

> [The words which I love and which I collect like precious gems are those whose meaning is a completely, or almost completely, closed book to me – vague words, dream-like sounds, marjorams [*sic*] and milloraines, flowers never ever seen. . . . What music can be compared to the pure resonance of obscure words, o cyclamor?]

It is an attitude which, as Gourmont implies, leads easily to a neglect of meaning for the sake of sound alone. A fourth and related feature is the Symbolists' search for allusiveness and suggestion in poetry, characteristics which they saw as being the opposite of the descriptiveness of Parnassian verse (and which they believed were present in the paintings of their idol, Gauguin). This aim was neatly expressed by Mallarmé in an interview with a naïve but earnest journalist, Jules Huret, in 1891: '*Nommer* un objet, c'est supprimer les trois quarts de la jouissance du poëme qui est faite de deviner peu à peu: le *suggérer*, voilà le rêve.' [To *name* an object is to take away three-quarters of the pleasure of the poem, which is made up of guessing little by little: to *suggest* it is the ideal.][24] Lastly, among the Symbolists a significant minority displayed an interest in other forms of 'language', or systems of 'signs'. Mallarmé was fascinated by the language of dance and mime, and by the 'abstract' language of music; Jarry's friend Marcel Schwob had a special interest in the *argot* of François Villon and the medieval *truands*; and Gourmont was passionately interested in the language of heraldry and in the medieval symbolism of precious stones and animals.

Thus far, Jarry follows unhesitatingly his Symbolist mentors. He adopts an elliptical prose style, and an idiosyncratic syntax involving frequent inversions of normal word order – in particular a tendency to place adjectives systematically before the noun. He enthusiastically joined in the game of word-creation, fearlessly employing in *Les Minutes de sable mémorial* and *César-Antechrist* such words as *florescence*, *aurité*, *firmamentaire*, *splendir*, *exorder*, *auditer*, and the (deliberately preposterous) Greco-Latin derivation *l'herpétologie ahénéenne* (= serpents of brass), used to designate Ubu's newly-devised system of sewage disposal. And he not only shared with Gourmont an interest in medieval religious symbolism and in the language of heraldry – whose arcane terminology inspired the title *Les Minutes de sable mémorial* and whose coats-of-arms, with their various shapes and colours, inspired the 'Acte héraldique' of *César-Antechrist*, in which not only the names of the characters but even the stage-directions are expressed in the language of heraldry – but had his own special interests in the even more abstract language of mathematics and in the gestural language of the puppet theatre.

But such features are relatively trivial by comparison with Jarry's views concerning the function of language. Here, he goes beyond all of his Symbolist contemporaries, including even his master Mallarmé, in two vitally significant respects. The first involves a development of the Mallarméan ideal of allusiveness or suggestion. This concept, pushed to its logical extreme, gives rise to an element of indeterminacy: the meaning attributed to, and the response evoked by, a poem or even a particular word may differ with each individual reader. Implicit in this ideal of suggestion is therefore the possibility of a cult of *deliberate* ambiguity, or 'polysemy' (that is, multiplicity of meaning). This is an idea which is central to Jarry's poetic theory, and which is explicitly formulated in the appropriately entitled 'Linteau' (or preface) to *Les Minutes de sable mémorial*. Not only does this offer us Jarry's clearest and most detailed formulation of his aesthetic principles but, as the word 'lintel' – the horizontal beam or stone slab above a door or window, which supports the structure above – suggests, it is crucial to an understanding not only of *Les Minutes* but of the works which follow as well.

After a preamble which clearly expresses his contemptuous dismissal of both accepted literary practices and philosophical systems, Jarry offers the following definition of his own aesthetic: 'Suggérer au lieu de dire, faire dans la route des phrases un carrefour de tous les mots.' ['To suggest instead of stating, to create in the highway of sentences a crossroads of all the words.']25 The opening words recall immediately the ambitions of Mallarmé; but the image of the crossroads gives to the idea of suggestion a more precise intellectual content. It implies that the work of literature does not merely allow of a number of vague possibilities of interpretation, but that each word of a text opens up a different line of signification. Every work of literature is thus susceptible of a multiplicity of interpretations; hence 'la dissection indéfinie exhume toujours des oeuvres quelque chose de nouveau' ['unending dissection always uncovers in works of literature something new']. But here a vital distinction occurs: whereas in 'l'oeuvre d'ignorance aux mots bulletins de vote' (a phrase which recalls Mallarmé's contemptuous reference to 'les mots de la tribu') the relationship existing between its various possible meanings is variable, in the 'œuvre de génie' it is constant. In Jarry's words:

Mais voici le critère pour distinguer cette obscurité, chaos facile, de l'Autre, simplicité* condensée, diamant du charbon, oeuvre unique faite de toutes les oeuvres possibles offertes à tous les yeux encerclant le phare argus de la périphérie de notre crâne sphérique: en celle-ci, *le rapport de la phrase verbale à tout sens qu'on y puisse trouver est constant*; en celle-là, indéfiniment varié.

[But here is the criterion which enables one to distinguish this obscurity, a facile chaos, from the Other, a condensed simplicity,* diamond made out of coal, the unique work made up of all the possible works offered to all the eyes which encircle the argus-like beacon of the periphery of our spherical skull: in the latter, *the relationship between the written phrase and any meaning which one may find therein remains fixed*; in the former, infinitely variable.][26]

In the 'work of genius', moreover, the author will at all times remain superior to the reader, however perceptive the reader may be, since the author has consciously created a synthesis of *all* possible meanings: 'Tous les sens qu'y trouvera le lecteur sont prévus, et jamais il ne les trouvera tous; et l'auteur peut lui en indiquer, colin-maillard cérébral, d'inattendus, postérieurs et contradictoires.' ['Every meaning which the reader may find therein is intentional, and he will never find them all; and the author can point out to him – a victim in a game of intellectual blind man's buff – unexpected, subsequent and contradictory meanings.'] The task of the reader must simply be to weigh conscientiously each word of a text: 'Qu'on pèse donc les mots, polyèdres d'idées, avec des scrupules comme des diamants à la balance de ses oreilles' ['Let him therefore weigh the words, polyhedra of ideas, as scrupulously as if they were diamonds, on the balance of his ears'].[27]

Not only, therefore, is *every* possible meaning of a text valid (because intended by the author), but all meanings are *equally* valid. The importance of this principle of polysemy for an understanding of Jarry's literary work cannot be overestimated. It is a principle which is exemplified in the very title of *Les Minutes de sable mémorial* itself. *Sable* refers both to the sand of the *sablier* or hourglass, which marks the passage of time, and which recurs in the title of the last poem in the volume, and to the term for the colour black in heraldry; and *mémorial* has the meaning of both 'in memory of' and 'of the memory'. The title as a whole therefore refers simultaneously to the passage of time whose 'minutes' are here recorded; to the movement of memory; and to the committal to paper of a series of moments of creative activity ('sable' referring to the ink-blackened pages) which memory has inspired or, alternatively and simultaneously, which are reproduced here as a 'memorial'. This is a principle which is exemplified throughout both *Les Minutes* and *César-Antechrist*, as we shall shortly see.

But Jarry's thought takes also a second and even more radical turn. Not only does he create, through the deliberate cultivation of polysemy, a multiplicity of levels of meaning. But in his work – to borrow the terminology of Saussurian linguistics – the *signifier* tends to detach itself from the *signified*; that is, language tends to break away from any reference to a 'real' world to assume an existence of its own. In this respect, more than in any other, he goes beyond his

Symbolist contemporaries. For one of the outstanding paradoxes of Symbolism is that, for all the boldness of certain of their ideas, the Symbolists did not depart by and large from a view of language as a fixed system of 'signs' whose function is to provide a vehicle of communication and a means of describing the real world. Only Mallarmé, in whose thought several impulses are at work simultaneously, departs significantly from this view. His aristocratic contempt for the 'mob', and his revulsion against literary commercialism – that is, against the idea of writing for a 'market' – together produce a tendency to reject the idea of writing for a 'public' at all. At the same time, in his reaction against the descriptiveness of Parnassianism and against anything which might be construed as mere *reportage*, he tends to turn away altogether from a conception of the writer as communicator to that exclusively of *creator*, writing for himself alone. Thus, in the thought of Mallarmé – at its most extreme point, at least – language ceases to be a medium of communication to become an object existing in its own right, autonomous and independent of the 'real' world, an object through which the artist (or writer) makes the supreme assertion of his creative freedom. His ambition was to create a language which would be in some way absolute – 'niant, d'un trait souverain, le hasard'.[28] Moreover, if language is, or is to become, autonomous and absolute, then the same must apply to literature: it, like music, in Mallarmé's view, ceases to be a form of communication or of representation, and is conceived of as existing alongside and independently of the 'real' world.

How is this seemingly impossible goal to be achieved? A key idea in Mallarmé's thought here is that of interrelationship or structure. Pursuing the analogy between poetry and music, he formulates the idea that, just as in a piece of music it is not the individual notes but their interrelationship which is all-important, so too in poetry it is not the individual word or image which matters, but the interrelationships between words and images – their place in the total context, or structure, of the work. The idea is most clearly formulated in the essay *Crise de vers* of 1896: the poet 'cède l'initiative aux mots, par le heurt de leur inégalité mobilisés; ils s'allument de reflets réciproques comme une virtuelle traînée de feux sur des pierreries' ['allows the words, spurred to action by the shock of their unequal force, to take the initiative; they blaze forth, lit up by their mutual reflections, like a potential flickering of flames over precious stones'].[29] Whether – as seems infinitely probable – Jarry was inspired at least in part by Mallarmé, or whether mere coincidence is responsible, the parallels between the ideas of the two men are striking. For it is just such a concept of a work of literature, in which the significance of words and images derives not from their conventional use but from their interaction with other words and images, resulting in the creation of an intricate and elaborate network of cross-references, that Jarry applies in *Les Minutes de sable mémorial* and *César-Antechrist*.

Les Minutes de sable mémorial comprises a collection of 33 separate pieces of verse and prose. The world which it opens up is a strange and esoteric one, revealing to a degree unusual even among the Symbolists the creation of a highly personal, individualistic world of the imagination. It is also a world situated outside both present time and space, either in a fantastical pseudo-medieval setting, or in an extra-terrestrial universe, or in a world of dream and nightmarish hallucination, indicative of Jarry's refusal to accept the world in which he lived. The volume encompasses a wide range of themes and subjects, from religious themes to horrific visions of catastrophe and death and scenes of sadistic cruelty. It contains allusions also to a host of strange and exotic objects, plants and animals – calvaries, gibbets, skulls, mandrakes, the passionflower, and such creatures as owls, snakes, slugs, toads, bats, crows, wolves, spiders and chameleons, to name but a few. And the tone of the volume is equally varied, ranging from poignant lyricism, through sardonic humour and deliberate blasphemy, to rhetorical declamation.

Though the technical skill and versatility of Jarry are striking, much in the volume is, inevitably, derivative, and some pieces are in the nature of literary exercises. Some poems are reminiscent of the work of poets such as Verlaine, Laforgue and Corbière, with their exploitation of changing rhythm, of acrobatic rhyming and of assonance and alliteration. Much too belongs to the conventional bric-à-brac of medievalism as reflected in the macabre Romanticism of writers such as Aloysius Bertrand. Much of the strange fauna, as well as the sometimes declamatory or hysterical tone, derives from Lautréamont's *Les Chants de Maldoror*; and other elements recall the sardonic humour and savage fantasy of Villiers de l'Isle-Adam. But much too is personal to Jarry. A number of poems take the form of 'word-paintings' which look forward to his *Gestes et opinions du docteur Faustroll, pataphysicien*: in them, he has attempted to capture in words the atmosphere of paintings by Gauguin and by the Norwegian painter Munthe ('Tapisseries. D'après et pour Munthe'). The choice of subjects is revealing: Gauguin's self-conscious primitivism is paralleled by Munthe's depiction, with a combination of skill and apparent naïvety, of the heroic exploits and magical world of Viking folklore. Other poems are (on one level, at least) memorable and quite moving pieces of lyricism. Such is 'Le Sablier', which closes the volume and which develops, through the image of the hourglass, the theme of the weeping or bleeding heart which is found also in the poem 'Berceuse du mort pour s'endormir' and in both the Prologue and Epilogue to *Haldernablou*.

A number of pieces are remarkable also for the visionary quality of their imagery. 'L'Opium' powerfully evokes a nightmarish vision (which purports to be opium-inspired, and which looks forward to both the work of the Surrealists and the world of Kafka) of an immense morgue through which the author wanders, a kind of lost paradise where the dead sleep in the posture of a foetus in a womb. (It looks forward also, on another level, to the association of the themes of death and murder with the Oedipus theme of *L'Amour absolu*.) 'Les Cinq Sens', though to some extent a literary exercise, is effective in rendering the sensations of touch, smell, hearing, sight and taste as the narrator makes his way through a weird museum of the dead carrying a foetus wrapped in a towel.[30] Even more striking is Jarry's ability to transform reality imaginatively, and in particular to attribute to inanimate objects the characteristics of living things. Almost any object, in fact, can be transformed into any other. Thus in 'Le Sablier' the three supporting vertical bars of the hourglass become first three stone pillars from which a heart is suspended, then the wooden bars of a pillory, three 'bras noirs calcinés' which count the hours of the damned, the trunks of trees, and finally a threefold gibbet. In *Haldernablou* (which was incorporated by Jarry into *Les Minutes*), a circular air-vent in a railway station is transformed into the mathematical symbol of zero and simultaneously attributed with both sexual and metaphysical properties, being addressed as 'Dieu métallique, essence et idole' and 'Onan du métal de ton sexe'.[31] In 'Phonographe', the second section of *Guignol*, there occurs a description of the recently invented phonograph as a metallic 'siren' who holds her lover by the head with her 'doigt unique'.[32] In *Haldernablou* and its attendant 'Paralipomènes', on the other hand, an inverse movement takes place, as objects and human features are translated into geometrical shapes in such images as 'dents triangulaires', 'crâne isocèle', 'les polyèdres d'une flûte', 'le trapèze du livre ouvert', 'figure hexagonale où s'inscrivent les cercles de deux yeux', 'la tour octogone' and 'l'hypoténuse de ses seins' ['triangular teeth', 'isoceles skull', 'the polyhedra of a flute', 'the trapezium of the open book', 'hexagonal face in which are engraved the circles of two eyes', 'the octagonal tower', 'the hypotenuse of his breast']. This tendency to transform objects in the world around him was a constant feature of Jarry's imagination, manifested throughout both his life and work, as testified by Louis Lormel looking back many years later:

Alfred Jarry était un grand chasseur d'images et d'analogies. Se trouvant un jour avec moi à la gare Saint-Lazare, sous la salle des Pas-Perdus, il voyait apparaître et disparaître, au plafond de verre, les pas des voyageurs. D'où l'idée d'un aquarium, évoqué dans l'*Amour absolu*. Il comparait aussi les machines à vapeur à de monstrueux insectes, aux pattes mouvantes, un train à un accordéon, etc. Ce genre de préoccupations, bien connu de tous les écrivains, était constant chez Jarry.

[Alfred Jarry was a great hunter after images and analogies. One day when we were together at the Gare Saint-Lazare, beneath the waiting-room, he saw the feet of passengers appearing and disappearing in the glass ceiling above our heads. Whence the idea of an aquarium, conjured up in *L'Amour absolu*. He also compared steam-engines to monstrous insects, with moving legs, a train to an accordion, etc. This kind of preoccupation, which is familiar to all writers, was an obsession with Jarry.][33]

The love of technical terms evident in *Les Minutes* and *César-Antechrist* was also to remain a characteristic of his work, extending beyond the mathematical, zoological, botanical and heraldic terminology and Greco-Latin neologisms[34] present here to embrace also the specialized vocabulary of philosophy, medicine, physics, cycling, fencing and military tactics.

Amidst the variety of themes and images in *Les Minutes de sable mémorial*, two groups dominate – those associated with death, and those associated with love or sex. Scenes of death are frequent, and there is barely a poem or prose passage which does not contain at least an oblique allusion to the subject. One of the most striking occurs in 'Les Paralipomènes de Haldernablou', which obscurely records a homosexual relationship between the narrator and a young 'éphèbe' which ends in the murder of the latter (whose eyes are then pecked out by the narrator's pet owls!), and the death-agony of a woman referred to variously as 'la moribonde', 'la Vieille Femme', and 'Centenaire Recluse', whose death occurs 'le 27 mars à trois heures du matin'.[35] The attitude expressed here and elsewhere in *Les Minutes* towards death appears to be a mixture of fear and fascination – fascination, since death (as *César-Antechrist* will make clear) brings a release from the restrictions of space and time. The theme of love, on the other hand, in addition to the central position which it occupies in *Haldernablou*, is the subject of numerous allusions, many of them implicit rather than explicit, being suggested by the recurrent images which the text contains. Sometimes a sexual connotation is suggested, rather facilely, by the shape of certain objects. Perpendicular shapes abound (the 'tour d'ivoire' of the 'Prolégomènes' of *Haldernablou*, the obelisks and columns of the latter, rapiers and pistols, and the vertical or oblique bars of heraldic coats-of-arms). The *pal* (the stake on which the unfortunate Achras is impaled, but also a heraldic form) becomes a sexual symbol as well as an instrument of sadistic torture, as also do Ubu's faithful henchmen, the *Palotins*, whose hirsute trinity 'jaillit en un élan phallique'.[36] Frequently, too, the explicitly formulated erotic or sexual associations of certain objects are implicitly transferred to other contexts in which those objects recur, leading to the creation of an increasingly elaborate pattern of cross-references. This is the case, for example, with the chameleon, originally identified with Léon-Paul Fargue, the model for 'Caméléo' in the original version of *Haldernablou* (the eyes of which are here compared to 'des pénis de nègres' and in 'Les Prolégomènes de Haldernablou' to a giant Phallus); with the bat, described as 'doublure de sexe tentaculaire retourné'; with the owl, through the description of a male sexual organ as 'beau comme un hibou pendu par les griffes'; and with the serpent, likened to a giant Phallus moving along the ground.[37]

Moreover, these two groups of images overlap and interact, intimately associating the two themes of sex and death. Most of the above-mentioned objects with sexual associations recur also in association with the theme of death. The same associations are present also, alongside its traditional significance, in the frequently recurring image of the mandrake. The closest identification of all occurs in 'Les Prolégomènes de Haldernablou', which contains a vision, inspired by the Biblical tale of Sodom and Gomorrah, of the destruction beneath a hail of sulphur and bitumen of a city whose inhabitants have violated the sexual 'Norm' of the Deity. Here, God himself takes on sexual attributes, as we witness his 'Phallus sacré, que les Indous appellent Lingam', crawl through a crumbling temple and slide across a sea of bitumen, bringing death and destruction to all those who 'rêvèrent des sexes plus purs que ceux par Dieu sortis du limon, et inventèrent les dièses et les bémols d'Éros, succédant au plain-chant brutal' ['dreamed of sexes purer than those created by God out of the primeval dust, and invented the sharps and flats of Eros, taking the place of primitive plain-song'].[38]

It is tempting to infer from this the existence of certain personal obsessions which Jarry is here endeavouring to exorcise. Indeed, the prominence throughout his work as a whole of sexual themes and of the theme of death, and their frequent association, suggests a picture of a young man struggling to surmount, and ultimately to control, these obsessions – in the case of *Les Minutes*, through their translation into symbolic and abstract terms. Whatever other conclusions one comes to concerning both this work and *César-Antechrist*, there is undoubtedly some measure of truth in this view. But at the same time, three factors exist which must prevent us from taking much in *Les Minutes entirely* at face value.

The first of these is the element of selfconscious imitation and patent exaggeration which much of the volume contains. For Jarry's borrowings are at times a little too obvious. Two examples will suffice: he himself draws attention, as we have seen, to the inspiration of Lautréamont; and the first part of the obscurely entitled poem 'La Régularité de la châsse', with its ludicrous superabundance of assonance and alliteration, reads like a pastiche of the work of Albert Samain, in such lines as:

Voler vers le ciel vain les voix vagues des vierges. . . .

Main maigrie et maudite où menace la mort! . . .

Naît une nef noyée en des nuits noires, nulles;
Puis les piliers polis poussent comme des pins . . . .

Mais ma main mince mord la mer de moire mauve . . .

> [*The vague voices of virgins flying futilely forth to heaven. . . .*
>
> *Shrivelled and cursed hand in which death threatens! . . .*
>
> *Appears a vessel drowned in the blackness of night, void;*
> *Then polished pillars spring up like pines . . .*
>
> *But the slim hand bites the sea of mauve rippling waters . . .*][39]

The second factor is the sudden intrusion into the apparently refined and poetic world of *Les Minutes* of the monstrous figure of Ubu, through the incorporation into the work of the *Guignol*. Here, in a scene of pure farce tinged with sadism, we are introduced first to M. Achras, the 'collecteur de polyèdres' whose peace and tranquillity are shattered by the arrival of Ubu and who ends by being impaled on the latter's portable 'pal nickelé'. And in the third section, 'L'Art et la Science', we witness Mère Ubu's secret tryst with her lover, the *vidangeur* Barbapoux, in the latrines, and their discovery by Ubu. The elevated-sounding title refers in reality to a comparison between the old 'artisanal' methods of sewage-disposal of Barbapoux and the shining new 'scientific' plumbing introduced by Ubu. Not only does the inclusion of these episodes shatter the hitherto prevailing tone of *Les Minutes*, but the reader is tempted (and no doubt intended by Jarry, if we are to believe the 'Linteau') to establish links between them and other parts of the volume – identifying for example the images of night and darkness, symbolizing death, in the 'Lieds funèbres' with the 'chute dans la nuit, dans l'humide et le noir' of 'L'Art et la Science' – and to see the insinuation of a fundamental 'equivalence' between the two.

The third factor relates to Jarry's aim of polysemy formulated in the 'Linteau' and manifested in the title of *Les Minutes de sable mémorial*. The key to an interpretation of *Les Minutes* is to be found not in the immediate subject or theme of individual poems or prose passages, but in the recurrence of a series of words and images throughout the volume. Thus, alongside the immediate or surface meaning apparent in any given text, words and images take on new 'meanings' deriving from their association with each other and from associations of ideas within the context of the volume as a whole (and sometimes also, indeed, from an interrelationship with other works of Jarry). In this way, Jarry deliberately and systematically creates a network of cross-references and allusions, and a multiplicity of different levels of meaning – realizing the ambition to 'faire dans la route des phrases un carrefour de tous les mots' and demonstrating the principle that 'le rapport de la phrase verbale à tout sens qu'on y puisse trouver est constant'.

This is not to say that all the poems and prose passages comprising *Les Minutes* were written with this complex scheme of cross-references and this principle of polysemy in mind. That this was not the case is revealed by Jarry himself in a disparaging reference in the 'Linteau':

Et il y a divers vers et prose que nous trouvons très mauvais et que nous avons laissés pourtant, retranchant beaucoup, parce que pour un motif qui nous échappe aujourd'hui, ils nous ont donc intéressé un instant puisque nous les avons écrits.

> [And there are various pieces of prose and verse which we consider very bad but which, whilst omitting a great deal, we have nonetheless retained, because for a reason which now escapes us they must have interested us at one time since we wrote them.][40]

Some, at least, of these 'vers et proses' were obviously written with quite a different intention in mind – indeed, there is much in *Les Minutes* which is undoubtedly deeply personal in inspiration – and were only subsequently incorporated into the overall scheme of the volume, becoming infused with new levels of meaning and new symbolic associations in the process.

Yet is it in fact correct here to speak of 'symbolism'? By definition, a symbol stands for or points to something beyond itself. But what, precisely, does this complex web of cross-references point to? What is it, ultimately, that is being 'signified'? Or does the world of *Les Minutes* realize, in a perhaps unexpected way, the ideal of Mallarmé of a work of literature independent and autonomous of the 'real' world, in which words do not 'refer' to objects or events in any such world but merely 's'allument de reflets réciproques'? The answer lies in an examination of Jarry's other major, and closely related, work of his 'Symbolist' phase, *César-Antechrist*.

César-Antechrist (as Jarry systematically writes the title) constitutes a kind of pivot in his literary output, linking *Les Minutes de sable mémorial* with, on the one hand, the *Ubu* plays and, on the other, *Gestes et opinions du docteur Faustroll, pataphysicien*. It is not simply a case of recurrence of the same patterns of imagery; these texts contain also explicit references to each other and even a degree of textual interpenetration. Alongside 'Les Prolégomènes de Haldernablou' (in which there occurs the telling phrase: 'César-Antechrist vous dira', thus linking *Haldernablou* with *César-Antechrist*), *Les Minutes* contains also 'Les Prolégomènes de César-Antechrist'; and *Faustroll* contains an explicit reference to *César-Antechrist*. Even more important is the element of textual interpenetration, or intertextuality. The *Guignol* incorporated into *Les Minutes* provides a first link with the *Ubu* cycle (and also, incidentally, a first introduction to Jarry's 'science of pataphysics', elaborated in *Faustroll*). The second part of 'Les Prolégomènes de César-Antechrist', sub-titled 'Ubu parle', consists entirely of a brief acknowledged quotation from *Les Polonais ou Ubu Roi*. And the 'Acte prologal' of *César-Antechrist*, originally published in *L'Art Littéraire* of July-August 1894, was subsequently incorporated into *Les Minutes* immediately before the 'Prologue de conclusion', and was *not* reprinted in the original edition of *César-Antechrist* in 1895: in its place was a note stating that the act 'ne sera point réimprimé ici' and referring the reader to *Les Minutes de sable mémorial* . . . Finally, the 'Acte terrestre' of *César-Antechrist* is none other than a shortened version of the play *Ubu Roi*.[41] In thus linking these – and, implicitly, other – works, Jarry was hinting at more fundamental relationships which profoundly affect the interpretation of each.[42]

César-Antechrist was published in November 1895 in an edition of 206 copies. It was illustrated by numerous woodcuts, only one of which was this time by Jarry himself. Its numerous stage-directions, indicating a keen concern for visual effects, suggest that Jarry may have hoped for an eventual staging of the play – an enterprise which was not wholly fantastical in view of the nature of the productions organized by the Théâtre d'Art a short time earlier, but which was certainly never realized. Amongst the manifold sources of the work, two are of particular importance. Much material is drawn directly from the *Apocalypse* with its portrayal of the 'Antichrist' of Christian tradition, popularly identified with the Emperor Nero – a work which had been in vogue since the days of Romanticism and whose popularity had been given a new impetus by the publication in 1873 of Renan's *L'Antéchrist* (which Jarry probably also drew upon). Much was also borrowed from Gourmont's *Le Latin mystique*, with its vast storehouse of medieval legend and symbolism which partly or wholly inspired such themes and motifs as the end of the world, the instruments of torture and martyrdom, the symbolic representation of Christ, the Tree-Cross, and the symbolism of such creatures as the Siren-Bird, the Dragon, the Leviathan, the Unicorn and the Lion. Even more, however, than the colourful legends and fantastic beliefs of this medieval Latin literature, it was the medieval attitude towards symbolism which fascinated Gourmont – and, in his wake, Jarry. For the world of *Le Latin mystique* is one in which symbolism has run riot, in which symbol is heaped upon symbol to the point of inextricability. Above all, Gourmont was delighted by the potential polysemy of many of these symbols, and by their inconstancy and even interchangeability – quoting with obvious relish, for example, the 'explanation' of Hugues de Saint-Victor of those symbols which represent both Christ *and* the Devil:

Si quelqu'un demande pourquoi le Christ est parfois signifié par des animaux immondes, tels que le serpent, le lion, le dragon, l'aigle et autres semblables: qu'il sache que le lion, quand il s'agit de fortitude, représente le Christ, quand il s'agit de rapacité, le diable . . . .

> [If anyone should ask why Christ is sometimes represented by base and vile creatures such as the serpent, the lion, the dragon, the eagle, and others of like kind: let him be told that the lion, when strength is signified, represents Christ, and when rapaciousness is signified, the devil . . . .[43]

But if the sources of *César-Antechrist* are relatively easy to establish, the 'meaning' of the work is less so. On the surface, it appears to be a poetic drama in the best rhetorico-symbolist manner, developing the Nietzschean theme of the 'death of God' and expressing a vision of a consequent rampant nihilism in the reign of an up-dated Antichrist. The idea was one very much in the air in these years, and Jarry is not alone in dramatizing it. His play begins with the death of the three Christs (crucified, in accordance with the traditions of the Black Mass, upside down), whose message of charity and humility is exhausted. Their death leaves Saint-Pierre-Humanité free but alone and abandoned ('Seul! – Seul. – Sans appui, sans barreaux. – Sans cage, sans maître.' ['Alone! – Alone. – Without support, without restraints. – With no shackles, and no master.']44), but as they die they salute the birth of Antichrist, who is to be the new and terrible master of Saint-Pierre-Humanité. For Antichrist is the antithesis of Christ; in the words of the former, 'Christ qui vins avant moi, je te contredis comme le retour du pendule en efface l'aller. Diastole et systole, nous sommes notre Repos.' ['Christ who came before me, I contradict you as each swing of the pendulum obliterates its predecessor. Systole and diastole, we are each other's rest.'] Where Christ is the Prince of Light and the embodiment of supreme Good, Antichrist is the Prince of Darkness and 'le souverain Mal'. Where Christ promised eternal life, Antichrist is the prophet and bringer of eternal Death. Both however are contained within a metaphysical framework symbolized by the above image of the pendulum:

Le jour et la nuit, la vie et la mort, l'être et la vie, ce qu'on appelle, parce qu'il est actuel, le vrai, et son contraire, alternent dans les balancements du Pendulum which is God the Father.]45

> [Day and night, life and death, being and living, that which, because it is of the present, is called truth, and its opposite, alternate in the swings of the Pendulum which is God the Father.]45

In conformity with this principle, the reign of Antichrist himself is not to last. At the end of the symbolic extravaganza of the 'Acte héraldique' (in which the various characters, symbolized by their heraldic escutcheons, move against the background of a set which itself represents various heraldic signs and which is impossible to understand without a knowledge of heraldry[46]), there appears the figure of ... Ubu. For Ubu is the earthly or physical 'Double' of Antichrist, the Beast of the Apocalypse, whose appearance heralds the beginning of his own reign. The 'Acte terrestre' (which is as long as the other three acts put together) recounts the ravages of Ubu, whose purely nihilistic and self-gratifying aims are neatly summed up in the brief quotation from *Ubu Roi* included by Jarry under the heading 'Ubu parle' in 'Les Prolégomènes de César-Antechrist': 'Quand j'aurai pris toute la Phynance, je tuerai tout le monde et je m'en irai.' ['When I have taken all the Phynance, I'll kill everybody and go away.']447] In the 'Acte dernier' – subtitled 'Du Jugement' – Antichrist reappears to announce his own impending death: 'J'ai dormi, mon âme a dormi, mon corps agissant a rampé, mon Double. Quand on voit son double on meurt.' ['I have slept, my soul has slept, my active body, my Double, has crawled over the earth. When one sees one's double, one dies.']448] And at the end of the work he does indeed die, 'calciné noir', as Christ descends from the Cross, the Holy Spirit soars on high, and God the Father reigns in triumph.

This, however, is only the most superficial interpretation of the drama, whose 'philosophy' Jarry deliberately and explicitly undermines from within. This is done, firstly, by the insertion of deliberately incongruous or even contradictory statements or details. For example, to Saint-Pierre-Humanité's anguished cry: 'Maître, Maître, pourquoi m'abandonnes-tu?', the Silver Christ explains simply that 'Dieu a sommeil'. In the final act, the words 'c'est ici mon fils bien-aimé, en qui j'ai mis toutes mes complaisances' ['this is my beloved son, in whom I am well pleased'] are spoken by 'God the Father' not with reference to Christ, but to Antichrist. And the title given to this final act – which opens with Antichrist inexplicably lowering a bull into a freshly dug grave – is 'Le Taurobole', in obvious memory of Rouget's Pump. Secondly, the protagonists themselves are made to comment (unfavourably) upon the religious and philosophical credibility of the drama, undermining that credibility as they do so. As the now dead [*sic!*] Christs salute the coming of Antichrist, the Silver Christ exclaims: 'Que le scepticisme, crédulité bourgeoise, ne s'indigne point d'entendre parler les morts.' ['Let scepticism, that bourgeois form of credulity, not be scandalized at hearing the dead speak.'] And Antichrist addresses Christ with the words: 'les littérateurs sans génie ni talent parlent de toi' ['literary hacks devoid of genius or talent speak of you'], and, even more clearly, states in reference to the religious and metaphysical framework of the work that 'la stupidité de ces théories est vieille comme Ormutz et Ahriman' ['the stupidity of these theories is as ancient as Ormuzd and Ahriman'].[49]

Thirdly, this effect of subversion is achieved even more fully through the 'symbolism' of the work. The heraldic extravaganza of Act II is overlaid with a mathematical symbolism, and both are subsumed into a phallic symbolism. At the centre of this extravaganza is the *bâton à physique* – originally the subject of a crude schoolboy joke at the Lycée de Rennes, where it was one of the objects intimately associated with 'Père Heb'. In *César-Antechrist* it constitutes at one and the same time a heraldic sign, a mathematical symbol forming both the sign minus and, by juxtaposition with itself, the sign plus, and a phallic symbol which is not only addressed in such mathematico-sexual terms as 'Phallus perpendiculaire au sourire de l'Ithyphalle en ta lateralité' ['Phallus perpendicular in your laterality to the smile of the Ithyphallus'], but is also the object of the invocation borrowed from Lautréamont and repeated here once again: 'Phallus déraciné, NE FAIS PAS DE PAREILS BONDS!' ['Uprooted Phallus, DO NOT LEAP ABOUT SO!'][50] Moreover, this sexual symbolism is extended also to the religious and 'apocalyptic' aspects of the drama. Not only is the birth of Antichrist portrayed by means of a fertility symbolism, but the figure of Antichrist is itself transformed, by an elaborate process of association, into a phallic symbol – as is also the Cross, and with it Christ as well. All are subsumed into the 'symbol' of the *bâton à physique*, which is addressed by the Templar and Fasce in the 'Acte héraldique' in the terms:

Tu es une roue dont la substance seule subsiste . . . . Tu es la roue, tu es l'oeil, demi-Saint-Esprit, Éternel. . . . Squelette, en tes culbutes d'ara, tu es le Christ ou Saint-Pierre. . . . MOINS-EN-PLUS, tu es le hibou, le sexe et l'Esprit, l'homme et la femme.

> [You are a wheel whose substance alone remains . . . . You are the wheel, you are the eye, semi-Holy Spirit, Eternal one. . . . Skeleton, in your macaw-like somersaults, you are Christ or Saint Peter. . . . MINUS-IN-PLUS, you are the owl, sex and the Spirit, man and woman.][51]

Even more than in *Les Minutes de sable mémorial*, symbol is here heaped upon symbol to the point where all become inextricable. And this extraordinary web of 'symbols' becomes in reality merely a symbolism of symbols, turning indefinitely – like the *bâton à physique* – in a closed circle upon itself and 'signifying' nothing but itself. Everything is here 'décor', and nothing but 'décor'.

Finally, the *bâton à physique* is the object of a further development also, which is hinted at in the systole/diastole image and in that of the pendulum, and by the elaborate series of antitheses to which these images give rise. It symbolizes (and, in the case of the signs minus and plus, whose 'contradiction' it resolves, demonstrates) the principle of the 'identity of opposites', a principle which is to be found in other works of Jarry also and which is central to his pataphysics. (He draws attention to this fact in *Gestes et opinions du docteur Faustroll, pataphysicien* where we are referred to 'un grand livre qui a pour titre *César-Antechrist*' in which is to be found 'la seule démonstration pratique, par l'engin mécanique dit *bâton à physique*, de l'identité des contraires' ['the only practical demonstration, by means of the mechanical device called *physick stick*, of the identity of opposites'].[52] Thus not only are the signs plus and minus identical, but so too, ultimately, are the concepts of day and night, light and darkness, good and evil, Christ and Antichrist. This is made explicit in the long invocation addressed by Fasce and the Templar to the *bâton à physique*, in the midst of which there suddenly enters ... the pataphysician:

Axiome et principe des contraires identiques, le pataphysicien, cramponné à tes oreilles et à tes ailes rétractiles, poisson volant, est le nain cimier du géant, par delà les métaphysiques; il est par toi l'Antechrist et Dieu aussi, cheval de l'Esprit, Moins-en-Plus, Moins-qui-es-Plus, cinématique du zéro restée dans les yeux, polyédrique infini.

[Axiom and origin of identical opposites, the pataphysician, clinging to your ears and your retractile wings, flying fish, is the dwarf on the crest of the giant, beyond all systems of metaphysics; he is through you Antichrist and God also, Pegasus of the Mind, Minus-in-Plus, Minus-which-is-Plus, kinematics of Zero remaining in the eyes, polyhedral infinity.][53]

Far from being resolved in some Hegelian 'higher synthesis', the religious, metaphysical, heraldic and mathematical antitheses of *César-Antechrist* are all, in equal measure, figments of the writer's – or of the pataphysician's – own imagination.

In short, the universe of *César-Antechrist* is a purely *verbal* universe, self-contained and wholly independent of any 'reality' outside of itself. This is indeed hinted at by Jarry in the text itself. At the very beginning of the 'Acte prologal', Saint-Pierre-Humanité explicitly states that it is his threefold *denial* which has brought into being the trinity of Christs whom he addresses: 'J'ai renié Dieu à trois reprises, et par mon reniement, triple foi, j'ai créé cette trinité renversée dont les bras amoureux m'étouffent.' ['I have denied God three times, and by my denial, threefold faith, I have created this inverted trinity whose loving arms stifle me.'][54] His words clearly indicate the purely verbal existence of this trinity of Christs (and illustrate at the same time the principle of the identity of opposites: denial = affirmation of existence). Whilst the Templar declares in the 'Acte héraldique' that 'le signe seul existe ... provisoire' ['the sign alone exists ... provisionally'].[55] To revert once again to the Saussurian distinction between *signifier* and *signified*, Jarry has simply abolished the latter term of the equation: the world of *César-Antechrist* is one in which the sign – or the word – is its own object.

Inevitably, such an interpretation of *César-Antechrist* influences our understanding of the works which precede and follow it with which it has explicit intertextual links. The purely verbal, imaginary character of the universe of *César-Antechrist* forces us to conclude that the strange and at times disturbing world of *Les Minutes de sable mémorial* may well also be, in the last resort, a purely imaginary one, 'signifying' nothing but itself. Moreover, the principle of polysemy which underlies both these works is implicitly extended to the text of *Ubu Roi* as well: the incorporation of the greater part of this into *César-Antechrist* confers upon the figure of Ubu a sexual significance which is wholly absent from the play in its original and independent form.[56] And, conversely, the presence of Ubu in the midst of such apparently 'poetic' works as *Les Minutes* and *César-Antechrist* has far-reaching consequences aesthetically, forcing us – by virtue both of the principle of association and of that of the 'identity of opposites' – to place the farce of *Ubu Roi* on the same level as the religious, philosophical and heraldic considerations of the former, and vice-versa. It is small wonder, therefore, that in *Guignol* Ubu is able to define himself as the epitome of 'Beauty':

La sphère est la forme parfaite. Le Soleil est l'astre parfait. .... Plus parfait que le cylindre, moins parfait que la sphère, du Tonneau radie le corps hyperphysique. Nous, son isomorphe, sommes beau.

> [The sphere is the perfect shape. The sun is the perfect star. .... More perfect than the cylinder, less perfect than the sphere, it is from the Barrel that the hyperphysical body irradiates. We, its isomorph, are beautiful.][57]

One can measure from this the gulf which separates Jarry from the great majority of his Symbolist colleagues. For all his numerous pronouncements on the subject, his own conception of 'Beauty' was clearly radically different from theirs. Nor did he share the widespread mystical belief that behind the phenomena of the visible world there lay some hidden 'meaning' or 'correspondence' with an ideal world, or some mysterious 'essence', which it was the task of poetry to reveal. It is this, ultimately, which causes him to part company with Mallarmé. For, despite Mallarmé's occasional dream of the creation of a literature which would be in some way 'absolute', autonomous, an end in itself, he does most of the time cling to the notion of poetry as the 'expression' of something. At times, this something is merely an evanescent and indefinable *état d'âme*, which can only be expressed by and through the interaction of the words and images of the poem itself. But at other times, Mallarmé clings tenaciously to a notion of poetry as the mysterious expression of 'the universe' itself, conceiving of poetry as fulfilling a metaphysical function which consists of endowing man's existence with its only possible meaning. This is the view expressed in the memorable definition:

La Poésie est l'expression, par le langage humain ramené à son rythme essentiel, du sens mystérieux des aspects de l'existence. Elle doue ainsi d'authenticité notre séjour et constitue la seule tâche spirituelle.

> [Poetry is the expression, through the language of man reduced to its basic rhythm, of the hidden meaning of aspects of existence. It thus endows our presence on this earth with authenticity and constitutes the only spiritual task.][58]

And the same fundamental idea is to be found in his meditations on the 'Grand Oeuvre' or 'le Livre', which will constitute 'l'explication orphique de la terre'. Such a conception, and such an ambition, are totally absent from Jarry's work. And to read *César-Antechrist*, as has frequently been done, as a 'mystical' work is to be guilty of a gross (if pardonable) naïvety.

Yet it would be equally wrong to dismiss *César-Antechrist*, as has also been done, as wholly or simply a piece of 'mystification' or sheer nonsense – a judgment identical with that which has been frequently, but wrongly, applied to *Ubu Roi*. For, strangely, this is also one of the most secret and revealing of the works of Jarry, whose most cherished conceptions and beliefs are all too often expressed, by a supreme paradox, in a deliberately derisory or even comic form. Behind – and through – the grandiose verbiage of *César-Antechrist*, and in spite of the satirical or spoofing intention which the work undoubtedly embodies, it contains also the expression of a number of ideas (concerning time, memory, 'God', imagination, power, and the relationship between the 'self' and the 'world') which are central to his thought, and which will be taken up again and developed in such works as *Les Jours et les Nuits*, *Le Surmâle* and *La Dragonne*. And it announces also a number of key ideas which are to be developed and illustrated in *Gestes et opinions du docteur Faustroll, pataphysicien*.

Lastly, there is one other crucial respect in which it would be wrong to see Jarry's intentions in *Les Minutes de sable mémorial* and *César-Antechrist* as wholly satirical or subversive, or to see in these two works a total inversion of the concepts and conventions of Symbolism. For the paradoxical, purely imaginary world which Jarry has here created has a positive value also. His creation of a purely imaginary, verbal universe, and of a wholly 'self-contained', 'autonomous' work of literature, represents the ultimate consequence of the Symbolist flight from realism and from reality – a shining example of 'pure' literature, in the most rigorous sense of the word.

A postscript to Jarry's early years in Paris and his early literary career is provided by the episode of his military service. He had tried, in August 1894, through the *député* Le Troadec, to get himself recruited into a Paris-based regiment, but was unsuccessful. And so, on 13 November 1894, his long hair was cut and he was enlisted in the 101st Infantry Regiment in Laval, with the prospect of a three-year stint in the army ahead of him. Scarcely surprisingly, he rebelled against the petty stupidities of military discipline – not directly, but by a minute and pedantic observance of regulations which had the effect of reducing all actions to apparent absurdity. He was also, in his over-large uniform, with his short legs unable to keep in step with the rest of the company on parade, and carrying the long, heavy army rifle which caused him to perform stiff gestures like a puppet, a born comic, whose effect upon the other troops was, in the eyes of the authorities, demoralizing to say the least.[59]

In all, he spent just over a year in the army. Despite a loathing of military discipline and regulations which he was to vent many times over in the course of the next few years, Alfred Jarry 'soldat de 2e classe' does not seem to have had too hard a time of it. He was generally popular with both officers and men; he ate in the officers' mess and was addressed by his corporal as 'Monsieur';[60] and Laval was after all the town of his birth, where his father and sister still lived and where he was able to visit them regularly. He also managed frequent periods of leave (often on grounds of ill-health – he was an almost chronic victim of influenza during this period) during which he was able to visit Paris. Being frequently left behind during parades and manoeuvres, he also spent a good deal of time reading and writing, and was able to continue from Laval his co-direction with Gourmont of *L'Ymagier*. All in all, in fact, the interruptions to his literary activities caused by the army seem to have been minimal. Indeed, in one respect the army actually proved to be a source of inspiration: during part of his time there he was busy observing and making notes for what was to be one of his finest novels, *Les Jours et les Nuits, roman d'un déserteur*, which was published in 1897. But the call of Paris and of freedom was too strong. Sometime in the Autumn of 1895, he swallowed a dose of picric acid, the effect of which was to turn his whole body yellow and to land him in hospital. After a period of convalescence he was given an honourable discharge from the army on 14 December 1895 (perhaps in part due to the intervention of Berthe de Courrière, as Rachilde maintained[61] – an intervention for which Jarry showed not the slightest gratitude). The discharge was officially on the grounds of 'chronic biliary lithiasis';[62] the story soon got around, however, perhaps encouraged by Jarry himself, that his certificate of discharge had described his condition as 'imbécillité précoce'.[63]

With his return to Paris at the end of 1895, Jarry, with two books – *Les Minutes de sable mémorial* and *César-Antechrist* – already published, was beginning to make something of a name for himself in the small but close-knit literary world of the capital. The end of his period of military service, together with his break with Gourmont some time during these months, marks a watershed in his literary career. For the early months of 1896 witness a marked change of direction, a turning away from the Symbolist influences and models which had helped to shape his work of the few years preceding, and a turning away also from poetry towards a concentration on prose works. Although there is evidence of a brief abortive attempt in the years following to recapture the vein of *Les Minutes* (some time around 1898 or 1899 he planned to publish a second volume of verse, to be entitled *Naviga-tions dans le miroir*, a title obviously inspired by Lewis Carroll's *Through the Looking Glass*),[64] it was above all to the novel and, more immediately, to the theatre that he now turned. For it was from the very beginning of 1896 onwards that a major campaign was to be launched for an eventual live production of *Ubu Roi*.

Chapter Four

Ubu

THE PREMIÈRE of *Ubu Roi* on 10 December 1896 had the effect of a bombshell (even if, artistically, it was a delayed-action bomb) in the French theatre. Never since the heyday of Romanticism, with the staging of Victor Hugo's *Hernani* in 1830, had the performance of a play produced such an outraged reaction on the part of critics and public alike. Yet the celebrated 'battle of *Hernani*' was a mere skirmish compared with the violence and furore to which Jarry's play gave rise. Why should this be? How was it that a simple farce, a mere schoolboy spoof upon a grotesquely incompetent teacher, could produce such a reaction? Why should this one play have had such an impact not just on contemporary audiences and critics, but upon the whole subsequent development of the French theatre? And why should Jarry (who after all wrote a great many other works – other plays, poetry, journalism and half-a-dozen novels) be remembered above all, rightly or wrongly, for just one play of which he was neither the sole nor even the principal author?

The answer to these questions is to be found partly in an examination of the state of the French theatre at the end of the nineteenth century, and partly in the aims and stratagems of Jarry himself. For the eventual production of *Ubu Roi* in December 1896 not only represented a deliberate attempt to revolutionize totally the theatre of its time, but was the culmination of a long, carefully prepared and intensely single-minded campaign of propaganda and subtle persuasion on the part of its author – a promotion campaign which can surely have few parallels in the history of the theatre.

Let us begin with a (necessarily brief) examination of the state of the French theatre at this time. There are two outstanding features of this theatre which concern us here. Firstly, it was above all a theatre of entertainment, catering to an overwhelmingly *bourgeois* public (for many members of which it was, quite literally, simply a form of 'after-dinner entertainment'). It was also an essentially Parisian theatre: in 1900, here were more theatres in Paris alone – some 50 in all – than in the whole of the rest of France. Technically, the theatre

1. 'Véritable Portrait de Monsieur Ubu', woodcut by Jarry first published in *Le Livre d'Art*, no. 2, April 1896, then in the original edition of *Ubu Roi*. Note the umbilical spiral, the walking stick pushed into the pocket and the stylized moustache, all features of the original figure of 'le P.H.' (Reproduced from *Peintures, Gravures & Dessins d'Alfred Jarry*, ed. Michel Arrivé, Collège de 'Pataphysique, 1968.)

2. The original woodblock from which the previous woodcut was printed. (Reproduced from *Peintures, Gravures & Dessins d'Alfred Jarry*, ed. Michel Arrivé, Collège de 'Pataphysique, 1968.)

3. 'Autre Portrait de Monsieur Ubu', pen-and-ink drawing by Jarry published in the facsimile edition of *Ubu Roi* (1897). The bowler hat is also a feature of the prototype of Ubu. (Reproduced from *Peintures, Gravures & Dessins d'Alfred Jarry*, ed. Michel Arrivé, Collège de 'Pataphysique, 1968.)

4. Woodcut by Jarry published in *Les Minutes de sable mémorial* (1894). The subject of the Passion of Christ and the associated Instruments of the Passion fascinated Jarry: the highly stylized motifs represented here are to be found scattered throughout *Les Minutes*, *Haldernablou* and *César-Antechrist*. (Reproduced from *Peintures, Gravures & Dessins d'Alfred Jarry*, ed. Michel Arrivé, Collège de 'Pataphysique, 1968.)

5. Jarry, with Leon-Paul Fargue, in 1893, from a group photo taken at the Lycée Henri IV. (Reproduced from *Peintures, Gravures & Dessins d'Alfred Jarry*, ed. Michel Arrivé, Collège de 'Pataphysique, 1968.)

6. Jarry photographed by Nadar in 1896, around the time of the first performance of Ubu Roi. (Reproduced from *Peintures, Gravures & Dessins d'Alfred Jarry*, ed. Michel Arrivé, Collège de 'Pataphysique, 1968.)

7. Jarry on his celebrated racing cycle in front of the Phalanstère. (Reproduced by permission of the Collège de 'Pataphysique.)

8. Jarry and Vallette with the *as* by the Seine at Corbeil. (Reproduced by permission of the Collège de 'Pataphysique.)

9. Jarry at the Phalanstère in Corbeil in 1898, the year in which *Gestes et opinions du docteur Faustroll, pataphysicien* was completed. (Reproduced from *Cahiers du Collège de 'Pataphysique*, no. 22–3 (1955), 3.)

10. Jarry and Alfred Vallette at the Phalanstère in 1898. Vallette is painting
the fishing boat which they jointly owned, prototype for the *as* of
Dr Faustroll. (Reproduced from *Peintures, Gravures & Dessins d'Alfred
Jarry*, ed. Michel Arrivé, Collège de 'Pataphysique, 1968.)

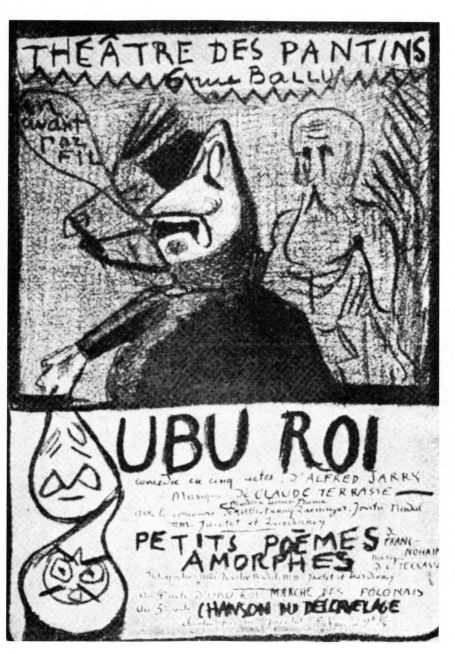

11. Lithograph by Jarry for the programme of the Théâtre des Pantins, published in December 1897. (Reproduced from *Peintures, Gravures & Dessins d'Alfred Jarry*, ed. Michel Arrivé, Collège de 'Pataphysique, 1968.)

12. Lithograph by Jarry for the cover of *La Chanson du Décervelage*, published by the Éditions du Mercure de France in the series *Répertoire des Pantins* in 1898. (Reproduced from *Peintures, Gravures & Dessins d'Alfred Jarry*, ed. Michel Arrivé, Collège de 'Pataphysique, 1968.)

was dominated by the traditions of the *pièce bien faite*, the well-made play, whose originator, the prolific dramatist Eugène Scribe, had roundly declared on his election to the Académie Française in 1836 that the theatre was a place for 'relaxation and amusement, not for instruction or correction', and that what amused audiences was 'not truth but fiction'. Scribe and his successors had provided not only France but the whole of Europe with a constant supply of technically skilful but thematically uncontroversial, if not utterly mindless, plays. Indeed, so entrenched were the traditions of the 'well-made play' that they were skilfully parodied by Jarry's friend Georges Polti in 1895 in his *Les Trente-six situations dramatiques,* a sort of compendium of stock situations. Such a generalization of course obscures individual differences: there were a minority of playwrights, such as Alexandre Dumas *fils* and Emile Augier, who attempted to write serious 'moral' dramas and 'problem plays', and others, such as Labiche and Feydeau, who developed the art of farce. Nor should one overlook the efforts of André Antoine, whose 'naturalist' Théâtre Libre (1887–94), inspired by Zola's literary theories and writings on the theatre, accomplished, albeit in a limited sphere, a minor revolution in production and acting techniques, rejecting the decorativeness and artificiality of the conventional, bourgeois theatre in favour of a scrupulously exact reproduction on the stage of the world at large, and limiting the hitherto dominant role of the actor in favour of that – virtually created by Antoine – of the *metteur en scène* or director. But the fact remains that where as in the seventeenth and eighteenth centuries the theatre had been considered the most noble of literary forms, by the end of the nineteenth it had, considered from an artistic point of view, on the whole fallen to probably the lowest ebb ever in its history. Much of the revolt which we witness in the theatre all over Europe in the closing years of the nineteenth century and the early decades of the twentieth springs first and foremost quite simply from an attempt to restore to the theatre the status of a serious art form.

The second dominant trend in this theatre which concerns us is that towards 'realism'. In broad terms, in fact, realism is the dominant trend not only in the theatre of the nineteenth century, but in almost all art-forms – including, most notably, the novel and, up to and including the Impressionists, in painting also. We have already seen, in the previous two chapters, something of the philosophical basis of this 'realism', and of the reasons for the revolt against it in Symbolist milieux, and we have also seen evidence of Jarry's clear preferences for non-realistic forms of painting. For the novelists of the nineteenth century, realism – social realism is perhaps a more apt term – meant not only the attempt to make us 'believe in' the reality of their characters' existence, but also the presentation of a set of representative figures firmly embedded in a specific *social* context. In the theatre, the term took on an additional dimension of meaning: it signified not only the portrayal by playwrights of 'realistic' or plausible characters and situations, but above all the attempt to make the audience believe by means of a variety of scenic artifices that the actors out there on the stage *were* the characters they were pretending to be, that the stage was a *real* drawing-room, or street corner, or shop interior. To this end, stage sets became, in the closing decades of the century, increasingly elaborate and detailed, with whole armies of designers and craftsmen being employed, and with real doors, real windows, real furniture being used in place of the earlier painted backdrops. These considerations apply both to the commercial, bourgeois theatre and to the naturalist theatre of Antoine and of such playwrights as Zola and Henry Becque in France, or Ibsen, Strindberg and Hauptmann, whose works were beginning to become known in France from the early 1890s onwards; although the naturalist theatre was in open revolt against the slick superficiality and comfortable idealism of the commercial theatre, producing – in Antoine's case – stark 'slice of life' dramas with brutal frankness, in terms of the attempt to create on the stage a convincing 'photographic' portrayal of the 'real' world, naturalism was simply a form of hyper-realism.

There is, however, something inherently paradoxical, if not self-contradictory, about the notion of 'realism' in art. And it is the awareness or intuition of this fact which lies behind the often violent rejection of all forms of realism by the Symbolists, including Jarry, and by their successors. Even such an arch-'realist' as Maupassant revealed an awareness of the problem when he declared that the great 'realist' novelists of the nineteenth century ought really to be called 'illusionists', since their aim was to create a convincing *illusion* of reality. All art is based upon convention, and the conventions of realism are directed towards the creation of an acceptable and implicitly accepted illusion. Nowhere, moreover, is the importance of convention greater than in the theatre, which is a hybrid art-form, neither appealing exclusively (as does the novel) to the imagination nor to the senses. The point was made emphatically by the playwright Thornton Wilder: 'The theatre lives by conventions: a convention is an agreed-upon falsehood, a permitted lie.'[1] It is the gradual recognition of this fact, followed by the deliberate and conscious exploitation of conventions other than those of realism, which lies at the root of the revolution in theatrical theory and practice which has taken place in the twentieth century, and which culminated, in France, in the so-called 'avant-garde' theatre or 'theatre of the absurd' of the post-War period. And it is at the fountainhead of this revolution that Jarry and the events of 10 December 1896 stand.

From the moment of his arrival in Paris, Jarry had lost no opportunity of promoting the cause of Ubu. With Henri Morin, and then with friends and fellow-students at the Lycée Henri IV, Fargue amongst them, he had recited, mimed and acted extracts from the two Ubu 'cycles' which were to become eventually *Ubu Roi* and *Ubu Cocu*, first in his lodgings on the Boulevard de Port-Royal, then in his luxurious apartment on the Boulevard St Germain. At the same time, he continued to work on and to revise the two plays. Sometime between 1891 and early 1893, the magnificently resonant name 'Ubu' was discovered. And at some time, too, the idea of an eventual performance in the live theatre, before a wider public, took root in Jarry's mind.

But first, Ubu's existence had to be revealed to the public at large through the medium of publication. Two extracts from the future *Ubu Cocu* formed, as we have seen, the major part of Jarry's second published text, *Guignol,* which appeared in the *Écho de Paris littéraire illustré* on 23 April 1893, having won for its 19-year-old author a *prix de prose* in the paper's *concours* for the previous month. Ubu's presence was further manifested in both *Les Minutes de sable mémorial* and *César-Antechrist* (the 'Acte terrestre' of which is simply an abridged version of the text of *Ubu Roi*). The first of these gave rise to an enthusiastic review by Gourmont in the *Mercure de France* which contained the (Jarry-inspired?) prophecy: 'De M. Ubu, encore à l'état d'ébauche, on .pourrait traire, je crois, un personnage d'un sinistre largement comique; M. Ubu a certainement beaucoup de choses à dire qu'il a tues et qu'il dira.' ['From M. Ubu, for the moment still in the early stages of elaboration, one could, I think, extract a character who would be both sinister yet highly comic. M. Ubu certainly has a great many things to say which he has not divulged, but which he will.']² Nor was Jarry's promotion of Ubu solely by means of the written word: the first issue of *Perhinderion* announced as being 'in preparation' (though in fact the volume never appeared) an 'album en couleurs' entitled *Petits Crayons des gestes les plus notoires de M. Ubu, maître des phynances.* Moreover, following his entry into the milieux of the *Mercure* in 1894, he was soon giving readings of the text of *Ubu Roi* at the regular Tuesday evening gatherings in the Vallettes' *salon* in the rue de l'Échaudé (a name immortalized in the *Chanson du décervelage*). That such readings were frequent is indicated by a letter to Jarry from Jean de Tinan, one of the *Mercure* faithful, following the publication of the play in June 1896 (the letter also makes it clear that Jarry continued to revise the text right up to the moment of its publication):

J'ai relu hier le *drame* en son intégrité (avec pas mal de petits changements, et très heureux, m'a-t-il semblé. Il m'a semblé vous l'entendre lire une fois de plus – avec accompagnement du rire de Rachilde, du rire de Moréno, du rire de Fanny, du rire de Vallette, du rire de Schwob, du rire de Hérold et du rire de tout le monde – selon les belles sonorités de l'admirable voix du maître des phynances.

[I read the *drama* yesterday in its entirety (with, it seemed to me, quite a lot of minor, and very successful, changes). It seemed to me that I could hear you reading it yet again – to the accompaniment of the laughter of Rachilde, of Moréno, of Fanny, of Vallette, of Schwob, of Hérold and indeed of everybody – in the sonorous tones of the master of phynances' admirable voice.][3]

The complete text of the play, with the title *Ubu Roi ou les Polonais*, had been published (along with a reproduction of a woodcut by Jarry entitled 'Véritable portrait de M. Ubu') in two parts in April and May 1896 in the monthly review *Le Livre d'Art*, co-edited by the poet Paul Fort,[4] and then in a single volume with the title and subtitle *Ubu Roi. Drame en cinq Actes en prose. Restitué en son intégrité tel qu'il a été représenté par les marionnettes du Théâtre des Phynances en 1888* [*Ubu Roi. Play in Five Acts in Prose. Restored in its entirety as it was performed by the marionettes of the Théâtre des Phynances in 1888*] by the Éditions du Mercure de France the following June. Its publication by the Mercure was greeted by a number of enthusiastic reviews in the young literary journals – among them those of Émile Verhaeren in *L'Art Moderne* of 19 July and Francis Viélé-Griffin in the August issue of the Mercure. While Viélé-Griffin enthusiastically put forward the usual contemporary 'political' interpretation of the play, the long article by Verhaeren (whose *Les Campagnes hallucinées* was to be one of the 27 'livres pairs' of Faustroll) was remarkable on the other hand for its sympathy and penetration. Picking up the hint contained in Jarry's subtitle, he sought a key to the understanding of the play in the world of the marionette, with its 'dérèglements des événements que les esprits enfantins si étrangement imaginitifs substituent avec un sérieux inconsciemment comique à la réalité' ['topsy-turvy view of the world which the minds of children, so oddly imaginative, substitute, with an unconsciously comic seriousness, for reality'], concluding his review with the memorable characterization of the figure of Ubu: 'Ah, le sale, ah l'aimable bonhomme!' ['Oh, the rotten, oh the lovable fellow!'].

But valuable as such publicity was, all this was still a far cry from a realization of Jarry's hopes for a live production of the play. The opportunity for this came with the deepening of his friendship, and then his association, with the young actor-director Aurélien Lugné-Poe. Lugné-Poe (who liked to write his name Poë and also to hint that he was related to Edgar Allan Poe, well known in France through the translations of Baudelaire and Mallarmé, and whose manner and sombre dress earned him the nickname 'le clergyman somnambule') had been for a time stage manager of Antoine's Théâtre Libre. Then, tiring (so he tells us) of the unpoetic 'vulgarity' of naturalism, he quit the Théâtre Libre to become for a time a moving spirit of the short-lived Symbolist Théâtre d'Art, founded in 1890 by Paul Fort, then still a schoolboy.[5] The Théâtre d'Art performed the works of playwrights such as the Belgian Symbolist Maurice Maeterlinck – another of Faustroll's authors – as well as poetic dramas by or adaptations of Laforgue, Verlaine, Mallarmé, Rimbaud and others. (Its most famous, or notorious, production was an adaptation of the Biblical *Song of Songs*, complete not only with incomprehensible chanting but also with the use of brilliantly coloured lighting, and perfumes wafted around the auditorium.) When Paul Fort retired – owing to poor health and the demands of 'poetic creation' – in the Spring of 1893, Lugné-Poe took over the theatre's artistic direction, renaming it the Théâtre de l'Oeuvre, and resolving once and for all to 'affranchir la scène de l'élan naturaliste qui . . . retardait toutes les possibilités théâtrales' ['free the stage from the upsurge of naturalism which . . . was hindering the exploitation of all the possibilities of the theatre'].[6] This aim was to be achieved partly by performing the works of playwrights from as many different countries and centuries as possible, partly through an exploitation of the full scenic possibilities of the stage, involving the creation of *spectacles* which would incorporate elements of dance, mime and music. In reality, the scope of Lugné-Poe's achievements was much more modest: these amounted primarily to a continuation of the efforts of the Théâtre d'Art to create a 'magical' theatre of dream and poetic fantasy, and productions of plays by leading Scandinavian playwrights, particularly Ibsen, already performed by Antoine. The fusion of these two aims, and the resolute hostility to naturalism, led to one of the more curious perversions in the history of the theatre: the creation of a 'Symbolist' Ibsen, whose characters were made to appear as shadowy creatures moving in a half-real, half-fantasy world.

Despite these limitations, Lugné-Poe's efforts quickly aroused the interest and sympathy of the whole Symbolist *avant-garde*, Jarry included. In October 1894, the latter sent to the young director a copy of the first issue of *L'Ymagier*, with a note expressing 'toute [sa] sympathie d'art',[7] and soon afterwards the two met through the agency of A.-Ferdinand Hérold, one of the faithful of the *Mercure*. Sympathy soon became mutual; Jarry was attracted by the director's youth (he was only four years older than Jarry himself), his poverty, and above all his artistic boldness: in February 1896 he scandalized respectable public opinion – already shocked by the revelations in England the previous year of the trial of Oscar Wilde – by staging Wilde's French drama *Salomé*. The action brought him further respect and support from the young *littérateurs* of the Symbolist movement, many of whom on the occasion of the performance staged a demonstration in favour of Wilde – Jarry prominent amongst them. On his side, Lugné-Poe wrote of Jarry that he 'excitait [sa] curiosité'.[8] The friendship deepened, and from the beginning of 1896 Jarry began submitting to Lugné-Poe proposals for a staging, during the next season of the Oeuvre, of *Ubu Roi* and then of *Les Polyèdres* (the future *Ubu Cocu*) – appearing to hesitate between the two plays, perhaps secretly hoping that Lugné would agree to produce both. His letters of this period reveal a subtle but unrelenting effort to ingratiate himself with the young director in order to achieve his aims. Oddly, perhaps, it is the first of these letters which is the most detailed, containing (in a deliberately casual tone) a long list of ideas for a production of *Ubu Roi*, which would be 'd'un effet comique sûr'; the letter is worth quoting at length:

Il serait curieux, je crois, de pouvoir monter cette chose (sans aucun frais du reste) dans le goût suivant:
1° Masque pour le personnage principal, Ubu, lequel masque je pourrais vous procurer au besoin. . . .
2° Une tête de cheval en carton qu'il se pendrait au cou, comme dans l'ancien théâtre anglais, pour les deux seules scènes équestres, tous détails qui étaient dans l'esprit de la pièce, puisque j'ai voulu faire un 'guignol'.
3° Adoption d'un seul décor, ou mieux, d'un fond uni, supprimant les levers et baissers de rideau pendant l'acte unique. Un personnage correctement vêtu viendrait, comme dans les guignols, accrocher une pancarte signifiant le lieu de la scène. (Notez que je suis certain de la supériorité 'suggestive' de la pancarte écrite sur le décor. Un décor, ni une figuration ne rendraient 'l'armée polonaise en marche dans l'Ukraine'.)
4° Suppression des foules, lesquelles sont souvent mauvaises à la scène et gênent l'intelligence. Ainsi, un seul soldat dans la scène de la revue, un seul dans la bousculade où Ubu dit: 'Quel tas de gens, quelle fuite, etc.'
5° Adoption d'un 'accent' ou mieux d'une 'voix' spéciale pour le personnage principal.
6° Costumes aussi peu couleur locale ou chronologiques que possible (ce qui rend mieux l'idée d'une chose éternelle), modernes de préférence, puisque la satire est moderne; et sordides, parce que le drame en paraît plus misérable et horrifique.

[It would be interesting, I think, to be able to stage this thing (without incurring any costs, what's more) in the following manner:
1° A mask for the main character, Ubu, which I could obtain for you if need be. . . .
2° A cardboard horse's head which he would hang around his neck, as in the old English theatre, for the only two equestrian scenes, all details which were in the spirit of the play, since I wanted to write a 'Punch and Judy' show.
3° Adoption of a single set or, even better, of a plain backdrop, doing away with the raising and lowering of the curtain during the single act. A character in evening dress would come, as in a Punch and Judy show, and hang up sign-boards indicating the scene of the action. (Note that I am sure of the superiority of the 'suggestive' power of a sign-board over that of a set. Neither a set, nor the use of extras, could convey 'the Polish army marching through the Ukraine'.)
4° Doing away with crowds, which are often clumsy on stage and impede understanding. Thus, a single soldier in the review scene, a single soldier in the jostle and scramble in which Ubu says: 'What a mob, what a rush, etc.'

5° Adoption of an 'accent', or even better of a special 'voice', by the main character.
6° Costumes as lacking in local colour or historical accuracy as possible (which conveys more clearly the idea of something eternal), modern, preferably, since the satire is modern; and squalid, because the play appears all the more wretched and horrendous as a result.][9]

These proposals – which all would-be producers of the play would do well to meditate upon and take note of – reveal clearly that Jarry had thought long and hard about a production of *Ubu Roi*, and knew exactly the effect which he wished to achieve. And in the event, almost all of these proposals were in fact implemented.

In the months that followed, Jarry continued alternately to badger and to coax Lugné-Poe. His next major step forward came with the retirement, for health reasons, some time in the Spring of 1896, of the Oeuvre's stage-manager, Van Bever. In May of that year, at the latest, Jarry entered the administration of the theatre with the title of *secrétaire-régisseur*, responsible for (amongst other things) day-to-day administration, advice concerning the programme for the following season, forwarding Lugné's mail while he was holidaying in Brittany, and writing his business letters – the young director was an atrocious speller, and was not much better on syntax. Lugné describes the zeal of his new recruit thus:

Installé dans ses fonctions, il les prend au sérieux. En costume de cycliste, sa tenue normale et régulière . . ., Jarry m'aide en tout, et m'évite les obstacles. . . . Il ouvre le courrier et me l'envoie, élude les difficultés d'une façon fraternelle et avisée. Mieux, il organise la publicité de la saison qui vient.
Et toujours, il fait avancer le pion *Ubu*.

> [Installed in his new post, he takes his duties seriously. In cyclist's attire, his normal and habitual dress . . ., Jarry helps me with everything, and removes obstacles in my way. . . . He opens the mail and sends it on to me, dodges problems in a brotherly and sensible way. Even better, he organizes the publicity for the forthcoming season.
> And at every point, he advances King *Ubu*'s pawn.][10]

Jarry's labours were not in vain. The programme for the fourth season of the Théâtre de l'Oeuvre was finally decided upon: it was to begin with the first French production of Ibsen's *Peer Gynt*, which was to be followed by a production of *Ubu Roi*. Small wonder that Jarry wrote to his still hesitant director to assure him that 'tout le monde s'accorde à trouver que le programme de cette année est incomparablement mieux que jamais' ['everybody is united in finding this year's programme incomparably better than ever'].[11]

The former production was undoubtedly much closer to Lugné's heart than that of *Ubu*. Yet even here, Jarry played a major role, throwing himself into the task with enthusiasm, advising, organizing, adapting Ibsen for French audiences and even partially rewriting the play, in particular the scene of the trolls, whose humour was, in the eyes of Lugné, 'si malaisé à suivre en français'.[12] Making a virtue of financial stringencies, he suggested the performance of Ibsen's fairy-tale extravaganza along lines he had in mind for Ûbu: 'Il est de ce drame comme de ceux de Shakespeare [*sic*], qui gagnent à être montés *d'une façon simple et sordide* et autrement ressembleraient au *Tour du monde en 80 jours* et autres pièces du Châtelet.' ['The same applies to this play as to those of Shakespeare [*sic*]: they benefit from being staged in a simple and squalid fashion and would otherwise be like *Around the World in 80 Days* and other plays performed at the Châtelet.'][13] He seems in fact to have been virtually co-director of the play with Lugné, as well as acting the role of king of the trolls – in which his success was, according to the latter, 'énaurme'.[14]

If Jarry was effectively co-director of *Peer Gynt*, he appears to have been almost solely responsible for the production of *Ubu Roi*, to the frequent exasperation of his nominal director. The uneasy relations between the two young men can be inferred from a number of passages in Lugné-Poe's memoirs: 'Jarry, entêté comme un mulet de son pays'; 'puis ses exigences d'auteur m'excèdent'; and 'Finalement, je m'attelle à *Ubu*, mais comme Jarry est animé d'une sorte de génie tourmenté, mille difficultés plus irritantes les unes que les autres naissent sous nos pas.' ['Jarry, as stubborn as a Breton mule'; 'and then, his demands as an author exasperate me'; 'Finally, I buckle down to *Ubu*, but as Jarry is driven by a kind of tormented genius, a thousand difficulties each more irritating than the last arise at every step.'][15] Yet Lugné candidly admits that from the start he had not the slightest idea what to make of the play. When he had asked Jarry to join him at the Oeuvre, he writes, 'j'étais à mille lieues de m'imaginer le genre de pièce qu'il me préparait' ['I never dreamed for a moment what kind of play he was about to put before me']; and, confronted with the text of *Ubu Roi*, he did not know 'par quel bout [le] prendre pour le réaliser à la scène' ['how on earth to set about staging it'].[16] At one point he had even wanted to act it as a tragedy! It was Jarry who, as his letters to Lugné-Poe make clear (perhaps it was for this reason that the latter neglected to publish the more revealing of these letters in his memoirs), more and more took charge of the production, choosing and seeking out potential actors, designing and ordering props, sounding out favourable critics, and even, it seems, on occasions conducting rehearsals.[17] When Lugné responded to his ideas for dispensing with large numbers of 'extras' on the stage with the suggestion that 'il faudrait dénicher des mannequins que l'on puisse habiller' ['we ought to track down some life-size models that we can dress up'],[18] Jarry promptly went ahead and ordered a total of

40 life-size wicker *mannequins* to represent the nobles and magistrates committed to Ubu's *trappe*.[19] He also had made a huge belly of cardboard and wicker for Ubu, together with a heavy pear-shaped mask, and a life-sized *cheval à phynance* – the latter alone costing 100 francs. (His extravagances, according to Lugné, 'plunged' the theatre 'blindly' into debt; the total takings for the two performances of the play were only 1,300 francs.) He also engaged his friend-to-be, the composer Claude Terrasse (brother-in-law of the painter Pierre Bonnard), to write incidental music for the play. It was even Jarry's own speech mannerisms which were imposed upon the performance, this time with the aid of Lugné: when a bewildered Firmin Gémier, engaged to play the main character, confessed that he did not know how to speak his lines, Lugné advised him to imitate Jarry's own brusque, staccato diction.

Meanwhile, Jarry conducted an equally vigorous campaign on behalf of the performance in the press. Following preliminary announcements in the *Mercure de France* and the *Revue Blanche*, he contacted a number of leading theatre reviewers for the daily press – Armand Silvestre, Aurélien Scholl, Jean Lorrain, and the 'big guns' Catulle Mendès and Henry Bauer. At the same time, he himself published a number of articles in the young literary reviews directed towards the production, which are invaluable in helping us to determine his own views on the theatre at this time. In September, Vallette gave pride of place in the *Mercure* to an article by Jarry with the enigmatic but significant title 'De l'inutilité du théâtre au théâtre' – an article whose forthcoming publication was announced in an enthusiastic review of *Ubu Roi* by Louis Dumur, the future dedicatee of Book VIII of *Faustroll*, in the very same issue of the *Mercure*. After registering the birth of Ubu as a 'type', Dumur went on 'prophetically':

Il y aurait une étude curieuse à faire sur la manière dont l'auteur d'*Ubu Roi* comprend le théâtre et spécialement le théâtre de marionnettes, car c'est à celui-ci que semblent surtout se rattacher de pareilles excentricités dramatiques. M. Jarry nous exposera un jour, je l'espère, ses idées à ce sujet. En effet, M. Jarry ne se borne pas . . . à mettre la caricature uniquement dans l'aspect extérieur et dans les gestes: il la met dans les caractères, dans l'âme, dans le langage.

[An interesting article could be written studying the way in which the author of *Ubu Roi* conceives of the theatre and in particular the puppet-theatre, for it is to the latter above all that such eccentric dramatic concepts seem to be linked. M. Jarry will one day outline for us, I hope, his ideas on this subject. As a matter of fact, M. Jarry does not restrict himself . . . to introducing caricature solely into the physical appearance and gestures; he introduces it also into the character, into the soul, into language.]

The purpose of Jarry's article was twofold: to prepare the public, and to overcome the hesitations of Lugné-Poe. A number of ideas, including the then widely mooted notion of an open-air theatre, were aimed directly at Lugné, who unhesitatingly swallowed the bait. The following month the *Mercure* published an article written by him as a follow-up to that of Jarry, entitled 'A propos de "l'Inutilité du théâtre au théâtre"'. Basing himself on recent contacts with the Elizabethan Society (he had spent part of September in London), and bowing for the most part to the authority of Jarry, he attempted to establish analogies between the 'bref et lumineux article' of the latter, particularly as regards the simplicity of sets, and the frank acceptance by the Elizabethan theatre of non-realistic conventions, which contrasted with 'la sottise *vraisemblable* de notre théâtre moderne' ['the stupid concern of our modern theatre with *verisimilitude*']. He went on to add, in explanation of Jarry's aims: 'Remonter à l'antique, à cette naïveté savante, me semble bien le secret du nouvel art pour lequel M. Jarry écrit et que je voudrais défendre par la technique de toutes les forces de mes moyens. [sic]' ['A return to the art of past ages, to that studied naïvety, seems to me to be the secret of the new art to which M. Jarry's efforts as a writer are directed and which I wish to defend by the technique of all the strength of my means.']20 A final touch was added to Jarry's campaign in the press with the publication, in the *Revue Blanche* for 1 December, of 'Les Paralipomènes d'Ubu'. Here, under the pretext of 'liquidating' the *bonhomme* once and for all, he gave details from his past contained in other Ubu texts which supposedly 'explained' the character, and which were in reality designed to whet further the public's appetite. (A third important article, 'Questions de théâtre' – an answer to his critics – was published in the *Revue Blanche* for 1 January 1897, following the performance.)

Yet still, at the eleventh hour, Lugné-Poe hesitated – 'pris', he tells us, 'de je ne sais quelle appréhension de l'effet d'*Ubu*' ['stricken with a vague but terrible apprehension as to the impact of *Ubu*'].21 This time it was Rachilde who persuaded him to go ahead with the production, arguing that 'toute la jeune génération (y compris quelques vieux aimant la blague)' ['the whole of the younger generation (including a few old folks who like a good joke)'] was anxiously awaiting the performance. Her letter, however, reveals her to have had no illusions about the nature of the play's impact: 'success' is 'quelquefois, simplement un grand *tapage*' ['sometimes, simply a terrific *uproar*']. It was also Rachilde who (with Jarry at her elbow?) finally persuaded Lugné to agree to perform the play as its author wished – as a *guignol*, or Punch and Judy show:

Poussez au *guignol* le plus possible, et, au besoin, j'ai cette idée depuis que je connais la pièce, faites relier vos acteurs (si possible) aux frises de votre théâtre par des ficelles ou des cordes, puisqu'ils sont de plus gros pantins que les autres.

> [Emphasize as much as possible the *Punch and Judy* aspect, and, if need be (I have had this idea in mind for as long as I've known the play), have your actors tied (if possible) to the borders of your theatre with strings or ropes, since they are even bigger puppets than the others.][22]

The final production of *Ubu Roi* at the Théâtre de l'Oeuvre was thus far more the work of Jarry himself than of anyone else, at least as far as the limitations imposed by inadequate rehearsals, the forced cutting of several scenes, and the unruly interruptions of the audience permitted. Gémier undoubtedly exaggerated when he claimed that there had been *no* time for rehearsals; but Jarry himself referred in a letter to Henry Bauer to 'les coupures auxquelles nous a forcés notre insuffisante préparation' ['the cuts which our inadequate preparation forced upon us'],[23] and stated with bitter irony in his speech to the audience before the performance that he had made 'toutes les coupures qui ont été agréables aux acteurs (même de plusieurs passages indispensables au sens de la pièce)' [*sic*] ['all the cuts which the actors wanted to be made (including even of several passages essential to the meaning of the play)']. These restrictions aside, however, the first performance of *Ubu Roi* in December 1896 – in terms of acting, costumes, set, musical accompaniment, movement and gesture, and above all the spirit of the production – accords in almost every respect with Jarry's own ideas for the play's staging, as contemporary accounts clearly reveal.[24]

In his letter to Lugné-Poe of January 1896, Jarry had called for the adoption of a single set or, preferably, a plain backdrop, scene-changes being indicated by the use of placards. In the actual production, an old man with a long white beard (in whom contemporaries insisted on seeing a symbol of time), wearing evening dress, crossed the stage on tiptoes and hung placards indicating the scene on a nail at the side of the stage. In place of a plain backdrop, however, Jarry had eventually decided in favour of a composite one, in which contemporaries saw the ultimate example of what was then known in artistic circles as 'synthesis', but which can equally be seen as a *reductio ad absurdum* of 'realism'. The work of a team of artists, all of them friends of the playwright and most of them associated with the group of painters who called themselves the 'Nabis' – Sérusier, Bonnard, Vuillard, Toulouse-Lautrec and Ranson –, it was described thus by the British critic Arthur Symons:

> the scenery was painted to represent, by a child's conventions, indoors and
> out of doors, and even the torrid, temperate and arctic zones at once.
> Opposite to you, at the back of the stage, you saw apple-trees in bloom,
> under a blue sky, and against the sky a small closed window and a fireplace
> . . ., through the very midst of which . . . trooped in and out these clamorous
> and sanguinary persons of the drama. On the left was painted a bed, and at
> the foot of the bed a bare tree, and snow falling. On the right were palm trees,
> about one of which coiled a boa-constrictor; a door opened against the sky,
> and beside the door a skeleton dangled from a gallows.[25]

The lighting was the responsibility of A.-F. Hérold, designated by
Jarry as his 'metteur en trappe', who used his powers to plunge the
theatre into darkness whenever the need arose to silence the audience, while Terrasse's incidental music for the play – described by
Arthur Symons as fairground music befitting a puppet-play – was
performed single-handedly by the composer who, in the darkness
behind the stage, strained his ears to hear through the furore of the
audience and struck piano, cymbals and drums more or less at
random.

The appearance and diction of the actors seem also to have been
generally in conformity with Jarry's wishes. He had called for the use
of masks, and the actors playing the main parts, at least, were indeed
masked, Gémier wearing (albeit reluctantly) the heavy pear-shaped
or triangular mask which Jarry had designed for him, as well as an
enormous cardboard belly.[26] He had called for costumes 'as lacking in
local colour and historical accuracy as possible' (adding that this
conveyed more accurately the idea of something 'eternal'). Correspondingly, the actors were, according to one report, 'en civil, à
quelques menus accoutrements près' ['wearing everyday dress, apart
from a few minor details of their get-up'].[27] Thirdly, Jarry had called
for the adoption by the actors of a special 'voice' appropriate to each
role, and each of the leading actors did in fact adopt a distinctive
'voice' or accent – Gémier speaking in the staccato manner he had
learned from Jarry, Mère Ubu (brilliantly played by Louise France) in
patois, Bordure with an English accent, the Tsar with a heavy Russian
accent, and the Queen with an Auvergnat accent.

Lastly, the use of props and 'extras', and the style of the acting,
seems to have been largely in accordance with Jarry's wishes. He had
intended props and 'extras' to be reduced to a minimum and to be
purely schematic; in the event, a life-sized cardboard horse seems to
have been used for the equestrian scenes in place of his suggested
cardboard horse's head, while crowds were indeed 'represented' by a
single actor, one soldier, for example, portraying the Polish army.
Even more striking was the use, in the performance, of actors to
replace props: thus an actor was used to represent the door of a
prison-cell. Finally, Jarry had wanted the actors to perform like

puppets, which they did, or attempted to do; if they did not actually have strings attached to their limbs, as Rachilde had suggested (an idea rejected somewhat contemptuously by Jarry), they nevertheless imitated in their bearing and movements the stiffness and jerkiness of marionettes, much to the bewilderment and disgust of most critics (Symons described them as playing 'the part of marionettes, hiding their faces behind cardboard masks ..., and mimicking the rigid inflexibility and spasmodic life of puppets by a hopping and reeling gait').[28] In these and in other respects, the *spirit* of the performance (insofar as it was allowed by the audience to manifest itself) was very much that which Jarry himself had envisaged – resulting in a new and quite revolutionary use of the stage of the live theatre, and in the creation of an entirely new form of humour.

There was one other, perhaps less happy, respect also in which Jarry had had his way. Despite Rachilde's advice to Lugné-Poe in the above-quoted letter: 'Evitez la conférence!', he had insisted, in conformity with the fashion of the day, on making a speech to the audience. Dressed like a circus clown in a white shirt with a huge starched front and an enormous bow-tie, his face completely whitened and his hair stuck down on his forehead he spoke from behind a table covered with a coal sack. According to Gémier, he was nervous and frightened; according to Rachilde – who knew him far better – he was 'sec et froid'.[29] Of the speech, delivered in the clipped tones of Ubu, the audience heard little and understood less. The speech over, Jarry bowed with the brusque, mechanical motion of a puppet, and disappeared.

The scenes that followed in the theatre have been described many times over. To Lugné-Poe, the performance amounted to 'un scandale'. To the writer Laurent Tailhade, it was 'une date qui fit époque dans l'histoire du symbolisme', a veritable 'bataille d'*Hernani* entre les jeunes écoles, décadentes, symbolistes, et la critique bourgeoise' ['a milestone in the history of Symbolism', 'a battle of *Hernani* between the young literary schools – Decadents, Symbolists – and the bourgeois critics'].[30] To the less partial W. B. Yeats, the spectacle was at once a source of bewilderment and apprehension (all the more so as Yeats understood little French):

> Feeling bound to support the most spirited party, we have shouted for the play, but that night at the Hôtel Corneille I am very sad, for comedy, objectivity, has displayed its growing power once more. I say: 'After Stéphane Mallarmé, after Paul Verlaine, after Gustave Moreau, after Puvis de Chavannes, after our own verse, after all our subtle colour and nervous rhythm, after the faint mixed tints of Conder, what more is possible? After us the Savage God.[31]

A distinction, however, needs to be made between the dress

rehearsal of 9 December and the *première* of 10 December – a distinction frequently blurred in the memories of those participants who later recalled the scene (including Lugné-Poe), and perpetuated by many writers on the subject since. The violence of the *générale*, attended by an audience made up mainly of friends and colleagues from the world of letters, many of whom knew the play already, was in fact far less great than that of the *première*. The performance ran fairly smoothly until Act III, Scene 5, where Ubu, who has been King for five days, visits his former ally Bordure in the prison at Thorn. Here, in place of the door of the prison cell, an actor stood with one arm outstretched; Gémier 'inserted' a key into his hand, made a clicking noise, and turned the arm as if opening a door. Suddenly tumult broke out on all sides, the audience apparently having decided at this point that 'the joke had gone on long enough'.[32] With the actors submerged beneath a deluge of shouts, insults, stamping and whistling, the performance came to a complete stop until Gémier, furious, had the idea of dancing a jig on stage to distract the audience. The audience broke into laughter, and the performance was able to continue, although further periodic interruptions occurred until the end.

It was at the *première*, the following evening, that the real explosion occurred. All the leading celebrities in the worlds of politics, journalism and letters were present, howling, shouting, stamping or applauding, from the very first word of the performance. Such was the uproar following Gémier's opening 'Merdre!' that it was 15 to 20 minutes before the play could continue and the second word be spoken. Not only was it the first time that the word had been pronounced (at least in such a prominent position in a play) on the French stage, but, according to Rachilde, Jarry's deformation of it – his addition of a magnificently sonorous 'r' to the celebrated *mot de Cambronne* – at one and the same time mystified the audience and was felt as an additional insult, provoking it to a paroxysm of fury. Further tumult broke out again and again as the performance proceeded, with Gémier trying to silence the audience by blowing into a tramway horn. To cries of 'Vive M. Scribe!', someone in the audience countered with: 'Vous ne comprendriez pas davantage Shakespeare!' ['You wouldn't understand Shakespeare any better!'], while Courteline stood on a *strapontin* and shouted at the audience: 'Vous ne voyez pas que l'auteur se fout de nous?' ['Can't you see that the author is taking us for a bunch of damned fools?'] The general feeling amongst this overwhelmingly bourgeois audience was one of outrage at this 'mystification' and 'blague informe'.

In the days following the *première*, the whole of the Parisian press howled, occasionally with glee, far more often with fury and indignation. The performance of *Ubu Roi* released a torrent of abuse and condemnation whose violence can rarely have been equalled in the history of the theatre. It was also the occasion of a celebrated journalistic duel between Henry Bauer, theatre critic of the influential *Écho de Paris* and the most eloquent and vociferous supporter of the play, and Henry Fouquier of *Le Figaro*, the epitome of bourgeois 'common sense' and the play's most persistent and tenacious critic (who managed to identify his rival Bauer as at one and the same time a Robespierre-like tyrant of letters, a literary anarchist, and Ubu himself!).[33] Yet the expressions of almost paroxysmic rage on the one hand, and of glee on the other, to which the performance of *Ubu Roi* gave rise cannot be explained solely in terms of the play itself. In fact, those who even attempted to judge it on its own terms, as a piece of theatre, were few indeed. Almost alone, Romain Coolus (pseudonym of René Weil) in the *Revue Blanche* of 1 January 1897 suggested briefly and tentatively that certain features of the set and acting constituted 'une sorte de langage théâtral nouveau sur lequel il y aura lieu de revenir' ['a kind of new theatrical language which merits further discussion']. For the majority of Jarry's contemporaries, *Ubu Roi* and its performance constituted above all a symbol, a bludgeon, an instrument of attack and counter-attack in an artistic, political and ideological struggle.

At the performance, and in the press during the weeks that followed, three main accusations were levelled against the play. Firstly, it was its alleged 'vulgarity' and 'obscenity' – typified by the opening 'Merdre!' – which provoked fury and indignation. One critic began his review with the words: 'Malgré l'heure tardive, je viens de prendre une douche. Mesure préventive indispensable quand on sort d'un pareil spectacle.' ['Despite the late hour, I have just taken a shower. An absolutely essential preventive measure when one has been subjected to such a spectacle.'] (*L'Événement*, 11 December 1896). Other typical comments were: 'Cet excès d'ineptie et de grossièreté' ['This excess of ineptitude and vulgarity'] (*Le Temps*, 14 December), 'cette allusion grossière et scatologique' ['this vulgar and scatological allusion'] (*La Critique*, 20 December), and 'cette insanité scatophile' ['this scatophile piece of insanity'] (*Le Petit Parisien*, 11 December).

Secondly, the play was condemned on political grounds. In the atmosphere of the time, it was inevitable that a large section of the public would interpret it as an 'anarchist' outrage, a theatrical equivalent of the bombs which only two years earlier had the citizens of Paris trembling with fear. This fact goes a long way towards explaining the frenzy of rage and hatred aroused by the performance; for despite the apparent frivolity that superficially characterizes these years around the turn of the century in France – symbolized in the nickname of 'la Belle Epoque' – this was also an age of High Seriousness, of the reign of a middle-class determined to preserve its political, social and cultural values against the attacks of those who sought to undermine them. Twenty-five years after the event, the memory of the Paris Commune of 1871 was still vividly present in the minds of France's *bourgeoisie*. This 'anarchist' interpretation was most eloquently formulated by Henry Fouquier in his duel with Henry Bauer (was it a mere coincidence that Fouquier's rival was himself a former *communard*?), who developed out of it, in an article of 13 December in *Le Figaro*, the notion of a literary 'Terror' which had reigned in recent years:

Or, ces anarchistes de l'art . . ., ces anarchistes renouvellent dans le monde des lettres ce que j'ai vu, de mes yeux désolés, se passer au moment de la Commune. . . . ces hommes . . . exercent sur le public une véritable terreur. Et cette terreur spéciale, toute littéraire, est de celles que l'opinion se laisse le plus aisément imposer.

> [Now, these anarchists of art . . ., these anarchists are repeating in the world of letters what I saw happening, with my own sorry eyes, at the time of the Commune. . . . these men . . . exercise over the public a veritable terror. And this special, wholly literary, form of terror is of the kind that public opinion most easily submits to.]

Yet if Fouquier's and others' outraged condemnation of *Ubu Roi* was intended as a condemnation of the literary 'anarchism' of the whole Symbolist movement, a no less political or 'anarchist' interpretation of the play was all too frequently put forward by Jarry's friends and supporters also, whose incomprehension often rivalled that of his most bitter critics. Almost without exception, they saw the figure of Ubu in terms of a political satire directed against the *bourgeois* and his allegedly unscrupulous craving for and exercise of political power. Thus Catulle Mendès, in his resounding and influential article in *Le Journal* of 11 December, saw Ubu as made up in part 'de Mayeux et de Joseph Prudhomme, de Robert Macaire et de M. Thiers', and as a satire upon 'les vertus, les patriotismes et l'idéal des personnes qui ont bien dîné' ['the virtues, the patriotism and the ideals of people who have dined well']. Jarry's friend A.-F. Hérold, writing in the *Mercure de France* of January 1897, quoted with obvious approval the comparison recently made by the journalist Henri Rochefort between Ubu and the country's then Prime Minister, Méline, and his colleagues, concluding his observations with the words: 'Et, en somme, Ubu n'est-il pas, professeur ou politicien, l'homme du gouvernement?' ['And, in short, is not Ubu, whether teacher or politician, the very model of our rulers?'] The most telling case of all is that of Henry Bauer who, in three long and resounding articles in *L'Écho de Paris* (of 23 November, 12 and 19 December) put the whole weight of his very considerable authority behind a similarly political interpretation. In the first of these articles, Bauer argued that the play was:

un pamphlet philosophico-politique à gueule effrontée, qui crache au visage des chimères de la tradition et des maîtres . . . . Ubu est l'extrême produit des dynasties de muflerie, engendré par la Révolution française et l'état de bourgeoisie civile et militaire, qu'il se désigne sous les noms de César, de Bonaparte, de Louis-Philippe, de Joseph Prudhomme, de Chauvin ou de Napoléon, qu'il soit revêtu par le coup d'État, l'émeute ou la turpitude des suffrages.

> [an impudently outspoken philosophico-political pamphlet which spits in the face of the myths of tradition and of our masters . . . . Ubu is the end-product of the dynasties of boorishness brought into being by the French Revolution and the civilian and military rule of the bourgeoisie, whether it goes by the name of Caesar, of Bonaparte, of Louis-Philippe, of Joseph Prudhomme, of Chauvin or of Napoleon, whether its rule hides behind the cloak of the *coup d'État*, the riot or the turpitude of the ballot-box.]

And in his articles of 12 and 19 December he argues the same interpretation, adding in the latter a significant twist in the interesting comment:

De cette énorme figure d'Ubu, étrangement suggestive, souffle le vent de destruction, l'inspiration de la jeunesse contemporaine qui abat les traditionnels respects et les séculaires préjugés.

> [From this huge, strangely suggestive, figure of Ubu there blows a wind of destruction, the inspiration of today's youth, which destroys everything once respected and centuries-old prejudices.]

It is perhaps small wonder that Fouquier and other hostile critics reacted as they did, and small wonder also that generations of Frenchmen and others have been nourished on the myth that *Ubu Roi* constitutes *simply* a satire on the 'bourgeoisie'.[34]

The third major accusation levelled against the play and its performance was that it was in no way a 'serious' piece of theatre, but rather that the whole enterprise was a gigantic *hoax* – 'une grandiose fumisterie' ['an elaborate fraud'] (*La Patrie*, 12 December), a 'mystification qui n'a rien d'artistique' ['a hoax lacking in any artistic value'] (*Le Soleil*, 11 December), 'une mystification de fort mauvais goût' ['a hoax in extremely bad taste'] (*Paris*). This view was summed up admirably by Francisque Sarcey, a leading theatre critic and the epitome of bourgeois self-satisfaction, who wrote in *Le Temps* on 14 December: 'C'est une fumisterie ordurière qui ne mérite que le silence du mépris. . . . La mesure est comble.' ['It is a filthy hoax which deserves only the silence of contempt. . . . This is the *limit*!'] A similar reproach was made, in less outspoken terms, even by many of Jarry's supporters and fellow-*littérateurs*. Jules Renard wrote in his *Journal* following the performance: 'Si Jarry n'écrit pas demain qu'il s'est moqué de nous, il ne s'en relèvera pas' ['If Jarry does not publicly state tomorrow that he has been making fun of us, his reputation will never recover']³⁵ And Henry Bauer asked in the second of his three articles: 'Comment certains spectateurs ne se rendaient-ils pas compte qu'A. Jarry se moquait et de lui et de nous?' ['How on earth did certain members of the audience not realize that A. Jarry was poking fun both at himself and at us?'

Where then does Jarry stand in relation to these charges and interpretations of the play? Was *Ubu Roi* intended as an assault upon the public's moral susceptibilities? Did Jarry conceive of the play in terms of political satire, or of any other form of satire, whether 'anarchist' in inspiration or not? And was the whole enterprise simply a gigantic hoax, a huge and elaborate practical joke?

There can be no doubt that one – but only one – of Jarry's aims was to shock and outrage his audience. Not only can this be deduced from his writings on the theatre, which display a near-absolute contempt for the bourgeois theatre-going public of his day, which he consistently refers to as 'the mob' (*la foule*) and contemptuously describes as 'illettrée par définition', understanding and appreciating 'non de soi, mais d'autorité' ['not by virtue of its own efforts, but through blind acceptance of received opinion'], and from the circumstances and content of his speech to the audience, but more direct and explicit evidence exists also. Among his papers deposited in the offices of the *Mercure de France* at his death was found a collection of press cuttings, carefully pasted onto sheets of blue and pink notepaper and assembled into a *dossier* of 14 pages, of reviews exclusively *hostile* to the play and its performance – the more obtuse reviews, such as those of Fouquier, receiving particular attention. In this aim to defy and to outrage, moreover, Jarry succeeded beyond all possible expectations: as an example of theatrical provocation and aggression, symbolized in the opening 'Merdre!', the first performance of *Ubu Roi* is outstanding in the history of the theatre, and it is small wonder that Antonin Artaud (who in 1927 founded with Roger Vitrac the Théâtre Alfred Jarry) was to find in the play a source of inspiration for his conception of a 'theatre of cruelty'.³⁶

It is also true that the performance represented, in part, an assault upon, if not the political and social, at least the cultural values of his public. For the violence and obscenity of the play's language represented an attack upon the linguistic conventions of the existing theatre just as surely as the deliberate incoherence of its set and the incongruities of the acting represented an attack upon the rationalistic world-view of Jarry's contemporaries. His writings manifest a supreme contempt not only for the ideas and values of the theatre-going public of his time, but more generally for the political and cultural values of the ruling bourgeoisie as a whole. But, as we saw in Chapter Three, he was equally contemptuous of the anarchist (or anarchosocialist) ideas of many of his literary friends and colleagues, and it is quite erroneous to assume that he intended *Ubu Roi* to be seen – as was all too often done and has, alas, continued to be done – in terms of a mere satire upon certain *specific* social and political forms and values. It is certainly the case that he intended the audience to see *itself* (or, as he puts it, its 'Double') in the person of Ubu, as he states explicitly in 'Questions de théâtre':

J'ai voulu que, le rideau levé, la scène fût devant le public comme ce miroir des contes de Mme Leprince de Beaumont, où le vicieux se voit avec des cornes de taureau et un corps de dragon, selon l'exagération de ses vices; et il n'est pas étonnant que le public ait été stupéfait à la vue de son double ignoble . . . .

> [I wanted the stage facing the public, from the moment the curtain rose, to resemble that mirror in the fairy-tales of Mme Leprince de Beaumont, in which the depraved man sees himself with the horns of a bull and a dragon's body, and so on according to the extent of his wickedness; and it is not surprising that the audience was dumbfounded at the sight of its ignoble Double . . . .]

(Moreover, he maintains, the anger of the public – 'la foule' – arose precisely from its recognition of itself: 'elle s'est fâchée parce qu'elle a trop bien compris, quoi qu'elle en dise' ['it grew angry because it understood all too clearly, whatever it may say'].) But the very terms of the comparison indicate that Jarry sees this identification of the public in moral, rather than political and social, terms. It is true also, notwithstanding this, that once or twice he allowed the enthusiasm of Ubu's supporters and apologists to carry him along in the direction of a socio-political satirical interpretation, for example quoting in 'Questions de théâtre', with explicit approval, Mendès' view that Ubu was 'fait [. . .] des pudeurs, des vertus, du patriotisme et de l'idéal des gens qui ont bien dîné'.[37] But such utterances run counter to the majority of his pronouncements on the subject, and in 'Les Para-lipomènes d'Ubu', published on the eve of the performance, Jarry had warned in advance against all such 'anarchist' and specifically anti-'bourgeois' interpretations, referring to Ubu in the words:

Ce n'est pas exactement Monsieur Thiers, ni le bourgeois, ni le mufle: ce serait plutôt l'anarchiste parfait, avec ceci qui empêche que *nous* devenions jamais l'anarchiste parfait, que c'est un homme, d'où couardise, saleté, laideur, etc.

> [*He is not* exactly Monsieur Thiers, nor the bourgeois, nor the epitome of boorishness: he would be, rather, the perfect anarchist, were it not for the fact, which prevents *us* from ever becoming the perfect anarchist , that he is a man, whence cowardice, filth, ugliness, etc.]

Similarly, in his speech to the audience, while thanking those critics who had supported the play, he nonetheless protested against the fact that 'leur bienveillance a vu le ventre d'Ubu gros de plus de satiriques symboles qu'on ne l'en a pu gonfler pour ce soir' ['their benevolence has caused them to see the belly of Ubu swollen with more satirical symbols than it has been possible to inflate it with for this evening']. And in the programme notes distributed to the audience, he implied that the very absence of historical realism in the play, its setting in a universal and eternal 'Nowhere', invalidated all such specific satirical interpretations: 'Si diverses satires se laissent voir, le lieu de la scène en fait les interprètes irresponsables.' ['If various satirical possibilities can be seen, the setting of the play removes any responsibility for these from the actors.'] In Jarry's own conception, therefore, the figure of Ubu is clearly not a satirical figure (in the sense of a satire upon a specific social class or historical period) and *Ubu Roi* is not on the whole a satirical play, any more than – as we shall see – it is a play which relies on verbal *wit* as a source of humour.

What of the third of the accusations levelled against Jarry, that of hoaxing? Again, it is undeniable that this was in part his aim – though not quite in the way that a majority of the audience believed. Over and over again, the accusations of hoaxing are linked to complaints concerning the play's total lack of wit (*esprit*) or humour, revealing in the process a total failure to appreciate the true nature of its comedy. (Indeed, a number of reviewers mention the fact that *Ubu Roi* was originally 'une farce de guignol' and yet still fail to draw from this any conclusions concerning the nature of that comedy, as well as continuing to try to judge it by such conventional dramatic criteria as psychological motivation of characters, or coherence of plot, and the like.) For the critic of *La République française* (12 December), 'il y aurait .... fallu de l'esprit, et je n'ai pas même découvert de vraie drôlerie dans *Ubu Roi*, sauf en une ou deux répliques' ['what was needed ... was some wit, and I didn't even find anything that was really funny in *Ubu Roi*, except in one or two lines']. For the critic of *Paris*, the play, intended as a pastiche of *Macbeth*, failed lamentably through its total lack of 'wit'. While the reviewer of *Le Petit Parisien* (11 December) summed up a host of similar accusations in the exasperated outburst: 'Avec cela pas un mot d'esprit!' ['To top it all, not a single witticism!'] Indeed, a number of analyses by those present of the audience's reactions make it clear that the public had come in the expectation of being treated to a display of verbal wit, in particular in the form of *risqué* sexual jokes and innuendoes.[38] Yet in Jarry's own conception, *Ubu Roi* was never intended to be a 'witty' play; on the contrary, most of the apparent attempts at verbal wit – typified by the jokes that Ubu time and again tries to make – are deliberately feeble, and Catulle Mendès was right when he spoke in *Le Journal* of 11 December of 'les drôleries pas drôles, les grotesqueries désolantes' ['the unwitty witticisms, the devastatingly unfunny lines'] of the play. In 'Questions de théâtre', Jarry emphasized that: 'Vraiment, il n'y a pas de quoi attendre une pièce drôle, et les masques expliquent que le comique doit en être tout au plus le comique macabre d'un clown anglais ou d'une danse des morts.' ['Really, there is no reason to expect a witty play, and the masks clearly indicate that the comedy must at the very most be the ghoulish comedy of an English clown or of a Dance of Death.'] And the audience ought to have realized from Mère Ubu's repeated refrain: 'Quel sot homme ...! quel triste imbécile ...!' ['What a stupid man ...! what a sorry fool ...!'] that 'Ubu ne devait pas dire "des mots d'esprit" comme divers ubucules en réclamaient, mais des phrases stupides, avec toute l'autorité du Mufle' ['Ubu was not intended to come out with "witticisms", such as various ubushites demanded, but stupid remarks, with all the authority of the *Mufle*']. The real element of hoaxing, in fact, lay elsewhere – and the joke was not only upon the 'bourgeois' members of the audience but also upon Jarry's Symbolist colleagues in the world of letters. For one of the characteristics of Symbolism was a profound belief in the 'mystery' of the world and a mania for searching for hidden 'meanings' and symbols in both life and art (it was this which led the audience to see in the character of the 'old man' whose task was to indicate scene-changes a symbol of Time). In their efforts to read a symbolic meaning into what was in origin and in essence a grotesque schoolboy farce, let alone the attempts of some to see in *Ubu Roi* a profundity comparable with the plays of Shakespeare, both bourgeois and Symbolists were sorely deceived. The hoaxing was compounded by the presence, and Jarry's retention, in the text of the play of a series of allusions or expressions – the repeated 'de par ma chandelle verte', the mysterious exploding 'palotins', the 'côtes de rastron' served at the banquet, the 'chiens à bas de laine' referred to in Act III, Scene 7, and even the deformation enshrined in the word 'merdre', to mention just a few – deriving from the original schoolboy folklore of the Lycée de Rennes and quite incomprehensible to all but its initiates. In this respect, at least, if Rachilde and others are right in their analysis of the impact of Ubu's opening 'Merdre!', the audience's reaction was plainly justified.

However, having conceded that there is some substance in all three accusations levelled against Jarry and the play's performance, it has to be said that, for its author, *Ubu Roi* and its staging were very much more than simply a deliberate act of aggression, or a mirror held up to his contemporaries, or a sustained and elaborate hoax. Over and above these aims, the performance represented, for Jarry, the launching of the haunting figure of Ubu himself and, even more importantly, an experiment in radically new dramatic techniques and the practical realization of a new and revolutionary conception of the theatre.

It is clear from all of Jarry's writings on the theatre[39] that his starting-point is a total rejection of *all* existing theatrical forms. This rejection applies first and foremost to the prevailing trend of 'realism' in the theatre of the nineteenth century: the attempt to reproduce on the stage a supposed 'copy' of the real world outside the theatre. For Jarry, the two concepts of 'nature' and 'art', far from being compatible, are diametrically opposed – a contrast made explicit in his programme notes for *Ubu Roi* which were distributed to the audience. He was not the first to revolt against the dominance of realism and naturalism in the theatre, and he was certainly not to be the last: both the Symbolist Théâtre d'Art, and then Lugné-Poe at the Oeuvre, had done so before him, whilst more generally a revolt against the conventions of realism and naturalism was to be the starting-point of all the great innovators in theatrical theory and practice from the late nineteenth century onwards, from the Swiss designer and theorist Adolphe Appia, through the brilliant English director and designer Edward Gordon Craig, and the half-mad, half-genial Frenchman Antonin Artaud, to the dramatists of the last 30 years. But his own revolt against these conventions was among the most radical and uncompromising. Thus, for example, the costumes of *Ubu Roi* are to represent the very reverse of historical realism ('aussi peu couleur locale ou chronologiques que possible' ['as lacking in local colour or historical accuracy as possible']). Would-be realistic sets are, he argues, hybrid and self-contradictory, 'ni naturel ni artificiel'. In fact, elaborate stage sets and their constituent elements come at the very top of Jarry's list of 'objets notoirement horribles et incompréhensibles' which 'encombrent la scène sans utilité' ['notoriously hideous and incomprehensible objects' which 'quite pointlessly clutter up the stage'].[40] These should be replaced by mobile and 'representative' props (such as tables, chairs and lamps, but including also windows which are to be opened or doors to be smashed in) which can be brought on to the stage or moved about as and when required, in full view of the audience, thereby effectively shattering any illusion of 'reality'.

Such ideas as these, though revolutionary at the time, have since become part of the stock-in-trade of much of twentieth-century theatre. More radical, and less easy for his successors to follow, is his treatment of the actor who, alongside the use of elaborate sets, is another of the 'objets ... qui encombrent la scène sans utilité'. He argues that the actor should, as in the ancient Greek theatre, deny his individuality to the extent of having his face hidden behind a mask, and that he should adopt a special and, in the literal sense of the term, monotonous 'voice', 'la voix du rôle', particular emotions being conveyed by the play upon the mask of the spotlights (a recent invention, of the possibilities of which Jarry shows himself keenly aware). By these and other means, the actor is to become merely 'une fantoche', a simple puppet. This dislike of, and indeed contempt for, actors, which he shares with many of his fellow writers, is a theme which runs through all Jarry's writings on and later references to the theatre. In part, it is simply a reaction against the exaggeratedly elevated status of the actor in the theatre – and indeed in the fashionable society – of the late nineteenth century, in which theatrical 'stars' (Sarah Bernhardt is no doubt the outstanding example) reigned supreme, fêted by all, dominating productions to the extent of choosing their own costumes and imposing their will and whims upon the rest of the cast. But in part also this dislike arises from resentment on the part of the creative writer of the freedom of *interpretation*, and therefore of distortion, which – inevitably, since no actor can totally efface his own personality or modify his physical appearance – the actor enjoys. A passage in Jarry's 'Conférence sur les pantins' of 1902 makes this point clearly, and expresses also his view of the superiority of the marionette-theatre in this regard:

Nous ne savons pourquoi, nous nous sommes toujours ennuyés à ce qu'on appelle le Théâtre. Serait-ce que nous avions conscience que l'acteur, si génial soit-il, trahit – et d'autant plus qu'il est génial – ou personnel – davantage la pensée du poète? Les marionnettes seules dont on est maître, souverain et Créateur, car il nous paraît indispensable de les avoir fabriquées soi-même, traduisent, passivement et rudimentairement, ce qui est le schéma de l'exactitude, nos pensées.

[We do not know why, but we have always been bored in what is known as the Theatre. Could it be because we were conscious of the fact that the actor, however brilliant he may be – and all the more so the more brilliant – or personal – he is – further betrays the ideas of the writer? Puppets alone, of which one is master, sovereign lord and Creator, for it seems to us essential to have made them oneself, translate, in passive and rudimentary fashion, which constitutes the very height of accuracy, our thoughts.][41]

This view of actors makes clear the extent of Jarry's opposition to the theatre of his time. For his revolt goes further than that of any of the great theatrical reformers of the late nineteenth or early twentieth century, to a rejection not just of contemporary forms but of the whole theatrical heritage of the preceding two and a half centuries and, beyond even this, to a rejection of the very *concept* of 'theatre' as currently understood. The deliberately provocative title of his article 'De l'inutilité du théâtre au théâtre' is of the utmost significance here. Even more emphatic is a statement in the Oeuvre's *Manifesto* published in the summer of 1896 for the forthcoming season, in which Jarry undoubtedly had a big hand, which explicitly rejects altogether the term 'theatre', affirming that 'si, dans le vocabulaire, un autre mot que le terme "théâtre" existait, nous l'aurions pris' ['if, in our language, a word other than "theatre" existed, we would have used it'].[42]

In his attempt to create a totally new form of theatre, Jarry turned back for inspiration to older, more 'naïve', and more popular, forms of the art. Above all else, he found a source of inspiration for the kind of theatre he wished to create in the puppet-theatre which he had so loved in his childhood. It was no coincidence that he chose to give to the published text of *Ubu Roi* the 'subtitle' 'Restitué en son intégrité tel qu'il a été représenté par les marionnettes du Théâtre des Phynances en 1888' ['Restored in its entirety as it was performed by the marionettes of the Théâtre des Phynances in 1888'] – a description which was not strictly accurate, since, whatever the exact extent of Jarry's contribution to the play, it had undergone some measure of re-working and re-writing at his hands, beginning with the name Ubu itself, but which he obviously chose in order to emphasize its 'naïve' and marionette-like character. In his letter to Lugné-Poe of January 1896, he pointed out that such suggestions as the use of masks, of special 'voices' for the characters, and the 'symbolic' representation of crowds by a single actor were all in the spirit of the play, 'puisque j'ai voulu faire un *guignol*'. Similarly, both his speech to the audience and the acting itself in the production of the play reveal his intention to have his actors perform as giant marionettes. Throughout his life Jarry continued to be fascinated and inspired by the example of the puppet-theatre, as we shall see in subsequent chapters. His later writings express also a continuing admiration for the clowns and acrobats of the circus and music hall – whom he finds superior to actors in their skill and unselfconsciousness – as well as for the gestural language of mime and dance.[43]

This turning back to older, more 'naïve' forms of expression in order to create something radically new is only superficially a paradox. In all revolutions, whether political or cultural, when men set out to create anew, they tend to turn back to a more distant past for inspiration. Thus the French revolutionaries of 1789–94 adopted many of the forms and symbols of the Roman Republic of the 1st century BC (and the Napoleonic empire which followed adopted those of the Roman Empire which succeeded it), the revolutionaries of 1848 in France looked back to the glorious days of 1792–3, and the Bolsheviks in 1917 looked back to the revolutionary traditions of France. Similarly, those dramatists who have been most responsible for the revitalization of the French theatre in the last 30 years have often turned back to older and simpler forms of 'theatre' for inspiration: Ionesco has never forgotten his childhood fascination with the *guignol*, and Beckett makes enormous use in his plays of the techniques of the circus and music hall. Moreover, Jarry was not alone among contemporaries in his fascination with the puppet-theatre, nor in his view that puppets could more effectively and faithfully translate the intentions of an author than live actors. An almost identical point of view was expressed by Oscar Wilde in 1892, following a production of *The Tempest* by Maurice Bouchor's Petit Théâtre des Marionnettes in the Galerie Vivienne, which was extremely popular among men-of-letters of the time:

> There are many advantages in puppets. They never argue. They have no crude views about art. They have no private lives . . . They recognize the presiding intellect of the dramatist, and have never been known to ask for their parts to be written up. They are admirably docile, and have no personalities at all.[44]

And quite independently, but parallel with Jarry, Edward Gordon Craig not only argued the need for 'abstract', non-realistic sets and advocated the use of masks, but spoke also of the need for the puppet to become once again 'the faithful medium for the beautiful thoughts of the artist' and dreamed of replacing live actors with all their limitations by a kind of 'über-marionnette'.[45]

What form of theatre, then, emerges from Jarry's revolt and from the above sources of inspiration? From his suggestions and instructions for the original performance of *Ubu Roi*, and from his various articles on the theatre, four fundamental aims can be deduced.

Firstly, he wanted to create a theatre based on stylization, or extreme simplification, even going so far as to speak of the creation of an 'abstract' theatre. This is what lies behind his advocacy of masks which, as he told the audience at the *première* of *Ubu Roi*, make the actors 'impersonal', the mask constituting 'l'effigie du PERSONNAGE' (Jarry's capitals). It is this also which lies behind his rejection in 'De l'inutilité du théâtre au théâtre' of 'realistic' sets in favour of a deliberately simplified or stylized backdrop which will depict the 'substance' of a scene. The same idea also lies behind his designation of the setting of *Ubu Roi* as 'Nowhere' (an end-result which the actual set of December 1896 attempted to achieve through the mutual cancelling-out of contradictory elements). And, carrying this line of thought to its logical conclusion, he even at one point suggests the use simply of a plain backdrop (supplemented by written placards to indicate the scene) into which the audience – in this instance clearly made up of members of the artistic 'élite' – can project its own vision of the scene: it would be 'dangerous', he argues, for the 'poet' to impose upon 'un public d'artistes . . . le décor tel qu'il le peindrait lui-même . . . il est juste que chaque spectateur voie la scène dans le

décor qui convient à *sa* vision de la scène' ['an audience made up of
artists ... a set such as he would paint it himself ... it is right that
each member of the audience should see the stage in terms of the set
which corresponds to *his* vision of the play'].[46] Such a 'théâtre
ABSTRAIT' (Jarry's capitals) would thus involve the 'élite' also in the
act of creation. It would be a theatre not of distraction or amusement,
still less of demonstration or exposition, but one (on the level of the
imagination at least) of *action*, in which the élite will participate in 'la
réalisation de la création d'un des siens, qui voit vivre en soi-même en
cette élite l'être créé par soi, plaisir actif qui est le seul plaisir de Dieu'
['the actualization of a work created by one of its own members, who
sees the work which he has created itself coming alive in this élite,
experiencing thus an active pleasure which is the only pleasure
experienced by God'].[47] In purely theatrical terms, such a conception
is perhaps best realized in the plays of Beckett (most obviously in a
play such as *Waiting for Godot*), where the audience is implictly invited
to actively project its own 'meaning' or interpretation into the abstract
or semi-abstract framework created by the playwright. On the more
general plane of aesthetic theory, Jarry is giving here the first
enunciation of a conception of literature in which the reader (or, in
the theatre, the spectator), far from merely passively absorbing or
registering the ideas of the writer, becomes in effect a co-creator
alongside the latter – re-creating in his own imagination the vision
which the writer has sought to embody in the written text. It is a
conception to which we shall have cause to return in examining a
number of Jarry's later works.

Whilst the dominant source of inspiration in Jarry's view of the
theatre is to be found in the *guignol* of his childhood, it seems highly
probable that he found a further source of inspiration for the above
ideas in the work of a number of painters whom he greatly admired.
If realism is the dominant trend in the literature of the nineteenth
century, it is no less dominant in the painting of the same period, up
to and including the Impressionists. As noted in Chapter Two, however, in the wake of the Impressionists we find the beginnings of a
move away from the explicit attempt to reproduce 'nature' on the canvas and towards a growing emphasis upon the personal vision of the
artist and the evolution of techniques which will lead, ultimately, to
the non-representational or 'abstract' art of the twentieth century.
Foremost among the painters whose work was moving in this
direction were Gauguin and his friends and disciples, among them
the Nabis, a number of whom were close friends of Jarry and
collaborated to produce the painted backdrop of *Ubu Roi*. It would of
course be absurd to pretend that either *Ubu Roi* or the work of the
Nabis is wholly 'abstract' (and it is, moreover, debatable whether any
work whose medium is language can achieve the degree of abstrac-

tion of painting); nevertheless, painters such as Sérusier, Denis, Bonnard and Vuillard were all strongly influenced by the 'cloisonnist' style which – originally evolved by Anquetin and Emile Bernard before being adopted in 1888 by Gauguin, who then passed it on to the young Sérusier in Brittany in the autumn of the same year – became a source of inspiration and a starting point for all these young painters in their search for a path away from naturalism. With its use of flat planes with firm outlines and of sharply contrasting, non-realistic colours, the style subsequently adopted by these painters was a highly schematic one, involving extreme simplification and stylization, which also imparted to their work, intentionally or not, an air of deliberate unsophistication or even, in some cases, of apparent crudeness and naïvety. The parallel between such a conception of art and Jarry's view of the theatre, similarly based on the principles of simplification and stylization, tending towards 'abstraction', is too great to be ignored. And given the profound interest of Jarry in contemporary painting and his known admiration for, as well as personal links with, many of the above painters, it is difficult to avoid the conclusion that he was at least in part inspired by their ideas and example.

The second of Jarry's overriding aims was the creation of a theatre which, alongside its use of techniques of simplification and styliza-tion, would aim to express themes which were not particular and transitory, but universal and eternal, resulting in the creation of archetypes and of 'myth'. In this, he was in part simply echoing the general anti-historical bias of the Symbolist movement, with its interest in myth and legend. Here, too, a parallel can once again be seen with Mallarmé, whose ideas on the theatre exercised an enor-mous influence upon the young Symbolists, and who went so far as to see Shakespeare's Hamlet in such archetypal and 'mythical' terms as an embodiment of the eternal adolescence of man, 'juvénile ombre de tous, ainsi tenant du mythe' ['youthful shadow of all men, belonging thus to the realm of myth'].[48] But at the same time, a concern with the universal and the eternal runs through all of Jarry's work, and nowhere is this more in evidence than in his conception of Ubu. For the 'Nowhere' of the play's setting is also a universal 'Everywhere': as he put it in the programme notes of December 1896, 'Nulle Part est partout, et le pays où l'on se trouve d'abord.' ['Nowhere is everywhere, beginning with the country in which one finds oneself.'] Moreover, according to a theory cherished by Jarry, just as geographical or physical contradictions cancel each other out to produce an abstract 'Nowhere-Everywhere', so too historical or chronological contradictions (such as the firing of a pistol in the year 1000) cancel each other out to produce a kind of abstract 'Eternity', as he explained in his speech to the audience:

Nous aurons d'ailleurs un décor parfaitement exact, car de même qu'il est un procédé facile pour situer une pièce dans l'Éternité, à savoir de faire par exemple tirer en l'an mille et tant des coups de revolver, vous verrez des portes s'ouvrir sur des plaines de neige sous un ciel bleu, des cheminées garnies de pendules se fendre afin de servir de portes, et des palmiers verdir au pied des lits, pour que les broutent de petits éléphants perchés sur des étagères.

> [We shall have, moreover, a perfectly accurate set, for just as there is an easy technique for situating a play in Eternity, namely, to have pistol-shots fired in the year 1000 or thereabouts, so you will see doors open onto snow-covered plains beneath a blue sky, fireplaces bedecked with clocks split down the middle to serve as doors, and palm trees growing at the foot of beds, so that little elephants perched on shelves can nibble away at their foliage.]

It is, in the last resort, because of this universal and eternal setting that we must reject any interpretation of *Ubu Roi* as a satire upon a specific historical period or social class. And although we can choose, in defiance of the author's own views, to interpret the play as a satire of the bourgeoisie, or a prophetic embodiment of the totalitarianism of the twentieth century, in Jarry's own conception Ubu is simply his own version of Everyman – an embodiment of the greed, the gluttony, the brutality, the treachery, the cowardice and the stupidity of Mankind as a whole.

That such a conception betrays a particularly bleak and pessimistic view of the world is undeniable. It is a conception which Jarry seems to have formed as early as during adolescence, if we are to believe him when he told the audience that the prototype of Ubu, his physics master at the Lycée de Rennes, M. Hébert, represented for him everything that was grotesque in human nature – 'tout le grotesque qui [fut] au monde'. And the same bleak view of mankind is expressed several times over in his writings on Ubu, a further striking example being the contemptuous reference in 'Les Paralipomènes d'Ubu', quoted above, to his creation in the terms: 'ce serait ... l'anarchiste parfait, avec ceci qui empêche que *nous* devenions jamais l'anarchiste parfait, que c'est un homme, d'où couardise, saleté, laideur, etc.' ['he would be ... the perfect anarchist, were it not for the fact, which prevents *us* from ever becoming the perfect anarchist, that he is a man, whence cowardice, filth, ugliness, etc.'].

Moreover, alongside the aim to create a radically new form of theatre, it is the projection of this 'archetypal' image onto the stage which is the chief 'point' of the play. A crucial passage in 'Questions de théâtre' – which expresses also a view of Ubu as a rampaging monster about to be released on the stage – makes this point emphatically: 'Je pense qu'il n'y a aucune espèce de raison d'écrire une oeuvre sous forme dramatique, à moins que l'on ait eu la vision d'un personnage qu'il soit plus commode de lâcher sur un scène que d'analyser dans un livre.' ['I think that there is absolutely no reason whatsoever to write a work in dramatic form, unless one has experienced a vision of a character whom it is more fitting to let loose on a stage than to analyse in a book.']⁴⁹ Where both 'bourgeois' and naturalist playwrights were agreed on the overriding importance of a strong and compelling plot, Jarry, in conformity here also with Mallarmé, contemptuously rejects the importance of the story or 'anecdote', declaring in his reply to a questionnaire on the theatre that 'toute "histoire" est si ennuyeuse, c'est-à-dire inutile' ['Every "story" is so boring, that is to say useless.']. He conceives of the theatre not primarily in terms of the development of a plot or the portrayal and analysis of character – both of which belong more properly to the novel – but as above all a visual medium, a place for the projection of powerful visual images which will strike the imagination of the spectator and imprint themselves on his memory. This desire to restore to the theatre its visual impact is common to all the great reformers of the twentieth century, reaching its climax in the violent attacks of Artaud upon the pre-eminence of the text and the written word in Western theatre. And, in the wake of Artaud and Jarry, it is an important aspect of the work of the so-called 'absurd' dramatists also; thus Ionesco, for example, sets out to 'concrétiser les symboles',⁵⁰ creating in the Killer of *Tueur sans gages* a concrete symbol of the brutal fact of death, while Beckett, in *Waiting for Godot*, provides us in the spectacle of his two tramps standing alone in a wasteland (a setting every bit as 'abstract' as that of *Ubu Roi*) with a powerful image of the human condition.

In this respect at least the reactions of Jarry's contemporaries were unanimous. However diverse or erroneous their interpretations of the significance of Ubu, all were agreed on the powerful impact of the figure. Mendès' brief assertion: 'Le Père Ubu existe', and Rachilde's assessment a few months later that 'Le type d'Ubu devint légendaire. Il l'est encore et le restera.' ['The figure of Ubu became legendary. He is still, and will remain so.']⁵¹ are but two typical comments. Less terse, but of no less weight, was the appreciation of Mallarmé, in a letter of congratulation sent to Jarry:

Vous avez mis debout, avec une glaise rare et durable aux doigts, un personnage prodigieux et les siens, cela, mon cher ami, en sobre et sûr sculpteur dramatique.
Il entre dans le répertoire de haut goût et me hante; merci.

[You have created, with a rare and lasting clay at your fingertips, a prodigious figure and his retinue, and that, my dear friend, with the skill of a sober and sure dramatic sculptor.
He enters the repertoire of high taste and haunts me; thank you.]⁵²

Jarry's third basic aim in the staging of *Ubu Roi* was quite different. It was the creation of a form of comic theatre based not on verbal wit, but on the exploitation of both older and new forms of humour – something which he believed he had found in the grotesque school-boy farce of the play, and which his production of December 1896 was designed to accentuate. (This is an aim which distinguishes him sharply from the majority of his fellow-Symbolists and from reformers such as Craig who similarly sought inspiration in the marionette-theatre, all of whom wished ultimately to restore to the theatre its former ritualistic and even religious function. Jarry's aim is, by contrast, purely secular and artistic.) For Ubu is not just the embodiment of gluttony, brutality and treachery; he is also, a fact which critics sometimes tend to forget, the embodiment of unutterable stupidity – a stupidity so colossal that we cannot but laugh at it and at him. It is true that that laughter may be tinged with a certain apprehension before the devastating effects of that stupidity, to say nothing of Ubu's cruelty and sadism. But it is laughter nonetheless, and in the figure of Ubu Jarry is inviting us to laugh at the grotesque stupidity of Mankind as well as deploring its moral ugliness. In his very first letter to Lugné-Poe concerning the staging of the play, he maintained that it would be 'd'un effet comique sûr', and the reaction of modern audiences amply testifies to the accuracy of his judgment. Indeed, it is arguable that the play has lost much of its power to shock and outrage modern audiences, and that its power to make us laugh is therefore all the greater – provided that the production understands and respects Jarry's wishes.[53]

In the absence of verbal wit, what are the main sources of the play's comedy? Its humour derives from four main sources, in ascending order of importance. Firstly, it derives from the element of parody. The basic 'plot' of *Ubu Roi* derives from a parody upon Shakespeare's *Macbeth*, whose ambitious wife urges her husband to assassinate the King and usurp the throne, only to be overthrown in turn. There are other elements of parody, too, for example upon the classical monologue in Mère Ubu's long speech at the beginning of Act V, together with other borrowings from Shakespeare, such as the banquet scene where the assassination plot is elaborated (*Julius Caesar*) and the bear of Act IV, Scene 6 (*The Winter's Tale*).[54] This is not satire – which implies the affirmation of values the opposite of those attacked – but simply parody or spoofing for its own sake, born of a schoolboy disrespect for the 'great' and the revered, and a source of impish delight for many. Secondly, by a strange paradox, the very obscenities of the play are a source of humour, at least for most modern audiences. To be able to use, or hear, 'taboo' words in an unexpected context offers a release from normal constraints, a release which expresses itself in laughter – all the more when those obscenities are compounded by word play and linguistic invention. For although the play may be characterized by an absence of witticisms, verbal humour of other kinds is present in abundance. Thirdly, much of the humour derives from the exaggeration, the slapstick, the sheer unreality of farce, in which the real is blown up to quite implausible proportions. The monstrously fat belly of Ubu, the slapstick of the battle scenes and fights, even the implausible rapidity with which events follow one another, all of these partake of the exaggeration and unreality of farce. This is a form of comedy which was exhaustively analysed by Jarry's former philosophy teacher at the Lycée Henri IV, Henri Bergson, in *Le Rire* (1900), in which he saw the sources of comedy as lying above all in the reduction of the living, the spontaneous and the human to the level of the mechanical and the inhuman. Whether Bergson, who as we saw in Chapter Two certainly outlined his ideas to his pupils, was indirectly responsible for confirming Jarry in his estimation for the *Ubu* plays must remain an open question. But in any case, Jarry – and *Ubu Roi* – go beyond the analysis of Bergson to the creation of a fourth source of humour, the most important of all. Alongside the techniques of dehumanization and reification examined by Bergson, which are characteristic of the art of farce, the comedy of the play derives also from an almost systematic exploitation of incongruity, an incongruity which is frequently pushed to the point of outright logical contradiction and sheer absurdity. This is a form of humour which has become widespread in our time, but which Jarry's first audiences almost totally failed to appreciate, and in the use of which he himself was a trail-blazer. Time and time again in *Ubu Roi* we encounter instances of incongruity, or of sheer logical contradiction, which provoke laughter: the juxtaposition of totally incongruous or contradictory elements in the set, such as the sun shining in the midst of a snow-storm, or a tree growing at the foot of a bed; the frequent alternation, in the dialogue, of different registers, from coarse slang and obscenities to deliberate archaisms, then to a pseudo-'noble' style, and back to slang again, in rapid succession (the opening scene offers a good example); the deformation of language, and the use of words as mere blocks of sound hurled at an adversary (as in the battle between the Ubus and Bougrelas in Act V, Scene 2); such statements as Ubu's pronouncement that he will light a fire while waiting for the others to bring wood (Act IV, Scene 6), in which the law of causality is stood on its head; the incongruity of using a single actor to 'represent' a crowd, and even more strikingly the use of actors as props, as in the scene set in the prison of Thorn (Act III, Scene 5); and, not least, the simple fact of human actors performing as marionettes. Examples of this type of humour can be found on almost every page of the text (though it is only in performance that many of the play's incongruities can be appreciated to the full), and together make of Jarry in this as in so many other respects a precursor of our own age.

Why precisely we should respond to such incongruity and illogicality with laughter – or, in the case of Jarry's original audience, with anger and indignation, perhaps born of fear – is another matter. And here too Jarry implicitly goes beyond the teachings of Bergson. For where Bergson sees humour as having an essentially social and morally corrective function, constituting a means of implicitly rejecting deviations from an accepted social norm, the humour of *Ubu Roi*, if it has any function at all, has a metaphysical rather than a social one. In so far as a relationship exists between literary or artistic forms and values and the wider context of social and philosophical forms and values, Jarry's audience in 1896 was right to feel itself somehow vaguely threatened by the play and its performance: for the 'anarchic' humour, as it has been called, of *Ubu Roi* was intended deliberately to shatter the cosily coherent, rationalistic view of the world of his contemporaries – and of many of our own.

This discussion of the nature of the comedy of *Ubu Roi* brings us to the fourth and final aim of Jarry in his presentation of the play. For this delight in the incongruous and the illogical – in what some would call sheer nonsense – together with a delight in wordplay and verbal inventiveness, is one of the characteristics of the mentality of children. Indeed, the world of the play is in many respects the world of childhood, in which the 'rules' of logic and propriety simply do not (or do not yet) exist. And Ubu himself is in many respects simply an overgrown child, whose reluctance to assassinate the King can be swept away by the inducement of wearing a big cape and eating lots of chitterlings (*andouilles*), whose resistance to distributing money to his Polish subjects can be overcome by the argument that they would not otherwise pay their taxes, and whose childish logic is summed up in the simple declaration: 'Je veux faire des lois maintenant'. Throughout *Ubu Roi*, Ubu himself behaves very much in the manner of a stupid, cruel, vindictive child – a child, moreover, whose simple-mindedness can be terrifying as well as comic, a characteristic summed up in the words: 'Avec ce système, j'aurai vite fait fortune, *alors je tuerai tout le monde et je m'en irai.*' [With this system I'll soon be rich, *then I'll kill everybody and go away.*']⁵⁵ It was something of this childlike quality that Jarry set out to capture in the production of 1896 – whence, for example, Arthur Symons' description (which was not intended to be complimentary) of the set as painted 'according to a child's convention'. Even if we did not know of the play's origins, it would be impossible to imagine *Ubu Roi* as anything other than the product of an unruly and disrespectful schoolboy imagination. As Albert Thibaudet rightly observed at the time of the controversy over its authorship: '*Ubu* est marqué au coin du génie enfantin .... Morin

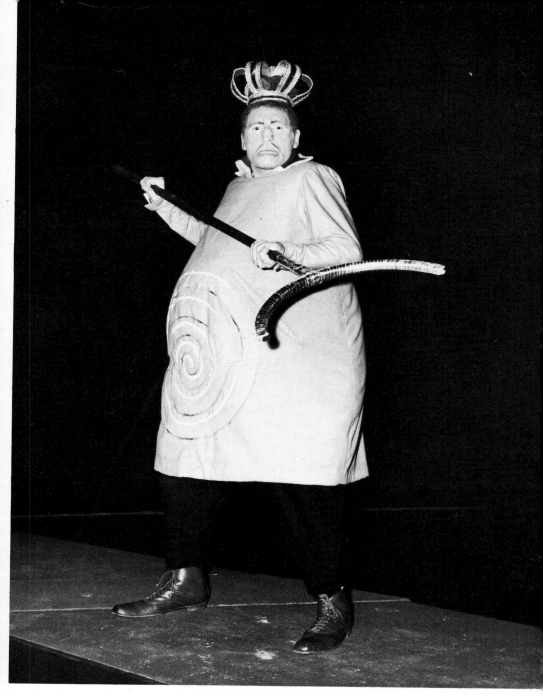

13. Ubu (Georges Wilson) and his *croc à merdre* in menacing posture in Jean Vilar's production of *Ubu* (a fusion of *Ubu Roi* and *Ubu Enchaîné*) at the Théâtre National Populaire, Paris, 1958. (Photo Agence de Presse Bernand, Paris.)

14. Ubu and his fellow-convicts in front of the prison in Jean Vilar's *Ubu* at the Théâtre National Populaire. (Photo Agence de Presse Bernand, Paris.)

15. Max Wall as Père Ubu and John Shepherd as Mère Ubu in Iain Cuthbertson's
production of *Ubu Roi* at the Royal Court Theatre, London, 1966. Sets
designed by David Hockney. (Photograph: Zoë Dominic.)

16. Ubu as warrior king astride his Phynancial Horse, leaving to fight the Russians in the Royal Court production of *Ubu Roi*, 1966. (Photograph: Zoë Dominic.)

17. Captain Bordure (Bernard Gallagher) confronts Ubu's Polish forces in the Ukraine (represented by Hockney's miniature windmill and letters forming 'Polish Army in the Ukraine' across the front of the stage) in the Royal Court production of *Ubu Roi*, 1966. (Photograph: Zoë Dominic.)

18. & 19. Allan Edwall as Père Ubu and Ing-Mari Tirén as Mère Ubu in Michael Meschke's production of *Kung Ubu*, Stockholm, 1964. The production, designed by Franciszka Themerson, combined live actors with two-dimensional puppet-like cut-outs animated by actors hidden behind them. It was subsequently performed in well over a dozen countries around the world. (Reproduced by permission of Franciszka Themerson.)

20. Père Ubu (Andreas Katsulas) holding lavatory brush, with Mère Ubu (Michèle Collison), Bordure (François Martouret) and fellow-conspirators in Peter Brook's production of *Ubu* given at the Bouffes du Nord, Paris, in 1977, the Young Vic, London, 1978, and subsequently in many countries around the world. The cable-reel ingeniously served as table, throne and instrument for demolishing the peasants' house in Act III, Sc. 4. (Photo Agence de Presse Bernand, Paris.)

21. Ubu in chains and fellow-convicts in Peter Brook's production of *Ubu*. (Photograph: Nicolas Treatt.)

22. (*facing*) Père Ubu with *palotins* in Peter Brook's production of *Ubu*. The enormously long flat rubber hose was wound by Ubu around his body when he became king, unravelling itself across the stage in the battle scenes.

23. Père and Mère Ubu overheard by Bordure in Peter Brook's production of *Ubu*. The enormous rug also served as the bear in Act IV, Sc. 6. (Photo Nicolas Treatt.)

ou Jarry, l'œuvre ne pouvait sortir que d'un cerveau d'enfant.' ['*Ubu* bears the imprint of the genius of childhood . . . . Morin or Jarry, the work could only have issued from the mind of a child.']⁵⁶ Around the same time, the philosopher Alain wrote of Jarry and Ubu: 'Jarry fut artiste en ceci surtout qu'à ses vingt ans il sut n'ajouter rien à cette œuvre d'enfance. Ainsi Ubu est vivant à la manière des contes.' ['Jarry was an artist above all in this, that at the age of 20 he was wise enough not to add anything to this work of childhood. Thus Ubu lives, in the manner of a fairy-tale.']⁵⁷ And Jarry himself, in one of his later *chroniques*, goes even further, implicitly equating the childlike, and even the 'puerile', with the 'eternal'.⁵⁸

If this is indeed a characteristic of the play, then the attitude towards childhood of most of Jarry's contemporaries goes a long way towards explaining the total failure of the audience to understand the true nature of its comedy. For this was an age of High Seriousness, in which it was considered essential, upon entering the 'serious' world of adulthood, to leave behind the attitudes and values of childhood. Whence the contempt displayed by Jarry's co-authors, Charles and Henri Morin, for this 'bêtise' and 'couillonnade' of their childhood years.⁵⁹ Whence also, perhaps, part of the explanation of the audience's outraged reaction to the element of alleged 'mystification' in the performance, frightened by that which they failed to understand: as Jarry shrewdly observed in *Ubu Enchaîné*, 'ce qui fait rire les petits enfants risque de faire peur aux grandes personnes' ['what causes children to laugh risks frightening grown-ups']. Today, 80 years and more on, we are much more prepared to admit the value of that state of mind of wonder and sheer delight in the absurd out of which *Ubu Roi* was born. Nevertheless Jarry was alone at the time in realizing the true value and true potential of the work, and in carrying it with him into his adult life and onto the Parisian stage. It is perhaps the greatest of all Jarry's claims to fame that, whatever his own contribution to the elaboration of the text of *Ubu Roi*, it was he and he alone who rescued this crude, naïve, grotesque yet fascinating and delightful work from the oblivion into which it would otherwise have fallen, and who saw in it possibilities commensurate with those of the highest art.

Chapter Five

Further manifestations of Ubu

THE REVERBERATIONS from the riotous first performance of *Ubu Roi* in December 1896 were to make themselves felt throughout the remainder of Jarry's brief existence – in spite of the apparent indifference of his initial reaction. Rachilde, looking back on the affair some months later, described his attitude thus: 'Alfred Jarry sortit de là sans étonnement. Ce nouveau jeune, *palotin* correct de la Providence, réintégra sa boîte, ne se souciant pas plus de cette affaire que d'une partie de quilles.' ['Alfred Jarry emerged from it all without any sense of surprise. This young newcomer, one of Providence's proper *palotins*, returned to his box, as unconcerned about the affair as about a game of skittles.'][1]

Such indifference provoked the resentment of Catulle Mendès who felt slighted that Jarry had failed to thank him for his enthusiastic defence of Ubu, and it was only at Rachilde's prompting that he eventually sent to Mendès the following note, in which gratitude was carried to the point of hypocritical obsequiousness:

Mon cher Maître,

Je vous remercie aussi infiniment que possible de ce que vous avez bien voulu dire d'*Ubu roi*. Personne n'a su délimiter aussi exactement ce qui était et n'était pas dans ce bonhomme et définir ce que j'avais du moins tâché d'y mettre. Je suis beaucoup plus heureux de votre bienveillance pour la pièce que de tout ce bruit, que j'espérais à peine autour.

Croyez à ma respectueuse reconnaissance.

[My dear Master,

I wish to thank you as infinitely as possible for what you were kind enough to say about *Ubu Roi*. Nobody has succeeded in determining so precisely what was and was not contained in the fellow and in defining what I had at least tried to convey through him. I am much more pleased by your kindness towards the play than by all the fuss surrounding it, which I scarcely hoped for.

Please accept my respectful gratitude.]

One immediate consequence of the performance was a marked

cooling in relations with Lugné-Poe. In the face of the scandal created by the performance, and perhaps more importantly of a bill for 1,300 francs in production costs which Jarry had run up, the young director was reduced to despair. Only many years later did he recognize the significance of the performance in the history of the French theatre (indeed, of all the plays first performed at the Oeuvre, *Ubu Roi* was to prove the most celebrated in both the short and long term); for the moment he saw only insurmountable debts and the desertion of the Oeuvre by its regular public. A few months after the event, Lugné left with his troupe for a tour of the provinces, determined to carry the gospel of Ibsen to the 'manichaeans' and 'Protestants' of the Languedoc.[3] On his return, in June 1897, he issued a manifesto declaring his intention of breaking off all relations with his former Symbolist associates: the Symbolists, with the sole exception of Maeterlinck, having failed to create any works which were dramatically viable, the Oeuvre would henceforth turn its attention to an exclusively international repertoire. The Symbolists replied a few days later with an open letter, drawn up by Pierre Quillard, which denied Lugné the right to break off 'purely fictitious' relations, and declared contemptuously that: 'Le Symbolisme – si Symbolisme il y a – n'a donc rien à voir avec M. Lugné-Poe, entrepreneur de représentations théâtrales.' ['Symbolism – if Symbolism exists – therefore has nothing to do with M. Lugné-Poe, organizer of theatrical performances.'][4] The letter was signed by twelve writers (sarcastically dubbed by Lugné 'les douze pères nobles du Symbolisme'[5]): Quillard, Henry Bataille, Romain Coolus, Louis Dumur, Paul Fort, A.-F. Hérold, Gustave Kahn, Rachilde, Henri de Régnier, Saint-Pol-Roux, Auguste Villeroy and . . . Alfred Jarry. The affair resounded through the pages of the press for more than a month, with letters, interviews, insults and counter-insults following each other in rapid succession – one such exchange even resulting in a farcical and inconsequential duel between Lugné-Poe and Catulle Mendès.

For all the abrasiveness of his opening attack, Lugné-Poe's disavowal by the Symbolists carried with it a considerable measure of ingratitude. Of the twelve signatories of the above letter, over half had had plays first produced by the young director – Jarry, of course, among them. No doubt wounded pride played its part in the violence of their reaction; Lugné-Poe had after all declared that none of them had written dramatic works of any value. But the contemptuous terms in which Lugné was dismissed as a mere 'entrepreneur de représentations théâtrales' revealed also the existence, all too characteristic among the Symbolists, of a haughty and even arrogant sense of the superiority of the creative writer over a mere actor and producer.[6]

A second, more far-reaching consequence of the performance of

Ubu Roi was a meteoric rise on the part of Jarry from relative obscurity to sudden fame – a fame which increasingly took the form of an identification, in the minds of his contemporaries, between creator and literary creation. It became customary among friends, and even among casual acquaintances, to refer to him and even to address him as '(le) Père Ubu'; a newspaper report some years later of an incident in which he was involved referred not to Alfred Jarry, but simply to 'le Père Ubu en personne'. It was a game with which Jarry appears, on the whole, to have willingly played along, although a discordant note is struck by Camille Mauclair, who described him as bitterly resenting the role forced upon him.[7] The process of 'identification' had begun soon after his arrival in Paris, though it was at this stage far from complete: Fargue later described his voice at this period as being soft and natural, and his intonation as having nothing of the harsh, 'ubuesque' delivery which he later adopted.[8] Now, his dress, speech and public behaviour became increasingly extravagant and eccentric. The result is that, for the next ten years of his life, one finds in the views and reminiscences of friends and contemporaries an extraordinary jumble of colourful anecdotes which, indiscriminately taking incidents and developments from different periods of his life without any attempt to place them in context, lead to the creation of a confused and complex picture of one of the most colourful eccentrics of an age which saw many such. In his own lifetime, Jarry became a legend, with all that that term denotes of both truth and fantasy. It is in fact necessary to read the reminiscences of many of his friends and contemporaries, looking back from a period often many years after his death, when the legend was all that remained in their minds, with the greatest of circumspection. Nevertheless, it is worth outlining briefly the main themes of this legend, which focus in particular upon his dress, his speech and conversation, his lodgings, his eccentricities of behaviour, and his love of pranks and practical jokes.

Many of Jarry's contemporaries have left behind a record of the vivid impression which he made upon them. Though small in stature, he was stocky and muscular, and his muscularity was emphasized by the cyclist's attire which he preferred to wear. His long dark hair was frequently plastered down by rainwater as he cycled about Paris in all weathers. According to Henri de Régnier, his gestures and movements were brusque and seemingly mechanical: 'D'où qu'il vînt . . . Alfred Jarry avait toujours l'air d'un pantin sorti d'une boîte à surprise. Il y avait en lui quelque chose de mécanique et d'articulé.' ['Wherever he happened to come from . . . Alfred Jarry always resembled a jack-in-the-box which had just sprung up. There was something mechanical and articulated in his movements.'][9] But the most striking features of all in his physical appearance were his extraordinarily dark, brilliant eyes. Régnier described them as shining 'd'un éclat métallique'[10] in his pale face, while Rachilde recalled his 'yeux noirs lui trouant largement la face, des yeux d'une singulière phosphorescence, regards d'oiseau de nuit à la fois fixes et lumineux' ['dark eyes, set in cavernous sockets, eyes of a strange phosphorescence, with the gaze, at once fixed and luminous, of a night bird'].[11]

Equally memorable was his peculiar intonation. Rachilde spoke of 'la rapidité de son débit, martelant les syllabes comme s'il les frappait au poinçon' ['the rapidity of his delivery, hammering out each syllable as if striking them with an awl'].[12] André Gide referred to 'son élocution bizarre, implacable, sans inflexions ni nuances, avec une accentuation égale de toutes les syllabes, y compris les muettes. Un casse-noisette aurait parlé, il ne l'eût point fait autrement' ['his bizarre, relentless manner of speaking, without inflexion nor nuance, with an equal emphasis upon every syllable, including the mute 'e's. Had a nutcracker spoken, it would have done so in exactly the same way.'][13] Another characteristic of his speech was his habitual adoption – as befitted Ubu's regal status – of the royal plural, *nous*. To this he added a periphrastic style, referring to the wind as 'celui qui souffle', to a train as 'celui qui se traîne', and so on, a device which delighted many of his friends. To these idiosyncracies, he added a verbal abundance which astonished his listeners. He was a compulsive talker, given to relating apparently fantastic tales and to engaging in lengthy demonstrations of strange and seemingly absurd paradoxes. Lormel's account of his love of paradox was quoted in a previous chapter. And Jean Saltas, who was to be a valuable source of support in his later years, recalled the apparently fantastic 'science fiction' tales he heard on the occasion of their first meeting (in 1897):

Il . . . s'assit et tout de suite très entouré commença à raconter, avec une verve étonnante, une de ces histoires merveilleuses et invraisemblables dont il avait le secret. D'ailleurs, pas toujours si invraisemblables. Je me rappelle en effet que celle qu'il raconta ce soir-là avait pour sujet une ville où c'étaient les trottoirs qui marchaient au lieu que ce fussent les hommes, et où les maisons avaient leur entrée au dernier étage. Alors qu'il n'était nullement question de trottoirs roulants ni d'aéroplanes, Jarry, on le voit, concevait déjà dans son imagination les uns et les autres.

> [He . . . sat down and, immediately surrounded by a large number of listeners, began recounting with an amazing verve one of those marvellous and improbable tales which he had the knack of telling. Not always so improbable, moreover. I remember, in fact, that the one he told that evening was about a town in which it was the pavements which moved instead of men, and in which the houses had their entrance on the top floor. At a time when there was absolutely no question of moving pavements or of aeroplanes, Jarry, as one can see, conceived of them both in his imagination.][14]

His lodgings too, from this time onwards, became legendary. In 1897, his inheritance used up, he was expelled from his apartment on the Boulevard de Port-Royal. After a brief period of refuge with his fellow Lavallois, the *douanier* Rousseau, towards the end of 1897 he moved into his last lodgings, at no. 7 rue Cassette. Here, an enterprising landlord, finding the ceilings of this ancient building too high, had divided the second floor into two horizontally, thus creating an extra floor. And here Jarry lived, in a garret on the second-and-a-half floor ('au deuxième et demi', as the *concierge* told visitors) which he named 'Notre Grande Chasublerie', on account of a manufacturer of ecclesiastical vestments who occupied part of the building.[15] No doubt the prospect of mystifying all who asked his address was as important as the modest rent in determining this choice of abode. André Salmon and Guillaume Apollinaire (who mistakenly refers to the 'troisième et demi'), among others, have both left vivid accounts of this dwelling and of the sparseness of furniture and incredible disorder of books and papers which reigned there. The ceiling was so low that all but the midget Jarry were forced to bend double, and he himself frequently had plaster-dust in his hair from touching the ceiling.[16]

As to his eccentricities of behaviour and his love of pranks and practical jokes, these ran the gamut from oddities such as eating meals in reverse order – beginning with the dessert and finishing with the *hors-d'oeuvre* – to decidedly less innocent and more danger-ous activities. Of the host of stories told about him, three groups stand out in particular: those concerning his sporting feats, his love of fire-arms, and his drinking.

He was one of the first and most enthusiastic practitioners of a cult which was only just beginning to catch the European imagination, that of sport. He was a fanatical cyclist, his pride and joy being a new, fabulously expensive 'Clément luxe 96' racing cycle, obtained on credit in Laval in November 1896, and in fact never paid for (at his death the sum of 545 francs was still owing).[17] On this magnificent machine he cycled everywhere in all weathers, forever boasting of the record speeds at which he travelled (he used to attempt to race the train from Corbeil to Paris, a distance of some 20 miles).[18] He was no less passionately fond of fishing. Most of his fishing was done at or near Corbeil, on the Seine south of Paris, where he succeeded in catching quantities of pike and gudgeon where all others had failed to catch anything. It was for this purpose that he purchased in July 1897, probably second-hand, a magnificent mahogany canoe – prototype of the *as* of Dr Faustroll.

Jarry's exploits with fire-arms have given rise to even more sensa-tional tales. Rachilde recounts how, at the Phalanstère at Corbeil, a house rented by the Vallettes for the Summer of 1898, he claimed to shoot nightingales whose singing prevented him from working or sleeping.[19] On another occasion at the Phalanstère, he once engaged in target practice with his revolver against the wall separating the house from that next door, where lived their landlady; when the stricken landlady came to complain, protesting that her children were playing on the other side of the wall and might easily be killed, Jarry allegedly replied in his staccato manner: 'Eh, Ma-da-me, si ce malheur arrivait, nous vous en ferions d'autres!' ['Oh, Ma-dam, if such a misfortune were to occur, we should beget others by you!'].[20] Referring to a period a few years later, André Salmon recalled him walking through the streets of Paris at night carrying, in brazen defiance of the law, a carbine rifle and a pair of revolvers, one of which he fired in the air when asked by an innocent passer-by for a light – 'du feu'![21] On another occasion, somewhat the worse for drink, he fired at the sculptor Manolo in a crowded café, and missed, doubtless on purpose, for he was an excellent shot. The incident, recounted many times over with suitable embellishments and used by Gide in his novel *Les Faux-Monnayeurs*, is typical of the daredevil brinkmanship in which Jarry so often engaged.

Finally, his devotion to alcohol was no less legendary. His favourite drink was the now-outlawed absinthe, which he characteristically re-named 'l'herbe sainte' and in the name of which he conducted a crusade against the drinking of water. His aversion to water was such, according to Rachilde, that it made him feel ill: when once her daughter, wanting to play a trick on Jarry, filled his glass with water which he took to be one of his colourless *marcs*, he 'l'avala d'un trait et fit la plus horrible des grimaces. Positivement, il en fut malade toute la journée.' ['he swallowed it in one gulp and pulled the most horrible of faces. It made him positively ill the whole day.'][22] He had, moreover, an astonishing capacity for absorbing alcohol – in ever-increasing quantities as the years went by – without, apparently, becoming drunk. Rachilde describes his consumption at a point probably some time in his last half-dozen years, in the terms:

Jarry commençait la journée par absorber deux litres de vin blanc, trois absinthes s'espaçaient entre dix heures et midi, puis au déjeuner il arrosait son poisson, ou son bifteck, de vin rouge ou vin blanc alternant avec d'autres absinthes. Dans l'après-midi, quelques tasses de café additionnées de marcs ou d'alcools dont j'oublie les noms, puis, au dîner, après, bien entendu, d'autres apéritifs, il pouvait encore supporter au moins deux bouteilles de n'importe quels crus, de bonnes ou mauvaises marques. Or, je ne l'ai jamais vu vraiment ivre, qu'une seule fois où je l'ai mis en joue avec son propre revolver, ce qui le dégrisa immédiatement.

[Jarry began the day with two litres of white wine, three absinthes followed at intervals between ten o'clock and midday, then at lunch he washed down his fish, or his steak, with red or white wine alternating with further absinthes.

In the course of the afternoon, a few cups of coffee laced with brandy or other spirits whose names I have forgotten, then, with his dinner, after, of course, further apéritifs, he could still take at least two bottles of any vintage, whether good or bad. Now, I never saw him really drunk, except on one occasion when I took aim at him with his own revolver, which sobered him up instantly.][23]

Such was the Jarry seen by his contemporaries, whom they chose to identify with 'le Père Ubu'. To what extent were they deceived by a sustained 'act' on Jarry's part and bedazzled by the legend which they themselves had helped to create? How much in all this was the 'real' Jarry, and how much the product of a deliberate *fabrication* – an 'imposture manifeste', in the words of Achras in *Ubu Cocu*, transformed into (in the terms of Ubu's reply) 'une posture magnifique'?[24] For André Gide, there was no doubt: Jarry had succeeded in destroying his own personality and adopting in its place a totally and all-consuming fictitious *persona*:

Ce Kobold, à la face plâtrée, accoutré en clown de cirque et jouant un personnage fantasque, construit, *résolument factice et en dehors de quoi plus rien d'humain ne se montrait*, exerçait au *Mercure* (en ce temps) une sorte de fascination singulière.

> [This Kobold, his face plastered white, got up as a circus clown, and playing a fantastic, fabricated, *resolutely artificial role outside of which no human characteristics could any longer be seen*, exercised (at that time) a kind of weird fascination at the *Mercure*.][25]

In part Gide is right: the role of Ubu (or what Jarry's contemporaries chose to see as such, although there is little enough in common between his impish pranks and eccentricities and the blundering monstrosity of Ubu) was a totally fabricated one. Yet the 'real' Jarry had not been destroyed, but continued to exist beneath and behind the mask; or rather, a number of other, different Jarrys continued to exist simultaneously, together perhaps constituting the 'real' man. This complexity is immediately apparent the moment we look beneath the surface. The Jarry who wrote *Les Jours et les Nuits* had little in common with the colourful eccentric whom his contemporaries identified with Ubu. Yet he was working on this novel at the same time as he was preparing for the staging of *Ubu Roi*, in 1896, and it was completed in April 1897, only four months after the performance. Further, the year 1899 saw the completion within a few months of each other of both *L'Amour absolu* – his most 'poetic' and in many ways most deeply personal work – and *Ubu Enchaîné*, the 'contrepartie' of *Ubu Roi*. An examination of Jarry's correspondence, sparse though it is, reveals, moreover, that in his letters at least it was above all with Rachilde and Vallette that he took on the attributes of 'le Père

Ubu'. His letters to other correspondents reveal that this supposed *farceur* and iconoclast was also a sincere and enthusiastic lover of literature. He could also be a loyal friend, and was a warm-hearted and devoted companion to the Vallettes' daughter, Gabrielle,[26] and to the children of his friend Claude Terrasse. And though at a profound level an essentially solitary person, he was also at the same time a lively companion who frequently enjoyed cycling excursions, fishing trips and drinking sprees with his friends.

In short, one of the most striking aspects of Jarry's life and work is this very complexity made up of so many different facets. Both his life and work reveal a gamut of different, and at times apparently conflicting, attitudes, and pose, in a way that few writers can have done to the same degree, the problem of the relationship between 'authenticity' and 'inauthenticity' in literature as well as in life. This is a problem to which we shall return in later chapters; for the present, we must examine those other literary manifestations of the figure of Ubu produced by Jarry. These 'further manifestations of Ubu' fall into four groups: the various versions of *Ubu Cocu*; the 'counter-part' of *Ubu Roi* to which Jarry gave the name *Ubu Enchaîné*; the 'musical comedy' *Ubu sur la Butte*; and his *Almanachs du Père Ubu*.

The history of the different versions of *Ubu Cocu* is an extraordinarily complicated one, which can be only briefly summarized here. Two versions of the play have been published: *Ubu Cocu*, first published in 1944 by the Éditions des Trois Collines in Geneva, from a manuscript in the possession of the poet Paul Éluard; and *Ubu Cocu ou l'Archéoptéryx*, a complete version of which was not published until 1972. When each version was written has been the subject of a great deal of debate and controversy.[27] As we saw in Chapter 1, a 'primitive' version was written during 1888–9 at the Lycée de Rennes in the form of *Onésime ou les Tribulations de Priou*. It is possible that this split into two plays in a reworking of the original thematic material the following year, 1889–90: Jarry in any case, in 'Les Paralipomènes d'Ubu' of 1896, refers to three plays, *Les Cornes du P.U.*, *Prophaiseur de Pfuisic* and *Les Polyèdres*, the third of which, at least, from his description of it, is obviously an earlier version of the first *Ubu Cocu*, while the first clearly contains a first draft of the eventual first act of *Ubu Cocu ou l'Archéoptéryx*. All of these early plays or playlets were performed, along with *Les Polonais*, by Jarry's marionette-theatre in Rennes. He continued to work on this body of plays after his arrival in Paris, and it was an extract from *Les Polyèdres* which formed the first and third parts of *Guignol*, published in the *Écho de Paris* in April 1893 and later incorporated into *Les Minutes de sable mémorial*. These scenes are little changed in the first *Ubu Cocu*, suggesting that he had produced a substantially complete version of this play, under the title *Les Polyèdres*, sometime during his early years in Paris. It is in any case certain that he worked on the play again at the very end of 1895 and beginning of 1896, submitting the manuscript of this revised version to Lugné-Poe early in 1896 in the hope of having it performed at the Théâtre de l'Oeuvre.[28] It is in all probability this revised version of the play, rebaptized *Ubu Cocu* sometime in 1896, which was published by the Éditions des Trois Collines in 1944. Two factors in particular would seem to support this argument. Firstly, there is evidence in this version of a concern on Jarry's part with the practical problems of staging (in particular, a relative concern for the unity of time and place). Secondly, the title *Ubu Cocu* is immediately followed by the phrase 'restitué en son intégrité tel qu'il a été représenté par les marionnettes du Théâtre des Phynances' ['restored in its entirety as it was performed by the marionettes of the Théâtre des Phynances'] – almost identical with, and clearly intended as a parallel to, the subtitle given to *Ubu Roi* on the occasion of its publication in June 1896. (In neither case is the description to be taken at face value.)

Following his failure to have *Ubu Cocu* performed at the Oeuvre, Jarry's attitude to the play seems to have undergone some fluctuation. In 'Les Paralipomènes d'Ubu' (the very title derives from the Greek for 'that which is left aside') he referred to a number of manuscripts of the Hébert/Ubu cycle which were now 'of little importance' to him, and of which only 'a few lines' – those extracts contained in 'Les Paralipomènes' – were worth publishing 'for curiosity's sake'.[29] A few years later, however, he again turned his attention to the play and produced a second finished version with the title *Ubu Cocu ou l'Archéoptéryx*, probably around the time of writing *Ubu Enchaîné* in 1899, or shortly afterwards. For this version, he transposed a number of scenes, fused the former Acts IV and V into one, and wrote a new first act set *inside* Ubu's *gidouille*. A note found among his papers indicates that he planned – or hoped – to publish this play along with the texts of *Ubu Roi* and *Ubu Enchaîné* in a single volume.[30] This project failing to reach fruition, either because of a refusal by publishers, or because Jarry had not in fact completed the rewriting of the play to his satisfaction, he may have conceived the idea of a facsimile publication as had been done for *Ubu Roi* in 1897: the care with which the manuscript had been written out would support such a hypothesis. Again, the project came to nothing, as did also a plan to publish one or other version of the play under the title *Ubu intime* in the context of his 'Théâtre Mirlitonesque' in 1906. Whence the frustration expressed in the dedication borne by the manuscript which he presented to Thadée Natanson some time during these years: 'A Thadée Natanson, hommage de cet Ubu clandestin, qui devait, dans l'intention de l'auteur, être "Ubu détruit par le feu".' ['To Thadée Natanson, with the compliments of this clandestine Ubu, which the author had intended to be "Ubu destroyed by fire".']³¹

A number of mysteries surround this rewriting of *Ubu Cocu*. Why, for one thing, did Jarry feel the need to produce yet another version of the play? It may be that he felt that the theme of Ubu's cuckoldry was insufficiently developed. But, strangely, although this theme is given greater prominence in *L'Archéoptéryx*, this remains in other respects a less coherent and unified work than the earlier *Ubu Cocu*, its final act in particular tending to fall apart into barely connected fragments. (There is also relatively little concern for the 'stageability' of the play, compared with *Ubu Cocu*.) It may be also that the rewriting of the play was to meet the demands of a genre much practised by Jarry between 1897 and 1906, that of the musical comedies of his Théâtre Mirlitonesque: though in *Ubu Cocu* there are as many songs as in *L'Archéoptéryx*, they are not evenly distributed throughout the play, whereas in the later version each act (with the exception of the first) ends with a song, in conformity with the rules of the genre. A further curious feature of *L'Archéoptéryx* is that Jarry seems to have gone back to earlier manuscript versions rather than basing himself on the text of 1895–6 (thus, for example, the names of a number of characters – Barbapoux in place of Memnon, Prayou in place of Rebontier – revert back to their original Rennes form or a close approximation of it). A number of plausible hypotheses have been put forward to explain this fact, among them the suggestion that Jarry was no longer in possession of the manuscript of *Ubu Cocu*, but no certain explanation exists. What is in any case certain is that he was not only willing to go back to the original source material in rewriting the play (as was the case, most strikingly, with the new first act), but that he deliberately *stressed* its schoolboy origins. Most if not all of the songs are only slightly adapted versions of texts written by the Morin brothers; but far from trying to hide this fact, Jarry, in copying out the poem 'Le Maître des Finances' for the conclusion of *L'Archéoptéryx*, carefully dated his copy 'octobre 1887', thereby indicating that its composition went back to a period 12 months *prior* to his own arrival at the Lycée de Rennes.

The history of *Ubu Cocu* suggests the enormous complexity of the raw material on which Jarry was working, and the extreme difficulty he found in welding its disparate themes into a coherent whole. Despite the differences between the two versions, however, the similarities are sufficiently great to enable us to discuss the play as a single unit and to see immediately the differences which it presents from *Ubu Roi*.

The themes upon which *Ubu Cocu* draws – satire or spoofing upon teachers at the Lycée de Rennes, in the form of Achras and his obsession with Polyhedra, and of Ubu's Conscience; Ubu's cruelty and rapacity, and the ferocious activity of his henchmen, the *Palotins*; his cuckoldry; the faecal theme – all derive from the same common 'fund' of schoolboy themes as *Ubu Roi*. Indeed, they exist here in a rather more 'raw' state than in the latter, where pure fantasy has taken over and the original models of the chief protagonists have been left far behind. But whereas *Ubu Roi* presents a unified vision of the cruelty and stupidity of the adult world, *Ubu Cocu* offers no such unified vision: we are offered simply a series of brief, mocking glimpses into that world. This is a consequence partly of the relative lack of unity of the play, partly of the character of Ubu himself. Though the structure of both versions of *Ubu Cocu* is considerably more unified than that of *Onésime*, both remain looser in construction than *Ubu Roi*. In the latter, a basic coherence is provided by the framework of the parody upon *Macbeth*: the conspiracy against the King, his murder and the seizure of the throne, Ubu's abuse of power and the subsequent revolt against his rule leading to defeat and flight from Poland, all form part of a strong and unified dramatic action. (Similarly, in *Ubu Enchaîné* the progressive degradation of Ubu – his descent into slavery – provides a coherent and unifying thread to the play.) In *Ubu Cocu*, on the other hand, no such unifying thread exists, and the links between the various themes of the play remain fairly tenuous. The Ubu of this play, moreover, is a rather different character from that of *Ubu Roi*: equally cruel and rapacious, but much more self-possessed, sophisticated and articulate, with little of the contemptible coward and imbecile of his first, more 'primitive' incarnation. The Ubu who introduces himself as a 'docteur en pataphysique' and who goes on to define pataphysics in a memorable passage is a far cry from the character whose childish terrors cause him to lose control of his bodily functions in Act IV of *Ubu Roi*:

PERE UBU: Ceci vous plaît à dire, Monsieur, mais vous parlez à un grand pataphysicien.
ACHRAS: Pardon, Monsieur, vous dites? . . .
PERE UBU: Pataphysicien. La pataphysique est une science que nous avons inventée et dont le besoin se faisait généralement sentir.
ACHRAS: Ô mais c'est qué, si vous êtes un grand inventeur, nous nous entendrons, voyez-vous bien; car entre grands hommes . . .
PERE UBU: Soyez plus modeste, Monsieur! Je ne vois d'ailleurs ici de grand homme que moi. Mais puisque vous y tenez, je condescends à vous faire un grand honneur. Vous saurez que votre maison nous convient, et que nous avons résolu de nous y installer.

> [PERE UBU: It pleases you to say so, Sir, but you are speaking to a great pataphysician.
> ACHRAS: I beg your pardon, Sir, you said . . .?
> PERE UBU: Pataphysician. Pataphysics is a science which we have invented and for which a general need was felt.

ACHRAS: Oh, but then, if you are a great inventor, we shall get along, look you; for between great men . . .
PERE UBU: Be more modest, Sir! I see here, in any case, no other great man but myself. But since you wish it, I condescend to do you a great honour. You shall know that your house suits us, and that we have resolved to take up residence in it.][32]

He is also a more selfconsciously (and successfully) comic character, indulging in wordplay as he discourses on the subject of brain physiology and quotes from a learned treatise by Théodule Ribot on *Les Maladies de la mémoire*:

PERE UBU: Ceci est sale. Il ne peut répondre, car il est tombé sur la tête. Son cerveau s'est endommagé sans doute à la circonvolution de Broca, en laquelle réside la faculté de discourir. Cette circonvolution est la troisième circonvolution frontale à gauche en entrant. Demandez au concierge . . . Messieurs, pardon! demandez à tous les philosophes: 'Cette dissolution intellectuelle a pour cause une atrophie qui envahit peu à peu l'écorce du cerveau, puis la substance blanche, produisant une dégénérescence graisseuse et athéromateuse des cellules, des tubes et des capillaires de la substance nerveuse!

[PERE UBU: This is dirty. He cannot answer, because he has fallen on his head. His brain has probably been damaged at the convolution of Broca, in which is located the faculty of discourse. This convolution is the third frontal convolution on the left after entering. Ask the caretaker . . . Gentlemen, I beg your pardon! ask any philosopher: 'This intellectual disintegration has as its cause an atrophy which progressively takes over the cortex of the brain, then the grey matter, producing a fatty and atheromatous degeneration of the cells, the tubes and the capillaries of the nervous system!][33]

There are other differences also between *Ubu Cocu* and *Ubu Roi*. The language of the play is very much less violent, although the scatological element is greater here than in *Ubu Roi* in other ways. This is partly through the presence of the theme of the conflict between the old 'artisanal' methods of sewage disposal and Ubu's new, scientific 'pompe à merdre', and partly through an identification of the *trappe* of both plays with a cess-pit: the unfortunate 'ouvrier ébéniste' who is seized by the Palotins is 'précipité la tête la première/Dans l'grand trou noir d'ousqu'on n'revient jamais' ['hurled head first/Into the big black hole what yer never returns from'],[34] while Ubu's Conscience is unceremoniously flung 'la tête la première dans le trou entre les deux semelles de pierre' ['head first into the hole between the two stone footrests'] [of an old-style seatless W.C.].[35] (The 'Pince-Porc' which the character of Rebontier/Prayou is condemned to frequent obviously has the same attribution.) In *Ubu Cocu*, moreover, to this scatological material is added the presence of explicit sexual themes – as the title of the play suggests. It is true that sexual allusions are not wholly lacking in *Ubu Roi*: whether or not we accept Charles Morin's assertion that, in the original conception of the play, *Ubu Roi* is 'la pièce la plus chaste *in the world*'[36] – and one may well doubt such a claim – it is certain that Jarry, through clever wordplay and by virtue of the principle of association, has incorporated into the play a number of implicit sexual allusions, as Michel Arrivé has pointed out.[37] But in *Ubu Roi* such elements remain implicit, whereas in *Ubu Cocu* they are wholly explicit; indeed scatological and sexual themes are linked in a striking way, as Mère Ubu and her lover meet in the latrines and together take refuge from an advancing Ubu (coming to make use of their hiding place) down the W.C. Linked to these developments is a disturbing element of sadism, as the shrieking Achras is impaled upon Ubu's shining 'pal' and hoisted into the air in the centre of the stage.

The atmosphere of the play, and its comedy, also present differences from those of *Ubu Roi*. *Ubu Cocu* contains a considerable number of songs (mostly sung in chorus by the Palotins), a feature wholly lacking in the 1896 version of *Ubu Roi* which contributes to the generally more jovial atmosphere of this play. Most if not all of these go back to the original fund of the Lycée de Rennes and many were originally intended to be sung to popular airs of the time (for example, the Palotins' refrain: 'Ce tonneau qui s'avance, neau qui s'avance, neau qui s'avance, c'est le Père Ubu' is modelled on the line from Offenbach's *La Belle Hélène*: 'Ce roi barbu qui s'avance, bu qui s'avance . . .', and was to be sung to the same tune). They were a feature also of *Onésime*, and, by their presence in these plays, create a link between some of Jarry's earliest works and his later Théâtre Mirlitonesque. The comedy tends also to spring from sources different from those of *Ubu Roi*. There is less exploitation of incongruities, and in its place an element of 'situation comedy' (in Ubu's and Achras' reversal of roles as the former takes over the latter's house) and above all that of wordplay. The transformation of the inanimate into the animate in Achras' 'polyhedra', and such plays on words as the 'grand homme' quoted above and Ubu's feigned mistaking of 'imposture manifeste' for 'posture magnifique' in Act I, Scene 3, are typical and amusing examples. Some of this wordplay, moreover, is of a kind comprehensible only to the initiates of the Lycée de Rennes, for example the puns upon *bourdonner* put into the mouth of Ubu's Conscience:

Ouf! quel choc! mon crâne en bourdonne! . . . Le vôtre ne bourdonne pas?

[Ow! what a blow! my head's buzzing from it! . . . Isn't yours buzzing?][38]

There are elements too of satire, as in the interview between Ubu and his Conscience where Ubu, being assured by his Conscience that Achras is harmless, resolves to make him a sacrificial victim of his cruel experiments. And there are, lastly, elements which derive from the antics and conventions of the *guignol*: the Conscience suspended by the feet in mid-air, and, most notable of all, the *dénouement* of the play. At the end of both versions, Ubu interrupts a dialogue with Achras and his Conscience to remark that 'la pièce dure depuis assez longtemps'; whereupon suddenly, and without the least semblance of logic or preparation, a crocodile enters and crosses the stage, bringing the dialogue – and the play with it – to an abrupt and quite arbitrary end. Borrowed originally from the conventions of the *guignol*, this crocodile was part of the folklore of the Lycée de Rennes; Jarry refers to it in 'Les Paralipomènes d'Ubu' as a device which can be adapted to any play in which a *dénouement* of an 'inextricable situation' is required. It is a device also which, in its deliberate flouting of logic and coherence, looks forward to the 'anti-plays' of the so-called 'theatre of the absurd'.

If the circumstances of composition and dating of *Ubu Cocu* are complex and uncertain, those of *Ubu Enchaîné* are extremely simple and clear. The play was written during the Summer of 1899 at La Frette, near Corbeil (a note at the end of the text gives the date of completion as September 1899), and was published in a joint edition with *Ubu Roi* by the Éditions de la Revue Blanche in 1900. In a publicity notice in the *Revue Blanche* of 1 January 1901 for his *Almanach illustré du Père Ubu (XXe Siècle)*, Jarry stated that the play was the 'contre-partie' of *Ubu Roi*. Its title was originally to have been *Ubu esclave*: the *Mercure de France* announced in May 1899 that a play by Jarry entitled '*Ubu esclave*, drame pour marionnettes' was 'in preparation'. Though this title implies a more direct opposition with *Ubu Roi* than that finally chosen, the latter has the advantage of imitating *Ubu Roi* in its parody of the classics: where *Ubu Roi* obviously refers to Sophocles' *Oedipus Rex* (*Oedipe Roi*, in the French translation), *Ubu Enchaîné* refers to Aeschylus' *Prometheus Bound* (*Prométhée Enchaîné*).

Although the play is in many respects an 'adult' work (in distinction from the schoolboy drama *Ubu Roi*), a good deal of the thematic material, and even the names of some of the characters (Pissembock and Frère Tiberge certainly, Pissedoux very probably), go back to the original schoolboy 'fund' of the Lycée de Rennes. It is even possible, as a passage in 'Les Paralipomènes d'Ubu' would seem to suggest, that an earlier version of the play itself existed at the Lycée. At the very least, Jarry has incorporated into *Ubu Enchaîné* scenes which derive from an earlier play or plays: the scene in Pissembock's house in which Ubu empties the dregs from 12 wine bottles derives from his own satirical sketch of 1889–90, *Le Futur malgré lui*. A number of place-names probably refer to the town of Rennes, where a Champ-de-Mars and adjacent Boulevard de la Liberté – both an integral part of the military and libertarian themes of the play – are to be found only a short distance away from the Lycée. And a number of scenes, particularly those involving the Turkish Sultan and his Grand Vizier, were very likely inspired by Lesage's *Gil Blas de Santillane*, an important source – acknowledged by the Morin brothers – of both *Les Polonais* and other works in the Ébé cycle.

The play was seen by many of Jarry's contemporaries as a satire upon the army and upon the official ideology of the Third Republic, enshrined in the motto 'Liberty, Equality, Fraternity' (of these three terms, the third has always been a very junior partner; only the first two have been of real importance in French political thought). Just as contemporary 'political' interpretations of *Ubu Roi* were to some extent understandable in the light of the 'anarchist' ferment of the period, so too the background of the Dreyfus Affair, which placed the army in the forefront of the nation's political life and called into question the very values upon which the Republic was supposedly founded, goes a long way towards explaining such an interpretation of *Ubu Enchaîné*. The national crisis provoked by the Dreyfus Affair was in fact at its height at the moment of Jarry's writing of the play: September 1899, when he finished the manuscript, was the month of the re-trial of Dreyfus in Rennes by a military court-martial (which once again found him guilty, though with extenuating circumstances). In addition to this circumstantial evidence, in the literal sense, Jarry's other works, in particular the novel *Les Jours et les Nuits* and his *chroniques* collected in *La Chandelle verte*, provide ample evidence of his loathing for and capacity for satire upon the army, while his *chroniques* express also a frequent contempt for the official ideology of the Third Republic.[39] There are undoubtedly elements of satire in the play, upon the courts and the emotional pleading of barristers, upon the hypocrisy of *dévotes* and the silliness of English tourists – although the exaggeration of the caricature in each case is such that one wonders how 'seriously' such satire is to be taken. Equally undoubtedly there is some measure of satire in the play upon the army: Ubu's exclamation of 'Vive l'armerdre!', repeated later in the play, cannot but have been intended as a gross insult to all who espoused militaristic values, and was felt as such by many. There are also many passages which seem, at first glance, to contain a satire upon the much-vaunted concept of 'freedom'; the first scene in which we encounter the 'Hommes Libres' is a typical example:

LES TROIS HOMMES LIBRES: Nous sommes les hommes libres, et voici notre caporal. – Vive la liberté, la liberté, la liberté! Nous sommes libres. – N'oublions pas que notre devoir, c'est d'être libre. Allons moins vite, nous arriverions à l'heure. La liberté, c'est de n'arriver jamais à l'heure – jamais,

jamais! pour nos exercices de liberté. Désobéissons avec ensemble . . . Non!
pas ensemble: une, deux, trois! le premier à un, le deuxième à deux, le
troisième à trois. Voilà toute la différence. Inventons chacun un temps
différent, quoique ce soit bien fatigant. Désobéissons individuellement – au
caporal des hommes libres.
LE CAPORAL: Rassemblement!
  Ils se dispersent.
Vous, l'homme libre numéro trois, vous me ferez deux jours de salle de
police, pour vous être mis, avec le numéro deux, en rang. La théorie dit:
Soyez libres! – Exercices individuels de désobéissance . . . L'indiscipline
aveugle et de tous les instants fait la force principale des hommes libres.

> [THE THREE FREE MEN: We are the Free Men, and here is our corporal. –
> Long live freedom, freedom, freedom! We are free. – Let us not forget that it
> is our duty to be free. Let's walk less quickly, otherwise we'll arrive on time.
> Freedom is never arriving on time – never, never! – for our freedom drill.
> Let's disobey all together . . . No! not all together: one, two, three! the first on
> one, the second on two, the third on three. That makes all the difference.
> Let's each invent a different tempo, even though it's very tiring. Let's disobey
> – individually – the corporal of the Free Men!
> THE CORPORAL: Fall in!
>   *They disperse.*
> You, Free Man number three, you'll do two days in the guard-house for
> having fallen in beside number two. The theory states: Be free! – Individual
> disobedience drill! . . . Blind and unflagging indiscipline is the chief source of
> strength of Free Men.][40]

Looked at closely, however, this passage reveals itself to be not so
much satire as a piece of elaborate nonsense – a *reductio ad absurdum* of
the concept of freedom. 'Freedom' here consists of doing systematically and compulsorily the opposite of what one is ordered to do, and
in its very systematization becomes simply another form of (self-
imposed) enslavement and tyranny. In order to understand more
fully Jarry's aims in *Ubu Enchaîné*, we must look more closely at his
designation of the play as the 'contre-partie' of *Ubu Roi*.

The opposition, and at the same time the parallel, between the two
plays is hinted at by Jarry from the very beginning of *Ubu Enchaîné*.
Where *Ubu Roi* begins with Ubu's resounding 'merdre!', here –
despite momentarily appearing to be on the point of doing so – Ubu
twice *fails* to pronounce 'the word':

Père Ubu s'avance et ne dit rien.
MÈRE UBU: Quoi! tu ne dis rien, Père Ubu. As-tu donc oublié le mot?
PÈRE UBU: Mère . . . Ubu! je ne veux plus prononcer le mot, il m'a valu trop
de désagréments.

> [*Père Ubu steps forward and says nothing.*
> MÈRE UBU: What! you say nothing, Père Ubu. Have you forgotten the word
> then?
> PÈRE UBU: Sh . . . ilence, Mère Ubu! I don't want to utter the word any more,
> it has brought too many troubles upon me.][41]

The opening 'merdre!' of *Ubu Roi*, together with its frequent repetitions throughout the play, sums up, in its combination of violence, aggressiveness and vulgarity, the schoolboy rejection of the adult world and its values expressed in *Ubu Roi*. In *Ubu Enchaîné*, therefore, Ubu's repeated refusal to pronounce 'the word' might be taken as an implicit acceptance of the world and values formerly rejected. But Ubu's obvious failure to pronounce the word serves, in fact, to remind us of it, and to make it implicitly present through the very conspicuousness of its absence. In this way, *Ubu Enchaîné* becomes both the opposite of *Ubu Roi*, and at the same time its 'double'.

This complex relationship is demonstrated by Jarry in a variety of ways. The presence and absence of the term 'merdre' symbolizes the opposition between the basic situation in the two plays: where the use of 'merdre' is associated with Ubu's rise to power and kingship, acting as a means of silencing all opposition and affirming his authority, its absence signifies the state of servitude which he seeks in *Ubu Enchaîné*. Similarly, the action of the two plays seems to move in opposite directions: where in *Ubu Roi* there is an upwards movement as Ubu seizes the throne and makes himself ruler of Poland (followed, it is true, by a fall due to his own excesses, though he ultimately escapes to continue his adventures elsewhere), in *Ubu Enchaîné* there is a steady movement downwards, as he becomes first a domestic servant, then a jailed convict, and lastly a galley-slave. At the same time, the opposition between kingship and servitude requires that the attributes of power and royalty give way to those of servitude and slavery: thus the crown, throne, *grande capeline*, umbrella and *cheval à phynance* of *Ubu Roi*, to say nothing of a long list of instruments of aggression or torture – the Palotins (extensions of Ubu's rapacious lust for *finance*), the *croc à finance, croc à merdre, sabre à finances, ciseau, couteau* and *balai innommable* – are replaced by the *tablier d'esclave, balai d'esclave, crochet d'esclave, boîte à cirer d'esclave*, etc. [respectively, 'finance hook', 'shite hook', 'finance sword', 'scissors', 'knife', 'lavatory brush'; 'slave's apron', 'slave's broom', 'slave's hook', 'slave's shoe-shine box']. This dissimilarity of situation, plot and attributes, however, masks a fundamental similarity between the two plays. The character and aims of Ubu himself remain basically identical throughout. In both cases, he actively engages in the pursuit of some goal which will bring self-gratification. Though in *Ubu Enchaîné* he is a much more cunning, articulate and self-possessed character than in *Ubu Roi*, having relatively little of the childish stupidity of his earlier incarnation – indeed, it is he, and not Mère Ubu, who here hatches the scheme which provides the main plot of the play, whereby he will progressively 'sink' into slavery – he remains equally rapacious, cruel, greedy and gluttonous. With the exception of *merdre* and its composite forms, he continues to utter the same oaths, exclamations and hideous threats – 'cornegidouille', 'corne d'Ubu', 'de par ma chandelle verte', 'tudez, décervelez', 'à la poche', 'je vous fous à lon poche', and the like [respectively, 'hornbelly', 'Ubu's horn', 'by my green candle', 'killa, disembrain', 'in the sack', 'I'll shove yer in the sack'].[42] He continues also to use the royal 'we', a usage ultimately justified by the fact that his prison becomes his 'palace', in which he is clothed, housed, regularly fed by attentive and devoted prison warders, all free of charge, and is finally elected 'king' by his fellow-convicts, who faithfully follow him and attempt to emulate him. Even in this topsy-turvy world, therefore, it is still Ubu who comes out on top: king or slave, he carries all before him. His exclamation in *Ubu Roi*: 'Eh! je m'enrichis', is echoed by an identical statement in *Ubu Enchaîné*: 'Eh! je m'enrichis ... comme d'habitude. Je continue mon travail d'esclave.' ['Eh! I'm getting rich . . . as usual. I'm continuing my work as a slave.'][43] Most telling of all are the words in which he announces his plans to Mère Ubu, in a passage which, through wordplay, parodies the semantic universe of the play:

Puisque nous sommes dans le pays où la liberté est égale à la fraternité, laquelle n'est comparable qu'à l'égalité de la légalité, et que je ne suis pas capable de faire comme tout le monde et que cela m'est égal d'être égal à tout le monde *puisque c'est encore moi qui finirai par tuer tout le monde*, je vais me mettre esclave, Mère Ubu!

> [Since we are in the country in which liberty is the equal of fraternity, which in turn is comparable only to the equality of legality, and since I am incapable of acting like everyone else and since being equal with everyone is equally indifferent to me *since it is still I who will end up killing everyone*, I'm going to become a slave, Mère Ubu!][44]

– a passage which recalls irresistibly to mind the lines from *Ubu Roi*: 'Avec ce système, j'aurai vite fait fortune, alors je tuerai tout le monde et je m'en irai.' ['With this system I'll soon be rich, then I'll kill everybody and go away.'][45] What could more aptly sum up the anarchic, and even nihilistic, destructiveness of Ubu in both plays?

Jarry's creation of parallels between the two plays does not, however, stop there. Just as Ubu the king is paralleled by Ubu the servant, prisoner and galley-slave, so too the fortunes of Mère Ubu follow a similar pattern. Parallels exist between the roles of other characters also. The role of Captain Bordure (as well as that, later in *Ubu Roi*, of Bougrelas) is fulfilled by Pissedoux, and the three Palotins are replaced by the three Free Men. Other relationships are less obvious, but the function of a number of the characters within each play is, in some respects at least, similar: King Wenceslas is replaced by Pissembock, Queen Rosemonde by Éleuthère, the Tsar by Soliman (the Turkish Sultan), while even the roles of minor characters such as Nicolas Rensky (the messenger who tells of the flight of Mère Ubu) find an equivalent in those of *Ubu Enchaîné*.

Alongside these parallels in the roles of the *dramatis personae* of the two plays, a great many scenes of *Ubu Enchaîné* simply transpose situations and events of *Ubu Roi*. In addition to the non-pronunciation and pronunciation respectively of 'the word', the opening scene is devoted in each case to outlining the scheme which will provide the main plot of the play. Ubu's subsequent assault on Éleuthère (whose wholly symbolic name means 'freedom' in Greek), which involves polishing her bare feet, parallels the attack on the Tsar, whose feet Ubu treads on, and, a few scenes later, Ubu's attack on the nobles also – his injunction to Mère Ubu: 'apporte le crochet à cirer et la boîte à cirer et la brosse à cirer' ['bring the polishing hook and the polishing box and the polishing brush'] clearly recalls the earlier 'Apportez la caisse à Nobles et le crochet à Nobles et le couteau à Nobles et le bouquin à Nobles!' ['Bring the Nobles case and the Nobles hook and the Nobles knife and the Nobles book!']. The ball at Pissembock's recalls the banquet-scene of *Ubu Roi*, and the trial of the Ubus that of the trial of the nobles and magistrates in *Ubu Roi*. The scene set in the *salon des dévotes*, which is visited by Ubu's chaplain, Frère Tiberge, collecting alms, and is subsequently invaded and demolished, parallels that in the peasants' house, which is visited by Ubu collecting taxes and then demolished (in fact the only possible justification for this otherwise inexplicable scene can be the creation of a parallel). The visit by Pissedoux to Ubu in prison parallels that by Ubu to Bordure in the fortress of Thorn, while at the same time inverting both the roles and the intentions of the protagonists, since Pissedoux wishes to get Ubu *out* of prison, while the latter wishes to remain. And in both plays Père and Mère Ubu, after a scene of farewell, are for a time separated and then reunited at the end. Act V of *Ubu Enchaîné* follows the action of *Ubu Roi* particularly closely. Scenes 1–2, which show the invasion of the prison by Pissedoux, his men and the people in a state of revolt, and the subsequent expulsion of Mère Ubu, parallel the action of Bougrelas, his supporters and the Polish people in revolt in attacking the royal palace in Warsaw and expelling Mère Ubu. Scenes 3 and 4, which show Ubu at the head of a convoy of convicts marching through 'Slavonia' (*la Sclavonie*), and the arrival of the jailer from Paris with news of the revolt, exactly parallel the scenes of Ubu at the head of the Polish army marching through the Ukraine and the arrival of Nicolas Rensky with identical news (in fact, Ubu's two speeches in Scene 3 transpose almost word for word those of the corresponding scene (Act IV, Scene 3) in *Ubu Roi*). Scene 5, in which Pissedoux and his men, in chains, attack Ubu and his convoy, beginning with an artillery barrage, exactly parallels Act IV, Scene 4 of *Ubu Roi* in which Ubu's Polish forces are attacked by the Russian army led by Bordure (who is knocked senseless by Ubu as Pissedoux is in the later play) and the Tsar, the attack again beginning with artillery fire and both scenes ending in a general *sauve-qui-peut*. Finally, the play ends with Ubu on a Turkish galley, sailing off to a new and unknown destination, just as in *Ubu Roi* he was on a ship being taken through the Baltic to France to begin his adventures anew.

In addition to these extensive parallels in the roles and scenes of the two plays, Jarry also draws attention to the relationship between them through a whole series of allusions in *Ubu Enchaîné* – many of them explicit, others implicit – to details, incidents and even in some cases words of the earlier play. These are far too numerous to list in detail here, and a few examples must suffice. Thus the first scene of *Ubu Enchaîné* contains a summary, in the dialogue between Père and Mère Ubu, of the plot of *Ubu Roi*. Reference is made at one point or another elsewhere in the play to the palace of Wenceslas, to the Polish army marching through the Ukraine, to Ubu's earlier 'crimes', to the hill and windmill in the Ukraine where he took up position, to his 'cheval à phynances', to the drunken crowds in Poland, to Ubu's earlier distribution of money, and so on. As Ubu momentarily forgets his new role, involuntary allusions to his earlier methods of torture occur: 'Enfoncement du petit bout de bois dans les oneilles'; 'je vous ferai passer par votre propre casserole' ['Driving of little wooden stick into the nearholes', 'you'll end up in your own stewpot'];[46] and the like. Whilst there is also an interesting reference to Ubu's 'science en physique' whose function here is the reverse of its earlier function: where in *Ubu Roi*, Ubu spoke of his invention of a system 'pour faire venir le beau temps et conjurer la pluie' ['to ward off rain and bring fine weather'], here, in order to make life in prison as uncomfortable as possible, he has invented by the same means 'un dispositif ingénieux pour qu'il pleuve tous les matins à travers le toit' ['an ingenious contraption for making rain come in every morning through the roof'].[47]

Ubu Enchaîné is thus the 'counterpart' of *Ubu Roi* in every possible sense of the word, both the 'double' of the text of the earlier play and its inversion. It transposes and at the same time inverts the basic situation of the earlier play (monarchy/republic, kingship/slavery, 'the word'/silence); it transposes and in many cases inverts the roles of the leading characters; it creates a detailed series of parallels with the dramatic structure and many of the scenes of the earlier play; it contains a long list of allusions to, and creates or implies parallels with, incidents and details of that play; and it contradicts by these means the 'political' or 'anarchist' interpretations which many contemporaries had read into *Ubu Roi* through showing that Ubu remains faithful to himself in every society and under any régime.

At the same time, the play is constructed upon a series of semantic oppositions (freedom *versus* tyranny; power *versus* submission; kingship *versus* slavery) which end by becoming indistinguishable from, and even explicitly identical with, each other. In this general switching of 'signs', everything becomes its opposite.[48] Not only does Ubu discover himself at the end of the play to be 'king' once more, but all along the line he has made the discovery that his power as a slave exceeds that which he enjoyed as king. As he tells Pissedoux in Act II, Scene 5: 'Et d'abord, qui êtes-vous pour donner des ordres? Ici ne commandent que les esclaves.' ['And for a start, who are you to give orders? Here only slaves command.'] And, invited in the closing scene to take over command of the ship (something which he had forcibly tried to do in *Ubu Roi*), he refuses in the words:

O non! Si vous m'avez mis à la porte de ce pays et me renvoyez je ne sais où comme passager sur cette galère je n'en suis pas moins resté Ubu enchaîné, esclave, et je ne commanderai plus. On m'obéit bien davantage.

> [Oh no! Even if you have thrown me out of this country and are sending me away goodness knows where as a passenger on this galley, I still remain Ubu Enchained, a slave, and I won't give orders any more. That way, people obey me far more.]

The reversal is complete on the other side also. Eventually the Free Men revolt and demand for themselves the benefits of imprisonment and slavery, pursuing and attacking the convoy of convicts on its way to embark on Soliman's galleys in order to take its place, and Pissedoux exclaims as with his men he invades the prison: 'Vive la liberté! ... La liberté, c'est l'esclavage!'[49] This is not satire, but a systematic reduction to a common level of meaninglessness of all concepts and values, providing yet another application of Jarry's concept (central to his 'science of pataphysics') of the 'identity of opposites'.

What, if anything, remains amidst this general *débâcle* of concepts and values?[50] The answer is: only Ubu himself, unconquered, undaunted, now fully aware of his own self-sufficiency. It is clearly a very different Ubu from that of *Ubu Roi*, and even from that of *Ubu Cocu* (in which, as here, he also declares himself 'docteur en pataphysique'), who, at the end of the play states that he no longer needs to play the role of either master or slave, but will devote himself henceforth, Buddha-like, to the contemplation of his own *gidouille*: 'Je commence à constater que Ma Gidouille est plus grosse que toute la terre, et plus digne que je m'occupe d'elle. C'est elle que je servirai désormais.' ['I am beginning to realize that My Gidouille is bigger than the whole world, and more worthy of my attention. It is she whom I shall serve henceforth.']⁵¹ Far from being a new idea in Jarry's work, however, this doctrine of withdrawal from the 'external' world in order to devote oneself to a contemplation and enjoyment of one's own, inner riches, was clearly formulated in *César-Antechrist*, a work whose links with *Ubu Roi* have been discussed in Chapter Three, and which is now implicitly linked to *Ubu Enchaîné* as well. In the words of Antichrist, 'Je n'ai que faire de cette extérieure représentation et je passe aveugle et sourd sur la terre, me contemplant moi-même, sûr qu'on ne peut rien m'adjoindre d'externe . . . ' ['I have nothing to do with this outward appearance and I pass blind and deaf over the earth, contemplating my own self, certain that nothing external can be added to me . . .'].⁵²

Such then is the 'meaning' (or non-meaning) of *Ubu Enchaîné*. What of its success as a piece of comic writing, since it must, today, ultimately stand or fall as such? As in *Ubu Roi*, the comedy does not on the whole derive from verbal witticisms: Ubu continues to make feeble jokes and puns which meet with the same scathing response from Mère Ubu (although a few other characters do engage in mildly amusing wordplay, for example Pissembock, or the Public Prosecutor in the trial scene). Some of the comedy does, on the other hand, spring from parody: just as part of the comedy in *Ubu Roi* arises from its parody upon *Macbeth*, here also the creation of unexpected parallels with the earlier play is a source of humour. There is parody too, bordering this time upon satire, in the portrayal of the English tourist, Lord Catoblepas, in the scene of Pissedoux's and Pissembock's reconciliation at Ubu's trial, and in the heart-rending *adieux* of Père and Mère Ubu (although the parody in these three cases is so gross that it is difficult to see it as 'serious' satire); and, more pointedly, in Ubu's 'Vive l'armerdre!'. There is the same exploitation for comic effect of vulgarity or obscenity in the names Pissembock and Pissedoux (rendered doubly comic by their attempts to hide the names). Much of the comedy derives also from the exaggeration to improbable or monstrous proportions which is characteristic of farce – for example, in Pissedoux's attempts to whip Ubu, which he gives up in despair before the sheer size of his victim's back; in the impossibility of executing Ubu because of the exorbitant cost of building a large enough guillotine; or in the revelation at the end of the play that Ubu is the Sultan's long-lost brother. There is a similar, though less extensive, exploitation of incongruity as in *Ubu Roi*: for example, in Éleuthère's cutting of Mère Ubu's chains with a tiny pair of scissors, or in the jailer's cry when it is time for prison visitors to leave of 'On ferme!', or Ubu's surprise failure to pronounce 'the word' which creates a hiatus between speech and action. As in *Ubu Roi*, much of the action is puppet-like, and such actions as Mère Ubu's splitting into two of Pissembock (immediately preceded by her exasperated and punning exclamation: 'Frappez, et l'on vous ouvrira!') cry out for a marionette-style performance, as does also the extreme rapidity of scene changes (which would necessitate the use of placards to indicate the scene, though Jarry does not explicitly call for these). There is comedy born of incongruity also in Ubu's occasional lapses as he momentarily falls back into his previous role of brutal and sadistic monster, offering for example to Éleuthère in Act I, Scene 6, the service of 'torsion du nez, extraction de la cervelle . . . non, je me trompe: cirage des pieds . . .' ['tweaking of the nose, extraction of the brain . . . no, I'm wrong: polishing of the feet . . .']. Above all else, however, the comedy in *Ubu Enchaîné* derives from the systematic inversion of situations, relationships and values, including semantic values, which the play portrays: Ubu *imposing* his services upon Éleuthère, the Free Men rising in revolt and demanding to be put in prison and in the galleys, and Ubu emerging through servitude and slavery to be 'king' once more. Far from having a reforming or corrective aim, the end result of Jarry's humour in *Ubu Enchaîné* is one of total negation – that of, as Henri Béhar nicely expresses it, 'la destruction de la réalité par la dérision absolue'.[53]

All of these characteristics make of *Ubu Enchaîné* a lively and entertaining play – all the more so if performed in conjunction with *Ubu Roi*, an enterprise which, given the length of the two plays, is perfectly feasible. The action is rapid and at times violent, albeit in comic fashion (in fact, it is faster moving on the whole than in *Ubu Roi*, the scenes being generally shorter; and even those scenes which transpose episodes from *Ubu Roi* are on the whole considerably abridged). It calls for a great deal of physical movement on the stage as well as containing an abundance of lively and rapidly changing dialogue. But in one fundamental way it cannot be put on the same plane as *Ubu Roi*, simply because it is a different *kind* of play: though successful as a comedy, *Ubu Enchaîné* is a much more sophisticated, clever work, whereas much of the appeal of *Ubu Roi* lies in its very crudeness and naïvety.

In addition to *Ubu Cocu* and *Ubu Enchaîné*, Jarry continued during these years to occupy himself with *Ubu Roi* also, in a way which was to lead to a fundamental change in the character of that play and to inaugurate a new *genre* in his literary production. *Ubu Roi* had been published in a second, luxurious, facsimile edition in 1897, together with the incidental music written for the play by Claude Terrasse and a plan giving the 'composition' – almost wholly fanciful – of its 'orchestra'.[54] In January 1898, the play was again performed, to the rapturous acclaim of audiences drawn largely from the world of letters, by the 'Théâtre des Pantins', a marionette-theatre set up in December 1897 in the huge *atelier* adjacent to the Terrasse apartment at no. 6 rue Ballu by, amongst others, Jarry, Pierre and Charles

Bonnard and Claude Terrasse, and placed under the direction of Georges Roussel, brother of the Nabi painter K.-X. Roussel. Ironically, where the performance of December 1896, being given in a 'private' subscription-theatre, escaped the clutches of the theatrical censor, for its performances at the Théâtre des Pantins Jarry was obliged to submit the text in advance to the censor, who promptly demanded the deletion of every single 'merdre' (and its various combinations) appearing in the text.[55] The marionettes themselves were furnished by Pierre Bonnard, the voice of Père Ubu was provided by Jarry himself and that of Mère Ubu by Louise France, who had played the role in 1896. Musical accompaniment was provided by Terrasse, playing on the piano the overture he had written in 1896 together with the *Marche des Polonais* in Act IV and the *Chanson du Décervelage* (which especially delighted audiences) at the end of Act V. The last was added to the printed text of the play as a conclusion on the occasion of its republication, jointly with *Ubu Enchaîné*, in 1900, and words and music of all three pieces were published in 1898 by the Éditions du Mercure de France as part of a series of brochures entitled 'Répertoire des Pantins', the cover of each featuring an original lithograph by Jarry himself.

As is the case with *Ubu Cocu*, this intrusion of songs into the text of *Ubu Roi* profoundly modifies the atmosphere of the play, making it at once both more jovial and even more puppet-like in character. This evolution was accentuated a few years later when, in November 1901, an abridged two-act version of *Ubu Roi* complete with songs was performed at the Cabaret des 4-Z'Arts in Montmartre by the marionettes of the Guignol des Gueules de Bois under the direction of the celebrated Antoine (the name 'gueule de bois' embodies a play upon words: it means a hangover, as well as referring to the wooden jaws, or faces, of the marionettes). Interestingly, although the action is simplified and the number of characters reduced, Jarry has in this version retained many of the best lines of *Ubu Roi* by changing the context in which they are spoken or attributing them to other characters, thus accentuating the element of verbal humour in the play; and he has also added a number of minor characters or details in conformity with the traditions of the *guignol*. The text of this two-act version, together with the addition of a prologue between the characters of Guignol and the Director, was published by Sansot in 1906 under the title of *Ubu sur la Butte* (a reference to the Butte Montmartre where it was first performed) as part of a proposed collection entitled 'Théâtre Mirlitonesque'.

Apart from *Ubu sur la Butte*, the last major manifestation in Jarry's work of the figure of Ubu is to be found in his two *Almanachs*. Such almanacs were numerous and immensely popular at the time, and Jarry may well have seen in the idea amongst other things a means of restoring his diminished fortunes. At the beginning of 1899, he produced an *Almanach du Père Ubu*, illustrated by Pierre Bonnard. A volume of 92 pages in small format, it bore the date January-February-March 1899 and was intended to be the first of a series appearing quarterly. Although no second issue followed, the idea was briefly revived with the publication two years later, in January 1901, by the art dealer and art publisher Ambroise Vollard of a 56-page quarto volume entitled *Almanach illustré du Père Ubu* (*XXe Siècle*), to which Jarry, Bonnard and, to a lesser extent, Vollard, Terrasse and Fagus all contributed. Lavishly (and, in places, salaciously) illustrated by Bonnard, it was described by Jarry in a publicity notice in the *Revue Blanche* of 1 January 1901 as a 'revue des plus récents événements politiques, littéraires, artistiques, coloniaux, par-devant le Père Ubu' ['review of the most recent events in the fields of politics, literature, art and colonial affairs, as seen through the eyes of Père Ubu']. The work was composed, according to Vollard, during drinking sprees and discussions between its five contributors in his cellar; one of its special features was a new calendar incorporating a new series of saints' days, using little known or purely fictitious names, the work largely of Fagus, who worked in the *bureau des déclarations de naissance* in one of the Paris *mairies*.[56] (The tradition was revived some 50 years later by the Collège de 'Pataphysique with its Pataphysical Perpetual Calendar.) Alas for Jarry's *phynances* and literary reputation, neither *Almanach* proved to be commercially successful: a letter of February 1902 to Terrasse indicated that some 800 copies of the first *Almanach* remained unsold, while Vollard testified in his memoirs to a similar fate which befell the second volume.[57]

The first *Almanach* contains, in addition to the obligatory calendar and various 'practical' hints and pieces of information, a number of humorous or satirical commentaries (in the form of dialogues between Ubu and other characters) upon current events in politics and the arts, a moving homage to the recently deceased Mallarmé, the statutes of Ubu's newly founded 'Grand Ordre de la Gidouille' (also revived by the Collège de 'Pataphysique), and even a number of pages of advertisements for published or forthcoming works by Jarry and his friends. The whole is a mixture of parody, pastiche, satire and plain nonsense, with the occasional fragment of serious information. While much is perhaps mildly amusing, a good deal also falls rather flat. A notable exception, however, is provided by a short 3-act dramatic sketch entitled *L'Île du Diable* which, by means of a transposition and adaptation of several scenes from *Ubu Roi* and *Ubu Cocu*, constitutes a biting satire upon the Dreyfus Affair, Captain Bordure representing the unfortunate Dreyfus and Ubu, together with his gagged Conscience, the civil and military establishment of France. It is interesting to note that Jarry's satirical barbs are here directed exclusively at the *anti-dreyfusards* – in particular at the army General Staff and at the cynicism of a government prepared to sacrifice an innocent man for the sake of the maintenance of order – and that there is no trace here of the antisemitism which is to be a prominent feature of *La Dragonne* a few years later. Noteworthy also is the humorous attempt to capture the essential quality or chief activity of a writer, painter, musician or politician by means of the formula 'celui qui' ('he who'): thus Vallette becomes 'celui qui Mercure', the Natanson brothers 'ceux qui Revuent Blanche', the novelist J.-K. Huysmans 'celui qui digère par la trappe' (a double allusion to Huysmans' susceptibilities and career), Rousseau 'celui qui douanait', and so on in a list of some 136 names.

In outline, the second *Almanach* roughly follows the first. However, whereas in the latter the political satire focussed chiefly upon the Dreyfus Affair, here, even more markedly, it is the 'colonial' theme which dominates, inspired by the growth of France's colonial empire, particularly in Black Africa. This satirical commentary upon the nation's colonial adventures, together with a comic presentation of the customs and habits of 'les nègres' (as Jarry, following the accepted usage of the time, calls them), reaches a culmination in the sketch *Ubu colonial* and in the delightfully obscene poem, set to music by Terrasse, *Tatane* – subtitled 'Chanson pour faire rougir les nègres et glorifier le Père Ubu' ['A song to make niggers blush and to glorify Père Ubu']. (A second version of *Tatane*, presumably intended for a third *Almanach*, was written but remained unpublished.) On the whole the satire is quite effective and entertaining; much of the remainder, however, is again rather disappointing, and it is a pity that Jarry did not give further rein here (though he was to do so in his *chroniques* collected in *La Chandelle verte*) to his obvious satirical talents.

In both of these *Almanachs* the character of Ubu is again different from that of the plays (though in his cunning he bears some resemblance to that of *Ubu Enchaîné*). Gone is the blundering monstrosity which characterized the hero of *Ubu Roi*; in its place is a would-be wit and entertainer (though one who is still capable of lapsing into egregious stupidity), brimming over with real or invented knowledge and with opinions – an embodiment of the role which Jarry himself took on to satisfy the wishes of his friends and contemporaries in his own supposed incarnation of 'le Père Ubu'. For these and other reasons, on the whole these two *Almanachs* must rate as relatively minor works. In two important respects, however, they look forward to the much more important texts included in *La Chandelle verte*, the beginning of which is roughly contemporary with the publication of the second *Almanach*. For here Jarry, in the guise of Père Ubu, has moved far away from the apparent aestheticism of his early works, with their expression of contempt for the 'contingent' and purely ephemeral, to become a *commentator* upon contemporary events, casting, in the words of the subtitle of *La Chandelle verte*, many 'lumières sur les choses de ce temps'. At the same time, the viewpoint from which such events are to be observed is hinted at, in the first *Almanach*, in Ubu's invention of his 'Tempomobile'. Although the function of this device, invented with the aid of his 'science en physique' (and which looks forward also to his *Commentaire pour servir à la construction pratique de la machine à explorer le temps*), is here given as that of 'exploring time' and of revealing to his readers 'toutes choses futures',[58] it looks forward to Jarry's attempt in *La Chandelle verte* to adopt a point of view outside of the space-time sphere of his contemporaries.

Such an evolution in Jarry's work still lay many years in the future, however, at the time of the publication and production of *Ubu Roi* in 1896. But the production of that play was contemporary with the writing of one of Jarry's most secret and personal works, *Les Jours et les Nuits*, which opens up a new vein in his literary production. We must now leave this 'public' side of Jarry's work to concentrate on an examination of the secret world of *Les Jours et les Nuits* and of the novels which immediately followed it.

Chapter Six

Dream, hallucination, love and death

THE YEARS 1896 to 1899 were a period of extraordinary creative activity for Jarry. They were a period also in which he turned away from poetry and – with the exception of his activity in and for the theatre described in the last two chapters – from the writing of plays to the novel. Two of the four novels, moreover, which he wrote in the course of these four years rank among his most personal works, offering us a profound insight into the emotional life of their creator. Indeed, for those who wish to identify Jarry solely with Ubu, such works as *Les Jours et les Nuits* and *l'Amour absolu* are a profound embarrassment, revealing a Jarry who could scarcely be further removed from the grotesque distorting mask of Ubu.

In one other important respect, too, the work of these years differs from that of his 'Symbolist' period. Although some of the poems and prose pieces of *Les Minutes de sable mémorial* have an interest and an appeal for the general reader, much also in *Les Minutes*, and even more in *César-Antechrist*, is of interest essentially in terms of the writer's own ideas and of their evolution. It is not until the publication of *Ubu Roi* in 1896 and of *Les Jours et les Nuits* a year later that we meet works which, though their biographical interest may still be strong, offer a more general appeal and interest to the reader.

Jarry had begun work on what was to be *Les Jours et les Nuits, roman d'un déserteur* in 1895, during his period of military service. It was completed by April 1897 at the latest, and published by the Éditions du Mercure de France in July of that year. As so often happens with Jarry, however, the themes with which it deals may go back even further: a line in one of the fragments included in *La Revanche de la Nuit* – 'Toutes mes Heures égales, rêve ou veille' (which replaced a previous version: 'Toutes mes heures, jour et nuit, rêve et sommeil') – suggests that the theme of the fusion of day and night may have been present in his mind at least as early as 1894.[1] The novel recounts, in a dense and at times 'poetic' style, the spiritual and temporal adventures of its singular and solitary hero, Sengle – a name which Jarry derives from the Latin *singulum*, *via* Rutebeuf: 'Sans avoir m'a laissié tout sengle'.[2] A complementary aim is that of a ferocious satire upon the cruelties and absurdities of life in the army, into which Sengle is conscripted.

Both the title and sub-title of the novel are characterized by the polysemy embodied in *Les Minutes de sable mémorial* and *César-Antechrist*, while the title also hints at the existence of a series of antitheses expressed throughout the novel. 'Day' and 'night' can be understood on at least three different levels. First of all, there is the literal sense of periods of external light and darkness. A second meaning, however, is hinted at in an explicit, if perversely paradoxical, reference in the text itself to the title of the work:

Et il [Sengle] pensait surtout qu'il n'y a que des hallucinations, ou que des perceptions, et qu'il n'y a ni nuits ni jours (malgré le titre de ce livre, ce qui fait qu'on l'a choisi), et que la vie est continue . . . .

> [And he [Sengle] believed above all that there are only hallucinations, or only perceptions, and that there are neither nights nor days (despite the title of this book, which is why it was chosen), and that life is continuous . . . .][3]

As the reference to 'hallucinations' and 'perceptions' makes clear, 'day' is to be understood also as signifying the waking consciousness, 'rational' thought and perception of the external world; while 'night' stands for dream and hallucination – the world of the imagination, the rich inner world of the 'self'. The title of the opening chapter of *L'Amour absolu* – 'Que la ténèbre soit!' – parodies the Book of Genesis in expressing a desire for the dominance of 'night'; here, on the contrary, it is the ambition of Sengle to obliterate the distinction between 'day' and 'night' by realizing a fusion of these two states. Within this broad framework, the first three chapters of the novel (entitled 'Premier jour', 'Première nuit' and 'Autre jour') suggest a third level of meaning. 'Night' is here the 'night of the soul' of Sengle, separated from his brother Valens, while 'day' with its attendant illumination stands for the peace and spiritual contentment Sengle feels in Valens' presence. This identification is made clear at the end of the first chapter: 'Son frère l'avait accompagné partout parce que cette chère tête devant lui et non un astre plus jaune ou plus blanc distinguait de la nuit le jour, afin qu'il ne fût très malheureux.' ['His brother had accompanied him everywhere because, for him, this beloved head and not a whiter or more yellow star distinguished day from night, so that he might not be very miserable.'][4] This symbolism reappears at the end of the novel, where Valens' face appears to Sengle illuminated by the light of his lamp, and where he finally stumbles towards the absolute night, or total darkness, of madness.

As for the subtitle, *roman d'un déserteur*, this refers not only to Sengle's attempts to escape physically from the grim absurdities of life in the army, with its 'ablation des cervelles' and 'enlaidissement des corps',[5] in order to return to the freedom of civilian life. It refers also to his efforts to escape from what Jarry likes to call 'l'Extérieur' into his own private world of dream and hallucination – to 'l'évasion vers soi'.[6] His 'desertion' is from reality itself, or at least from the awareness of that reality through the normal waking consciousness, into a *continuum* of dream and hallucinatory awareness. The novel traces Sengle's efforts to achieve this dual 'desertion' to their final tragic conclusion.

Not surprisingly, the novel draws heavily upon Jarry's own experiences, both in the army and in his private life. A number of real events and personages appear to have been incorporated directly into *Les Jours* with little attempt at fictional disguise, and to a small extent the novel has something of the aspect, with regard to its minor characters, of a *roman à clef*,[7] whilst Jarry's hero, Sengle, undoubtedly contains a good deal of his creator. The external resemblances are immediately obvious: both are writers devoted to the cause of Art, both are Bretons, and both wear long hair, are fervent cyclists and fencers, and are of unusually small stature. More important than these, however, are the intellectual and spiritual resemblances which the novel suggests. There also seems little doubt that the intensely intimate if strange relationship between Sengle and his brother Valens owes much to the relationship between Jarry and Léon-Paul Fargue. Jarry lays great stress on the gap of two and a half years which separates Sengle from his younger brother (at one point the precise difference in age is mentioned three times in as many pages), the exact difference in age between himself and the younger Fargue also. But, at the same time, Valens is a much idealized Fargue, since Fargue is also clearly alluded to as the subject of an earlier 'friendship' who is now savagely spurned, dismissed as a mere literary hack who had simply plagiarized his friend, Sengle, and further as lily-livered and uninterested in sporting feats:

Avant Valens, il eut plusieurs amitiés qui s'égarèrent, des faute-de-mieux, qu'il reconnut plus tard avoir subies parce que les traits étaient des à peu-près de Valens, et les âmes, il faut un temps très long pour les voir. L'une dura deux ans, jusqu'à ce qu'il s'aperçut qu'elle avait un corps de palefrenier et des pieds en éventail, et pas d'autre littérature qu'un amiévrissement de la sienne, à lui Sengle; laquelle fit des ronds des mois après avec des souvenirs rapetassés dans la cervelle de l'ex-ami. Il trouvait mauvais également, fervent d'escrime, qu'on eût peur des pointes et ne sût pas cycler assez pour jouir de la vitesse.

[Before Valens, he experienced several friendships which went astray, cases of for-want-of-something-better, experiences which, he later recognized, he had undergone because the physical features bore a vague resemblance to those of Valens and, as for souls, it takes a long time before one can see them. One of these lasted for two years, until he noticed that the object of his affections had the body of a stable-groom and splayed feet, and no other literature than a mawkish imitation of his, Sengle's; which made ripples for months afterwards along with botched up recollections in the mind of the ex-friend. Sengle, who was a devotee of fencing, disapproved also of those who were afraid of rapier points and who were not good enough cyclists to enjoy speed.][8]

No less surprisingly, Jarry's savage portrait of army life owes much to his own experiences. Such satirical barbs were not, however, without precedent. Though Jarry is writing out of deep personal indignation and resentment, the novel must be seen also against the background of a spate of anti-militaristic novels and tracts published in the 1880s and 1890s in France and of a strain of anti-militarism (and even explicit anti-patriotism) widespread in intellectual circles at this time. Indeed, one of the most outspoken and provocative of such publications was Gourmont's pamphlet *Le Joujou patriotisme* of 1891 – so provocative in fact that its publication lost its author his post at the Bibliothèque Nationale. Heaping sarcasm on the idea of *la patrie* and describing patriotism as a 'virus' and as 'la sottise suprême', Gourmont haughtily declared in response to the demands of nationalists such as Déroulède for a war of revenge upon Germany in order to win back the 'lost provinces' of Alsace–Lorraine:

Personnellement, je ne donnerais pas, en échange de ces terres oubliées, ni le petit doigt de ma main droite: il me sert à soutenir ma main, quand j'écris; ni le petit doigt de ma main gauche: il me sert à secouer la cendre de ma cigarette.

[Personally, I would not give, in exchange for these forgotten lands, either the little finger of my right hand: it serves to support my hand when I write; or the little finger of my left hand: it serves to flick the ash from my cigarette.][9]

The tone could not but have appealed to the young Jarry, many of whose pronouncements on the army and on questions of national prestige and honour are in similar vein.

In *Les Jours et les Nuits*, however, his concern is less with such broader issues than with a vivid and stark account of conditions and activities in the conscript army into which he had been drafted. Though the style retains much of the self-conscious contortions of his Symbolist phase, the descriptive quality of the writing is 'realistic' enough. We are introduced to scenes of rifle practice in the freezing cold of a winter's morning, the forced taking of cold showers in the bitter open air, the torments of exercises in the gymnasium, midnight alerts and manoeuvres, and marches through mud, frost and water. We witness a comrade's attempted suicide, and the callous incompetence of army doctors who lightheartedly succeed in killing a patient through faulty diagnosis (Jarry's contempt for the medical profession generally is second only to that he holds for the army). The army is satirized in particular for its filth and squalor (in fact a deep horror of dirt and, one is tempted to add, of material reality generally runs through the novel); for its brutal harshness and indifference to physical and mental comfort; and for its cultivation of a 'herd' mentality. It is the latter above all, the mindless regimentation practised by the army, which offends Sengle's aristocratic and individualistic instincts. In a chapter characteristically entitled 'De l'abrutissement militaire', Jarry states categorically that the first aim of army discipline is to 'abolish intelligence' and to substitute for it a small number of animal instincts deriving from the crude instinct for self-preservation. (What Sengle wishes to put in place of this reduction to a common denominator we shall see shortly.) Though in the main satirical, however, it would be wrong to see Jarry's portrait of army life in *Les Jours* as wholly negative: the novel contains also a number of purely descriptive passages (evocations of the countryside through which the troops march, snatches of marching songs) in which he sets out to record impressionistically certain of the sights and sounds associated with army life.

As for the form of the novel, *Les Jours et les Nuits* is loosely structured, even anecdotal at times, and contains numerous digressions in the form of recollections of past events or philosophical discourses, while characterization, in the conventional nineteenth-century sense of the term, is reduced to a minimum: though he subtitled the work a 'novel', Jarry had no intention of following the conventions of the realist novel of the time. A number of chapters are also made up of accounts of dreams or other 'hallucinatory' experiences of the hero Sengle. And inserted into the text are also several poems; one of these, it is important to realize (as the compilers of an anthology of Jarry's verse once failed to do), along with a similarly extravagant prose passage, is *not* by Sengle, who dismisses both of them contemptuously: Jarry is here parodying the excessively 'erudite' and convoluted Symbolist manner which he had himself at times adopted in *Les Minutes* and *César-Antechrist*. Most of the poems, however, contain no such satirical intention, and constitute some fine examples of lyrical and evocative verse devoid, on the whole, of the self-conscious artificiality of much of the earlier work, though frequently drawing upon the same fund of images. One expresses in a simple and direct manner the regret and longing of Sengle separated from his brother Valens; the first stanza runs:

Je ne sais pas si mon frère m'oublie
Mais je me sens tout seul, immensément
Avec loin la chère tête apâlie
Dans les essais d'un souvenir qui ment.

> *[I do not know if my brother has forgotten me*
> *But I feel alone, immensely alone*
> *With far away the pale, beloved face*
> *Lost amidst the failings of a fickle memory.]*[10]

Four lines in the chapter entitled 'Le Tain des mares', which is devoted to an account of a childhood pilgrimage to Sainte-Anne-d'Auray, evoke the church of Sainte-Anne and its statue of the saint:

Le clocher est semblable à un peuplier.
À la cime perche la Sainte dorée
Dans l'ombre, rose des vents mélancolique
Avec sa Fille, et sous leurs pieds les Reliques.

> *[The steeple is like a poplar tree.*
> *At its summit perches the gilded Saint*
> *In the shadows, pink from the winds and melancholy*
> *With her Daughter, and beneath their feet the Relics.]*[11]

In the same chapter, a poem of 16 lines, 'Parmi les bruyères, penil des menhirs', evokes a half-real, half-imaginary landscape of the Brittany of Sengle's (and Jarry's) childhood.

Despite the novel's looseness of structure, however, three 'threads' provide either something in the way of a plot or, failing that, at least an element of thematic continuity. These are the account of Sengle's initiation into army life and of his various attempts at 'desertion'; the gradual revelation of the true nature of the 'love' between Sengle and Valens; and Sengle's attempts to overcome the dualism of reality and dream, perception and hallucination, matter and mind, in order to achieve a fusion of differing and frequently opposed states of being. An account of each in turn will help to throw light on the true subject of *Les Jours et les Nuits*.

The first of these provides the chief narrative element in the novel. After Sengle's appearance before the recruiting board, we see him being issued with an over-large uniform (a source, together with an account of his inability to handle the long, heavy army rifle, of considerable comedy) and his installation in the barracks, where literary-minded officers attempt both to turn their newly conscripted poet to account socially and to profit from his literary advice. Book I ends with the frustration of his initial plans to desert to Belgium, whilst Book II recounts Sengle's first vain attempts to have himself discharged as medically unfit. Gradually, the idea takes hold of him that he must make himself gravely ill in order to obtain the shelter of the army hospital, where at least he can enjoy the peace and freedom to read, sleep and dream at will. In Book III, a faked high temperature followed by the swallowing of a dose of pure caffeine succeed in obtaining for him 15 days 'convalescent' leave in Paris, followed, eventually, by permanent residence in the hospital. Even this degree of freedom proves ultimately to be unsatisfactory, however, and Sengle finally succeeds at the end of Book IV – thanks to the deviousness of his medical student friend, Nosocome, and the connivance of a sympathetic doctor – in obtaining a discharge from the army on medical grounds.

The novel does not, however, end here. In Book V, two and a half years after Sengle's discharge, it is the turn of Valens similarly to long for escape from the army into which he has now been conscripted. In an effort to help him obtain a discharge through illness, Sengle sends Valens a sample of the scarlet-fever bacillus with which he is to infect himself. Whether or not the scheme succeeds we do not know, for at the end of the novel a tragic end befalls Sengle himself. As he sits at his writing desk, Valens' face appears amidst a flood of recollections from the past, seeming to smile at him from out of a section of plaster on the wall above his head illuminated by his lamp. He imagines that Valens, like himself two and a half years previously, has regained his liberty, and that the face of Valens, and with it his whole soul, is beckoning to him. Sengle rises in an effort to embrace his brother:

Et pour revivre ce passé il se haussa vers le masque . . . . Sengle se pencha
vers son frère, désormais deviné, à travers la distance, libre, pour lui rendre
toute l'affection du bon baiser de lumière sonore.

> [And to relive this past he raised himself up towards the face . . . . Sengle
> leaned towards his brother, henceforth divined, through the distance, to be
> free, in order to return all the affection contained in the kiss of resonant light.][12]

The table overbalances, and Sengle crashes to the floor, his skull smashed by the fall of a heavy lump of plaster which had broken away from the wall, reduced by the impact to a state of idiocy.

Such, at least, is the interpretation of the cause of Sengle's madness explicitly formulated in the official report quoted in the last chapter. But this is only the most superficial of several possible levels of interpretation – worthy, Jarry implies, of the 'common sense' view of the 'bourgeois' (this final chapter is ironically entitled 'Selon Monsieur Prud'homme'). In order to understand fully the implications of the novel's ending, we need to examine more closely the exact nature of Sengle's 'desertion' and of the relationship between Sengle and Valens.

Sengle's determination to liberate himself from the clutches of the army is not born solely of a revulsion against the latter's petty stupidities and brutality. Much more important is the desire to preserve his own individuality intact in the face of official efforts to cultivate a herd mentality. In support of this deep-seated desire, Jarry draws a distinction between two 'instincts of self preservation', the 'noble' and the 'ignoble', the former being defined as 'l'instinct de conserver son moi et de maintenir son individualité impénétrable aux forces extérieures' ['the instinct to preserve one's self and to keep one's individuality impenetrable to outside forces'].[13] (His words are curiously reminiscent of Maurice Barrès' 'Culte du moi', though the resemblance derives not from any direct influence, but from the common roots of the ideas of both men in the 'egotism' of the Symbolist generation.) Moreover, Jarry even attempts to enlist the support of Christian doctrine to justify this egotism of Sengle and of the spiritual and intellectual élite to which he belongs. Sengle accepts, in his idiosyncratic way, the practices of Catholicism; but his true 'religion' is a devotion to the cultivation of the 'self', which is justified – in a chapter entitled, with characteristically self-conscious irony, 'Un peu de sacrilège' – by a highly personal reinterpretation of the moral injunctions of the Bible:

Ceux dont l'intelligence et le corps sont élus, à moins d'imprévu détraquement, se laissent aller dans la gravitation de leurs actes autour de leur synthèse intérieure, et ne désobéissent à aucune prescription du Décalogue, *respectant en Dieu soi.* Les commandements altruistes: 'Le bien d'autrui . . .' sont d'aristocratiques formules d'isolement.

> [Those whose minds and bodies are of the elect, barring unforeseen breakdown, freely allow their actions to gravitate around their inner synthesis, and disobey not a single of the Ten Commandments, respecting in God themselves. The altruistic commandments: 'The good of others . . .' are aristocratic expressions of the right to isolation.][14]

It is in the light of this fundamental egotism that the relationship between Sengle and Valens must be seen. For as well as his 'brother', Valens is also the 'double' of Sengle, in whom the latter sees himself – or, more precisely, the self that he was two and a half years previously – now reflected, just as the future of Valens two and a half years hence is now mirrored in the present of Sengle. Thus the duality, but at the same time complementary nature, of night and day in the novel is reflected in the relationship between the two young men. This theme of the 'double' or Doppelgänger, whose origins are to be found in German Romanticism, fascinated Jarry. According to the legend, every man has a double, the sight of whom heralds the approach of death. Jarry had made brief use of the idea in *César-Antechrist*, where Ubu appears as the 'double' of Antichrist, his appearance heralding the latter's death. Here, however, the theme of the 'double' is both more complex and more mysterious. Sengle's need of his brother is such that the separation caused by his conscription appears as a form of 'death' (symbolically, 'night'). Moreover, the need for Valens' actual physical presence is all the greater, we are told, since Sengle lacks all powers of recollection:

Sengle était dépourvu de toute mémoire des figures et ne pouvait reconstruire, même en s'imaginant les calquer dans l'air, les traits de sa mère morte deux jours après la mort.

> [Sengle was lacking in any memory for faces and could not recall to mind, even by imagining himself tracing them in the air, the features of his dead mother two days after her death.][15]

Indeed, such is this absence of memory that, after the separation has lasted for some months, he is no longer even sure that Valens had ever really existed. Yet, despite this need for Valens' physical presence, and for all the intimacy of their relationship, Jarry is at pains to stress that the amorous bond linking the two young men is of a spiritual and emotional rather than a physical nature:

Le mot Adelphisme serait plus juste et moins médical d'aspect qu'Uranisme, malgré son exacte étymologie sidérale. Sengle, pas sensuel, n'était capable que d'amitié.

> [The word Adelphism would be more accurate and less medical in appearance than Uranism, despite the latter's exact sidereal etymology. Sengle, who was not sensual, was capable only of friendship.][16]

Indeed, the physical reality of Valens is needed by Sengle *solely* in order to provide a mirror to himself, to make up for the deficiencies of his own memory:

Et Sengle, amoureux du Souvenir de Soi, avait besoin d'un ami vivant et visible, parce qu'il n'avait aucun souvenir de Soi, étant dépourvu de toute mémoire.

> [And Sengle, in love with the Memory of Self, needed a living and visible friend, because he had no memory of his own self, being devoid of all faculty of remembering.][17]

But at the same time, and paradoxically, as the above quotation suggests, Sengle is in fact less in love with an independently existing Valens, physical or spiritual, than with the image, and the memory, of his own 'self'. His need is in reality a purely narcissistic one. Thus Valens comes ultimately to constitute for Sengle in his self-absorption (as the title of the penultimate chapter, 'Sur la route de Dulcinée' – a

reference to the idealized and half-imaginary beloved of Don Quixote
– suggests) simply the imagined incarnation of his own past, which
Valens mirrors in every respect from earliest childhood onwards.
When, in the penultimate chapter, Valens' face appears to Sengle, it
is in the midst of a host of memories of his own past, memories of his
experiences in the army, memories in particular of childhood experiences recalled earlier in the novel, Valens' 'soul' being described in
terms of images which equate it clearly with those childhood experiences. Sengle attempts to embrace Valens 'pour revivre ce passé';
and, after his fall, which precipitates him into a state of idiocy, we are
told that: 'Sengle tâtonnait dans la nuit vers son Soi disparu comme le
coeur d'une bombe, la bouche sur son meurtre.' ['Sengle remained
groping in the darkness for his Self, vanished like the heart of a
bomb, his mouth pressed to its murder.']¹⁸

This mysterious reference to 'murder' hints at a significant departure, in Jarry's use of the myth of the 'double', from his original
source. In *Les Jours et les Nuits*, it is not the seeing by Sengle of his
'double', Valens, which precipitates death; it is, rather, the attempt to
embrace him – that is, to establish *physical* contact. On one level,
therefore, the novel appears to express the same deep-seated fear of
physical contact which we saw in *Haldernablou*, in which the development of the love between the two protagonists into a physical
relationship leads ultimately to the murder by Duke Haldern of his
page Ablou. The implication is clearly that love must remain a purely
spiritual experience, and that any attempt to translate it into physical
terms must result in the destruction not only of that love but also of
one or other of the lovers. Indeed, even more radically, if Valens is
ultimately merely an ideal projection of Sengle's own 'self' or imagination, then the implication would seem to be also that any
attempt to translate that ideal into a lived experience is similarly
doomed to disaster. Love is, and must remain, an ideal, purely
imaginary (or narcissistic) experience.

Jarry's elaboration of the strange relationship between Sengle and
his brother Valens involves us, however, not only in an exploration of
the nature of 'love' as he conceives of it. It leads us also to the central
subject of *Les Jours et les Nuits*, which is that of the nature of time and
consciousness. For the novel records, in a partly fictionalized form,
the explorations of Jarry himself into differing states of consciousness
and his experiments and experiences in the realms of memory, of
perception, of dream and of hallucination, which culminate, in the
novel, in the attempt by Sengle to achieve within himself a fusion of
past and present, of memory and imagination, of perception and
hallucination, of the waking consciousness and dream, of matter and
spirit, in a continuum of hallucinatory awareness.

Where, in *Haldernablou*, the two protagonists dreamed of the 'union' of their two beings (symbolically expressed in the fusion of their two names in the title of the work), here the idea of 'la communion de deux êtres devenus un' is explicitly rejected by Sengle (or Jarry) in favour of a 'communion' of past and present, which Sengle is able to realize through his contemplation of Valens, two and a half years his junior. 'Love' itself is ultimately conceived of as the attempt to recapture one's own past in the present, to achieve a fusion of past and present: Sengle is not only 'amoureux du Souvenir de Soi' but indeed 'vivait (et mourrait ...) de souvenir'.[19] Such a simultaneous experience of a moment of past and a moment of present time constitutes, moreover, according to Jarry, an experience of 'eternity', which is 'pour l'être qui pense la plus haute jouissance':

Sengle découvrait la vraie cause métaphysique du bonheur d'aimer: non la communion de deux êtres devenus un . . .; mais la jouissance de l'anachronisme et de causer avec son propre passé (Valens aimait sans doute son propre futur, et c'est peut-être pourquoi il aimait avec une violence plus hésitante, ne l'ayant pas encore vécu et ne le pouvant tout comprendre). Il est admirable de vivre deux moments différents du temps en un seul; ce qui est suffisant pour vivre authentiquement un moment d'éternité, soit toute l'éternité, puisqu'elle n'a pas de moment.

> [Sengle was discovering the true metaphysical cause of the happiness of love: not the communion of two beings become one . . . ; but the enjoyment of anachronism and of conversing with one's own past (Valens, no doubt, was in love with his own future, and that was perhaps why the violence of his love was more hesitant, since he had not yet lived it and was unable to understand it fully). It is admirable to live two different moments of time in a single one; such an experience is sufficient to allow one to live authentically a moment of eternity, indeed the whole of eternity, since it is undivided into moments.][20]

Such a concept bears a fascinating resemblance to the ideas of Proust (Jarry's premature death tends to obscure the fact that both men belong to the same generation: only two years separate their dates of birth). For Proust, the simultaneous experience of past and present (involving the coincidence also of imagination and memory) is similarly 'un peu de temps à l'état pur', an experience of eternity (and also of the hidden 'essence des choses').[21] This similarity of ideas should not, however, cause us to assume a direct influence of one writer upon the other. On the contrary, it is adequately explained by the intellectual roots of both men in the Symbolist movement, and in particular by their common interest in, and the influence upon them of, the ferment of ideas in philosophy and psychology which was taking place in France in the last two decades of the nineteenth century, which in turn helped to shape the ideas of the Symbolists – a subject which, in the case of Proust, has been studied in detail by

Elizabeth Czoniczer in *Quelques antécédents de 'A la recherche du temps perdu': (Tendances qui peuvent avoir contribué à la cristallisation du roman proustien).*[22]

At the same time, however, Jarry, unlike Proust, appears to hesitate to expound such ideas with complete conviction. This at least seems to be the implication of the deliberately fanciful examples which he puts forward of this supposed experience of 'eternity' through the fusion of moments of the past and present:

C'est aussi énorme que le vraisemblable sursaut de Shakespeare, revenu dans tel musée de Stratford-on-Avon, où l'on montre encore 'son crâne à l'âge de cinq ans'. C'est la jubilation de Dieu le Père un et deux dans son Fils, et la perception qu'a le premier terme de son rapport avec le second n'a pu donner moins que l'Esprit-Saint.

> [It is as whopping as the probable start which Shakespeare would experience, where he to return to some museum or other in Stratford-on-Avon where they still exhibit 'his skull at the age of five'. It is the jubilation of God the Father, one with, yet separate from, his Son, and the perception by the former of his relationship with the latter could not have engendered anything less than the Holy Spirit.][23]

Something of the same hesitation (expressed again through self-conscious irony) pervades Jarry's discussion of the curious relationship which exists between Sengle and the 'external world' to which reference is made at several points in the novel. In a chapter entitled, significantly if obscurely, 'Pataphysique', which looks forward to some of the ideas expounded in *Gestes et opinions du docteur Faustroll, pataphysicien,* Jarry tells us that Sengle (very much an idealized version of his creator and an expression of wish-fulfilment here) believes that he is able to demonstrate the influence of mind over matter and to control physical events by an act of will. He can, for example, control the fall of the dice (with the result that his friends refuse to play with him any longer: 'Personne ne joua plus aux dés avec lui, car il dépouillait de sommes considérables.' ['Nobody would play at dice with him any longer, for he divested them of substantial sums.']) At one point in the novel, even, his experiments in controlling events by a pure act of will result in the unforeseen murder of a hospital orderly in a quarrel. So successful are his experiments in this field that 'Sengle s'était cru le droit, de par son influence expérimentée sur l'habitus de petits objets, d'induire l'obéissance probable du monde' ['Sengle had come to believe, as a result of testing his influence over the behaviour of small objects, that he had the right to infer the probable obedience of the world'].[24] And as a result of these 'rapports réciproques avec les Choses, qu'il était accoutumé à diriger avec sa pensée' ['reciprocal relationships with Things, which he was accustomed to direct with his mind'], he comes to conceive of the world as a huge ship with himself as its captain: 'Le monde n'était qu'un immense bateau, avec Sengle au gouvernail' ['The world was simply a huge ship, with Sengle at the helm'].[25] Yet here too Jarry withholds from committing himself totally to such ideas and identifying wholly with his hero: in an alternative metaphor, the world is seen as a huge windmill whose sails turn at Sengle's command – an implicit reference to Don Quixote and his fantasies, which is backed up by two other references: Book IV, in which this chapter occurs, has as an epigraph a quotation from Cervantes' novel: 'Voyons donc quels sont ces contes que tu veux me faire'; and the chapter ends with the cryptic statement:

Don Quichottisme un peu que la conception de ce grand moulin à vent, mais il n'y a encore que les imbéciles qui ne les connaissent que par la mouture.
Et Sengle avait dulcinifié ou déifié sa force.

[There was an element of quixotism in the idea of this giant windmill, but it is only imbeciles who still only know them from the milling.
And Sengle had dulcineified or deified his strength.][26]

Alongside these attempts to abolish the dichotomy of past and present and mind and matter, and even more central to the novel, are Sengle's experiments in the field of perception and his efforts to obliterate the distinction between 'reality' and 'dream', or between perception and hallucination; that is, in the symbolism of the novel's title, between 'day' and 'night'. Here Jarry is not only drawing upon his own experiences but reveals himself also as having a profound knowledge of the work of contemporary psychologists and philosophers. As a result of the influence which he believes he is able to exercise over events in the world around him, Sengle arrives at a point at which

il ne distinguait pas du tout sa pensée de ses actes ni son rêve de sa veille; et perfectionnant la leibnizienne définition, que la perception est une hallucination vraie, il ne voyait pas pourquoi ne pas dire: l'hallucination est une perception fausse, ou plus exactement: *faible*, ou tout à fait mieux: *prévue* (*souvenue* quelquefois, ce qui est la même chose). Et il pensait surtout qu'il n'y a que des hallucinations, ou que des perceptions, et qu'il n'y a ni nuits ni jours . . ., et que la vie est continue. . . .

[he no longer in the least distinguished his thoughts from his actions nor his state of dreaming from that of wakefulness; and perfecting the definition of Leibniz according to which perception is a hallucination which is true, he saw no reason not to say: hallucination is a perception which is false, or more precisely: *weak*, or even better: *foreseen* (*remembered* sometimes, which is the same thing). And he believed above all that there are only hallucinations, or only perceptions, and that there are neither nights nor days . . . , and that life is continuous . . . .][27]

If a parallel can be established between the ideas expressed in *Les*

Jours et les Nuits concerning time and eternity and the work of Proust, no less strikingly the above passage looks forward to the ideas of the Surrealists, whose high priest André Breton declared in his first *Manifeste du surréalisme* of 1924: 'Je crois à la résolution future de ces deux états, en apparence si contradictoires, que sont le rêve et la réalité, en une sorte de réalité absolue, de *surréalité* . . . .' ['I believe in the future reconciliation of those two states, which seem so mutually contradictory, of dream and reality, in a kind of absolute reality, of *super-reality* . . . .'] Sengle's ambition to achieve a fusion of these two states together with that of perception and hallucination, past (memory) and future (imagination) – the latter two being, he implies, on a psychological plane at least, equivalents – into a continuum of hallucinatory awareness is exemplified at numerous points in the novel. *Les Jours et les Nuits* reveals, for example, a fascination with various drug-induced states of consciousness, a fascination shared by many at the time and which found expression in a long literary tradition going back to the Romantics and exemplified by such writers as Baudelaire, Gautier, Nerval, De Quincey and Coleridge. Baudelaire (whose *Les Paradis artificiels* deals with the subject) and De Quincey (whose *Confessions of an English Opium Eater* directly inspired Baudelaire) are both alluded to in *Les Jours*, in the form of the famous invocation from the *Confessions*, translated by Baudelaire: 'O juste, subtil . . .', used as the title of chapter 1 of Book III, 'Le Rêve cyanique'. Chapter 3 of the same Book contains a vivid account of Sengle's hallucinations caused by his swallowing of a large dose of pure caffeine; and a later chapter entitled 'Les Propos des Assassins' (etymologically, *assassin* = *hashishin* or taker of hashish) records the actions and dialogue of three friends of Sengle during a night-long orgy of hallucinations induced by hashish and other drugs, Sengle remaining quietly to one side carefully observing and taking notes, in less need than the others of artificial stimulants since 'l'état de haschisch est le plus semblable à son état normal, puisque c'est un état supérieur' ['the state induced by hashish is the one which bears most resemblance to his normal state, since it is a higher state'].[28] If a key to the structure of this chapter, as Michel Arrivé has shown at length,[29] is to be found in a free association of ideas, images and above all sounds, resulting in a disintegration followed by a reconstitution of language, its underlying theme is that of time – in particular, the way in which the distinction between past, present and future is obliterated and in which time becomes expanded almost infinitely in a state of drug-induced hallucination:

Les propos se répliquaient avec une vitesse exagérée, coupés de silences inévaluables, les haschischins n'ayant pas de notion du temps, sans doute à cause du nombre des images, et payant sans pose, riches d'années à milliards, par trois cents ans les minutes et les secondes.

[This exchange of remarks took place at an exaggerated speed, broken by incalculable periods of silence, those under the influence of hashish having no notion of time, no doubt because of the superabundance of images, and, with billions of years at their disposal, quite naturally treating the minutes and seconds as periods of three hundred years.]

Whilst Sengle 'écoutait dans l'éternité'.[30]

Not only, moreover, does Sengle's attempt to achieve a fusion of past and present, waking consciousness and dream, perception and hallucination, constitute the central theme of *Les Jours et les Nuits*, but the text of the novel itself endeavours to suggest and to perpetuate this fusion of past and present, 'dream' and reality (dream being understood here in a broad sense to include remembrance and imagination – everything in fact which is the opposite of immediate perception, an equivalence suggested by Jarry himself in Book IV, Chapter 4). Scenes from the present and from the past of Sengle alternate and even merge with each other. And whereas scenes from the past are described with an abundance of precise detail, scenes from the present are recorded with a deliberate vagueness, particularly in regard to such details as time and place and the links between events; frequently this is achieved by presenting Sengle's experiences simply in the form of brief notations of sense-impressions, with a predominance of nouns and adjectives and a minimum of verbs and conjunctions, which would serve to indicate the relationships between objects and events and to impose a rational order upon the world. The result is a series of fleeting impressions, as in a dream – a technique exemplified by the following passage, in which scenes from the present and the past are superimposed one upon the other (Sengle is observing the surrounding countryside during early-morning manoeuvres):

Les talus avec les haies rousses et la mousse bleue, où il poursuivait les grillons avec un couteau pour boucher le trou derrière eux, quand il était libre. La rivière où glisse un patineur libre. Par delà les peupliers, une croix ancienne qu'il a cherchée longtemps, comme en rêve, la sachant là avant de la découvrir, où au lieu du Christ sont crucifiés les accessoires de sa passion . . . . Le hammerless qu'on tient sous le bras, comme les soldats ne font qu'après qu'un uniforme est mort, et qui porte infaillible, parce qu'épaulé librement.

[The embankments with the russet hedges and the blue moss, on which he pursued crickets with a knife used for blocking up the hole behind them, when he was free. The river over which a free skater glides. Beyond the poplars, an ancient cross which he spent a long time searching for, as in a dream, knowing it to be there before discovering it, on which in place of Christ are crucified the objects associated with his Passion . . . . The hammerless rifle which one carries under one's arm, as soldiers do only after a uniform is dead, and which infallibly hits its target, because aimed in freedom.][31]

It is of course in Sengle's attempt to escape from present reality and active life into memory, imagination, dream and the 'dark' world ('night') of the subconscious that his ultimate 'desertion' lies. But at the same time, the tragic conclusion of the novel shows Jarry to be aware of the dangers of such a quest in a way in which his hero was not. The fragility of the link which Sengle endeavours to establish between conscious and unconscious, between 'day' and 'night', and which is finally broken is made clear through Jarry's use of a curious legend drawn from an ancient Chinese source, which he found in a book entitled *Ethnographie des peuples étrangers à la Chine*, recently translated by the Marquess d'Hervey de Saint-Denys from a thirteenth-century Chinese work (published in Geneva, 1877–82). This concerns the 'flying heads' of the Leao people, whose heads were able to detach themselves from the body at nightfall and to fly away, returning only at morning. The legend is first referred to in Chapter 3 of the novel, in which Sengle, during a walk in a forest with Valens 'dans un état d'esprit tel que s'il avait pris du haschisch' ['in a state of mind such as if he had taken hashish'], experienced the hallucinatory sensation of his soul having detached itself from his body and flying like a kite in the air, attached only by a fragile thread:

'Mon frère, dit-il à Valens, ne me touche pas, car le fil s'interrompra aux arbres, comme lorsqu'on court avec le cerf-volant sous les poteaux du télégraphe; et il me semble que si cela arrivait, je mourrais.'
    Et il avait lu dans un livre chinois cette ethnologie d'un peuple étranger à la Chine, dont les têtes peuvent voler vers les arbres pour saisir des proies, reliées par le déroulement d'un peloton rouge, et reviennent ensuite s'adapter à leur collier sanglant. Mais il ne faut pas qu'un certain vent souffle, car, le cordon rompu, la tête dévolerait outre-mer.

[' Brother', he said to Valens, 'do not touch me, for the thread will get caught in the trees, as when one runs with a kite beneath telegraph poles; and I have the feeling that, if that happened, I should die.'
    And he had read in a Chinese book this ethnology of a people foreign to China, whose heads can fly up towards the trees in order to seize their prey, attached by the unwinding of a red ball of thread, and then return to fit back onto their bleeding necks. But it is essential that a certain wind should not blow, for, were the thread to break, the head would fly away over the sea.][32]

(The same chapter contains reference also to the occultist concept of the 'astral body', a form of being intermediate between body and soul, first found in the section of *Les Minutes de sable mémorial* entitled 'L'Opium', where it serves to suggest the sensation of 'dédoublement', or splitting of the personality into two, to which the use of opium can give rise. And there may also be in that order given to Valens not to 'touch' his brother an implicit allusion to the beliefs of spiritualism, according to which irreparable damage can be done to a medium if suddenly seized during a seance.) The legend is again referred to twice in the two final chapters of *Les Jours*. As Sengle stretches up towards the imagined face of Valens in an effort to embrace him, Jarry inserts the words, recalling the earlier reference: 'L'ethnographie chinoise d'un peuple étranger à la Chine . . . il ne faut pas qu'un certain vent souffle . . .' ['The Chinese ethnography of a people foreign to China . . . it is essential that a certain wind should not blow . . .']. And the closing words of the book are: 'Sengle avait lu dans un livre chinois l'ethnographie d'un peuple . . . Dévolerait outre-mer.' ['Sengle had read in a Chinese book the ethnography of a people . . . Would fly away over the sea.']³³

This symbolism of the 'flying heads' is used in conjunction with another piece of symbolism (this time ironical) in order to underline the inherent dangers, and ultimate failure, of Sengle's quest. After his accident, Sengle is taken to the psychiatric hospital of Sainte-Anne where he is certified insane. But Saint Anne – patron saint of the basilica and town of Auray to which Sengle made a childhood pilgrimage – was also the patron saint of his childhood, as we are explicitly reminded in the penultimate chapter amidst a flood of childhood memories which come back to him as he rises to embrace Valens: 'Sengle était amoureux des mares et des bêtes qui volent sur les mares; on ne sait jamais, pensait-il *sur la route* de Sainte-Anne, si l'on retrouvera des mares ou les mêmes mares.' ['Sengle loved ponds and the creatures which fly about above ponds; one never knows, he thought, *on the road* to Sainte-Anne, if one will find any ponds or the same ponds again.']³⁴ The highly pessimistic implication to be drawn from this juxtaposition is clear: the attempt to achieve a fusion of dream and reality, of past and present, of conscious and unconscious as desired by Sengle, can end only in the splitting apart of the personality; the search for spiritual and temporal unity can only end in madness: 'Et Sengle tâtonnait dans la nuit vers son Soi disparu . . .' ['And Sengle remained groping in the darkness for his vanished Self . . .'].

Though a difficult and complex work, *Les Jours et les Nuits* is at the same time a fascinating one. The passages of remembrance of Sengle's childhood are imbued with a tenderness and a nostalgia which give them a great deal of charm. The account of conscript life, for all the harshness of Jarry's portrayal, possesses a quality of vividness which makes the reading of it an impressive and memorable experience; and the account of Sengle's spiritual adventures has a fascination which goes far beyond any purely autobiographical interest which the novel may hold.

Shortly after the completion of *Les Jours et les Nuits*, Jarry began work on another novel to which he gave the suggestive title of *L'Amour en visites*. At first glance, this novel could not appear more different from the highly personal and partly autobiographical *Jours*. Jarry's motives in writing it are not wholly clear, though it is probable that one of them was financial. By 1897, the inheritance he had received from his father had long since been dissipated, and the publication of *Jours* had been a financial disaster. Vallette thereafter refused to allow any further works by his former protégé to be published by the Mercure de France as a financial venture. By way of compensation, and perhaps out of a feeling of obligation, Rachilde put Jarry in touch with Pierre Fort, a publisher of erotica of dubious quality: a letter of Fort to her of 18 September 1897 speaks of her recommendation of one of her 'camarades', and indicates that Jarry had by this time already submitted a plan for the novel to Fort, who published it in May of the following year.[35]

In view of the circumstances of its publication, *L'Amour en visites* has sometimes been seen as a piece of hack-writing in which Jarry exploited, for purely financial reasons and with a considerable degree of success, the *veine grivoise* – a popular taste for mild (by modern standards, very mild) pornography. On the other hand, it is certain that the book's publisher got something rather different from what he had been expecting. For though Jarry is here undoubtedly exploiting a popular vein, he does so in a very idiosyncratic fashion. One can only suppose that Fort was misled by the title and the ostensible content of certain chapters – though if his degree of literacy, as evidenced by the spelling and syntax of the following letter, is an indication of his literary acumen then the task can hardly have been difficult:

Mon cher Monsieur Jarry,
Je vients de téléphoner à M. Lépice [the printer] qu'il ma répondu qu'il avait
tirer 4 feuilles et que les autres 2 qu'il vous les avait envoyer pour être corriger
et il ma fait entendre qu'il y auraient peut être un peu trop de copie je
voudrais que sa ne fasse pas plus de six feuilles je désirerais que vous me le
portiez demain matin nous pourrions arranger cela ensemble. [*sic.*]

> [Dear Mr Jarry,
> I've just telephone M. Lépice [the printer] what told me that he had print
> you 4 sheets and that the other 2 that he had send them to you for
> proof-reeding and he give me to understand that maybee there is a bit two
> much copy I'd like the hole lot not too go over six sheets I'd like you to bring it
> to me tomorrow morning we could sort it out together.][36]

Fort may have been misled in another way also. Of the 11 chapters making up *L'Amour en visites*, two had been published previously and considerably antedated the conception of the novel – Chapter X, 'Au Paradis ou le Vieux de la Montagne', and Chapter XI, 'Chez Madame Ubu', which is none other than the third section (originally entitled

'L'Art et la Science') of *Guignol*. (The same is true of another chapter which Jarry had intended to include, making the number of chapters up to 12, but which was sacrificed to the publisher's demand that the novel be shortened, namely, the short five-part narrative originally published as *L'Autre Alceste* in the *Revue Blanche* of 15 October 1896.[37]) Jarry's original plan was altered in two other respects also. An intended chapter entitled 'Chez Margot' was replaced by the existing Chapter VIII, 'La Peur chez l'Amour', which Rachilde later claimed to have written in response to a challenge from her young friend to 'faire du Jarry';[38] and the intended final chapter, 'Chez Dame Jocaste ou l'Amour Absolu', also disappeared to become the starting point for an entirely separate and quite different novel, being replaced by the above-mentioned extract from *Guignol*, which portrays the secret tryst of Mère Ubu with her lover in the latrines.

L'Amour en visites thus consists of a rather motley collection of episodes, or 'visits', as Jarry chooses to call them. The first seven feature a young hero named Lucien, who offers certain superficial resemblances with Jarry himself: he is Breton, from a solidly bourgeois provincial background, small of stature, a keen athlete, with a dark complexion and large, flashing, dark eyes – eyes whose 'sombre largeur', as Jarry self-indulgently puts it, are 'pleine des choses inquiétantes attestatrices de la race dont on fait les déserteurs ou les assassins; la race . . . de ces aventuriers écumeurs des océans de jadis' ['full of those disquieting things which are a sign of the race of which deserters and murderers are made; the race . . . of those buccaneering adventurers of former times'].[39] These chapters recount, successively, the prelude to the would-be sexual initiation of the young Lucien as a 15-year-old schoolboy with the family chambermaid ('Chez Manette'); his visit, as a very drunken young conscript, to a high-class courtesan in her luxurious *hôtel* ('Chez Manon'); his efforts, as a young writer, to escape the attentions of a lecherous 'old lady' ('Chez la Vieille Dame'); Lucien's attempts to seduce a duchess ('Chez la grande dame'); his involvement, in an embarrassing *malentendu*, with a naïvely precocious young cousin ('Chez la petite cousine'); and his attempts to elude the manoeuvres used by women to ensnare their chosen partner ('Chez la fiancée'). The seventh chapter, 'Chez le médecin', is a strange monologue addressed to a doctor, revolving around the theme of purity (in which Lucien paradoxically lays claim to an absolute purity of sexlessness).

One can perhaps understand, from this brief résumé of the content of these chapters, how Pierre Fort was led into believing that he had before him a simple *roman grivois*. Not only the subject-matter, moreover, but also many features of the book's style appear on the surface to belong to a conventional vein. Jarry reveals himself an expert in the art of racy narrative (though punctuated by some very

Jarryesque imagery), alternating with rapid exchanges of conventional dialogue. So expert, in fact, that one soon realizes that he is here
parodying the style of the conventional theatre and *vaudeville* as well
as that of the popular *roman feuilleton*. Far from being intended to
titillate, the whole tenor of Jarry's style is satirical. Moreover, the
satire goes beyond that of conventional literary forms to embrace the
entire *bourgeois* social world in which Lucien's adventures take place;
each of these first seven chapters expresses their author's loathing of
bourgeois conventions and hypocrisy, and indeed of a whole social
milieu.

This attack reaches its climax in Chapter III, 'Chez la Vieille Dame',
a brilliant and ferocious piece of satire based on an episode in his own
life. For the 'Old Lady' in question is none other than Berthe (de)
Courrière, former mistress of such men as the sculptor Clésinger and
General Boulanger and currently mistress and housekeeper of Remy
de Gourmont, who had set her lecherous sights on Jarry as well as
upon a host of other young men attached to the Symbolist movement. Though she is not named (all her letters are in fact signed 'La
Vieille Dame' or 'L.V.D.'), the allusion must have been clear to all of
Jarry's friends; moreover, Jarry actually reproduces a series of letters
and telegrams from Berthe to himself, as well as the text of a long,
appallingly bad poem in the best rhetorical mystico-symbolist manner
which she had once hidden within the pages of a book which she had
lent to him. Small wonder that the publication of this chapter almost
landed its author in prison.

Chapter III exudes in almost every line Jarry's utter loathing of the
person of Berthe. The following extract is a good example:

LA VIEILLE DAME: J'ai changé devant vous cinq fois de robe, et vous n'avez
pas regardé. J'ai des robes fendues sur le côté, afin qu'on aperçoive dessous
mes caleçons jaunes, et il suffit de défaire une seule agrafe pour que
s'évanouisse toute la robe. Et je les ai fait construire spécialement pour
l'adultère.

Je ne me lave jamais, sinon avec de la vaseline. Je l'achète à bas prix chez
un pharmacien suburbain, lequel me fournit aussi de la pommade anti-
herpétique.

Ces soins m'ont permis de conserver la finesse de ma peau. Oh! ne me
regardez pas ainsi à la lumière. Ce ne sont que de petits boutons rouges.

> [THE OLD LADY: I have changed my dress five times in front of you, and
> you have not looked. I have dresses split up the sides, so that my yellow
> drawers can be seen beneath them, and it needs only a single hook to be
> undone for the whole dress to slide off. And I had them made especially for
> adultery.
> I never wash, except with vaseline. I buy it cheaply from a back-street
> chemist, who also supplies me with anti-herpetic ointment.
> By these means I have been able to keep my skin in good condition. Oh!
> do not look at me like that in the light. They are only little red spots.][40]

This attitude of disgust expressed here, moreover, extends far beyond the immediate context. In all seven of these above-mentioned chapters there is evidence of the same ferocious misogyny, the same revulsion felt towards women in general, at least as physical beings. It would be going too far to see in *L'Amour en visites* evidence for Roger Shattuck's allegation of 'psychological impotency in the presence of any woman he [Jarry] might have loved':[41] one cannot really draw too general a conclusion from the terrors of the 15-year-old Lucien in Chapter I. Nevertheless, Lucien's adventures (with the possible exception of Chapter IV, 'Chez la grande dame') betray a curious reluctance on his part to capitalize upon a situation and to consummate a relationship.

The remaining four chapters move away entirely from Lucien and from more-or-less conventional narrative and dialogue first to allegory, then to poetic drama, and finally to scatological farce. Rachilde's claim to have been the author of Chapter VIII, 'La Peur chez l'Amour', may well be true; it is impossible to tell from an analysis of the text whether it is authentic Jarry or the result of a very skilful imitation. In any case, it matters little, since the chapter is almost purely a rather laboured literary exercise, making use of wordplay and elements of imagery reminiscent of *Les Minutes de sable mémorial* and other of Jarry's early works. Chapter IX, 'Chez la Muse', also features an allegorical dialogue, this time between the poet ('Lui') and his Muse ('Elle'), in which Jarry satirizes the Romantic concept of the female Muse and continues his ferocious onslaught on womankind as a whole and, by implication, upon heterosexual love – the imagery recalling at times the savage onslaughts of 'Les Prolégomènes de Haldernablou' in *Les Minutes*. Here the wordplay exhibits a lightness of touch and occasional flicker of humour absent in the previous chapter, as well as a skilful use of rhyme and rhythm. Finally, *L'Amour en visites* is brought to a close with the poetic drama 'Le Vieux de la Montagne' and 'Chez Madame Ubu'.

For all the suggestiveness of the title and the apparent content of certain chapters, therefore, *L'Amour en visites* is a very different work from that which it first appears to be. The prelude to a number of sexual encounters (whose outcome remains uncertain); a piece of virulent satire; allegory and poetic drama; and the conjunction of the pseudo-sexual and the scatological in a scene of pure farce, the whole underscored by a savage anti-feminism, in which sex is associated with sordidness and squalor – all this is a far cry from the book which Pierre Fort believed he was publishing. So far, in fact, that one ends up wondering whether *L'Amour en visites* can really be regarded as a work of 'erotica' at all, in any sense of the word. Indeed, just as the inclusion in *Les Minutes* of the text of *Guignol* served to 'depoeticize' the work as a whole, so too the inclusion of its third part here as the last chapter of the novel serves to provide a final eloquent comment upon the volume and its subject matter as a whole.

As the last chapter of *L'Amour en visites* suggests, the relationship between this and other of Jarry's works is much closer than might at first sight appear; Jarry indeed underlines the link – while at the same time indulging in a spot of self-publicity – by quoting from both *Ubu Roi* and *Les Jours et les Nuits* in the body of the text, and explicitly acknowledging these sources in footnotes. In particular, a link exists, both through the obvious similarity of their titles and on the level of themes and imagery, between *L'Amour en visites* and Jarry's next and emotionally most highly charged novel, *L'Amour absolu*. It seems probable, in fact, that the latter arose out of his idea for the original concluding chapter of *L'Amour en visites*, entitled 'Chez Dame Jocaste ou l'Amour Absolu', the theme of incest (Jocasta, wife of Laius, was the mother of Oedipus) upon which this chapter was to turn opening up such imaginative possibilities to its author that he preferred to incorporate it into a larger work. Alongside the theme of incest, moreover, the starting point for another of the key ideas developed in *L'Amour absolu* can be seen in Lucien's paradoxical claim, in his monologue to the bemused doctor in Chapter VII, to being the product of a Virgin birth and hence, by implication, the 'Son of God'.

An element of mystery surrounds the circumstances of the publication of *L'Amour absolu*. Jarry completed the work in February 1899, and it was published the same year in a limited facsimile manuscript edition without any indication of publisher. It is probable that he had hoped for publication by the Éditions du Mercure de France, but that Vallette expressed doubts about both the form of the book and in particular about its intelligibility. Jarry, however, stuck to his guns, refusing to countenance any alteration whatsoever to his text – an attitude in striking contrast to his stance over the composition of *L'Amour en visites*, as the following extract from a letter to Vallette reveals:

J'ai oublié de vous dire hier au sujet de mon in-18 et ce matin je me suis levé beaucoup trop tard pour venir vous en informer, qu'il est bien entendu que même s'il paraît invendable au Mercure, je n'y change rien du tout dans l'ordre des chapitres ni en rien.

> [I forgot to tell you yesterday à propos of my book and this morning I got up too late to come and let you know, that it goes without saying that even if at the Mercure it seems unsaleable, I shan't change anything at all in the order of the chapters or in any respect.][42]

Did he then undertake – rashly, since he had no money – to publish the work at his own expense, Vallette subsequently coming to his rescue as a friend rather than publisher and paying the bill out of his own pocket? Whatever the case, the Editions du Mercure de France subsequently became the depository for the 50 copies of the novel that were printed.

L'Amour absolu is the most difficult of Jarry's works both to summarize and to characterize by reference to conventional literary forms. On the simplest, and most banal, level it relates the life story of a man condemned to death for the murder of his mother with whom he had had an incestuous relationship. But such a bald summary can give only a hopelessly distorted view of a work which, though its author subtitled it a 'novel', might just as aptly have been called a 'prose poem'. Though there is a narrative element present in the work, it is far from being continuous, while the notion of 'characters' in any conventional sense is even less appropriate. For if the action revolves around a single 'character' (to whom Jarry gives the name Emmanuel Dieu), his identity is not single but multiple. On one level he is simply a man awaiting execution for the crime of murder at the coming dawn. But on another level he is, as Jarry informs us,' un homme dans le genre de Dieu'.[43] Indeed, he is doubly 'God', since Emmanuel – a name given, in the Book of Isaiah, to the coming Messiah and applied in the Gospel of Matthew (1.23) to Jesus – means in Hebrew 'God with us'. Emmanuel is thus at one and the same time man and God, the Son of God, the Holy Ghost, as well as simultaneously the son, husband and lover of Miriam/Varia, an identity formulated by him in the words:

Femme, il y a un seul Dieu en trois personnes, je suis un seul Dieu en trois personnes, j'ai huit cent sextillions de siècles, avec tout ce qu'il y a dedans, parce que c'est moi qui les ai faits, et j'avais l'éternité quand j'ai créé le premier siècle! Je suis le Fils, je suis ton fils, je suis l'Esprit, je suis ton mari de toute éternité, ton mari et ton fils, très pure Jocaste!

> [Woman, there is one God in three persons, I am one God in three persons, I am eight hundred sextillion centuries old, with everything that they contain, because it is I who made them, and my age was eternity when I created the first century! I am the Son, I am your son, I am the Spirit, I am your husband from all eternity, your husband and your son, most pure Jocasta!][44]

Similarly, his mother and mistress, if not multiple, at least takes on two distinct identities. She is at one and the same time Varia, the wife of Emmanuel's (adoptive) father Maître Joseb, the flesh-and-blood living woman who nurses and who is incestuously attracted to Emmanuel; and Miriam (Hebrew form of the name Mary), wife of Joseph the carpenter and the 'Mother of God' – the opposite of the living Varia, indeed almost the unconscious identity of the latter, who comes into existence only when Varia is sleeping or unconscious ... or dead: 'Miriam, pour *être*, anéantissait Varia.'[45] Like Emmanuel,

Miriam is ageless, existing from all eternity, identifiable (in part at least) not only with the Virgin Mary of Christianity but with Venus and other pagan goddesses, representing something of an eternal woman and mother figure.

Lastly if, on one level, Emmanuel is a murderer awaiting execution at the coming dawn, and on another he is the 'Son of God' reliving the story of his Passion, on a third level he is quite simply a man dreaming 'assis près de sa lampe', whose 'imprisonment' is merely within the confines of his own 'skull'. As Jarry tells us at the end of the first chapter, 'S'il n'a pas tué, pourtant, ou si *l'on n'a pas compris qu'il tuait*, il n'a d'autre prison que la boîte de son crâne, et n'est qu'un homme qui rêve assis près de sa lampe.' ['If he has not killed, however, or if *they have not understood that he has killed*, he has no other prison than the shell of his skull, and is only a man sitting dreaming by his lamp.']⁴⁶ The novel is therefore, on this level, simply a projection of his own dreams or fantasies – or, as Jarry puts it, the 'creation' of his own 'desire':

La Vérité humaine, c'est ce que l'homme veut: un *désir*.
La Vérité de Dieu, ce qu'il *crée*.
Quand on n'est ni l'un ni l'autre – Emmanuel –, *sa* Vérité, c'est *la création de son désir*.

> [Human Truth is what man wishes: a *desire*.
> The Truth of God, that which he *creates*.
> When one is neither the one nor the other – Emmanuel – , *his* Truth is *the creation of his desire.*]⁴⁷

Far from awaiting execution, Emmanuel is merely awaiting the onset of sleep – though a sleep which itself (insofar as it obliterates consciousness and opens the door to the world of dreams) resembles a 'temporary' death: we are told in Chapter I that 'Emmanuel Dieu se sert du sommeil, vieux Léthé, comme d'éternité provisoire' ['Emmanuel Dieu makes use of sleep, that old Lethe, as temporary eternity'];⁴⁸ and Chapter III bears the significant title 'Ô sommeil, singe de la mort' ['Oh sleep, mimic of death'].

It is the complexity, and ambiguities, of these identities and relationships which determine the complexities of the novel's development, and which explain also the significance of the title. For the 'love' with which *L'Amour absolu* deals is 'absolute' in every sense of the word, being a fusion of several different kinds of love: that of the child for its mother, that of the sexually maturing adolescent for that same mother, and that – eternal, in the person of Emmanuel Dieu – of 'God' himself.

At the centre of the novel stands Emmanuel's relationship with his mother, the corollary of which is a hatred of and contempt for his father which leads to a wish for the murder of the latter. In his exploration of what Freud was to baptize the 'Oedipus complex', as of other ideas in the novel, there is a striking similarity between the insights of Jarry and those of Freud. That Jarry could not, for purely chronological reasons, have known the work of Freud is beyond doubt; but he did have a profound knowledge of the work of the French school of psychology which flourished in the 1880s and 1890s and he was keenly interested in particular in the researches of psychologists such as Pierre Janet and Alfred Binet into such phenomena as split personality, hypnosis and catalepsy, and in the work of Charcot on the subject of hysteria; these researches were themselves a major source of inspiration to the young Sigmund Freud during his years of study in Paris in the 1890s.[49] But if Jarry borrows ideas from such sources, the use to which he puts them, as in *Les Jours et les Nuits*, is peculiarly his own. The same applies, moreover, to the autobiographical data which the novel contains: those details from Jarry's own early life which are used in tracing the career of Emmanuel Dieu are transformed and incorporated by him into an imaginative whole which far surpasses the banal circumstances of the life of the work's author.

Indeed, in its fusion of autobiographical data, psychological theory and insights, mythology, religion and literary references, *L'Amour absolu* is one of the densest and richest of Jarry's works, opening up a wealth of possible allusions and interpretations. In it, the ambition expressed in the 'Linteau' of *Les Minutes de sable mémorial* to 'faire dans la route des phrases un carrefour de tous les mots' combines with the Mallarmean ideal of 'l'Oeuvre' or 'le Livre', a work which in its density and multiplicity of allusion will constitute a résumé of existence as a whole.

If the main part of *L'Amour absolu* traces the life-story – or the 'Passion' – of Emmanuel, the first three chapters constitute a kind of prologue to the work, introducing its dominant themes and images. The dominant imagery is, as in *Les Jours et les Nuits*, one of light and darkness, the title of the opening chapter offering us Jarry's own variation upon the divine injunction of *Genesis*: 'Let there be light!', in the form: 'Que la ténèbre soit!' Where, therefore, in the earlier novel, Sengle sought – in part at least – to achieve a fusion of 'night' and 'day', of the waking consciousness and of dream, here 'day' and 'light' are rejected entirely in favour of darkness: the darkness of night, as Emmanuel Dieu in his prison cell awaits the coming dawn and execution; the darkness of sleep and oblivion; and the darkness of Emmanuel's own inner world of memories and dreams. This darkness is illuminated only by the harsh electric light of his prison cell (likened to a glaring sun or star), or by the 'lamp' of his own awareness (which perhaps owes something to the magic lamp of Aladdin in *The Thousand and One Nights*).

Barely less important is the imagery of imprisonment. The two sets of images are in fact juxtaposed in the opening lines of the book:

Il habite une des branches de l'étoile de pierre.
La prison de L A S A N T É.
Comme il est condamné à mort, la branche où se cataloguent les condamnés à mort.

> [*He* lives in one of the arms of the stone-built star.
> The prison of L A S A N T É.
> As he is condemned to death, the arm in which are catalogued those condemned to death.][50]

Emmanuel Dieu is 'l'éternel incarcéré, de qui toutes les paroles répondent à des interrogatoires' ['the eternally incarcerated one, all of whose words are a reply to a constant questioning'].[51] Images of enclosed spaces abound in the novel, while closely related to such images are the themes of strangulation and suffocation, echoed in the tale of Sindbad and the Old Man of the Sea, which culminate in the attempted strangulation of Emmanuel's father. In this respect also one can see a parallel between *L'Amour absolu* and earlier works, in particular *Les Minutes de sable mémorial*, suggestive of the existence within their author of an obsessive sense of 'imprisonment' within the confines of his own 'self'.

For Jarry, however, the withdrawal into the closed if infinite world of the 'self' has other attributes also. It constitutes a movement towards 'God', towards 'Being' (that is, the philosophical opposite of 'Living'), and towards 'eternity' – whence in *L'Amour absolu* the identification of Emmanuel, a man 'qui rêve assis près de sa lampe', with 'God'. For if Emmanuel is imprisoned within his own 'skull', he is also free to wander at will through the realms of imagination and memory and to *create* anew within those realms, enjoying the infinite creativity of God. But at the same time, this state of being which Jarry identifies with 'God' and with 'eternity' is also, according to a definition put forward in *César-Antechrist*, a form of, or an approach towards, 'death':

La mort est le ressaisissement concentré de la Pensée; elle ne s'étoile plus infiniment vers le monde extérieur; sa circonférence, nyctalope pupille, se rétrécit vers son centre; c'est ainsi qu'elle devient Dieu, qu'elle commence d'être.

> [Death is the concentrated re-possession of itself by Thought; it no longer radiates out infinitely towards the external world; its circumference, nyctalopic pupil, contracts towards the centre; it is thus that it becomes God, that it begins to be.][52]

Thus the theme of 'absolute' love merges with the theme of death, which, more than any other single theme, comes to dominate the novel. This idea of death, moreover, is obscurely linked to that of murder. Emmanuel (and, through him, no doubt, Jarry) identifies, 'avec redoutable et désirée certitude', with '*les grands criminels* et LES CONDAMNÉS À MORT' ['with formidable and wished-for certainty', with '*the great criminals* and THOSE CONDEMNED TO DEATH'],[53] while Jarry also cryptically hints at the theme of murder in the line: 'S'il n'a pas tué, pourtant, ou si *l'on n'a pas compris qu'il tuait*' ['If he has not killed, however, or if *they have not understood that he has killed*']. What private obsession this series of parallel themes hints at in Jarry himself will become clear in an analysis of the remaining chapters of the novel.

The following 11 chapters of *L'Amour absolu* relate the 'confession' of Emmanuel, or the various stages of his 'Passion', 'de l'enfance à trente-trois ans'.[54] He is able to relive these various stages of his existence in the space of one night thanks to the infinite elasticity of the time of memory: 'nous vivons un temps infiniment *condensé*, un instant nous suffit à vivre toute notre vie' ['we live an infinitely *condensed* time, a moment suffices to enable us to live our whole life'].[55] His confession is based, not surprisingly, on the reminiscences of the childhood and youth of his creator. It is, however, important to remember that we are dealing here with a fictionalized transposition and not with simple autobiography. Thus Jarry's own commercial-traveller father is transmuted into the Lampaul notary, Maître Joseb, who, if he contains something of Anselme Jarry (his identification with the traveller Sindbad, for example, suggests something of his profession), contains elements also of Alfred's maternal grandfather (a *juge de paix* and descendant of a long line of *notaires*) and of his property-owning but uncultured cousins, the Gorvels. Similarly the Lycée Henri IV, which Jarry attended, becomes the Lycée Condorcet; whilst the Gare Montparnasse, at which he caught the train for Laval and Rennes, becomes the Gare St-Lazare. Other details, however, insofar as we can believe the testimony of his sister Charlotte, are straightforwardly autobiographical, amongst them those concerning his early schooling, his love of solitude and of the Breton countryside. And others again, such as the games and fantasies of the child, we can reasonably assume to be based directly on his own early life. With these reminiscences, Jarry intermingles a wealth of allusions and images drawn from his past and present reading: from his eternal favourite Rabelais; from Dumas' *Comte de Monte Christo*; from Quinet's *Ahasvérus*, with its tale of the Wandering Jew ('Le Juif errant', which he transforms into 'le Christ-Errant', the title of the second chapter); from the Gospels, Christian tradition and the Catholic liturgy; from classical history and mythology; from Norse mythology (the figure of the God Odin and his wolf companions); from French folklore (the fairy Mélusine); and from *The Thousand and One Nights*, one of his favourite books then appearing in the translation of Dr Mardrus (the Giant Roc, Scheherezade, Aladdin, Sindbad).

Linking these various episodes and allusions are the twin themes of Emmanuel's love for his mother and his utter contempt for and loathing of his father: in purely human terms Varia and Joseb, Breton forms of Mary and Jóseph. His father, Maître Joseb, as he is called by the simple folk of Lampaul, is satirized for his false pretensions to superiority over his fellow-citizens, for the futility of his occupations, and for his ignorance and lack of culture:

Mais Me Joseb était notaire à la mode de Bretagne.
Notaire y signifie généralement toute personne qui écrit. . . .
Or, Me Joseb écrivait et lisait à peine . . . .

> [But Maître Joseb was a notary after the Breton fashion.
> In Brittany, notary generally means any person who writes. . . .
> Now, Maître Joseb only barely wrote and read . . . .]

He is also dismissed contemptuously at one point, through the identification with Sindbad, as 'un vieux colporteur à barbe blanche'.[56] The novel however goes beyond the mere expression of contempt to that of sexual jealousy and hatred, as Emmanuel meditates upon his parents' lovemaking – a jealousy which leads ultimately to the conception of a scheme for the murder of his father (although, curiously, it is not himself but his mother whom he wills to commit this act).

Much more important, however, than Emmanuel's hatred and jealousy of his father is the account of his incestuous relationship with his mother, Varia. Chapter VIII recounts Varia's visit to her 15-year-old son in an isolated customs officer's hut above the cliffs along the Breton coast,[57] passing on her way through a host of plants and living creatures which take on clearly erotic, and particularly phallic, associations. Though this episode ends in flight (followed by the sudden arrival of a customs officer, whom Varia treacherously silences with a kiss on the mouth), other encounters follow. One of these, related in the following chapter, 'De sinople à une hermine en abîme', even has a ring of *vaudeville* about it worthy of *L'Amour en visites*: the first time Emmanuel addressed his mother – visiting her son in Paris and waiting for him outside the Lycée Condorcet – no longer as 'maman' but as 'Madame', 'elle lui proposa, à la sortie de Condorcet, le "fiacre au Bois et à l'heure", ou le cabinet particulier' ['meeting him as he left Condorcet, she offered him the alternative of "a carriage in the Bois by the hour", or a private dining-room'].[58] Subsequent chapters recount their clandestine embraces under the very nose of the drunken notary, as well as further visits by Varia to her *lycéen* son in Paris.

Up to this point, Emmanuel's drama would seem to constitute a classic example of what Freud was to call the Oedipus complex – love for one's mother coupled with sexual jealousy of and a desire to kill one's father. But a significant departure from this pattern occurs as the note of farce gives way to an atmosphere of dramatic intensity. For closely allied to the theme of incestuous love is that of *fear*. Varia, on her way to seek out Emmanuel in his *cabane de douanier*, and again when confronted with her son's sexuality, is seized by a panic of fear. And in the course of one of their encounters a look of fear, described as 'the dregs of Love', passes from Emmanuel's eyes to those of his mother:

Mais soudain quelque chose de noir . . . choit des pupilles d'Emmanuel dans les pupilles de Varia.
La lie de l'Amour, qui est la Peur.
Varia tremble comme sous une neige, dans une nuit à voir la neige noire.

> [But suddenly something black . . . falls from the pupils of Emmanuel into the pupils of Varia.
> The dregs of Love, which are Fear.
> Varia trembles as if under a blanket of snow, in a blackness so intense as to make snow appear black.][59]

Fear leads to violence, as Varia in a frenzy seizes a dagger and attempts – unsuccessfully, thanks to his hypnotic powers – to stab her son. And incestuous attraction turns ultimately to hatred and contempt not only of his father, but of his mother as well, leading finally to the murder of his mother, for which Emmanuel is, at the beginning of the novel, awaiting execution.[60]

But Varia is only one of the identities of Emmanuel's mistress or lover, who is also Miriam, the embodiment of eternal woman- and motherhood, who has existed alongside Emmanuel Dieu from all eternity and whose existence, far from being annulled by the death of Varia, is on the contrary all the more fully affirmed:

Emmanuel Dieu savait si bien que par le *meurtre* de Varia (meurtre plus réel que la radiation de l'univers selon la chair, l'expulsion hors de l'Absolu – à tout le poignard qui est l'épée de feu de l'Ange qui ferme les Paradis . . .) il n'avait pas tué Miriam!
AU CONTRAIRE.
La vraie Miriam était en dehors de Varia.

> [Emmanuel Dieu knew perfectly well that by the *murder* of Varia (murder more real than the radiation of the universe experienced by all flesh, the expulsion from the Absolute – at the point of the dagger which is the sword of the Angel who closes the gates of Paradise . . .) he had not killed Miriam!
> ON THE CONTRARY.
> The true Miriam existed outside of Varia.][61]

Where, moreover, Varia is obliged to submit to the sexual demands of her husband, thus provoking her son's jealousy, Miriam has no part in these sordid encounters; her relationship with Emmanuel remains a purely spiritual, ideal one:

'Mais ils font des choses, quoiqu'il soit très vieux.
Pourvu qu'on fasse ça avec elle, ça lui est bien égal qu'on soit beau ou laid.
Il ne m'a jamais connue, *moi*.
Il ne connaît que *l'autre*.'

> ['But they do things together, even though he is very old.
> Provided that men do it with her, she doesn't care whether they are handsome or ugly.
> He has never known *me*.
> He knows only *the other*.']⁶²

Miriam is also, by implication, the embodiment of 'absolute' truth whereas Varia – whose name, on one level the Breton form of Mary, also enables Jarry to make of her 'celle qui ment' – is the embodiment of falsehood and deceit, which is seen as a compulsion of the female sex: women lie 'par le chemin des écoliers. Avec détails. Analytiquement.'; 'le sexe du Mensonge' is itself 'femelle' ['by the path of schoolboys. With details. Analytically.'; 'the sex of Lying' is itself 'female']; or, as Jarry also puts it in a lapidary phrase: 'Le sexe de Varia est l'oeillère d'un masque' ['The sex of Varia is the eyehole of a mask'].⁶³ Most important of all, however, is the opposition between life and death embodied by the contrast between Varia and Miriam. For Varia is 'celle *qui est vivante*',⁶⁴ implicitly identified with the figure of Eve whose name, according to the Book of Genesis (3.20), means 'the mother of all living' and who therefore constitutes a symbol of human life itself. Whereas Miriam, through repeated play on the part of Jarry upon the phonetic similarity of the three words *Miriam, myrrhe* (one of the three precious gifts brought to the Infant Jesus by the Three Wise men, but used also in the ancient world in the embalming of corpses) and *mort*, becomes at first implicitly, and then explicitly, identified with death: 'ma petite Miriam, MYRRHE plutôt, toi qui est morte'.⁶⁵ Thus the theme of 'absolute' love, as embodied by the love of Emmanuel Dieu for his wife and mistress Miriam, is indissolubly associated with that of death.

It is easy to see in *L'Amour absolu* a fictionalized transposition of Jarry's own relationship with his parents, and in particular of his deep and lasting attraction to his mother. It is also possible to see in the dissociation of Varia and Miriam, and in the mysterious association of Miriam with death, both something of his attitude towards his mother and an oblique allusion to the circumstances of her death. For weeks on end, in the early spring of 1893, Caroline Jarry had remained by her son's bedside during a grave illness, nursing him back to life and health from the brink of death, only to die herself, a short time later, as a result of illness and exhaustion. Jarry never got over the sense of loss which her death produced; and it is possible also that he was afflicted by a lifelong sense of guilt born of the idea that she had given her life for his and that he was as a result – albeit unwittingly and unwillingly – responsible for her death, or 'murder'. It may be that it was in an attempt to expunge this intolerable sense of guilt that he created the figure of Miriam, representative of the 'eternal' love between mother and son extending beyond the grave: 'Emmanuel Dieu savait ... que par le *meurtre* de Varia ... il n'avait pas tué Miriam! AU CONTRAIRE.' Thus devotion to his mother became a devotion to the *memory* of her love, beyond death – and a cult, almost, of Death itself.

Such an interpretation must, however, remain conjectural. And, much more important, it restricts the significance of *L'Amour absolu* to a purely autobiographical plane. For the novel is not, as has been made clear, simply a transposition of Jarry's own life: it is also an attempt to give expression to themes which its author saw as having a universal significance. Emmanuel is not only (in part) Jarry, he is identified, implicitly and explicitly, with the figure of Christ, whose career his own life parallels in a number of respects. Further, on another plane again, his 'Passion', multiplied a millionfold and perpetually renewed, is that of mankind itself: 'et il y a à toutes les aubes autant de millions de Dieux intermittents semblables à moi qu'il y a de milliers d'autels, de myriades de messes et de milliards d'hosties consacrées.'['and there are at every dawn as many millions of intermittent Gods like me as there are thousands of altars, myriads of masses and billions of consecrated hosts.']⁶⁶ In the abundance of its religious, literary and other images and allusions, *L'Amour absolu* evokes resonances which go far beyond the life of its author to become also something in the nature of a meditation upon the universal theme of death: the closing lines of the novel, which occur amidst a cluster of religious images as Emmanuel descends from his 'mansarde' to pray at the feet of the statue of the Virgin, constitute a quotation (slightly, but significantly, modified) of the last two lines of the *Ave Maria*:

'... Priez pour nous ...
À présent, qui est l'heure de notre mort.'

['... Pray for us ...
Now, which is the hour of our death.']⁶⁷

In the complexity of its imagery and allusions, as in the terseness and lapidary quality of its short, single-sentence paragraphs, *L'Amour absolu* has something of the richness, density of meaning and sonorous quality of the finest verse. It contains also a wealth of phonetic and imaginative associations, as Jarry plays endlessly upon both the form and meanings of words, creating a parallel to the complex network of relationships which the novel portrays in the complexity and polysemy of its language also. Emotionally, too, the novel embraces a vast range of registers, from the sardonically or whimsically humorous, through the ribald, the declamatory, the nostalgic and tenderly evocative to the pathetic and intensely passionate. If some parts, moreover, have a ring of deliberate blasphemy about them, others in turn are suffused with a deep (if unorthodox) religious feeling. Though a difficult work, *L'Amour absolu* stands as one of the richest and finest of Jarry's creations, as well as one of the most revealing of the secret recesses of the mind of its creator. No less revealing of that mind, but in a totally different way, representing a very different side of his outlook and personality, is a work which was completed only a few months before the writing of *L'Amour absolu* and to which we must now turn: his monumental *Gestes et opinions du docteur Faustroll, pataphysicien*.

Chapter Seven

Faustroll and pataphysics: from cabbage-leaves to the surface of God

JARRY'S *Gestes et opinions du docteur Faustroll, pataphysicien*, which he subtitled 'roman néo-scientifique', is the densest, most complex and, at first sight, most bewildering of all his works. In it, even more than in *L'Amour absolu*, he set out to realize the ambition formulated in the 'Linteau' of *Les Minutes de sable mémorial* to 'suggérer au lieu de dire, faire dans la route des phrases un carrefour de tous les mots' ['to suggest instead of stating, to create in the highway of sentences a crossroads of all the words']. By such means he has attempted, in *Faustroll*, to create a synthesis of his own wisdom, or at least of his views in the fields of literature, art, science and philosophy. As we are told in the novel, in the manuscript 'entrusted' by Dr Faustroll to the bailiff, Panmuphle,

Faustroll avait noté une toute petite partie du Beau qu'il savait, et une toute petite partie du Vrai qu'il savait, durant la syzygie des mots; et on aurait pu par cette petite facette reconstruire tout art et toute science, c'est-à-dire Tout . . . .

> [Faustroll had noted down a tiny part of the Beauty which he knew, and a tiny part of the Truth which he knew, during the syzygy of words; and it would have been possible to reconstruct from this tiny facet all art and all science, that is to say the Totality . . . .][1]

Faustroll is thus a work almost encyclopaedic in character, opening up, through its multiple allusions and cross-references, a vast field of speculation. As such, it is seen by many devotees of Jarry as the pinnacle of his achievement, and indeed constitutes the 'Bible' of all good pataphysicians. But *Faustroll* can also easily appear to be the most incoherent of all Jarry's works – lacking in structure and juxtaposing the most disparate elements, a work in which the account of an imaginary journey is interspersed with the scrupulously exact reproduction of legal documents, with literary, artistic and musical 'homages' in the form of descriptive tableaux of a series of 'imaginative universes', with descriptions of 'imaginary' paintings, and with passages of (pseudo-) scientific analysis and philosophico-metaphysical speculation!

It was the latter impression, alas, which determined the reaction of contemporary publishers, and the history of the book's publication is a sorry one. It was completed in the spring of 1898 at the Phalanstère in Corbeil. Jarry fully expected it to be published by the Editions du Mercure de France and prepared his manuscript accordingly. But after the fiasco of *Les Jours et les Nuits,* Vallette prudently refused to publish so diffuse and bewildering a work. Jarry then offered it to Thadée Natanson, co-editor of the *Revue Blanche,* who also, courteously but no less firmly, declined to publish it. Thereupon Jarry cut his losses and accepted the compromise of a partial publication in the pages of the *Mercure* review, Chapters VI and X to XXV appearing in the issue for May 1898. He had to content himself with using these printed pages from the *Mercure* intercalated with manuscript pages to make a number of private copies of the work which he presented to a few chosen friends – and wrote with wry humour at the end of one such copy the 'prophetic' note: 'Ce livre ne sera publié intégralement que quand l'auteur aura acquis assez d'expérience pour en savourer toutes les beautés.' ['This book will only be published in full when the author has acquired enough experience to savour all its beauties.']² It was not until 1911, four years after Jarry's death, that *Faustroll* was finally published, thanks to the efforts of his friends Gaston Danville and Jean Saltas, by the publisher Eugène Fasquelle. The poet Guillaume Apollinaire was alone in (briefly) reviewing the book, hailing its appearance as 'la plus importante publication de 1911'.³

Though *Gestes et opinions du docteur Faustroll, pataphysicien* was completed early in 1898 (the first chapter opens with the bailiff's statement: 'L'an mil huit cent quatre-vingt-dix-huit, le huit février'),⁴ when Jarry was still only 24 years of age, the idea of a work which would contain an outline of his pataphysics goes back several years earlier. It seems that he at first thought of writing a 'theoretical' treatise on the subject: the back of the title page of *Les Minutes de sable mémorial,* published in 1894, announced, along with the forthcoming publication of *César-Antechrist,* 'On prépare: *Éléments de pataphysique'.*⁵ It is probable, in fact, that the first chapter of Book II, 'Éléments de Pataphysique', and the three concluding chapters, 'Selon Ibicrate le Géomètre', 'Pantaphysique et catachimie' and 'De la Surface de Dieu', were originally written quite independently of the later work, in 1894 or 1895, since all three of the latter betray the same mathematical obsession as *César-Antechrist,* in particular that concerning the signs Plus and Minus. Jarry's reasons for abandoning this initial project are unknown, although the most probable explanation is that he came to realize that the invention of a personage such as Dr

Faustroll would convey the *spirit* of pataphysics far more effectively than any purely theoretical presentation.

What, indeed, could be more 'pataphysical' (leaving aside for a moment a discussion of the precise meaning of that term) than Jarry's portrait of Faustroll? –

Le docteur Faustroll naquit en Circassie, en 1898 (le XXe siècle avait [−2]ans), et à l'âge de soixante-trois ans.

À cet âge-là, lequel il conserva toute sa vie, le docteur Faustroll était un homme de taille moyenne, soit, pour être exactement véridique, de $(8 \times 10^{10} + 10^9 + 4 \times 10^8 + 5 \times 10^6)$ diamètres d'atomes; de peau jaune d'or, au visage glabre, sauf unes moustaches [*sic*] vert de mer, telles que les portait le roi Saleh; les cheveux alternativement, poil par poil, blond cendré et très noir, ambiguïté auburnienne changeante avec l'heure du soleil; les yeux, deux capsules de simple encre à écrire, préparée comme l'eau-de-vie de Dantzick, avec des spermatozoïdes d'or dedans.

> [Doctor Faustroll was born in Circassia, in 1898 (the 20th century was −2 years old), at the age of sixty-three.
> At that age, which he retained all his life, Doctor Faustroll was a man of medium height, namely, to be absolutely accurate, of $8 \times 10^{10} + 10^9 + 4 \times 10^8 + 5 \times 10^6$ atomic diameters; with golden-yellow skin, his face being clean-shaven apart from a pair [*sic*] of sea-green moustaches, such as King Saleh wore; the hairs of his head alternately ash-blond and jet black, producing an auburn ambiguity which changed according to the angle of the sun; his eyes, two capsules of ordinary writing ink, prepared in the same way as Danzig schnapps, with the addition of golden spermatozoa.][6]

In its combination of elements of parody (on Hugo's pompous allusion, in the opening line of the first poem of *Les Feuilles d'automne*, to the year of his own birth, 1802: 'Ce siècle avait deux ans ...'), of deliberate (but wryly comic) nonsense ('naquit ... à l'âge de soixante-trois ans ..., lequel il conserva toute sa vie'), of the juxtaposition of weirdly incongruous details (in the description of Faustroll's complexion, moustaches, hair and eyes), and in its mania for precise and pedantic mathematical calculation, the passage is a microcosm of the novel as a whole.

It goes almost without saying that Faustroll far more truly and fundamentally represents Jarry himself than the mindless monster, Ubu. Ubu is a *persona*, a role adopted by Jarry for the purpose of keeping the world at arm's length; but such a role constitutes an alienation from his true self. Faustroll, too, is in part a role – but a role which, in its very fabrication, represents the essence of the mind of its creator. This identity is broadly hinted at by Jarry in the course of describing Faustroll's adventures, and even through the name he has chosen. 'Faustroll' is a fusion of 'Faust' and 'troll', a Scandinavian goblin or imp and the role which Jarry played in Lugné-Poe's production of Ibsen's *Peer Gynt* in 1896: the name suggest an impish, mischievous, inverted Faust-figure. Among the objects seized by the bailiff Panmuphle is 'un portrait du sieur Faustroll, par AUBREY BEARDSLEY',[7] who is believed to have painted a portrait of Jarry of which all trace has been lost. The library of Faustroll, also seized by Panmuphle, is in part at least that of Jarry himself. And certain of Faustroll's adventures parallel Jarry's own experiences: *inter alia*, the former's expulsion from his lodgings in the rue Richer in 1898 parallels Jarry's own expulsion from his 'Calvaire du Trucidé' on the Boulevard de Port-Royal the previous year; Faustroll's yellow complexion recalls that of his creator after he had poisoned himself with picric acid in order to escape from the army in 1895; and his navigation in a skiff (*as*) through the seas of Paris recalls the numerous fishing and boating expeditions undertaken by Jarry and Vallette on the Seine south of Paris in their *as*.

Faustroll is accompanied on his adventures by two companions, the bailiff, Panmuphle, and the 'dog-faced baboon', Bosse-de-Nage. Both figures, and their names, are satirical. 'Panmuphle' combines the Greek prefix *pan* with the word *mufle*; literally the muzzle or snout of an animal, and metaphorically a boorish and stupid person, the word had been given a new impetus as a term of abuse for the unthinking and uncultured 'bourgeois' by Jarry's friend Laurent Tailhade in his savagely satirical volume of verse, *Au Pays du Mufle* (1891). Panmuphle represents, in part, the commonsensical, naïve 'outsider's' point of view, faithfully if uncomprehendingly recording the *gestes* and *opinions* of Faustroll. But, more than this, he represents the epitome of that 'positivistic' or 'rationalistic' viewpoint of which Faustroll himself – and Jarry's whole science of pataphysics – is the antithesis. Who could be a more perfect spokesman for that viewpoint than a *huissier*, the legalistic dogsbody of a 'rationally' ordered world? Panmuphle's *style*, moreover, is essential in this respect to Jarry's purpose: for what could better symbolize that world than the incomparably rigid formalism of legal documents – documents which are reproduced by Jarry with scrupulous exactitude, extending even to the official seals and stamps.

Bosse-de-Nage, on the other hand, who suffers from a lack of intelligence, being 'moins cyno- qu'hydrocéphale' and who 'ne savait de parole humaine que 'Ha Ha''', is a satire upon Jarry's friend Christian Beck, an aspiring young Belgian writer, contributor to the *Mercure* and butt of Jarry's private jokes partly on account of his unfortunate stutter. (The name – in Old French *nage* or *nache* = buttock – might be translated as 'Bum-Face'.) Faustroll had undertaken to teach his companion to speak, with the result that 'il prononçait assez correctement quelques mots belges . . ., mais le plus souvent il proférait un monosyllabe tautologique: ''Ha Ha'', disait-il en français; et il n'ajoutait rien davantage.' ['he spoke more-or-less correctly a few words of Belgian . . . , but most of the time he uttered a tautological monosyllable: "Ha Ha", he said in French; and he added not a word more.']8 This 'tautological monosyllable' is proferred by Bosse-de-Nage at intervals throughout the novel, as the final comment on all matters.

Gestes et opinions du docteur Faustroll, pataphysicien is essentially the story of a journey, or *périple*, as Jarry calls it (borrowing the word along with many another detail of the work from Rabelais), through the imaginative worlds of literature, painting, music, science, philosophy and theology. The various episodes of the book are loosely tied together by the 'narrative' of Panmuphle. This narrative begins with the bailiff serving an expulsion order on Dr Faustroll for non-payment of rent, and then effecting a distraint upon the good doctor's library, consisting of a total of 27 assorted volumes described 'les 27 livres pairs', 'pairs' being used in the sense of equal in value or status (as in 'parity'), implying the (pataphysical) equivalence of all 27.9 In addition to these books, Panmuphle also seizes two *affiches*, by Toulouse Lautrec and Bonnard, an old picture of the Breton Saint Cado, and a portrait of Faustroll by Aubrey Beardsley. Thereupon Faustroll obliges the bailiff and Bosse-de-Nage to undertake with him a strange circumnavigation 'from Paris to Paris by sea', a journey made in the doctor's skiff, which is in reality a sieve. The idea of the sieve probably derives from Edward Lear's 'Jumblies' (further evidence of Jarry's wide knowledge of foreign literatures, as well as of his predilections) – a piece of amusing nonsense which, however, Jarry attempts to render plausible by means of a lengthy scientific discourse on capillary action and surface tension borrowed from *Soap Bubbles, Their Colour And The Forces Which Mould Them* (1890) by the English physicist C. V. Boys, to whom the chapter is dedicated.10 From his library of 27 volumes, Faustroll conjures up to accompany him on his journey elements from each, described as 'les vingt-sept plus excellentes quintessences d'œuvres qu'aient rapportées les gens curieux de leurs voyages'. ['the twenty-seven most excellent quintessences of works brought back by curious people from their travels'.]11 In their company, rowed by the unfortunate Panmuphle and guided by the light radiating from the glabrous cheeks of Bosse-de-Nage, Faustroll begins his journey.

In the course of this navigation, in Book III, 'De Paris à Paris par mer ou le Robinson belge' – which comprises roughly one-third of the total book – Faustroll visits a series of 'islands'. Each of these islands is the object of a description which is in fact an evocation of the particular 'imaginative universe' constituted by the work of the poet, novelist, artist or composer to whom the corresponding chapter is dedicated. These include the poets Franc-Nohain, Gustave Kahn, Stéphane Mallarmé, Henri de Régnier and Laurent Tailhade; the novelists or prose writers Léon Bloy, Marcel Schwob and Rachilde; the artists Aubrey Beardsley, Émile Bernard and Paul Gauguin; and the composer Claude Terrasse. In these evocations of the work of each man, Jarry, developing and perfecting a technique first employed in his early art-criticism, has succeeded in creating a new literary *genre*, for which such terms as 'prose poems' and 'word pictures' can only be very approximate. Most offer a remarkably vivid, and sometimes very beautiful, 'synthetic' vision of the imaginative world of men whom he admired greatly and with whom he was closely associated. In some instances, in his evocation of the world of a particular artist he makes use of elements drawn from several works, fusing them into a single imaginative whole; his evocation of the imaginative world of Aubrey Beardsley, in a chapter aptly entitled 'Du pays de Dentelles', is a typical example:

Le roi des Dentelles l'étirait [i.e. the light] comme un cordier persuade sa ligne rétrograde, et les fils tremblaient un peu dans l'obscurité de l'air, comme ceux de la Vierge. Ils ourdirent des forêts, comme celles dont, sur les vitres, le givre compte les feuilles; puis une madone et son Bambin dans de la neige de Noël; et puis des joyaux, des paons et des robes, qui s'entremêlaient comme la danse nagée des filles du Rhin. Les Beaux et les Belles se pavanèrent et rouèrent à l'imitation des éventails, jusqu'à ce que leur foule patiente se déconcerta dans un cri. De même que les junoniens blancs, juchés dans un parc, réclament avec discordance quand la menteuse intrusion d'un flambeau leur singe prématurément l'aube leur miroir, une forme candide s'arrondit dans la futaie de poix égratignée; et comme Pierrot chante au brouillamini du pelotonnement de la lune, le paradoxe de jour mineur se levait d'Ali-Baba hurlant dans l'huile impitoyable et l'opacité de la jarre.

[The king of Lace drew the light out just as a rope-maker plaits his reluctant fibres, and the threads quivered a little in the dimly-lit air, like gossamer. They wove themselves into forests, like those which, on window-panes, the hoar-frost creates with a myriad of leaves; then into a Madonna and Child amidst the Christmas snow; and then into jewels, peacocks and gowns, which intermingled like the swimming dance of the Rhine Maidens. The Beaux and the Belles strutted about and swept to and fro in imitation of fans, until their patient host broke up with a cry. Just as white Junonians, roosting in a park, protest discordantly when the lying intrusion of torchlight prematurely apes the dawn, their mirror, so the round shape of a white-clad figure is seen amidst the raked over pine-pitch of a slender copse; and as Pierrot sings to the tangle of the moon's entwined ball, the paradox of sunrise in a minor key saw Ali Baba screaming in the pitiless oil and the opaqueness of the jar.][12]

In other instances, Jarry attempts to capture the essential qualities of a writer by translating these into pictorial terms, through images of his own invention. This is pre-eminently the case in his evocation of the world of Mallarmé, which is worth quoting at some length. The chapter is entitled 'De l'île de Ptyx', an allusion to Mallarmé's sonnet 'Ses purs ongles très haut . . .', familiarly known as the 'Sonnet en -yx', one of whose lines ends with the (non-existent) word *ptyx*. The first of its three paragraphs evokes the essential qualities of Mallarmé's verse – its precision, its exquisiteness, its imagery of light, fire and warmth – qualities which seem to capture the very essence of things, 'the substance of the universe'; the second paragraph evokes the familiar objects and customs of Mallarmé's Tuesday evening receptions in the rue de Rome which Jarry attended:

L'île de Ptyx est d'un seul bloc de la pierre de ce nom, laquelle est inestimable, car on ne l'a vue que dans cette île, qu'elle compose entièrement. Elle a la translucidité sereine du saphir blanc, et c'est la seule gemme dont le contact ne morfonde pas, mais dont le feu entre et s'étale, comme la digestion du vin. Les autres pierres sont froides comme le cri des trompettes; elle a la chaleur précipitée de la surface des timbales. Nous y pûmes aisément aborder, car elle était taillée en table et crûmes prendre pied sur un soleil purgé des parties opaques ou trop miroitantes de sa flamme, comme les antiques lampes ardentes. On n'y percevait plus les accidents des choses, mais la substance de l'univers, et c'est pourquoi nous ne nous inquiétâmes point si la surface irréprochable était d'un liquide équilibré selon des lois éternelles, ou d'un diamant impénétrable, sauf à la lumière qui tombe droit.

Le seigneur de l'île vint vers nous dans un vaisseau: la cheminée arrondissait des auréoles bleues derrière sa tête, amplifiant la fumée de sa pipe et l'imprimant au ciel. Et au tangage alternatif, sa chaise à bascule hochait ses gestes de bienvenue.

[The island of Ptyx is made up of a single block of the stone of that name, which is priceless, for it has never been seen except on this island, which is entirely composed of it. It has the serene translucency of white sapphire, and it is the only precious stone which is not ice-cold to the touch, but whose fire enters one and spreads out as wine is absorbed into the body. Other stones are cold like the cry of trumpets; it has the sudden warmth of the surface of kettledrums. We were easily able to land there, for it was hewn in the shape of a table, and it seemed to us that we were setting foot on a sun purged of the opaque or too-shimmering parts of its flame, like the burning lamps of old. Here one no longer perceived the accidents of things, but the substance of the universe, and it was for this reason that we did not bother to enquire whether its flawless surface was composed of a liquid held in equilibrium according to eternal laws, or a diamond impenetrable to all except light falling directly from above.

The lord of the island came towards us in a vessel: the funnel puffed out neatly rounded blue haloes behind his head, magnifying the smoke from his pipe and imprinting it upon the sky. And as the ship alternately pitched and tossed, his rocking chair nodded gestures of welcome.][13]

The passage admirably expresses Jarry's utter veneration for the figure of Mallarmé, in whom he saw the perfect artist. Mallarmé was to die later in the year in which *Faustroll* was written, and Jarry, as a tribute to his master, added to his unpublished manuscript the note:

'Le fleuve autour de l'île s'est fait, depuis ce livre, couronne mortuaire.' ['The river which surrounds the island has been transformed, since this book was written, into a funeral wreath.']¹⁴ He also republished this chapter from *Faustroll* in his *Almanach du Père Ubu* of January-February-March 1899, adding to the text an evocation of Mallarmé's funeral on 11 September 1898 which he had himself attended (wearing a pair of 'canary yellow'-coloured shoes borrowed from Rachilde at the last moment for the ceremony), and which is here attended by Faustroll who witnesses the crowd kneeling down 'devant le *catholique* (puisque ce veut dire quelquefois universel) de la gloire' ['before the *catholic* (since it sometimes means universal) of glory']. The conclusion to the passage implicitly compares Mallarmé to the God Pan, in an allusion to the ancient cry: 'Great Pan is dead!'¹⁵

Not all the evocations in *Faustroll*, however, are of exquisite beauty and shining light, and nor are all of them admiring. Denigration is directed, in Book V, at France's wealthy 'academic' painters, and praise bestowed – in ascending order – upon Monet, Degas, Whistler, Cézanne, Renoir and Manet. And Jarry's favoured devices of scatology and wordplay come together in three chapters of *Faustroll* which are savagely satirical. The first is Chapter XII, in which Faustroll begins his navigation by skirting around but refusing to land on an island: it is entitled 'De la mer d'Habundes, du Phare olfactif, et de l'île de Bran, où ne bûmes point' ['Of the Sea of S'Hitt', of the olfactory Beacon, and of the Ile of Cack, where we drank not']. The chapter was dedicated, in the *Mercure de France* publication of May 1898, to 'Louis Lermoul', an insulting reference to Louis Lormel, editor of *L'Art Littéraire*, in whose pages Jarry had begun his literary career. It was a reply to the allegorical short story entitled 'Entre soi' which his former friend and associate had published in *La Plume* in 1897, in which Jarry and Léon-Paul Fargue were viciously caricatured under the names of 'la Tête de Mort' and 'l'Androgyne'. But Jarry's scatology, though it may deliberately fly in the face of contemporary 'good taste', is never gratuitous: his portrayal of Lormel and his new associates as a hideous half-dead and putrefied creature feeding on its own excrement is a damning comment on the attempts of a number of young *littérateurs* parasitically to live off the 'putrefied' doctrines of Symbolism and Catholicism.

The second example of scatology and wordplay combined occurs in Chapters XXX and XXXI, directed against the popular novelist Pierre Loti (who made a brief appearance earlier in the guise of a legless cripple, or *cul de jatte*), whose work evidently constituted for Jarry the epitome of falseness and sentimentality. He was certainly not the first to attack Loti for these characteristics of his work: Gourmont, in an article in the *Mercure de France* of July 1896, had stressed the abundance of clichés and platitudes which comprised Loti's style. But in *Faustroll* Jarry launches a far more scurrilous attack, portraying Loti in a scene which recalls Ubu's disappearance down the lavatory in *Ubu Cocu* and which is doubtless intended to convey the idea that Loti's work (to paraphrase a well-known popular French idiom) provokes defecation.

Faustroll's 'visits' are followed by a variety of adventures, among them, a fit of homicidal madness provoked by the sight of a horse's head (the epitome, for him, of ugliness), during which he is responsible for a universal annihilation; and the invention of a curious 'Machine à peindre', which he commits to the charge of the painter Henri Rousseau. After the total devastation of the world and the annihilation of all its inhabitants, the Machine continues its random work, producing a series of purely 'accidental' canvases, which are described in Chapter XXXIV, 'Clinamen'. There is still confusion and uncertainty among Jarry scholars not only over the identity of these 13 paintings, but even over whether they describe 'real' works of art or works merely 'imagined' by Jarry.

In the final stages of this universal destruction, Faustroll himself dies. His death enables the secrets of his knowledge to be revealed to Panmuphle, as the roll of wallpaper designed by Maurice Denis in which he had draped his body unfolds, revealing, like a musical score, 'tout art et toute science' written between the lines of its spiral decorations.[16] Faustroll's death also enables him to continue his explorations in the ethereal realms beyond the physical world. Here, as in Book II of the novel, Panmuphle's narrative gives way to excerpts from the good doctor's own writings, in the form of two 'telepathic letters' addressed by Faustroll to the celebrated English physicist Lord Kelvin, along with three 'fragments' from two of his future books. These lead us back from literature and art to the fields of scientific and philosophical speculation, and to the principles and practice of Jarry's 'science' of 'pataphysics', to which a number of earlier chapters have already opened the door. In fact, whatever the interest and value of the literary and artistic parts of the book, it is to Jarry's other chief aim in *Faustroll*, his outline of pataphysics, that the interest of the modern reader is most likely to be drawn.

Jarry's pataphysics, as outlined in *Gestes et opinions du docteur Faustroll, pataphysicien*, has given rise to a bewildering variety of interpretations. It has been seen as everything from an elaborate philosophical joke to a form of exalted mysticism. It has also been seen as an attempt to create, out of the ruins of existing values, *new* values of a transcendental order; thus Roger Shattuck, the author of a study of Jarry and three other prominent figures of 'la belle époque':

In a grotesque symmetry, *Faustroll* moves in the opposite direction from the *Ubu* plays and forms their complement. Beneath the highly congested surface, and in spite of its desultory structure, one senses in *Faustroll* the search for a new reality, a stupendous effort to create out of the ruins Ubu had left behind a new system of values – the world of pataphysics.[17]

Shattuck sees a justification for this view in the epigraph to *Ubu Enchaîné* of 1899:

Cornegidouille! nous n'aurons point tout démoli si nous ne démolissons même les ruines! Or je n'y vois d'autre moyen que d'en équilibrer de beaux édifices bien ordonnés.

[Hornbelly! we won't have demolished everything if we don't demolish the ruins as well! Now, I see no other means of doing so than by using them to erect fine, harmonious new edifices.]

But a close examination of this epigraph reveals that Jarry's true purpose as implied here is less positive than negative. Ubu's ultimate objective remains to 'demolish everything'; and the 'fine new edifice' which is to be constructed is to be an instrument for completely sweeping away even the remaining ruins; it is a 'construction' designed to complete the task of destruction. A correct interpretation of Jarry's aim here is crucial, not only for an understanding of his pataphysics, but for an understanding of his whole philosophical outlook.

In endeavouring to determine the exact nature of Jarry's pataphysics, it is first necessary to look at its origins. Like the figure of Ubu, the *term* 'pataphysics' goes back to the Lycée de Rennes, and to the common fund of schoolboy terminology upon which Jarry drew so abundantly. According to Charles Morin, 'le P.H.', predecessor of Ubu, was baptized with 'essence de pataphysique'.[18] Initially, therefore, pataphysics was intimately bound up with the person of Père Heb: it seems that the unfortunate M. Hébert was in the habit of invoking his 'science en physique', which became rapidly transformed into 'science en pataphysique' – a 'science' which seems to have given Père Heb the power to act upon phenomena in a peremptory and miraculous way, and even to have constituted an occult or magical source of knowledge. This is the meaning which the term still has as it survives into both the *Guignol* of 1893 and *Ubu Cocu*:

N'oubliez pas non plus de dire à votre cuisinière qu'elle a l'habitude – nous le savons par notre science en pataphysique – de servir la soupe trop salée . . . .

Ce n'est pas que nous ne puissions, par notre science en pataphysique, faire surgir de terre les mets les plus exquis . . . .

[Don't forget also to tell your cook that she is in the habit – as we know by means of our science of pataphysics – of putting too much salt in the soup . . . .

It is not that we cannot, by means of our science of pataphysics, cause the most exquisite dishes to spring up out of the ground . . . .][19]

Associated with pataphysics was another schoolboy concept which Jarry chose to retain, that of the 'bâton-à-physique' of M. Hébert. Originally a crude sexual symbol, it becomes in *César-Antechrist* the subject of an elaborate mathematico-sexual development in which (amongst other things) it represents in one position the sign Minus (−) and, juxtaposed with itself at an angle of 90 degrees, the sign Plus (+) – thereby demonstrating the principle of the 'identity of opposites'. The concept recurs briefly in Chapter XXXIX of *Faustroll* (one of those chapters possibly written around 1894), where the reader is referred to 'un grand livre qui a pour titre *César-Antechrist*, où se trouve la seule démonstration pratique, par l'engin mécanique [*sic*] dit *bâton à physique*, de l'identité des contraires' ['a big book entitled *César-Antechrist*, in which is to be found the only practical demonstration, by means of the mechanical [*sic*] device called *physick stick*, of the identity of opposites']. The author of this work is given as 'le R. P. Ubu, de la Cie de Jésus' – partly a piece of amusing nonsense, but partly also a means of drawing the reader's attention to the close links existing between *Faustroll*, *César-Antechrist* and the *Ubu* plays.[20] Indeed, it was through the figure of Ubu that, as we saw in Chapter Two, Jarry first chose to reveal his 'science' of pataphysics to the world, pataphysics being defined in the *Guignol* of 1893 as 'une science que nous [i.e. Ubu] avons inventée et dont le besoin se faisait généralement sentir' ['a science which we have invented and for which a general need was felt']. Further cryptic references to pataphysics occurred in the early text 'Visions actuelles et futures', published in *L'Art Littéraire* in May-June 1894, and in the 'Linteau' which preceded *Les Minutes de sable mémorial*, where the word is twice used. Further, one of the chapters of *Les Jours et les Nuits* is also, as we have seen, entitled 'Pataphysique'.

What lies behind Jarry's strange and persistent attachement to these schoolboy concepts? He himself provides a clue when, in 'Les Paralipomènes d'Ubu', speaking of the origins of *Ubu Roi* and its schoolboy authorship, he draws attention to 'le principe de synthèse que trouve l'enfant créateur en ses professeurs' ['the principle of synthesis which the imaginatively gifted child finds in its teachers'].[21] The particular teacher in whom this 'synthesis' was embodied was, of course, a physics master. And thus it was that through him, or more exactly through his blundering incompetence, the *potache* Jarry came to call into question not only the authority and moral values of adult society, but also, in the second half of the nineteenth century, its most vaunted product: Science. And thus from M. Hébert's 'science of physics' was born the antithesis and negation of that science: pataphysics.

Such, then, are the origins of pataphysics. But it was not merely capriciousness, or blind adolescent revolt, or even deliberate mystification, which led Jarry to the detailed elaboration of his new 'science'. We saw in Chapter Two how, at the moment of obtaining his *baccalauréat*, he hesitated, according to Henri Morin, between preparing himself for the École Normale Supérieure and the École Polytechnique. Far from being ignorant in scientific matters, Jarry was on the contrary keenly interested in and aware of the latest scientific and technological developments of his age. He read (and reviewed) a considerable number of newly published scientific works, and kept abreast of the latest theories, which he often cited or employed in his own literary works, not least in *Faustroll*. (He also had something of a mania for translating abstract concepts into algebraic or geometrical symbols, and for expressing large numbers, in the manner of the physicist, in terms of powers of ten.) In his detailed knowledge of and his interest in contemporary science, moreover, Jarry was almost unique among those writers associated with the Symbolist movement, most of whom deliberately turned their back upon such manifestations of the modern world.

Perhaps most important of all, Jarry was also fully aware of an important shift in the philosophical basis of contemporary science. He was familiar, at least in general terms, with the ideas of philosophers such as Ravaisson, Lachelier, Émile Boutroux (whose influential *De la contingence des lois de la nature* appeared in 1874), and the man who had been his philosophy teacher at the Lycée Henri IV, Henri Bergson, all of whom had contributed to a growing and influential *critique* of the nature and pretensions of nineteenth-century science. This 'anti-positivist reaction', as it is sometimes called, took a number of different forms and was motivated by a variety of factors, some disinterestedly scientific, others social, religious or philosophical. Three main criticisms of the claims of nineteenth-century 'science' were formulated. Firstly, the movement questioned the methods of science, pointing out (a) that science deals not in certitudes but merely in useful hypotheses containing a greater or lesser degree of 'probability'; and (b) that science deals not in literal descriptions but in 'working models' or 'symbols' of reality. Secondly, it questioned the equation of 'reality' with the merely scientifically observable and measurable, arguing that it is only a part of total reality which is accessible to such observation and measurement. Thirdly, it questioned the doctrine of epistemological realism (or 'naïve realism') – the view accepted, at least implicitly, by the great majority of scientifically-minded thinkers in the third quarter of the nineteenth century, that through our senses we perceive the world exactly *as it is*.

As a result of these criticisms, a number of key ideas had, by the 1890s, become fairly well established even among non-scientifically-minded, educated men. The first of these was that science dealt not in literal descriptions of reality, but in abstract representations and symbols. To this was added, in some minds, the notion that the progress of science, far from producing an ever more accurate picture of reality, was on the contrary leading further and further away into a realm of increasingly pure abstraction. Much of the impetus behind such thinking was provided by the contemporary conflict between 'science' and 'religion', and by a desire to reaffirm the values and beliefs of Christianity (and, with them, in some cases, the existing social order which they were seen to uphold). A typical example is the case of the literary critic and editor of the influential, conservative *Revue des Deux Mondes*, Ferdinand Brunetière, who was shortly afterwards to proclaim his allegiance to the doctrines of Catholicism; in an article of 1896 entitled 'Les Bases de la croyance', Brunetière triumphantly quoted the words of a Christian apologist, Jules Payot: 'Ma science n'empêche point mon ignorance de la réalité d'être absolue . . . . Langage symbolique, admirable système de signes, plus la science progresse, plus elle s'éloigne de la réalité pour s'enfoncer dans l'abstraction.' ['My knowledge of science does not prevent my ignorance of reality from being absolute . . . . A language of symbols, an admirable system of signs, the more science develops, the more it moves away from reality to plunge into abstraction.'][22] Alongside this notion, the idea was also taking root that the scientist, in constructing his model of reality, actually *selects* facts and events out of the totality of events or phenomena making up the universe, and in this way imposes his own, perhaps purely arbitrary, interpretation upon those events.[23]

Jarry takes up and develops many of the ideas of this 'anti-positivist reaction'. He is scathing in his attacks on the 'vulgar' faith in science of his 'bourgeois' contemporaries, for whom science has become a new 'supersitition'. More surprisingly, his contempt for the scientist (*le savant*) is only slightly less virulent than that for the bourgeois or *le vulgaire*. One can distinguish in his work four main criticisms of this 'science'. Firstly, he argues that the 'laws' of science have no real existence; they are but descriptive generalizations, existing only in the mind of the scientist, by means of which he tries to link together particular, isolated, unique events and phenomena. Or as Jarry puts it: 'les lois que l'on a cru découvrir de l'univers traditionnel' are but 'des corrélations d'exceptions . . . , de faits accidentels' ['the laws

which it is believed have been discovered in the traditional universe'
are but 'correlations of exceptions ... , of purely accidental
phenomena'].[24] Secondly, he maintains that the interpretations which
the scientist imposes upon events in the physical world – the
'explanations' which science puts forward – are chosen *arbitrarily*.
This is the idea which lies behind such an apparently perverse
argument as the following, in which the attack is given a twist at the
end by a stab at Jarry's lifelong enemy and despoiler of his beloved
absinthe – water:

Au lieu d'énoncer la loi de la chute des corps vers un centre, que ne
préfère-t-on celle de l'ascension du vide vers une périphérie, le vide étant pris
pour unité de non-densité, hypothèse beaucoup moins arbitraire que le choix
de l'unité concrète de densité positive *eau*?

> [Instead of formulating the law of the fall of a body towards a centre, why not
> give preference to that of the ascension of a vacuum towards a periphery,
> the vacuum being considered a unit of non-density, a hypothesis which is far
> less arbitrary than the choice of the concrete unit of positive density, *water*?][25]

Thirdly, and more radically, in his reaction against the naïve 'scient-
ism' that characterizes popular thought in the late nineteenth century, Jarry goes beyond these two not uncommon criticisms
apparently to reject the very basis of the scientific method itself,
namely, the principle of induction and the law of causality. Science is
based on the assumption that if a given event is seen to occur under
the same conditions a sufficient number of times, then it is possible to
induce from this that that event will always occur in the same way,
and to formulate a general 'law' accordingly. But the principle of
induction, according to Jarry, is nothing but the simple 'prejudice' of
'universal consent' which, with his aristocratic contempt for all such
'democratic' notions, he dismisses out of hand:

La science actuelle se fonde sur le principe de l'induction: la plupart des
hommes ont vu le plus souvent tel phénomène précéder ou suivre tel autre, et
en concluent qu'il en sera toujours ainsi. D'abord ceci n'est exact que le plus
souvent, dépend d'un point de vue, et est codifié selon la commodité, et
encore! . . . Le consentement universel est déjà un préjugé bien miraculeux et
incompréhensible.

> [Modern science is founded upon the principle of induction: most men have
> seen a certain phenomenon most often precede or follow some other
> phenomenon, and conclude therefrom that this will always be the case. For a
> start, this is true only in a majority of cases, depends upon a certain vantage
> point, and is codified only for the sake of convenience, if even that! . . . The
> principle of universal assent is already in itself a quite miraculous and
> incomprehensible prejudice.][26]

Finally, closely linked to this rejection of the principle of induction is Jarry's rejection of the evidence of the senses: the 'knowledge' revealed by or acquired through the senses is entirely *relative* to the perceiver. And scientific instruments of measurement, far from correcting the defects and distortions of the senses, merely magnify them and increase their relativity. As he puts it in a passage in *Les Jours et les Nuits*: 'l'organe des sens étant une cause d'erreur, l'instrument scientifique amplifie le sens dans la direction de son erreur' ['the sense-organ being a cause of error, the scientific instrument magnifies the error of the sense-organ'].[27] And in *Faustroll*, speaking of notions of attraction and repulsion of bodies, Jarry declares with aristocratic contempt that the very concept of a 'body' is

un postulat et un point de vue des sens de la foule, et, pour que sinon sa nature au moins ses qualités ne varient pas trop, il est nécessaire de postuler que la taille des hommes restera toujours sensiblement constante et mutuellement égale.

[a postulate and a point of view deriving from the senses of the mob, and, in order that, if not its nature, then at least its qualities should not vary too greatly, it is necessary to postulate that the size of men will always remain more-or-less constant and uniform.][28]

It is this concept of the relativity of knowledge – its relativity to the sense-organs of the perceiver and also, in this instance, to his physical dimensions – that Jarry sets out to demonstrate in Chapter IX, 'Faustroll plus petit que Faustroll':

Le docteur Faustroll . . . se voulut un jour plus petit que soi-même, et résolut d'aller explorer l'un des éléments, afin d'examiner quelles perturbations cette différence de grandeur apporterait dans leurs rapports réciproques.

[Dr Faustroll . . . decided one day that he wanted to be smaller than himself, and resolved to go and explore one of the elements, in order to examine in what ways this difference of size would upset their mutual relationships.][29]

And so, having reduced himself to the size of a mite, Faustroll travelled along a cabbage-leaf until he encountered a drop of water, in the form of a ball twice his size, through whose transparency the universe appeared magnified to gigantic proportions. The example, and Faustroll's subsequent adventures with this 'ball' of water, are borrowed from an address given by the eminent scientist Sir William Crookes (to whom the chapter is dedicated) to the Society for Psychical Research in London, of which a translation had appeared in the *Revue scientifique* in Paris in May 1897. Crookes' aim was also to convince his audience of the relativity of all knowledge, by means of a demonstration of the changes which would appear to occur in the laws of the universe following a simple change in the size of the observer. To this end, he invented a minuscule human being, a *homunculus*, whom he placed in the middle of a cabbage-leaf covered with drops of dew, where, Crookes maintained, amongst other things he would have difficulty in retaining his belief in the universality of the law of gravity. Crookes' conclusion was therefore: 'Cette science dont nous sommes fiers, n'est-elle pas simplement conditionnée par les circonstances accidentelles, ne comprend-elle pas une grande part de subjectivité . . . ?' ['Is not this science of which we are so proud simply conditioned by fortuitous circumstances, does it not contain a large measure of subjectivity . . . ?']^{30}

What then are the principles of pataphysics which will replace this defective 'science'? The classic definition occurs in Book II of *Faustroll*, 'Éléments de pataphysique', in a chapter entitled, appropriately, 'Définition':

Un épiphénomène est ce qui se surajoute à un phénomène.
La pataphysique, dontl' étymologie doit s'écrire " $\varepsilon\pi\iota(\mu\varepsilon\tau\grave{\alpha}\ \tau\grave{\alpha}\ \varphi\upsilon\sigma\iota\chi\grave{\alpha})$ et l'orthographe réelle *'pataphysique*, précédé d'un apostrophe, afin d'éviter un facile calembour, est la science de ce qui se surajoute à la métaphysique, soit en elle-même, soit hors d'elle-même, s'étendant aussi loin au-delà de celle-ci que celle-ci au-delà de la physique. Ex.: l'épiphénomène étant souvent l'accident, la pataphysique sera surtout la science du particulier, quoiqu'on dise qu'il n'y a de science que du général. Elle étudiera les lois qui régissent les exceptions et expliquera l'univers supplémentaire à celui-ci; ou moins ambitieusement décrira un univers que l'on peut voir et que peut-être l'on doit voir à la place du traditionnel, les lois que l'on a cru découvrir de l'univers traditionnel étant des corrélations d'exceptions aussi, quoique plus fréquentes, en tous cas de faits accidentels qui, se réduisant à des exceptions peu exceptionnelles, n'ont même pas l'attrait de la singularité.
DEFINITION: *La pataphysique est la science des solutions imaginaires, qui accorde symboliquement aux linéaments les propriétés des objets décrits par leur virtualité.*

[An epiphenomenon is that which is superinduced upon a phenomenon.
Pataphysics, whose etymology should be written as " $\varepsilon\pi\iota(\mu\varepsilon\tau\grave{\alpha}\ \tau\grave{\alpha}\ \varphi\upsilon\sigma\iota\chi\grave{\alpha})$ and whose real spelling should be *'pataphysics*, preceded by an apostrophe in order to avoid a simple pun, is the science of that which is superinduced upon metaphysics, either within, or outside of, the confines of the latter, extending as far beyond metaphysics as metaphysics extends beyond physics. E.g., the epiphenomenon often being the accident, pataphysics will be above all the science of the particular; even though it is said that the only science is that of the general. It will study the laws governing exceptions and will explain the universe supplementary to this one; or, less ambitiously, will describe a universe which can be seen, and which perhaps should be seen, in the place of the traditional one, the laws which it is believed have been discovered in the traditional universe being also correlations of exceptions, albeit more frequent ones, or in any case of accidental phenomena which, since they are at bottom only unexceptional exceptions, do not even possess the attraction of singularity.

DEFINITION:*Pataphysics is the science of imaginary solutions, which symbolically attributes to the lineaments of objects the properties described by their virtuality.*][32]

The passage begins on an apparently serious note; but immediately the reader is cautioned by Jarry's proposal of an obviously fanciful etymology for 'pataphysics' and his reference to a 'facile pun' (that is, 'patte à physique', reminiscent of 'bâton-à-physique' and other similar *ubuesque* constructions). We begin to move towards a definition with the statement that pataphysics is 'la science de ce qui se surajoute à la métaphysique, soit en elle-même, soit hors d'elle-même'. But what is metaphysics? Jarry goes to great lengths to point out the arbitrary and imaginary nature of the 'truths' of physics; metaphysics – literally, 'beyond physics' – amplifies and extends these 'truths' to even greater heights of fancifulness. Therefore pataphysics, 's'étendant aussi loin au-delà de celle-ci [metaphysics] que celle-ci au-delà de la physique', carries us, it would seem, into a realm of pure and boundless imaginative speculation.

It is in the next sentence, however, that we come to the first of Jarry's two key definitions. Pataphysics is 'la science du particulier'; it will study 'les lois qui régissent les exceptions', the 'laws' of science and of the 'traditional universe' being merely 'des corrélations d'exceptions ... , de faits accidentels'. The statement takes us to the heart of Jarry's anarchistic view of the world: rejecting all scientific 'laws', and with them – on an ethical and philosophical plane – all norms, standards and values, pataphysics will concern itself solely with the particular and the exceptional, treating all phenomena as purely 'accidental' or 'epiphenomena'. Everything, for pataphysics, is an exception (beginning with Dr Faustroll himself, who in his idiosyncracies and eccentricities is perhaps the supreme exception, and who for his part defined 'the universe' as *'ce qui est l'exception de soi'*.[32])

But the 'laws' of science – the vast body of human knowledge laboriously accumulated over the centuries – are not to be totally discarded. For all their arbitrariness and 'imaginary' quality, these 'laws' are no less interesting than the 'exceptions' which they claim to govern. And they too, together with *all* propositions concerning the nature of reality, will be the subject of 'study' by pataphysics. Taking up, implicitly, the Kantian distinction between the 'thing-in-itself' (the 'virtualité' of objects), which is unknowable, and the perceivable 'phenomenon' (their 'linéaments'), Jarry declares that pataphysics, by 'symbolically' attributing to the phenomenon the properties of the thing-in-itself, accepts all such propositions; and it accepts them by virtue (he implies) of treating them all as equally valid or invalid – as equally 'imaginary'. Thus pataphysics is also, in the second of Jarry's two key definitions, the 'science of imaginary solutions': 'La pataphy-

sique est la science des solutions imaginaires, qui accorde symboliquement aux linéaments les propriétés des objets décrits par leur
virtualité.'

But what are we to make of Jarry's claim that pataphysics 'expliquera l'univers supplémentaire à celui-ci', or at least 'décrira un
univers que l'on peut voir et que peut-être l'on doit voir à la place du
traditionnel' ['will explain the universe supplementary to this one' . . .
'will describe a universe which can be seen, and which perhaps
should be seen, in the place of the traditional one']? And indeed, how
'seriously' are we take this whole 'pataphysical' argument? Is Jarry
simply referring, when he speaks of 'l'univers que l'on peut voir . . .',
to his own anarchistic view of the world? Or is it the case, as Roger
Shattuck, for example, argues, that Jarry is here pointing the way to
some new, non-rational, mystical philosophy: 'Behind the double-
talk, Jarry is aiming not merely at the limit, but beyond the limit of
man's conceptual powers, and this without ever abandoning the
pretense of reason.'[33] The question can be decided only by a detailed
examination of the practical demonstrations to which Jarry's pataphysical 'logic' is applied.

A great deal of the scientific material in *Faustroll*, as we have
already in part seen, is borrowed directly from leading English
physicists of the time. In Chapter VI, the whole of the theoretical
material (though not necessarily its application) relating to capillary
action, surface tension, the floating sieve, the quartz thread, and
other concepts, is borrowed directly from C. V. Boys' *Soap Bubbles,
Their Colour And The Forces Which Mould Them*, and the incident of the
'jet musical' in Chapter XXXI is borrowed from the same work; in
Chapter IX, Jarry borrows heavily from an address by Sir William
Crookes; and the material of Chapters XXXVII, 'De la règle de
mesure, de la montre et du diapason', and XXXVIII, 'Du soleil, solide
froid' – the two 'telepathic letters' sent by Faustroll after his death to
Lord Kelvin – is drawn from Kelvin's *Popular Lectures and Addresses,
vol. I: Constitution of Matter*, translated into French as *Conférences
scientifiques et allocutions* and published by Gauthier-Villars in 1893.
Kelvin's work in particular seems to have been a source of delight to
Jarry, who adapts the material of the scientific original, transposing
and combining different details in a way not unlike his evocations of
literary and artistic worlds in Book III. With all three scientists,
moreover, he borrows not only ideas but words, phrases and even
whole sentences, to the point where, were his intentions not wholly
otherwise, one might be tempted to speak of blatant plagiarism.[34]

But it is not sufficient simply to state that Jarry has borrowed this
material. The question remains: why has he done so? To a minor
degree, it is merely for humorous effect: the use to which he puts
this scientific data often contains a touch of eccentric originality, as

when he transforms the 'bons yeux magnétiques' of Kelvin into Faustroll's 'bons yeux pataphysiques', or when he makes the situation of Kelvin's hypothetical observer lost in time and space and deprived of all instruments for measuring these dimensions the very definition of 'death': 'Je crois, Monsieur, que c'est bien cet état qui constitue la mort.' ['I think, Sir, that it is indeed this state which constitutes death.']³⁵ In fact, the nature of Jarry's sources lends itself to such treatment and helps to explain the reason for his attraction to these scientists: all three seem to have brought to their researches and theories a touch of wry humour. But there is also a further, more important reason for Jarry's attraction to and borrowing from them, which explains also the detail and the extent of his borrowing which, far from justifying accusations of plagiarism or lack of originality, is essential to his purpose. He was delighted by works in which profound scientific knowledge was allied to great imaginative powers, and which without abandoning a solid factual basis reached out into the realms of imaginative speculation, towards the unusual, the bizarre and even the (apparently) fantastical. It is precisely this that one finds in the hypotheses and speculations of a Boys, a Crookes or a Kelvin. What, in fact, could have been better suited to appeal to Jarry's imagination than Kelvin's speculations on the plight of a man lost in time and space, or on the composition of the 'ether', or on the possibility that the sun is in reality a cold, homogeneous, solid mass? How much more delighted would he have been with the science of more recent times, with its superabundance of such metaphors to describe the universe as 'black holes', 'anti-matter', 'curved space', the 'big bang' theory, and the like. He would doubtless have seen much of twentieth-century physics as soaring into the realms of pure pataphysics, extending 'as far beyond metaphysics as the latter extends beyond physics'.

However, Jarry's use of this scientific material in *Gestes et opinions du docteur Faustroll, pataphysicien* goes beyond mere humour and a love of the bizarre and fantastical, to a rejection of the normal processes of logical reasoning. Though he may appear never to abandon 'the pretence of reason', he in fact makes only a half-hearted attempt to refute the claims of science on its own ground of logic. A typical example is his statement that science has the disadvantage that it deals with merely unexceptional exceptions which, because they are unexceptional, are therefore not even interesting ('n'ont même pas l'attrait de la singularité'). Further on in the same chapter, the effect of his diatribe against the senses of 'the mob' (which includes 'les petits enfants et les femmes') and the 'prejudice' of 'universal consent' is largely cancelled out by the nature of the examples he puts forward in support of his argument: for all that 'the mob' is incapable of perceiving ellipses, nevertheless 'les bourgeois mêmes conservent leur vin dans des tonneaux et non des cylindres' ['even the *bourgeois* keep their wine in barrels and not cylinders'].[36] Moreover, the whole argument of Chapter IX, in which Jarry (or rather Faustroll), following Crookes, sets out to demonstrate the relativity of all knowledge, is secretly undermined from within by being placed under the heading of 'pataphysics'. The reason is clear enough: after all, who is trying to demonstrate the relativity of the human view of things and to describe a possible non-human view but ... a human being? The demonstration is 'rigged' from the start: everything is relative to the human view-point – including demonstrations of its relativity.

But the true nature and purpose of Jarry's pataphysical logic can be most clearly seen in Book VIII of *Faustroll*, 'Éthernité'. The title is another play on words, a fusion of 'eternity' and the 'ether' which some scientists of the time regarded as the medium through which waves or particles of light travelled in space (and which also conjures up, with unconscious but ironic prophecy, the ether which Jarry was reduced to drinking at the end of his life). The first two chapters are taken up with Faustroll's 'telepathic' communication of his discoveries in time and space to his 'colleague' Kelvin. The main subject of Book VIII, however, is not physics but theology and metaphysics. The Book begins with the following epigraph, attributed to 'François Bacon':

> Leves gustus ad philosophiam movere fortasse ad atheismum, sed pleniores haustu ad religionem reducere.

Jarry's quotation is of the celebrated dictum of Sir Francis Bacon (one of the founding fathers of the principles of modern science) found in his essay on 'Atheism', from his *Essays* published simultaneously in Latin and English in 1625, the English text of which reads: 'A little philosophy inclineth a man's mind to atheism; but depth in philosophy bringeth men's minds about to religion.' But if the English text in no way lends itself to ambiguity, the Latin text certainly does: it can be taken (and was doubtless intended by Jarry to be taken) to read: 'A slight sip ...' and 'a fuller draught ...', being thereby transformed into an implicit reference to drink. This epigraph sets the tone for what is to follow.

After Faustroll's two letters, two further brief chapters. 'Selon Ibicrate le Géomètre' and 'Pantaphysique et Catachimie', introduce us to fragments of the 'pataphysical' teachings of Ibicrate and of his 'divine master', Sophrotatos the Armenian. These re-echo many of the themes, as well as the manner, of *César-Antechrist*, whereby theological and metaphysical concepts are neatly reduced to heraldic and mathematical symbols. But the crowning point of the whole work is the final chapter, 'De la surface de Dieu'. This chapter, as with many passages in *Faustroll*, is a marvellous piece of wryly comic writing. But to read it as a 'serious' attempt to affirm 'beliefs', new or old, would be a total misunderstanding of Jarry's purpose. The tone of the argument, and the manner of reasoning, are no less 'pataphysical' than those which enabled Jarry (or Faustroll) in the preceding chapters to 'discover' that eternity takes the form of a 'motionless ether', that the sun is a 'cold solid', and that the author of *César-Antechrist* is 'le R. P. Ubu de la Cie de Jésus'.

Just as by writing 'ethernity' Jarry was able to perform a physiochemical analysis of that 'dimension', so here, by reducing 'God' to a hypothetical geometrical form, he is able to proceed to calculate his 'surface':

Dieu est par définition inétendu, mais il nous est permis, pour la clarté de notre énoncé, de lui supposer un nombre quelconque, plus grand que zéro, de dimensions, bien qu'il n'en ait aucune, si ces dimensions disparaissent dans les deux membres de nos identités. Nous nous contenterons de deux dimensions, afin qu'on se représente aisément des figures de géométrie plane sur une feuille de papier.

[God is by definition without extension, but it is permissible, for the sake of the clarity of our exposition, for us to suppose that he has any number of dimensions greater than zero, even though he possesses none, if these two dimensions disappear in the two halves of our equation. We shall content ourselves with two dimensions, in order that one may easily visualize figures of plane geometry on a sheet of paper.][37]

These mathematical calculations are 'verified' by reference to the visions of Anne-Catherine Emmerich (1774–1824), a German nun and mystic whose visions describing the life and Passion of Christ were recorded by Clemens Brentano in a work translated into French as *La Douloureuse passion de Notre-Seigneur Jésus-Christ*, first published in Munich in 1833.[38] Eventually, via a long series of algebraic equations, Jarry arrives at the following series of propositions:

DEFINITION: *Dieu est le plus court chemin de zéro à l'infini.*
Dans quel sens? dira-t-on.
– Nous répondrons que Son prénom n'est pas Jules, mais *Plus-et-Moins.*
Et l'on doit dire:
± *Dieu est le plus court chemin de 0 à ∞ , dans un sens ou dans l'autre.*

And finally:

Donc, *définitivement:*
DIEU EST LE POINT TANGENT DE ZÉRO ET DE L'INFINI.
La Pataphysique est la science . . .

[DEFINITION: *God is the shortest distance between zero and infinity.*
In what direction? one may ask.
We shall reply that His first name is not Johnny, but *Plus-and-Minus.* And one should say:
± *God is the shortest distance between 0 and* ∞ , *in one direction or the other.*]

[Therefore, *definitively:*
GOD IS THE TANGENTIAL POINT BETWEEN ZERO AND INFINITY.
Pataphysics is the science . . .][39]

Must we conclude, then, that the whole of Jarry's pataphysics is simply a gigantic spoof, a huge and elaborate practical joke? There is certainly some point in Jarry's criticisms of the pretensions of nineteenth-century science. But his 'absolutist' mentality causes him to pass from one extreme to the other, from a view of the absolute 'truth' of the propositions of science to that of their absolute 'un-truth'. Instead of accepting the view to which the mathematician Henri Poincaré was to give the name *le commodisme*, the view that the 'explanations' of science are merely the most 'convenient', if not most 'probable', representations of reality, Jarry declares all such explana-tions to be equally relative, equally arbitrary, equally 'imaginary'. It is this view of science and philosophy which ultimately explains and justifies the presence within *Faustroll* of such apparently diverse subjects as literature, art, physics, theology and metaphysics, and which, despite any initial impression which the book may give, ensures its essential unity. For in Jarry's eyes the world of the sciences and of philosophy is just as much an 'imaginary' world as that of literature and the other arts: all are equally constructions of the human imagination. Indeed, commenting in an article in *La Plume* some years later on the term 'l'imagination scientifique', he declared categorically that he conceived of no other form of imagination.[40] And in another article in the same journal a few months later devoted to the 'roman scientifique' – precursor of the 'science-fiction' of today – he presented the modern scientist as simply the successor to the alchemist and sorcerer of a bygone age:

Le roman scientifique remonte, en ligne directe, aux *Mille et Une Nuits*, dont beaucoup des contes sont alchimiques, et au *Cabinet des Fées*. L'usage des baguettes des fées s'est seulement un peu vulgarisé, ou agrandi, et l'on ne brûle plus les sorciers: on les décore.
    Le ruban rouge [i.e. of the *Légion d'Honneur*] serait-il le dernier vestige d'une tradition qui s'est perdu, et la réduction d'une flamme d'auto-da-fé?

[The scientific novel goes back, in a direct line of descent, to *The Thousand and One Nights*, many of the tales of which are alchemistical, and to *Le Cabinet des Fées*. The use of magic wands has simply become a little more commonplace, and widespread, and we no longer burn sorcerers at the stake: we decorate them.

Could it be that the red ribbon [of the *Légion d'Honneur*] is the last
surviving vestige of a now lost tradition, and a miniaturization of the flame of
an *auto-da-fé*?][41]

For Jarry, the principles of pataphysics underlie all domains of human
thought and creativity, as they underlie the whole of his own work:
all creations of the human mind are purely 'imaginary solutions', all
are equally 'pataphysical'. But at the same time pataphysics, by
placing all such manifestations of human creativity on the *same* level,
is able to *accept* them all with the same dispassionate detachment.
Total scepticism, by a supreme paradox which lies at the centre of
Jarry's thought and work, opens the door also to total 'belief'. And
thus it is that pataphysics can call itself the 'science' of these
'imaginary solutions', or, as Jarry puts it on the last page of *Faustroll*,
simply 'the science . . .'.[42]

Thus the 'universe supplementary to this one' is not a mystical or
transcendental one, but merely the private, personal world of dream
and fantasy of Jarry himself, and of each one of us – a universe whose
autonomy the weapon of pataphysics, with its absurd logic, is
designed to preserve from the encroachments of a hostile world. And
thus it is that Jarry plays endlessly, here and elsewhere in his work,
with the ideas of physicists, mathematicians, philosophers and
theologians. Yet, in spite of the above, there does remain behind all
the apparent nonsense and spoofing an element of fundamental
seriousness. In a sense, what Jarry wishes to do in his playful attacks
upon contemporary science is to go back several centuries to the point
at which modern science was born, and at which it first asserted itself
in opposition to the principles of medieval scholastic philosophy.
Scholasticism was essentially metaphysical in nature, being concerned with the 'why', as opposed to the 'how', of things: it was
concerned to establish (by a process of deduction from first principles
taken as given) the ultimate *reason* for events, the 'why' of their
occurrence; a reason which was found ultimately, of course, in God,
the 'prime mover' of the universe. Modern science, on the other
hand, explicitly turned its back on such considerations, declaring
them to be insoluble, and set about instead the laborious, piecemeal
and painstaking task of establishing *how* the universe functioned. It
was Jarry's intuition that, for all the progress of scientific knowledge,
the fundamental question of the *why* of existence remained un-
answered. Moreover, not only could science not provide an answer to
the problem of the ultimate purpose of the universe (which, it
seemed, admitted of no answer, the traditional religious explanations
having been relegated to the domain of mere myths); it was incapable
also of establishing the philosophical *necessity* of all phenomena, and
of existence itself, the question which is the central preoccupation of

existentialist philosophy from Heidegger to Sartre. Long before (to take perhaps the best known fictional example) Sartre's Roquentin, but in common with a small but growing number of other men of his time, Jarry seems to have realized that the mere fact that a given event habitually preceded or followed another offered no guarantee that it would invariably and necessarily do so. For practical purposes, of course, we can usually safely assume that events will conform to pattern; but the absence of any necessity, in absolute philosophical terms, remains. And the intuition which lies behind the 'illogicalities' of the behaviour of Jarry's Faustroll is that of the ultimate illogicality – or 'gratuitousness' – of existence itself.

Gestes et opinions du docteur Faustroll, pataphysicien is a work which presents many difficulties for the reader, and particularly for readers of later generations, difficulties which arise partly as a result of Jarry's technique of allusion, but partly also as a result of the enormous erudition which the book displays. Moreover, though Jarry's literary taste was as sure as that of any of his contemporaries, several of the writers whose work is evoked here have faded in importance or were included for reasons of personal homage, and the wealth of contemporary allusions runs the risk of rendering much of the text obscure for present-day readers. This is the danger of any *roman à clef*, and it is this that *Faustroll* at times comes close to becoming. The excellent work done by members of the Collège de 'Pataphysique, upon which later editors have been able to build, goes a long way towards providing the key which a reading of *Faustroll* requires. But the question remains: ought a work to have need of such erudite elucidation in order to be comprehensible to the average educated reader? There are several other works of Jarry, among them *Les Jours et les Nuits*, *L'Amour absolu* and the *Ubu* plays, which meet his own requirement of 'universality' more fully than does *Faustroll*.

It has to be admitted also that, for all that *Faustroll* is the Bible of all good pataphysicians, as a 'Bible' it remains slight: that part of the work given over to a theoretical outline of Jarry's pataphysics remains small, and the vast majority of its chapters are concerned with an evocation of the various 'islands' visited by Faustroll. Jarry has in fact given us only the sketchiest outline of his philosophy of pataphysics, leaving it to later generations, notably in the form of the Collège de 'Pataphysique, to elaborate upon his brief indications.

But such reservations must not be allowed to blind us to the enormous positive qualities of the work. It does at least contain an outline, however sketchy, of Jarry's pataphysics. It contains some extremely vivid, memorable and, in some cases, moving evocations of the work of major figures in French literature and painting. And it remains, amongst its other qualities, a great comic work. Comic elements in fact abound, running the gamut from parody, through savage satire, the pedantic reproduction of the (unconsciously comic) legalistic style of Panmuphle, and the juxtaposition of grotesquely incongruous or contradictory elements, to the spoofing and burlesque of the final chapters. These comic elements, moreover, are an essential part not only of the novel itself but of the whole attitude to the world which it expresses. For there is a further and final dimension to Jarry's pataphysics: pataphysics is not just a set of concepts, or a view of the world; it is also a particular state of mind, an *attitude to life*. And though the 'theoretical' exposition of pataphysics may be slight, Jarry has abundantly demonstrated, through the figure of Dr Faustroll himself, the spirit of pataphysics which he himself sought to maintain throughout much of his own life. Pataphysics involves an attitude which is neither one of commitment nor refusal, of acceptance nor rejection, but of a combination of each – a mixture of fascination and detachment akin to the amused playfulness of the child. Indeed, Jarry's rejection of the values and beliefs of contemporary society does not involve any form of 'dropping out', or physical withdrawal from that society. On the contrary, he remained keenly interested in and fascinated by the kaleidoscopic spectacle of the world around him; and nowhere can this better be seen than in his reviews and 'journalistic' writings, to which the next chapter turns.

Chapter Eight

The art of 'speculative' journalism

IT MAY AT FIRST seem strange to find in Jarry, given his frequent expressions of contempt for the institutions and values of contemporary society, a commentator upon the social and political *mores* of his age. It was not a role, in fact, to which he came easily. He protested at the *première* of *Ubu Roi* against the almost universal attempts of contemporaries to read a socio-political interpretation into the play, warning the audience that the 'bienveillance' of certain critics 'a vu le ventre d'Ubu gros de plus de satiriques symboles qu'on ne l'en a pu gonfler pour ce soir' ['has seen the belly of Ubu swollen with more satirical symbols than it has been possible to inflate it with for this evening'].[1] He also refused the solicitations of Georges Bans, director of the review *La Critique* (which published the 'Présentation' of the play distributed to the audience), who urged him to become a regular contributor to the review as the creator of 'ce genre nouveau auquel vous me semblez destiné: la critique politique' ['this new genre for which you seem, to my mind, cut out: political commentary'].[2]

By a curious quirk of fate, however, it was via the figure of Ubu, and the role of 'le Père Ubu' foisted upon him, that Jarry came to social and political commentary. There are traces of social satire in earlier works, from the youthful playlets contained in *Ontogénie* to the satirical vein of parts of *Les Jours et les Nuits* and of *L'Amour en visites*. But it was only with the publication of the first *Almanach du Père Ubu* at the beginning of 1899, followed by the second Almanach at the beginning of 1901, that the role of social and political observer became a dominant element in his work. From his 'revue des plus récents événements politiques, littéraires, artistiques, coloniaux, par-devant le Père Ubu' ['review of the most recent events in the fields of politics, literature, art and colonial affairs, as seen through the eyes of Père Ubu'],[3] it was but a small step to the 'lumières sur les choses de ce temps' of his contributions in the field of journalism.

A small step, moreover, not only in content but also in style. For the style, and perhaps even more appropriately the tone and 'voice' of his journalism, which differs so markedly from the highly mannered, rhetorical style of his Symbolist phase, owes a great deal to the manner and voice of Ubu as portrayed by Jarry both on the stage of his puppet-theatre and in his own life. Above all else, it owes its tone of sovereign authority to Jarry's use throughout of the first person plural, 'nous' – the 'nous' of Ubu's regal person. But at the same time it would be wrong to exaggerate the importance of the contribution made by Ubu to Jarry's journalism; for that contribution remains essentially formal in nature, and the point of view which Jarry, at his best, expresses here is radically different from that of the *Almanachs*.

If Jarry himself was slow to adopt the role of journalistic commentator, the task was not rendered any easier by his relations with editors. After the débâcle of his attempts to have *Faustroll* and *L'Amour absolu* published at the expense of the Éditions du Mercure de France, his relations with Vallette – at least on a literary or professional plane, for the two men continued to be fishing and boating companions in their retreat on the Seine south of Paris – seem to have undergone a distinct cooling. From this point on, his contributions to the *Mercure* review became increasingly rare, and ceased altogether after the publication of his *Commentaire pour servir à la construction pratique de la machine à explorer le temps* in February 1899.[4] This disaffection of the *Mercure* for Jarry is particularly striking in view of the fact that, at the very point at which his contributions ceased and he turned to other, in some cases rival, journals, the *Mercure* was itself transformed by Vallette from a mainly literary review to a much more broadly-based publication. Roughly ten years after its foundation, the leading Symbolist review of its day, though not abandoning literature, widened its scope to become also, in the words of Vallette's new prospectus, a 'revue documentaire d'actualité' catering to the aspirations and demands of a much wider readership. To meet the requirements of its new role, Vallette freely distributed responsibilities for a wide range of subjects among the *Mercure*'s regular contributors and the *habitués* of Rachilde's *salon*, responsibilities which, in accordance with a common practice of the time, often had little in common with the particular interests or specialized knowledge of the reviewer in question. Jarry alone appears to have been left out.

By this time, it is true, he did have a regular column in the *Revue Blanche*, with the *Mercure* the most solid and enduring of the 'avant-garde' literary reviews of the day, though more orientated towards politics than the latter, having a pronounced leaning towards liberal and socialist ideas and in particular towards the currently fashionable 'anarchism'. Jarry's first contribution to the review had been *Le Vieux de la Montagne* in 1896, followed shortly afterwards by *L'Autre Alceste*,

'Les Paralipomènes d'Ubu', and, in January 1897, 'Questions de théâtre'. Although he had gained the friendship of Thadée Natanson – nominally co-director, with his brother Alexandre, but in reality the director of the review – his staunchest friend at the *Revue Blanche* was Félix Fénéon, who must rank as one of the most discreet and unobstrusive, but also perspicacious, critics and editors of his time. Though he refused all titles other than that of 'Administrateur', Fénéon was the real guiding spirit of the Revue Blanche. Meticulous and correct in all matters, he was also open and generous in his dealings with penurious young writers in whom he discerned talent: the poet Jules Laforgue had benefited from his generosity in the last year of his life, and Jarry too was to do so on a number of occasions.

For all Fénéon's interest in Jarry, however, other members of the editorial board of the review were less enthusiastic about such a 'difficult' and 'obscure' young author, and it was not until the publication of Jarry's two *Almanachs* that Fénéon again found the opportunity to come to the assistance, other than momentarily, of his *protégé*. Realizing the potential contained in the latter's newly assumed role of 'commentator' upon contemporary events, Fénéon lost no opportunity of putting work his way. It was as a simple book reviewer that Jarry began his new series of contributions to the *Revue Blanche*. Over the next three years, from 1 July 1900 to 1 April 1903, he reviewed a total of 72 separate published volumes and, in the 'Chronique des Théâtres' from 1 January to 15 April 1903, 25 performances of plays. Alongside appreciative reviews of books by authors whom he admired, several of whom – Rachilde, Verlaine, Kahn, Maeterlinck, Péladan and Henri de Régnier – figure in Faustroll's list of 'livres pairs' (to which one must add J. C. Mardrus' translation of *The Thousand and One Nights*, the publication of successive volumes of which Jarry greeted with unbounded and almost ecstatic enthusiasm), the *Revue Blanche* also published reviews by him of such diverse non-literary works as *Code-manuel du Pêcheur* and *Code-manuel du Chasseur*, *État actuel de nos connaissances sur l'origine de l'homme*, *L'Arbre gnostique*, *Supériorité des animaux sur l'homme*, *Le Golf en Angleterre et les Golf-clubs de France*, *La Natalité en France en 1900*, *Étude médico-légal du meurtre rituel*, *Prêtres et Moines non conformistes en amour*, and *La Psychologie de l'amour*. Whether these titles represent Fénéon's or Jarry's choice is uncertain; in either case, they give rise to learned and serious discussions which testify to the range of Jarry's interests and the profundity of his knowledge over a vast field. Here and there, however, a typically 'Jarryesque' point of view emerges, as he seizes the opportunity to point out inconsistencies in the law, as he reveals his delight in the bizarre and the grotesque, or as he attempts to combat the anthropocentrism of his contemporaries and their conviction of the superiority of European civilization over all others. A number of these reviews also provide the inspiration for some of his 'speculative' articles: for example, De Quincey's essay *On Murder as one of the Fine Arts* (translated as *De l'assassinat considéré comme un des beaux-arts*) is the starting-point for the article 'L'Homme au sable'; a review of a play entitled *Looping the Loop* gives rise to 'Loubing the Loub', a satire upon the travels of France's President, Émile Loubet; and Léon Walras' *Éléments d'économie politique pure* provides the inspiration for an article on 'L'Échéance dans ses rapports avec le suicide' ['Settlement dates and their relationship to suicide']. On the whole, however, revealing as many of these reviews are, in them Jarry is limited, both in his manner of treatment and in the point of view expressed, by the very need to 'review'. As expressions of the personality of their author, they are much less revealing than his other articles.

It was his *Spéculations* and *Gestes*, comprising a total of 86 articles published sometimes singly, sometimes in groups of two, three, four or even five in the fortnightly *Revue Blanche* between 15 January and 15 December 1901 and 1 January and 15 December 1902 respectively, which constituted Jarry's most important contribution to that journal. It was they, too, which were responsible for making of these two years the most secure of his life, thanks to the regular and generous remuneration which he received from the *Revue Blanche* for his articles. For though the status of journalist may have been a lowly one at the time, that of *chroniqueur*, or commentator upon current events and issues, was both prestigious and well-paid, attracting the contributions of many well-established as well as aspiring writers. Indeed, Jarry was fortunate to live in a period when a wealthy and flourishing press paid its literary contributors handsomely and enabled many of them, as a result, to survive by their pen alone.

Alas, after 11 years of vigorous existence, towards the end of 1902 the *Revue Blanche* announced its forthcoming demise. Jarry was subsequently successful in negotiating with the editor of *La Renaissance Latine*, Binet-Valmer, a continuation of his series of articles under the title *Le Journal d'Alfred Jarry* – evidence, indeed, of his growing personal fame as a *chroniqueur*. The series came, however, to an abrupt end after the first two articles (published in November and December 1902) when Prince Bibesco, the review's financial backer, took objection to the third article Jarry had submitted. To compensate for the loss of his column in *La Renaissance Latine*, Fénéon managed to secure for his protégé the 'Chronique des Théâtres' in the last eight issues of the *Revue Blanche*. In the meantime, *La Plume* had agreed to publish a new series of articles under the title *Le Périple de la littérature et de l'art*, which ran from 1 January 1903 to 15 January 1904, comprising a total of 21 articles. Though *La Plume*'s remuneration was relatively meagre, Jarry was able once again to enjoy a regular income, and to profit from the gaily sociable atmosphere that pre-vailed among contributors to the review, which reached its climax in the regular banquets organized by *La Plume*, over one of which Jarry himself, in the person of 'le Père Ubu', presided and at which he first recited the delightful obscene sonnet 'Le Bain du Roi'.[5] At the same time, he contributed also to *Le Canard Sauvage*, an illustrated weekly satirical journal founded by his friend Franc-Nohain, which began publication on 21 March 1903 immediately after the demise of the *Revue Blanche*. Most of its 31 issues (the last one appeared on 18 October 1903) are devoted to a particular current event, social, political or judicial. Beginning life with a large band of contributors, many of them taken over from the *Revue Blanche*, it rapidly became the work of only three men, Franc-Nohain, Jarry and Charles-Louis Philippe. The first two of these also contributed to *L'Oeil*, a second short-lived satirical weekly founded by Franc-Nohain which for a time ran concurrently with *Le Canard Sauvage*. Jarry's articles in these two papers number 39 and 7 respectively.

The demise of *Le Canard Sauvage*, followed shortly afterwards, at the beginning of 1904, by that of *La Plume*, left Jarry in increasingly desperate straits. With the exception of half a dozen more articles, these two events were to mark the end of his journalistic career. The articles in question comprise four 'Fantaisies parisiennes' written for *Le Figaro*, in which he attempted, with only moderate success, to recapture the vein of his *Spéculations*, and of which only the first was published, on 16 July 1904. Why the others remained unpublished is not known (though there was certainly little in common between Jarry's brand of humour and the august *Figaro*), but at least their existence in manuscript form gives the lie to the tale according to which, following a disobliging remark made to him in the offices of the newspaper, he tore up his second article and stormed out uttering only the single-word reply: 'Merdre!' The other two articles (which, in contrast, show that something of his old inspiration did remain) were published – as 'Poèmes en prose'! – in the issues for June–July and September 1905 of the Milanese review *Poesia* directed by the founder-to-be of Futurism, F. T. Marinetti.

An epilogue to Jarry's career as journalist was provided by his various plans, in the last two years of his life, to publish a collection of these articles. Towards the end of 1905, he drew up a plan in the form of a complete list of the titles of his *Spéculations* and *Gestes*. All but a tiny minority of these he numbered, from 1 to 77 (though these two series consist of 86 articles, several on the same subject were bracketed together). Of these, he then selected a small quantity (varying from 35 to 22) for inclusion in an anthology to be published by Sansot as part of a series of 'six petits volumes baroques', with the title *Siloques, superloques, soliloques et interloques de Pataphysique*.[6] This project having failed to reach fruition, he finally, in the last few months of his life, seems to have conceived the idea of a much broader collection of articles, which was to be called *La Chandelle verte, lumières sur les choses de ce temps*.[7] From Jarry's own references to the 'manuscript' of this work,[8] and from Vallette's description of it in his obituary notice following his death as 'le texte très abondant des *Spéculations*',[9] it seems probable that he intended it to include, in addition to his *Spéculations* and *Gestes*, at least those articles published in *La Plume*, and perhaps even his articles from other journals. Alas, these plans had to wait another 62 years for their complete realization, with the publication by Maurice Saillet in 1969 of *La Chandelle verte*, a complete collection of all Jarry's articles of these years together with his book reviews, in a volume of almost 700 pages.

For all Jarry's hesitations, however, it is clear from these plans that he regarded his *Spéculations* and *Gestes* in the *Revue Blanche* as the kernel of this collection and as the peak of his achievement. This is a judgment with which one cannot but agree. For there are noticeable, and in some cases notable, differences in both manner and quality between the various series of articles. His supreme creation in this field, and one in which, yet again, Jarry invented virtually a new literary form, is that of the 'speculation'. (The change of title from *Spéculations* to *Gestes* in the *Revue Blanche* seems to have been in response to a remark made by Thadée Natanson, to which he alludes in the first of his articles under the new title, concerning the multiplicity of 'gestes' – actions or exploits – making up the kaleidoscopic spectacle of life, and may have been intended to flatter Natanson; it does not indicate any real difference between the two series.) The name suggests immediately the character of these articles, which distinguishes them from the 'chroniques' of previous writers. Where previous 'chroniques' were simply commentaries, sometimes witty or satirical, sometimes serious, upon current events or issues, Jarry's 'speculations' differ first and foremost in that, for him, these events are no more than a *point de départ*; starting from the most banal of subjects, many of them commonplaces of popular journalism – acts of petty crime, court proceedings, road and railway accidents and similar news items – Jarry's articles rapidly become the vehicle for the development of his own 'speculative' ideas or for the expression of a personal and highly idiosyncratic point of view. He was fortunate in this respect in enjoying a freedom in regard to both choice and treatment of subject which few previous *chroniqueurs* had enjoyed: even on the liberal *Revue Blanche*, the extreme liberty accorded to Jarry had been granted to only two previous contributors: Mallarmé, whose *Variations sur un sujet* appeared in 1894, the year in which Fénéon had joined the review, and Tristan Bernard, both authors whom he held in high regard.

While Jarry's two articles in *La Renaissance Latine* continue in the same vein, those in *La Plume*, under the heading of *Le Périple de la littérature et de l'art*, present a number of differences: much more space is given over to straightforward literary discussions (though the visual arts are, surprisingly, almost wholly neglected), and the point of view expressed is more direct and 'serious'. The differences are even greater in *Le Canard Sauvage* and *L'Oeil*. In conformity with the policy of the two papers, these articles are mostly satirical commentaries upon contemporary events, varying greatly in quality from the brilliantly successful to the rather anodyne. It is particularly towards the end of the series that the latter tend to occur – perhaps due to Jarry's inspiration drying up, but equally probably as a result of the absence of freedom which he had earlier enjoyed. There is another limiting factor, too, in these satirical articles, which applies to all satire which remains closely tied to particular events: however successful or brilliant they may have seemed at the time and may still seem to readers with a wide historical knowledge, their appeal to most present-day readers must necessarily be restricted.

But though the dominant tone and the ultimate objective of these different series of articles may vary, a great many subjects are common to all of them, and so too are a number of methods or techniques. Jarry's work as *chroniqueur* constitutes a fascinating guide to the range of interests and personal predilections of its author, as well as to the workings of his mind. It also offers a running commentary upon several of the themes expressed in his literary work, and in particular in the novels on which he was at work during this period, *Messaline, Le Surmâle* and *La Dragonne*. The subjects with which he deals can very roughly be grouped under five main headings, though the numbers in each category are of necessity only approximate, since many articles range over several fields at once.

The first of these groups, and by far the largest, comprising almost half of the total, but also the most diverse, is that of current events and issues (though excluding crime and politics). Jarry deals with such varied subjects as royalty (the funeral of Queen Victoria, the coronation of Edward VII), popular festivals (Mardi gras, 14 July), the issue of new postage stamps, the latest census, feminism, duelling, spiritualism, cannibalism, suicide, venereal disease and depopulation. To a considerable extent, his choice of subjects here is identical with that of other journalists and *chroniqueurs* of the period: all of these were subjects which aroused great public interest. But at the same time, Jarry is particularly drawn to a number of subjects, which run through most if not all of the different series. These are, in ascending order of frequency: religion; the use and abuse of alcohol; medical knowledge and practice; sports and 'sporting' events (from car-racing, horse-racing, fishing and shooting to the game of shuttlecock); and the subject of transport, in the form of cycling, the motor-car, the railways, the omnibus and even, in one article, aviation. Closely related to this subject of transport, and almost as frequent, is that of road and rail accidents, with which he shows a particular fascination.

The second group, in order of importance, is that concerning crime, the law, the police and the courts, comprising roughly one-fifth of all his articles, and over one-quarter in *Spéculations* and *Gestes*. He deals with a wide range of breaches of the law, from petty offences to acts of brutal and multiple murder; with the 'psychology' of the police and judges; and with the drama of court proceedings and confrontations. Matching his interest in road, rail and other accidents, he displays a particular interest in sensational and violent crimes (the article 'Les Sacrifices humains du 14 juillet', in *Spéculations*, is a catalogue of fatal accidents, murders and other acts of violence by means of which 'la fête nationale a été célébrée'[10]) and in sexual crimes or offences such as homosexuality, rape, prostitution and even necrophilia.

The next most important group, comprising almost half of those articles in *Le Périple de la littérature et de l'art*, though only about one-eighth of *Spéculations* and *Gestes* and about one-seventh of the total, are those articles dealing with language, literature and other art forms. Several of these are reviews of recently published or performed works by writers whom Jarry particularly admired; others discuss the relationship between literature and the plastic arts or literature and childhood; while a number express his fascination with the circus and with clowns, dance and mime, and his continuing dislike of actors. Several are also devoted to discussions of linguistic usage and form (syntax, style, orthography), or reveal his interest in theories of the origin of language and the relationships between languages.

The fourth group – about one-ninth of the total, and mostly in *Le Canard Sauvage* – deals with political subjects (apart from the Army): government policies, parliamentary debates, the institutions of the Third Republic, the unending Dreyfus Affair, and the like. Finally, there are those articles, comprising one-tenth of the total but over one-sixth of *Spéculations* and *Gestes*, devoted to the Army and to patriotism. In an age in which the Dreyfus Affair had brought the French Army into the forefront of national life and had made of it for many Frenchmen a symbol either of national honour or of injustice and unreasoning prejudice, Jarry never missed any opportunity, whether in the form of satirical broadsides or of innumerable passing stabs, to vent his feelings on the subject.

In his choice of almost all of these subjects, one overriding principle can be seen at work. Time and again, not only Jarry's treatment of them but the subjects chosen reveal an eye for the bizarre, the incongruous and the extraordinary, and for the paradoxes and inconsistencies in the thought and values of his contemporaries. Typical examples are the case of the conscript who was given a discharge from the Army because his ugliness caused 'une hilarité préjudiciable à la discipline' in the ranks;[11] his alleged discovery that, under the terms of the *Code militaire*, the practice of necrophilia constituted grounds for exemption from military service;[12] or his reference to the invention by a young Frenchman of a small cannon which fired simultaneously in opposite directions with horrific results.[13] But however fascinating and revealing the range and the nature of Jarry's subjects are, his manner of treatment is no less important. It is necessary to examine the techniques employed in *La Chandelle verte* before going on to discuss the underlying aims of these articles.

One of Jarry's favourite techniques involves taking a word or expression, used metaphorically, in a literal sense, or equating all the different meanings of a single word and treating all those objects to which it refers as the same kind of phenomenon. Thus, in 'Les Arbres français', he adds to his list of botanical species of trees such items as 'la potence' and 'les arbres généalogiques'.[14] He presents an argument for the infallibility of the Pope – addicted, he maintains, to drink – by a literal interpretation of the adage *in vino veritas*.[15] He plays upon the expression 'le métal conjugal', used figuratively to describe radium, recently discovered jointly by Pierre and Marie Curie,[16] and upon the term 'chambre' in a discussion of the Chambre des Députés.[17] By means of an initial semantic confusion of this kind, Jarry frequently puts forward and systematically develops an alternative account or 'explanation' of some commonplace or well-known event, or even deliberately confuses two distinct sets of circumstances, as for example in 'Le Monument de Boulaine', in which the pursuit of the corrupt financier Boulaine is systematically confused with the erection of a statue to the poet Baudelaire,[18] or in 'La Passion considérée comme course de côte', in which every detail of the Passion of Christ is carefully transposed into its equivalent in a bicycle-race.[19]

By far the most common of Jarry's techniques, however, is that of presentation of events from a particular point of view. More than anything else, the articles comprising *La Chandelle verte* are, in the language of literary criticism, exercises in point of view. What is most striking in these articles is the rigour and consistency with which Jarry develops his chosen viewpoint, pursuing his 'speculations' to their ultimate logical conclusions. Frequently he adopts the time-honoured satirical device of feigning to share the point of view of those he is attacking. Thus he poses as a typical worthy, serious-minded, respectable and responsible citizen, sharing the fears and moral indignations of his fellow-citizens. Delighting in clichés and conventional circumlocutions, he refers to 'nos lectures de feuilles publiques' or the stirrings of 'l'opinion publique', and feigns to identify with 'tout honnête homme', 'les contribuables' and the ubiquitous 'on'. He even poses as an upholder of the law – 'le législateur, en sa sagesse tant de fois par nous célébrée' ['the legislator, whose wisdom we have so often proclaimed']; as a 'bourgeois' – 'Quelques bourgeois pratiques, dont nous fûmes' ['A few practical-minded *bourgeois*, of which we were one'];[20] and as a loyal patriot and defender of the Army:

Nous ne manquerons point à notre coutume d'extraire de toute cérémonie patriotique l'enseignement qu'elle comporte.

[We shall not fail to observe our customary practice of drawing from every patriotic ceremony the lesson which it contains.][21]

Ce fait, pas plus qu'aucun autre, n'aura le pouvoir de nous faire dire quoi que ce soit d'irrévérencieux envers l'armée . . . .

[Neither this fact, nor any other, shall have the power to cause us to say things that are in any way irreverent about the army . . . .][22]

Similarly, in *Le Canard Sauvage*, he presents a satirical commentary upon current political events from the point of view of an honest, but naïve citizen. In the art of tongue-in-cheek irony, Jarry is without any doubt a master.

Most of the time, however, he uses the technique of adopting a point of view different from or even diametrically opposed to that of his contemporaries. One form which this frequently takes is the feigned adoption of a naïve, uncomprehending, 'outsider's' viewpoint, particularly that of someone who is a stranger to the customs and institutions of European civilization. By this means, Jarry attempts to make the familiar and commonplace appear strange and bizarre. A typical example is the first of his *Spéculations*, which he intended to open *La Chandelle verte*, 'Les Nouveaux timbres':

C'est une des superstitions humaines, quand on veut s'entretenir avec des proches momentanément éloignés, qu'on jette dans des pertuis *ad hoc*, analogues aux bouches d'égout, l'expression écrite de sa tendresse, après avoir encouragé de quelque aumône le négoce, si funeste pourtant, du tabac, et acquis en retour de petites images sans doute bénites, lesquelles on baise dévotement par derrière.

[It is one of the superstitions prevalent amongst men that, when one wishes to converse with those near to us who are momentarily far-off, one throws *ad hoc* into narrow openings, similar to sewer-vents, the written expression of one's affection, after having egged on with one's alms the baneful proprietor of the tobacconist's shop and received in return little pictures, which are no doubt holy, which one kisses piously on the back side.][23]

At other times, this technique involves a simple distortion of the perspective on events of his contemporaries – as when he chooses to regard hanging as a 'sport',[24] or in the 'explanation' that he gives of the massacre and devouring of a party of European explorers: far from being motivated by 'basse gourmandise et pur souci culinaire', the cannibals who devoured these Europeans were aiming at 'une sorte de communion avec leur civilisation'.[25] Similarly, in the article 'Paris colonie nègre', he waxes indignant at police attempts to track down a 'nigger' who had refused to pay for drinks in a café and had assaulted a waiter; far from being a petty criminal, the man was quite clearly an explorer from Africa who 'dégustait, dans l'intérêt de la science africaine, les produits de notre sol' ['was sampling, in the interests of African science, the products of our agriculture'], and who, in butting the waiter in the stomach, was merely courteously reproducing 'ce qu'il devait, non sans motif, conjecturer être le *salam du pays*' ['what he must have conjectured, not without good cause, to be the *salaam* of the country'].[26]

More frequently, one finds a deliberate inversion of the point of view and values of contemporary society – the adoption of a precisely opposite standpoint. Thus in 'Les Piétons écraseurs', we find him discussing the danger posed by pedestrians to cyclists and motorists.[27] His subtle attacks on the courts and the law result in a defence of 'illegal' and 'criminal' acts. And his reaction to the contemporary campaign against alcoholism takes the form of a defence not just of alcohol but of alcoholism: it is not alcoholics but anti-alcoholics who are ill, 'en proie à ce poison, l'eau, si dissolvant et corrosif qu'on l'a choisi entre toutes substances pour les ablutions et lessives' ['victims of that poison, water, so powerful a solvent and a corrosive that, of all possible substances, it has been chosen for the washing of our bodies and our clothes'];[28] moreover, it is 'l'usage, et à plus forte raison l'abus, des boissons fermentées' which distinguishes men from beasts ['the use, and even more the abuse, of fermented liquor'].[29]

But the most important of Jarry's techniques of presentation consists of the adoption, in various forms, of a 'scientific' point of view. Sometimes this takes the form of an attempt simply to adopt a rigorously 'objective', 'amoral' viewpoint. Most frequently, though, it consists in adopting the feigned point of view of an 'anthropologist' or a 'naturalist'. Writing as an anthropologist, he studies and cata-logues the curious customs and habits of contemporary European civilization. Combining this approach with wordplay based on simi-larity of form, in a discussion of cannibalism he makes of 'l'anthro-pophagie' a branch of 'l'anthropologie' and proceeds to treat it exactly as any other 'anthropological' phenomenon.[30] As an anthropologist-cum-naturalist, he treats of social phenomena in terms of biological 'functions', and of changing social patterns as biological 'adaptations to environment', speaking, in an article entitled 'Psychologie ex-périmentale du gendarme', of 'quelques beaux spécimens de cet organe préhensible de la société, le gendarme', of 'la morphologie externe de ces militaires', and of 'un état d'esprit spécial ... devenu propre à leur espèce' ['a number of fine specimens of that prehensile organ of society, the *gendarme'* ... 'the external morphology of these soldiers' ... 'a particular state of mind which ... has become a peculiarity of their species'].[31] While in the article 'Moeurs des noyés', he treats his subject, that of a drowned man, as a little-known biological species, carrying out (not without a touch of *humour noir*) the investigations of a naturalist into its habits and way of life.[32]

Such techniques reveal also a peculiar trait of Jarry's imagination, already commented on in the context of *Les Minutes de sable mémorial*: his tendency to see inanimate or mechanical objects in animate or biological terms. This tendency he puts to good effect in a number of his *Spéculations* and *Gestes*. In one of the most successful applications of the 'naturalist's' point of view, 'Cynégétique de l'omnibus', he transforms the omnibus into a wild beast akin to the rhinoceros and sets about a 'scientific' study of its appearance and habits and of the attempts of men to trap the animal.[33] No article in this vein, however, surpasses 'Le Drapaud' as a piece of comic writing. Beginning with a fusion of the words 'drapeau' (flag) and 'crapaud' (toad), and interpreting the exclamation 'au drapaud!' by analogy with 'au voleur!', 'à l'assassin!' and 'au loup!', Jarry makes of 'le drapaud', in a rollicking but light-hearted satire upon the Army, a wild creature to be hunted down and captured. An extract must serve to give the flavour of his application of this technique at its best:

La chasse au drapaud nous paraît, telle qu'elle se pratique actuellement, le monopole d'une société, nombreuse d'ailleurs sans cesser d'être choisie et qui a su concerver – nous l'en félicitons – les pittoresques traditions de l'ancienne vénerie. On se livre à ce sport cynégétique tant à pied qu'à cheval, les piqueurs ont des livrées d'azur par le haut et d'écarlate par le bas avec des boutons de métal partout. Des fanfares compliquées ont succédé au vétuste cor de chasse. Le fusil qui sert à abattre la bête est ingénieusement armé d'un épieu au bout. . . .

Le drapaud endormi dans sa bauge, d'après nos observations, se roule en boule à la façon du hérisson; mais ses piquants sont disposés autrement; à vrai dire il n'en porte qu'un, de couleur jaunâtre et métallique, dirigé le plus souvent vers le ciel: une sorte de corne. . . . il replie, autour de ce corps rigide et reposant sur le sol par le bout de sa queue, des ailes membraneuses, ou plutôt une aile unique, aussi mince que celles de la chauve-souris, et trilobée, quant à sa couleur, dont le bariolage flatte l'oeil presque autant que celui de certains escargots.

Il est assez fréquent que l'extrémité de la queue du drapaud se différencie en une excroissance singulière. . . . Quelques naturalistes appellent cet animal support *porc-drapaud* . . .

[Flog-hunting, as it is practised nowadays, appears to us to be the monopoly of an organization whose members are both numerous yet highly select and which has succeeded – we are delighted to say – in preserving the picturesque traditions of the ancient art of venery. The practitioners of this sport are both mounted and on foot, the livery of the whips consists of a sky-blue jacket and scarlet breeches covered all over with metal buttons. Complicated fanfares have taken the place of the time-honoured hunting horn. The rifle which is used to kill the beast is ingeniously equipped with a spike on the end. . . .

The flog asleep in its wallow, it would seem from our observations, rolls itself into a ball in the manner of the hedgehog; but its spines are arranged differently; in truth, it has only one, of a yellowish, metallic colour, which is most commonly pointed skywards: a kind of horn. . . . Around this rigid body supported by its tail which remains resting on the ground, it folds membranous wings, or rather a single wing, as thin as those of the bat and separated, as regards its colour, into three lobes, whose multicoloured aspect is almost as striking to the eye as that of certain snails.

It happens quite frequently that the tip of the tail produces a strange excrescence, differentiating it from the rest. . . . Some naturalists call this supporting creature a *flog-boarer* . . .][34]

'Le drapaud' is typical in other respects also: it provides an example not only of the workings of Jarry's imagination and of his treatment of language; it also displays one of the most characteristic features of *La Chandelle verte*: Jarry's sustained and systematic development or demonstration – appearing at times almost to border on mania – of a chosen idea or point of view. In these and other respects, *La Chandelle verte* offers a faithful portrait of the mind and character of its creator.

But what is the aim of these demonstrations? The most commonly accepted view of Jarry, even today, as well as that held by the great majority of his contemporaries, is that of a 'humorist', if not *farceur*, aiming purely at comic (or perhaps occasionally satirical) effects.[35] An exactly opposite point of view is expressed by Maurice Saillet in his introduction to *La Chandelle verte*; according to Saillet, this work shows that 'jamais Jarry ne bouffonne ni ne bafoue, et qu'il n'est pas de génie plus affirmatif ni plus résolument constructeur que le sien' ['never does Jarry jest or mock, and there is no more positive nor determinedly constructive mind than his'].[36] The truth is rather different; if the former view of Jarry's journalism is much too limited, Saillet, in reacting against it, patently flies in the face of the evidence.

One can distinguish, in *La Chandelle verte*, between four different aims or intentions. A small number of articles are perfectly 'serious' in intention, that is they are quite straightforward discussions, mainly of literary questions. A second group embraces those whose intention is purely humorous or comic, that is excluding satire. In normal usage, of course, irony and satire are generally considered to be forms of 'humour'; for the sake of clarity, however, the term is reserved here for that which is designed simply to create in the reader a reaction of amusement (ranging from a belly-laugh to merely a faint smile) as an end in itself, without the aggressive or hostile implications of satire. A third group comprises those articles whose aim is wholly or mainly satirical. Finally, a fourth group is made up of those articles in which Jarry goes beyond mere humour and satire to the expression, implicitly or explicitly, of a point of view which can be described as 'pataphysical'.

These divisions are, however, far from being clear-cut. Humour and satire often exist side by side in the same article and are sometimes inextricably intertwined; elements of spoofing and satire occur briefly in the midst of some of Jarry's most 'serious' reviews; and humour, satire and 'serious' discussions can all give rise, ultimately, to reflections which are 'pataphysical' in nature. The relative importance of each of these aims varies, moreover, from one series to another. In *Spéculations* and *Gestes*, in very rough terms, about two-fifths of the articles are wholly or mainly humorous in intention, just under a quarter are satirical, and about one tenth are 'serious' discussions, the remainder being a mixture of various aims. In *Le Périple de la littérature et de l'art*, just under half are 'serious' discussions, and roughly a quarter and a sixth are satirical and humorous respectively. In Le *Canard Sauvage* and *l'Oeil*, on the other hand, the proportions are approximately two-thirds satirical and the remainder mainly humorous in intention.

Jarry's serious articles deal with a variety of subjects. In 'Edgar Poe en action', for example, he demonstrates at some length that a recently published 'autobiographical confession' is the work of a mythomaniac who has simply plagiarized Poe's *The Adventures of Arthur Gordon Pym*. Several articles in *Gestes* ('Barnum', 'Juno Salmo au Nouveau-Cirque', 'Liane de Pougy aux Folies-Bergère') are frankly enthusiastic reviews of circus, dance and mime. On a number of occasions, he makes use of his own solid knowledge of Latin to give a lesson in translation to professional translators. In his literary criticism and discussions he adopts two main approaches: a detailed critical comparison of texts to reveal parallels between different works (a method which testifies to his critical acumen); and an 'impressionistic' approach, pointing out the abstract qualities of an author and translating those qualities into concrete images.

His efforts at humour scarcely need further illustration. Though occasionally his humour is laboured or rather feeble, on the whole the result is successful and sometimes brilliantly so. Frequently the very titles of the articles are a source of wry humour, as for example 'Le Comité directeur de l'Au-delà', 'Les Piétons écraseurs', 'Psychologie expérimentale du gendarme', 'Hommages posthumes' or 'Les Moeurs des noyés' ['The Management Committee of the Hereafter',

'Roadhog Pedestrians', 'Experimental Psychology of the *Gendarme*', 'Posthumous Homage', 'The Mores of the Drowned']. *La Chandelle verte* also contains some fine examples of *humour noir* – as in 'Le Tir dans Paris', in which Jarry recommends the streets of Paris at night for revolver practice, adding that in view of the relative inaccuracy of the revolver, 'il sera sage de ne pas ambitionner de cible de diamètre moindre qu'une tête humaine' ['it would be prudent not to aim at any target smaller in diameter than a human head'];[37] or his statements that it is because 'les noyés' are less aggressive than fish that the latter eat the former,[38] and that 'les noyés, comme les poissons, sont riches en phosphore, constituent donc un excellent engrais' ['the drowned, like fish, are rich in phosphorous, and therefore constitute an excellent fertilizer'].[39] There are also traces in *La Chandelle verte* of sadistic humour, both in a general and in a specifically sexual sense: discussing the recent invention of an automatic castigator intended for recalcitrant pupils, Jarry recommends its use to all wife-beaters and as a substitute for sexual intercourse, since that act constitutes 'une castigation intérieure' of the woman.[40] Lastly, a couple of articles in *Le Canard Sauvage*, 'La Passion considérée comme course de côte' and 'La Vierge au Manneken-Pis'., which are mainly humorous in intention and are among Jarry's most brilliantly successful comic pieces, might be construed by some as blasphemous and as evidence of a continuing hidden attachment to Christianity. It is certainly the case that Jarry's humour is here based on irreverence and disrespect for religion; but it is surely arbitrary to regard this as any more 'blasphemous' than his satirical treatment of the, for some, equally sacred secular principles of the French Republic.

As to his satire, the favourite targets of this are, not surprisingly, the Army, patriotism, the law, and the political institutions, principles and practices of the Republic; while numerous satirical barbs are directed also at such subjects as attempts at linguistic and orthographical reform, European colonialism, the institution of marriage, and doctors and the practice of medicine. Well over a dozen articles, and a vast number of passing remarks, are aimed at the Army and patriotism. A propos of a 'patriotic' newspaper article, he notes ironically that: 'nous n'aurions pas mieux dit, même aux heures où nous nous efforçons, pour garder notre cerveau plus libre, d'en évacuer toute intelligence' ['we could not have expressed it better ourselves, even in those moments in which we endeavour, in order to keep our mind clear, to vacate it of all intelligence'].[41] Satirizing the Army's blind adherence to tradition, he describes it as a relic of a bygone age, referring to 'les militaires actuels, chez qui on peut le plus commodément étudier les vestiges de l'âge de pierre, qu'ils conservent purs' ['soldiers of today, in whom one can most conveniently examine the vestiges of the Stone Age, which they preserve in their purest form'].[42] And à propos of the Lebel 86 army rifle which, he maintains, is universally known to jam when fired, he adds that: 'Il est permis de supposer que l'inventeur n'avait établi cet appareil que pour rendre, en cas de défaite, notre armement inutilisable par l'ennemi.' ['We have the right to assume that the inventor created this apparatus purely in order to render our arms unusable by the enemy in the event of defeat.'][43]

But scathing as Jarry's satire on the Army is, the follies, contradictions and absurdities (in his view) in the Law arouse even greater passion in him. The reason may well be that, though he had succeeded in escaping from the Army, he had not succeeded in evading the clutches of the State in its other forms. But his satire here goes beyond the demands of a conventionally 'commonsense' point of view, to the formulation of a much more profound and wide-ranging critique, as we shall see.

His satire on certain political issues is scarcely less virulent. The principle of universal suffrage is the object of a number of savage barbs. At several points in *La Plume* and *Le Canard Sauvage* he satirizes the anti-clericalism of Émile Combes and his dissolution of the religious Congregations. His levity at the expense of the beliefs of Christianity is more than balanced by his scorn for the secular 'religion' based on such idols as 'Progress', 'Science', and 'History'. With savage irony, in 'Le Discours de M. Combes', he accuses Combes of really adopting the philosophy that 'il faut une religion pour le peuple' and of merely substituting for Christianity this secular religion:

Dieu n'existe pas, et la preuve qu'il n'existe pas . . . *c'est qu'il s'appelle autrement*. . . . Plus de paradis, mais l'Avenir, la Vérité, la Justice, le Progrès, tous égaux, tous bourgeois, tous élus, comme dans le discours si neuf du compagnon Un Tel *sur le grand nombre des élus*, un paradis social, quoi!

> [God does not exist, and the proof that he does not exist . . . *is that he is called by another name*. . . . No paradise any more, but the Future, Truth, Justice, Progress, all equals, all *bourgeois*, all of the elect, as in the oh-so-novel speech of companion So-and-so *on the vast number of the elect*, a social paradise, what!][44]

He tends to regard the actions of governments as deriving from a policy of 'bread and circuses', with the emphasis on the latter: 'Le peuple ne se nourrit seulement pas de pain, mais aussi de parades militaires (*circenses*)' ['The populace does not live by bread alone, but by military parades (*circenses*) also'].[45] To some extent, the object of his satire in his *Spéculations* and *Gestes* is in line with the general political leanings of the *Revue Blanche* towards a 'socialist', 'anarchistic' and generally 'anti-Establishment' standpoint. But at times he diverges significantly from this line, as in 'Le Prolongement du Chemin de fer de ceinture' where he satirizes the ideas of a socialist parliamentary candidate.[46] And in *Le Canard Sauvage* he explicitly rejects the very basis of republicanism, scornfully translating the principles of 'liberty', 'equality' and 'fraternity' on which the Republic is – ostensibly – founded as 'Liberté, pour le plus fort, d'imposer à ses subordonnés ses principes fraternels, égaux et libres.' ['Freedom, for the strongest, to impose his fraternal, equal and free principles on his subordinates.'][47]

A less frequent, but no less significant, object of attack is provided by doctors, medicine and, through the latter, 'science' itself. He has a veritable loathing of doctors, whom he portrays as ignorant, superstitious, vile butchers, cutting up bodies for the sadistic pleasure of poking about inside them: 'Le curé est le médecin de l'âme. Les médecins font la curée des corps.' ['Priests make souls whole. Doctors hack bodies apart.'][48] 'M. le docteur Socquet . . . ayant soigneusement fouillé partout dans l'intérieur du cadavre, selon la coutume de ses pareils' ['Dr Soquet . . . having carefully rummaged around inside the corpse, as his kind are in the habit of doing'].[49] And in an attack on the contemporary crusade against alcoholism, which he presents as merely the modern form of a medieval crusade against heretics and witches (the threat of hell-fire having simply been transposed from the after-life into the bodily organs in the present), Jarry maintains that doctors are the new high priests of this cult: 'Les médecins sont les nouveaux prêtres qui bénéficient . . . auprès de la foule . . . du prestige d'être détenteurs de mystères. Les ignorants ont un mot pour définir les autres ignorants, spécialisés: ils les appellent des savants.' ['Doctors are the new High Priests who enjoy . . . in the eyes of the mob . . . the prestige of holding the key to mysteries. Ignorant people have a term for describing those of their kind who are specialists in ignorance: they call them scientists and scholars.'][50]

In one of his most wide-ranging attacks, bordering on direct denunciation rather than satire – 'Prix divers' in *Le Canard Sauvage* – Jarry deals with the different applications of the term 'prix' in modern society. Beginning with school prize-giving, which develops 'la vénalité des potaches', the article goes on to denounce the concept of 'price' in relation to works of art – the buying of works of art, and their consideration in terms of 'market value' – and to attack the institution of marriage, which in a previous article had been presented as legalized rape[51] and is here seen as legalized prostitution, the buying and selling (by men) of the bodies of young women: 'Une fille belle et vierge, cela se vend, comme on sait' ['A beautiful virgin is a saleable commodity, as everyone knows']. The article finally broadens out into an attack on the whole commercial ethic and basis of contemporary society: 'En matière de prix, la civilisation se présente comme un vaste bazar à treize' ['In matters of buying and selling, civilization takes on the appearance of a huge sixpenny bazaar'].[52]

There would seem to be little – if anything, in fact– outside of a small and restricted domain of literature and the arts in the society of his time of which Jarry does approve. Modern technology is dismissed, at least momentarily, simply as a complicated barbarism, 'l'âge de fer' representing little real advance upon 'l'âge de pierre'.[53] Medicine, and by implication, the whole of modern science, is regarded merely as a new superstition. Even teachers are explicitly likened to their 'Stone Age' equivalents: 'Le professeur de l'âge de pierre (imité par les professeurs modernes en des termes plus compliqués)' ['The teacher of the Stone Age (imitated by teachers of today in more complicated terms)'].[54] Almost all those values upon which contemporary society, and indeed the whole of modern civilization, is based would seem to be implicitly relegated by Jarry to the domain of myth, of a vast body of purely mythical conceptions. The question that must therefore be asked is what, if anything, he wishes to put in the place of the society and values which he condemns. Satire upon existing institutions and values generally implies the affirmation of other, opposite values. Is this the case with Jarry?

Underlying much of Jarry's satire is his utter hostility to all attempts to subordinate the individual to the State. 'Anarchistic' and 'negative' such an attitude may be, in the eyes of the State and those who uphold it. But this standpoint is also in a sense positive, in that it upholds the supreme value of the individual. In the great age of individualism represented by the France of the 'Belle Époque', Jarry stands out as one of the fiercest defenders of the status (one hesitates to say 'rights') of the individual and of the value of absolute, anarchistic individualism.

So much, at least, may be positive. But Jarry's position with regard to the society, and the civilization, of his time goes beyond mere satire to the expression of a 'pataphysical' point of view, that is, beyond the undermining of existing social institutions to a 'detachment' not only from these, but from all ethical values as well. This sometimes takes the form of the expression of a purely amoral or ahistorical point of view. A typical example (which Jarry pushes to the point of deliberate paradox) occurs in a discussion of the concept of 'judicial error':

On n'est pas encore très accoutumé à se dire qu'il y a *toujours* erreur judiciaire. Il n'est pas impossible que dans quelques douzaines de siècles, l'opinion devenant publiquement admise que les vertus et les crimes sont choses sociales et arbitraires, on comprenne qu'il n'y a qu'une erreur judiciaire aussi grave que celle de condamner un innocent: c'est celle de condamner un homme que nos modes disent coupable. Les délits ou les bonnes actions ne seront, dans ces temps utopiques, que différentes manières de vivre des honnêtes gens. Ainsi, on dira, pour la commodité du langage et pour éviter de faciles confusions: 'M. X . . ., l'honnête homme qui a fondé un prix de vertu; M. Y . . ., l'honnête homme qui a assassiné une vieille dame.'

> [People are still not very accustomed to the idea that there is *always* judicial error. It is not beyond the bounds of possibility that in a few thousand years, public opinion having come to accept that virtue and crime are purely social and arbitrary matters, people will understand that there is only one judicial error worse than the condemnation of an innocent man: it is the condemnation of a man whom fashion decrees to be guilty. Crimes and good deeds will simply be, in those utopian times, different ways of life of worthy people. Thus it will be customary, for the sake of linguistic convenience and to avoid simple confusions, to refer to 'Mr X . . ., the worthy citizen who created a prize for virtue; Mr Y . . ., the worthy citizen who murdered an old lady'.][55]

A similar point of view is expressed in a discussion of fatal accidents: 'Les accidents de métro, chemins de fer, tramways, etc., ont ceci de bon, comme les guerres, qu'ils éclaircissent le trop-plein misérable de la population.' ['Accidents on the underground, the railways, trams, etc., are, like wars, a good thing in this respect, that they thin out the wretched excess of population.'][56] For all Jarry's lack of pity and compassion, however, such statements (which are elsewhere contradicted by his satire on the massacres of warfare) smack of a degree of deliberate provocation. More frequent, and more revealing of his true attitude, are his comments on 'la justice', a term which, by a curious semantic trick of the French language, confuses 'the law' as laid down by legislators and enforced by police, magistrature and prison service, and 'Justice' as an ideal concept, always striven after but never attained. The gap which exists between the two is a time-honoured target of satirists and social critics, and Jarry similarly is quick to point out the arbitrariness and relativity of existing criteria of legality and illegality. It is no accident that, three times in *La Chandelle verte* and twice in the context of discussing criminal trials, he alludes to Pascal's celebrated phrase on the relativity of concepts of 'law' and 'justice': 'Vérité au deçà des Pyrénées, erreur au delà . . .' ['Truth on one side of the Pyrenees, error on the other . . .'].[57] This context goes a long way towards explaining his preoccupation with crime, and particularly sexual crimes, in which it would be wrong to see merely a morbid curiosity. For of all the actions considered at various points in history to be 'illegal' or 'immoral', none are more subject to variation, from one age and from one civilization to another, than sexual acts.

But Jarry goes beyond merely pointing out the 'absurdities' and 'incoherence' of the law,[58] to a denial of any valid basis for it whatsoever. The first of his *Gestes* expresses his intention to treat all acts as absolutely equal (though with the added implication here that they will be judged solely from an aesthetic point of view): 'Tous ces gestes, et même tous les gestes, sont à un degré égal esthétiques, et nous y attacherons une même importance.' ['All these acts, and even all acts generally, are aesthetic to the same degree, and we shall attach an equal importance to them all.']⁵⁹ Of more significance is his application, in his comments on the law, and on the claims of the State in general, of the principle referred to in the previous chapter of the 'identity of opposites'. Thus in 'L'Échéance dans ses rapports avec le suicide' he chooses to regard the 'rights' of the State and of the individual citizen to mint money freely as absolutely equal: 'nous avons esquissé une théorie de la fabrication de la monnaie fiduciaire en libre concurrence, opération dite irrévérencieusement par l'État faux-monnayage quand il ne la perpètre pas lui-même.' ['we have sketched out a theory of free and competitive printing of banknotes, an operation which the State irreverently calls forgery when it does not perpetrate it itself.']⁶⁰

Similarly, in 'De quelques viols légaux', he disputes the 'right' of the State to commit 'murder' either on an individual scale (executions) or on a mass scale (war) when that right is denied to the individual. Implicitly rejecting what one might call the 'social contract' view of society – the view that organized society is based upon the open or tacit agreement of a majority of its members to renounce and condemn certain acts for their own protection and mutual self-interest – Jarry adopts the point of view that the only 'right' which the majority holds in any context, whether law, politics, social behaviour or any other, is 'le droit du plus fort'. In 'De quelques viols légaux', this view is expressed in the form of an open denunciation of the *Code civil*: 'on lira avec plus de fruit le Code en rétablissant en toute son ampleur une expression écrite partout en abrégé: *la loi*. On doit bien lire: la loi [du plus fort].' ['A more fruitful understanding of the Code can be obtained by restoring to its full form an expression which is everywhere written in abbreviated form: namely, *the law*. It is necessary to read this as: the law [of the strongest].']⁶¹ In conformity with this view, in a number of articles Jarry presents the conflict between an accused individual and the law as a battle between equally legitimate, though unequally matched, forces. Thus in 'Le Tueur de femmes', the courtroom confrontation between a man accused of the murder of several women and the presiding judge is seen as a contest between two 'killers': 'M. Vidal, le Tueur de Femmes, et cet autre spécialiste M. Trinquier, président des assises, le Tueur d'Hommes'. The contest however is an unequal one and M. Trinquier must inevitably win:

Car M. Trinquier a groupé autour de lui des gendarmes à la meule . . ., et des
jurés à la douzaine. Tous ces préparatifs confirment la préméditation de son
attentat contre M. Vidal; mais peu lui en chaut. Quelle différence flagrante
n'y a-t-il pas en effet entre M. Vidal, qui assassine pour voler, et le Tueur
d'Hommes à qui l'État consent 'un fixe'?

> [For M. Trinquier has surrounded himself with masses of *gendarmes* . . . and
> jurors by the dozen. All these preparations confirm the premeditation of his
> attempt on the life of M. Vidal; but this matters little to him. What a glaring
> difference is there not, in fact, between M. Vidal, who kills in order to steal,
> and the Killer of Men to whom the State grants a stipend?][62]

Much, of course, in such articles as these smacks of deliberate and
wilful provocation. But behind the element of provocation, and
irrespective of any wryly comic intention, there lies also a fundamental seriousness. For Jarry's ultimate perspective in *La Chandelle
verte* is, at its most radical, one which, in conformity with the
principles of his pataphysics, not only regards all concepts, actions,
criteria and values as equal in value, but regards them as such
because all are equally arbitrary. He sees the whole of adult existence
as an extension and magnification of the *games* of childhood which
are governed by a set of, perhaps complex, but arbitrary rules:

Si l'homme adulte, comme on l'a dit, 'n'est qu'un enfant qui a grandi',
n'est-on pas à peu près certain qu'il a grandi *en tant qu'enfant*, et qu'il n'a fait
qu'exagérer ses tendances puériles?

> [If the adult human being is but, as has been said, 'a child who has grown
> up', is it not almost certain that he has grown up *as a child*, and that he has
> simply come to exaggerate his childhood [*or:* childish] tendencies?]

Indeed, the only real difference between the world of childhood and
that of adulthood is that in the latter,

Maintenant seulement tout est en jeu. Ce que les grandes personnes
appellent jeu, ce sont les occupations autres que les leurs, qui ne dérangent
point les leurs; les jeux autres que leurs jeux, et les seuls qu'elles permettent,
pour cette raison.

> [Only now, everything is part of the game. What grown-ups call games are
> occupations other than theirs, which do not interfere with theirs; games other
> than their games, and the only ones which they allow, for this reason.][63]

Beyond the humour and the satire, Jarry's ultimate aim in *La Chandelle
verte* is to jolt us out of our accepted view of the world and our
unconsciously accepted values, and to force us to share his own
perspective on life (or that which he endeavoured to adopt): that of
his 'science' of pataphysics. It was with complete seriousness,

moreover, that he wrote at the end of *Faustroll* that 'La pataphysique est la science ...'. For the pataphysical viewpoint – dispassionate interest, curiosity unmotivated by any *parti pris*, refusal to apply unwarranted ethical judgments – is also the theoretical ideal of the scientist. To this ideal, Jarry adds the attempt to view the events of history (which include those of the present) from a point outside and above 'history', from which even the most fundamental and sacred laws of society appear as merely transient conventions. For Jarry, and for pataphysics, life itself is a 'convention':[64] a vast, unending and extraordinarily elaborate *game*.

It is in this context that one can better understand also his preoccupation with language, and even his apparently most gratuitous humour and spoofing based on wordplay. Numerous articles in *La Chandelle verte* express his fascination with language, not as a medium of communication, but as form. Moreover his playing with knowledge or ideas is matched, for the very same reason, by his playing with language itself. Beyond the puns, the deliberate misinterpretation of metaphors, the tendency to treat words as autonomous objects divorced from meaning and context, lies Jarry's conviction that all the concepts and beliefs on which our civilization, and indeed 'civilization' itself, rests are mere constructions of language: that all 'reality' resolves itself, in the final analysis, into a purely linguistic reality, into autonomous linguistic structures, written forms, mere sounds. Though most of the time this idea remains implicit in *La Chandelle verte*, Jarry expresses it explicitly à propos of the concept of time. Under the guise of a humorous discussion of the arrival of the New Year, he develops the theme of the artificial or 'imaginary' nature of time (and, with it, of space): both are part of the fabric of purely 'imaginary' concepts by means of which mankind seeks to give form or structure to the shapelessness of existence, to create 'meaning' out of chaos:

l'homme pourrait-il vivre sans le secours des dates? La durée est chose trop transparente pour être perçue autrement que colorée de quelques divisions. . . .
La seule vérité actuelle est celle-ci: l'espace et le temps ne sont que des *formes* . . .

> [Could man survive without the help of dates? Time is something too transparent to be perceived in any other way than coloured by a few divisions. . . .
> The only truth here and now is this, that space and time are merely *forms* . . .][65]

Similarly, in Jarry's view, all the ideas and values which provide the motivation for our actions and by means of which we regulate and govern our lives and society – those of *la patrie*, 'flag', 'duty', 'right', no less than those of 'good' and 'evil', 'morality' and 'immorality' – are purely 'imaginary solutions', or 'myths', at bottom mere words.

La Chandelle verte, then, far from being, as it has sometimes been seen, the merely 'incidental' production, for financial reasons, of a writer whose real devotion was to 'pure' literature, is one of the most fascinating and most important of Jarry's works. These 'journalistic' articles are of value in three essential respects. They are valuable, first of all, simply as entertaining reading: though the quality is variable, many are good, and some are superb examples of humour, irony and satire. Secondly, in the context of Jarry himself, they are of immense value for the light they throw on his personality and interests, on the workings of his mind, and on the philosophical standpoint which he strove to make his own. And they are valuable, finally, in many instances, as expressions of that philosophical standpoint: as examples of the application to the events of, and the values and the assumptions underlying, everyday life of a 'pataphysical' point of view.

Chapter Nine

Sexual and sporting feats: 'Messaline' and 'Le Surmâle'

Messaline and *Le Surmâle*, published in 1901 and 1902 respectively, stand together in Jarry's work like the two halves of a diptych. The first, subtitled by its author 'roman de l'ancienne Rome', goes back for its subject to the first century AD; the second, subtitled 'roman moderne', is set amidst the technological wonders of the future, in the year 1920. Both novels centre around the theme of sexual exploits, not to say 'performance', the one female, the other male. And both are much more conventional in style and form than Jarry's previous novels: each tells a 'story', introduces a set of recognizable 'characters', and evokes a background to events. Both are, as a result, more accessible, at least superficially, to the average reader. These two novels, and Jarry's journalism which is contemporary with them, would seem to show a turning away from the highly idiosyncratic style and intensely personal themes of his earlier work, to a much greater awareness of writing for a public, and of the demands of that public.

But both *Messaline* and *Le Surmâle* are works which can, and which need to, be read on two levels: that of the 'uninitiated' reader who takes them at their face value, in the manner of Jarry's contemporaries who saw *Messaline* simply as another 'historical' novel and *Le Surmâle* as a 'science fiction', sporting and sexual extravaganza; and that of the reader (but how many were there outside of Jarry himself?) who has grasped the secret of his attitude to life and literature as expressed by the principles of pataphysics.

Given the central role of sexual themes in the two novels, it is important to trace Jarry's treatment of such themes hitherto and the evolution of his attitude. From the beginning, sexual themes and images are an almost constant feature of his work, from his first complete published text, *Haldernablou*, through *Les Minutes de sable mémorial*, *César-Antechrist*, *Les Jours et les Nuits*, *L'Amour en visites* and *Faustroll* to *L'Amour absolu*, completed in the year which preceded the writing of *Messaline*. Almost the only exceptions to this generalization are the plays of the *Ubu* cycle, though even here sexual themes do make a brief appearance, albeit in farcical vein. *Haldernablou*, with its savage misogyny, its frank treatment of the theme of homosexual love and its autobiographical content, provides us with a first sharp insight into the attitudes and the emotional life of its author, suggesting both an attraction to and a fear of love and physical contact, coupled with feelings of guilt and remorse in its young author. A similar personal obsession is even more clearly suggested by the apocalyptic rhetoric of 'Les Prolégomènes de Haldernablou' in *Les Minutes*. Here Jarry unites and personifies (in a manner which prefigures *Messaline*) sexual and divine forces in the image of the sacred Phallus, which here brings destruction and divine retribution to all who have 'violé la Norme' and dreamed of 'purer' forms of love. In *César-Antechrist*, the invocation in the 'Acte héraldique' – 'Phallus déraciné, NE FAIS PAS DE PAREILS BONDS!' – suggests a simultaneous fascination with and fear of unbridled sexual forces and instincts. The same Act contains also a strange dialogue between the signs Plus and Minus, whose translation of sexual forces (as, elsewhere, of other concepts) into mathematical and heraldic symbols illustrates a favourite technique of Jarry.

Les Jours et les Nuits presents the subject from a very different angle: here we see the rarefied and spiritualized love of Sengle for his brother Valens, which progressively reveals itself to be, in reality, a narcissistic self-love. Love, divorced from its physical basis, is associated here with the themes of recollection of the past, self-recognition and experience of 'eternity'. In *L'Amour en visites*, on the other hand, we find Jarry's first treatment of heterosexual love, but in a fiercely satirical vein which expresses the same savage misogyny as earlier works, and which associates sex with sordidness and squalor. In *Faustroll*, the subject makes a brief appearance in Book VI (whose title 'Chez Lucullus' looks forward to the Gardens of Lucullus in *Messaline*), in the form of the theme of ejaculation; this is associated firstly (in Chapter XXXIII, 'Du Termès') with the theme of death (Visité, the daughter of the Bishop Mensonger, falls victim to Faustroll, 'car elle ne survécut point à la fréquence de Priape'), and then, in the following chapter, 'Clinamen', with that of artistic creativity whose activity it parallels. Love again forms the dominant theme in *L'Amour absolu*, with its evocation of an incestuous and 'absolute' love with which, once more, the themes of fear and death are associated.

In almost all of these instances, then, alongside a persistent note of misogyny, love is associated with a revulsion from physical contact, and with fear. There is little if anything in Jarry's work prior to the two novels of 1901 and 1902 which would seem to presage a more favourable treatment of the subject. Yet *Messaline* (despite the opinion of many of Jarry's contemporaries, who saw in the novel a vilification of woman, reduced to the level of a mere courtesan or prostitute) and

Le Surmâle contain his first sustained and, so to speak, 'positive' treatment of heterosexual love. There are indications, though only slight ones, in his other writings of this period of a modification of his earlier attitude. Whilst some of his *chroniques* (such as 'Battre les femmes', in *Gestes*) continue to express the same savage misogyny as before, others (for example, 'Balistique de la danse' and 'Liane de Pougy aux Folies-Bergère', also in *Gestes*) reveal, if not an appreciation of women as sexual beings, at least an appreciation of their physical skill in dance and mime.[1] And there is even the suggestion, in a review of Verlaine's *Parallèlement*, of some erotic appreciation of the female form: after evoking the 'contours' of the printed text which are such a source of delight, Jarry notes that it is impossible 'de suivre les arabesques voluptueususes du texte ... sans être poursuivi, *agréablement d'ailleurs*, par des imaginations de choses arrondies: de petites femmes et de petites filles, de chairs blondes et de boucles noirs, de joues, de ventres, de seins et de cuisses ...' ['to follow the voluptuous arabesques of the text ... without being pursued, *pleasantly so moreover*, by visions of round forms: of young women and girls, of white flesh and dark curls, of cheeks, of bellies, of breasts and of thighs ...'].[2] Such a sentiment, if genuine, is a far cry from the savage reference in 'De l'inutilité du théâtre au théâtre' to the female body with its 'tissu adipeux – odieux parce qu'il est utile, générateur du *lait*' ['adipose tissue – odious because it is useful, the source of production of *milk*'].[3]

Jarry's journalistic writings reveal also another factor: his profound interest in the psychology, or more precisely the psycho-physiology, of sexual attraction and desire. A review dated 1 March 1903 of *La Psychologie de l'amour* by his friend Gaston Danville shows his acquaintance with the theories of philosophers, psychologists and physiologists, and his own erudition, in this field (as well as his particular attraction to Danville's attempts to formulate mathematically the laws of physical attraction). He asserts that novelists hitherto have concerned themselves only with the behaviour of lovers and not with love itself: 'Les psychologues du roman n'ont jamais observé l'amour, mais des amoureux' ['Novelistic psychologists have never studied love, but only lovers'].[4] His own interest, by implication, is therefore in the phenomenon of love or sexual attraction *in itself*, as a fundamental psychological and physiological force.

And yet, there is evidence at certain points in Jarry's work that his treatment of the themes of sex and love is not at all times to be taken wholly at face value. The outrageously declamatory tones of 'Les Prolégomènes de Haldernablou', no less than the mathematico-heraldico-sexual extravaganza of *César-Antechrist* or the composition of *L'Amour en visites*, are suggestive of an element of wilful exaggeration, of sheer playfulness, or of irony. It may be that Jarry, by giving free rein to his own obsessions, is attempting to come to terms with those obsessions by means of translating them into imaginative terms, which he then juggles with in an ironical, only semi-serious, or even purely farcical way.

An additional factor forming the background to *Messaline* is Jarry's interest in classical antiquity. Though his work from beginning to end reveals his thorough knowledge of the literature of classical Greece and Rome, he was by no means alone in his use of such sources. The ancient world had long been a fashionable subject amongst men of letters, and the 1880s and 1890s had seen a particular vogue for novels set in Graeco-Roman, and even Middle Eastern, antiquity. This interest had been fanned by the notion, which the 'Decadent' movement of the 1880s had helped to popularize, of a parallel between the 'aged' and 'tired' civilization of nineteenth-century Europe, threatened by a new invasion of 'barbarians' from without or within, and the Rome of the 'Decadence' (identified, somewhat inaccurately, with the first century AD when Roman power was actually at its height). The result had been the upsurge of a wide-spread popular interest in the subject of ancient Rome and the creation of an image of Roman civilization as brutal and cruel, given over to displays of gaudiness, to debauchery and to an orgy of self-indulgence, as exemplified by such figures as the Emperors Nero and Heliogabalus. Jarry himself refers also to a contemporary interest among artists in the Empress Messalina.[5]

Most of this interest in classical Rome, however, is greeted by Jarry with disdain. In one of his articles in *La Plume* entitled 'Héliogabale à travers les âges', he dismisses both the actions of the Roman Emperor and contemporary interest in the supposed 'orgies' of ancient Rome as puerile.[6] More significantly, he is contemptuous of those authors and works whose chief aim is historical 'reconstruction' – including the popular *Quo vadis?* by the Polish novelist Henryk Sienkiewicz, the first complete French translation of which appeared in 1900 just as the serialization of Jarry's *Messaline* began in the pages of the *Revue Blanche*.

It is necessary, therefore, to determine precisely Jarry's own position regarding the question of 'history' and historical reconstruction, since this is vital to an understanding of *Messaline*. Fortunately, supplementing his brief remarks in *La Chandelle verte* and elsewhere,[7] he has left us a lengthy and detailed discussion of the matter in a lecture delivered at the Salon des Indépendants in 1901, entitled *Le Temps dans l'art*. The chief ambition of the artist in any medium, Jarry states, is to 'mettre son oeuvre en dehors du temps'. Yet 'time', or history, is necessarily the raw material of all art. What then should the artist's attitude be towards this raw material? He admits the fascination of the past and the temptation of historical reconstruction, a fascination which lies, for the writer, above all in language:

La reconstitution historique a toujours séduit, comme prétexte à des oeuvres d'art. La couleur spéciale ou la forme bizarre des bijoux anciens charment le peintre, comme les mots des âges disparus paraissent à l'écrivain d'autant plus sonores et expressifs qu'ils sont, même à lui-même, plus incompréhensibles.

> [Historical reconstruction has always appealed to creative artists as a pretext for the creation of works of art. The peculiar colour or strange form of the precious stones of antiquity fascinate the painter, just as the words of past ages seem to the writer all the more sonorous and expressive the more incomprehensible they are, even to himself.][8]

But should the primary aim of the artist be historical reconstruction as an end in itself, the establishment of historical 'truth'? In order to examine this question, Jarry takes as an example Breughel's *Massacre of the Innocents*, a work which is totally anachronistic, showing Roman soldiers in sixteenth-century dress in the streets of a typical Flemish town. This anachronism, he maintains, is totally irrelevant. The true qualities of Breughel's painting – its 'horreur tragique' – are independent of historical veracity. Besides, the true subject of the painting is an eternal one, which is re-enacted in every war.[9]

Not quite content with this as a final answer, however, Jarry also looks briefly at the argument that the very uniqueness of certain elements of the past may cause a painter or a novelist to modify significantly his conception of his subject – and that art and literature have a role to play in restoring and recreating lost civilizations. His implied answer to this argument is a denial of any essential difference between past and present, or indeed between different cultures and civilizations – a view made explicit in a book review of 1 August 1901, in which he declares that all travel literature proves 'que dans les temps les plus anciens et chez les peuples les plus lointains c'est exactement la même chose qu'aujourd'hui chez nous' ['in the most ancient times and amongst the most distant peoples, things are exactly the same as they are today amongst us'].[10] But the example chosen in *Le Temps dans l'art* (that of the omnibus, which arouses in modern man the same fears as some prehistoric monster did in our Stone Age ancestors) here turns the whole issue into farce, sidestepping the question (it may well have been this, together with Jarry's diatribes against soldiers who, he claims, set out deliberately to massacre small children, that provoked the consternation of the audience at this lecture).[11] His conclusion, however, which derives solely from his discussion of Breughel, is emphatic:

En somme, l'oeuvre d'art se passe assez bien de la notion de temps: le souci
de la reconstitution d'une époque n'a d'autre effet que de retarder le moment
où elle sera délivrée du temps, c'est-à-dire éternelle et dans la gloire. Si l'on
veut que l'oeuvre d'art devienne éternelle un jour, n'est-il pas plus simple, en
la libérant soi-même des lisières du temps, de la faire éternelle tout de suite?

> [All in all, the work of art is able to dispense quite happily with the concept of
> time: the attempt to recreate a particular era has no other result than that of
> delaying the moment at which it will be released from time, that is to say
> eternal and crowned with glory. If one wishes a work of art to become eternal
> some day, is it not simpler, by liberating it oneself from the contours of time,
> to make it eternal here and now?][12]

Whether based on reasoned argument or simply stubborn prejudice, therefore, Jarry's position is clear: he refuses to recognize any
uniqueness or particularity in the past, and chooses to regard history
solely as a *décor* and a pretext. The implications for *Messaline*, and
even for the 'futuristic' *Le Surmâle*, are far-reaching.

Messaline appeared in six successive issues of *La Revue Blanche* from
1 July to 15 September 1900, triumphantly marking the beginning of
Jarry's regular contribution to that review, and was published in
volume form by the Éditions de la Revue Blanche in July 1901. Jarry's
main source for the events of the novel is Book XI of Tacitus' *Annals*,
supplemented by details from Juvenal, Suetonius and other classical
authors.[13] These sources recount in censorious tones the scandalous
promiscuity of the Empress Messalina, wife of Claudius, her debauchery and corruption of the whole imperial court, her deplorable
influence on the Roman populace, and her eventual death on the
orders of Claudius, whose eyes were finally opened.

Jarry follows these sources closely for the main framework of
events in his novel. Part I, 'Le Priape du Jardin royal', begins with
Messalina, having left her husband sated and sleeping, descending
by night to the squalid suburbs of Rome, where she takes her place
alongside the professional prostitutes of a common brothel, 'la
maison du Bonheur', consumed by a desperate, compulsive desire
which even the brutal assaults of countless men are unable to satisfy.
We are next introduced to the eccentric and enigmatic figure of
Claudius, 'ce personnage falot et si incompréhensible qu'on n'a
jamais su si ce fut un homme de génie ou un idiot' ['this colourless, so
utterly incomprehensible character that no-one has ever known
whether he was a genius or an idiot'],[14] so concerned with his
innumerable volumes of history and his memoirs that he alone in the
imperial palace – most of whose male occupants have at some time or
other been her lovers – knows nothing of his wife's infidelities.
Claudius' dictating of his memoirs offers a convenient device for
sketching in his past life – his rejection by his family, the universal

belief in his idiocy, his debauchery, the circumstances of his access-
sion to the throne following the murder of Caligula – and for
conveying his blind attachment to Messalina. The same chapter
recounts also Messalina's awakening and rising, describing her train
of thoughts on the morning after her night spent in the brothel. We
see her cult of her own naked body, and above all her worship of her
chosen god, Phallus, together with her despairing belief that he has
fled from the house in which he seemed to have lodged and taken
refuge in some new, unknown place. Gradually the idea takes hold of
her that Phallus, a god who has many different names – 'Pan, Priape,
Phallus, Phalès (qui est son nom divin), Amour, Bonheur, le dieu de
qui elle sait le plus d'invocations!' ['Pan, Priapus, Phallus, Phales
(which is his divine name), Love, Happiness, the god for whom she
knows more invocations than any other!']¹⁵ – and one of whose forms
is that of Priapus, 'dieu des Jardins', has taken refuge in the vast and
magnificent Gardens of Lucullus, now in the hands of the mysterious
and exotic 'Valérius l'Asiatique'. In her desire to obtain for herself
both the key to the Gardens and 'la clé du dieu', she determines to
secure the death of Valerius through the services of Publius Suilius, a
professional denouncer. Valerius is dragged before Claudius by a
motley band of soldiers, where he is accused, amongst other charges,
of conspiracy against the Emperor. Condemned to death by a
reluctant Claudius, he is allowed the privilege of taking his own life:
that evening, he ceremonially cuts his throat, and his body is
cremated on a huge funeral pyre in a corner of the Gardens. That
same night, Messalina visits the Gardens of Lucullus in search of her
god. The visit is the occasion for a lengthy description of this vast and
mysterious domain, as seen through the eyes of the Empress, in
all the splendour of its weird and fantastic exoticism. After a long
search, Messalina encounters, in the centre of the huge 'hippodrome'
of Lucullus which is surrounded by precious objects, a human form
which she takes to be that of the god – and which turns out to be the
mime, Mnester, from whose attempted embrace she flees. But this
event is followed by the description of a performance by Mnester in
the circus to mark the Emperor's fifty-eighth birthday, during which
the fortuitous coincidence of his dance and song with an eclipse of the
sun convinces Messalina that Mnester is after all an incarnation of the
god she seeks.

Part II, 'Les Adultères légitimes', recounts Messalina's vain
attempts to make Mnester, who has sunk into a state of apparent
stupor, return her love, followed by her love for other men – for 'il
n'est du caractère d'aucune femme d'hésiter longtemps entre un dieu
unique, fût-il de l'amour, et un nombre pluriel d'hommes' ['it is not in
the nature of any woman to hesitate for long between a single god,
even were he the god of love, and a plurality of men'].¹⁶ She

conceives a passion for a dashing young patrician, Silius, whose facile eloquence had seduced her, and with cold-blooded venality organizes the mass sale of the privilege of citizenship and allows men to go to their death in order to attempt to buy Silius' love with a flood of costly gifts. By this means, and by the force of her own ardour, she succeeds in her designs. But Silius becomes increasingly jealous of her legitimate husband, and desires to have the exclusive possession of her. Bowing to his wish, Messalina, without divorcing Claudius, secretly marries him. The marriage is celebrated by Bacchanalian revelries, terminated by a gladiatorial combat during which Messalina, consumed by a sudden desire for a Negro gladiator, causes the death of his adversary and then, in a frenzy, calls upon the unwilling Negro to kill her. At last Claudius, absent from Rome, learns of his wife's adultery through the denunciation of his secretary, and Messalina's piqued former lover, Narcissus. Returning to Rome, he allows himself to be persuaded into ordering her death and that of Silius and his accomplices. Messalina is trapped by Claudius' soldiers in the gardens to which she has fled at night, reduced by her terror to a state of apparent idiocy and childishness. A dagger pushed into her hand brings her back to the present, but at this point she falls once again into her former religious frenzy, deploring the flight of her god. Before her refusal to take her own life, a soldier advances with drawn sword; and it is this object in which Messalina sees the final incarnation of the god whom she had sought in these same gardens, which she embraces and which she now implores to possess her entirely. Pierced by the soldier's blade, she falls to the ground, and the novel closes with Claudius, at first unable to convince himself that she is really dead, then succumbing to despair, finally meditating upon his next, and fourth, wife.

As a background to these events, Jarry presents us with a vivid and memorable portrait of Rome in the first century A.D., emphasizing such features as the venality of the soldiers, the ferocity, fickleness and barbarity of its crowds, the universal treachery and fear of treachery, and the barbarity of Roman 'justice' which appears as a mere travesty of justice. He also describes certain of the customs and laws, such as those relating to denunciation and marriage. Three features in particular stand out in this portrait of Imperial Rome. The first is the universal cruelty and bloodlust, whether in the form of the savagery of the crowd, of the frequency of bloody gladiatorial combats, of the numerous murders and executions ordered by Claudius (who, however, is less savage than his predecessors), or of the long list of murders and assassinations carried out at the instigation of Messalina. The second feature is the universal obsession with sexual pleasures, seen not merely in Messalina and her entourage, but in the Emperor and in Rome as a whole, which becomes 'la ville des adultères depuis l'exemple de l'impératrice' ['the city of adultery in the wake of the Empress's example'.][17] Prostitution, both male and female, abounds, while the omnipresence of erotic statues and other objects serves as a constant reminder of the preoccupation with sexual satisfactions. The third feature is the dominance of religious preoccupations. Everywhere we see images of Rome's pagan gods, in statues and other objects representing them, and everywhere we see evidence of religious cults and beliefs, from a preoccupation with auguries and fortune-telling to the worship of pagan deities.

The picture which Jarry paints of Roman life is thus a stark and impressive one. But his aim in creating this portrait is not historical reconstruction as an end in itself. On the contrary, these features remain subordinate to the needs of the narrative, and serve also to express and to echo the main themes of the novel. The same applies to Jarry's numerous descriptions of objects. Occasionally the extent of the detail in some of the novel's descriptive passages (for example, that of the fabulous Gardens of Lucullus) seems to reveal a measure of self-indulgence on the part of the author, a succumbing to the temptation, to which he referred in *Le Temps dans l'art*, of the fascination of strange and forgotten words. The same is true of the extreme detail of his descriptions of Mediterranean fish, or of Vectius Valens' learned reflections on the origins and varieties of absinthe and other potions distilled from plants. But though the detail may appear excessive, the underlying aim of the description is never either purely decorative or historical: all of these objects incarnate and symbolize the major themes of the novel.

These themes can be approached most directly through the characters themselves, of whom only two, Messalina and Claudius, are of major importance. Claudius appears as a weak, indecisive individual, wilfully blind or else too lost in his own erudition to see clearly into events around him, given to speech-making and play-acting in order to hide his own weakness, but dominated, like his wife (though to a lesser extent), by sexual needs. His portrayal is not without touches of humour, through such comic details as his stuttering, his nervous tics and trembling and his habit of lapsing in moments of distraction into Greek. His young wife, on the other hand, is a woman of limited intelligence, superstitious, jealous and vengeful, cruel, cynical and murderous in pursuit of her aims, relying on an almost animal cunning and on awareness of her own irresistible sexual power.

Neither character is fully 'rounded', though Messalina at least does 'live' through our seeing directly into and participating in her anguish. But Jarry's aim is not to create fully rounded characters: it is to show us a woman totally dominated by a single passion and idea. For the true subject of *Messaline* is not a woman, nor womankind in general, but the impersonal force of sex itself. Messalina is the incarnation of unbridled sexuality, the incarnation of the eternal prostitute whose shadow has hung over Rome from its foundation. This theme of sexuality takes on four main attributes in the novel. The first is that of insatiability. The brothel in Chapter I is described in images of overflowing and of things uncontainable, and Messalina's own insatiability is emphasized by a graphic detail borrowed from the poet Juvenal:

Et il vint des hommes, des hommes et des hommes.
Jusqu'à l'aube, où le *leno* congédia ses vierges.
La dernière, après même sa suivante, elle ferma sa cellule, *mais le désir la consumait encore.*

> [And there came men, and more men, and yet more men.
> Until the dawn broke, when the *leno* dismissed her virgins.
> The last of all to close her cell, after her attendant even, was Messalina, *yet she was still consumed with desire.*][18]

Secondly, sexuality is linked, through Messalina's association with images of darkness and night, with the dark and vaguely sinister hidden world of the subconscious. Messalina is a 'divinité des ténèbres', and as she descends to the brothel, and later goes to meet Silius, she is 'la Nuit elle-même'.[19] (Sex is also associated, briefly, with squalor and sordidness: the brothel is situated in a 'rue obscène' in 'l'un des plus bas bouges de Suburre', amidst 'les tas d'ordures du faubourg' and with 'des baquets d'excréments devant la porte' ['an obscene street' in 'one of the lowest hovels of the Suburra', amidst 'the piles of refuse of the suburb' and with 'buckets of excrement in front of the door'].[20] Thirdly, sexual desire is associated in the person of Messalina with rampant animality. Messalina is 'comme une bête en chasse' ['like a beast hunting its prey']; she prowls in search of her prey 'à pas de louve' ['with the stealthy footsteps of a she-wolf']; she is likened in her passion to an animal on heat', 'un monstre . . . infâme et . . . inassouvi' ['a vile and . . . unsated monster']; and she is the very incarnation of the She-wolf, symbol of Rome since its foundation and which, according to legend, suckled Romulus and Remus, the city's founders.[21] Finally, Messalina is the embodiment also of the irresistible power of sexual forces, a power which expresses itself in the universal cruelty and bloodlust of Rome, and which impels Messalina to commit a long series of bloody deeds. Thus her desire to obtain the key to the Gardens of Lucullus causes her to engineer the death of Valerius. Her sudden lust for the Negro gladiator leads her to disarm his opponent by the sheer force and irresistibility of her sexual magnetism. And her jealous passion has been responsible for countless murders, including those of numerous members of her own and Claudius' families.

But Messalina represents more than just the insatiability, unconscious force, animality and power of sexual passion. In her, the sexual
and the religious also are united. For the sexuality which she
incarnates is both animal and divine, and, ultimately, the whole
drama of *Messaline* is one acted out by 'the gods' themselves. The city
of Rome itself is regarded by its inhabitants and by tradition as divine
and even as a 'god'. Messalina, as Empress, enjoys from the outset
the status of a semi-divine being, while, even more clearly, she is
explicitly identified by the author and by Claudius, and identifies
herself, with the goddess Venus (whom Claudius worships above all
other gods). Thus it is that Messalina can address Phallus as her 'frère
dieu'. Through the novel's complex imagery, in fact, Jarry establishes
a three-way identification between the 'divinities' of Messalina, of
Rome and of Sex itself, the Empress and Rome both being seen as
incarnating the themes of love and of prostitution, which are in turn
embodiments of the universal, creative life-force itself:

Le plus vieux mythe du Latium renait dans cette chair de vingt-trois ans: la
Louve, nourrice des jumeaux, n'est qu'une figure d'Acca Larentia, déesse
tellurique, mère des Lares, la Terre qui enfante la vie, l'épouse de Pan qu'on
adore sous l'espèce d'un loup, la prostitution qui a peuplé Rome.

> [The oldest myth of Latium comes to life again in this twenty-three-year-
> old flesh: the She-wolf, who suckled the twins, is but an embodiment of Acca
> Larentia, the earth goddess, mother of the Lares, the Earth which gives birth
> to life itself, the wife of Pan who is worshipped in the form of a wolf, a
> symbol of the prostitution which has populated Rome.][22]

It is, however, above all through Messalina's cult of Phallus, in
which sexual passion and religious aspiration are inextricably inter-
woven, that this fusion of sexual and religious themes is developed.
Of the many representations of gods in Rome, it is those of Phallus, in
his manifold forms and under his various names, which predomin-
ate. The huge phallus which stands above the entrance to the 'maison
du Bonheur' is at once 'animal et divin'; it is 'la bête-dieu', 'le dieu
roide', a symbol of the 'dieu générateur, dieu suprême aux temps
antiques', 'l'emblème de vie universelle, le dieu solaire [qui] fulgure
... au fronton de son temple' ['the god-beast', 'the rigid god'; 'the
god of reproduction, the supreme god of ancient times'; 'the symbol
of universal life, the sun god [whose image] flashes forth from the
pediment of his temple'].[23] It is to this, her god, that Messalina cries
out in a frenzy of longing:

Où es-tu, Phalès, Priape, fils de Bacchus et de Vénus? et de ton seul nom
qui ne change point, où es-tu, dieu des Jardins? Ma contemplation est de toi
si absolue, mon désir si certain, que je sais que tu existes quelque part ailleurs
que dans le saint de l'étable ou la parure morte des femmes.

[Where are you, Phales, Priapus, son of Bacchus and of Venus? And by your only unchanging name, where are you, god of the Gardens? My adoration of you is so absolute, my desire so certain, that I know that you exist somewhere else other than in the holy statues of the cowshed or the lifeless finery of women.][24]

In her worship of Phallus, sexual passion is transformed, or sublimated, into a religious ardour, and her passionate search for the god extends far beyond merely sexual longing to become a truly religious quest.

Messaline is in fact as much a religious as an erotic work, in which Jarry has raised the theme of sexuality to the level of myth, and in which the true protagonists are the forces of male and female sexuality respectively. The novel expresses his own fascination with this subject, and perhaps hints at a more general relationship between sexual desire and religion. In elevating his subject to this plane however, Jarry is also following the time-honoured procedure of religion and myth; for outside of the monotheistic cultures of Judaism, Christianity and Islam, sexual and reproductive forces have from time immemorial been personified and worshipped as gods, and their power has seemed a no less evident and no less essential factor of existence than that of other natural forces.

Alongside this myth, Jarry also makes use of that of the phoenix, the mythological bird which is consumed by fire but rises again from the ashes. The god Phallus or Priapus, symbol of male sexuality, is likened first to a bird and then implicitly to the phoenix with its cycle of death and resurrection, as Messalina recalls to mind her brief encounter with the god in Chapter I:

Elle l'a vu.
Il est favorable aux hommes d'une faveur brève et il meurt dès qu'il touche une femme . . .
Et s'il ressuscite c'est pour mourir encore . . .

> [She has seen him.
> He favours men with a short-lived favour and he dies the moment he touches a woman. . . .
> And if he rises again it is to die yet once more. . . .][25]

But the theme of death has another, starker and more definitive application. As in earlier works of Jarry, the theme of love is once again associated with that of death, and the one seems inevitably to lead to the other. A relationship between the two themes is suggested at several points in the novel through its imagery: in Chapter I, the brothel is situated between 'la maison du charcutier et celle du bourreau' ['the house of the pork-butcher and that of the executioner']; the twin attributes of Priapus are his sex, and his scythe

– symbol of death, which, 'en même temps que l'*autre* geste du dieu qui féconde, *semait* la mort par tout le champ' ['simultaneously with the *other* act of the god which fecundates, *sowed the seeds* of death throughout the whole field']; and the flames which consume the body of Valerius are likened to the wing-feathers of birds, which become ruffled at mating-time.[26] There is also the curious episode of the *murrhins* – goblets carved from a rare and precious stone which surround the arena of Lucullus, one of which lodges in a fold of Messalina's cloak during her search for her god and is rediscovered by Silius. The detailed description of these *murrhins* suggests that they constitute a symbol of the female sexual organ; while the name given to them recalls phonetically the word *myrrhe*, associated both in the embalming practices of the ancient world, and in *L'Amour absolu*, with *la mort* (death). The association of love and death also has a more direct expression. Twice before the final chapters Messalina reveals a wish for death, when she envies Valerius his fate and when she calls upon the gladiator to kill her; and in the penultimate chapter, she seizes the sword of the tribune, which she identifies with the god Phallus, in an ecstatic and frenzied embrace, exclaiming as she does so:

Emporte-moi, Phalès! L'apothéose! Je la veux tout de suite, avant d'être vieille! Ou fais-moi vieillir tout de suite, jusqu'à la divinité. Emporte-moi chez nous, au plus haut ciel! le plus haut! le premier! Tu es le premier, ô Immortel! tu vois bien que je suis vierge! . . . Bonheur, ô comme tu me fais mal! Tue-moi, Bonheur! La mort! donne . . . la petite lampe de la mort. Je meurs . . . je savais bien qu'on ne pouvait mourir que d'amour!

[Carry me away, Phales! Oh apotheosis! I want it here and now, before I grow old! Or else make me old at once, so that I may attain the status of divinity. Carry me away to our home together, in the highest heavens! the highest! the first! You are the first, oh Immortal One! you can see that I am a virgin! . . . Oh Happiness, how you hurt me! Kill me, Happiness! Death! give me . . . the little lamp of death. I am dying . . . I *knew* that one could die only of love!][27]

One of the greatest problems confronting any novelist aiming to portray characters drawn from a culture or civilization distant in time or space from our own, and motivated by beliefs and ideas foreign to us, is to render psychologically convincing the behaviour and mental processes of such individuals. In *Messaline*, Jarry to some extent sidesteps the problem by attempting to fuse psychology with symbolism. The marriage is, on the whole, a successful one, though there are occasional false notes. But alongside this, the novel contains a number of elements which damage, no doubt deliberately, the credibility of the world it creates, reminding us that this is after all a purely imaginary construction. Certain of his occasional comparisons with the contemporary world create just such a jarring effect, as for example the statement that the façade of the brothel would appear to 'un passant d'aujourd'hui' as 'une gendarmerie provinciale, quand il n'est pas dimanche', or his comparison of the cramped cells of the prostitutes with a modern water-closet.[28] There is also the incident of Messalina's (unconscious?) playing upon the word 'absolument', which she enunciates – repeating a pun already used in *L'Amour absolu* – as 'ab-so-lu-ment' [absolute-lie]. But whether or not these details are deliberately intended to detract from the fictional 'illusion' and to shatter the total plausibility of the novel, reminding us of the art, or artifice, which it entails, one episode certainly is: that surrounding the strange character of 'Valerius the Asiatic'.

Valerius is an historical figure, the details of whose role in Roman politics, fabulous gardens, denunciation and suicide Jarry found, along with the other main events of the novel, in Tacitus. But other details of his portrayal strike a totally and intentionally false note. The name 'the Asiatic' probably derived from the exploits of Valerius or of other members of this family in Asia Minor; but Jarry, inspired by the name (and while keeping the historically accurate but deliberately contradictory detail of his birthplace, Vienna), makes of him a native of the most distant country known to Roman civilization: China. Though Rome did have tenuous trading links with China, the existence in Rome itself in the first century A.D. of such a figure is historically inconceivable. Moreover, Jarry makes of Valerius not just a native of China, but a caricature of the Chinaman. Every detail of his description (Valerius' shaven head with one long jet-black pigtail, his long blue and gold silk robe, his long fingernails, his stance 'dans l'attitude d'une idole rare, exotique et incompréhensible' ['in the stance of a rare, exotic and inscrutable idol'][29] as well as that of the objects with which he surrounds himself (the giant porcelain dogs, one paw resting on a ball, which guard his palace, his 'artificial fingers' – i.e. chopsticks – with which he eats, the rice paper on which his will is written by a scribe, his concubines with their tiny feet, and the cymbals which resound in his palace) goes to make of Valerius an embodiment of the popular nineteenth-century image of a Chinese mandarin!

But there is another dimension also to the figure of Valerius, which shatters even further the 'historicity' of Jarry's portrait of the ancient world: he contains certain resemblances to Jarry himself. Accused by Publius Suilius of having prostituted himself 'au mépris de son sexe', he replies in the following manner: "Interroge tes fils, Suilius, *vibra une voix qui isolait toutes les syllabes* .... Si tu ne m'a jamais vu, leur chair a eu toutes les preuves que je suis un homme!'" ["'Question your sons, Suilius", *vibrated a voice which clearly separated each syllable* .... "If you have never seen me, their flesh has suffered abundant

proof that I am a man!'''].[30] This idiosyncracy of speech establishes a
clear identity between the novelist (whose peculiar speech mannerisms were described in Chapter Five above) and his protagonist, as
well, perhaps, as constituting a defence of the former's sexual powers.
Similar remarks apply, moreover, to the enigmatic figure of the mime
and acrobat, Mnester, with his tiny feet 'plus courts que des sabots de
chèvre' – reminiscent of those of his creator as well as those of both
Sengle and Faustroll – and his 'jambes de Pan',[31] which look forward
to Jarry's description of the hero of *Le Surmâle* whose feet are
'extraordinairement petits, comme les vases antiques figurent ceux
des faunes' ['extraordinarily tiny, like the feet of fauns which figure
on antique vases'].[32]

Neither figure, however, is merely the subject of a spoof on Jarry's
part; for both Valerius and Mnester have a crucial role to play in the
complex sexual symbolism of the novel, a symbolism which they
ultimately reveal to be utterly aberrant. Both figures are associated at
one point or another with the phallus, and also, implicitly or
explicitly, with the image of the sun-god with which it is identified.
But Mnester is also associated, both symbolically and in the mind of
Messalina, with the moon, a symbol in the ancient world (popula-
rized by Flaubert's *Salammbô*) of the female principle and of fecundity.
Whence Messalina's declaration to Claudius at the end of Part I of the
novel: 'Claude, mon mari, empereur, dieu ...: *je veux* LA LUNE.'
['Claude, husband, emperor, god ...: *I want* THE MOON.'][33] Not
only does the culmination of Mnester's acrobatic performance before
the Emperor and Messalina coincide with the eclipse of the sun by the
moon, but the shape which he himself finally assumes – that of a ball –
itself suggests the sphericity of the full moon. Or rather, in the course
of the acrobatics and gyrations which he performs his body takes on
both the shape of the perpendicular, symbol of male sexuality, and of
the circle or sphere:

car le mime, après *un saut et demi* périlleux, est retombé sur les mains, en
posture de cubiste .... Le mime saute sur un seul bras par bonds énormes ...
et le voici qui tourne très vite et de plus en plus vite sur sa main, ouverte à
terre .... Quelque chose avait roulé à bas de l'estrade du théâtre, et occultait
encore la lumière par terre: une boule aussi parfaitement ronde que le disque d'une
planète chue, le corps inextricablement *pelotonné* de Mnester à la fin de sa danse.

> [for the mime, after a perilous somersault and a half, has landed on his
> hands, in the position of a Greek acrobat .... The mime, supporting himself
> on one arm only, performs huge leaps in the air ... and now he spins around
> very quickly and more and more quickly resting on his open hand which
> alone touches the ground .... Something had rolled to the bottom of the
> rostrum of the arena, and still occulted the light upon the ground: a ball as
> perfectly round as the disk of a fallen planet, the inextricably *ravelled* body of
> Mnester at the end of his dance.][34]

Mnester thus implicitly unites both male and female sexuality in his own person, and comes to suggest, symbolically, the figure of the Androgyne (indeed, he is described, when first seen by the Empress, as performing 'le baiser de Narcisse'), whose *self*-sufficiency therefore explains his failure, or inability, to respond to Messalina's amorous advances. That the Empress should thus fall in love with such a sexually ambiguous figure is itself odd, to say the least; but even more remarkable is the resemblance which exists between the terms in which his acrobatics are described in the above passage and those used some years earlier in both *Visions actuelles et futures* and *César-Antechrist* to describe the gyrations of the *bâton-à-physique*, which similarly unites the shapes of both the perpendicular and the circle, and which is addressed in the words: '*Ne fais pas de pareils bonds*, demi-cubiste sur l'un et l'autre pôle de ton axe et de ton soi ['*Do not leap about so*, demi-acrobat resting upon both poles of your axis and of your self'].[35]

The complexities of the novel's symbolic associations do not by any means stop here, and it is not possible in this brief account to do more than hint at those complexities. But, as the above example of Mnester suggests, there is much in the sexual and religious 'symbolism' of *Messaline* which reveals itself to be, ultimately, as aberrant as that of *César-Antechrist*, with which it is implicitly linked. As with the latter, too, the nature of this 'symbolism' serves to point to the underlying character of the work as a whole: far from representing the fruits of an effort at historical 'reconstruction', or even of an attempt to create a coherent network of symbolism, *Messaline* is first and foremost an imaginative, or more exactly *verbal*, construction. No less than in *Les Minutes de sable mémorial* and *César-Antechrist*, words are here 'polyèdres d'idées', and Jarry has sought to create a complex and intricate network of correspondences between words and images which echo back and forth throughout the work, from his description of Messalina in Chapter I descending to the brothel *à pas de louve* (instead of the usual *à pas de loup*), which enables him to establish a link with the she-wolf which symbolizes Rome and with the word *lupa* (prostitute), through the palindrome Amor/Roma in Chapter II, to the play on words between the name of the goddess Artemis and *artemisia* (absinthe) and dozens, if not hundreds, of other examples. In this way he has set out to make of the text of *Messaline* also 'un carrefour de tous les mots', and the embodiment of a self-contained imaginative and verbal universe, opening up an almost inexhaustible field of imaginative possibilities.

Thus *Messaline* is truly one of Jarry's most complex, but also most secret works. Nevertheless it remains, even for the reader who has failed to penetrate all its secrets, a powerful and impressive novel, containing moments of intense drama and a wealth of powerful imagery. The language, though still erudite and sometimes technical, is simpler than in some of his earlier works, and a comparison of surviving manuscripts shows his efforts to render both language and style more accessible to the reader.[36] As to the novel's dramatic structure, though unusual, this admirably reflects the development of its themes. It is the first chapter, describing Messalina's descent at night to the brothel in the suburbs of Rome, which constitutes the climax of dramatic intensity, and contains also the novel's richest and densest imagery; it is followed by a progressive fall in tension which corresponds to the Empress's failure to satisfy her insatiable longing, both sexual and religious. Only at the end does the narrative again approach the same level of dramatic intensity, thus describing a curve falling and then rising again, as Messalina believes that she is at last about to find the fulfilment of that longing and the object of her quest – in death.

The tone and the treatment of sexual themes in *Le Surmâle*, on the other hand, are radically different. If *Messaline* portrays the sheer power of sexual forces, *Le Surmâle* portrays the attempt to control and to channel those forces, in a vein which on the whole moves away from the dramatic intensity of *Messaline*. It has popularly been regarded as the best of Jarry's novels, a view implicitly echoed by Rachilde in the subtitle of her biography of Jarry, 'le Surmâle des Lettres'. It is also, after *Ubu Roi*, the work which has seen the largest number of editions.

The novel was completed, according to the date at the end of Jarry's manuscript, on 18 October 1901 and was published by the Editions de la Revue Blanche the following year (the dedication on the manuscript presented to Thadée Natanson 'en hommage amical' bears the date 2 May 1902). Its writing is thus contemporary with Jarry's articles in the *Revue Blanche*, several of which, together with those in *La Plume* the following year, provide a commentary on three important themes or features of the novel.

The first of these is the 'futuristic' or 'science fiction' aspect of *Le Surmâle*. Jarry was an enthusiast of what was then known as the 'scientific' novel and was later to be called 'science fiction'. He included Jules Verne's *Voyage au centre de la terre* among Faustroll's 'livres pairs', no doubt as a joint tribute to a favourite author of his boyhood and a precursor of the *genre*, and throughout his adult life he remained a passionate admirer of H. G. Wells, whose *The Time Machine* inspired his own (or Dr Faustroll's) *Commentaire pour servir à la construction pratique de la machine à explorer le temps* and whose work provided a constant point of reference for Jarry. *La Chandelle verte* contains several references to Wells's novels,[37] while the important article published in *La Plume*, 'De quelques romans scientifiques' (which also lists as precursors of the genre Cyrano de Bergerac and Villiers de l'Isle-Adam), brackets Wells together with Lord Kelvin in a common admiration: Wells is 'le maître d'aujourd'hui' in the field of the 'roman scientifique, *ce répertoire de l'irréalisé actuel*', which constitutes 'un voyage vers l'avenir' ['the present-day master' . . . 'scientific novel, *that repertoire of what is as yet unrealized*' . . . 'a journey into the future'].[38]

A second group of comments in *La Chandelle verte* relates to Jarry's defence of alcohol, which in one article he extends to other substances regarded by medical opinion as 'poisons', and notably to strychnine. (The five-man cycling team in *Le Surmâle* is fed on the miraculous new 'Perpetual-Motion-Food' whose secret formula is 'à base d'alcool et de strychnine!') In certain circumstances, he argues, such poisons constitute 'une nourriture excellente': 'la strychnine . . . tue au centigramme, et, en bonne quantité, tonifie' ['an excellent form of sustenance': 'strychnine . . . taken by the centigramme, kills, and, in large quantities, tones up']. Besides, 'il faudrait doser selon les capacités différentes des individus' ['one ought to adjust the dose according to the varying capacities of individuals']. 'Poison' is simply 'the unexpected'; and, in the case of alcohol, it is *lack of habit* which produces alcoholism: 'il n'y a d'alcoolique que celui qui n'a pas bu et dont les ancêtres n'ont pas bu' ['the only alcoholics are those who have never drunk and whose ancestors did not drink'].[39]

This paradoxical notion, that the effect of a substance on the human organism is in inverse ratio to its quantity – and, by analogy, that the potential of muscular and sexual energy increases with expenditure, with the result that 'les forces humaines n'ont pas de limites' – is one of the key ideas of *Le Surmâle*. It is related by Jarry to the argument that physical capability can also be increased indefinitely through 'training'. This notion is first suggested in Book V, Chapter II of *Les Jours et les Nuits*, where 'M. Sisyphe' finally succeeds in carrying his *boule* to the top of the mountain thanks to the steady muscular development resulting from years of continuous effort, and where Jarry relates this idea, in turn, to the biological principle (actually expounded by Lamarck, but incorrectly attributed here to Darwin, and since rejected by scientific opinion) that 'la fonction fait l'organe ou le développe s'il existe déjà' ['function creates the bodily organ, or develops it if the latter already exists'].[40]

A third aspect of *Le Surmâle* on which *La Chandelle verte* provides a commentary is Jarry's passion for sport, and in particular for the sport of cycling. He was an almost fanatical devotee of cycling, which experienced its golden age in the last decade of the nineteenth century, when machines for two, three, four and even more riders were commonplace. In the article 'La Mécanique d'Ixion' in *La Plume* he includes himself, implicitly, among those who '[ont] tenu sur ses fonts baptismaux le cyclisme' ['were gathered around the font at the baptism of cycling'].[41] Jarry himself used to race the train between Paris and Corbeil, according to the Vallettes' daughter: 'Il aimait faire la course avec le train, et quand il rentrait, il annonçait pompeusement: "Nous avons battu un record"' ['He loved to engage in a race with the train, and when he returned he announced pompously: "We have broken a record".'][42] It is possible also that he witnessed as a youth one of the celebrated Paris-Brest-Paris races to which he refers in *Le Surmâle*, and which, along with Paris-Bordeaux-Paris (races which, incidentally, were then dominated by English and American cyclists) provided a model for the 'Course des dix mille milles' of *Le Surmâle*.[43] This passion for 'sport', moreover, provides a further link with *Messaline*. The concept of limitless and record-breaking physical, and particularly sexual, 'performance' is foreshadowed in that novel, where the insatiable appetite of Messalina leads to 'une joute d'amour prolongée' ['a prolonged love-joust'][44] and to whose record-breaking performance of having 'essuyé en un jour plus de vingt-cinq amants' ['suffered the assaults of more than twenty-five lovers in one day'] the hero of *Le Surmâle* refers.[45] At the same time this theme of insatiability, as formulated in a passage such as the following, also looks forward to the concept of indefinite lovemaking put forward by Jarry's 'supermale': 'On est époux de Messaline pendant le moment d'amour, puis encore et toujours à cette condition que l'on puisse vivre une ininterruption de moments d'amour' ['One is Messalina's husband during the moment of sexual encounter, then again and forever on this condition only, that one can sustain without interruption an unending series of such moments'].[46]

The plot of *Le Surmâle* is a deceptively simple one. Its dominant themes are all stated clearly in the opening chapter by Jarry's hero, André Marcueil. The novel opens with Marcueil's claim that 'L'amour est un acte sans importance, puisqu'on peut le faire indéfiniment' ['The act of love is of no importance, since one can perform it indefinitely'], which he generalizes a few pages later into the assertion that 'Les forces humaines n'ont pas de limites' ['Human strength and endurance know no limits'].[47] These claims are made in the course of a *soirée* at his elegant château de Lurance near Paris. Amongst Marcueil's guests, who include (we are in the year 1920) several wealthy Americans prominent in the fields of science and technology, four play a particularly significant role in the events of the novel. These are the celebrated American chemist, William Elson, a devotee of the virtues of alcohol; his daughter Ellen; the fabulously rich engineer and motor- and aircraft-manufacturer, Arthur Gough; and Marcueil's best friend, Dr Bathybius, an impatient and irritable, but not unsympathetically portrayed, figure who serves as a counterfoil to the extravagant ideas put forward by his friend, embodying the rationalism of scientific opinion and replying to Marcueil's assertions with the solid 'facts' of medical science and physiology.

The reaction of Marcueil's guests to these extravagant claims is one of universal scepticism bordering on hostility. Nevertheless, the conversation turns to the physical possibilities of the 'machine' that is the human body. Elson, who claims to have invented, with his 'Perpetual-Motion-Food', a form of nourishment which will indefinitely stave off muscular fatigue, invites Marcueil to watch a race which has been organized between a team of cyclists from America nourished exclusively on this substance, and a high-speed locomotive designed by Arthur Gough. Marcueil, however, continues to insist that the human body has no need of such artificial stimulants. The conversation returning to the theme of love and sexual 'performance', the guests vie with each other to recall the most outstanding examples from the literature and legend of the past. It is Marcueil who makes the highest 'bid' with the example, quoted from Rabelais, of the Indian whose exploits were celebrated by Theophrastus, Pliny et Athenaeus, who 'avec l'aide de certaine herbe le faisait en un jour soixante-dix fois et plus' ['with the aid of a certain Herb, did it in one Day three-score times and ten, and More'].[48] In a subsequent discussion with Bathybius later that night in an English bar in Paris, Marcueil, amidst a great display of medical and physiological knowledge, pursues his claims, extending his view of human potential to all fields of activity: 'un homme qui ferait l'amour indéfiniment n'éprouverait pas plus de difficulté à faire n'importe quoi d'autre indéfiniment: boire de l'alcool, digérer, dépenser de la force musculaire, etc. Quelle que soit la nature des actes, le dernier est pareil au premier ....' ['a man who could make love indefinitely would not experience any greater difficulty in doing anything else indefinitely: drinking alcohol, eating, expending muscular energy, etc. Whatever the nature of the acts performed, the last is identical with the first ....'][49] But once again, Marcueil's claims are met by scepticism; all the more so when he quotes in support of his convictions the example of the extraordinary adventures of Baron von Münchausen. There is, however, one exception among his guests: at the close of the conversation which she had overheard, Elson's virgin daughter, Ellen, whispers to Marcueil the words: 'Je crois à l'Indien.'[50]

The remainder of the novel is devoted to a demonstration by Marcueil of these apparently extravagant claims. Jarry's hero is a curious figure. A recluse, of aristocratic lineage and considerable wealth, he is at first introduced to us as a weak and insignificant creature. Thirty years old, of pale complexion, possibly balding, with feeble eyesight behind a gold lorgnette, stooped, short of breath, his whole body seems to evoke an air of physical debility and ill-health: that of a man who 'réalisait si absolument le type de l'homme ordinaire que cela, en vérité, devenait extraordinaire' ['embodied so completely the characteristics of ordinariness that the very fact itself became extraordinary'].[51] But there is another, hidden side to Marcueil, as a recapitulative chapter reveals. Born with a mysterious deformity which he seems to have owed to a distant ancestor, he determined at an early stage to be 'fait comme tout le monde'. The effect of his peculiar diet and extraordinarily strenuous exercises had been to develop in him a strength far surpassing that of other men, but which he went to extraordinary lengths to hide, in order to 'se confondre avec la foule'.[52]

A first glimpse of his superhuman strength is provided by his demolition, in a state of rage provoked by his conversation with Bathybius, of a 'dynamometer' in an amusement park late at night. The next morning Marcueil is visited by Ellen Elson, who hints at her feelings for him but is rebuffed. The visit is followed by one of the two dramatic climaxes of the novel. The fifth and longest chapter – 'La Course des dix mille milles' – is one of Jarry's most successful pieces of writing, mingling fantasy, drama and humour in a colourful and racy narrative. The event, a five-day race from Paris to Siberia and back again at speeds of over 300 kilometres an hour between an express train carrying William Elson, his daughter and Arthur Gough, and a team of cyclists on a five-man tandem who are nourished exclusively on cubes of 'Perpetual-Motion-Food', is narrated by one of the participants, Ted Oxborrow, and quoted from the *New York Herald*. The drama and mystery are heightened by the existence of a mysterious object following them and the appearance of enormous garlands of red roses, similar in all respects to those which Ellen Elson had seen in the gardens of Lurance, which appear overnight draped over the window of her compartment of the train. These events are followed by the episode of the death and 'resurrection' of one of the team of cyclists, Jewey Jacobs. Jacobs' feet, like those of his team-mates, are fixed to the pedals of the machine; and gradually, the energetic pedalling of the others reinvigorates his body:

Petit à petit il prend goût à la chose, et voilà ses jambes qui suivent les nôtres, l'*ankle-play* qui revient, jusqu'à ce qu'il se mît à tricoter follement. . . .

En effet, non seulement il régularisa, mais il emballa, et le *sprint* de Jacobs mort fut un sprint dont n'ont point d'idée les vivants.

> [Bit by bit he took a liking to it, and then his legs began to follow ours, his ankle-play returned, until his legs began to move frantically in a knitting motion. . . .
>
> Indeed, not only did he catch us up, but his speed increased beyond ours, and the sprint of the dead Jacobs was a sprint the like of which the living cannot even conceive.][53]

But still the mysterious object pursues them. Uncertain whether he is observing real events or merely experiencing hallucinations, Oxborrow imagines that the team is overtaken at night by a fantastic apparition, which is witnessed from the train only by Ellen Elson, who watches with a 'curiosité surexcitée' and then, seemingly, 'avec amour'. Gradually, the apparition takes on the shape of a solo cyclist astride a racing cycle of a model never before seen, which its rider 'actionnait en se jouant et en effet comme s'il eût pédalé à vide' ['rode without really trying and indeed as if he were pedalling in the void']. The struggling locomotive is at last overtaken by the team, which arrives at the finishing post – only to find that someone or something has beaten them to it: the post is 'couronné de roses rouges, les mêmes obsédantes roses rouges qui avaient jalonné toute la course ... Personne n'a pu nous dire ce qu'était devenu le fantastique coureur.' ['crowned with red roses, the same haunting red roses which had lined the whole route of the race ... Nobody could tell us what had become of the fantastic cyclist.']⁵⁴

Back in Paris, Marcueil announces to Bathybius that the 'Indian' has been found who will 'break the record' of Theophrastus' Indian. His astonishing cycling feat has been merely a dress rehearsal for what is to follow. One other event also constitutes a rehearsal for it (and provides an example of Jarry's taste for 'humour noir'): in the grounds of Lurance, the body of a young girl is discovered, who has been inexplicably 'violée à mort'. For the purposes of his demonstration, which is to take place in the great hall of the château during a period of 24 hours from midnight that night, Marcueil invites to Lurance the seven most celebrated courtesans of the day, and a select company of male friends, including Bathybius, who is to act as 'scientific' witness in an adjoining room. Marcueil's disappearance on a pretext is followed by the appearance of 'the Indian' – in the shape not of a Hindu, but of a North American 'red-skin' straight out of the novels of Fenimore Cooper, complete with bearskin, moccasins, peace-pipe and tomahawk. After a hearty but silent supper, he withdraws to the great hall to await the courtesans.

But then an unexpected event occurs. The seven women are mysteriously locked in a room together, and the startled 'Indian' finds himself confronted by the naked form of ... Ellen Elson. Watched by the observant eye of Bathybius, the couple begin their record-breaking endeavour. All that night and the next morning they continue, breaking off at midday for a gargantuan repast; at two o'clock, having equalled the figure of seventy reached by Theophrastus' Indian, they sleep until 11.28 p.m. – and, awakening, in the 30 minutes that remain before midnight raise that figure to a breath-taking and record-breaking 82.

Met by the enthusiastic acclaim of his guests, the 'Indian' escapes from their presence to return to the hall, where Ellen determines that now, at last, they will make love for their own sake. To the jeers of the courtesans, who have at last discovered and broken a window overlooking the hall, the couple begin their passionate embrace. To silence the women, Marcueil sets going a phonograph which, by chance, begins to play an old romance the words of which seem to parallel their own adventure, and in which the theme of love is, once again, associated with death. Hypnotized by the words of the song, the couple are unable to cease their embrace even though the force of it is killing Ellen. And Ellen dies, leaving Marcueil in a state of stupor, regretting the rashness of his boast:

La phrase d'où était née la prodigieuse aventure se représenta à son esprit telle que, personnage volontairement et falot et quelconque, il l'avait par caprice proférée:
– L'amour est un acte sans importance, puisqu'on peut le faire indéfiniment.
Indéfiniment . . .
Si. Il y avait une fin.
La fin de la Femme.
La fin de l'Amour.

> [The statement out of which the whole incredible adventure was born came back into his mind, in the very form in which, playing a deliberately droll and indifferent role, he had on a whim uttered it:
> 'The act of love is of no importance, since one can perform it indefinitely.'
> Indefinitely . . .
> On the contrary, there was an end.
> The end of Woman.
> The end of Love.][55]

Only now does Marcueil realize that he loves Ellen, and only now does he discover her beauty. Halfway between sleep and waking, he muses on the nature of their love, which he conceives now in universal and mythological terms; and, succumbing to sentimentality, he composes a long poem which identifies Ellen with Helen of Troy, the traditional incarnation of feminine beauty and love.

But the charm is broken by the discovery that Ellen is not dead after all: she had merely fainted. Her outraged father, learning of the event, insists that Marcueil marry his daughter, and, before the reluctance of the dazed Supermale, conspires with Bathybius and Arthur Gough to force him to love Ellen. Inspired by Bathybius' chance remark that Marcueil is not a man but a machine, Gough, 'le mécanicien capable de tout construire' ['the engineer capable of building anything'], sets out to construct 'la machine la plus insolite des temps modernes', designed to 'influencer des forces considérées jusqu'à ce jour comme insaisissables: la Machine-à-inspirer-l'amour'

['the strangest machine of modern times' . . . 'influence forces hitherto regarded as completely beyond reach: the Love-Inspiring
Machine'].[56] Marcueil is tied to this electro-magnetic monstrosity and
a strange 'crown', in which are embedded a pair of electrodes, is fixed
to his head. The current is switched on – to produce a phenomenon
which no-one had foreseen. Instead of Marcueil being influenced by
the machine, the current is reversed, and it is he who influences the
machine:

Donc, ainsi qu'il était mathématiquement à prévoir, si la machine
produisait véritablement de l'amour, c'est LA MACHINE QUI DEVINT
AMOUREUSE DE L'HOMME.

> [Thus, just as was mathematically predictable, if the machine did truly
> inspire love, it was THE MACHINE THAT FELL IN LOVE WITH THE
> MAN.][57]

The experiment ends, however, tragically. Marcueil's 'crown' over-
heats, its glass melts, and the metal, 'devenue mâchoire incandes-
cente', bites into the temples of the struggling Supermale. He breaks
free of his bonds, but it is too late; and his twisted and naked body is
found wrapped around the bars of the iron grill of the park: 'Le
Surmâle était mort là, tordu avec le fer.' ['The Supermale had died
there, twisted around the iron bars.'][58]

Le Surmâle appears on the surface, then, as a rollicking tale of
alternately fantastic, dramatic, spectacular, passionate and finally
tragic events. It is easy to see why it has popularly been regarded as
the best and most accessible of Jarry's novels. The language is
relatively simple and straightforward, the style is fairly conventional,
characterization is clear-cut, and the narrative moves forward quickly
thanks to an abundance of dramatic events interspersed with lively
dialogue.

The underlying 'moral' of the novel would seem, at a glance, to be
equally straightforward. The most common interpretation of *Le
Surmâle* is that put forward by Bathybius in the last chapter of the
novel, namely that in an increasingly technological world man can
only survive by becoming superior to the machines which he has
created:

en ce temps où le métal et la mécanique sont tout-puissants, il faut bien que
l'homme, pour survivre, devienne plus fort que les machines, comme il a été
plus fort que les fauves . . . Simple adaptation au milieu . . . Mais cet
homme-là est le premier de l'avenir . . .

> [in this age in which metal and machines are all-powerful, man must, in order
> to survive, become stronger than the machines, just as he was stronger than
> the beasts . . . A simple matter of adaptation to environment . . . But this man is
> the first of a new era . . .][59]

Bathybius' remarks would seem to constitute the logical conclusion of a number of references in the novel to the 'machine' that is the human body, which is forced to compete with other machines. Thus Jarry's 'Surmâle' can be seen as a precursor of a popular twentieth-century myth embodied in a host of 'superman'- and 'supermale'-type figures. It is also possible to see in Marcueil's tragic end (following Jarry's description of the 'crown' which is fixed to his head and his explicit comparison a page later between Marcueil and the crucified Christ) a 'martyrdom' to the inhuman demands of science and technology – a *dénouement* which, for all its tragedy, is a reassuringly moral one. Superhuman excess and *hubris* are punished (albeit by means of an accident), wise limitation and 'common sense' win the day, and the fabric of a 'rational' science and a stable bourgeois society is preserved.

Thus for once, it would seem, Jarry, while continuing to indulge his own fantasies has given the public what it wants; pampering, in the 'science-fiction' aspect of *Le Surmâle*, to its superstitious belief in the wonders of 'science'; catering, in its spectacular, not to say theatrical, side to that public's love of 'spectacles'; providing, in the novel's ending, the moral reassurance it desired; and, on a stylistic plane, responding positively to Rachilde's challenge to 'écrire comme tout le monde'.

But, beneath the surface, all is not quite what it seems. There can be no doubt that the idea of an existence which was not bound by normal limitations exercised a fascination over the mind of Jarry (who, characteristically, saw its darker and more sinister implications), a fascination echoed in the comments of Marcueil and Ellen Elson inspired by the fantastic exploits of Baron von Münchausen:

Car peut-on imaginer l'existence insupportable que mènerait dans la société envieuse et malveillante des hommes celui qui aurait dans sa vie de tels miracles! – toujours puisqu'il paraît que ce sont des miracles. On le rendrait responsable de toutes les actions inexpliquées et de tous les crimes impunis, comme on brûlait jadis les sorciers . . .
– On l'adorerait comme Dieu, dit Ellen Elson. . . .
– Et de quelle liberté ne jouirait-il pas, achevait Marcueil, si l'on pense que, commît-il des crimes, l'incrédulité universelle lui fournira ses alibis!

['For can one imagine the intolerable existence which would be led, in a jealous and spiteful society, by a man whose life contained such miracles! – precisely because they appear to be miracles. He would be held responsible for every unexplained act and every unpunished crime, just as people used once to burn sorcerers . . .'
'He would be worshipped as a God', said Ellen Elson . . . .
'And think of the freedom which he would enjoy', concluded Marcueil, 'when one reflects that, even were he to commit crimes, the universal incredulity of his contemporaries would provide him with alibis!'][60]

Dreams of such 'absolute' freedom and power occur, moreover, elsewhere in the work of Jarry. But fascination is not of course belief, and the choice by Marcueil of Baron von Münchausen as an illustration of his ideas is typical of his creator's deliberately paradoxical logic. For the view which Marcueil expounds of the 'limitless' nature of human physical achievement is based ultimately not on experimental evidence, but on examples drawn from the realms of literature and legend and, even more paradoxically, upon a peculiarly abstract and mathematical conception of the progression of 'les forces humaines'. Speaking to Bathybius of the sexual potential of both men and women, Marcueil claims that:

cette manifestation [devient] permanente et plus exaspérée à mesure que l'on s'éloigne, les ayant franchies vers l'infini numérique, des forces humaines; et [il y a] avantage, par conséquent, à les franchir dans le plus court délai possible, ou, si l'on veut, *imaginable*.

> [this manifestation [becomes] permanent and more pronounced the further one moves beyond human strength and endurance towards numerical infinity; and [it is] consequently advantageous to do so in the shortest time possible or, if you prefer, *conceivable*.][61]

No less paradoxically, Jarry's apparent indulgence of the literary and moral preferences of his public gives rise to a series of internal contradictions. That same public can scarcely have appreciated (if it had understood) his contemptuous reference, through the words of Ellen Elson, to 'la SCIENCE avec une grande SCIE ...', or his scathing remark that Marcueil's sacrifice was made 'pour la plus grande sauvegarde de la science, de la médecine et de l'humanité bourgeoises' ['for the greater safeguard of bourgeois science, medicine and culture'].[62] Moreover, the public's taste for 'spectacles' was an object of repeated attack in Jarry's writings on the theatre. Could it be that the whole of Jarry's elaborate demonstration of the proposition on which the novel is based (and, with it, the novel itself) is yet again purely a 'solution imaginaire'?

It is certainly remarkable to find Jarry, in view of his work hitherto, employing all the techniques of a typical nineteenth-century realist novelist. He adopts the standpoint of the omniscient narrator, sketching in the background of his characters, analysing their hidden motives and secrets, and revealing in his hero the existence of two contradictory natures fighting for dominance:

Puis il ricana malgré lui, quoiqu'un moi obscur lui chucotât en dedans qu'il avit lieu de pleurer; puis il pleura quoiqu'un autre moi, qui paraissait nourrir une haine individuelle contre le précédent, lui expliquât copieusement, bien qu'en un instant, que c'était la belle heure pour rire aux éclats.

[Then he sniggered in spite of himself, even though a hidden self whispered inside him that he had reason to weep; then he wept even though another self, which seemed to harbour a particular hatred of the previous one, explained to him in detail, although in a flash, that this was the moment to roar with laughter.][63]

He records the conversations of polite society with apparent 'objectivity', and describes the nascent love of Ellen for Marcueil in a manner worthy of any writer of sentimental romances. In his gradual presentation of the secret nature of his hero, he makes use of all the conventional devices for creating an air of mystery. At the same time, Jarry plays, chameleon-like, with authorial viewpoint. In discussing the apparently extravagant claims of Marcueil, he makes himself a spokesman for conventional wisdom: 'C'est un fait souvent observé, que les êtres les plus débiles sont ceux qui s'occupent le plus – en imagination – des exploits physiques.' ['It is a frequently observed fact that it is the most feeble individuals who are most obsessed – in their imagination – with physical exploits.'][64] He poses as a moralist, mildly deploring the constricting influence of social conventions on the sincere expression of opinion and, in even more moralistic vein, reproaches his hero for his 'ironie froide' and admonishes 'cet homme si anormal qu'il n'avait pu échauffer son coeur qu'à la glace d'un cadavre'. ['this man who was so abnormal that he had only been able to warm his heart on the icy coldness of a corpse'][65]

Even more striking is the range and diversity of tones which the narrative expresses. Beginning on an 'objective' note the narrative then evokes an air of mystery and expectancy surrounding the person of Marcueil, which is followed by the drama mingled with fantasy of the 'Course des dix mille milles'. Then, after the black humour of the episode of the discovery of Marcueil's rape victim, the tone changes in the account of Marcueil's and Ellen's lovemaking to one never before encountered in the work of Jarry, in such passages as:

Il n'y avait plus qu'un homme et une femme, libres, en présence, pour une éternité. . . .

C'était l'*Enfin seuls* de l'homme et de la femme reconçant à tout pour se cloîtrer dans les bras l'un de l'autre. . . .

Ils commencèrent de s'aimer, et ce fut comme le départ d'une expédition lointaine, d'un grand voyage de noces qui ne parcourrait point de villes, mais tout l'Amour.

Quand ils s'unirent d'abord, Ellen eut peine à ne pas crier, et son visage se contracta. Pour étouffer sa souffrance aiguë il lui fallait quelque chose à mordre, et ce fut la lèvre de l'Indien. Marcueil avait eu raison de dire que pour certains hommes toutes les femmes sont vierges, et Ellen en souffrit la preuve, mais elle ne cria point, quoique blessée. . . .

Le second baiser, mieux savouré, fut comme la relecture d'un livre aimé. . . .

Ils continuèrent, et chacun de leurs baisers fut une escale dans un pays différent où ils découvraient quelque chose et toujours une chose meilleure.

[Nothing remained but a man and a woman, free, in the presence of each other, for all eternity. . . .

It was the *Alone at last* of man and woman, abandoning everything in order to cloister themselves in each other's arms. . . .

They began to make love, and it was like departing on a distant expedition, on a long honeymoon journey which would not pass through towns, but the whole of Love.

When they first came together, Ellen found it hard not to cry out, and her features contracted. To stifle the sharp pain, she felt the need for something to bite, and it was the Indian's lip which she found. Marcueil had been right in saying that for some men all women are virgins, and Ellen suffered the proof of this, but she did not cry out, even though wounded. . . .

The second embrace, better savoured, was like the re-reading of a favourite book. . . .

They continued, and each of their embraces was like a halt in a different country in which they discovered something and always something better.][66]

Jarry treats his subject with a lyricism, a discretion, and even an apparent tenderness and sympathetic understanding into the joys and sufferings of love, which seem quite extraordinary in such an author, while the episode of Ellen's 'death' seems to touch a depth of poignancy and understanding (not to say sentimentality) never before reached by Jarry, in its account of the mingling of love and suffering in Ellen and of Marcueil's belated discovery of her beauty and of his love for her:

Il rit encore, mais pleura nerveusement en regardant Ellen.
Elle était très belle . . . .
Le marbre de la vivante était encore pur et lumineux: à la gorge et aux hanches, les mêmes nielles imperceptibles qu'a l'ivoire fraîchement coupé.
Marcueil découvrit en soulevant les paupières d'un index délicat, qu'il n'avait jamais vu la couleur des yeux de sa maîtresse. Ils étaient obscurs jusqu'à défier toute couleur . . . .
Les dents étaient de minutieux joujoux bien en ordre. . . .
Les oreilles, à n'en pas douter, avaient été 'ourlées' par quelque dentellière.

[He laughed again, but wept hysterically upon looking at Ellen.
She was very beautiful . . . .
The marble of the living woman's flesh was still pure and luminous: around her bosom and her hips, the same imperceptible flaws as one finds in freshly cut ivory.
Marcueil discovered upon gently raising her eyelids with his index finger that he had never seen the colour of his mistress's eyes. They were darker than any colour imaginable . . . .
The teeth were minute and neatly arranged toys. . . .
The ears, beyond any shadow of doubt, had been 'hemmed' by some lacemaker.][67]

But this mood of lyrical tenderness is shattered at several points. At the end of the 24-hour contest the tone turns briefly to farce, in

Marcueil's reception by his astonished and jubilant guests, who see in the performance of 'the Indian' the answer to France's depopulation problem! The mood created by Ellen's death is shattered, moreover, by the curt and cynical lines:

Ellen n'était pas morte.
Évanouie ou pâmée seulement: les femmes ne meurent jamais de ces aventures-là.

> [Ellen was not dead.
> She had merely fainted or swooned: women never die from such adventures as these.][68]

The apparent lyricism of Jarry's treatment of love in the above scenes is also counterbalanced by the savagery of his portrayal of the seven courtesans whom Marcueil invites to Lurance. In frustration at being deprived of the promise of the 'Indian', the women turn to each other and indulge in an orgy of masturbation and lesbianism. Every detail of their portrayal reveals an attitude of contempt and revulsion, perhaps more indicative of the author's true attitude towards the sexual being of women. Lastly, the final episode, that of the 'Machine-à-inspirer-l'amour', is, for all its apparently tragic ending, a scene of pure farce, in which Jarry's detailed description of the Machine resembles that of his *Commentaire pour servir à la construction pratique de la machine à explorer le temps* and the calculations of Book VIII of *Faustroll*, revealing the same love of the technical details of physics directed towards purely fantastic ends.

Jarry's narrative, in fact, is shot through with contradictions. In such abrupt transitions as Marcueil's sentimental musing on the death of Ellen to the discovery that she has merely fainted, or from the epoch-making sexual feats of this 'Supermale' to his strange submission to the voice of a phonograph and to the banal prospect of a conventional bourgeois marriage, the bathos and incongruity really is too great for credibility. At the same time, the apparent lyricism and sentimentality is undermined from within by the inclusion of a number of incongruous details: the song played by the phonograph – a 'vieille romance populaire ... fort connue et imprimée dans plusieurs recueils de folklore' ['an old popular romance ... very well known and printed in several collections of folklore'][69] – is distinguished chiefly by its stereotyped sentiments and imagery, while Marcueil's poem resembles a literary exercise whose banality is matched only by that of the song.

In short, for all the variety of tones which the narrative espouses, the events of *Le Surmâle* – from Marcueil's extravagant claims in Chapter I, through the episode of his obsession with his 'deformity', his feats in the 10,000-mile cycling race, the death and revival by his team-mates of Jewey Jacobs and Marcueil's attempt to break 'le record de l'Indien', to his death at the hands of a machine – are really pure farce. Behind a variety of disguises, Jarry *plays* with narrative technique, authorial viewpoint and tone just as, in *La Chandelle verte* and elsewhere, he plays with ideas. This theme of disguise is suggested, moreover, in the novel itself, in a remark which, though it refers immediately to Marcueil's attempts to hide his difference and to be 'fait comme tout le monde,' applies equally well to Jarry's own appearance of conformity to accepted literary models and his presentation of *Le Surmâle*, 'roman moderne', in the guise of a 'science-fiction' extravaganza:

La conformité avec l'ambiance, le 'mimétisme' est une loi de la conservation de la vie. Il est moins sûr de tuer les êtres plus faibles que soi que de les imiter. Ce ne sont pas les plus forts qui survivent, car *ils sont seuls*. C'est une grande science que de modeler son âme sur celle de son concierge.

> [Conformity with one's environment, 'mimetism', is a law of self-preservation. One is less sure of killing those weaker than oneself than of imitating them. It is not the strongest who survive, for *they are alone*. Knowing how to model one's soul upon that of one's *concierge* is a very great art.][70]

This theme of disguise, moreover, is present throughout the novel also in the actions and costumes of its protagonists. Not only Marcueil's 'Indian' with his 'red' skin and nudity, but also his counterpart in Marcueil's customary 'habit noir', as well as his 'manteau espagnol' resembling a monk's cowl, his cyclist's attire and even his martyr's 'crown', are all forms of disguise. The same applies to Ellen Elson, who wears a pink mask when driving and later, matching Marcueil's 'Indian,' dons a black mask to hide her identity from the watching Bathybius. And the theme is embodied also in the courtesans, who disguise their vulgarity and lubricity beneath the most unconvincingly innocent and pure names – Adèle, Blanche, Eupure, Herminie, Irène, Modeste and Virginie – and who appear as the counterpart to the distinguished and aristocratic society constituted by Marcueil's guests at Lurance. So prolific, in fact, is this theme of disguise that *Le Surmâle* comes to take on something of the appearance of a fancy-dress parade, or of a comic opera of changing identities.[71]

The same theme of 'disguise', or 'mimetism', can be seen in the relationship between Jarry himself and several of his characters, beginning with his 'hero', Marcueil. Marcueil's age (he is 30, only two years older than Jarry at the time of his completion of *Le Surmâle*), his smooth black hair, his small feet, his eccentricities, a number of traits of character including his 'ironie froide' and his 'cruelty' towards women, together with the adoption of a *persona* to hide his true nature, all suggest elements of an identity between author and protagonist, while his aristocratic lineage (which Jarry was later to lay claim to), his immense wealth (which Jarry certainly never enjoyed), and above all his superb physique, his fantastic cycling prowess and his sexual potency, might lead us to see in him a case of wish-fulfilment on Jarry's part. But other aspects of his portrayal, particularly in his role of 'the Indian', reduce this identity to the level of farce and constitute part of a private joke. His regular diet of raw mutton recalls a hollow boast made by Jarry to eat raw mutton chops, which Rachilde put to the test and exposed.[72] And according to Rachilde, 'l'Indien' was the name by which their terrified maid-servant at the Phalanstère referred to Jarry, and the name which he himself used in the signature of a photograph showing him astride his fabulous 'Clément luxe 96 course sur piste' bicycle.[73] Nor does the identification end with Marcueil. Jarry attributes to William Elson his own zeal in defence of alcohol. Elson has been appointed president of all the new temperance societies of the United States 'du jour où, par un revirement prévu de la mode scientifique, il fut proclamé que la seule boisson hygiénique était l'alcool absolu' ['from the moment when, as a result of a predicted reversal of scientific fashion, it was proclaimed that the only healthy drink was pure alcohol'], and was also responsible for the 'philanthropic' invention of a means of rendering the domestic water supply undrinkable, but still suitable for washing in.[74] He is also made to re-enact an episode of Jarry's own life: the firing of a revolver in a restaurant, in order to prove that the steadiness of his aim is not impaired by alcohol. His fanaticism culminates in the act of pouring a bottle of excellent rum into the furnace of the ailing locomotive – with predictably disastrous results. And Dr Bathybius, acting strangely out of character, produces during his long vigil of observation a bizarre 'élucubration scientifico-lyrico-philosophique' which develops a number of Jarryesque ideas on the nature of 'God' and which recalls the speculations upon the 'surface of God' of *Faustroll*. Reflecting on the 'dimensions' of God, Bathybius concludes that 'Dieu est infiniment petit', or, more exactly, 'un point' – a 'point' which he identifies with the only 'imperishable' part of man, the microscopic *germen*, which becomes a 'God in two persons', 'ce Dieu qui naît de l'union des deux plus infimes choses vivantes, les *demi-cellules* qui sont le Spermatozoaire et l'Ovule' ['this God who is born of the union of the two tiniest living things, the *half-cells* constituted by the spermatozoon and the ovum']. 'Love' is simply the uniting of this 'god' and 'goddess' – or the illusion of choice produced by their irresistible attraction to each other:

Quand le dieu et la déesse veulent s'unir, ils entraînent chacun de leur côté, l'un vers l'autre, le monde où ils habitent. L'homme et la femme croient se choisir . . . comme si la terre avait la prétention de faire exprès de tourner!

[When the god and the goddess wish to unite, they each draw towards the other, simultaneously, the world which they inhabit. Men and women believe that they choose each other . . . as if the earth were to claim to rotate by an act of will!][75]

No less striking than the diversity of attitudes and tones expressed in *Le Surmâle* is the multiplicity of literary, historical and mythological references and quotations which the novel contains, numbering over 30 in all. Few novels can ever have contained such a profusion of diverse allusions and quotations, whose sources range from Rabelais and Lesage to Cato, Pliny and St Jerome. The first chapter alone, which sets the scene for the events which are to follow, contains over a dozen such references or quotations; while even in the midst of their lovemaking, Marcueil quotes to Ellen from Aristotle and the fables of Florian, and greets the intruding Bathybius, at the end of their 24-hour ordeal, with a quotation from *The Thousand and One Nights*: 'Qui est-tu, être humain?'.[76] This abundance of references has a dual function. They serve, on the level of the narrative, as a source of inspiration to Marcueil, who sets out to pit himself against and to surpass these 'models' from the past. The crucial reference here is of course that to 'l'Indien tant célébré par Théophraste, Pline et Athénée' (which is in fact a double reference: Marcueil quotes from Rabelais, who is in turn citing these three authors). But another 'model' is also proposed: that of Hercules, who is referred to in Chapter I, and again in Chapter III by the General – the Hercules not immediately of the legend, however, but of the legend at one remove, Hercules as he figures in the comic opera *Les Travaux d'Hercule* by Flers and Caillavet, set to music by Jarry's friend Claude Terrasse. And behind these two shadowy figures are references to a host of mythological, legendary and fictional 'supermen' from Jupiter and Achilles through Samson and Mohammed to the incomparable Baron von Münchausen.[77]

On another level, however, these references and models serve a different function: through them, the figure of Marcueil is made to sum up and to prefigure, and at the same time to deflate and to debunk, all the legendary 'supermen' and 'supermales' of the past, present and future, just as Marcueil's idyllic and belated 'découverte de la Femme', translated by Jarry into universal and mythological terms, sums up and simultaneously parodies the forms and traditions of a whole literature of love.

This wealth of literary allusions and quotations, moreover, extends to Jarry's own previous work. Chapter I contains an unacknowledged quotation from *Ubu Enchaîné* in the form of a satirical quip by one of Marcueil's guests: 'Portez . . . arme! Une, deux, trois.' The incident in Chapter IX in which Ellen, in a rage, attempts to stab Marcueil with a long hairpin and is put to sleep by Marcueil by hypnosis (a source of great fascination in Jarry's day) almost exactly parallels a scene in *L'Amour absolu* in which Varia attempts to stab Emmanuel and is similarly put to sleep. Marcueil's dazed translation of the words of the song played by the phonograph into chemical formulae bears a distant resemblance to the nonsense-chemistry of 'le P.H.' in *Oné-sime*. And Jarry's translation of the drama of Marcueil and Ellen into mythological terms in Ellen's identification with Helen of Troy parallels Messalina's identification with Venus.[78]

Of these various parallels, it is that with *Messaline* which is the most extensive and significant. Ellen's expressed belief that Marcueil must have been, in a previous existence, 'quelque part dans les temps anciens, une très vieille reine courtisane' ['somewhere, in ancient times, a very old courtesan queen'][79] establishes a vital link between Jarry's hero and the heroine of his previous novel. But even more compelling are those suggestions of a parallel between Jarry's 'Sur-mâle' and Messalina's god, Phallus. A reference by Marcueil in Chapter III to 'la rigidité phallique' and, even more clearly, the shape and colour of the 'poteau couronné de roses rouges' at the end of the cycling race, recall the terms of the description of Phallus/Priapus or of his various representations. Jarry's emphasis upon the colour of his 'redskin', who appears to Bathybius as 'une forme écarlate, nue, musclée et obscène', similarly recalls those representations, as well as the definition of *Messaline* that 'le chauve écarlate tend vers l'absolu'. It is even possible that the 'coldness' of Marcueil – whose extravagant claims at the beginning of the novel create 'un froid' among his guests – is intended to recall the remark in *Messaline* that 'Priape est un homme froid'. In short, Jarry's 'Supermale' is as much a figure of myth as Phallus/Priapus; or rather, both are incarnations of the same fundamental myth – in all senses of the word. And both ultimately, in fact, bear a curious resemblance to that other central 'myth' of Jarry's work, 'Père Ubu', who since the primitive days of the Lycée de Rennes and *Ubu Roi* has acquired new attributes, both intellectual (in Jarry's *Almanachs*) and sexual, and who in Jarry's poem 'Le Bain du roi' published in *La Revue Blanche* on 15 February 1903 adopts the 'redskin' and phallic-technological attributes of the hero of *Le Surmâle*: on the inadequate 'caleçon vulgaire' covering the 'redondance illus-tre' of his 'cul' are

portraicturés en or, au naturel,
Par derrière, un Peau-rouge au sentier de la guerre
Sur un cheval, et par devant, la tour Eiffel

> [portrayed in gilt, in the raw,
> Behind, a Red-skin on the war-path
> Riding a horse, and, in front, the Eiffel Tower.][80]

Finally, a series of detailed parallels exists between the two major events of *Le Surmâle*, the 'Course des dix mille milles' and Marcueil's attempt to 'battre le record de l'Indien', which further illuminate Jarry's attitude towards his subject. For all the apparent differences of subject and tone, in reality both episodes recount a *race*, in the first instance against a train and a five-man tandem, in the second against the clock – the limit of 24 hours. Both sequences begin at a leisurely pace (relatively speaking) and end with a 'sprint' (Marcueil and Ellen make love 11 times in the last 30 minutes; the tandem reaches a speed of close to 400 kilometres per hour) at a speed almost four times that of the early stages. And both contests involve also a 'death' which is followed by a 'resurrection': those of Ellen, and of Jewey Jacobs. Both record-breaking feats are preceded (at least in the order of narration) by a minor example of physical prowess: the first by the 'killing' of the 'dynamometer', the second by the killing through rape of a young girl. Even more obviously, Jarry's description of the race allows of an interpretation in sexual terms: the 'poteau couronné de roses rouges', ['the finishing post crowned with red roses'] and the 'grand sphinx atropos' ['big death's-head hawkmoth'] of Oxborrow's boyhood recollections which 'alla chercher, dans une passion guerrière, au plafond sa propre ombre . . ., et la cogna, à heurts répétés, de tous les béliers de son corps velu: toc, toc, toc . . .' ['flew up, with warlike passion, towards its own shadow on the ceiling . . . , and banged against it, with repeated blows, with all the battering rams of its hairy body: knock, knock, knock . . .'],[81] are two among several details which lend themselves to such an interpretation. The lovemaking contest also contains a number of specific allusions to the race: in a vase on the table are 'quelques-unes des roses du Mouvement Perpétuel'; Marcueil, in addressing Ellen, repeats a phrase from Oxborrow's narrative, 'l'ombre grinçait'; and, meditating on the death of Ellen, he formulates a comparison with Arthur Gough and his racing cars: 'Il avait mis sept femmes, en réserve, dans la galerie, pas autrement qu'Arthur Gough n'aurait emmené sept automobiles de rechange . . . en cas de *panne*' ['He had placed seven women in the gallery, in reserve, in exactly the same way as Arthur Gough would have brought with him seven spare automobiles . . . in case of *breakdown*.'][82] The similarities between the two episodes extend even to the imagery used. The idea of a journey is twice expressed or suggested in the second sequence, in a description of Marcueil's and Ellen's love as a voyage to distant lands, and in a reference to that love as the 'étapes' of a 'parcours'. The metaphor of a railway carriage from which one looks out recalls the behaviour of Ellen during the race; and Bathybius' allusion a few pages later to the 'fanal double' of a locomotive recalls the lights of Arthur Gough's locomotive. Parallels can even be found between the thorns which burst the tyres of the tandem and Marcueil's 'crown of thorns', and between the 'machine volante en forme de trompette' which pulls the team and the horn of the phonograph.

The purpose of these parallels is unmistakable: they point to the fact that, for Jarry, the episode of Marcueil's and Ellen's love and of the attempt to break the record of 'the Indian' is, every bit as much as that of the cycling race, a sport, or a game. The concept of 'game', moreover, is expressed several times over in the novel itself. The first chapter, in which Marcueil's guests attempt to 'outbid' each other in quoting examples of outstanding sexual feats, is entitled 'La Manille aux enchères' – the name of a popular card-game. And in the course of this bidding, one of the guests quotes from the comic opera *Les Travaux d'Hercule* a line which describes one of the hero's legendary sexual exploits as being 'à peine un jeu'. The same phrase is repeated by Marcueil at the end of the chapter; it is recalled by Oxborrow's description of the phantom cyclist who rode his machine 'en se jouant'; and it is repeated verbatim at the very end of the novel in the context of Ellen Elson's finding of a husband. Its meaning is clear: if in *La Chandelle verte* Jarry reveals his tendency to regard the whole of life as a vast and elaborate 'game', *Le Surmâle* provides an example of literature treated as a no less intricate game.

Like *Messaline*, therefore, *Le Surmâle*, despite its apparent accessibility, is also actually one of Jarry's most secret works. Appearing to recount dramatic and spectacular events in the fields of sport and love, its real, hidden subject, no less than that of *Messaline*, is to be found in the negation or cancelling out of its own imaginative world by itself. Jarry, while appearing to write for a public, is in reality mocking that public at every turn of the narrative, and writing only for a select few; perhaps even for himself alone. In both *Messaline* and *Le Surmâle*, the 'imaginary' world created by the novelist is undermined from within. This is not to say that both novels cannot provide gripping and entertaining reading; on the contrary, this they certainly can and do. But both reveal themselves to be, ultimately, works of pure 'imagination' – 'des solutions imaginaires'.

This conclusion has an important bearing on Jarry's treatment of the theme of love. It is difficult to accept the view of J.-H. Sainmont, repeated several times over in the publications of the Collège de 'Pataphysique, that right from the beginning of his literary career Jarry *plays* with sexual themes. It is rather the case that, throughout his literary work, one can see Jarry *trying* progressively to come to terms with subjects which are surrounded for him by a number of personal obsessions and complexes, trying to adopt the attitude of detachment and playfulness suggested by Sainmont, and at last, in *Le Surmâle*, succeeding in that aim.

Chapter Ten

Musical comedies and return to the past

IN THE BACKGROUND of such works as *Le Surmâle* and the articles comprising *La Chandelle verte*, one can sense a change in the intellectual climate of the age in which Jarry was living, a growing awareness of the scientific and technological developments which were gradually transforming Western society, and a spirit of acceptance of this evolution very different from the outlook of Symbolism with its tendency to reject the values and institutions of the modern world and to flee from it. This change is in accord with the evolution of modern art and literature as a whole from the aestheticism of the 1880s and 1890s to what has come to be known as 'modernism'. The change is reflected, moreover, in the circle of Jarry's own friends and acquaintances during this period. Around the turn of the century he was becoming popular with a group of young poets and artists who were destined to make a significant name for themselves in the twentieth century, among them the poets Guillaume Apollinaire, Max Jacob and André Salmon. According to Salmon, they looked upon Jarry as one with them in spirit – 'un grand frère génial'.[1] It was with Apollinaire that relations were closest, the two men frequently meeting to talk, play billiards, drink or dine together. Though their friendship seems to have been fraught with a series of missed rendezvous, they shared a deep sympathy and mutual respect, as well as a boyish love of pranks and practical jokes (to say nothing of a taste for mystification): in a letter of October 1903 Jarry, excusing his earlier failure to write, stated in a letter to Apollinaire: 'Je crois que quand deux littérateurs sympathisent, il y a toujours rencontre, sans correspondance postale.' ['I think that when two men-of-letters are in sympathy with each other, their minds will always meet, without postal correspondence.'][2] Some time in the early years of this century, too, he made the acquaintance of the Milanese poet and founder-to-be of Futurism, F. T. Marinetti, who published a number of texts by Jarry (and his sister Charlotte) in his review *Poesia* – a further indication of his responsiveness to the changing literary climate of these years.

The most important of the texts published (in this case after Jarry's death) by Marinetti was the comic opera *L'Objet aimé*, a fragment of which had already appeared in Apollinaire's *Le Festin d'Ésope* in November 1903. This was one of at least ten such works which have been unearthed to date, only two of which (and a fragment of a third) were published during Jarry's lifetime. Variously designated by their author as *opéra-bouffe*, *opéra-comique*, *opérette-bouffe* and *opérette*, they were written between the end of 1897 and 1905 or 1906. They are: *Par la taille* (written in December 1898 and published by Sansot, along with *Ubu sur la Butte*, under the collective title of *Théâtre Mirlitonesque*[3] in 1906), *Le Moutardier du Pape* (published in 1907), *L'Objet aimé*, *Pantagruel*, *Léda*, *Le Manoir enchanté*, *Jef*, *Pieter de Delft*, *L'Amour maladroit* and *Le Bon Roi Dagobert*. Written occasionally in collaboration with other authors, they were also in most if not all cases written in close collaboration with the composer Claude Terrasse, who had composed and performed the incidental music for *Ubu Roi* in 1896 and with whom Jarry had worked closely in the Théâtre des Pantins in 1897–8. Prolific and imperious, Terrasse recognized Jarry's talents as a librettist and bombarded him with requests for libretti which he could, and no doubt did, set to music. Most of these scores are, alas, now lost, although it is known that a number of their joint works were performed: for example *Léda* in May 1900 and *Le Manoir enchanté* in January 1905. The longest and most ambitious of all, however, the comic opera *Pantagruel*, based of course on Rabelais, on which Jarry worked from late 1897 to sometime in 1905, was not even completed until after his death (by Eugène Demolder, with whom he had worked on the libretto) and was first performed at the Grand Théâtre in Lyons in 1911.

The status of these musical comedies, and their place in Jarry's literary production as a whole, has been a subject of confusion and debate amongst Jarry scholars hitherto. Some have seen such works as mere trivia which he wrote purely for financial gain and which provide a witness to his increasingly desperate financial situation and rapidly declining inspiration. It is true that Jarry himself, perhaps defensively, in response to criticism from Rachilde of his planned *Théâtre Mirlitonesque*, referred to its 'petits bouquins verts' as having 'juste l'importance d'une pipe en sucre'.[4] Members of the Collège de 'Pataphysique, on the other hand, have argued eloquently that these works are no less an expression of Jarry's 'pataphysics' than any other which he wrote, and ought to be treated with equal regard. The truth probably lies somewhere between these extremes. That Jarry, recognizing in himself a talent for this kind of writing, did hope for quick financial returns from it, seems certain (in this, alas, he was sorely abused). On the other hand, parts of *La Dragonne*, and in particular the episode entitled 'La Bataille de Morsang', published in the *Revue*

Blanche in April 1903, show that, far from declining, his creative powers at this time were at their height. Moreover, rather than being the product of a supposed 'decline', these musical comedies were produced over a period of some eight or nine years while he was working on such different and diverse books as *L'Amour en visites*, *Faustroll*, *L'Amour absolu*, *Messaline*, *Le Surmâle* and *La Dragonne*. In addition, during this period Jarry must have devoted a great deal of time to these works, since several exist in more than one version while as many as eight different versions of *Pantagruel* are known to exist.[5]

What is in any case certain is that clear and important links exist between Jarry's 'théâtre mirlitonesque' and the remainder of his literary output. There is a link not only with the verse-playlets which he wrote at both St-Brieuc and Rennes, but also with parts of the early Hébert/Ubu 'cycle' which contain numerous songs. A link too is provided through the medium of marionettes, for *Ubu Roi* was performed by Jarry, almost from the first, as a puppet-play, and was so performed once again at the Théâtre des Pantins in 1897–8; and the characters of these musical works, in their extreme simplification and stylization, are also puppets, dangling from the strings of their creator – indeed, *Pantagruel* was originally conceived, in its first version, as a play for marionettes. A further bridge is provided by *Ubu sur la Butte*, Jarry's own abridged version of *Ubu Roi* complete with songs which was specifically written for performance as a *guignol* and which constituted one of the two published volumes of his *Théâtre Mirlitonesque* in 1906. Throughout his life, in fact, Jarry displayed and expressed a deep love for the 'popular', supposedly naïve, and even childlike forms of art and literature of the past and of his own time. Foremost among the Symbolists he had, first with Gourmont in *L'Ymagier* and then independently in *Perhinderion*, set about rehabilitating the popular art of the *image d'Épinal* and of old engravings and woodcuts (as well as expressing an unbounded admiration for the sophisticated 'naïvety' of the art of such men as Gauguin, Filiger, Émile Bernard and the *douanier* Rousseau). In addition to this activity in the artistic field, he had included amongst the *livres pairs* of Faustroll, placed on the same plane as recognized literary masterpieces, such works as the *Théâtre* of Florian and the ineffable *Le Serment des petits hommes* of Marceline Desbordes-Valmore. Indeed, Rimbaud's words in *Une Saison en enfer* might apply equally well to Jarry:

J'aimais les peintures idiotes, dessus de porte, décors, toiles de
saltimbanques, enseignes, enluminures populaires; la littérature démodée,
latin d'église, livres érotiques sans orthographe, romans de nos aïeules,
contes de fées, petits livres de l'enfance, opéras vieux, refrains niais,
rythmes naïfs.

[I loved idiotic paintings, inscriptions over doors, stage sets, showmen's back-cloths, signboards, popular coloured prints; old-fashioned literature, Church Latin, erotic books full of spelling mistakes, novels read by our grandmothers, fairy tales, children's books, old operas, silly refrains, naïve rhythms.][6]

Furthermore, many a passage in *La Chandelle verte* testifies to his lifelong love of such 'popular' forms of artistic expression and entertainment as the circus, mime and dance.

At the same time other, more subtle links exist between certain of these musical comedies and such novels as *Faustroll*, *Messaline* and *Le Surmâle*. *Léda*, written around the same time as *Messaline*, expresses – admittedly in a very much lighter vein – the same fundamental view of womankind and the same grimly pessimistic vision of the impossibility of satisfying desire. The deliberate confusion of 'real' and 'imaginary' in *Faustroll* (for example, the death and resurrection of Bosse-de-Nage) looks forward to the successive 'deaths' suffered by M. Vieuxbois in *L'Objet aimé*. *Le Surmâle*, with its abundance of lively dialogue and its dramatic and spectacular action, is not only the most 'theatrical' of Jarry's novels, but represents a bridge between these and his musical comedies in another, more fundamental way also; in its playing about with reality and illusion, its narration of spectacular or tragic events which are neither wholly 'real' nor wholly 'unreal' (for example, the 'death' and 'resurrection' of Jewey Jacobs, or the 'death' of Ellen Elson), it looks forward to the spirit of his 'théâtre mirlitonesque' in which, in the words of J.-H. Sainmont, 'rien n'est tout à fait "pour de vrai" (ni "pour de faux")' ['nothing is completely "for real" (nor "unreal")'].[7] It may well be that these musical comedies play the same role, in relation to the 'serious' works of Jarry's later years – *Messaline*, *Le Surmâle*, *La Dragonne* – as the *Ubu* plays and excerpts from them perform in relation to works of an earlier period, in particular *Les Minutes de sable mémorial*, *César-Antechrist* and *L'Amour en visites*; namely, they constitute a kind of 'counterpoint' to such works, putting them into perspective and revealing on Jarry's part a broader and more subtle concept of literature.

What are the dominant characteristics of these comic operas or operettas, as their author calls them? Jarry's 'théâtre mirlitonesque' shares with the *Ubu* plays and with his expressed views on the theatre a total and resolute hostility to the conventions of the realist and naturalist theatre. There is not the slightest effort to create 'realistic' plots or 'rounded' characters; on the contrary, the plots are deliberately contrived, while Jarry's characters are almost all stereotypes if not caricatures, lacking in individuality and often designated either simply by pronouns (*Lui* and *Elle*, in the case of his pair of lovers in *Le Manoir enchanté* and *L'Amour maladroit*) or by their function (*l'objet aimé, le rival heureux, le maire*). In some cases, too, they are characterized by elements of dress or physical attributes (*le Géant, le Bossu*), just as Ubu was characterized by his repeated exclamations (*merdre, de par ma chandelle verte*, etc.) or his paraphernalia (*la machine à décerveler, le croc à phynances, le bâton-à-physique*). Even where they possess a personal name, it is frequently that of a personage of legend or history (Leda, Good King Dagobert). Verbal distortions and inventions, spoonerisms, puns and other forms of wordplay abound, together with acrobatic rhyming and sudden and unexpected changes of rhythm and metre, while the exigencies of the musical score give rise to a series of verbal acrobatics which, in their ingenuity and novelty, are a source of delight. To this deliberate air of falseness created by extreme simplification and verbal fantasy, moreover, Jarry adds an almost systematic exploitation of anachronism: in *Léda*, we learn that a feminist newspaper, *Le Gynécée*, has just been founded in ancient Sparta; the Salvation Army makes an appearance in *Le Moutardier du Pape*, set in the ninth century; and in the same play, the Pope's *moutardier* makes a telephone call 'sans fil provisoirement en attendant qu'on en invente' ['without a line, for the time being, pending its invention']. Further, the musical score, and in particular the singing – as opposed to speaking – of lines adds a further dimension of unreality to an already deliberately false and unreal world. Lastly, for all their apparent frivolousness, a common moral emerges from these musical comedies: the dreams of an idyllic love, or of the satisfying of an overwhelming passion, are doomed to failure; at the end there must be a return to the grey banality of everyday life. As the Chorus puts it at the end of *Léda*:

L'idéal,
C'est fatal,
Fait envie;
Mais de déception
La folle passion
Sera toujours suivie.

Il faut n'aimer que $\begin{cases} vous, \\ nous, \end{cases}$

Prosaïques époux!

> [*The ideal,
> Inevitably,
> One longs for;
> But by disappointment
> Mad Passion
> Will always be followed.
> You must love only each other,
> Oh prosaic couple!*]

Such 'moral' overtones, however, are amongst the least important aspects of these works, in which artificiality, fantasy and light-heartedness reign supreme as in all such manifestations of the genre. Indeed, Jarry's conformity to the 'rules' of the genre of the comic opera is striking. Where in his poetry, in his novels, and in his earlier plays, he takes existing forms and radically transforms them, either overtly and explosively, as in *Ubu Roi*, or through subtly undermining them, as in *Les Minutes de sable mémorial*, here paradoxically he sets out to remain deliberately within the rules laid down by such established masters of the genre as Meilhac and Halévy, Flers and Caillavet, or Offenbach, and even skilfully to exploit those rules to the full. The reason is simple: the genre of the comic opera and operetta is already universally recognized to be a totally artificial one, of which there is no need to reveal the hidden 'strings'. The world of Jarry's 'théâtre mirlitonesque' is one of *pure* theatre, or more exactly pure theatricality, in which he found once again a spontaneous delight in fun and nonsense and wordplay characteristic of childhood, and in which he saw a mirror-image of – in his view – the essential 'theatricality' of life itself.

Jarry's failure to have all but two of these musical comedies published, and his failure even to complete *Pantagruel*, were to have disastrous consequences for his financial situation. The demise of *La Plume* at the beginning of 1904, in fact, left him without a regular source of income, and inaugurated a period of increasingly desperate poverty which was to last until his death. For a time, however, the effects of this poverty were muted by a number of factors. He was persuaded by Claude Terrasse, anxious as Jarry himself was to finish *Pantagruel* once and for all, to spend the winter of 1903–4 with him in the Bonnard family property at Le Grand-Lemps in the Isère, to the north-west of Grenoble. Here, from November 1903 to May 1904, Jarry enjoyed the benefits of family life and home cooking. He was a charming companion to the Terrasse children, and he also made a lasting impression upon the small provincial town: this unusual visitor with his *ubuesque* 'grande capeline' quickly became popular, and even left his mark upon the very bourgeois *habitués* of the billiard room of the Café Brosse, who adopted his own manner of address: 'Monsieuye et vénéré ami et bougre d'âne'![8] Though he was soon bored with provincial life, the experience provided the material for the first chapter of a new novel, *La Dragonne*, a first draft of which was probably written at Le Grand-Lemps.

A further escape from the effects of poverty was provided by his favourite retreat near the Barrage du Coudray, on the Seine near Corbeil, where he could catch fish in abundance. Here, from 1900 to around 1905, he lodged in a simple shack belonging to the owner of the nearby Auberge du Barrage, a short distance away from the

Vallettes' country villa. Though originally a summer retreat, Jarry came to spend ever longer periods at Le Coudray. Here, away from Paris and the harrassment of creditors, fishing, cycling with Eugène Demolder or other friends, or drinking with the fishermen and bargees who frequented the neighbouring inn, he spent his happiest moments in his 'bon royaume du Barrage'[9] – at least until the demands of local creditors also became too insistent to be ignored. Apollinaire captured the spirit of this existence admirably in a description of Jarry in terms of a young river-god:

Alfred Jarry . . . m'apparut comme la personnification d'un fleuve, un jeune fleuve sans barbe, en vêtements mouillés de noyé. Les petites moustaches tombantes, la redingote dont les pans se balançaient, la chemise molle et les chaussures de cycliste, tout cela avait quelque chose de mou, de spongieux; le demi-dieu était encore humide, il paraissait que peu d'heures auparavant il était sorti trempé du lit où s'écoulait son onde.

> [Alfred Jarry . . . appeared to me as the personification of a river, a young beardless river, dressed in the sodden clothes of a drowned man. The thin, drooping moustache, the frock coat the tails of which swung to and fro, the floppy shirt and the cyclist's shoes, all had something soft and spongy about them; the demi-god was still wet, it seemed as if only a few hours earlier he had arisen soaking wet from the bed where his stream flowed.][10]

In 1904 and 1905, Jarry purchased two small adjoining plots of land on which he had built his famous 'Tripode' – so-called because it stood on *four* supports – a square wooden hut whose sides measured exactly 3.69 metres. Despite the legends surrounding it, the 'Tripode' was not built until shortly before his long illness of 1906, and as a result he barely lived in it. Neither its construction nor even the land were ever fully paid for; in 1908, after Jarry's death, the builder, Dubois, was still claiming some 1200 francs in payment.[11]

From 1904 onwards, illness born of privations was an increasingly recurrent feature of Jarry's life. The winter of 1904–5 was a particularly severe and difficult one, and that of 1905–6 was even worse. With increasing poverty and ill-health, he sank also into the grip of depression; though his friends were seldom aware of it, Jarry himself spoke a short time later of his 'dépression morale', while Rachilde, looking back, referred to his 'solitude farouche' during these years when he spent long periods alone in his 'Grande Chasublerie' or working at the Bibliothèque Nationale.[12] From November 1905 he was kept in bed for long periods with influenza, without any form of heating in his lodgings and weighed down by fatigue and debt. Jean Saltas, whom he had met some years earlier, described Jarry arriving at his home, often having cycled through bad weather, with holes in his shoes or wearing only slippers on his soaked feet, under which his host would quietly slip a warm brick. A letter to Saltas of May 1906, recapitulating upon the events of the preceding two years, is even more eloquent:

A) Début de la maladie: fin de la terrible besogne du *Pantagruel*, six mois en Dauphiné (novembre 1903-mai 1904). Je n'aime pas la montagne et n'être pas chez moi.

B) Retour dudit Dauphiné. Représentation remise à l'hiver prochain. Dépression morale. Dettes, etc . . . Ne plus pouvoir, sous peine de dérangement par les créanciers, séjourner tranquille au Coudray. Perdu l'habitude ancienne des douches dans la rivière; des livres de poissons excellents mangés à profusion, etc.

C) Hiver terrible à Paris, sans feu . . . et quelquefois les pieds dans l'eau (Merci de vos briques). . . .

Total: deux ans de privations où tout autre aurait . . . claqué.

> [A) Beginning of the illness: end of the terrible task of composing *Pantagruel*, six months in the Dauphiné (November 1903–May 1904). I don't like the mountains and not being at home.
>
> B) Return from the said Dauphiné. Performance put off until the following winter. Psychological depression. Debts, etc . . . No longer able, for fear of being disturbed by creditors, to sojourn peacefully at Le Coudray. Lost the old habit of taking showers in the river; of pounds of excellent fish eaten in abundance, etc.
>
> C) Terrible winter in Paris, without any heating . . . and sometimes with wet feet (Thanks for your bricks). . . .
>
> In short: two years of privations in which anyone else would have . . . snuffed it.][13]

So desperate had his situation become by 1904–5 that he had even ceased to eat regularly. In his letters from Laval in 1906, he was at pains to convince his correspondents that it was malnutrition that had been the cause of his illness, and to deny the widespread belief – which he himself had helped to encourage, and which had been put about by Saltas, amongst others – that the true cause was excessive drinking. He wrote to Fénéon, for example:

Le bruit a été répandu, par une 'coquetterie inconsidérée' de ma part, que le 'Père Ubu' buvait comme un templier. A vous je puis avouer comme à un vieil ami . . . que j'avais un peu perdu l'habitude de *manger* et que c'était ma seule maladie.

> [The rumour has been put about, as a result of a piece of 'ill-considered coquetry' on my part, that 'Père Ubu' drank like a fish. I can admit to you, as an old friend . . ., that I had somewhat lost the habit of *eating* and that that was my only illness.][14]

But though it may not have been a major cause of his illness, he was during these years drinking more and more. He continued to imbibe vast quantities of his beloved absinthe, and then, towards the end, of ether (a sad and ironic reminder of the *éthernité* of *Faustroll*). Rachilde refers to 'cet état d'ivresse permanente dans lequel il semblait trépider au lieu de vivre normalement' ['that state of permanent drunkenness in which he seemed to quiver instead of living normally'].[15] Though the description smacks of moral censure and may be exaggerated, a fragment of the uncompleted *La Dragonne* entitled 'Descendit ad inferos', which was probably written early in 1905 and which undoubtedly reflects a great deal of Jarry's own experience, powerfully evokes his hero's utter destitution and his 'descent' through solitary drinking into the depths of semi-consciousness:

Il but seul et méthodiquement, sans jamais parvenir à se griser, et sans aucune chance de jamais devenir ce qu'il est de mode d'appeler aujourd'hui un alcoolique: ses doses étaient trop formidables pour qu'elles ne glissassent point sur ses cellules comme un fleuve se perd et se filtre à travers un sable éternel et indifférent: sinon depuis longtemps Erbrand eût été mort. . . .

Et il but l'essence même de l'arbre de science à 80 degrés, l'alcool qui garde le goût de la pomme, et il se sentit chez lui dans le Paradis retrouvé . . .

Mais bientôt il ne put boire davantage dans les ténèbres, car pour lui il n'y eut plus de ténèbres, et comme sans doute Adam avant la faute et à coup sûr les grands anthropomorphes, il voyait clair dans l'obscurité. . . .

Et il n'achetait jamais ou presque de vêtements . . . . Il n'avait à ménager personne, ne dépendant de personne.

Et il se priva souvent de nourriture, parce qu'on ne peut pas tout avoir à la fois et que boire à jeun profite davantage.

[He drank alone and methodically, without ever succeeding in reaching a state of drunkenness, and without any hope of ever becoming what it is fashionable these days to call an alcoholic: his doses were too huge for them not to slide over his cells as a river filters through an eternal and indifferent bed of sand and disappears: otherwise Erbrand would have long since been dead. . . .

And he drank the very essence of the tree of knowledge at 80° proof, the spirit which retains the taste of the apple, and he felt at home in a Paradise regained . . .

But soon he could drink no more in the darkness, since for him there was no longer any darkness, and no doubt like Adam before the Fall and certainly like the great anthropoids, he could see in the dark. . . . And he never or scarcely ever bought any clothes. . . . He needed to show consideration to no-one, depending upon no-one.

And he often went without food, because one cannot have everything at once and drinking on an empty stomach does more good.][16]

While working on *La Dragonne*, Jarry agreed to collaborate with Saltas on a translation of *Pope Joan* by the modern Greek novelist Emmanuel Rhoïdes. A first, anonymous French translation had appeared in 1878 and had enjoyed a *succès de scandale*. Perhaps Jarry saw in the translation a possibility of quick financial returns. Though he must have enjoyed the novel's ribald humour and ferocious anticlericalism, he found the task of translation itself tedious, and longed to put it aside in order first to complete *La Dragonne*. The two men worked together during the 'terrible winter' of 1905–6 and the following Spring, Saltas (who was of Greek origin) dictating a rough draft which it was Jarry's task to put into '[un] français correct et même littéraire'.[17] He also planned partly to rewrite Rhoïdes' novel in order to eliminate its sometimes rather tedious digressions, urging Saltas to accept the advice of the poet Jean Moréas that it was necessary to 'arranger le plus possible et dans le sens humoristique le texte de Rhoïdis, qui souvent vraiment ne serait pas drôle en français' ['modify as much as possible and in a humorous direction Rhoïdes' text, which often would really not be funny in French'].[18] But his part in the joint task was never quite completed, and it was not until after his death, in 1908, that *La Papesse Jeanne* (subtitled, according to the fashion of the time, *roman médiéval*) finally appeared.[19]

In addition to working on these two novels, Jarry also planned, as mentioned earlier, to have published by Sansot in 1906 the six volumes comprising his *Théâtre Mirlitonesque*. Only the first two were in fact published, and their financial return was negligible. As a further source of support for his friend, therefore, Vallette, aided by Félix Fénéon, organized the publication of a *de luxe* subscription edition of *Le Moutardier du Pape*. Though it did not appear until the following year (and less than 100 copies were sold), Jarry was able to obtain an advance upon the subscription money as early as July 1906; on his own admission, it literally saved his life. After some hesitation, in April 1906 he also accepted the idea of a second performance of *Ubu Roi*, to be preceded by an address given by Laurent Tailhade. But feet were dragged, and it was not until 1908, perhaps owing to consciences having been pricked by Jarry's death, that the performance eventually took place, with Gémier once again in the leading role.

But the project which occupied Jarry most during his last years was the novel *La Dragonne*, the history of whose writing is inseparably bound up with the vicissitudes of his own life in these years. (The title of the work is, once again, polysemic: *la dragonne* is at one and the same time the feminine form of dragoon, implying that its subject will be a female soldier; the leather thong attached to the handle of a sabre; and a term applied – at least by Molière – to a shrewish woman.) The conception of the novel goes back to at least the beginning of 1903, and probably earlier. Originally, it revolved around the subject of the army: the novel was to relate its hero's refusal of or incapacity for a military career, his betrothal, the abduction of his fiancée by a handsome army officer, and his surprising and spectacular revenge upon the army. It is perhaps characteristic of Jarry that he wrote this last episode, which was to comprise the whole second half of the novel, first, in the form of the self-contained *nouvelle* or long short story entitled 'La Bataille de Morsang', which was published in the penultimate issue of the *Revue Blanche* on 1 April 1903.

Jarry's visit to Le Grand-Lemps in the winter of 1903–4 brought about the first major modification of these plans. He decided to transpose the events surrounding the birth and upbringing of his hero's fiancée to the mountains of Dauphiné, and to include in the first part of the novel a portrayal of the small-town provincial life and café society which he came to know and love. He was working on these early chapters again around December 1905, and what was to constitute the first chapter in the published version of *La Dragonne* appeared under the title 'Omne Viro Soli' in the review *Vers et Prose* in April 1906. Other modifications and additions followed, inspired by other events in his own life and by a desire to accentuate the identity between his already partly autobiographical hero and himself. Increasingly, *La Dragonne* came to reflect the life of its author: almost everything that Jarry loved or experienced or encountered between the years 1903 and 1906 found its way into the novel, from his fishing on the Seine and his love of fencing to his apology for alcohol, his illness, and his eventual religious conversion. Increasingly, too, the 'adventure' of its hero became that of his creator: a voyage of discovery back into the past and a 'descent', through illness and delirium, towards death.

Though he continued to work on *La Dragonne* until only a few weeks before his death, the novel was never finished. Its publication in 1943 by the Éditions Gallimard with the subtitle 'roman' (the text of which was reproduced by the *Oeuvres Complètes* of 1948) was a totally misconceived and misleading enterprise, compounded by an extraordinary number of printing errors, including the omission or repetition of whole pages, and of misreadings of the manuscript. For the manuscript on which the publication was based is not only incomplete, but also incoherent and even to an extent unintelligible. A majority of chapters exist only in the form of fragments or rough drafts, while others were never even begun. Even worse, there is a fundamental lack of unity between the three parts of the novel: both as a result of illness and the accident of death, and of the fundamentally irreconcilable nature of his material, Jarry has not only failed to weld that material into a coherent whole, but probably never even succeeded in satisfactorily conceiving it as such. Thirdly, and in some ways most disturbing of all, sections of the novel are either partly or even wholly the work not of Jarry himself, but of his sister Charlotte.

But for all its shortcomings, *La Dragonne* remains one of the most fascinating and revealing of Jarry's works, in part for the role which it played in his own life, but above all for the light which it throws on his evolution both as a writer and as a man. The published text is less interesting in this respect than the surviving *dossier* of carefully classified drafts and fragments of chapters, chapter headings, roughly scribbled notes and (sometimes mutually contradictory) sets of plans. This *dossier* suggests that *La Dragonne* was to have been a work radically different from the published version, a work of which the latter is only a pale reflection.

Part I of the novel – the most complete of its three parts – recounts the frustrated dreams of military glory of the provincial *juge de paix*, Martin Paranjeoux-Sabrenas, his hopes for a son who will realize those dreams, and the birth of a daughter to whom he transfers all his hopes and whom he baptizes with the appropriately martial name of Jeanne. The account of her upbringing is followed by that of her father's attempts to find a suitable husband for her. His plans for her marriage to a young *polytechnicien* named Erbrand Sacqueville were to be frustrated however by Jeanne's abduction by a handsome Jewish officer variously named Dreyfus, Zweifuss, Schweinfuss, Schwynfuss, Gontran de Sainte-Croix, and finally modified, in the manuscript sent to Thadée Natanson, to Durand, Baron de Saint-Crucifix.

The style of this part of the novel is different yet again from that of any previous novel of Jarry. Though the tone is wryly comic and the narrative is underscored throughout by irony (except in those passages dealing with Erbrand), there is no trace here of any such subversive intention as secretly undermines, for example, *Le Surmâle*. The irony is contained *within* the narrative, which conforms wholly to the conventions of nineteenth-century descriptive realism. An abundance of details concerning the rituals and customs of everyday life in a small provincial town, extending even to explanations of local idiosyncracies of speech and habits, testify that Jarry's intention here is in large part descriptive and informative. Similar remarks apply to his slightly self-indulgent descriptions of the Seine south of Paris. These chapters express his own fond memories of his stay in Le Grand-Lemps and of his fishing expeditions, as well as his fascination with the comic rituals surrounding the most banal events. Though Jarry may have felt certain regrets at having chosen to write in such a manner (in a letter to Fénéon he described the opening chapter as 'le plus vulgaire' of the novel[20]), these pages are nonetheless a fine example of the genre of descriptive realism, enlivened by a vividness of observed detail and the mildly ironical or mocking tone which turns through them.

Part I of *La Dragonne* was to end with a chapter entitled first 'Le Dîner', and then 'Si Monsieur veut'. Its function was to present the 'ideas' and to portray the psychology or character of the hitherto rather shadowy figure of Erbrand, in the course of a conversation over dinner (and hence without the support of actions through which character can be revealed). It was also to contain a complementary presentation of the character of the Jewish officer who was to seduce Jeanne, thereby preparing the way for subsequent events: her moral decline, Erbrand's solitary drinking, and his ultimate revenge. This chapter was thus a pivot of the whole action of the novel – and one of the major reefs on which it foundered. Jarry's failure to write more than a few fragmentary lines of dialogue for this chapter may well be due to more than just accidental causes: for the portrayal of character or individual psychology is undoubtedly one of the weakest points in his work, or at least a task which did not interest him and from which he preferred to shy away.

The majority of Part II in the published version of *La Dragonne* is given over to an account of the battle of Morsang, preceded, more or less incoherently, by a scene showing a regiment on the march and by the poem 'Le Mousse de la Pi-ouït'. Both of these are mere fragments: the first Jarry intended to fill out by the inclusion of a small collection of marching songs; the second (a long, rather facile and repetitious poem about the misfortunes of a cabin-boy who falls overboard into the Seine) is only a caricature of what he had in mind and was intended merely as a pretext for further vast developments. A fourth chapter entitled 'Le Roi boit', which was to describe Erbrand's frantic drinking, is not even represented in the published text.[21]

'Le Mousse de la Pi-ouït' was to have been sung in the midst of a crowded *bistrot* frequented by the fishermen and bargees of the Seine, and to have been punctuated by a series of interjections and interruptions. Through these Jarry aimed to create a stylized evocation of this jovial, ribald and hard-drinking world which he knew and loved, and of the river which was its life-blood. These interjections were also to have suggested a number of different levels of interpretation (among them, sexual) of the song itself, involving a technique of polysemy characteristic of their author. The whole episode was also to have prepared the way for the account of the battle of Morsang, through the discovery by the drunken bargees of the corpses floating down the river. These and other developments in *La Dragonne* would seem to confirm a trend already noted in Jarry's other works of the same period, a move progressively away from the highly 'poetic', esoteric style of his early years to increasingly conventional, and, more importantly, popular forms of expression: marching songs, popular ballads or *complaintes*, elements of popular speech, and the like. But at the same time, the organization of this material leads to the creation of forms of expression no less highly stylized than those of earlier years. Had Jarry succeeded, in the case of the 'Mousse', in realizing this vast 'orchestration' of themes and effects, he would have created a completely new literary form; alas, his failure even to approach a realization of the scheme is a testimony both to the magnitude and complexity of the task, and to the exhaustion of his own creative powers.

'La Bataille de Morsang', on the other hand, is one of his most remarkable pieces of writing, testifying to the fact that, at the beginning of 1903 at least, he was at the height of his creative powers. It is also the only part of the novel which can be regarded as substantially complete and definitive: Jarry's subsequent modifications to the text of the *Revue Blanche* were minor and relatively insignificant, and he himself described it, in a letter to Fénéon, as a 'nouvelle faisant un tout, empruntée au roman'.[22] It recounts the episode of Erbrand's symbolic revenge upon the army and upon Jeanne (who has become the regimental whore), in which, by a brilliant piece of military strategy, he causes a whole regiment to bring about its own annihilation.

The genesis of this account is characteristic. Erbrand chooses the site for his intended massacre on account of the name of a nearby village: *Morsang* (suggestive of both *mort/sang* and *mord/sang*). Morsang-sur-Seine was the name of a village near Jarry's favourite fishing spot on the Seine, and it is probable that he himself was inspired to conceive not only the title but also this whole grandiose episode by the imaginative power of the name itself. Having chosen his location, Erbrand begins his work by the murder of the regiment's two scouts and the cutting of the telegraph wires which, followed by the fall of night, throws the marching troops into a state of panic. When the regiment, arms at the ready and moving laboriously around a horse-shoe bend in the Seine some 600 to 700 metres in diameter, has almost formed a circle, Erbrand, in the centre of the circle, impersonating the general in command shouts an order to halt. A shot released by a startled trooper, transformed by its echo into an apparent volley, precipitates a general terror, and, in the midst of the ensuing confusion, Erbrand signals the order to commence firing. The soldiers begin to fire frantically into the darkness across the river at the invisible and imaginary enemy. At the centre of the panic-stricken and murderous circle, Sacqueville alone is safe, the trajectory of the bullets passing over his head – a situation likened by Jarry to that of the still point at the centre of a cyclone:

Cyclone est cercle. La mort y est centrifuge. La mort est toujours centrifuge, ce qui explique l'explicable longévité de Dieu et de quelques hommes. Le cyclone est un trou avec de la mort autour.

> [Cyclone is circle. In it, death is centrifugal. Death is always centrifugal, which explains the inexplicable longevity of God and of some men. A cyclone is a hole with death all around.][23]

All night the grisly rhythm of the slaughter continues, until the death of the last man.

Such a brief résumé can give only the vaguest idea of the atmosphere and quality of Jarry's writing. 'La Bataille de Morsang' is an outstanding example of what might be called his 'speculative realism'. Though the narrative contains occasional elements of irony and humour, and though it depends for its effect in part upon an abundance of vivid, striking and sometimes wryly comic imagery, Jarry's description of the battle, taken as a whole, is far from being purely fanciful. On the contrary, the narrative contains a wealth of precise tactical, strategic and ballistic details, almost every one of which, taken individually, is strictly plausible. The events portrayed are the result of a rigorous *deduction* from an initial set of circumstances, pushed to the absolute limits of possibility (a fact to which Jarry himself drew attention retrospectively in referring to this episode in his notes as 'une possibilité' and through his intention to subtitle this section 'Le Possible'[24]). The style of 'La Bataille de Morsang (to say nothing of its themes) relates it closely to his *Spéculations*, the whole episode being in fact a greatly expanded 'speculation' in narrative form. Indeed, as if to stress this fact, Jarry had intended to add to it, à propos of Jeanne's corpse floating down the river, an adaptation of his article on 'Les Moeurs des noyés' which had appeared in the *Revue Blanche* in May 1902.[25]

'La Bataille de Morsang' expresses with a force and clarity not found in his work since *Les Jours et les Nuits* the essence of Jarry's feelings towards the army, a symbol here and elsewhere, in the rigidity of its organization and its attempted regimentation of the individual, of the State or society as a whole. The difference between the two novels is revealing: where Sengle 'deserted', preferring the negative solution of escape from the army, Erbrand Sacqueville, the supreme strategist, after rejecting the army brings about its annihilation – by itself. But his actions also go beyond this: he is 'personally' responsible for a further three murders with his sword: those of Captain Canon, one of Jeanne's lovers; of the regimental chaplain, who bears the unlikely name of 'de Rayphusce' and who is the brother of the Jewish officer who first seduced Jeanne; and finally, of Jeanne herself.

In a scene with clear sexual implications, the nymphomaniac Jeanne is pierced by Erbrand's sword, and her body, like that of the chaplain, is carried away by the Seine, which throughout has appeared as the accomplice of Erbrand in his murderous designs. Its later discovery by the bargees confirms and reinforces her portrayal as the embodiment of the lubricity and perversity of womankind:

Son sexe émergea le premier boire l'air que respirent les hommes, et au petit bruit de baiser qu'il fit, en crevant la surface, comme un cyprin gobe une miette de gateau, on vit qu'il leur disait: 'Bonjour'.

> [Her sexual organ emerged first to drink in the air which men breathe, and from the little kissing noise which it made as it broke surface, like a carp gulping down a crumb of cake, it could be seen that it was saying to them: 'Hello'.][26]

The death of the *abbé* – the sole survivor, along with Jeanne, of the battle – has an equally clear symbolic significance. His duel to the death with Sacqueville is preceded by a number of allusions to the 'death' of God:

– Et maintenant Dieu n'est pas, et l'homme est l'être humain, dit Sacqueville. . . .
    L'abbé le contempla avec des yeux qui s'égaraient, ne cria point, car sa voix s'étrangla. Sacqueville crut percevoir, au fond de sa gorge, les deux mots hébreux qui expriment: Dieu est mort!

> ['And now God is not, and man is man', said Sacqueville. . . .
>   The priest looked at him wild-eyed, did not cry out, for his voice caught in his throat. Sacqueville thought that he could make out, in the depths of his throat, the two Hebrew words which signify: God is dead!][27]

And as he hands to Erbrand the bottle to which Jarry's hero consigns his 'confession', the chaplain embarks upon a long, rambling meditation in which, through punning upon the word 'Spirit', God is replaced by Alcohol, and the 'afterlife' is reinterpreted as being merely the dreams of the disintegrating brain:

Au commencement, l'Esprit de Dieu flottait sur les eaux. . . .
Mais il n'y a point de Père, sinon dans l'Esprit: le Père est soluble dans l'Esprit: l'Esprit est l'arche du Père sur les eaux. . . . Nous, prêtres, avons catalogue en trois classes les vagabondages de la fantaisie des morts. Nous, disciplinons leurs rêves, qui sont le seul Autre Monde. La décomposition de leur cerveau organise l'Éternité. . . . Il importe que la digestion des morts soil légère. Le cordial de l'Esprit est santé souveraine et ce que les hommes traduisent: la vie future. . . .
L'Esprit est ce Dieu futur et éternel, le même qui engrosse les vierges et qui, au commencement, flottait et sous l'espèce de qui l'homme communiera, quand il n'y aura plus besoin de communion, ou que Dieu, resté en arrière, communiera de l'homme . . . dès que l'homme aura 'battu le record' de Dieu.

> [In the beginning, the Spirit of God moved upon the face of the waters. . . .
>   But there is no Father, other than in the Spirit: the Father is soluble in the Spirit: the Spirit is the ark of the Father upon the water. . . . We priests have classified into three groups the wanderings of the imagination of the dead. We discipline their dreams, which are the only Other World. The disintegration of their brain organizes Eternity. . . . It is important that the

food of the dead should be light and easily digested. The stimulant of the Spirit is the sovereign source of health and what men translate as: the life hereafter. . . .

The Spirit is this future and eternal God, the same one which gets virgins pregnant and which, in the beginning, moved over the waters and in whose kind man will receive Holy Communion, when there is no longer any need for Communion, or when God, having remained behind, will receive Communion of man . . . as soon as man has 'broken the record' of God.][28]

'La Bataille de Morsang' testifies to an important aspect of Jarry's imagination, already noted: namely, his sadistic predilection for scenes of murder and bloodshed. But it casts an even more revealing light on another side of that imagination: his dreams of power – culminating in the power of total destruction – over his fellow human beings. Erbrand here represents a projection of Jarry himself into absolute terms; he wields an absolute power and ability of which his creator could only dream. His revenge upon the army through the annihilation of a whole regiment and (by the killing of Canon, the *abbé* and Jeanne) through the ritual murder of Authority, God and Womankind respectively, represents on the part of Jarry the dream of a total destruction of society itself, if not a 'revenge' upon existence as a whole.

After such dizzy heights, anything else must of necessity involve a fall into relative banality. By its very nature, 'La Bataille de Morsang' must constitute a conclusion: the logical culmination of the events of the novel. Jarry's decision to add a third part to *La Dragonne* was to have disastrous consequences.

As he worked on the novel, Jarry was seized more and more by the desire to accentuate the identity between his hero and himself, and to make of *La Dragonne* a compendium of his own life and experiences. The urge to recapitulate upon and take stock of one's past grows stronger in most men as they advance in years; yet Jarry was still only in his early thirties. Did he have a premonition, born of his successive illnesses, that the end was fast approaching? Whatever the answer, it is certainly the case that in him the urge to recapture the past and to 'rediscover' his spiritual roots grew in intensity as his health declined.

Autobiographical details are nothing new in Jarry's work. In *Haldernablou, Les Jours et les Nuits, L'Amour absolu, Faustroll* and even possibly in certain chapters of *L'Amour en visites* he had used elements of his own character and experiences, appropriately transposed into fictional form. It is therefore not surprising to find features in common between Erbrand Sacqueville and his creator. He shares with Jarry his smallness of stature; he has a passion for fishing and a love of the Seine, with a particular predilection for the region around Le Coudray; as a boy, he had a passion for marionettes (in which he –

or Jarry – saw an interesting analogy with fishing: 'C'était encore de la pêche, tenir les pantins au bout d'un fil' ['It was yet another form of fishing, holding puppets on the end of a string']²⁹); after brilliant studies in the provinces, he had gone to Paris to continue his education; his mother had died while he was a student there, quickly followed by his father; and he had broken off all contact with his surviving family.

But *La Dragonne* contains more than just autobiographical parallels and personal reminiscences transposed into fiction. It does not merely present Jarry's life and character as they were, but also as they *might have been*; Erbrand represents a kind of 'alternative existence', in which the defects and inadequacies of real life are corrected and compensated for. For Erbrand Sacqueville is an idealized Jarry, and the circumstances of his life, in particular his family circumstances, are those which Jarry, at this stage of his career at least, would have wished for himself. *La Dragonne* is thus a work not merely of fictionalized, but of 'idealized' autobiography; and it is these auto-biographical elements, real or imagined, which confer an extra dimension upon the novel and which give a poignancy and an interest to its otherwise mediocre, and in parts banal and hackneyed, final part.

The differences are striking. Erbrand is 'né sur les côtes bretonnes', where Jarry was born in Laval. His mother and father leave Brittany to live in Paris while their son studies there. His mother, 'de vieille noblesse bretonne' (an ancestry which Jarry came to claim for his own mother), is an expert horsewoman, swimmer and fencer. His father, a doctor of laws, had (unlike Anselme Jarry) in deference to his wife's wishes given up the idea of a career in industry, managing 'une filature ou une usine', in favour of a 'chaire de législation' at the local *lycée*.³⁰ While Erbrand himself passes, albeit somewhat nonchalantly, through the prestigious École Polytechnique – a course which was taken by a number of his schoolfriends, among them Henri Morin, and which Jarry himself, according to the testimony of Morin quoted in Chapter 1 above, was for a time on the point of taking. Most striking of all, although as a young man he had passed under the influence of prevailing intellectual fashions – 'il s'était "emballé" ... sur les théories qu'il lui était impossible ... de ne point sentir ambiantes: anarchisme, ibsénisme, etc ...' ['he had got himself "worked up" ... about theories which it was impossible for him ... not to be aware of around him: anarchism, Ibsenism, etc ...'] – Erbrand is emphatically *not* a writer, and in fact abhors 'men of letters': 'bien qu'il ne fût point homme de lettres, il avait ces gens en horreur' ['although he was no man-of-letters, he detested such people'].³¹ Had Jarry come to regret the turning which he had taken at the age of 20, and the path that he had followed ever since?

In particular, he came to place a dominant emphasis on Erbrand's Breton origins and spiritual roots. In the early chapters, this ancestry had been only one of several strains (il avait autant d'atavismes vendéens, normands ou manceaux que bretons' ['he had as many ancestors from the Vendée, from Normandy or from Le Mans as from Brittany']), and in 'La Bataille de Morsang' it is his Norman ancestry which is most stressed.[32] But at some point, possibly even as early as February 1905, on the occasion of a visit to Lamballe, Jarry conceived the idea of making Erbrand return to the land of his Breton ancestors, a journey which would also be a voyage of rediscovery into his own past.

Jarry's collapse from exhaustion and undernourishment in April 1906 and his subsequent return to Laval were crucial events both in his own life and in the history of *La Dragonne*. Feverish, debilitated, in rags, on 11 May he was put by his friends Gastilleur and Van Bever on the train to Laval and entrusted to the care of his sister Charlotte. Though he had made a number of return journeys to both Laval and Lamballe in the previous 15 months, such a journey must have seemed to Jarry in his feverish state a return to his own past, as well as to the most conservative and backward-looking region of France; if his own return did not first suggest the idea of a similar journey on the part of Erbrand, then it certainly confirmed it in his mind. And in a desperate effort to complete the long overdue manuscript of *La Dragonne*, he set about, in the week following his arrival, converting his own impressions into those experienced by his hero. His imagination excited by fever, he dashed off a number of pages relating Erbrand's return to the land of his ancestors deep in the heart of Brittany (which Laval was certainly not), a journey of return both into his own past and into 'la Nuit des temps'; for Erbrand's return mysteriously leaps across a period of seven centuries to the year 1206 and into a mystical and legendary past.[33] Never before in his work had the identity between novelist and protagonist been so great. Confidently announcing to Rachilde a few days after his arrival his imminent complete recovery, he relates his intention to *use* his experiences for *La Dragonne*:

La 'Vie Posthume' du Père Ubu, Madame Rachilde, est extraordinaire, mais il n'a mal nulle part et peut-être (j'écris toujours peut-être quand je pense assurément) cette fatigue anormale n'était-elle qu'un prétexte fourni par la nature pour qu'il vive – en l'écrivant d'ailleurs à mesure, ô littérature – la dernière partie de la Dragonne: la Nuit des Temps. Il croyait disparaître . . ., ainsi qu'il l'a décrit dans les chapitres faits avant l'aventure, en trouant derrière lui le rideau de velours noir . . . . Il se documente actuellement comme un simple Zola . . . .

[The 'Posthumous Existence' of Père Ubu, Madame Rachilde, is extraordinary, but he has no pain anywhere and perhaps (I always write perhaps when I think undoubtedly) this abnormal fatigue was only a pretext provided by nature to enable him to live – while writing it down, moreover, bit by bit, oh literature – the last part of *La Dragonne*: the Night of Time. He thought he was going to vanish . . . in the manner he described in the chapters written before the adventure, leaving a hole behind him in the black velvet curtain . . . . At present he is documenting himself like a mere Zola . . . .][34]

The letter suggests also a new idea: whether through exaggeration of the gravity of his condition, or through a strange premonition of events to come, the expression 'la Nuit des Temps' had come to take on a new meaning for Jarry. Through a symbolism common in his work, it became identified in his mind with the eternal 'Night' of death. The real crisis, however, was yet to come, between 25 and 28 May – curiously accompanied by a fever of letter-writing which increased in intensity with his illness. A series of letters and postcards kept his friends in Paris informed of his condition. On 27 May he also dictated to Charlotte a vast and detailed plan for *La Dragonne* embodying his now radically revised conception of the novel; to the plan in Charlotte's handwriting, he added the note: 'Le lendemain commence la fièvre cérébrale, qui indique [?] le dernier chapitre' ['The next day there begins the cerebral fever, which points to [?] the last chapter'], followed by another note which ends with the words: 'Ceci est le dernier manuscrit autographe du Père Ubu il va s'arrêter dans la nuit des temps. Bonsoir. Monsieuye/AJ' ['This is the last manuscript in the hand of Père Ubu he is going to come to a stop in the night of time. Goodnight. Sirrah/AJ'].[35] At the height of his fever, he experienced a vision of Saint Michael and came to believe also that he himself, like Christ, had experienced a descent into Hell followed by a 'resurrection'. Whilst there, moreover, he had done 'ce que le Christ n'a point osé faire aux enfers': he had 'liberated' the fallen angel, Lucifer, who had been placed in his power for two days.[36] He also received the last rites, and on 28 May dictated the following letter to Rachilde which reveals a strange mixture of heroic bravado and pathetic self-deception:

Madame Rachilde,

Le père Ubu, cette fois, n'écrit pas dans la fièvre. (Ça commence comme un testament, il est fait d'ailleurs.) Je pense que vous avez compris, il ne meurt pas (pardon, le mot est lâché) de bouteilles et autres orgies. Il n'avait pas cette passion et il a eu la coquetterie de se faire examiner partout par les 'merdecins'. Il n'a aucune tare ni au foie, ni au coeur, ni aux reins, pas même dans les urines! Il est épuisé, simplement (fin curieuse quand on a écrit *Le Surmâle*) et sa chaudière ne va pas éclater mais s'éteindre. Il va s'arrêter tout doucement, comme un moteur fourbu. Et aucun régime humain, si fidèlement (en riant en dedans) qu'il les suive, n'y fera rien. Sa fièvre est peut-être que son coeur essaye de le sauver en faisant du 150. Aucun être humain n'a tenu jusque-là. Il est, depuis deux jours, l'extrême oint du Seigneur et, tel l'éléphant sans trompe de Kipling, plein d'une insatiable curiosité. Il va rentrer un peu plus *arrière* dans la nuit des temps. . . .

> [Dear Madame Rachilde,
>
> Père Ubu, this time, is not writing in a state of fever. (This is beginning like a last will and testament, it is written moreover.) I think that you have understood, he is not dying (forgive me, the word has slipped out) as a result of bottles and other orgies. He did not have a passion for such things and he has made a point of having himself examined all over by the 'medicsh'. He has no flaw, neither in the liver, nor the heart, nor the kidneys, nor even in the urinary tract! He is exhausted, quite simply (a curious end when one has written *Le Surmâle*), and his boiler is not going to burst but simply to go out. He is going quite simply to stop like a worn-out engine. And no human form of treatment, however faithfully (whilst laughing inwardly) he may follow it, will do anything about it. His fever perhaps comes from the fact that his heart is trying to save him by producing a rate of 150. No human being has ever held out to that point. He has been, for the last two days, the extreme anointed of the Lord and, like Kipling's trunkless elephant, is filled with an insatiable curiosity. He is going to return a little further *back* into the night of time. . . .][37]

In all this there is an undoubted element of posturing, something of the attitude expressed in Jarry's statement to Apollinaire after he had fired his revolver at the sculptor Manolo: 'N'est-ce pas que c'était beau comme littérature?' Jarry was not just making literature out of life, but selfconsciously turning life itself into 'literature'. A letter of 29 May to Vallette in fact described those letters of the day before as 'un peu exagérées', and a telegram of 30 May, also to Vallette, sought to excuse his 'littérature exagérée' due to his 'grande crise cérébrale'.[38] Nevertheless, what he took to be his own brush with death had given him, or so he believed, the material for the conclusion of *La Dragonne*. He wrote to Fénéon on 8 June: 'Le petit tourisme que je viens de faire, sans "blague", au-delà des portes de la mort, m'a donné le chapitre final, j'en suis très content' ['The little tourist excursion which I have just undertaken, all "joking" aside, beyond the gates of death, has given me the final chapter, I'm very pleased with it'].[39] Erbrand, like Jarry, was to fall gravely ill and, like the hero of an ancient epic, was to undergo his 'descent into Hell', followed by a 'resurrection' 'on the third day'. These episodes he planned to entitle 'Descendit ad inferos' – used previously to describe Erbrand's descent into alcoholism, but now imbued with a new, starker meaning – and 'Tertia Die'.[40]

The transmutation of this experience into the pages of *La Dragonne* is, however, disappointing. Part III contains an account of Erbrand's return to his native Pell-Bras which he had left behind ten years previously, imagining, in his former naïvety, 'que sa vie était dans la grande ville'.[41] But the Erbrand who makes this journey is radically different from the character we have known hitherto: faithful to the memory of his parents, and imbued with a sense of the values of family, tradition and continuity with the past. The tone is solemn if not sombre, and the opening pages of Part III are charged with an emotion which is wholly lacking in the previous two parts of the novel. Was the emotional force of Jarry's own return to Laval really that experienced by Erbrand? Or is he here somewhat unscrupulously simply making literary capital out of his impressions, forcing them into a conventional mould? The question is impossible to answer with complete certainty. But the heavy emphasis upon Erbrand's recollections of his childhood, some of which are almost certainly Jarry's own, suggests at least that the tone reflects something of the latter's own feelings towards the familiar scenes and places of his early years. It is even possible that Erbrand's discovery of the virtues of family, tradition and bourgeois solidity reflects a secret longing on his creator's part, at this stage of his life, for an assurance and a stability which he had either never enjoyed or had at one time rejected.

Less convincing are other episodes in the fragmentary and incoherent text. The account of the marriage of Jeanne and Erbrand is maudlin and conventional in the extreme ('tous les deux d'un grand caractère, et si bien faits l'un pour l'autre ...' ['both of them of outstanding character, and so well suited to each other ...']ary[42]). This is followed by a visit to the Forest of Paimpont, transformed for the purpose into the mysterious and magical Forest of Brocéliande of Arthurian legend. Here, in a confused hotch-potch of themes, Arthurian romance mingles with elements of family history, of druidism and astronomy, in the depths of a mystical and mythical past. Here, too, Erbrand falls victim to a mysterious 'fièvre cérébrale', closely if clumsily based on the illness of Jarry himself, and is tended by the devoted Jeanne, who is made to play the role performed in Jarry's own life by Charlotte. The banality of much of this derives from the superficiality of its Breton and Arthurian themes. Far from expressing any deeply personal themes or meditation, the final part of the novel simply mingles personal reminiscences with a mishmash of literary and historical clichés hastily culled from secondary sources – above all from Maurice Duhamel's recently published *Essai sur la littérature bretonne ancienne* of 1905, from which Jarry took five pages of notes which he incorporated into the novel. Though he could legitimately claim Breton (if not noble) ancestry on his mother's side,[43] in reality his own 'discovery' of his Breton past and spiritual roots was at least as much a conscious invention as a true discovery. And although part of his childhood was spent in Brittany, in

Saint-Brieuc and Rennes, the town of Laval to which he had now returned, though staunchly Catholic and conservative, was not and never had been either politically or linguistically a part of Brittany, despite Jarry's claims to the contrary.

The mediocrity of Part III of *La Dragonne* provides a sad comment upon the decline of Jarry's own creative powers and critical judgment. But its banality and incoherence are not wholly attributable to Jarry himself. Charlotte's correspondence with the Vallettes after her brother's death provides convincing external evidence that, under the guise of carrying out his last wishes, she 'completed' parts of the novel. It is also possible that she has 'arranged' parts of the manuscript, with less than happy results. The difficulty of identifying her contribution is complicated by the fact that much of Jarry's text was dictated to or copied out by her, and is thus, in the original manuscript, in her handwriting. On thematic and stylistic grounds, however, it is certain that she is wholly or mainly responsible for the last ten pages of Chapter IV, which recount the childhood of Erbrand's mother – an idealized portrait of Caroline Jarry. The style of these is broken and incoherent (her characteristic technique of linking phrases by a series of dots and dashes could not be more different from the involved syntax of her brother), the imagery hackneyed and the sentiments maudlin; while the Brittany evoked here is so obviously the stereotyped land of mystery and romance as to seem almost a caricature. Charlotte obviously believed that vagueness, not to say incoherence and confusion of ideas, was in itself sufficient to create 'poetry'. As to the final part of the novel, though many of the themes, motifs and even individual phrases are undoubtedly Jarry's, recurring elsewhere either in his notes or in other works, the style, and the existence of a number of patently nonsensical statements, suggest that up to half of the published text has been 'reworked' by Charlotte. It is difficult to find any excuse for the arrogance of Charlotte in thus presuming to tamper with the work her brother had left behind.

Much more interesting than these Arthurian and related developments, however, are two other episodes of which fragments exist both in the published text and in the *dossier* of *La Dragonne* and which throw light on Jarry's religious and political evolution. Perhaps due to the effects of his illness, perhaps as a result of an intellectual evolution which was taking place regardless and was accelerated by the influence of the staunchly Catholic milieu of Laval, Jarry seems to have undergone a religious conversion. Rachilde at least believed so, adding to one of her letters the sarcastic comment: 'Mais j'oublie que vous êtes catholique et que vous croyez en l'intervention de l'Autre' ['But I am forgetting that you are a Catholic and that you believe in the intervention of the Other'].[44] At some point, he scribbled upon a blank sheet of paper a statement of belief which paraphrases (while giving it a significant and unexpected twist) Tertullian's celebrated phrase 'Credo quia absurdum', in the form: '*Credo, quia absurdum . . . non credere.* Alfred Jarry'.[45] If it is difficult to accept wholly Maurice Saillet's interpretation of this as simply the expression of a 'précaution éminemment scientifique' on Jarry's part[46] (that is, of the 'scientific' viewpoint of pataphysics, which neither completely accepts nor completely rejects any belief or proposition, placing them all on the same plane), it is difficult also to take Jarry's apparent conversion wholly at face value. It may be that, even at such a crucial moment of his life, something of his irrepressible love of paradox which caused him to argue that 'truth' is to be found solely in the creations of the imagination is once again present. And perhaps the above statement has to be read in the light of Ellen Elson's profession of her belief in the existence of Marcueil's 'Indian' in *Le Surmâle*: 'j'y crois parce que personne n'y croira . . . *parce que c'est absurde . . . comme je crois en Dieu!*' ['I believe in him because nobody will believe in him . . . *because it's absurd . . .* as I believe in God!']*[47] Whatever the case, the fact remains that Jarry's conversion, if such it was, was certainly not to any orthodox form of Christianity. In the midst of his profession of belief in God is to be found the same fundamental egoism which characterizes his work and thought throughout, here causing him in his feverish and hallucinatory state to believe that his own exploits had been greater even than those of Christ. And in his above-quoted letter to Rachilde of 28 May, he went on to profess the same very un-Catholic and un-Christian view of the after-life and of heaven which he had already expressed in 'La Bataille de Morsang', as merely the by-products of a disintegrating brain:

Il [i.e. le Père Ubu] croit que le cerveau, dans la décomposition, fonctionne au delà de la mort et que ce sont *ses rêves* qui sont le Paradis.

> [He [i.e. Père Ubu] believes that the brain, in its decomposition, continues to function beyond death and that it is *its dreams* which constitute Paradise.][48]

Whatever the nature and status of his religious beliefs, however, the fact remains also that Jarry's relationship to the Catholic faith of his childhood is a complex one, and is closely bound up with his real or assumed sense of identity with the ultra-Catholic province of Brittany. There are traces throughout his work, alongside elements of what might be construed as deliberate blasphemy, of a certain sympathy for the beliefs and practices of Catholicism, particularly in a Breton context. And though an attitude of hostility towards the Church was noted in *La Chandelle verte*, this is less anti-Catholic than anti-clerical and is counterbalanced by an equally, if not even more, fierce hostility towards the 'secular' religion of his contemporaries and the demands of the State. In any conflict opposing the forces of traditional religion and the secular authorities, one can well imagine him, despite a latent anti-clericalism, feeling more sympathy for the former than for the latter; all the more so as support for Catholicism was a means of affirming the strength of his Breton identity. And in fact, Brittany was engulfed at the time of the Separation of Church and State in 1905 by a passionate campaign of protest and civil disobedience: the attempts of the authorities to carry out an inventory of Church property were met by virulent denunciations from the pulpit, popular demonstrations and riots resulting at times in bloody confrontations, and widespread resignations among Catholic army officers and magistrates. In all these events Jarry took a lively if passive interest, identifying fully with his outraged compatriots, boasting to Rachilde from Laval that he was there in the 'whitest' Department in France,[49] and reaffirming his position in *La Dragonne* through the figures of Erbrand's grandfather, General de l'Ermelinaye, and his cousin, who bears the distinctively Breton name of Marie-Guy.

This evolution goes hand in hand with the development of a virulent and even sadistic antisemitism. Jeanne's seducer of Part I of *La Dragonne*, Dreyfus, Zweifuss, Schweinfuss, etc., *alias* Durand de Saint-Crucifix, makes a final appearance with his wife and young son in the guise of a simple bourgeois tourist in Part III. All three members of the family were to be trapped in the treacherous sands of the Bay of Mont St-Michel and were to be eaten by foraging pigs, their blood supposedly being shed for the blood of Christ crucified by the Jews! Further if slight evidence of his changing attitude is the claim of Henry de Bruchard that Jarry, on his return to Paris from Laval, had confided to him his intention of becoming a writer of 'reactionary' antisemitic polemics.[50] The origins of this antisemitism may lie in the influence of his newfound Breton and Catholic compatriots, to whom the events surrounding the Separation of Church and State appeared as the work of a conspiracy of Jews and Freemasons. But it may also have a broader and more disturbing basis. For Jarry's intellectual evolution runs parallel in this respect to that of a great many writers and intellectuals of his time, amongst them his close friend Franc-Nohain, his one-time mentor Remy de Gourmont, and almost the whole group associated with the *Mercure de France*, who moved progressively from the free-thinking and provocative 'anarchism' of the early 1890s to the reactionary and intransigent nationalism of 1914.

By means of these developments, Jarry believed that he was at last on the point of finishing the unending *La Dragonne*. The truth was exactly opposite: the creation of a third part split the already loosely constructed novel definitively into two. The recurrence in his notes and letters of the terms 'à raccorder' and 'raccord' points to his awareness of the incoherence of the novel, and at the same time to his inability to weld its disparate parts together. Alongside the decline of his former creative powers, this inability suggests also two further factors: Jarry's discomfort within the confines of the conventional novel, with its demands of unity and coherence, which he had set himself to write; and the total incompatibility of his material.

This incompatibility exists on three different levels. There is first of all the contrast of tone and style between the light-hearted, slightly mocking narrative of Part I and the speculative extravagances of Part II, on the one hand, and the solemn and 'poetic' final part on the other. Secondly, on the level of plot, the presence together of Erbrand and Jeanne in Part III is in blatant contradiction with the outcome of the battle of Morsang. To resolve this contradiction, Jarry fell back upon the 'solution' of making the battle a dream experienced by the drunken Erbrand, the corpses which float down the Seine and are mistaken by the drunken bargees for crocodiles being simply empty bottles carried along by its waters. But such a solution has the effect of largely destroying the impact of Part II of the novel; for the battle loses not only much of its imaginative force, but ultimately its whole point, if it is regarded simply as a dream. Its ultimate impact on the reader depends upon its being presented not as an imaginary, but as a real, event – or at the very least as an event which, by virtue of an inherent logic, *might* have occurred. Thirdly, there is an incompatibility on the level of character. The pure, devoted and passive Jeanne of Part III is in blatant contradiction both with the self-willed figure of Part I, who was indifferent both to Erbrand and to the prospect of marriage, and with the Jeanne of 'La Bataille de Morsang'; even if one accepts that the battle is merely a dream, Erbrand's imagining of his fiancée as a regimental whore contrasts strangely with her subsequent nature. Most revealing of all is the contradiction within the character of Erbrand himself, between the 'Exterminator' of the battle of Morsang, and the new Erbrand of Part III who repudiates his former bohemian and wayward existence and rediscovers the virtues of an aristocratic, military, Breton and Catholic past. The former represents a projection of Jarry himself into absolute terms; the latter is a purely relative figure, reflecting a Jarry weakened by illness and ground down by constant poverty and destitution.

That Jarry himself was aware of the contradiction is shown by a number of hesitations and uncertainties. Successive drafts of a scene describing the Breton resistance to the secular authorities' attacks on the Church show a progressive backing-away from his initial extreme position: Erbrand's cousin, Marie-Guy, ordered to break down the doors of the Church of Notre-Dame de Pritz near Laval, refuses, and at first offers his sword to the Bishop in symbolic submission, then hangs it in the Church as an *ex-voto*, and finally calmly replaces it in its scabbard.[51] Some months later, Jarry further distanced himself from his earlier beliefs, replying to Rachilde's taunts with the words: 'Nous avons eu tous les joujoux: notre descente aux enfers – ça peut toujours distraire un littérateur. Il faut aller un peu dans tous les [endroits?].' ['We have had all the toys: our descent into hell – that can always provide a writer with a source of entertainment. One has to pay a visit to some extent to all [places?].'][52]

In short, Jarry was no longer sure *who* Erbrand was, and, correspondingly, who he himself was. Life was moulding itself upon literature in a new and unconsciously ironical way, as he found himself being progressively 'taken over' by his fictional but autobiographical hero. His identification with Erbrand and exploitation of the novel's 'Breton' themes with all that they implied were dragging him along a path leading to religious and political extremes which a few years earlier he would have condemned out of hand, and to the adoption of a standpoint which represented a total abandonment of the principles and outlook of his pataphysics. But at the same time, part of him at least, aware of what was happening, resisted and fought against this evolution. Was it in order to flee the Catholic atmosphere of Laval and the new identity which he felt was in process of creation that, a mere few weeks before his death, he abandoned work on Part III of *La Dragonne* and took the fateful decision to return permanently to Paris?

The story of Jarry's attempts to finish *La Dragonne* is a sad one. His correspondence of the last two years of his life reveals an extraordinary capacity for naïve optimism and self-delusion. Yet this capacity for self-delusion at least enabled him to achieve a measure of serenity and detachment in the midst of his misery and suffering. Did it constitute a final, ironic instance of the application of his 'science of imaginary solutions'? He set himself tasks to fulfil which he was now quite incapable of accomplishing. He engaged upon a lengthy battle with Saltas in order to gain time to complete *La Dragonne* before *La Papesse Jeanne*. His awareness of the incoherence of *La Dragonne* in its existing form even led him in February 1907 to conceive the idea of amputating part of it (probably the whole of Part II) in order to form a new, separate novel: the 'troisième roman' whose imminent creation he at once triumphantly announced to his friends Vallette, Saltas and Gastilleur.[53] It was an idea which might just have succeeded in saving *La Dragonne*; but such schemes were now beyond his capability. Yet over and over again in letters to friends and publishers he confidently announced the novel's completion as imminent, while probably secretly intending, as he had proposed to Saltas concerning *La Papesse*, to present the manuscript to Fasquelle unfinished, convinced that the latter would not read it, and to complete it at the proof stage.[54]

Meanwhile, the problems of grinding poverty and illness remained. For all his blind optimism, his strength was slowly draining
away. His first serious illness in Laval in May 1906 had kept him
bedridden for around 40 days. Return to Paris at the end of July was
followed by relapse and a further return to Laval. His visits to Paris
were becoming increasingly brief, and he was spending more and
more time in Laval. A further serious bout of illness kept him
confined to bed there for 45 days, from May to July 1907. Early in July
he made a brief visit to Paris to see the *concierge* of the rue Cassette,
who found him 'fort débilité physiquement et . . . amaigri'.[55] He was
so weak, in fact, that he was unable even to walk short distances. Yet
all the while he continued to dream of returning to his beloved
'Tripode', of his neighbours at Le Coudray and of fishing in the Seine.

His debts, too, were becoming increasingly urgent while his
financial situation became daily more hopeless. (The extent of his
debts was not fully realized until after his death, when Vallette did his
best to sort out the mess and to help Charlotte, as far as was possible,
in discharging her brother's debts.) His creditors were lying in wait
for his return both to Paris and to Le Coudray. He was incapable of
managing his financial affairs successfully, continuing always to hope
for some miraculous solution to all his problems. Even if he had
succeeded in completing *La Dragonne* and *La Papesse Jeanne*, the
advances which he had already obtained on these meant that he
could expect little or nothing more from their publication. The sale of
Le Moutardier du Pape had not brought in as much as he had hoped.
He even tried to obtain from Terrasse (who had already lent him
some 3,000 francs) an advance on the future royalties from *Pantagruel*,
the only effect of which was to provoke a temporary quarrel between
the two friends which further delayed the eventual publication and
performance of the work. Threatened with expulsion from his lodgings in the rue Cassette (which at one point he thought of countering
by taking out a new lease in the name of Ubu!), he was only able to
save the situation thanks to a loan of 100 francs by Thadée Natanson.
His attitude towards such charity is sadly indicative of the extent to
which destitution had worn down his former pride and susceptibility;
where in June 1906 he had written to Fénéon concerning the money
from *Le Moutardier*: 'grâce à Vallette je n'ai rien à demander à
personne, ce que je n'ai jamais fait, d'ailleurs' ['thanks to Vallette I
have nothing to ask of anyone, something which I have never done,
what's more'],[56] he now calculatingly played off his two chief benefac-
tors, Vallette and Natanson, one against the other.

Some time towards the middle of 1907 he had abandoned work on
Part III of *La Dragonne* and turned his attention to the chapter entitled
'Le Mousse de la Pi-ouït'. In September he abandoned this and set
about 'classifying' the texts of his journalistic anthology, now re-

named *La Chandelle verte*. None of these schemes was completed. His last published work was a brochure entitled *Albert Samain, Souvenirs* which appeared in May 1907, a brief study of the work of the Belgian Symbolist poet whom Jarry may have met in the offices of the *Mercure de France* but with whom he had few affinities. Probably the result of a commission accepted to earn a few francs – Jarry himself stated in a letter to Rachilde that the work 'n'est qu'une besogne . . . bâclée'[57] – its chief interest lies in its autobiographical reminiscences, though even these are not always accurate, Jarry's memory being obviously distorted by illness.

At the beginning of October 1907 Jarry, fully aware of what awaited him there but tired of family life and longing for the intellectual stimulus of the capital, returned definitively to Paris. Here, he dragged himself along for several weeks amidst wretched poverty, desperately weak physically but continuing to drink heavily. A note scribbled on a visiting card to Thadée Natanson on 26 October, requesting ten francs to enable him to carry on for another week to the 'completion' of the 'manuscrits Fasquelle', reveals him to be bedridden again: ('Ce n'est d'ailleurs pas très pénible au milieu des livres et des paperasses' ['Besides, it's not very hard in the midst of my books and papers'][58]). On 29 October Vallette and Saltas, alarmed at not having seen him for several days, went to the rue Cassette where, after obtaining the services of a locksmith to open the door, they found Jarry lying half-conscious and with his legs paralysed on his bed. He was taken to the Hôpital de la Charité, where numerous friends called to visit him. Even in the face of death, according to witnesses, he retained something of his old spirit of amused detachment: seeing his friend Georges Polti pale and shaken at the sight of his condition, he asked challengingly: 'Eh! Polti, ça ne va donc pas que vous êtes si pâle?'.[59] He even asked for a bottle of wine to 'fortify' himself,[60] while his last wish, according to Saltas, was for a toothpick.[61] His last words, reported by Léautaud, were: 'je cherche, je cherche . . .', finally becoming muffled into a repeated 'j'ch, j'ch, j'ch . . .'.[62]

Jarry died, without the sacraments, and in a state of mind, according to all those who witnessed him, of calm and even amused detachment, on All Saints Day, 1 November 1907. The autopsy performed by Dr Stéphen-Chauvet revealed the cause of death to be not chronic alcoholism, as Saltas and others thought, but tuberculous meningitis, a then fatal disease, probably the consequence of a pulmonary infection brought on by exposure to cold and damp.[63] After a brief funeral service organized by members of his family at Saint-Sulpice, he was buried on 3 November at the Cimetière de Bagneux. The burial was attended by, amongst others, Vallette, Rachilde, Octave Mirbeau, Jules Renard, Maurice Beaubourg,

Charles-Louis Philippe, Paul Valéry, Paul Léautaud, Fagus, Thadée Natanson, Louis Lormel (with whom Jarry had been reconciled shortly before), Remy de Gourmont and Guillaume Apollinaire. It was described by Apollinaire in the terms:

... nous étions une cinquantaine à suivre son convoi. Les visages n'étaient pas très tristes, et seuls Fagus, Thadée Natanson et Octave Mirbeau avaient un tout petit peu l'air funèbre. Cependant, tout le monde sentait vivement la disparition du grand écrivain et du charmant garçon que fut Jarry. Mais il y a des morts qui se déplorent autrement que par les larmes. ...

Non, personne ne pleurait derrière le corbillard du Père Ubu. Et comme c'était un dimanche ..., la foule de ceux qui avaient été au cimetière de Bagneux s'était, vers le soir, répandue dans les guinguettes des alentours. Elles regorgeaient de monde. On chantait, on buvait, on mangeait de la charcuterie: tableau truculent comme une description imaginée par celui que nous menions en terre.

> ... there were about fifty of us at his funeral. The faces were not very sad, and only Fagus, Thadée Natanson and Octave Mirbeau looked just the tiniest bit gloomy. Nevertheless, everyone felt very keenly the disappearance of the great writer and the charming fellow that Jarry had been. But there are some whose death one laments in other ways than with tears. ...
>
> No, nobody wept behind the hearse carrying Père Ubu. And as it was a Sunday ... the crowd of those who had been at the Bagneux cemetery had, towards evening, scattered amongst the open-air cafés in the area. These were full to overflowing with customers. People were singing, drinking, eating cold meats: a colourful scene which might have been imagined by the very man himself whom we had just buried.[64]

It was an event such as Jarry himself would doubtless have wished.

Chapter Eleven

Language, truth and meaning

TO MOST of his contemporaries, Jarry remained an enigma. The reminiscences of friends and acquaintances stress the apparently contradictory elements in his character, describing him as cynical yet naïve, timid but intensely proud and fiercely independent, wishing to shock and scandalize yet capable of great tact, consideration and warmth of feeling. Some found his combination of penetrating intelligence, remarkable powers of retention and enormous erudition with an impish sense of humour and a childlike delight in pranks and mystification to be somehow vaguely sinister. André Gide saw behind his spoofing an essentially negative attitude to life: 'On ne pouvait pousser plus loin que lui la négation, et cela dans des écrits de forme souvent dure et durable' ['It was impossible to be more negative than he was, and that in works written in a form which was often solid and lasting'].[1] Others, however, were struck by the admirable, and even 'noble', aspects of his character: his generosity, his sense of dignity, and his detachment and equanimity in the face both of fame and of poverty and misfortune – a poverty which was itself to a considerable extent the result of his own pride, of a refusal to compromise with the values of the world in which he lived. This web of contradictions is best summed up in the obituary published by Vallette in the *Mercure de France* a few days after his death:

Alfred Jarry aimait à rappeler qu'il était venu au monde le jour de la Nativité de la Vierge, le 8 septembre 1873; il est mort le jour de la Toussaint, avec une grande précision, dirait-il lui-même. C'est une des plus singulières figures de la jeune génération, et l'être le plus contradictoire qui soit. Très intelligent et d'une inclairvoyance rare; original assurément, et assimilateur jusqu'à la singerie; nul plus que ce chercheur d'absolu ne fut à la merci du contingent; extraordinairement compréhensif, il ignora la vie comme personne; délicat souvent, discret, plein de tact en mainte circonstance, il aimait à prendre des attitudes cyniques. . . . Volontaire, tenace, hâbleur un peu, il s'illusionnait facilement et toujours dans le sens de l'optimisme – d'où quelques bonnes sottises qui lui furent préjudiciables. Ses désirs furent des impulsions d'enfant: un livre en caractères alors rares en France, un canot, une cabane au bord de la Seine: il les réalisa immédiatement – incontinent eût-il dit – sans souci des possibilités, envers lui-même et contre tous. Il fut charmant, insupportable et sympathique.

[Alfred Jarry liked to remind people that he was born on the feast-day of the Nativity of the Virgin, 8 September 1873; he died on All Saints' Day, with great precision, he would himself have said. He was one of the strangest figures of the younger generation, and the most contradictory being imaginable. Very intelligent and lacking in perspicacity to a rare degree; of great originality, certainly, yet assimilating other men's ideas to the point of imitativeness; no-one more so than this seeker after absolutes was at the mercy of the purely contingent; of an extraordinary depth of understanding, he was more ignorant of life than anyone; often thoughtful, discreet, full of tact in many a situation, he liked adopting cynical attitudes. . . . Headstrong, stubborn, a bit of a braggart, he easily deluded himself and always in an optimistic direction – whence a few pieces of utter foolishness which rebounded to his detriment. His wishes were the impulses of a child: a book printed in a typeface which was then rare in France, a rowing boat, a shack on the banks of the Seine: he achieved them instantly – forthwith, he would himself have said – without concern for the possible consequences, for himself and for everyone else. He was charming, unbearable and likeable.][2]

At the same time, however, Vallette's sympathetic tribute to his former friend and *protégé* as a man went hand-in-hand with an uncomprehending dismissal of his work as a writer. Indeed, for most of his contemporaries Jarry remained above all simply 'le Père Ubu' – the self-willed incarnation of his own monstrous creation. Baffled by his literary works, they preferred to fall back upon the more colourful aspects of his life, which they chose to interpret in turn as manifestations of a kind of 'lived' literature. Thus Apollinaire – basing himself on the incident in which Jarry had fired his revolver at the sculptor Manolo in a crowded café, and afterwards exclaimed: 'N'est-ce pas que c'était beau comme de la littérature?' – two years after his death, in 1909:

Alfred Jarry a été homme de lettres comme on l'est rarement. Ses moindres actions, ses gamineries, tout cela, c'était de la littérature. C'est qu'il était fondé en lettres et en cela seulement.

[Alfred Jarry was a man-of-letters to an extent rarely achieved. His most insignificant deeds, his childish pranks, everything he did was literature. The reason was that his whole life was steeped in literature, and only in literature.][3]

The same theme was taken up and given even wider circulation by André Breton:

Nous disons qu'à partir de Jarry, bien plus que de Wilde, la différentiation tenue longtemps pour nécessaire entre l'art et la vie va se trouver contestée, pour finir anéantie dans son principe.

[We maintain that from Jarry, even more than from Wilde, onwards, the distinction long regarded as necessary between art and life is going to be challenged, before being finally totally destroyed.][4]

Though there is an element of truth in Breton's view (there is an obvious parallel between Jarry's adoption of a purely fictitious *persona* and the equally 'contrived' nature of a novel such as, say, *Le Surmâle*), it obscures the fact that behind this façade, which some took to be the only reality, Jarry was the most secretive of men. Worse, it has had disastrous consequences for the appreciation of his literary work by focussing attention on the legend of Jarry to the detriment of that work. Yet it is ultimately on the basis of his literary work that Jarry must be judged and on account of that work that he remains important today; indeed, that he can be seen as one of the most important figures in the vanguard of the literature and the theatre of this century.

All the same, it remains the case that the attempt to come to grips with the 'real' Jarry is bedevilled by not just the one, but the series of 'poses' which he adopted throughout his life and literary career. Nothing could be more revealing in this respect than the dialogue between Ubu and Achras from the *Guignol* of 1893, in which Jarry hinted, at the very beginning of his literary career, at what was to follow – a dialogue in which Ubu, through a feigned misunderstanding, transforms Achras' protestations that his (Ubu's) actions constitute 'une imposture manifeste' into the affirmation of a 'posture magnifique'. The episode points simultaneously to two essential features of Jarry's character and literary work: his chameleon-like nature, which caused him to espouse an extraordinary variety of literary forms, from the most esoteric Symbolist verse through apparently rollicking tales of adventure to crude and scatological farce, and which poses, in a way which few writers can have done to the same extent, the question of 'authenticity' in literature and in life; and his obsessive love of paradox (and even, at times, of apparent deliberate contradiction). It is this latter tendency which is to a large extent responsible for making of Jarry a great comic writer: of his several attempts to formulate a theory of comedy, none applies better to his own work than the statement that 'le rire naît de la découverte du contradictoire' ['laughter is born of the discovery of contradiction'].[5] But the same tendency is responsible also for making of him one of the most self-revealing, but also most secretive, of writers. Through a deliberately paradoxical formulation of ideas which are close to his heart, which prevents us from taking almost *any* statement he makes wholly at face value, Jarry at one and the same time reveals, and hides, his true self.

Nevertheless, as this study has tried to show, behind the paradoxes and apparent contradictions there is a basic continuity running through Jarry's life and work: the rebelliousness of the precociously intelligent schoolboy, which expressed itself in the crude violence of Ubu, was transformed into the irreverence and love of nonsense of

Faustroll; while the child's sense of wonder at the strangeness and unfamiliarity of the world developed into an awareness of the arbitrariness of all attempted explanations of that world and a love of the infinite riches of the imagination. And, when all possible allowance has been made, a number of themes do remain which recur and dominate Jarry's work, and which enable us to piece together something of an intellectual and spiritual portrait of its creator.

The first of these is Jarry's fierce defence of a philosophy of absolute individualism, and of his own individuality. The chief reason for his loathing of the army – which in this and other respects represents to him a microcosm of society as a whole – is that it demands the suppression of individual identity, the reduction of the individual to the level of the common herd. Both Sengle and Erbrand Sacqueville not only defend their individuality and right to solitude in the face of the army's attempted regimentation, but are temperamentally incapable, since the army is by definition the mass, of being soldiers; as Jeanne says to Erbrand: 'tu n'es pas soldat, puisque tu es tout seul'.[6] This fierce defence by Jarry of his own individuality takes the form also of a sense of the inviolability of his own 'self', physical as well as intellectual, which probably lies behind his life-long loathing of men of the medical profession (expressed in particular through his disgust at the idea of the surgeon's cutting open and 'poking around inside' the body of his victim). Indeed, this loathing for the medical profession goes hand in hand with a seeming expression of horror of physical existence generally; a horror which has a profound bearing upon Jarry's attitude towards sexuality and sexual relations, and must have played some role in the sexual and emotional solitude which characterized most of his adult life, and which his boasts of superhuman achievements in other fields were perhaps in part designed to hide.

This individualism takes the form also of the expression throughout his work of a real or feigned egocentrism, albeit one which frequently manifests itself in the form of spoofing or *badinage*. He was fond of asserting his ability to perform superhuman feats in the fields of writing, drinking, eating, fishing and cycling, and, like his hero André Marcueil, he liked to imagine himself as a 'superman' (if not actually 'supermale'). And, although such claims are always couched in the language of irony, behind the irony and *badinage*, as so often happens, there is an element of conviction in such claims as that made to Rachilde and Saltas at the time of his illness in May 1906 that 'Aucun être humain n'a tenu jusque-là' ['No human being has held out to that point'], that 'Un autre aurait pu très bien devenir fou' ['Anyone else might easily have gone mad'], and that 'On n'a pas écrit pour rien le *Surmâle*' ['It's not for nothing that we wrote *Le Surmâle*'].[7]

This egocentrism, and Jarry's individualism generally, were no doubt encouraged and reinforced by the egotistical and individualistic tendencies of Symbolism. The Symbolists' tendency to regard literature and art as essentially self-projection (or the translation into words or onto the canvas of the individual's own inner imaginative world), no less than Gourmont's definition of Symbolism as simply 'l'expression de l'individualisme dans l'art', were both powerful influences in the shaping of his aesthetic views at least. Equally important was the reinforcement by Symbolism of an inherent tendency towards a form of spiritual narcissism. Indeed, A. G. Lehmann aptly remarks, in his study of *The Symbolist Aesthetic*, that 'symbolism has enriched the repertory of modern civilisation by only one myth, and that a renovated one – Narcissus'.[8] From Mallarmé's *Igitur*, through Laforgue's *Hamlet*, Barrès' *Culte du Moi*, Villiers de l'Isle-Adam's *Axël*, Gourmont's *Sixtine*, Gide's *Traité du Narcisse*, and Valéry's *Monsieur Teste* (whose hero stands in the same relation to the intellect as Ubu does to physical appetite and desire) to the preoccupation with time and memory of Proust, one finds running through the literature of the Symbolist movement and of its precursors and heirs a preoccupation with the introspective, self-absorbed individual. Perhaps the ultimate incarnation of the Narcissus-myth is to be found in the caricatural resolve of the figure of Ubu, at the end of *Ubu Enchaîné*, to devote himself henceforth to the contemplation of his own *gidouille*.

But Symbolism is not, of course, the only influence helping to mould Jarry's view of the world. Over and above that influence lies his own intuitive response to existence which is reinforced by developments in the scientific and philosophical thought of the age and which leads to the formulation of his own anarchical, individualistic 'science' of pataphysics. Pataphysics – the 'science of the particular' in one of Jarry's two celebrated definitions – claims to regard all phenomena as 'exceptions' and to relegate all ethical, scientific or philosophical laws or norms to the domain of equally arbitrary 'imaginary solutions'. But at the same time it claims neither to accept nor to reject any of these same 'imaginary solutions' but to regard them all with the same 'scientific' impartiality. Thus pataphysics becomes, as we have seen, not just the formulation of a philosophical view of the world, but at the same time a carefully cultivated attitude to life, an attitude of amused but disinterested detachment from all things. Pataphysics comes therefore to constitute a form of spiritual freedom, born of a detached contemplation of the kaleidoscopic spectacle of life (or of the essential 'theatricality' of existence) and of a detachment, ultimately, from one's own 'self'.

The second dominant theme in Jarry's work is the exaltation of the artist, who is not only seen as an equal with, but indeed replaces

'God'. Here too the influence of Symbolism is paramount, though few can have surpassed Jarry in the haughtiness, if not arrogance, of his pronouncements on this subject. In a universe left empty by 'the death of God', in Nietzsche's melodramatic phrase, only man remains. But Jarry, far from turning like a majority of his contemporaries in the nineteenth century to such substitute absolutes as Progress, Science or History or to some other form of humanistic faith, tends to turn instead to the idea that, in the absence of a transcendental deity, it is man himself, in the form of the creative artist, who 'becomes God'. Faustroll, Emmanuel Dieu, Sengle and César-Antechrist – all of them representing different facets of the mind of their creator – all lay claim, implicitly, to such divine status.

What are the attributes of 'God' so conceived, or the qualities of the creative writer which enable him to lay claim to such a status? God, like the artist, is first of all creator, endowed with an infinite creativity which enables him to bring into being a myriad of autonomous and self-sufficient worlds of the imagination (thus Antechrist is made to exclaim: 'Dieu – ou moi-même – a créé tous les mondes possibles, ils co-existent, mais les hommes ne peuvent même en entrevoir un.' ['God – or I myself – have created all possible worlds, they co-exist, but men cannot even catch a glimpse of one of them.'].[9] Alongside this infinite creativity, a further attribute is the enjoyment of an absolute freedom – absolute within the realms of that same world of the imagination. A third is the enjoyment of absolute power over that world. Yet at the very centre of this threefold claim is a deliberate paradox: for this enjoyment by the artist of the attributes of deity can be achieved only by a total exclusion of the outside world and by a denial of its claims. Here again speaks the hero of *César-Antechrist*, a work in which, just over the threshold of his literary career, Jarry states in a derisorily grandiloquent and rhetorical form many of the ideas which will be central to his work as a whole:

Je n'ai que faire de cette extérieure représentation et je passe aveugle et sourd sur la terre, me contemplant moi-même, sûr qu'on ne peut rien m'adjoindre d'externe . . . . Je suis César il est vrai, non des hommes que je méprise et pour qui je ne veux user les courts moments de mon séjour terrestre, mais de l'Univers et de l'Absolu, car, grâce à cet oubli mon esclave, ce que je veux existe ou n'existe pas selon qu'il me plaît.

> [I have nothing to do with this outward appearance and I pass blind and deaf over the earth, contemplating my own self, certain that nothing external can be added to me . . . . I am Emperor, it is true, not over men whom I despise and on whose behalf I have no wish to expend the brief moments of my earthly sojourn, but of the Universe and the Absolute, for, thanks to this faculty of forgetfulness which is my slave, what I desire exists or does not exist according to my own pleasure.][10]

But power is also the power of total destruction as well as of creation; a power of destruction which is a further attribute of God. There is considerable truth in Jean Rostand's statement: 'Tuez un homme, vous êtes un assassin; tuez-en des millions, vous êtes un conquérant; tuez-les tous, vous êtes Dieu.' ['Kill one man, you are a murderer; kill millions, you are a conqueror; kill them all, you are God.']¹¹ The ultimate manifestation in Jarry's work of this theme of power and of the associated claim to be 'God' is to be found in a series of visions of a universal annihilation – real or symbolic – which are to be found, spanning his work as a whole, in *César-Antechrist*, in *Faustroll* and in *La Dragonne*. Such a total annihilation of (in Faustroll's words) 'ce qui est l'exception de soi' constitutes the ultimate affirmation of the 'self' and its freedom, and the ultimate identification with God. For all that such dreams in Jarry's work must remain dreams, their occurrence throws a fascinating light on the inner imaginative world of their creator.

A third major theme is that of the nature of 'truth'. The idea of the relativity of conceptions of 'truth', as well as of 'justice', was a common theme of Jarry's journalistic writings collected in *La Chandelle verte* (see Chapter Eight above). This conception of the relativity of 'truth' seems to have haunted him from his early years. A passage in *César-Antechrist*, spoken by the Golden Christ, presents truth and falsehood as alternating in the pendulum-like movement of history: 'Le jour et la nuit, la vie et la mort, l'être et la vie, *ce qu'on appelle, parce qu'il est actuel, le vrai*, et son contraire, alternent dans les balancements du Pendule qui est Dieu le Père.' ['Day and night, life and death, being and living, *that which, because it is of the present, is called truth*, and its opposite, alternate in the swings of the Pendulum which is God the Father.']¹² Most telling of all, however, are two passages from *L'Amour absolu* (the first from a chapter entitled, significantly, 'Le Droit au mensonge'). The first passage seems to assert that Truth is one and absolute, relating it implicitly to the Platonic idea of the One, or divine fountainhead of all being:

Il n'y a qu'une Vérité.
Et des myriades, exactement toute la série indéfinie des nombres – tous les nombres qui ne sont pas l'Un – de choses qui ne sont pas cette Vérité.

> [There is only one Truth.
> And myriads, to be precise the whole infinite series of numbers – all those numbers which are other than the One – of things which are not this Truth.]

In the second, which is even more cryptic, Jarry plays upon the word 'absolument':

Absolu-ment.
C'est une charade.
Ce que ne qualifie pas le premier mot est le sujet du second.
Tout dans l'univers de définit par ce verbe ou cet adjectif.

> [Absolute-ly [lie].
> It's a riddle.
> That which is not qualified by the first word is the subject of the second.
> Everything in the universe is defined either by this verb or by this
adjective.][13]

Over and above the wordplay, and in spite of the love of paradox
which manifests itself yet again here, Jarry is implying that *every*
'truth' which is not absolute is a 'lie'. For such an 'absolutist'
mentality as his, a mentality which reveals itself also in his rejection
of the purely relative 'truths' of science and in the elaboration of his
pataphysics, in the absence of God or of any other metaphysical
absolute, there are and can only be 'lies'.

A fourth important theme is that of time, which runs through the
whole of Jarry's work. His aesthetic and philosophical views are here
fundamentally in accord: just as he argues, in his lecture on *Le Temps
dans l'art*, that the artist should reject all attempts at historical realism
and should aim directly at the creation of the 'eternal', so too
elsewhere does he assert (adopting implicitly the distinction made by
Bergson and, in his wake, by twentieth-century phenomenologists
between 'cosmic' or 'clock' time and the time of inner experience) that
the inner imaginative world of the artist is the domain of 'eternity'
here and now: 'Il viendra un temps universel, qui existe déjà de toute
éternité pour plusieurs' ['There will come to pass a universal age,
which already exists from all eternity for several of us'].[14] The whole
of Jarry's work, in fact – from *Les Minutes de sable mémorial* with its
deliberately anachronistic settings; through *Les Jours et les Nuits* and
L'Amour absolu in which he attempts to fuse, respectively, past and
present, time and 'eternity'; *Faustroll*, in which the good doctor
pataphysically explores the 'geography' of time; the *Commentaire pour
servir à la construction pratique de la machine à explorer le temps* which
comes to the unexpected conclusion that the true 'machine à explorer
le tempts' is memory; *La Chandelle verte*, which contains a number of
reflexions on the purely 'pataphysical' or imaginary nature of time;
Messaline and *Le Surmâle*, in which he embarks upon the creation of an
imaginary past and future respectively; to *La Dragonne*, in which his
autobiographical hero returns to a mystical and legendary past –
can be seen as the expression of an attempt to 'deny' time, and to
escape from its eternally revolving wheel; an escape which can only
be found ultimately, of course, in death.

Such a conclusion brings us to the last major theme which it remains to examine, namely that of death itself. Together with its corollary, that of sex (that is, the instinctive, self-perpetuating force of life), it dominates much of his poetry and other works, from his earliest writings included in *Ontogénie* onwards. The themes of death and sex are the object of a fascination, if not obsession, on the part of Jarry, and much in his work can be seen as the expression of an attempt to deny the claims of the latter, coupled with almost a hymn of praise to the former. To what extent did he succeed in mastering this twin obsession, and to what extent did his cultivation of an attitude of pataphysical detachment extend also to this domain? Looking at his work as a whole, it is impossible to accept the view, formulated many times over in the writings of the Collège de 'Pataphysique, that Jarry *at all times* simply plays with these two themes. It is rather the case that, throughout his work, we can see him wrestling with them, trying progressively to come to terms with and ultimately to exorcise a deep-seated personal obsession: transforming sexual realities into abstractions and elevating sexual forces to the level of Myth (which, by a semantic trick, he then places on the same level as other 'myths'), and juggling with the theme of death to the point where it comes to appear unreal and inoffensive, if not farcical. If a novel such as *Le Surmâle* suggests that Jarry may at last have succeeded in exorcising the phantom of his sexual obsessions, the circumstances of his death (in contrast to the melodramatic posturing which accompanied his expectations of death in May 1906) suggest at last a resigned and calm acceptance of that reality.

And so we return to the theme with which we began this examination of the man behind the façade: freedom, in the form specifically of a detachment not only from 'the world' but from one's own 'self' as well. The logical end of such a process can only be, of course, death. And just as Jarry's use of alcohol played a role in his attempts to liberate himself from the bonds of time through the creation of a state of mind in which past and present, memory and present awareness, dream and the waking consciousness were fused into a continuum of hallucinatory experience, so too it plays a significant if different role here as well. Though it is certainly not true, as Saltas and others maintained, that Jarry's drinking was in the end directly responsible for his death, it is certain that, in the last few years of his life at least, his drinking took on an element of wilful self-destructiveness. But, paradoxically, this would-be self-destruction through drink, if such it is, represents the ultimate possible affirmation of freedom. Jarry's repeated defence, in his *chroniques* and elsewhere, not just of alcohol but of alcoholism is not merely an automatic response to the criticisms of 'responsible' and 'right-thinking' contemporaries, but the consequence also of a deeply held conviction of the absolute right of the individual to choose his own fate, whatever the circumstances. In short, his individualism goes to the logical extreme of a defence of the right to suicide; and, in his own life, the affirmation of his own total freedom extends even to a destruction of himself.

What sort of literature emerges from the 'vision du monde' outlined above? Just as a number of key themes enable us to piece together a portrait of the man himself, so too a number of key ideas or tendencies are present which help to shape his literary work. The first of these is his consistent and fierce hostility towards all forms of 'realism' and 'naturalism', whether in literature, painting or the theatre. In this hostility he is in line with the most outstanding artists of his own time – the Nabis, Gauguin, Van Gogh, Cézanne and the founders of Cubism – and with the dominant trend of modern art as a whole. He is also very much in tune, as we have seen, with the ideas of the major theatrical reformers of the turn of the century, men such as Edward Gordon Craig. In Jarry's own work, this opposition to realism takes four main forms. It takes the form, firstly, in his critical writings and pronouncements, of an open expression of contempt for all attempts to create a convincing 'illusion' of reality whether on the stage, in the novel or on the canvas, together with a contemptuous rejection of any art which concerns itself with the merely particular or historical. It takes the form, secondly, in novels such as *Messaline* and *Le Surmâle*, of a subtle undermining of apparent realism from within. Thirdly, it takes the form of a glorying in all that is purely 'imaginary' or even 'fantastical'. No work better exemplifies this tendency than the short poetic drama *Le Vieux de la Montagne* of 1896 which, alongside its central theme of the exercise of absolute power over men's minds through hallucinogenic drugs, combines legend with deliberate anachronism and with a largely fanciful geographical setting, and contains a wealth of sumptuous imagery of brilliant lights and colours, of liquids, of hard and precious stones and of mythical beasts. Lastly, Jarry's hostility to realism leads to a championing of the universal, the eternal, the stylized and purely schematic, and (in his own theatre) to the creation of his own unforgettable archetype, Ubu. As he put it succinctly in the conclusion to his lecture on *Le Temps dans l'art*: 'Si l'on veut que l'oeuvre d'art devienne éternel un jour, n'est-il pas plus simple, en la libérant soi-même des lisières du temps, de la faire éternelle tout de suite?' ['If one wishes a work of art to become some day eternal, is it not simpler, by liberating it oneself from the contours of time, to make it eternal here and now?']¹⁵

The second major determining factor in Jarry's literary work is a fascination, which he everywhere reveals, with form. Here, too, his thought is in line with the major trends of the last hundred years. From Flaubert's dream of writing 'un livre sur rien . . ., un livre qui se tiendrait de lui-même par la force interne de son style' ['a book about nothing . . ., a book which would hold together by the inner strength of its own style']¹⁶ onwards, a dominant tendency in French literature has been that towards an ever-increasing emphasis on form – a tendency which, in Jarry's own time, reached a climax in the work of the contemporary writer most revered by him, Mallarmé. In part, this emphasis on form arose simply from a growing awareness on the part of writers of the *art* which they practised and a desire to achieve formal perfection. But in part also it sprang from an ambition to bring literature into line with the other arts: with the already 'abstract' art of music, and with that of painting which was currently embarking upon the path which would ultimately lead to the 'abstract' art of the twentieth century. The example of painting was, for Jarry, a particular source of inspiration. Although the work of none of those painters whom he knew and admired could in any way be described as 'abstract', they were all nonetheless moving, in their various ways, away from a conception of the work of art as the reproduction of a 'reality' external to the artist and towards an affirmation of its own autonomous and self-contained 'reality'.

Such a conception Jarry endeavoured to transpose into the domain of literature. Following the lead given by Mallarmé, who had spoken of the need for the poet to '[céder] l'initiative aux mots' which 's'allument de reflets réciproques comme une virtuelle traînée de feux sur des pierreries' ['[allow] the words to take the initiative' which 'blaze forth, lit up by their mutual reflections, like a potential flickering of flames over precious stones'],¹⁷ his work reveals a conception of literature as a self-contained imaginative and verbal construction in which words and images refer to each other rather than to a supposedly 'real' world outside of the work of literature itself – in which the *signifier* becomes its own *signified*. In this he goes beyond the preoccupations and aims of his Symbolist contemporaries to point the way forward to much of the literature of the twentieth century. The point is nicely made by Michel Décaudin, speaking of Jarry's poetry, in a detailed study of the poetry of the post-Symbolist era:

Jarry ne renonçait pas aux recherches de langage et de sonorités rares de l'école symboliste; mais . . . il les vidait, en les utilisant, de leur fonction esthétique pour ne les justifier que par la fantaisie qui préside à leur création. En libérant ainsi l'expression poétique et l'image de toute signification – disons mieux, de toute signifiance – il leur reconnaissait . . . une autonomie presque totale. Le poème tend à ne devenir qu'un jeu d'images qui tire sa fin de sa seule existence . . . .

[Jarry did not give up the researches of the Symbolists into language and unusual sound-patterns; but . . ., in making use of them, he emptied them of their aesthetic function to end by justifying them solely by the fantasy which gave rise to them in the first place. In thus freeing poetic language and imagery from all meaning – or even more precisely, from all significance – he accorded them . . . an almost total autonomy. The poem tends to become merely an interplay of images whose very existence alone constitutes its end . . . .][18]

Examples can be multiplied from his novels and other works as well as from his poetry, from the deliberately facile puns of his 'théâtre mirlitonesque', through the polysemy of much of *Les Minutes de sable mémorial* and *César-Antechrist*, the sophisticated wordplay and linguistic distortion of *La Chandelle verte*, the complex wordplay upon such terms as *fils, mère, époux, épouse* and *vierge* which structure much of *L'Amour absolu*, the examples of Valerius 'the Asiatic' in *Messaline* and the 'Indian' of *Le Surmâle*, to the *éthernité* of *Faustroll*. Time and again in Jarry's work, the word or image takes on a life of its own, no longer referring to any object or reality outside the text but merely to the *text* itself, or to other words and images of that text. The result is at times something in the nature of a verbal delirium which, at one end of the literary spectrum, recalls the delight in words of Jarry's other great mentor, Rabelais, and, at the other, looks forward to the Joyce of *Finnegan's Wake* and beyond. Before all else comes the word, and the word is absolute, autonomous, an end in itself. As Jarry expressed it through the words of the Templar in *César-Antechrist*: 'Le signe seul existe ... provisoire' ['The sign alone exists ... provisionally.'].[19] Or, as he stated also in a lapidary phrase in one of his *chroniques*: 'il n'y a que la lettre qui soit littérature' ['there is only the letter which constitutes literature'].[20]

None of this, however, is the result of mere perversity or quirkishness on Jarry's part. Underlying the verbal games played by him lies a persistent and profound reflection on the nature of language itself which, explicitly or implicitly, runs through his work, not least in the pages of *La Chandelle verte*. It is an interest which manifests itself, moreover, not just in language as a system of verbal signs, but in such other systems of 'signs' as the abstract language of mathematics, the language of heraldry, or the religious symbolism of medieval Christian writers. Behind his incessant wordplay and verbal clowning lies a deep-seated intuition that all 'reality' (other of course than material reality) is at bottom a linguistic reality – that all statements of a philosophical, religious, ethical or scientific order are not just (in the language of pataphysics) 'imaginary solutions' but, in the final resort, mere words.

A further striking characteristic of Jarry's work is that which has come to be known in recent years as intertextuality – that is, the recurrence of the same elements within more than one text, or the incorporation of part or parts of one text into another. The point is nicely made in an article by Noël Arnaud:

Sans conteste, l'oeuvre de Jarry offre un champ particulièrement fécond à l'étude de l'"intertextualité" (à tous les sens, et les plus divers, que lui donnent aujourd'hui les linguistes), à la mise à jour du collage textuel et de la réalimentation d'un texte par un autre, non point seulement dans ses 'thèmes' ou son lexique (ce qui est au demeurant le lot de beaucoup d'écrivains, et de toutes époques) mais dans son fonctionnement . . . .

> [Indisputably the work of Jarry provides a particularly fruitful domain for the study of 'intertextuality' (in every one of the many and varied meanings given to that word these days by linguists), for the elucidation of the processes of textual collage and the feeding of one text upon another, not merely with regard to its 'themes' or its vocabulary (which is the case after all with a great many writers, from all periods of history) but with regard to its basic operation . . . .][21]

As Arnaud implies, Jarry does not just incorporate elements from one of his own works into another, or even simply 'quote' from his own works; he includes also 'quotations' – acknowledged or unacknowledged – from the works of other writers in his own, calling into question in the process the concepts of originality and of literary 'proprietorship'. At the very beginning of his literary career stands an apparent act of 'plagiarism' in his appropriation of the text of *Les Polonais*, written by Charles and Henri Morin. He goes even further in his appropriation of the various songs from the original Hébert 'cycle', which he incorporates largely unaltered into the *Ubu* plays. Another striking example of the same process is to be found in *Haldernablou* and in its links with *César-Antechrist*, as we saw in Chapters Two and Three above: the injunction 'Phallus déraciné, NE FAIS PAS DE PAREILS BONDS!', which occurs in the latter, refers back to a mysterious phase in *Haldernablou*, which itself alludes to a line from *Les Chants de Maldoror* of Lautréamont. Moreover, not only has Jarry in *Haldernablou* taken over wholesale much of the imagery and language of *Les Chants de Maldoror* (rescued from oblivion and revealed to the literary world at large by his then friend and mentor, Gourmont) but he implicitly acknowledges the fact (and attributes the 'paternity' of the work to a third person) in his carefully worded dedication: '*Appartient à* Remy de Gourmont'.[22] *Les Minutes de sable mémorial* and *César-Antechrist* offer further examples of the same process of intertextuality: Jarry includes in the former the first act of *César-Antechrist* and excerpts from the future *Ubu Cocu*, as well as 'quoting' from both *Ubu Roi* and *César-Antechrist*; while in the latter, not only is much of the imagery and phraseology 'borrowed' from such works as the *Apocalypse* and Gourmont's *Le Latin mystique*, but the 'Acte terrestre', which forms the longest part of the work, is an abridged version of the text of *Ubu Roi*. Similar instances of cross-referencing and quotation can be found in *Les Jours et les Nuits*, in *L'Amour en visites* (where quotations from the previous novel and from *Ubu Roi* are explicitly acknowledged), in *L'Amour absolu* and in *Faustroll* (in which Jarry quotes, with implicit acknowledgment, from the works of eminent scientists of the day such as Crookes, Boys and Kelvin). Lastly, paradoxically, it is two of his most seemingly 'open' and accessible works which most fully exemplify this technique: *Messaline* is virtually one long series of quotations, or paraphrases, from beginning to end, producing what has been described as a 'collage' and/or 'montage',[23] and the text of *Le Surmâle* contains some 30 or so literary, historical or mythological references and quotations, and probably many times more as yet undetected.

The principle of intertextuality is thus central to the whole of Jarry's work. In a sense, that work is made up in considerable measure of a series of 'quotations' from beginning to end. If we choose to label such a procedure 'plagiarism' then we must admit, paradoxically, that Jarry time and again 'plagiarizes' his own work also. In reality, however, such a label obscures his real intentions. Implicit in Jarry's work is a prolonged reflection upon the very nature of the act of literary creation, and upon the questions of originality and of authorship or 'proprietorship' in literature. Despite his nominal adherence to the Symbolist doctrine of absolute originality, Jarry realized that creation is never, for man, 'out of nothing'. The very words we speak are learned from others, are the fruit of a process of conscious or unconscious imitation. And what is true of language must be true also, *ipso facto*, of the art form whose medium it constitutes, that is, literature. Total originality is therefore impossible, and all literature is to a greater or lesser extent a result of 'quotation' from the words and works of other men. The original contribution of the individual writer lies in his transposition, transmutation and organization of this material; the point is made explicitly by Jarry himself in a *chronique* entitled 'Toomai des Éléphants':

un cerveau vraiment original fonctionne exactement comme l'estomac de l'autruche: tout lui est bon, il pulvérise des cailloux et tord des morceaux de fer. Qu'on ne confonde point ce phénomène avec la faculté d'assimilation, qui est d'autre nature. Une personnalité ne s'assimile rien du tout, elle déforme; mieux, elle transmute, dans le sens ascendant de la hiérarchie des métaux. Mise en présence de l'insurpassable – du chef-d'oeuvre – il ne se produit pas imitation, mais transposition: tout le mécanisme de l'association d'idées de l'oeuvre qui, selon une expression sportive ici fort juste, sert d'"entraîneur'.

> [a truly original mind functions in exactly the same way as the stomach of the ostrich: it will accept everything, it pulverizes stones and twists pieces of iron. Let us not confuse this phenomenon with the faculty of assimilation, which is different in nature. A personality does not assimilate unto itself anything at all, it transforms; even better, it transmutes, in the sense in which

one uses that word in reference to an ascending hierarchy of metals. When it finds itself confronted with the unsurpassable – the masterpiece – it is not imitation which takes place, but transposition: the whole mechanism of the association of ideas inspired by the work, which functions, to use a sporting expression which is particularly apt here, as a 'coach' or 'trainer'.][24]

And a different, but equally illuminating, image is to be found in his article 'La Mécanique d'Ixion'; in the legend of Ixion bound, as a punishment, to a perpetually revolving wheel he finds a metaphor for, amongst other things, the circular movement of memory, and the nature of artistic creativity:

Heureusement, la roue d'Ixion, de par l'éternité qu'elle dure, 'prend du jeu':
Ixion ne tourne plus *dans le même plan*: il revit, à chaque circuit, son expérience
acquise, puis pousse une pointe, par son centre, dans un nouveau monde
liséré d'une courbe fermée; mais après il y a encore d'autres mondes!

> [Fortunately, Ixion's wheel, as a result of the eternity of its rotation, develops a degree of 'play': Ixion no longer rotates *in the same plane*: with each new rotation he relives his past experience, then moves outwards from its centre, by a mere fraction, into a new world bordered by a closed circle; but after that there are yet further worlds!][25]

Behind the phenomenon of intertextuality in Jarry's work, and over and above this reflection on the nature of literary creation, one can see also a further idea: the dream of a literature which would be in some way 'absolute'. In his articles and reviews collected in *La Chandelle verte* we find frequent expression of the idea that all literature contains only a limited number of situations and human types which are repeated, with an infinite number of variations, over and over through the ages, making it possible therefore to reduce all works of literature to a small number of basic *schémas* or models and perhaps even, ultimately, to a single 'archetypal' form. The same fundamental idea underlies his discussion of other areas of human activity and thought also. Behind his denial of the importance of history lies a belief in the fundamental sameness of all civilizations, which can be reduced to a single 'abstract' model. A review of a book on economics reveals his attraction to the idea of a 'science' of economics (science being for Jarry at its most 'perfect' when it is at its most abstract – the most perfect science therefore being geometry) almost mathematical in its precision and abstraction; and a review of an erudite study of gnostic religions gives rise to the suggestion that the similarities in myth and ritual between different religions offer proof of the existence of 'une religion absolue, dont les autres ne seraient que des facettes incomplètes et déformées'[26] – that is, that there exists a kind of abstract 'framework' into which all particular religious concepts and practices can be fitted.

But Jarry's thought goes beyond these domains to that of language also, and to the dream of the existence of an absolute or universal language; not, that is, an artificially created one, such as the contemporary Esperanto or Volapük, for which he expressed only contempt, but one which would somehow underlie and underpin all existing languages. Behind his innumerable puns and other forms of word-play lies the notion, fanciful or not, of a secret affinity between words which such games reveal or hint at. The idea is expressed several times over by him. For example, in a review of a work by his friend Franc-Nohain, who similarly indulges in wordplay, he states that 'Les allitérations, les rimes, les assonances et les rythmes révèlent des parentés profondes entre les mots. Où dans plusieurs mots, il y a une même syllabe, il y a un point commun.' ['Alliterations, rhymes, assonances and rhythms reveal deep-seated kinships between words. Where there exists, in several words, the same syllable, there is an element of common ground.']27 And in *La Dragonne*, he writes that 'les paronymes ont un sens mystérieux et clair pour qui sait les lire, et les jeux de mots ne sont pas un jeu' ['paronyms have a mysterious and clear meaning for anyone who knows how to read them, and wordplay is not just a game'].28 Even more radically and clearly, Jarry actually goes so far as to deny the underlying diversity of all languages, symbolized in the myth of the tower of Babel:

Babel est un mythe populaire et la confusion des langues n'existe que pour le populaire, lequel se plaît à s'en imaginer plusieurs parce qu'il ne connaît même pas toute la sienne.

[Babel is a myth of the common people, and the confusion of tongues exists only in the minds of the common people, which likes to imagine that there are several of them because it does not even have a thorough knowledge of its own.]29

And speaking of Erbrand Sacqueville's tutor in *La Dragonne*, he writes that:

son oncle et premier précepteur l'abbé Saint-Pligeaux lui avait enseigné que pour qui sait lire il n'y a qu'une langue au monde et que pour celui-là il n'y a jamais eu de Babel.

[his uncle and first tutor, the Abbé Saint-Pligeaux, had taught him that for anyone who knows how to read there is only one language in the world and that for such a person Babel never existed.]30

Vallette was indeed right in describing Jarry as 'ce chercheur d'abso-lu'. For alongside this dream of an 'absolute' and universal language is to be found also that of an 'absolute' work of literature. Jarry here offers a final parallel with Mallarmé, who was similarly haunted by the ill-defined notion, to which he gave the name 'le Livre' or 'l'Oeuvre', of a kind of absolute work which would in some way subsume and replace all others. Could it be that in this is to be found a further and final explanation of the diversity of Jarry's literary work – each volume constituting an element in the construction of his own form of 'le Livre'?[31]

But if this is so, it expresses only a part of the totality of Jarry's intentions and aims as a writer. As we have seen at several points in this study, he also, at least at times, conceives of literature as a vast, elaborate and intricate game, and nowhere more so than in his two seemingly most 'limpid' and popular works, *Messaline* and *Le Surmâle*. Such a conception of literature provides a link, of course, with the 'games' and playfulness of childhood, which is itself an important and recurrent theme in his work. Even Jarry's pataphysics, which provides a key to so much of his attitude to both literature and life, has its origins in childhood, in the ill-applied 'science of physics' of the grotesquely incompetent M. Hébert. And in the perspective of pataphysics, as exemplified in *Faustroll* and expressed in many a passage of *La Chandelle verte*, it is not only literature but life itself which is seen as a 'game', governed by complex and elaborate, but ultimately arbitrary, rules.

It is too easy to say in response to such a philosophy that Jarry himself never really grew up. The continuity which is such a striking feature of his whole work in this regard – the recurrence of themes and motifs first found in the works of his childhood and adolescence, the love of linguistic invention and distortion which are present from the start, his love of the simplification and stylization of the puppet-theatre and his life-long fascination with the figure of Ubu – is the result of a conscious policy on his part and the expression of a deeply rooted philosophical intuition. Moreover, that intuition is in tune with a broader shift of ideas which has led to a radical transformation of our own culture. Jarry's championing of the spirit of childhood in his work (and not least in his theatre), in which he was almost alone amongst men of letters of his time, forms part nonetheless of a broader philosophical evolution, to which men such as Freud, Bergson and others all in their diverse ways contributed and to which a parallel can be seen, in the world of art, in the 'naïvety' of a painter such as Rousseau or in the fascination of the Cubists with the alleged 'primitivism' of African folk-art: an evolution away from the dominant rationalism of the latter part of the nineteenth century towards a new interest in and a rehabilitation of the values of dream, the subconscious, intuition, spontaneity and, last but not least, childhood. Jarry is part of a movement which would eventually break down forever the once-rigid barriers between the supposedly 'serious' world of adulthood and the 'playful' universe of childhood.

Notes

INTRODUCTION:
THE JARRY REVIVAL

1. Rachilde, *Alfred Jarry ou le
   Surmâle des Lettres* (Paris:
   Grasset, 1928), 211; Guillaume
   Apollinaire, 'Les
   Contemporains pittoresques:
   Feu Alfred Jarry', in *Les Marges*
   (November 1909), 854; André
   Salmon, 'Alfred Jarry ou le Père
   Ubu en liberté', in *L'Ami du
   Lettré* (Paris, 1924), 256.
2. Essay entitled 'Alfred Jarry',
   subsequently included in *Les
   Pas perdus* (Paris: Gallimard,
   1924).
3. *Manifestes du surréalisme* (Paris:
   Gallimard, Collection 'Idées',
   1963), 39.

CHAPTER ONE
CHILDHOOD AND YOUTH

1. According to Jarry's friend
   Charles-Henry Hirsch, quoted
   by Fernand Lot, *Alfred Jarry.
   Son Oeuvre* (Paris, 1934). The
   very facts here are far from
   accurate: two years actually
   separated the deaths of his
   parents.
2. Noël Arnaud, *Alfred Jarry d'Ubu
   Roi au docteur Faustroll* (Paris:
   La Table Ronde, 1974).
3. Quoted by Rachilde, *Alfred Jarry

ou le Surmâle des Lettres (Paris,
1928), 30.
4. Alfred Jarry in *La Dragonne*, and
   Charlotte in her 'Souvenirs sur
   Alfred Jarry', in *O.C.*, Éditions
   du Livre, I, 30, 34–5).
5. *O.C.*, Pléiade, I, 932. Jarry's
   italics.
6. *O.C.*, Pléiade, I, 933.
7. Charlotte Jarry, 'Souvenirs sur
   Alfred Jarry', in *O.C.*, Éditions
   du Livre, I, 28.
8. *O.C.*, Pléiade, I, 25–6.
9. 'Souvenirs sur Alfred Jarry', in
   O.C., Éditions du Livre, I, 29,
   31.
10. *O.C.*, Pléiade, I, 797.
11. *O.C.*, Éditions du Livre, V, 134.
12. *O.C.*, Pléiade, I, 797.
13. According to Arnaud, *op. cit.*,
    310.
14. In his last published text, the
    brochure *Albert Samain,
    Souvenirs*, reproduced in *O.C.*,
    Éditions du Livre, VII, 320.
15. *O.C.*, Pléiade, I, 127.
16. *O.C.*, Pléiade, I, 89.
17. In a paper read at the Jarry
    Colloquium at Cerisy-la-Salle in
    1981, Michel Arrivé suggested
    that the name Roupias derived
    from a juxtaposition of each
    letter in turn in the two halves
    of the Latin phrase *ruis, o pater*.
18. According to Arnaud, *op. cit.*,
    274.
19. Henri Hertz, 'Alfred Jarry, *Ubu

Roi et les professeurs', in
Nouvelle Revue Française, 1 Sept.
1924, 263–73.

20. (Paris: Floury, 1921). Chassé
     had a mania for hyphens and
     insisted on systematically
     writing *Ubu-Roi*.

21. Quoted by Chassé, *Dans les
     coulisses de la gloire: D'Ubu-Roi au
     douanier Rousseau* (Paris:
     Éditions de la Nouvelle Revue
     Critique, 1947), 73.

22. *Mercure de France*, 16 Nov. 1907,
     374.

23. In *O.C.*, Pléiade, I, 467–74.

24. Letter to Chassé quoted in *Les
     Sources d'Ubu-Roi*, 46n.

25. 'Ubu ou la création d'un
     mythe', in *C.C.P.*, no. 3, 61n.

26. Quoted by Chassé, *Les Sources
     d'Ubu-Roi*, 86. The word *cornes*
     is ambiguous: it means both
     horns – symbol of, amongst
     other things, cuckoldry – and
     patches of hard skin.

27. *O.C.*, Pléiade, I, 467.

28. In his speech to the audience at
     the *première* of *Ubu Roi*, in *O.C.*,
     Pléiade, I, 399. My italics.

29. In 'Les Paralipomènes d'Ubu',
     in *O.C.*, Pléiade, I, 467.

30. This source was first identified
     by André Lebois in his *Alfred
     Jarry l'irremplaçable* (Paris: Le
     Cercle du Livre, 1950). The key
     words here are *la pompe*, which
     means both 'pump' and
     'pomp'; *les lieux*, sometimes
     used in jocular fashion as an
     abbreviation for *lieux d'aisance*
     (lavatory or toilet); and *cabinet*,
     used by Racine in all innocence
     to designate an inner private
     room, but which also has the
     meaning, in the plural, of
     water-closet.

31. These speech mannerisms gave
     rise to a curious example of
     transposition on Jarry's part.
     According to the reminiscences
     of a former pupil of the Lycée
     de Rennes, Guillaumin (cited
     by André Lebois in *Alfred Jarry
     l'irremplaçable*), M. Périer spoke
     in a monotonous, staccato
     manner, involving a
     pronunciation of the mute 'e'.
     This speech pattern was later
     adopted by Jarry, and given not
     to Achras but to Ubu.

32. *Ubu Cocu*, Act I, Scene 1, in
     Ubu, ed. N. Arnaud and H.
     Bordillon (Paris: Gallimard,
     Collection 'Folio', 1978), 135. In
     the later version of the play,
     Ubu Cocu ou l'Archéoptéryx
     (reproduced in *O.C.*, Pléiade, I)
     this scene is transposed to Act
     II, Scene 1.

33. *Ubu Cocu*, Act IV, Scene 3, in
     Ubu, ed. Arnaud and Bordillon,
     173. In the later version of the
     play, this scene is transposed to
     Act V, Scene 6.

34. In a review of *Toomai des
     Éléphants*, in *La Plume*, 1 Jan.
     1903, reproduced in *La Chandelle
     verte*, ed. M. Saillet (Paris: Livre
     de Poche, 1962), 261.

35. In the brochure *Albert Samain.
     Souvenirs*, reproduced in *O.C.*,
     Éditions du Livre, VII, 320.

36. 'Le Groupement littéraire
     qu'abritait le "Mercure de
     France"', in *Mercure de France*,
     vol. 298, no. 1000 (1 July 1940 –
     1 Dec. 1946), 169.

37. This story was told by Jarry to
     Léon-Paul Fargue, who related
     it in turn to E. Peillet. Cf. J.-H.
     Sainmont, 'Occultations et
     exaltations d'*Ubu Cocu*', in
     C.C.P., no. 3–4, 30.

38. *Ubu Cocu*, Act I, Scene 4, in
     Ubu, ed. Arnaud and Bordillon,
     139–40; *Ubu Cocu ou
     l'Archéoptéryx*, Act II, Scene 4.

39. The process was explained by
     Henri Morin in a letter to
     Charles Chassé. Cf. Chassé, *Les
     Sources d'Ubu-Roi*, 50–1.

40. *Ubu Cocu*, Act I, Scene 6.

41. *Ubu Cocu*, Act III, Scene 3. In the later version of the play, *Ubu Cocu ou l'Archéoptéryx*, this scene is transposed to Act I, Scene 2.
42. The original version of the song, published by Chassé, gives Thorigné, a commune nine kilometres from Rennes, as the scene of the *décervelage*.
43. According to Charlotte Jarry, 'Souvenirs sur Alfred Jarry', *O.C.*, Éditions du Livre, I, 29.
44. *Ibid.*, 32, and letters of Henri and Charles Morin to Chassé quoted in *Les Sources d'Ubu-Roi*, 56 and 60.
45. Henri Hertz, 'Alfred Jarry collégien et la naissance d'*Ubu Roi*', in *Les Écrits Nouveaux*, Nov. 1921, 74.
46. Henri Hertz, 'Alfred Jarry, *Ubu Roi* et les professeurs', in *Nouvelle Revue Française*, 1 Sept. 1924, 263–73.
47. *Les Sources d'Ubu-Roi*, 30.
48. 'Souvenirs sur Alfred Jarry', in *O.C.*, Éditions du Livre, I, 33–4.
49. Henri Hertz, 'Alfred Jarry collégien et la naissance d'*Ubu Roi*', in *Les Écrits Nouveaux*, Nov. 1921, 75.
50. *La Chandelle verte*, 261. The same method of study is employed by the hero of *La Dragonne*.
51. Letter to Chassé, quoted in *Les Sources d'Ubu-Roi*, 85.

CHAPTER TWO
PARIS, POETS AND ARTISTS

1. Gandilhon Gens-d'Armes [*sic*], 'Alfred Jarry au Lycée Henri IV', in *Les Marges*, Jan. 1922, 43.
2. *Albert Samain. Souvenirs*, in *O.C.*, Éditions du Livre, VII, 320.
3. Gandilhon Gens-d'Armes, *op. cit.*, 44.
4. Quoted by Noël Arnaud, *Alfred Jarry d'Ubu Roi au docteur Faustroll* (Paris: La Table Ronde, 1974), 22.
5. Cf. Louise Rybko-Schub, *Léon-Paul Fargue* (Geneva: Droz, 1973).
6. In an interview with Frédéric Lefèvre, 'Une heure avec Léon-Paul Fargue', in *Les Nouvelles Littéraires*, 12 Jan. 1929.
7. Quoted by Rybko-Schub, *op. cit.*, 25.
8. Letter to Fargue of 1 Apr. 1893, quoted by Rybko-Schub, *op. cit.*, 25.
9. Interview with Frédéric Lefèvre, *Les Nouvelles Littéraires*, 12 Jan. 1929.
10. *O.C.*, Pléiade, I, 769.
11. Interview of Fargue with Frédéric Lefèvre, *Les Nouvelles Littéraires*, 12 Jan. 1929, and Léon-Paul Fargue, *Le Piéton de Paris* (1932) and *D'après Paris* (1939), published as one volume (Paris: Gallimard, 1964).
12. Louis Lormel, 'Alfred Jarry. Souvenirs', in *La Phalange*, 15 Sept. 1907, 557; Georges Rémond, 'Souvenirs sur Jarry et autres', *Mercure de France*, 1 Apr. 1955, 662.
13. Fargue, in an interview with E. Peillet shortly before his death, quoted in J.-H. Sainmont, 'Occultations et exaltations d'*Ubu Cocu*', *C.C.P.*, no. 3–4, 30.
14. *Albert Samain. Souvenirs*, in *O.C.*, Éditions du Livre, VII, 320–1. Jarry's quotation (from *The Book of Revelation* 6:14) is not wholly accurate.
15. Charlotte Jarry, 'Souvenirs sur Alfred Jarry', in *O.C.*, Éditions du Livre, I, 34.
16. Document described in *C.C.P.*, no. 10 [Catalogue of the 'Expojarrysition' of 1953 organized by the Collège de 'Pataphysique], 62.

17. According to Fargue in his interview with Frédéric Lefèvre, in *Les Nouvelles Littéraires*, 12 Jan. 1929.
18. Fargue, *Portraits de famille* (Paris: Janin, 1947), 147–8.
19. Lormel, 'Alfred Jarry. Souvenirs', in *La Phalange*, 15 Sept. 1907, 556–7. Lormel's account of Jarry's speech mannerisms is suspect; other witnesses testify to the fact that it was not until the period 1896–7 that he began to adopt this *ubuesque* manner.
20. The document is described in *C.C.P.*, no. 10, 62.
21. Fargue, *Portraits de famille*, 150.
22. Cf. *La Chandelle verte*, ed. M. Saillet (Paris: Livre de Poche, 1969), 314, 551–2.
23. *Alfred Jarry ou le Surmâle des Lettres* (Paris: Grasset, 1928).
24. Fargue, interview in *Les Nouvelles Littéraires*, 12 Jan. 1929, and Jarry, *La Chandelle verte*, 604.
25. The list is given by Fargue, *Portraits de famille*, 145–54.
26. 'De l'imagination et de l'expression chez M. Alfred Jarry', in *La Revue Blanche*, 1 June 1902.
27. Cf. the letter of Jean de Tinan to Jarry of 3 July 1896, published in 'Le Souvenir de Jean de Tinan', *Le Divan*, no. 98, Apr. 1924, 258–9.
28. Interview with Frédéric Lefèvre, in *Les Nouvelles Littéraires*, 12 Jan. 1929.
29. According to Dr Albert Haas, 'Souvenirs de la vie littéraire à Paris', in *Les Soirées de Paris*, May 1914.
30. List given by Michel Arrivé in his introduction to *Peintures, Gravures et Dessins d'Alfred Jarry*, Collège de 'Pataphysique, 95 E.P. [1968].
31. Cf. the letters published by

Arnaud in *Alfred Jarry d'Ubu Roi au docteur Faustroll*, 154–5, 157–9. Filiger's letters to Jarry were also published in the *Dossiers du Collège de 'Pataphysique*, no. 22–4, 7–18.
32. Cf. Jarry's two letters to Vallette from Pont-Aven, in *O.C.*, Pléiade, I, 1038–9.
33. The first of these was included in *Les Minutes de sable mémorial*. The three poems were first published together by Maurice Saillet in *La Revanche de la Nuit* in 1949. They are included in *O.C.*, Pléiade, I, 252–5.
34. *Le Piéton de Paris*, 116.
35. The extract was kept by Rousseau among his papers. It is quoted in *C.C.P.*, no. 26–7, 50. The 'pen' which the critic thought he saw was in fact the tongue of a chameleon. Cf. Lormel's description of it in *L'Idée Moderne*, 15 Apr. 1895, quoted in *C.C.P.*, no. 22–3, 104.
36. Dr Albert Haas, 'Souvenirs de la vie littéraire à Paris', in *Les Soirées de Paris*, May 1914, 270–1.
37. In his article on Filiger, *O.C.*, Pléiade, I, 1025.
38. Article in *Art et Critique*, 30 Aug. 1890, quoted by Jacques Robichez, *Le Symbolisme au théâtre. Lugné-Poe et les débuts de l'Oeuvre* (Paris: L'Arche, 1957), 108.
39. *O.C.*, Pléiade, I, 1024. Jarry's italics and capitals.
40. Both statements quoted by Denis Bablet, *Esthétique générale du décor de théâtre de 1870 à 1914* (Paris: Editions du C.N.R.S., 1964), 87.
41. *O.C.*, Pléiade, I, 1024.
42. 'Le Courrier des Arts', in *Paris-Journal*, 28 June 1914. Quoted in *C.C.P.*, no. 26–7, 48, and M. Arrivé (ed.), *Peintures, Gravures et Dessins d'Alfred Jarry* (Collège

de'Pataphysique and Le Cercle
Français, 1968), 8.

43. Publicity notice quoted in *O.C.*,
Pléiade, I, 1264.

44. *Perhinderion*, no. 1, in *O.C.*,
Pléiade, I, 995.

45. Published in *O.C.*, Pléiade, I,
905–6.

46. Rachilde, *Alfred Jarry ou le
Surmâles des Lettres*, 33, 59.

47. *Ibid.*, 21. Rachilde's italics.

48. Lormel, 'Entre soi', in *La Plume*,
no. 203, 1 Oct. 1897, 605–6.

49. Lugné-Poe, *La Parade*, II:
Acrobaties (Paris: Gallimard,
1931), 174, 163.

50. Letter of 27 May 1894, in *O.C.*,
Pléiade, I, 1036–7.

51. *O.C.*, Pléiade, I, 216.

52. *O.C.*, Pléiade, I, 216.

53. *O.C.*, Pléiade, I, 221, 222, 227.

54. 'Acte héraldique', Sc. 6. In
O.C., Pléiade, I, 289.

55. *O.C.*, Pléiade, I, 220.

56. *O.C.*, Pléiade, I, 227.

CHAPTER THREE
SYMBOLISM AND ITS
SUBVERSION

1. *Promenades littéraires*, III (Paris:
Mercure de France, 1963), 151.

2. 'Les Progrès de l'Apolitique en
France', *La Revue Blanche*, 1 July
1892, 18–19.

3. This question of the
contemporary *critique* of science
is most relevant to a discussion
of Jarry's own 'science' of
pataphysics, and will be
examined in more detail in
Chapter 7.

4. A detailed study of this ferment
of ideas in France and of its
impact on literary milieux has
been made by Elizabeth
Czoniczer, *Quelques antécédents
de "A la recherche du temps
perdu" (Tendances qui peuvent
avoir contribué à la cristallisation
du roman proustien)* (Paris &
Geneva: Droz, 1957).

5. In particular in his *De
l'intelligence* (1870). Whence the
anguished response of the
historian Michelet on reading
the work: 'Il me prend mon
moi!'

6. Quoted by Édouard Dujardin in
Mallarmé par un des siens (Paris:
Messein, 1936), 33.

7. The original German title was
*Die Welt als Wille und
Vorstellung*. A first French
translation appeared in 1886,
but the version which was to
become regarded as the
definitive French translation
was that of Auguste Burdeau,
*Le Monde comme volonté et comme
représentation*, published in
three volumes between 1888
and 1890.

8. First published 1874, 2nd edn
1885. By 1906 the work had
reached its 10th edition.

9. Gourmont, *L'Idéalisme*,
reproduced in *Le Chemin de
velours* (Paris: Mercure de
France, 1902), 215.

10. The supposed opposition
between Symbolists and
Naturalists existed in reality far
more on the level of aesthetic
theory than of practice.
Moreover, it was as much a
political as a literary opposition,
involving a rejection, as
Gourmont realized, not only of
Zola's alleged 'mépris de l'idée'
and 'dédain du symbole', but
also of his 'romantisme
populaire' and 'symbolisme
démocratique' (preface to *Le
Livre des Masques* of 1896). In
reality, the novels of Zola owe
almost as much to the
compelling force of his own
imagination and personal
obsessions as to the realities
and preoccupations of the

world around him – a fact which Zola criticism of the last 30 years or so has at last come fully to appreciate, but which only Mallarmé and, grudgingly, Gourmont among the Symbolists were perspicacious enough or impartial enough to recognize. Nevertheless, this theoretical opposition is vitally important in determining the artistic *aims* of the Symbolists – and of Jarry also.

11. Gourmont, preface to *Le Livre des Masques* (1896) (Paris: Mercure de France, 1963, 11–12). My italics.
12. Ibid., 12–13.
13. Gourmont, *L'Idéalisme*, in *Le Chemin de velours*, ed. cit., 220. Whatever the excesses to which their enthusiasm carried them, Gourmont and his colleagues were responsible for revolutionizing the field of literary criticism in France. By the late 1880s and early 1890s, opposition was growing to the predominantly biographical and sociological approach of earlier nineteenth-century critics such as Sainte-Beuve and Taine, who tended to regard a work of literature chiefly as a reflection of the life of its author or of the society in which he lived. Amongst a variety of new approaches, that of Gourmont and his fellow-Symbolists, who argued in favour of a view of the work of art as a self-contained imaginative construction, as a projection of the inner imaginative world of the artist, was undoubtedly the most penetrating. Although another 50 years were to elapse before it was to become widely accepted in French academic circles, their approach pointed the way forward to much of the

literary criticism of the last 30 years. Theirs was a lesson well learned by the young Jarry.
14. Published under the title of 'Autre présentation d'*Ubu Roi*', in *O.C.*, Pléiade, I, 401–3.
15. *O.C.*, Pléiade, I, 1024.
16. *Ibid.*, 329–30. The reference to the world as an 'extérieure représentation' recalls, of course, the language of the Symbolists' favourite philosopher, Schopenhauer. Jarry is also here playing with ideas juggled with by Gourmont in an essay of February 1894 entitled 'Dernière conséquence de l'idéalisme': here Gourmont maintains that 'poussée à son extrême, la théorie idéaliste [aboutit], pratiquement, au néronisme ou au fakirisme, selon qu'elle évolue en des intelligences actives ou en des intelligences passives; socialement . . . au despotisme ou à l'anarchie' ['pushed to its ultimate limits, the theory of idealism [leads], in practical terms, to neronism or fakirism, depending upon whether it works itself out in active or in passive minds; and, on a social plane . . ., to despotism or to anarchy']. (Reproduced in *La Culture des Idées* (Paris: Mercure de France, 1964, 258.)
17. Jarry's sneering reply to a survey of opinion concerning Zola immediately after the latter's death in 1902 ran as follows: 'Il n'y a rien de si propre que la m . . . bien lavée, dit un proverbe. Le mettre en action comme écrivain et comme citoyen, telle fut la tâche héroïque et naïve d'Émile Zola: il s'employa à lessiver l'âme populaire et à décorer l'honneur de l'armée.' [' "There

is nothing so clean as well washed sh . . .'', runs a proverb. To illustrate this as writer and citizen was the heroic and naïve task undertaken by Émile Zola: he devoted himself to scrubbing clean the working-class soul and to decorating the honour of the army.'] (*La Plume*, 15 Oct. 1902. Quoted in *Réponses à des enquêtes par Alfred Jarry*, Collège de 'Pataphysique, 97 E.P. [1969/70], 21.)

18. In *O.C.*, Pléiade, I, 341–4.
19. *Ibid.*, 963. My italics.
20. A detailed discussion of the relations between anarchist and literary milieux can be found in Jean Maitron, *Histoire du mouvement anarchiste en France (1880–1914)* (Paris: Société universitaire d'éditions et de librairie, 1955).
21. Quoted by Jean Bossu, *Laurent Tailhade et son temps* (n.p., Editions 'L'Idée libre', n.d. [1945?]). By an irony of fate Tailhade was himself to be the victim of such terrorist acts: he lost an eye when a bomb exploded in the Restaurant Foyot in April 1894.
22. *O.C.*, Pléiade, I, 337, 340. Jarry's italics.
23. *Ibid.*, 1012–13.
24. Reply to the *Enquête sur l'évolution littéraire* of Jules Huret, reproduced in Mallarmé's *Oeuvres Complètes* (Paris: Gallimard, Bibliothèque de la Pléiade, 1945), 869. Mallarmé's italics.
25. *O.C.*, Pléiade, I, 171.
26. *Ibid.*, 172. Jarry's italics. Corresponding to the asterisk placed against the word *simplicité*, Jarry added the following footnote: 'La simplicité n'a pas besoin d'être simple, mais du complexe resserré et synthétisé (cf.

Pataph.).' ['Simplicity does not need to be simple, but consists of complexity compressed and synthesized (cf. *Pataph.*).']
27. *O.C.*, Pléiade, I, 172–3. The same view is expounded in the novel *Les Jours et les Nuits*, published in 1897. Speaking of its hero Sengle's 'littératures', 'curieusement et précisément équilibrées', with their 'combinaisons mathématiques', Jarry tells us that 'on pouvait [les] anatomiser et atomiser indéfiniment, chaque molécule étant cristallisée selon le système de la masse, avec des hiérarchies vitalisantes, commes les cellules d'un corps' ['one could dissect and atomize [them] indefinitely, each molecule forming part of a crystalline structure determined by the whole, with life-sustaining hierarchies, like the cells of an organism'] (*O.C.*, Pléiade, I, 793–4). The mathematical or geometrical imagery – reminiscent of the 'crossroads' and 'polyhedra of ideas' of the 'Linteau' of *Les Minutes* – is characteristic of Jarry, suggesting both the 'mathematical' precision of the relationships between words and images in his work, and the tendency in that same work towards 'abstraction'.
28. Did Mallarmé mean by 'le hasard' something akin to the Saussurian notion of the 'arbitrary' nature of the relationship between 'signifier' and 'signified'? Saussure, the father of modern linguistics, pointed out that the relationship between a particular word or sound, e.g. 'book', and the object or idea to which it refers is a purely conventional, and not a

necessary one; it is a relationship which varies from one language and even from one moment of history to another. Mallarmé's pronouncements on the subject of language would seem to suggest that this or something akin to it was the meaning that he had in mind.

29. Mallarmé, *Oeuvres Complètes*, 366. A number of passages in this essay had already appeared in earlier writings. In any case, the question of chronology is here relatively unimportant, since Mallarmé's ideas were conveyed to his young disciples as much verbally as through his writings.

30. The theme of the foetus preserved in alcohol has already been noted in Jarry's *Ontogénie*. Its presence here provides a further instance of the recurrence and interpenetration of themes – or 'intertextuality' – which is characteristic of his work as a whole.

31. *O.C.*, Pléiade, I, 217.
32. *Ibid.*, 185.
33. 'Les Débuts du Symbolisme: Remy de Gourmont, Alfred Jarry et l'*Art littéraire*', in *Le Gaulois*, 3 Dec. 1921, 4.
34. Two such terms particularly cherished by Jarry are 'paralipomena' and 'prolegomena', which signify respectively 'that which is omitted' (or 'left aside'), and a preliminary discourse or introduction.
35. *O.C.*, Pléiade, I, 238. The significance of the date is not known.
36. *Ibid.*, 184.
37. *Ibid.*, 215, 212, 224 and 212 respectively.
38. *Ibid.*, 212.

39. *Ibid.*, 199.
40. *Ibid.*, 173.
41. Apart from the abridgement, a few other, minor changes have been made also. The main character is referred to throughout as 'Ubu' instead of 'Père Ubu' (which renders him slightly less comic), Captain Bordure becomes simply 'Bordure', and the three 'Palotins' become Pile, Giron and Cotice – the last four names all being heraldic terms, which provide a link with Act II, the 'Acte héraldique'.
42. A number of motifs provide a link also with the novels *Les Jours et les Nuits* (the reference to 'le jour et la nuit', and the theme of the 'Double') and *L'Amour absolu* (the customs officer's hut which 'sert de repos . . . au Dieu qui attend son heure', and the Giant Roc from *The Arabian Nights*). Whilst the play's reflections on the subject of 'truth' look forward to passages in other works by Jarry, in particular to some of the texts collected in *La Chandelle verte*.
43. *Le Latin mystique* (Paris: Mercure de France, 1892), 171.
44. *O.C.*, Pléiade, I, 279.
45. *Ibid.*, 281, 276.
46. These problems are elucidated in the erudite article of J.-H. Sainmont, 'Petit Guide illustré pour la visite de *César-Antechrist*', *C.C.P.*, no. 5–6, 53–65. According to Sainmont, for all his pretentions to a knowledge of heraldry, Jarry merely dabbled in the science, remaining ignorant even on elementary points and producing a nonsensical description of his own supposed coat-of-arms. His interest in the subject was

probably inspired by Gourmont, whose own knowledge of it was far more solid.

47. *O.C.*, Pléiade, I, 241.
48. *Ibid.*, 327.
49. *Ibid.*, 276, 331, 325 and 280–1 respectively. Ormuzd and Ahriman are the two opposing principles of Good and Evil in the Zoroastrian religion.
50. *O.C.*, Pléiade, I, 289.
51. *Ibid.*, 289.
52. *Ibid.*, 730.
53. *Ibid.*, 290.
54. *Ibid.*, 274.
55. *Ibid.*, 292.
56. The enormously elaborate network of sexual and other connotations conferred by these intertextual links upon elements of the text of *Ubu Roi* is painstakingly and lovingly explored by Michel Arrivé in *Les Langages de Jarry. Essai de sémiotique littéraire* (Paris: Klincksieck, 1972).
57. *O.C.*, Pléiade, I, 188.
58. In *La Vogue*, 18 Apr. 1886, quoted by A. G. Lehmann in *The Symbolist Aesthetic in France, 1885–1895* (2nd edn, 1968), 90.
59. According to the former friend of his army days Géroy, 'Mon ami Alfred Jarry (Souvenirs)', in *Mercure de France*, 1 July 1947, 493–509.
60. Charlotte Jarry, 'Souvenirs sur Alfred Jarry', in *O.C.*, Éditions du Livre, I, 34.
61. Rachilde, *Alfred Jarry ou le Surmâle des Lettres* (Paris, 1928), 66.
62. According to his certificate of discharge, reproduced in *C.C.P.*, no. 26–7, 53.
63. Jean Saltas (who was one of the victims of this story), 'Souvenirs sur Alfred Jarry', in *O.C.*, Éditions du Livre, I, 23.
64. Fragments of four of a planned

12 poems making up this collection were published by Maurice Saillet in 1949 in *La Revanche de la Nuit*. They can be found also in *O.C.*, Pléiade, I, 267–8.

CHAPTER FOUR
UBU

1. Cited by John Fletcher (ed.), *Forces in Modern French Drama* (London, 1972), 7.
2. *Mercure de France*, Oct. 1894, 177–8.
3. Letter of 3 July 1896, published in 'Le Souvenir de Jean de Tinan', *Le Divan*, no. 98 (Apr. 1924), 258.
4. In an article published in *Commoedia* in 1922, provoked by Chassé's attack on Jarry's authorship of *Ubu Roi*, Paul Fort told a curious tale of how he had to *force* Jarry – who wanted to burn the manuscript – to let him publish the text of the play. According to Fort, he and a number of friends were obliged to go to Jarry's lodgings on the Boulevard St Germain, tear the manuscript from his very hands, and themselves put the disordered pages into some sort of order (cited by Rachilde, *Alfred Jarry ou le Surmâle des Lettres* (Paris, 1928), 112). The same story is told in Fort's *Mémoires* (Paris: Flammarion, 1944, 52), complete with even more colourful details: 'Pendant une nuit entière, et sans Jarry, nous mîmes les scènes en un ordre à peu près logique, et cet ordre, par miracle [*sic*], se trouva être le bon.' ['We spent a whole night, without Jarry, arranging the scenes into a more-or-less logical order, and, by a miracle [*sic*], this order

turned out to be the right one.']
The story of Jarry's reluctance
to publish *Ubu Roi* is patently
nonsense. Is the rest therefore
pure fantasy – an example of
pure invention not untypical in
the memoirs of writers (Fargue
is a case in point)? Or was Jarry
playing some sort of game
which Fort failed to see
through?

5. Fort was thereupon promptly
expelled from his Parisian lycée
by its headmaster, scandalized
at the idea of a schoolboy
founding a theatre, let alone
one which performed works by
such men as the sodomitic and
alcoholic Verlaine and the
outrageously obscure
Mallarmé.

6. Lugné-Poe, *La Parade*, II:
Acrobaties (Paris: Gallimard,
n.d.), 42.

7. Letter of 30 Oct. 1894, cited by
Lugné-Poe, *ibid.*, 160.

8. *Ibid.*, 159.

9. Letter of 8 January 1896, cited
by Lugné-Poe, *ibid.*, 161–2 and
reproduced in *O.C.*, Pléiade, I,
1042–4.

10. Lugné-Poe, *op. cit.*, 163.

11. Letter of 1 Aug. 1896, cited by
Lugné-Poe, *ibid.*, 166.

12. *Ibid.*, 170, 172.

13. Letter of August 1896, cited by
Lugné-Poe, *ibid.*, 168. My
italics.

14. *Ibid.*, 170.

15. *Ibid.*, 163, 174, 175.

16. *Ibid.*, 160.

17. See those letters of Jarry
published by N. Arnaud and
H. Bordillon as an appendix to
their edition of *Ubu* (Paris:
Gallimard, Coll. Folio, 1978),
410–33.

18. Letter cited by P. Lié (pseud.),
'Comment Jarry et Lugné-Poe
glorifièrent Ubu à l'Oeuvre', in
C.C.P., no. 3–4, 42.

19. Lugné-Poe, *op. cit.*, 176.

20. It may well have been such
references to the alleged
simplicity of sets and costumes
in the Elizabethan theatre – in
which Lugné-Poe sought a
justification for the necessary
simplicity of his own
productions – which, together
with Jarry's facetious epigraph
to the published text of *Ubu Roi*,
was responsible for the play's
being regarded by hostile critics
as no more than a parody of
Macbeth and by supporters as an
original creation comparable in
its sublimity to Shakespeare.
Needless to say, neither view is
tenable.

21. Lugné-Poe, *op. cit.*, 174.

22. Letter cited by Lugné-Poe, *ibid.*,
174.

23. Letter of 15 Dec. 1896, cited by
Arnaud and Bordillon in *Ubu,
ed. cit.*, 437.

24. These accounts include, in
addition to the reminiscences of
Lugné-Poe, Gémier and others,
the numerous press reviews of
the performance. A valuable
anthology of these can be found
in H. Robillot, 'La Presse d'*Ubu
Roi*', *C.C.P.*, no. 3–4, 73–88.

25. Arthur Symons, 'A Symbolist
farce', in *Studies in Seven Arts*
(London: 1906), 373. Other
details can be added to Symons'
description: for example, an
elephant riding on a red disk
(representing the sun), and a
chamber-pot visible under the
bed.

26. Jarry's comment in his speech
to the audience that 'Ubu n'a
pas eu le temps d'avoir son
masque véritable' ['Ubu has not
had time to have his true mask']
is surely to be understood
metaphorically. Numerous
contemporary descriptions
refer to Gémier's mask.

Rachilde (*op. cit.*, 80) describes him as 'orné d'un masque effroyable' ['bedecked with a hideous mask'], and Lugné-Poe in his memoirs recalls his 'masque en carton qui le gênait' ['cardboard mask which hampered his movements'] (*op. cit.*, 177). Jarry's friend Georges Rémond spoke of Gémier's 'masque en poire triangulaire qui obturait son nez' ['triangular pear-shaped mask which pinched his nose'] ('Souvenirs sur Jarry et autres: La Bataille d'*Ubu Roi*', in *Mercure de France*, 1 Apr. 1955, 668). And Gémier himself, in an interview published in *Excelsior* on 4 Nov. 1921 ('Deux représentations retentissantes: M. Firmin Gémier nous dit ce que furent la répétition générale et la première d'*Ubu Roi*', pp. 2–3), speaks of feeling hot and trapped beneath 'le masque lourd dessiné par Jarry' ['the heavy mask designed by Jarry'] and his huge belly. In the revival of the play in 1908, after Jarry's death, Gémier refused to wear this mask.

27. Valentin Mandelstamm, in *Fantasio*, 15 Apr. 1908, quoted by F. Caradec in *L'Étoile-Absinthe*, no. 7–8 (Dec. 1980), 66–9. It is unfortunately impossible to be sure of the details of the costumes, though it seems probable that here also Jarry's instructions, which reveal a desire to combine deliberate banality with incongruity, were carried out. According to these instructions, Ubu was to wear a steel-grey suit, with a walking-stick in his right-hand pocket, and on his head a bowler hat with a crown sitting on top when he becomes King; Mère Ubu was to be dressed as a flower-seller-cum-*concierge*; Bordure was to wear the tight-fitting garb of a Hungarian gipsy musician; Bougrelas, a baby's dress and bonnet; and so on. (Document published in *C.C.P.*, no. 3–4, 13–14.)

28. *Op. cit.*, 372.
29. Rachilde, *op. cit.*, 71.
30. Article cited by Rachilde, *op. cit.*, 70–1.
31. *Autobiographies* (London, 1955), 348–9.
32. Gémier, interview published in *Excelsior*, 4 Nov. 1921.
33. The story related by Lugné-Poe in *Acrobaties*, and repeated by Roger Shattuck in *The Banquet Years: The Arts in France, 1885–1918* (rev. edn, London 1969), according to which Bauer in the end lost the battle to the superior bombast of Fouquier who then took his place at the *Écho de Paris*, appears to be without foundation. Bauer was still writing for the paper in 1898, and it was in fact the conflict between his passionately pro-Dreyfus stand and the anti-Dreyfus policy of the paper in 1898–9 which led to his departure from the *Écho de Paris*.
34. The entries in the popular *Petit Larousse Illustré* are typical: '*Ubu Roi*, comédie caricaturale, satire énorme de la bourgeoisie' ['*Ubu Roi*, grotesque comedy, vast satire on the bourgeoisie'], and 'Le Père Ubu, caricature bouffonne de la stupidité bourgeoise' ['Père Ubu, grossly comic caricature of bourgeois stupidity'].
35. Jules Renard, *Journal* (Paris: Gallimard, Bibliothèque de la Pléiade, 1960), 363.
36. Further evidence of a conscious desire to create a scandal is

contained in a letter to Lugné-Poe of 1 Aug. 1896, in which Jarry suggests that the role of Bougrelas be played by a 13-year-old boy instead of by a young woman, as a century-old tradition would have demanded. Alongside the argument that 'ça ne s'est jamais vu et . . . il faut que ''l'Oeuvre'' monopolise toutes les innovations' ['that's never yet been seen and . . . the *Oeuvre* must secure a monopoly of all new ideas'], he advances also the argument that 'cela exciterait des vieilles dames et ferait crier au scandale certaines' ['it would excite a few old ladies and cause some of them to make a public outcry'] (cited by Lugné-Poe, *op. cit.*, 167). (Incidentally, Jarry had his way, and the role of Bougrelas was played by a boy.) There is also the story told by his friend Georges Rémond, according to whom Jarry organized his friends into a *cabale* with instructions to heckle if the audience was appreciative, and to cheer if the audience heckled: 'Le scandale, disait Jarry, devait dépasser celui de *Phèdre* ou d'*Hernani*. Il fallait que la pièce ne pût aller jusqu'au bout et que le théâtre éclatât.' ['The scandal, Jarry said, must surpass that of *Phèdre* or *Hernani*. The play must not be allowed to run to the end of its performance and the theatre must be in a state of uproar.'] ('Souvenirs sur Jarry et autres', in *Mercure de France*, 1 Apr. 1955, 664–5). These, however, are the recollections of a man looking back almost 60 years, and making his own contribution to the elaboration of the Jarry 'legend', in this

instance that of an amiable *enfant terrible*. Therefore there must be some doubt as to whether such an account can be taken absolutely literally.

37. *O.C.*, Pléiade, I, 416. (Jarry's quotation of Mendès' words is not wholly accurate.) A similar view is suggested in a letter of Jarry to Henry Bauer, thanking him for his articles in support of Ubu and appearing (though with doubtful sincerity?) to agree with Bauer's interpretation: 'Votre bienveillante chronique a fait naître les profitables polémiques qui suivent. Il est si amusant de voir la tête du mufle, amateur d'''esprit parisien'' à qui on a présenté sa propre image sur la scène . . . .' ['Your kindly article gave rise to the fruitful polemics which follow. It is so amusing to see the reaction of the *mufle* [epitome of boorishness], the lover of ''Parisian wit'' who has been confronted with his own reflection on the stage . . . .'] (*O.C.*, Pléiade, I, 1059).

38. This is the view of Rachilde, for example, in her *Alfred Jarry ou le Surmâle des Lettres*, and of the actor Jehan Adès in an interview with René Druart, published in *C.C.P.*, no. 20, 53: 'On attendait des énormités et on les désirait. Et les dames elles-mêmes n'étaient pas prêtes à s'en offusquer.' ['The audience was expecting, and wanting, to hear outrageous things spoken. And the ladies themselves were quite prepared not to take offence.']

39. The most important of these are 'De l'inutilité du théâtre au théâtre', 'Questions de théâtre', and his unpublished reply to a 'questionnaire sur l'art

dramatique'. Although Jarry referred to the first of these articles as being 'pas une théorie complète, puisque j'ai pensé surtout à la mise en scène d'*Ubu*' ['not a complete theory, since I have thought above all in terms of a production of *Ubu*'] (letter to Lugné-Poe, cited in *Acrobaties*, 169), *Ubu Roi* is itself so central to his conception of the theatre that the main ideas expressed in this and the other two articles can justifiably be taken as having a general application. From a later period in his career, the 'Conférence sur les pantins' of 1902 as well as a number of texts and passages in his *chroniques*, collected in *La Chandelle verte*, reveal the continuing existence of similar views and preferences.

40. 'De l'inutilité du théâtre au théâtre', in *O.C.*, Pléiade, I, 406.
41. In *O.C.*, Pléiade, I, 422–3.
42. Cited by Lugné-Poe, *op. cit.*, 170. There is a curious paradox (one of many) in Jarry's views here. His desire to revolutionize the theatre of his time is a real and deep-seated one, testified to both by his own efforts to have *Ubu Roi* performed in accordance with his precise wishes, and by his several important articles on the theatre. But at the same time, alongside his continuing contempt for the theatre and the theatre-going public of his time, there are occasional indications in his writings of later years that he regards the theatre *as an art form* as inferior to other, purely literary, forms, since in the latter the imagination is allowed a completely free rein, unhindered by the constraints of a specific visual and auditive representation. A passage in one of his *chroniques* is, despite the tongue-in-cheek humour, telling in this regard: 'C'est fort judicieusement que des critiques célèbres adoptèrent la coutume, on s'en souvient, d'assister aux premières représentations paupières closes, attitude d'après laquelle seuls des voisins inconsidérés ont cru pouvoir diagnostiquer le sommeil. Ils en usaient ainsi, les grands critiques, afin de *n'être point distraits de leurs impressions plus directes.* Dans une intention non moins louable, à Bayreuth et à Paris, des représentations furent données dans l'obscurité la plus profonde.' ['It was indeed judiciously that a number of famous critics adopted the habit, as the reader will recall, of sitting through first nights with closed eyelids, a posture which led only the more rash among their neighbours to diagnose sleep. These great critics acted in such a manner in order *not to be distracted from their more immediate impressions.* For a no less praiseworthy reason, in Bayreuth and in Paris, performances were given in the most total darkness.'] ('Le Droit de critique', in *La Chandelle verte*, 211. My italics.)
43. See in particular the articles 'Barnum', 'Juno Salmo au Nouveau-Cirque' and 'Liane de Pougy aux Folies-Bergères', in *La Chandelle verte*, 149–52, 154–7 and 162–3 respectively.
44. Cited by Denys Sutton, Introduction to *Pierre Bonnard*, Catalogue of the Royal Academy of Arts Winter Exhibition, 1966, 14. A similar enthusiastic response was

expressed by Paul Margueritte in a little brochure of 1888 introducing Bouchor's theatre, in which he praised – in terms which look forward to Jarry – 'les fantoches impersonnels, êtres de bois et de carton' which 'possèdent une vie falote, mystérieuse. Leur allure de vérité surprend, inquiète. Dans leurs gestes essentiels tient l'expression complète des sentiments humains.' ['these impersonal puppets, creatures of wood and cardboard' which 'possess a wan and mysterious life. Their air of truth is surprising, disturbing. In their schematic gestures is to be found the expression of the totality of human emotions.'] (*Le Petit Théâtre (Théâtre de Marionnettes)* (Paris: Librairie Illustrée, 1888), 7–8).

45. Edward Gordon Craig, 'The actor and the Über-marionnette' (essay written in 1907), in *On the Art of the Theatre* (London, 1911), 84–5.

There is something of a paradox in Jarry's artistic preferences here. On the one hand, he takes up a defiantly elitist and anti-democratic standpoint; yet at the same time, he champions such distinctly popular forms of expression as the *guignol*, the circus and the music hall (and, in the field of the visual arts, the *image d'Épinal*). Tempting though it may be, however, to see in the latter fact the expression of a political and social *parti pris* on his part, there is no evidence at all in his writings to support this view, and his attitude remains resolutely one of 'art for art's sake.'

46. 'De l'inutilité du théâtre au théâtre', in *O.C.*, Pléiade, I, 406.

47. 'Réponses à un questionnaire sur l'art dramatique', in *O.C.*, Pléiade, I, 412.

48. 'Hamlet', in *Crayonné au théâtre* (1887). Reproduced in Mallarmé's *Oeuvres Complètes*, (Paris: Gallimard, Bibliothèque de la Pléiade, 1945), 300.

49. *O.C.*, Pléiade, I, 415.

50. Eugène Ionesco, *Notes et contre-notes* (Paris: Gallimard, 1962), 16.

51. Rachilde, article in *Mercure de France*, Aug. 1897.

52. Letter of 27 Oct. 1896, published in Stéphane Mallarmé, *Correspondance*, recueillie, classée et annotée par Henri Mondor et Lloyd James Austin, tome VIII (Paris: Gallimard, 1983), 256.

53. Jarry's choice of *Ubu Roi* rather than *Ubu Cocu* for presentation at the Théâtre de l'Oeuvre may be of significance here. For *Ubu Roi* is at one and the same time a less 'personal' or original creation than *Ubu Cocu* (to which Jarry's own contribution is undoubtedly greater), and a less sophisticated play (in the latter, the character of Ubu undergoes a slight change, to become a much more self-conscious, more deliberately witty character). In other words, in giving precedence to *Ubu Roi*, Jarry chose to present Ubu to the public in his most crude and primitive form.

54. The 'plot' of *Ubu Roi* has been subjected to a detailed structural analysis by Henri Béhar in his *Jarry dramaturge* (Paris: Nizet, 1980). Béhar argues that, insofar as the plot of *Macbeth* can be seen as a paradigm of that of all historical tragedies, the plot of *Ubu Roi* in turn therefore becomes a spoof upon *all* such plays.

55. Act III, Sc. 4. My italics. This phrase was obviously of the utmost importance for Jarry in characterizing Ubu: in 'Les Prolégomènes de César-Antechrist' in *Les Minutes de sable mémorial*, it stands alone (in a slightly modified version) under the heading 'Ubu parle': 'Quand j'aurai pris toute la Phynance, je tuerai tout le monde et je m'en irai' ['When I have taken all the Phynance, I'll kill everybody and go away'] What purer expression could there be of total nihilism?

56. 'Réflexions sur la littérature: L'Affaire Ubu', *Nouvelle Revue Française*, 1 July 1922, 61–62.

57. *Les Libres Propos*, 17 Dec. 1921. Cited by H. Robillot, *C.C.P.*, no. 3–4, 88.

58. 'Livres d'enfants', in *La Chandelle verte*, 310–2.

59. Cited by Charles Chassé, *Sous le masque d'Alfred Jarry(?): Les Sources d'Ubu-Roi* (Paris: Fleury, 1921), 65.

CHAPTER FIVE
FURTHER MANIFESTATIONS
OF UBU

1. Article in the *Mercure de France* of Aug. 1897, quoted in *C.C.P.*, no. 26–7, 58.

2. Letter dated 15 Dec. 1896, in *O.C.*, Pléiade, I, 1060.

3. Lugné-Poe, *La Parade*, II: *Acrobaties* (Paris: Gallimard, n.d.), 184.

4. Quoted by Jacques Robichez, *Le Symbolisme au théâtre. Lugné-Poe et les débuts de l'Oeuvre* (Paris: L'Arche, 1957), 395.

5. Quoted by Robichez, *op. cit.*, 397.

6. The break between Jarry and Lugné-Poe did not prove to be definitive, however. On the occasion of the marionette performances of the Théâtre des Pantins in 1898, the Oeuvre offered its services as a booking office. While in a revival of *Peer Gynt* at the Oeuvre in 1901, it was again Jarry who took the part of the King of the Trolls, according to P. Lié (*pseud.*), 'Comment Jarry et Lugné-Poe glorifièrent Ubu à l'Oeuvre', in *C.C.P.*, no. 3–4, 51.

7. 'Je parlai un jour à Jarry. . . . Il me dit: "On m'écrase sous Ubu. Ce n'est qu'une fumisterie de potaches qui n'est même pas de moi, je l'ai faite avec des camarades, puis je l'ai raccommodée, corsée de traits burlesques et scatologiques, ça m'a paru pouvoir faire une pièce drôle. J'ai fait et surtout je faisais bien autre chose. Mais ils sont tous là à me boucher la route avec *Ubu*. Il faut que je le parle, que je le mime, que je le vive. On ne veut que ça!" . . . Il me fit l'effet d'un être au coeur froissé, très fin, et affreusement las de son personnage fictif dont il était devenu le prisonnier.' ['I spoke one day to Jarry. . . . He told me: "I am crushed beneath Ubu. It's only a schoolboy hoax which wasn't even written by me, I concocted it with school-friends, then I patched it up and spiced it with grossly comic and scatological details, it seemed to me that it could be a comic play. I have written, and I have continued to write, a great many completely different things. But they are all there, blocking my path with Ubu. I have to speak Ubu, mime Ubu, live Ubu. That's the only thing they want!" . . . He struck me as being a sensitive being, deeply wounded, and terribly tired of

his own fictitious creation whose prisoner he had become.'] (*Servitude et Grandeur littéraire*, Paris: Ollendorff, 6th edn 1922, 108–9).
It is difficult to know how much credence to give to Mauclair's testimony. Certainly the role of 'Ubu' was one encouraged, and even to a certain extent forced upon Jarry, by his contemporaries. But at the same time he does appear on the whole to have willingly 'played the game', although to a far lesser extent than most of his contemporaries acknowledged.

8. Interview with Frédéric Lefèvre, 'Une heure avec Léon-Paul Fargue', in *Les Nouvelles Littéraires*, 12 Jan. 1929.

9. *De mon temps* (Paris: Mercure de France, 4th edn 1933), 146.

10. *Ibid.*, 150.

11. *Alfred Jarry ou le Surmâle des Lettres* (Paris: Grasset, 1928), 15.

12. *Ibid.*, 149.

13. 'Le Groupement littéraire qu'abritait le "Mercure de France"', in *Mercure de France*, vol. 298, no. 1000 (1 July 1940 – 1 Dec. 1946), 168.

14. 'Souvenirs sur Alfred Jarry', in *Les Marges* (Jan. 1922), 28.

15. The building, though now demolished, still existed in this form in 1952. Cf. Jean Loize, 'La Grande Chasublerie d'Alfred Jarry', in *C.C.P.*, no. 5–6, 66–8.

16. Apollinaire in 'Les Contemporains pittoresques: Feu Alfred Jarry', in *Les Marges* (Nov. 1909), 851–6; Salmon, 'Le Père Ubu en liberté', in *L'Ami du Lettré* (1924), 239–64.

17. Jules Trohel, 'Alfred Jarry et les huissiers', *Mercure de France*, 1 May 1934, 626–36; T. Lecompte, 'Histoire d'une bicyclette gratuite (avec expertise)', in *C.C.P.*, no. 5–6, 69–70.

18. Cf. amongst others Géroy, 'Mon ami Alfred Jarry (Souvenirs)', in *Mercure de France*, 1 July 1947, 493–509.

19. *Alfred Jarry ou le Surmâle des Lettres* (Paris, 1928), 133. Cf. also Jarry's letter to Rachilde in *O.C.*, Pléiade, I, 1064–5.

20. Rachilde, *op. cit.*, 140–1.

21. Salmon, *op. cit.*, 257–8.

22. Rachilde, *op. cit.*, 182. There is a certain naïvety, not to say gullibility, manifest on Rachilde's part in her recounting of many of these anecdotes!

23. *Ibid.*, 180–1.

24. *Ubu Cocu*, Act I, Sc. 3.

25. 'Le Groupement littéraire qu'abritait le "Mercure de France"', in *Mercure de France*, vol. 298, no. 1,000 (1 July 1940 – 1 Dec. 1946), 168. My italics. It was for this reason that Gide chose to include the figure of Jarry in his novel *Les Faux-Monnayeurs*, which turns upon the themes of authenticity and falsehood; the 'real' but at the same time fictitious character of Jarry is cleverly juxtaposed with the novelist's own 'fictitious' characters who are searching for authenticity.

26. Cf. the interview with Mme Gabrielle Fort-Vallette published in *Le Magazine littéraire*, no. 48, Jan. 1971, 13.

27. See the two articles by J.-H. Sainmont, 'Occultations et exaltations d'*Ubu Cocu*', *C.C.P.*, no. 3–4, 29–36, and 'Rennes visions d'histoire', *C.C.P.*, no. 20, 27–36; Michel Arrivé's bibliographical note in the first volume of the Pléiade edition of Jarry's works, 1185–89; and the 'Notice' by H. Bordillon and N. Arnaud in *Ubu* (Paris:

Gallimard, Collection Folio, 1978), 466–84. Though the argument of Bordillon and Arnaud is in parts slightly abstruse, their discussion of the problem – the most recent and by far the most detailed – for the most part carries conviction.

28. Cf. Jarry's letters to Lugné-Poe of 8 Jan. and 12 March 1896, quoted in full in *Ubu*, ed. Arnaud and Bordillon, 412–14.

29. His intentions in 'Les Paralipomènes' are however ambiguous: these extracts were presented to the public by Jarry ostensibly in order to 'liquidate' completely the figure of Ubu through an explanation of him 'by his past'. Yet, published as they were on 1 December, only nine days before the *première* of *Ubu Roi*, they were surely also intended to whet the public's appetite for the performance. Was Jarry in 'Les Paralipomènes' testing reactions to Ubu, uncertain himself at this point of the exact status and value to give to this material?

30. See the 'Projet de réunion des trois *Ubu* en un volume', in *O.C.*, Pléiade, I, 521. *Ubu Cocu* is here given the title of *La Conscience*.

31. Quoted by M. Arrivé, in *O.C.*, Pléiade, I, 1179.

32. *Ubu Cocu*, Act I, Sc. 3.

33. *Ubu Cocu*, Act V, Sc. 2. The same passage occurs in both versions of *Ubu Cocu*. A footnote added in both cases gives the exact source of the quotation from Ribot, including even in the former a page number!

34. *Ubu Cocu*, Act III, Sc. 3, and *L'Archéoptéryx*, Act I, Sc. 2.

35. *Ubu Cocu*, Act II, Sc. 3, and *L'Archéoptéryx*, Act III, Sc. 3.

36. *Sic*. Quoted by Chassé, *Sous le masque d'Alfred Jarry (?): Les Sources d'Ubu-Roi* (Paris: Floury, 1921), 30.

37. In his *Les Langages de Jarry* (Paris: Klincksieck, 1972).

38. *Ubu Cocu*, Act IV, Sc. 3.

39. See in particular the scathing reference to the army in 'Ceux pour qui il n'y eut point de Babel', *La Chandelle verte*, 298–9, and his review of a speech by the anti-clerical Émile Combes in 1903, 'Le Discours de M. Combes', *ibid.*, 273–7.

40. Act I, Sc. 2. The last sentence cleverly parodies the view of discipline expressed in the army's own manual, quoted by Jarry in *Les Jours et les Nuits*: '"La discipline, qui est la force principale des armées", dit la théorie . . . .' (*O.C.*, Pléiade, I, 763.)

41. Act I, Sc. 1. A similar refusal to pronounce 'the word' occurs in the trial scene of Act III, Sc. 2. Here, however, Ubu gives a totally contradictory reason for his refusal, namely that it would bring him luck: 'il me porterait chance, il me ferait acquitter'. This contradiction points to the arbitrariness of the reasons given: what matters is the *fact* of Ubu's silence, and its juxtaposition with *Ubu Roi*.

42. Michel Arrivé argues that the sadism manifested in *Ubu Roi* gives way to masochism in the behaviour of the hero of *Ubu Enchaîné*. This is more the case in appearance than in reality: latent sadism continues to show in both Ubu's words and behaviour. It is also untrue, as Arrivé claims in his 'Notice' to *Ubu Enchaîné* in the Pléiade edition of Jarry's *Oeuvres Complètes*, that 'tous les instruments de l'agressivité

ubuesque' have disappeared. A number on the contrary continue to appear or to be referred to.

43. *Ubu Roi*, Act III, Sc. 2; *Ubu Enchaîné*, Act I, Sc. 7.
44. *Ubu Enchaîné*, Act I, Sc. 1. My italics.
45. *Ubu Roi*, Act III, Sc. 4.
46. *Ubu Enchaîné*, Act I, Sc. 3.
47. *Ubu Roi*, Act III, Sc. 7; *Ubu Enchaîné*, Act III, Sc. 1.
48. The function of the otherwise rather pointless scene with the English tourist, Lord Catoblepas, is presumably to underline this semantic inversion. The systematic misuse by Lord Catoblepas' manservant of the English-French dictionary gives such mistranslations as palace for prison, orb and chain of office for convict's ball and chain, and so on.
49. *Ubu Enchaîné*, Act V, Sc. 1.
50. The highly ambiguous, and much misinterpreted, epigraph of *Ubu Enchaîné* is worth examining in this context:

> PÈRE UBU: Cornegidouille! nous n'aurons point tout démoli si nous ne démolissons même les ruines! Or je n'y vois d'autre moyen que d'en équilibrer de beaux édifices bien ordonnés.

> [PERE UBU: Hornbelly! we won't have demolished everything if we don't demolish the ruins as well! Now, I see no other means of doing so than by using them to erect fine, harmonious new edifices.]

In so far as this epigraph refers to his new play, Jarry seems to be saying here (amongst other things), firstly, that the text of *Ubu Enchaîné* is built upon the 'ruins' of that of *Ubu Roi* (constituting the carefully constructed 'fine new edifice' referred to) and, secondly, that this construction is one which cancels itself out, leading, on a semantic plane, to its own destruction, the aim of this new construction being explicitly given as that of 'demolishing' even more thoroughly than before the existing or surviving 'ruins'.

51. *Ubu Enchaîné*, Act V, Sc. 7.
52. *O.C.*, Pléiade, I, 329.
53. *Jarry dramaturge* (Paris: Nizet, 1980), 95.
54. The sources of this fanciful orchestra are examined by Jacques Carelman in 'L'Orchestre d'*Ubu Roi*', in *Europe*, March-Apr. 1981, 160–71.
55. See the discussion of the censored manuscript in *Ubu*, ed. Arnaud and Bordillon, 453–4. It may well have been this forced deletion of 'the word', reducing Ubu on occasions to silence, which provided the starting-point in Jarry's mind for *Ubu Enchaîné*.
56. *Souvenirs d'un marchand de tableaux* (Paris: Albin Michel, 1937), 119–20.
57. *Ibid.* Vollard himself took over the character of Ubu after Jarry's death, making of him a wholly satirical figure in a series of illustrated commentaries upon current events: *Le Père Ubu à l'hôpital* (1916 and 1917) and *Le Père Ubu à l'aviation* (1918), both illustrated by Pierre Bonnard; *La Politique coloniale du Père Ubu* (1919), illustrated by Georges Rouault; *Le Père Ubu à la guerre* (1923); *Les Réincarnations du Père Ubu* (1925

and 1932), also illustrated by Rouault; and *Le Père Ubu au pays des Soviets* (1930).

58. *O.C.*, Pléiade, I, 536.

CHAPTER SIX
DREAM, HALLUCINATION,
LOVE AND DEATH

1. *O.C.*, Pléiade, I, 249, and notes, 1115.
2. *Ibid.*, I, 747.
3. *Ibid.*, I, 794.
4. *Ibid.*, 748.
5. *Ibid.*, 775.
6. *Ibid.*, 815.
7. An annotated edition of the text belonging to Jarry's friend Édouard Julia explicitly identifies a number of these figures (see Michel Arrivé's notes to *O.C.*, Pléiade, I, 1241–2). Jarry's transposition of names in the novel is often amusing, and reveals his sophisticated love of wordplay. Thus his friend and fellow-writer Ernest La Jeunesse becomes Severus Altmensch (Severus being a latinization of the German form of Ernest, *Ernst*, and Altmensch a transposition into German of the antonym of La Jeunesse), while the painter Léonard Sarluis becomes Raphaël Roissoy (Sar, *czar* = *roi*, and *lui* = *soi*). No less entertainingly, *Le Mercure de France* becomes *L'Iodure de Navarre*.
8. *O.C.*, Pléiade, I, 769. A pencilled note in the margin of Édouard Julia's copy of the novel explicitly identifies this former friend as 'Léon-Paul Fargue' (cf. *O.C.*, Pléiade, I, notes, 1243). Jarry's use of *elle* ('elle avait un corps de palefrenier'), while ostensibly justified by the feminine gender of *amitié*, is both ambiguous and deliberately insulting. It may also be that the name Valens (Latin for *strong*) was also chosen with deliberate irony.
9. *Le Joujou patriotisme* (Paris: J.-J. Pauvert, 1967), 58.
10. *O.C.*, Pléiade, I, 768.
11. *Ibid.*, 797.
12. *Ibid.*, 834–5.
13. *Ibid.*, 763.
14. *Ibid.*, 814. My italics.
15. *Ibid.*, 767.
16. *Ibid.*, 769.
17. *Ibid.* This same identification of 'love' with the contemplation of one's own past in the present of another person occurs briefly in the short prose narrative *L'Autre Alceste*, written in August 1896 (when Jarry was working on *Les Jours et les Nuits*), where the centenarian Solomon says of his son Rehoboam: 'Roboam, mon fils, est dans la force de l'âge du corps et de l'esprit; et j'ai pour lui un amour qu'il serait sacrilège de prostituer à une femme, car en lui je me remire en mon passé; j'observe avec ma sagesse centenaire la croissance de mon corps et de mon esprit de vingt ans . . . .' ['Rehoboam, my son, is in his prime physically and mentally; and I have for him a love which it would be sacriligious to prostitute to any woman, for in him I see my own past reflected back at me; I contemplate with my centenarian wisdom the growth of my body and my mind at the age of twenty . . . .'] (*O.C.*, Pléiade, I, 914).
18. *O.C.*, Pléiade, I, 834, 835.
19. *Ibid.*, 835.
20. *Ibid.*, 768.
21. Marcel Proust, *A la recherche du temps perdu* (Paris: Gallimard,

Bibliothèque de la Pléiade, 1954), III, 871–2.

22. (Geneva and Paris: Droz, 1957). Much of Czoniczer's discussion of the possible influence of the ideas of men such as Pierre Janet and Alfred Binet applies to Jarry too. See also the article by Catherine Stehlin based on an examination of Jarry's notebooks in which he recorded the lectures of his philosophy teacher at Henri IV, Henri Bergson: 'Jarry, le cours Bergson et la philosophie', in *Europe* (March-Apr. 1981), 34–51. Stehlin argues that Jarry adopts, but distorts in order to integrate them into his own thinking, a number of the ideas of Bergson.

23. *O.C.*, Pléiade, I, 768–9.
24. *Ibid.*, 793.
25. *Ibid.*, 794–5.
26. *Ibid.*, 795.
27. *Ibid.*, 794. Jarry is actually here confusing Leibniz with the nineteenth-century 'positivist' philosopher Hippolyte Taine in stating his view that 'la perception est une hallucination vraie'. In his preface to *De l'Intelligence* (1870), Taine stated his intention of regarding 'la perception extérieure ... comme une hallucination véridique' – a statement taken out of context and eagerly seized upon by certain of the Symbolists, who used it to develop and support their own solipsistic view of the 'subjective' nature of perception and of the consequent 'unreality' of the external world. Jarry's immediate source may well have been once again Gourmont, the hero of whose novel *Sixtine* (1890) declares

that: 'L'objet auquel je pense très fortement s'incorpore devant mes yeux en une forme visible .... J'ai senti des présences de personnes certainement bien loin de moi, selon le commun jugement, et cela ne m'étonne point, car *la sensation régulière n'est qu'une hallucination vraie.*' ['The object which I think about very intensely is embodied before my eyes in a visible form .... I have felt the presence of persons who were certainly far removed from me, according to the common judgment, and that in no way surprises me, for *normal sensation is only an hallucination which is true.*'] (Paris, Éditions du Mercure de France, 1918 edn, 66. My italics.) In his *Promenades philosophiques* a few years later (1905–9), Gourmont again refers to 'la sensation' as 'une hallucination vraie', attributing the view this time explicitly to Taine (Paris, Éditions du Mercure de France, 1963 edn, I, 84). It is equally possible, however, that Jarry developed some of the above ideas out of the teaching of Bergson, who in his lectures quoted Taine and at one point stated (though with a nuance that Jarry chose to ignore) that 'le souvenir d'une sensation passée, lorsqu'il est suffisamment précis, complet et isolé surtout, est encore une sensation. Les sensations dites imaginaires qu'on éprouve en rêve et même pendant la veille pour peu qu'on se laisse aller à sa fantaisie, en sont la preuve. Tout état de conscience passé ... imite la perception présente et devient en quelque sorte hallucinatoire.' ['the memory of a past sensation, when it is sufficiently clear, full and above all isolated, is still a sensation. The so-called imaginary sensations which one experiences in dreams, and even in the waking state if one but allows imagination to take over momentarily, are proof of this. Every past state of consciousness . . . imitates present perception and becomes, so to speak, hallucinatory.'] (Cited by Catherine Stehlin, 'Jarry, le cours Bergson et la philosophie', in *Europe* (March–Apr. 1981), 46.)

28. *O.C.*, Pléiade, I, 828.
29. See *Les Langages de Jarry*, part I, Ch. 2.
30. *O.C.*, Pléiade, I, 823, 825. The same fascination with drug-induced states of consciousness and their concomitant hallucinations and loss of sense of time can be seen in another work of the same period, the short five-act poetic drama *Le Vieux de la Montagne*. Written in March 1896 and originally published in the *Revue Blanche* of 1 May 1896, it was later incorporated by Jarry into *L'Amour en visites* where it forms Chapter X, 'Au Paradis ou le Vieux de la Montagne'. Its source is the medieval legend of the Old Man of the Mountains, inspired by the fanatical Islamic sect, founded in the eleventh century and encountered by the Crusaders, known as the 'Assassins' or 'Hashishins'.
31. *O.C.*, Pléiade, I, 761.
32. *Ibid.*, 749–50.
33. *Ibid.*, 835, 837.
34. *Ibid.*, 834. Jarry's italics. The passage reproduces both the imagery and phraseology of Chapter 4 of Book IV, 'Le Tain des mares'.

35. 'Lettres de Paul Fort', in *D.C.P.*, no. 22–4, 19–26.
36. *Sic.*: 'Lettres de Paul Fort', in *ibid.*, no. 22–4, p. 25, and *O.C.*, Pléiade, I, Notes, p. 1249.
37. The key idea of this dense (and frankly rather tedious) work, which relates it to *Le Vieux de la Montagne*, is the power of illusion. It is based on a passage from the Koran which relates the death of Solomon, who dies while supervising the work of reconstruction of a new palace. His body however remains upright for a full year, propped up on his stick, and the genies working under his command, believing him to be still alive and watching them, continue their labours. It is not difficult to see how Jarry conceived of the application of this idea to his own age.
38. According to Maurice Saillet, 'Relativement à *L'Amour absolu*', in *C.C.P.*, no. 8–9, 74.
39. *O.C.*, Pléiade, I, 854.
40. *Ibid.*, 862.
41. *The Banquet Years* (rev. edn, 1969), p. 197.
42. *O.C.*, Pléiade, I, 1075.
43. *Ibid.*, 920.
44. *Ibid.*, 924–5.
45. *Ibid.*, 951.
46. *Ibid.*, 921. Jarry's italics.
47. *Ibid.*, 950. Jarry's italics.
48. *Ibid.*, 920.
49. Jarry's interest in the work of contemporary psychologists has been studied in detail in the excellent article of Brunella Eruli, 'L'Immaculée Conception', in *L'Étoile-Absinthe*, no. 7–8 (1980), 49–60, and in the same author's *Jarry: i mostri dell'immagine* (Pisa: Pacini, 1982). The parallels between Jarry and Freud were discussed in 'Jarry er Freud', a paper read at the Jarry

Colloquium at Cerisy-la-Salle in Aug.-Sept. 1981 by Anne Clancier, who maintained that 'Jarry et Freud auraient tous deux, en même temps, en se référant aux mêmes sources, inventé la théorie psychanalytique' ('Jarry and Freud, it would seem, both invented simultaneously, inspired by the same sources, the theory of psychoanalysis'). Clancier also suggested, humorously, that Jarry had 'plagiarized Freud . . . by anticipation'!

50. *O.C.*, Pléiade, I, 919. Jarry's italics and capitals.
51. *Ibid.*, 922.
52. *Ibid.*, 281.
53. *Ibid.*, 923. Jarry's italics and capitals.
54. *Ibid.*, 922.
55. *Ibid.*, 923. Jarry's italics.
56. *Ibid.*, 929, 955.
57. A fascinating insight into the thematic interrelatedness of Jarry's work is provided by the occurrence of a cryptic reference to this customs officer's hut in *César-Antechrist* which seems to foreshadow *L'Amour absolu*: 'sert de repos, cahutte de douanier, au Dieu qui attend son heure' ['customs officer's hut, which serves as a place of rest for the God who is awaiting his appointed hour'] (*O.C.*, Pléiade, I, 292).
58. *O.C.*, Pléiade, I, 939.
59. *Ibid.*, 943.
60. The theme of murder is possibly obliquely suggested by Jarry's use of the word *meurtrière* in Chapter VIII; the word refers literally to the window or spyhole through which Emmanuel looks out from his customs officer's hut, but evokes also *meurtre* and *meurtrier*, thereby linking the themes of incestuous love and murder.
61. *O.C.*, Pléiade, I, 957. Jarry's italics and capitals.
62. *Ibid.*, 926–7. Jarry's italics.
63. *Ibid.*, 950, 949.
64. *Ibid.*, 926. Jarry's italics.
65. *Ibid.*, 928.
66. *Ibid.*, 922.
67. *Ibid.*, 958. Jarry's italics. The original lines, in the French version of the prayer, are: 'Priez pour nous pauvres pécheurs/Maintenant et à l'heure de notre mort.' ['Pray for us sinners now and at the hour of our death.']

CHAPTER SEVEN
FAUSTROLL AND
PATAPHYSICS

1. *O.C.*, Pléiade, I, 722.
2. Two – slightly differing – manuscript versions exist of *Gestes et opinions du docteur Faustroll, pataphysicien*. The first (subsequently given to Louis Lormel and generally known as the Lormel manuscript) was written in the spring of 1898 and was used as the basis for a partial publication in the pages of the *Mercure de France* in May 1898. It was on this manuscript that Jarry wrote the above note. The second version (known as the Fasquelle manuscript) includes the printed text from the *Mercure* supplemented by the remaining chapters which have been copied by hand by Jarry (though not including Chapter XXXIV, which was published separately in *La Plume* of 15 Nov. 1900 under the title 'Treize images' and dated 'November 1897'). This second version was probably produced towards the end of 1898 or early in 1899, a copy of it being sent

(presumably in the hope of publication by the Éditions de la Revue Blanche) to Thadée Natanson, who acknowledged its receipt in a letter to Jarry of 19 Jan. 1899 (reproduced in *O.C.*, Pléiade, I, 1217).

3. Cited in *C.C.P.*, no. 10, 11.

4. *O.C.*, Pléiade, I, 657.

5. An article by Sylvain-Christian David suggests that the title 'Éléments de pataphysique' may have been inspired by the *Elemente der Psychophysik* of the German philosopher, physicist and psychologist Gustav Theodor Fechner (1801–1887). Fechner, amongst other things an exceptionally lucid analyst of his own mind, was a major source of inspiration to the young Freud in the formulation of his theory of the Unconscious. It is certain that Jarry knew his work. See S.-C. David, 'Pataphysique et psychanalyse', in *Europe* (March-April 1981), 52–61.

6. *O.C.*, Pléiade, I, 658–9.

7. *Ibid.*, 661. Jarry's capitals.

8. *Ibid.*, 672. According to legend, it was the unfortunate Beck whom Jarry fired at with his revolver in the course of a dinner at the Taverne du Panthéon in 1897. Beck also went on to publish a number of novels under the pseudonym, curiously, of Joseph Bossi – a case of life imitating art?

9. In addition to these 27 'livres pairs', there are also 27 dedicatees of chapters of *Faustroll*. The reason for Jarry's choice of the number 27, according to Noël Arnaud and Henri Bordillon in their edition of *Faustroll* (Paris: Gallimard, Collection 'Poésie', 1980, 181), lies in the fact that the writings held by the Church to be canonical, and which make up the New Testament, also number 27. The claim implicitly being made by Jarry is that *Faustroll* constitutes a new 'Bible'!

10. A translation of Boys' work had appeared in France in 1892 as *Bulles de savon: quatre conférences sur la capillarité faites devant un jeune auditoire* (Paris: Gauthier-Villars). For this elucidation, as well as for many other details concerning Jarry's sources in *Faustroll*, I am deeply indebted to the excellent work done by the Collège de 'Pataphysique and published in its *Cahiers* and *Dossiers*, in particular the invaluable *Cahier Faustroll*, no. 22–3.

11. *O.C.*, Pléiade, I, 678.

12. *Ibid.*, 677–8.

13. *Ibid.*, 685.

14. *Ibid.*, 686.

15. *Ibid.*, 565.

16. *Ibid.*, 722. Jarry had a special fondness for the form of the spiral. It first figures in one of his sketches of Ubu, ornamenting the latter's *gidouille* or belly, before being transferred to Faustroll. He also uses it as a symbol of the workings of memory and of the 'time' of memory in his *Commentaire pour servir à la construction pratique de la machine à explorer le temps* of 1899. It has since been adopted by the Collège de 'Pataphysique as a symbol of *éthernité* and as the emblem of the Ordre de la Grande Gidouille.

17. The quotation is from Shattuck's introduction to *Selected Works of Alfred Jarry*, ed. R. Shattuck and Simon Watson Taylor (1965), 13.

18. Letter to Charles Chassé, cited in Chassé, *Sous le masque d'Alfred Jarry (?). Les Sources*

d'Ubu-Roi (Paris: Fleury, 1921), 35.

19.   *O.C.*, Pléiade, I, 182, and *Ubu Cocu*, Act II, Sc. 2. It is far from certain that, even at a later stage in his career, Jarry's use of the term 'pataphysics' is at all times consistent. A reference, in the publicity notice for his second *Almanach du Père Ubu* which he had published in the *Revue Blanche* of 1 Jan. 1901, to 'la "pataphysique" du personnage' (i.e. of Ubu), which is defined as 'son assurance à disserter *de omni re scibili*, tantôt avec compétence, aussi volontiers avec absurdité, mais dans ce dernier cas suivant une logique d'autant plus irréfutable que c'est celle du fou ou du gâteux' ['his self-confidence in holding forth *de omni re scibili*, sometimes in a competent, though just as readily in an absurd, manner, but in the latter case according to a logic which is all the more irrefutable in that it is the logic of the insane or the senile'] (*O.C.*, Pléiade, I, 1211), clearly indicates that Jarry is here using 'pataphysique' as a synonym for a simple tendency to spout nonsense.

20.   *O.C.*, Pléiade, I, 730. Also associated originally with Père Heb's pataphysics, and equally the subject of a schoolboy joke, were the *palotins* – originally the pupils of the Lycée de Rennes – who act as Ubu's henchmen. In the short text 'Visions actuelles et futures' of 1894, these creatures too are raised to philosophical 'significance': 'La Pataphysique est la science de ces êtres et engins actuels ou futurs avec le Pouvoir de leur Usage (*discipulus*) . . .' ['Pataphysics is the science of

these present and future beings and devices with the Power to Make Use of them (*discipulus*) . . .']. They are also described – significantly, in view of Jarry's concept of the relationship between the 'self' and 'reality' – as 'les seuls / Parfaits pour qui veut que sa *Volonté* s'érige loi souveraine' ['the only creatures / Perfect for he who wishes to erect his *Will* as sovereign law'] (*O.C.*, Pléiade, I, 341, 340. My italics in the latter case.)

21.   *O.C.*, Pléiade, I, 467.

22.   *La Revue des Deux Mondes*, 15 Oct. 1896, 880. Brunetière even goes on from this to proclaim the total inability of 'science' not only to guarantee the reality, but the very 'existence', of a world external to ourselves (*ibid.*, 882).

23.   A more sophisticated expression of this point of view was put forward by Bergson, following his separation of man's psychic functions into 'intuition' and 'intellect'. Intellect, Bergson argued, through its instrument of analysis, dissects, breaks up, 'spatializes' the raw material of experience into manageable 'quantities'; it is the instrument of science, by means of which it constructs its picture of reality in terms of quantitative numerical relationships.

24.   *Faustroll*, Bk II, ch. VIII, in *O.C.*, Pléiade, I, 668.

25.   *O.C.*, Pléiade, I, 669.

26.   *Ibid.*, 669.

27.   *Ibid.*, 795.

28.   *Ibid.*, 669.

29.   *Ibid.*, 670.

30.   Quoted by Bernard Gros, 'Des origines de la feuille de chou', in *C.C.P.*, no. 22–3, 52. Crookes' address was published in the *Revue*

scientifique, no. 20, tome VII, 609ff.

31. *O.C.*, Pléiade, I, 668–9. Jarry's italics. In the Lormel manuscript, the third sentence begins 'Et l'épiphénomène . . .'

32. *O.C.*, Pléiade, I, 722. Jarry's italics.

33. *The Banquet Years: The Arts in France, 1885–1918*, (rev. edn, 1969), 242.

34. Despite these borrowings, Jarry's 'scientific' data is not without its minor errors, mainly of mathematical calculation (though these might of course have been corrected in the event of a publication of *Faustroll* during his lifetime). Cf. Lutembi, 'De quelques mécomptes', *C.C.P.*, no. 22–3, 115.

35. *O.C.*, Pléiade, I, 726.

36. *Ibid.*, 669.

37. *Ibid.*, 731.

38. Jarry was fascinated by the imaginative profusion of these visions. He refers to her again in his lecture on 'Le Temps dans l'art', given at the Salon des Indépendants in 1901, where he speaks of an 'image étrange et assez belle que nous avons trouvée dans les révélations mystiques de Catherine Emmerich' ['strange and rather beautiful image which we found in the mystical revelations of Catherine Emmerich'] (*La Chandelle verte*, 564).

39. *O.C.*, Pléiade, I, 733, 734.

40. In a review of Rachilde's *La Princesse des Ténèbres*, 'Ce que c'est que les ténèbres, in *La Chandelle verte*, 296.

41. 'De quelques romans scientifiques', in *La Chandelle verte*, 320.

42. It has to be said that Jarry's viewpoint is far from being consistent in this respect – evidence perhaps of the extreme difficulty of upholding a 'pataphysical' viewpoint at all times. Many a passage in his 'journalistic' writings, and particularly in his work as a book reviewer, reveals his frank acceptance of the conclusions of modern science. Thus, to take just one example, he makes the following comment in reviewing a translation of a work by the German physicist and biologist Haeckel, entitled *État actuel de nos connaissances sur l'origine de l'homme*: 'La descendance de l'homme d'une série de primates tertiaires éteints n'est plus une vague hypothèse, mais bien un fait historique.' ['The descent of man from a series of now extinct Tertiary primates is no longer a vague hypothesis, but a firmly established historical fact.'] (*La Chandelle verte*, 539.)

CHAPTER EIGHT
THE ART OF 'SPECULATIVE' JOURNALISM

1. *O.C.*, Pléiade, I, 399.

2. Cited by Maurice Saillet, Introduction to *La Chandelle verte* (Paris: Livre de Poche, 1969), 7n.

3. Publicity notice for the second *Almanach* published in the *Revue Blanche*, 1 Jan. 1901; cited in *O.C.*, Pléiade, I, 1211.

4. This lengthy article – whose author was given, in the *Mercure*, as 'Dr Faustroll' – was inspired by H. G. Wells' *The Time Machine*, which had recently appeared in a French translation by Henry Davray. Where Wells was interested primarily in the uses to which

such a machine might be put, Jarry was fascinated by the *idea* of the machine. He was of course as aware as anyone of the inherent contradictions, not to say absurdities, of such a notion; but, far from wishing to expose such contradictions, he set out to play with them. Where in *Faustroll* his hero had undertaken to operate 'experimentally' upon the metaphors used by scientists, performing a physio-chemical analysis of the 'ether', here he sets about applying the same approach to the concepts of space and time, carrying to extreme lengths the customary confusion between the two concepts (the passage of 'time' being determined by such phenomena as the rotation of the earth or the movement through space of the earth around the sun, etc.). Thus Jarry (or Faustroll) is able to describe the movement of his machine through time as a movement through space. The final twist to the argument is equally characteristic, involving a return from physics to the sphere of psychology: the true 'machine à explorer le temps', we are told, is . . . memory.

5. According to André Salmon, 'Le Père Ubu en liberté', in *L'Ami du Lettré* (1924), 242, 248.

6. Cf. the plans published by Maurice Saillet as an appendix to his edition of *La Chandelle verte*, 680–5.

7. Cf. Jarry's postcard to Rachilde from Laval, 14 Aug. 1907, cited by Saillet in his Introduction to *La Chandelle verte*, 25. The title 'La Chandelle verte' re-establishes a link with the figure of Ubu, whose celebrated oath 'de par ma chandelle

verte!' is proferred no less than 14 times in *Ubu Roi*.

8. Cf. his letter to Rachilde of 7 Sept. 1907, cited by Saillet in *La Chandelle verte*, 26.

9. *Mercure de France*, 16 Nov. 1907, 374.

10. *La Chandelle verte*, 106.

11. 'Le Rire dans l'armée', in *Spéculations, ibid.*, 94.

12. 'Hommages posthumes', in *Spéculations, ibid.*, 127.

13. 'Les Sacrifices humains du 14 juillet', in *Spéculations, ibid.*, 107

14. In *Spéculations, ibid.*, 85.

15. 'L'Infaillible suffrage', in *Le Canard Sauvage, ibid.*, 347.

16. 'Le Métal conjugal', in *Le Périple de la littérature et de l'art, ibid.*, 333.

17. 'La Rentrée de la Chambre', in *Le Canard Sauvage, ibid.*, 385.

18. In *Le Journal d'Alfred Jarry, ibid.*, 245ff.

19. In *Le Canard Sauvage, ibid.*, 356ff.

20. *La Chandelle verte*, 222–3, 138.

21. 'La Mobilisation des touristes', in *Spéculations, ibid.*, 121.

22. 'Les Gardes civiques de Bruxelles', in *Spéculations, ibid.*, 90.

23. *La Chandelle verte*, 35.

24. 'Hanging', in *Gestes, ibid.*, 169.

25. 'Anthropophagie', in *Gestes, ibid.*, 175.

26. In *Spéculations, ibid.*, 59.

27. In *Spéculations, ibid.*, 99–100.

28. 'M. Faguet et l'alcoolisme', in *Spéculations, ibid.*, 46.

29. 'Le Cas de Madame Nation', in *Spéculations, ibid.*, 63.

30. 'Anthropophagie', in *Gestes, ibid.*, 174.

31. In *Spéculations, ibid.*, 112–13.

32. In *Gestes, ibid.*, 196–8.

33. In *Spéculations, ibid.*, 141–4.

34. In *Gestes, ibid.*, 190–1. The uniform described in paragraph one during the flag-saluting ceremony is of course the sky-blue tunic and crimson trousers of the French army before 1914.

35. This was the point of view argued by François Caradec in a paper on 'Jarry chroniqueur' given at the Jarry Colloquium at Cerisy-la-Salle in August-September 1981. Caradec maintained that Jarry's ambition was simply to be, in the jargon of the period, 'un auteur gai', a humorist, and saw a split within his creative writing between his 'literary' work on the one hand and his work as *chroniqueur* on the other.
36. Introduction to *La Chandelle verte*, 12.
37. In *Gestes, La Chandelle verte*, 166.
38. 'Les Moeurs des noyés', in *Gestes, ibid.*, 197.
39. 'Communication d'un militaire', in *Gestes, ibid.*, 203.
40. 'Battre les femmes', in *Gestes, ibid.*, 171.
41. 'La Mobilisation des touristes', in *Spéculations, ibid.*, 121.
42. 'Ceux pour qui il n'y eut point de Babel', in *Le Périple de la littérature et de l'art, ibid.*, 298–9.
43. 'Les Fusils transformés', in *Spéculations, ibid.*, 130.
44. In *Le Périple de la littérature et de l'art, ibid.*, 277. Jarry's italics.
45. 'L'Affaire Humbert-Dreyfus', in *Le Canard Sauvage, ibid.*, 329.
46. In *Gestes, ibid.*, 193–5. In two of his book reviews in the *Revue Blanche*, Jarry goes even further, hinting that the championing of 'le peuple pauvre' is as arbitrary as that of any other social class or cause (*La Chandelle verte*, 546), and suggesting that it is perhaps not 'bien urgent de faire de la littérature sur les pauvres, puisqu'il y en aura toujours' ['particularly urgent to write books about the poor, since they will always exist'] (*ibid.*, 672).

47. 'Le Tribunal de Dieu', *ibid.*, 380. Lest it be thought, however, that Jarry is arguing from a conventional conservative, anti-republican standpoint, it is worth noting that this satire on the principles of the Republic is counterbalanced by his interpretation, in the same article, of the term 'liberté religieuse' as 'liberté d'imposer aux petits enfants, quand ils n'ont point encore l'âge de raison, ses idées religieuses' ['freedom to impose upon small children, before they have reached the age of reason, one's own religious beliefs'] (*loc. cit.*).
48. 'Diagnostics', in *L'Oeil, ibid.*, 497.
49. 'De la douceur dans la violence', in *Le Journal d'Alfred Jarry, ibid.*, 256.
50. 'La Morale murale', in *Le Périple de la littérature et de l'art, ibid.*, 279.
51. 'De quelques viols légaux', in *Gestes, ibid.*, 206.
52. *La Chandelle verte*, 430–4.
53. 'Accidents de chemin de fer', in *Spéculations, ibid.*, 70.
54. 'Ceux pour qui il n'y eut point de Babel', in *Le Périple de la littérature et de l'art, ibid.*, 298.
55. 'L'Abbé Bruneau', in *Spéculations, ibid.*, 83.
56. 'L'Auto populaire', in *Le Canard Sauvage, ibid.*, 445–6.
57. 'Le Tueur de femmes', in *Gestes, ibid.*, 235; 'La Vérité bouffe', in *Le Périple de la littérature et de l'art, ibid.*, 303; 'L'Âme ouverte à l'art antique', in *Le Canard Sauvage, ibid.*, 427.
58. Cf. 'De quelques viols légaux', in *Gestes, ibid.*, 204.
59. 'Barnum', *ibid.*, 150.
60. In *Spéculations, ibid.*, 134.
61. In *La Chandelle verte*, 204–5.
62. In *Gestes, ibid.*, 236–7. Cf. also 'Hommages posthumes', in

Spéculations, ibid., 125–8, and 'De la douceur dans la violence', in *Le Journal d'Alfred Jarry, ibid.*, 251–7.

63. 'Livres d'enfants', in *Le Périple de la littérature et de l'art, ibid.*, 310–11. Jarry's italics.

64. Cf. 'Ce que c'est que les ténèbres', in *Le Périple de la littérature et de l'art, ibid.*, 296.

65. 'Livres d'étrennes: Le Calendrier du facteur', in *Le Périple de la littérature et de l'art, ibid.*, 267–8. My italics.

CHAPTER NINE
SEXUAL AND SPORTING
FEATS

1. *La Chandelle verte*, 169–73, 158–60 and 162–3 respectively.

2. Review of 15 Feb. 1901, in *La Chandelle verte*, 578. My italics.

3. *O.C.*, Pléiade, I, 409. Jarry's italics.

4. *La Chandelle verte*, 663.

5. A *Spéculation* of 15 Apr. 1901 refers to a recent exhibition of paintings on the subject of Messalina (*La Chandelle verte*, 71), and a review of 15 Apr. 1902 of the ninth 'Exposition de la Libre Esthétique' in Brussels singles out a painting of Messalina by Toulouse-Lautrec (*ibid.*, 621).

6. *Ibid.*, 317–19.

7. Cf. also his comments on Péladan's *Modestie et Vanité*, in *La Chandelle verte*, 661, and his haughty remark in the programme notes for *Ubu Roi*: 'Nous ne trouvons pas honorable de construire des pièces historiques.' ['We do not consider it honourable to write historical plays.'] This contempt for 'history' is, as we have seen, a trait which Jarry shares with the whole Symbolist generation.

8. *La Chandelle verte*, 561.

9. He also puts forward an argument which admits of no reply: whatever the circumstances, the artist of 'genius' is always right – 'du moment que le peintre a du génie, c'est le peintre qui a raison'! (*ibid.*, 563).

10. *Ibid.*, 598.

11. Cf. *C.C.P.*, no. 10, 126.

12. *La Chandelle verte*, 566.

13. Details concerning Jarry's sources and the use which he makes of them can be found in Thieri Foulc's notes to his edition of *Messaline* (Paris: Eric Losfeld, 1977), and in the article by Brunella Eruli, 'Sur les sources classiques de *Messaline*: collages et montages', in *L'Étoile-Absinthe*, no. 1–2 (May 1979), 65–83.

14. *Messaline* (Paris: Eric Losfeld, 1977), 45.

15. *Ibid.*, 54.

16. *Ibid.*, 121.

17. *Ibid.*, 143.

18. *Ibid.*, 40. My italics in last line.

19. *Ibid.*, 124, 38.

20. *Ibid.*, 35–6.

21. *Ibid.*

22. *Messaline*, 36.

23. *Ibid.*, 37–41.

24. *Ibid.*, 54–5.

25. *Ibid.*, 54.

26. *Ibid.*, 36, 70, 83. Jarrys italics.

27. *Ibid.*, 161.

28. *Ibid.*, 37, 39.

29. *Ibid.*, 68.

30. *Ibid.*, 65. My italics.

31. *Ibid.*, 91, 92.

32. *Le Surmâle*, ed. Thieri Foulc, (Paris: Eric Losfeld, 1977), 60–1.

33. *Messaline*, 107. Jarry's italics and capitals.

34. *Ibid.*, 103–7. Jarry's italics. The word *cubiste* used by Jarry refers to a Greek dance which involved acrobatic movements.

35. *O.C.*, Pléiade, I, 339 and, with minor but insignificant variations, 289.

36. See Brunella Eruli, 'D'une *Messaline* à l'autre', in *Europe*, March-Apr. 1981, 113–20.

37. *La Chandelle verte*, 155, 296, 598.

38. *Ibid.*, 321. My italics.

39. *Ibid.*, 271–2, 328.

40. *O.C.*, Pléiade, I, 818–19.

41. *La Chandelle verte*, 284.

42. Interview with Mme Gabrielle Fort-Vallette in *Le Magazine Littéraire*, no. 48 (Jan. 1971), 13.

43. For further details concerning Jarry's sources for this episode of *Le Surmâle*, as well as for a fascinating account of contemporary cycling races, see Paul Gayot, 'L'Odyssée et l'histoire', *Subsidia Pataphysica*, no. 19, 19–47. Almost every detail of Jarry's narrative (which includes an abundance of technical details) has its counterpart in reality – though the use to which he puts this material remains, of course, peculiarly his own.

44. *Messaline*, 38.

45. *Le Surmâle*, 47.

46. *Messaline*, 38.

47. *Le Surmâle*, 21, 24.

48. *Ibid.*, 32.

49. *Ibid.*, 51.

50. *Ibid.*, 37.

51. *Ibid.*, 23.

52. *Ibid.*, 42.

53. *Ibid.*, 76.

54. *Ibid.*, 83, 88, 87, 88 respectively.

55. *Ibid.*, 134.

56. *Ibid.*, 143.

57. *Ibid.*, 146. Jarry's capitals.

58. *Ibid.*, 148.

59. *Ibid.*, 147.

60. *Ibid.*, 36.

61. *Ibid.*, 49. My italics.

62. *Ibid.*, 113, 143.

63. *Ibid.*, 131.

64. *Ibid.*, 24.

65. *Ibid.*, 140.

66. *Ibid.*, 111–15.

67. *Ibid.*, 134–5.

68. *Ibid.*, 141.

69. *Ibid.*, 126.

70. *Ibid.*, 42. Jarry's italics.

71. It is probable that the names of some, if not all, of the characters of *Le Surmâle* have some hidden significance also, as so often happens in Jarry's work. Senator Saint-Jurieu derives from 'injurieux', while the name of his wife, the Baroness Pusice-Euprépie de Saint-Jurieu, is a spoonerism based on the obscene combination 'pisseux prépuce'. Bathybius derives from the Greek *bathos* (deep) and *bios* (life) – appropriate for a physiologist. As for the names of the five-man cycling team, Oxborrow was actually the name of an English professional cyclist, while the names of 'Corporal' Gilbey and Sammy White (a negro, whence 'Black and White') are intended to evoke popular brands of gin and whisky respectively. For a more detailed discussion of the origin and significance of names in *Le Surmâle*, see Paul Gayot, 'L'Odyssée et l'histoire', in *Subsidia Pataphysica*, no. 19, 19–47, and especially the article 'Fictions et moutures', *Subsidia Pataphysica*, no. 20–1, 77–81.

72. Rachilde, *Alfred Jarry ou le Surmâle des Lettres* (Paris: Grasset, 1928), 16, 139–40. Rachilde also liked to refer to Jarry as 'l'homme des bois', no doubt stressing his primitive savagery, as she saw it. The term is used by Jarry in a chapter of *Les Jours et les Nuits*.

73. Photograph reproduced in *C.C.P.*, no. 5–6, 69.

74. *Le Surmâle*, 67.

75. *Ibid.*, 108. It is difficult, in view of the context, to know how 'seriously' Jarry himself takes such ideas. In his review of Danville's *La Psychologie de l'amour*, he refers to his own use (obviously in this place in *Le Surmâle*) of the hypothesis of Delbeuf, according to which 'un homme et une femme seraient irrésistiblement jetés l'un vers l'autre par la volonté inconsciente d'un spermatozoaire et d'un ovule' ('a man and a woman are irresistibly thrown towards each other by the unconscious will of a spermatozoon and an ovum') (*La Chandelle verte*, 663). The hypothesis is rejected by Danville, and Jarry's own view here concerning it is unclear, although one can certainly understand his attraction, for both philosophical and personal reasons, to a theory which views 'love' as simply an unconscious and irresistible physiological attraction, everything else being purely 'imaginary'.
76. *Le Surmâle*, 120.
77. For further details of these references, cf. the article 'Des Sources, des Résurgences et des Filtres', *Subsidia Pataphysica*, no. 20–1, 61–72.
78. *Le Surmâle* contains another curious example of this 'imitation': Jarry's association of the themes of love and death through, firstly, the extraordinarily banal terms of the song reproduced by the phonograph (which itself offers an example of 'repetition'), and then in the farcical episode of Ellen's 'love-death', constitutes a case of parody of one of his *own* favourite ideas.
79. *Le Surmâle*, 63.
80. *O.C.*, Pléiade, I, 423.
81. *Le Surmâle*, 83.
82. *Ibid.*, 134.

Chapter Ten
Musical Comedies and
Return to the Past

1. 'Alfred Jarry ou le Père Ubu en liberté', in *L'Ami du Lettré* (1924), 256.
2. Letter of 27 Oct. 1903, in *O.C.*, Éditions du Livre, VII, 305.
3. The term 'mirlitonesque', which recalls the *mirliton* (reed pipe, or kazoo) presented by Ubu to King Wenceslas in *Ubu Roi*, is used to designate a form of popular verse or music which is trivial and facile, or inharmonious, a form of which Jarry asked in his *Conférence sur les pantins* of 1902: 'Et les vers voulus "*mirlitonesques*" ne sont-ils pas l'expression à dessein enfantine et simplifiée de l'absolu, sagesse des nations?' ['As for that verse intended to be "*mirlitonesque*", is it not the expression, deliberately childish and simplified, of popular wisdom?'] (In *Tout Ubu*, ed. M. Saillet, Paris: Livre de Poche, 1962, 496. Jarry's italics.).
4. Letter of 16 July 1906, quoted in *C.C.P.*, no. 10, 152.
5. Figure given by Noël Arnaud, 'Jarry et le mirliton', in *Europe*, March–April 1981, 62–80. Arnaud's excellent article contains a much fuller discussion of this and related questions.
6. 'Délires II: Alchimie du verbe', in *Oeuvres* (Paris: Garnier, 1960), 228. (Quoted by Noël Arnaud in 'Jarry et le mirliton',

in *Europe*, March-April 1981, 65.)

7. In *C.C.P.*, no. 10, 133.
8. According to Franc-Nohain, 'Pantagruel au Café Brosse', in *Comoedia*, 29 Jan. 1911.
9. Letter of 29 Apr. 1904, quoted in *D.C.P.*, no. 27, 52.
10. 'Les Contemporains pittoresques: Feu Alfred Jarry', in *Les Marges*, Nov. 1909, 851.
11. According to J.-H. Sainmont, in *C.C.P.*, no. 10, 122.
12. *Alfred Jarry ou le Surmâle des Lettres* (Paris: Grasset, 1928).
13. Letter of 25 May 1906 (incorrectly dated 8 May by Saltas), in *O.C.*, Éditions du Livre, VII, 280–1. On the dating of Jarry's letters to Saltas, see *C.C.P.*, no. 10, 150–1.
14. Letter of 8 June 1906, reproduced in *C.C.P.*, no. 26–7, 83–4. Cf. also Jarry's letters to Saltas of 19 May, 28 May and 19 June 1906, in *O.C.* Éditions du Livre, VII, 282–92.
15. Rachilde, *op. cit.*, 136.
16. Passage from Jarry's *dossier* of notes for *La Dragonne*, reproduced in *D.C.P.*, no. 27, 48–50. For the probable date of this passage, see *ibid.*, 14n.
17. Letter to Saltas, n.d., in *O.C.*, Éditions du Livre, VII, 294.
18. Letter to Saltas, n.d., *ibid.*, 295.
19. By an irony of fate, Jarry's and Saltas' translation has recently been republished without any mention on the cover not only of Saltas but even of the author. The book presents itself as '*La Papesse Jeanne*, par Alfred Jarry', ed. M. Voline (Paris: Éditions Neo, 1981).
20. Letter of 8 June 1906, reproduced in *C.C.P.*, no. 26–7, 83–4.
21. Fragments from it are reproduced in *D.C.P.*, no. 27, 48–50.

22. 28 Feb. 1903, in *O.C.*, Éditions du Livre, VII, 304.
23. *O.C.*, Éditions du Livre, V, 94. The text of the *Revue Blanche*, reprinted in *D.C.P.*, no. 27, 70–100, is here identical.
24. Cf. Plan of 27 May 1906 and Jarry's 'Plan de travail' of 1905–6, reproduced in *D.C.P.*, 27, 11–19 and 20–1 respectively.
25. Plan of 27 May 1906, reproduced in *D.C.P.*, no. 27, 15.
26. *O.C.*, Éditions du Livre, V, 128; *D.C.P.*, no. 27, 99–100.
27. *O.C.*, Éditions du Livre, V, 112–15; *D.C.P.*, no. 27, 89–91. The text of the *Revue Blanche* contains only one minor and insignificant variant.
28. *O.C.*, Éditions du Livre, V, 113–14; *D.C.P.*, no. 27, 89–90. The references to 'le seul Autre Monde' and to man having '"battu le record" de Dieu' are additions to the text of the *Revue Blanche*.
29. In *D.C.P.*, no. 27, 39n.
30. *O.C.*, Éditions du Livre, V, 51 and 48. Erbrand's father is a curious example of imaginative fusion, of Jarry's maternal grandfather, who was a *juge de paix* as well as teaching at Saint-Brieuc, and of one of his teachers at the Lycée de Rennes, a 'professeur de Morale, Législation et Économie Politique' named . . . Jarry. (cf. *C.C.P.*, no. 20, 32, and *D.C.P.*, no. 27, 7, n. 5). It is also probable that the description of the house of Erbrand's maternal grandfather, General de l'Ermelinaye, at Pell-Bras owes a good deal to that of Jarry's maternal grandfather.
31. *O.C.*, Éditions du Livre, V, 50.
32. Cf. *ibid.*, V, 49, 110.
33. Cf. Jarry's plans in *D.C.P.*, no. 27, 16, 21.

34. Letter of 15 May, quoted in *C.C.P.*, no. 26–7, 81.
35. *Sic.* Quoted in *D.C.P.*, no. 27, 18. The reading 'indique' is not completely certain.
36. Cf. the draft of an extraordinary letter to Rachilde, dictated to Charlotte but never sent, reproduced in *D.C.P.*, no. 27, 111–13.
37. Quoted by Rachilde in *Alfred Jarry ou le Surmâle des Lettres*, 220–3. Jarry plays upon the word *régime*: it means also the speed at which an engine operates – whence the reference to his heart-rate.
38. Letter quoted in *D.C.P.*, no. 27, 109. Telegram quoted in *C.C.P.*, no. 10, 150.
39. Quoted in *C.C.P.*, no. 26–7, 83.
40. Cf. plans in *D.C.P.*, no. 27, 113.
41. *O.C.*, Éditions du Livre, V, 129.
42. *Ibid.*, V, 136.
43. It was once assumed by Jarry scholars that he had simply invented a spurious noble ancestry, claiming descent through his mother from the dukes of Dorset. The researches of Noël Arnaud suggest that this belief, whatever its foundations, was widely held in his mother's family. Cf. *Alfred Jarry d'Ubu Roi au docteur Faustroll* (Paris: La Table Ronde, 1974), 286–96.
44. Letter of 5 May 1907, quoted in *D.C.P.*, no. 27, 43.
45. Quoted in *D.C.P.*, no. 27, 113. Jarry's underlining.
46. In his Preface to *La Chandelle verte* (Paris: Livre de Poche, 1969), 11.
47. *Le Surmâle* (Paris: Eric Losfeld, 1977), 62. Jarry's italics.
48. Quoted by Rachilde in *Alfred Jarry ou le Surmâle des Lettres*, 223. Jarry's italics. The passage from 'La Bataille de Morsang' is

to be found in *O.C.*, Éditions du Livre, V, 113–14.
49. Quoted in *D.C.P.*, no. 27, 42.
50. In his *Petits Mémoires du temps de la Ligue* (1912), quoted by J.-H. Sainmont in *D.C.P.*, no. 27, 42, n. 4.
51. Cf. *O.C.*, Éditions du Livre, V, 134–5, and *D.C.P.*, no. 27, 42–3.
52. Letter of June 1907, quoted in *D.C.P.*, no. 27, 110.
53. Cf. *D.C.P.*, no. 27, 25 and 65, and Jarry's correspondence in *O.C.*, Éditions du Livre, VII, 278–316.
54. Cf. for example his letter to Saltas, n.d., *ibid.*, VII, 295–6.
55. Letter of Jarry, quoted in *D.C.P.*, no. 27, 64.
56. Letter of 8 June 1906, reproduced in *C.C.P.*, no. 26–7, 83.
57. Letter of 1907 published in *Les Marges*, 12 Jan. 1922; quoted in *C.C.P.*, no. 10, 153.
58. In *O.C.*, Éditions du Livre, VII, 316.
59. According to Rachilde, *op. cit.*, 217.
60. According to Rachilde, *loc. cit.*
61. Preface to *Ubu Roi* (Paris: Fasquelle, n.d.), 14. Saltas' version of events has been disputed: it has been claimed that Jarry, whose speech was presumably becoming slurred, requested not *un cure-dents* but *un cureton* (a slang expression for a priest, or *curé*). Though plausible, such a view must remain forever purely speculative.
62. Paul Léautaud, *Journal littéraire*, II (Paris: Mercure de France, 1955), 75.
63. Dr Stéphen-Chauvet, 'Les Derniers jours d'Alfred Jarry', in *Le Mercure de France*, 242 (15 Feb. 1933), 77–86. According to Dr Stéphen-Chauvet's account of the progress of the disease,

Jarry's apparent equanimity may have been at least as much the result of its impact upon his brain cells as of a conscious philosophy.

64. 'Les Contemporains pittoresques: Feu Alfred Jarry', in *Les Marges*, Nov. 1909, 855–6.

CHAPTER ELEVEN
LANGUAGE, TRUTH AND MEANING

1. 'Le Groupement littéraire qu'abritait le "Mercure de France"', in *Mercure de France*, vol. 298, no. 1,000 (1 July 1940 – 1 Dec. 1946), 168–9.
2. *Mercure de France*, 16 Nov. 1907, 373–4.
3. 'Les Contemporains pittoresques: Feu Alfred Jarry', in *Les Marges*, Nov. 1909, 854.
4. *Anthologie de l'humour noir* (Paris: Gallimard, 1941).
5. *La Chandelle verte*, ed. M. Saillet (Paris: Livre de Poche, 1969), 630.
6. *O.C.*, Éditions du Livre, V, 122.
7. Letter to Rachilde of 28 May 1906, quoted in *Alfred Jarry ou le Surmâle des Lettres* (Paris: Grasset, 1928), 220–1, and letters to Saltas, n.d., in *O.C.*, Éditions du Livre, VII, 288, 285.
8. *The Symbolist Aesthetic in France, 1885–1895* (2nd edn, 1968), 114.
9. *O.C.*, Pléiade, I, 330.
10. *Ibid.*, I, 329.
11. Quoted by J.-H. Sainmont, in *D.C.P.*, no. 8, 27.
12. *O.C.*, Pléiade, I, 276. My italics.
13. *Ibid.*, 949, 951.
14. In *La Chandelle verte*, 313.
15. *Ibid.*, 566.
16. Letter to Louise Colet, Jan. 1852. In *Correspondance*, II (Paris: Gallimard, Bibliothèque de la Pléiade, 1980, 51.
17. 'Crise de vers', in *Variations sur un sujet. Oeuvres Complètes* (Paris: Gallimard, Bibliothèque de la Pléiade, 1945), 366.
18. *La Crise des valeurs symbolistes. 20 ans de poésie française, 1895–1914* (Toulouse: Éditions Privat, 1960), 254.
19. *O.C.*, Pléiade, I, 292.
20. 'L'Aiguillage du chameau', in *Gestes, La Chandelle verte*, 230.
21. 'De *Messaline* au Tsar de toutes les Russies', in *L'Étoile-Absinthe*, no. 1–2, 56.
22. *O.C.*, Pléiade, I, 214. My italics.
23. Cf. the article by Brunella Eruli, 'Sur les sources classiques de *Messaline*: collages et montages', in *L'Étoile-Absinthe*, No. 1–2, pp. 65–83. A similar point was made by Patrick Besnier in a paper entitled 'Point de Babel' read at the Jarry Colloquium at Cerisy-la-Salle in August–September 1981: '*Messaline* et *Le Surmâle* sont d'abord – et peut-être seulement – de méticuleux exercises de traduction: à bien des égards le prodigieux édifice de *Messaline* est un gigantesque montage de textes anciens; et les conversations aux premier et troisième chapitres du *Surmâle* sont un concours de traduction.' ['*Messaline* and *Le Surmâle* are first and foremost – and perhaps simply – meticulous exercises in translation: in many respects the prodigious edifice constituted by *Messaline* is a gigantic *montage* of classical texts; and the conversations in the first and third chapters of *Le Surmâle* constitute a competition in translation.']
24. In *Le Périple de la littérature et de l'art, La Chandelle verte*, 262.
25. In *ibid.*, *La Chandelle verte*, 285. Jarry's italics.

26. *La Chandelle verte*, 549–50.
27. 'Ceux pour qui il n'y eut point de Babel', in *Le Périple de la littérature et de l'art, La Chandelle verte*, 301.
28. *O.C.*, Éditions du Livre, V, 130.
29. 'Ceux pour qui il n'y eut point de Babel', *La Chandelle verte*, 298.
30. *O.C.*, Éditions du Livre, V, 130.
31. I am indebted to the above-mentioned paper by M. Patrick Besnier, 'Point de Babel', for a number of ideas expressed in this paragraph.

Appendix:

10 December 1896
: Performance of *Ubu Roi* by the Théâtre de l'Oeuvre at the Nouveau Théâtre, Paris. Directed by Aurélien Lugné-Poe (assisted by Jarry). Sets by Sérusier, Bonnard, Vuillard, Toulouse-Lautrec, etc. Music by Claude Terrasse. With Firmin Gémier as Père Ubu and Louise France as Mère Ubu.

10 November 1901
: Marionette performance of *Ubu sur la Butte* by the Guignol des Gueules de Bois at the Théâtre des Quatz'arts, Montmartre. Directed by M. Trombert.

22 September 1937
: Performance of *Ubu Enchaîné* by the Compagnie Le Diable Écarlate at the Comédie des Champs-Élysées, Paris. Directed by Sylvain Itkine. Sets by Max Ernst. With Jean Temerson as Père Ubu and Gabrielle Fontan as Mère Ubu.

21 May 1946
: Performance of *Ubu Cocu* at the Chambre de Commerce in Reims. Directed by Emmanuel Peillet. With Pierre Minet as Père Ubu.

August 1952
: First American performance of *Ubu Roi* by the Living Theater of Julian Beck and Judith Malina at the Cherry Lane Theater, New York. With Mungi Moskowitz as Père Ubu. (The translation used appears to have been an unpublished version by the directors, Beck and Malina.)

29 December 1952
: First stage performance in England of *Ubu Roi* (in the translation by Barbara Wright) at the Irving Theatre, London. Directed by William Jay. With Anthony Twite as Père Ubu and Jean Thorp as Mère Ubu. (This performance was preceded by a dramatic reading of the play, also in Barbara Wright's translation, at the Institute of Contemporary Arts, London, on 18 February 1952. Direction was also by William Jay. Père

Ubu was played/read by Harold Lang and Mère Ubu by Selma Vas Diaz.
The actors/readers wore masks designed by Franciszka Themerson.)

17 (? or 19) August 1963

Performance of *Ubu Roi* at the Traverse Theatre Club, Edinburgh, as part
of the 1963 Edinburgh Festival. Directed by Terry Lane. With Ian Trigger
as Père Ubu and Rosamund Dickson as Mère Ubu. (The production
continued to run for some time, and with great success, at the Traverse
Theatre Club.)

21 July 1966

Performance of *Ubu Roi* by the English Stage Company at the Royal
Court Theatre, London. Translated, adapted and directed by Iain
Cuthbertson. Designed by David Hockney. Music (for two pianos) by
Frank Spedding. Lighting by Robert Ornbo. With Max Wall as Père Ubu
and John Shepherd as Mère Ubu. (Though not the first performance in
England or the UK, it seems to have been this which chiefly established
the play on the path to fame in that country.)

Bibliography

WORKS BY ALFRED JARRY

[Place of publication is Paris unless otherwise indicated]

1. *Collective editions*

Oeuvres Complètes, ed. R. Massat. Monte Carlo: Éditions du Livre and
    Lausanne: Henri Kaeser, 8 vols., 1948. [A chaotic and generally rather
    faulty edition.]
Oeuvres Complètes, ed. Michel Arrivé. Gallimard, Bibliothèque de la Pléiade, I,
    1972. [Vol. II is in preparation.]
Tout Ubu, ed. Maurice Saillet. Livre de Poche, 1962.
Ubu, ed. Noël Arnaud and Henri Bordillon. Gallimard, Collection Folio, 1978.
    [The best edition of the *Ubu* plays in French.]

2. *Individual works*

Les Minutes de sable mémorial. Mercure de France, 1894.
César-Antechrist. Mercure de France, 1895.
Ubu Roi. Mercure de France, 1896.
Les Jours et les Nuits, roman d'un déserteur. Mercure de France, 1897.
L'Amour en visites. Pierre Fort, 1898.
Almanach du Père Ubu, illustré. Private publication, 1899.
L'Amour absolu. Mercure de France, 1899.
Ubu Enchaîné [with *Ubu Roi*]. Éditions de la Revue Blanche, 1900.
Almanach illustré du Père Ubu (XXe siècle). Ambroise Vollard, 1901.
Messaline, roman de l'ancienne Rome. Éditions de la Revue Blanche, 1901.
Le Surmâle, roman moderne. Éditions de la Revue Blanche, 1902.
Par la taille. Sansot, 1906.
Ubu sur la Butte. Sansot, 1906.
Albert Samain. Souvenirs. Victor Lemasle, 1907.
Le Moutardier du Pape. Private subscription edition, 1907.

3. *Posthumously published works*

Pantagruel [in collaboration with Eugène Demolder, music by Claude
    Terrasse]. Société d'éditions musicales, 1910 [libretto and score], 1911
    [libretto only].

Gestes et opinions du docteur Faustroll, pataphysicien, suivi de *Spéculations.*
　　Fasquelle, 1911.
Gestes, suivis des *Paralipomènes d'Ubu.* Éditions du Sagittaire, 1921.
La Dragonne. Gallimard, 1943.
Ubu Cocu. Geneva: Éditions des Trois Collines, 1944.
La Revanche de la Nuit, poèmes retrouvés, ed. M. Saillet. Mercure de France,
　　1949.
Commentaire pour servir à la construction pratique de la machine à explorer le temps.
　　Collège de 'Pataphysique, 1950.
Visions actuelles et futures. Collège de 'Pataphysique, 1950.
Autour d'Ubu. Collège de 'Pataphysique, 1951.
Les Alcoolisés. Collège de 'Pataphysique, 1952.
Les Nouveaux timbres. Collège de 'Pataphysique, 1952.
L'Objet aimé, ed. R. Shattuck. Éditions Arcanes, 1953.
L'Ouverture de la pêche. Collège de 'Pataphysique, 1953.
Le Futur malgré lui. Collège de 'Pataphysique, 1954.
Tatane. Collège de 'Pataphysique, 1954.
Soleil de Printemps [with drawings by Pierre Bonnard]. Collège de
　　'Pataphysique, 1957.
Être et Vivre. Collège de 'Pataphysique, 1958.
Le Temps dans l'art. Collège de 'Pataphysique, 1958.
Album de l'Antlium. Collège de 'Pataphysique, 1964.
Les Antliaclastes (2e version). Collège de 'Pataphysique, 1964.
Saint-Brieuc des Choux, ed. M. Saillet. Mercure de France, 1964.
Peintures, gravures et dessins d'Alfred Jarry, ed. Michel Arrivé. Collège de
　　'Pataphysique and Le Cercle français du livre, 1968.
La Chandelle verte, lumières sur les choses de ce temps, ed. M. Saillet. Le Livre de
　　Poche, 1969.
Réponses à des enquêtes. Collège de 'Pataphysique, 1970.
Le Manoir enchanté et quatre autres oeuvres inédites, ed. N. Arnaud. La Table
　　Ronde, 1974.
Correspondance avec Félix Fénéon. Société des Amis d'Alfred Jarry, 1980.
Léda, ed. N. Arnaud and H. Bordillon. Christian Bourgois, 1981.

4. *Other editions cited*

Messaline, roman de l'ancienne Rome, ed. Thieri Foulc. Eric Losfeld, 1977.
Le Surmâle, roman moderne, ed. Thieri Foulc. Eric Losfeld, 1977.

5. *Translations by Jarry*

La Papesse Jeanne d'Emmanuel Rhoïdès, traduit du grec moderne par Alfred Jarry
　　avec la collaboration de Jean Saltas. Fasquelle, 1908.
La Ballade du Vieux marin, d'après S. T. Coleridge. Ronald Davis, 1921.
Les Silènes, d'après C. D. Grabbe. Les Bibliophiles créoles, 1927.
Olalla de R. L. Stevenson. Collège de 'Pataphysique, 1958.

WORKS TRANSLATED INTO ENGLISH

Selected Works of Alfred Jarry, ed. Roger Shattuck and Simon Watson Taylor.
　　London: Methuen, 1965, paperback edition 1980. [Contains complete

texts of *Ubu Cocu*, trans. Cyril Connolly with original drawings by Siné,
of Jarry's writings on the theatre, and of *Gestes et opinions du docteur
Faustroll, pataphysicien*; a selection of his poems and essays and *chroniques*;
and excerpts from the *Almanachs du Père Ubu, Les Jours et les Nuits* [trans.
Days and Nights] and *Messaline*, together with a Portfolio of Illustrations.]

The Garden of Priapus [*Messaline*], trans. Louis Colman. New York: Black Hawk
Press, 1936.

The Supermale, trans. Barbara Wright and Ralph Gladstone. London: Jonathan
Cape, 1968; republ. Norfolk, Conn.: New Directions, 1977.

The Ubu Plays, ed. Simon Watson Taylor. London: Methuen, 1968. [Contains
Ubu Rex, trans. Cyril Connolly and Simon Watson Taylor; *Ubu Cuckolded*,
trans. Cyril Connolly; and *Ubu Enchained*, trans. Simon Watson Taylor.]

Ubu Rex, trans. David Copelin. Vancouver: Pulp Press, 1973.

Ubu Roi, trans. Barbara Wright, illus. Franciszka Themerson. London:
Gaberbocchus Press, 1951; 2nd edn 1961, 3rd edn 1966.

PRINCIPAL CRITICAL AND BIOGRAPHICAL WORKS DEVOTED TO JARRY

[The most useful of these are briefly indicated.]

Arnaud, Noël, *Alfred Jarry d'Ubu Roi au Docteur Faustroll*. Paris: La Table
Ronde, 1974. [Vol. one of a massive biography of Jarry. Chaotic, but
contains a mine of valuable information. The second and final volume is
in preparation.]

Arrivé, Michel, *Les Langages de Jarry. Essai de sémiotique littéraire*. Paris:
Klincksieck, 1972. [A brilliant semiological study, though limited in
scope.]

Arrivé, Michel, *Lire Jarry*. Paris: Presses Universitaires de France, 1976. [A
collection of articles along the same lines as the previous volume.]

Béhar, Henri, *Jarry: le monstre et la marionnette*. Paris: Larousse, 1973.

Béhar, Henri, *Jarry dramaturge*. Paris: Nizet, 1980. [A re-issue of the previous
volume with the addition of a long final chapter. A very detailed and
solid study of Jarry's theatre.]

Besnier, Patrick, *Les Bretagnes d'Alfred Jarry*. Rennes: Maison de la Culture de
Rennes, 1980.

Caradec, François, *A la recherche d'Alfred Jarry*. Paris: Seghers, 1974.

Chassé, Charles, *Sous le masque d'Alfred Jarry (?). Les Sources d'Ubu-Roi*. Paris:
H. Floury, 1921.

Chassé, Charles, *Dans les coulisses de la gloire: d'Ubu-Roi au douanier Rousseau*.
Paris: Éditions de la Nouvelle Revue Critique, 1947. [A re-issue of the
previous volume with the addition of new material. A misguided
denunciation of Jarry's authorship of the *Ubu* plays, though containing
valuable material on their genesis.]

Chauveau, Paul, *Alfred Jarry, ou la naissance, la vie et la mort du Père Ubu*. Paris:
Mercure de France, 1932.

Cooper, Judith, *Ubu Roi: An Analytical Study*. Tulane Studies in Romance
Languages and Literature, no. 6, 1974. [Detailed but very pedestrian
study of the play.]

Eruli, Brunella, *Jarry: i mostri dell'immagine*. Pisa: Pacini, 1982. [A useful study
of a number of key themes in Jarry's work.]

Europe, March-April 1981. Paris. [Special issue of 347 pp. devoted mostly to Jarry, containing a number of valuable articles.]

Giedion-Welcker, Carola, *Alfred Jarry, eine Monographie*. Zurich: Die Arche, 1960.

LaBelle, Maurice Marc, *Alfred Jarry. Nihilism and the Theatre of the Absurd*. New York/London: New York U.P., 1980.

Lebois, André, *Alfred Jarry l'irremplaçable*. Paris: Le Cercle du Livre, 1950.

Lévesque, Jacques-Henry, *Alfred Jarry*. Paris: Seghers, 1951.

Lot, Fernand, *Alfred Jarry. Son Oeuvre*. Paris: Éditions de la Nouvelle Revue Critique, 1934.

Le Magazine Littéraire, no. 48, Jan. 1971. Paris. [Special issue devoted mainly to Jarry. Contains some useful material, mainly biographical in nature.]

Perche, Louis, *Alfred Jarry*. Paris: Éditions Universitaires, 1965.

Rachilde (*pseud.* of Marguerite Eymery), *Alfred Jarry ou le Surmâle des Lettres*. Paris: Grasset, 1928. [The first biography of Jarry. Largely anecdotal, and patronizing in tone, but containing much valuable material.]

Shattuck, Roger, *The Banquet Years. The Arts in France, 1885–1918*. New York: Harcourt, Brace & Co., 1958; rev. edn, London: Jonathan Cape, 1969. [The first serious study in English of Jarry together with three other figures of the 'Belle Époque'. Useful, though now somewhat out of date.]

Stillman, Linda K., *La Théâtralité dans l'oeuvre d'Alfred Jarry*. York, S. Carolina: French Literature Publications Co., 1980.

What is 'Pataphysics? Special edition of the *Evergreen Review*, no. 13. New York: Grove Press, 1960.

To the above must be added also the numerous and invaluable critical studies published by the Collège de 'Pataphysique in its *Cahiers du Collège de 'Pataphysique* (1950–7), *Dossiers acénonètes du Collège de 'Pataphysique* (1957–65), *Subsidia Pataphysica* (1965–74) and (since the voluntary 'occultation' of the Collège) the *Organographes du Cymbalum Pataphysicum* (1975 onwards), together with the articles in the more recent *L'Étoile-Absinthe* published from 1979 onwards by the Société des Amis d'Alfred Jarry. The most useful of these studies are listed in the following section of the bibliography.

OTHER BOOKS AND ARTICLES CITED

Apollinaire, Guillaume, 'Les Contemporains pittoresques: Feu Alfred Jarry', *Les Marges*, Nov. 1909.

Arnaud, Noël, 'De *Messaline* au Tsar de toutes les Russies', *L'Étoile-Absinthe*, no. 1–2, 1979.

Bablet, Denis, *Esthétique générale du décor de théâtre de 1870 à 1914*. Paris: Éditions du CNRS, 1964.

Besnier, Patrick, 'Point de Babel', paper read at the Jarry Colloquium at Cerisy-la-Salle in Aug.-Sept. 1981.

Blum, Léon, 'Les Progrès de l'Apolitique en France', *La Revue Blanche*, 1 July 1892.

Bossu, Laurent, *Laurent Tailhade et son temps*. [n.p.] Éditions 'L'Idée Libre', n.d. [?1945].

Breton, André, 'Alfred Jarry', in *Les Pas perdus*. Paris: Gallimard, 1924.

Breton, André, *Anthologie de l'humour noir*. Paris: Gallimard, 1941.

Breton, André, *Manifestes du surréalisme*. Paris: Gallimard, Collection 'Idées', 1963.

Caradec, François, 'Jarry chroniqueur', paper read at the Jarry Colloquium at Cerisy-la-Salle in Aug.-Sept. 1981.

Clancier, Anne, 'Jarry et Freud', paper read at the Jarry Colloquium at Cerisy-la-Salle in Aug.-Sept. 1981.

Craig, Edward Gordon, *On the Art of the Theatre*. London: Heinemann, 1911.

Czoniczer, Élizabeth, *Quelques antécédents de 'A la recherche du temps perdu'* (*Tendances qui peuvent avoir contribué à la cristallisation du roman proustien*). Paris and Geneva: Droz, 1957.

Décaudin, Michel, *La Crise des valeurs symbolistes. 20 ans de poésie française, 1895–1914*. Toulouse: Éditions Privat, 1960.

Dossier de la Dragonne, no. 27 of *Dossiers acénonètes du Collège de 'Pataphysique*, devoted to a detailed analysis of Jarry's plans and manuscripts of *La Dragonne*.

Dujardin, Édouard, *Mallarmé par un des siens*. Paris: Messein, 1936.

Eruli, Brunella, 'L'Immaculée Conception', *L'Étoile-Absinthe*, no. 7–8, 1980.

Eruli, Brunella, 'Sur les sources classiques de *Messaline*: collages et montages', *L'Étoile-Absinthe*, no. 1–2, 1979.

Fargue, Léon-Paul, *Portraits de famille*. Paris: Janin, 1947.

Fargue, Léon-Paul, *Le Piéton de Paris/D'après Paris*. Paris: Gallimard, 1964.

Fletcher, John, (ed.), *Forces in Modern French Drama*. London: University of London Press, 1972.

Fort, Paul, *Mes Mémoires*. Paris: Flammarion, 1944.

Franc-Nohain, 'Pantagruel au Café Brosse', *Comoedia*, 29 Jan. 1911.

Gayot, Paul, 'Fictions et moutures', *Subsidia Pataphysica*, no. 20–1.

Gayot, Paul, 'L'Odyssée et l'histoire', *Subsidia Pataphysica*, no. 19.

Gémier, Firmin, interview published under the title of 'Deux représentations retentissantes: M. Firmin Gémier nous dit ce que furent la répétition générale et la première d'*Ubu Roi*', in *Excelsior*, 4 Nov. 1921.

Gens-d' Armes, Gandilhon, 'Alfred Jarry au Lycée Henri IV', *Les Marges*, Jan. 1922.

Géroy, 'Mon ami Alfred Jarry (Souvenirs)', *Le Mercure de France*, 1 July 1947.

Gide, André, 'Le Groupement littéraire qu'abritait le "Mercure de France"', *Le Mercure de France*, vol. 298, no. 1000, 1 July 1940 – 1 December 1946.

Gourmont, Remy de, *Le Latin mystique*. Paris: Mercure de France, 1892.

Gourmont, Remy de, *L'Idéalisme*, reproduced in *Le Chemin de velours*. Paris: Mercure de France, 1902.

Gourmont, Remy de, *Sixtine*. Paris: Mercure de France, 1918.

Gourmont, Remy de, *Le Livre des masques*. Paris: Mercure de France, 1963.

Gourmont, Remy de, *Promenades littéraires*, III. Paris: Mercure de France, 1963.

Gourmont, Remy de, *Promenades philosophiques*, I. Paris: Mercure de France, 1963.

Gourmont, Remy de, *La Culture des Idées*. Paris: Mercure de France, 1964.

Gourmont, Remy de, *Le Joujou patriotisme*. Paris: J.-J. Pauvert, 1967.

Gros, Bernard, 'Des origines de la feuille de chou', *Cahiers du Collège de 'Pataphysique*, no. 22–3.

Haas, Dr Albert, 'Souvenirs de la vie littéraire à Paris', *Les Soirées de Paris*, May 1914.

Hertz, Henri, 'Alfred Jarry collégien et la naissance d'*Ubu Roi*', *Les Écrits Nouveaux*, Nov. 1921.

Hertz, Henri, 'Alfred Jarry, *Ubu Roi* et les professeurs', *La Nouvelle Revue Française*, 1 Sept. 1924.

Jarry, Charlotte, 'Souvenirs sur Alfred Jarry', published in vol. I of Jarry's *Oeuvres Complètes*. Monte Carlo: Éditions du Livre and Lausanne: Henri Kaeser, 1948.

Ionesco, Eugène, *Notes et contre-notes*. Paris: Gallimard, 1962.

Léautaud, Paul, *Journal littéraire*, II. Paris: Mercure de France, 1955.

Lecompte, T., 'Histoire d'une bicyclette gratuite (avec expertise)', *Cahiers du Collège de 'Pataphysique*, no. 5–6.

Lefèvre, Frédéric, 'Une heure avec Léon-Paul Fargue', *Les Nouvelles Littéraires*, 12 Jan. 1929.

Lehmann, A. G., *The Symbolist Aesthetic in France, 1885–1895*. Oxford: Blackwell, 2nd edn, 1968.

'Lettres de Paul Fort à Alfred Jarry', *Dossiers acénonètes du Collège de 'Pataphysique*, no. 22–4.

Lié, P. [*pseud.*], 'Comment Jarry et Lugné-Poe glorifièrent Ubu à l'Oeuvre', *Cahiers du Collège de 'Pataphysique*, no. 3–4.

Loize, Jean, 'La Grande Chasublerie d'Alfred Jarry', *Cahiers du Collège de 'Pataphysique*, no. 5–6.

Lormel, Louis, 'Entre soi', *La Plume*, no. 203, 1 Oct. 1897.

Lormel, Louis, 'Alfred Jarry. Souvenirs', *La Phalange*, 15 Sept. 1907.

Lormel, Louis, 'Les Débuts du Symbolisme: Remy de Gourmont, Alfred Jarry et l'*Art littéraire*', *Le Gaulois*, 3 Dec. 1921.

Lugné-Poe, Aurélien, *La Parade*, II: *Acrobaties*. Paris: Gallimard, 1931.

Lutembi, 'De quelques mécomptes', *Cahiers du Collège de 'Pataphysique*, no. 22–3.

Maitron, Jean, *Histoire du mouvement anarchiste en France (1880–1914)*. Paris: Société universitaire d'éditions et de librairie, 1955.

Mallarmé, Stéphane, *Oeuvres Complètes*. Paris: Gallimard, Bibliothèque de la Pléiade, 1945.

Mallarmé, Stéphane, *Correspondance*, recueillie, classée et annotée par Henri Mondor et Lloyd James Austin, tome VIII. Paris: Gallimard, 1983.

Margueritte, Paul, *Le Petit Théâtre (Théâtre de Marionnettes)*. Paris: Librairie Illustrée, 1888.

Mauclair, Camille, *Servitude et Grandeur littéraire*. Paris: Ollendorff, 6th edn, 1922.

Quillard, Pierre, 'De l'imagination et de l'expression chez M. Alfred Jarry', *La Revue Blanche*, 1 June 1902.

Régnier, Henri de, *De mon temps*. Paris: Mercure de France, 4th edn 1933.

Rémond, Georges, 'Souvenirs sur Jarry et autres', *Le Mercure de France*, 1 Apr. 1955.

Renard, Jules, *Journal, 1887–1910*. Paris: Gallimard, Bibliothèque de la Pléiade, 1960.

Robichez, Jacques, *Le Symbolisme au théâtre. Lugné-Poe et les débuts de l'Oeuvre*. Paris: L'Arche, 1957.

Robillot, Henri, 'La Presse d'*Ubu Roi*'. *Cahiers du Collège de 'Pataphysique*, no. 3–4.

Rybko-Schub, Louise, *Léon-Paul Fargue*. Geneva: Droz, 1973.

Saillet, Maurice, 'Relativement à *L'Amour absolu*', *Cahiers du Collège de 'Pataphysique*, no. 8–9.

Sainmont, Jean-Hugues [*pseud.*], 'Occultations et exaltations d'*Ubu Cocu*', *Cahiers du Collège de 'Pataphysique*, no. 3–4.

Sainmont, Jean-Hugues [*pseud.*], 'Petit guide illustré pour la visite de *César-Antechrist*', *Cahiers du Collège de 'Pataphysique*, no. 5–6.

Sainmont, Jean-Hughes [*pseud.*], 'Rennes visions d'histoire (En marge d'*Onésime*)', *Cahiers du Collège de 'Pataphysique*, no. 20.

Sainmont, Jean-Hughes [*pseud.*], 'Ubu ou la création d'un mythe', *Cahiers du Collège de 'Pataphysique*, nos. 1 and 3–4.

Salmon, André, 'Alfred Jarry ou le Père Ubu en liberté', *L'Ami du Lettré*, 1924.

Saltas, Jean, Preface to *Ubu Roi*. Paris: Fasquelle, [n.d.].

Saltas, Jean, 'Souvenirs sur Alfred Jarry', *Les Marges*, Jan. 1922. Republished in vol. I of Jarry's *Oeuvres Complètes*. Monte Carlo: Éditions du Livre and Lausanne: Henri Kaeser, 1948.

Stéphen-Chauvet, Dr, 'Les Derniers jours d'Alfred Jarry', *Le Mercure de France*, 242, 15 Feb. 1933.

Sutton, Denys, Introduction to *Pierre Bonnard*, Catalogue of the Royal Academy of Arts Winter Exhibition, London, 1966.

Symons, Arthur, 'A Symbolist farce', in *Studies in Seven Arts*. London: Constable, 1906.

Taine, Hippolyte, *De l'intelligence*. Paris, 1870.

Thibaudet, Albert, 'Réflexions sur la littérature: L'Affaire Ubu', *La Nouvelle Revue Française*, 1 July 1922.

Trohel, Jules, 'Alfred Jarry et les huissiers', *Le Mercure de France*, 1 May 1934.

Vallette, Alfred, 'Mort d'Alfred Jarry', *Le Mercure de France*, 16 Nov. 1907.

Vollard, Ambroise, *Souvenirs d'un marchand de tableaux*. Paris: Albin Michel, 1937.

Yeats, William Butler, *Autobiographies*. London: Macmillan, 1955.

Index

[Major entries are indicated by italics.]